TEACHING LEARNERS WITH MILD DISABILITIES: INTEGRATING RESEARCH AND PRACTICE

Second Edition

Ruth Lyn Meese

Longwood College

Wadsworth
Thomson Learning™

Australia • Canada • Mexico • Singapore • Spain • United Kingdom • United States

Education Editor: Dianne Lindsay
Assistant Editor: Tangelique Williams
Editorial Assistant: Keynia Johnson
Marketing Manager: Becky Tollerson
Project Editor: Trudy Brown
Print Buyer: Tandra Jorgensen
Permissions Editor: Joohee Lee

Production Service: Graphic World, Inc.
Photo Researcher: Sue Howard
Cover Designer: Ellen Kwan
Cover Printer: Webcom Ltd.
Compositor: Graphic World, Inc.
Printer: Webcom Ltd.

Printed in Canada
6 7 08 07 06

For permission to use material from this text, contact us by
Web: http://www.thomsonrights.com
Fax: 1-800-730-2215 **Phone:** 1-800-730-2214

For more information, contact
Wadsworth/Thomson Learning
10 Davis Drive
Belmont, CA 94002-3098
USA
http://www.wadsworth.com

International Headquarters
Thomson Learning
International Division
290 Harbor Drive, 2nd Floor
Stamford, CT 06902-7477
USA

**UK/Europe/Middle East/
South Africa**
Thomson Learning
Berkshire House
168-173 High Holborn
London WC1V 7AA
United Kingdom

Asia
Thomson Learning
60 Albert Street, #15-01
Albert Complex
Singapore 189969

Canada
Nelson Thomson Learning
1120 Birchmount Road
Toronto, Ontario M1K 5G4
Canada

Library of Congress Cataloging-in-Publication Data
On file

ISBN: 0-534-57852-7

*To James W. Windle, my husband, who took care of everything
around the house during this revision and still managed
to give me abundant encouragement;*

*To my wonderful daughter, Katie Svetlana Windlemeese, who continues
to teach me more about teaching every day; and,*

To all those who teach children with mild disabilities,

Thank you.

BRIEF CONTENTS

CONTENTS

6 Assessing Student Progress   128

7 Planning for Successful Instruction   162

11 Reading Instruction   272

12 Written Language Instruction   328

One particularly thorny problem my colleagues and I continue to face is helping the preservice teacher see the relevance of theory and research for daily practice in the classroom. With only limited classroom experience, the teacher-to-be is often unable to connect topics covered in college "methods" courses to the many actions taken by teachers throughout the school day. Although our students participate in early, supervised field experiences and related classroom discussions, each assigned field placement is unique. Naive learners can easily become confused about their observations.

In an attempt to integrate theory and research with practice in my methods courses, I developed numerous activities, examples, and scenarios for our classroom discussions. However, this practical material lacked the cohesive framework needed to put it in perspective. In addition, although case approaches encourage reflective discussion, I have found that my preservice teachers first must acquire some fundamental information if they are to profit from these discussions.

This book, then, was born of necessity. To unify activities, examples, and cases for classroom discussion, I developed a set of hypothetical schools, students, and teachers with whom my preservice teachers could identify. These fictional students and their teachers have become the framework for relevant on-campus instruction in theory, research, and related practice. In the college classroom, for example, we can discuss decisions made by Ms. Kirk, a fourth-grade teacher, and Ms. Lopez, a special educator, who collaborate in the classroom and share responsibility for the instruction of Travis and Joey, two fourth-graders with mild disabilities. We can also assume the role of Mr. Abel, a secondary-level special educator, or that of Mr. McNally, a geography teacher, and conduct collaborative planning and teaching role-plays in our classroom. In addition, we can plan lessons and activities appropriate for the two fourth-graders, Travis and Joey; a sixth-grader, Susan; and ninth-grader, Robert—all students with mild disabilities. Moreover, because many students with learning and behavioral problems are never identified for special education programs, but nonetheless present instructional challenges for their classroom teachers, I have included four students without mild disabilities—Celie, Kevin, Leon, and Marcus—in our instructional framework.

This book, therefore, is most appropriate for the preservice teacher of students with mild disabilities, both the classroom teacher and the special educator. Inservice teachers new to the field of special education, however, may also find the book helpful in meeting their needs. Throughout the text, I have attempted to present not only research-based instructional methods, but also those shown to be effective by teachers engaging in reflective practice.

In this second edition of the textbook, therefore, I have updated all of the research in each chapter to include important works occurring since the book's original publication. I have, for example, included research and practical tips regarding inclusion, a service model increasingly used by the public schools during the 1990s, as well as relevant requirements from IDEA (1997). In addition, I have added a new sixth-grade student, Taylor, to highlight the needs of "Section 504 students" in the classroom. Furthermore, a new chapter, Oral Language Instruction, will emphasize the importance of language development and phonological awareness for later success in reading. Throughout the text I have attempted to illustrate the importance of respecting cultural, ethnic, and linguistic diversity in the classroom.

Moreover, I have included two new features in every chapter of the book. First, each chapter contains a box titled "Web Watch" that lists a number of related sites on the World Wide Web to which students can go for current information, lesson plans, or resources. All chapters also end with at least one application exercise asking students to gather information from the Web sites given and use it to produce a handout, plan a workshop, modify a lesson, or engage in some other professional activity. Finally, every chapter contains an application exercise requiring students to use *InfoTrac College Edition* to locate current research through the web on topics covered in the chapter.

Part One still provides some basic foundations for instruction. In Chapter 1, I introduce our fictional schools, teachers, and students. These teachers and students then become the basis for examples, feature boxes, and application exercises in subsequent chapters. Although adequate introductory information about these students and teachers is presented in Chapter 1 (with details provided in Appendix A for the four students with mild disabilities), I would encourage the instructor who uses this text to personalize the hypothetical students and teachers to reflect local or regional needs of the schools he or she serves. Chapters 2 and 3 also provide foundations for instruction. Chapter 2 centers on the characteristics of learners with mild disabilities, while the focus of Chapter 3 is on historical and current approaches to teaching these learners.

In Part Two, Organizing for Instruction, we discuss the importance of communicating for student success in Chapter 4 and managing the classroom environment in Chapter 5. Chapter 6, Assessing Student Progress, and Chapter 7, Planning for Successful Instruction, offer beginning teachers the means to link the knowledge and data gained about students with relevant instructional objectives and lesson plans.

The content of Part Three, Providing Instruction, is sufficiently detailed to be of immediate practical classroom use. Effective teacher behaviors are the focus of Chapter 8, and techniques to promote student-mediated learning are introduced in Chapter 9. Chapters 10 through 15 provide the teacher with effective methods for oral language instruction, reading instruction, written language instruction, mathematics instruction, content-area instruction in the regular classroom, and instruction in social and independent living skills, respectively. Again, focus questions, examples, boxed material, Web resources, and application exercises are contained in every chapter, and most feature the students and teachers introduced in Chapter 1, whom the reader by now has come to "know."

I owe a debt of gratitude to the many indispensable people who have made a project of this magnitude possible. My graduate assistants, Carrie Chambers, Shannon Lavinus, and Amy Johnson, spent many hours obtaining resources and permissions and constructing materials in the Appendixes. Dianne Lindsay and her staff at Wadsworth and Mike Ederer and the compositors at Graphic World offered invaluable editorial advice and support. Finally, the following reviewers gave generously of their time to provide thoughtful comments and suggestions that strengthened the manuscript: Lyman W. Boomer, Western Illinois University; Kathy Boyle-Gast, University of Georgia; Steven Daley, Idaho State University; Rosa Gonzalez, California State University, Northridge; Michele Kamens, Rider University; Paul Malanga, University of South Dakota; Darcy Miller, Washington State University; Lewis Putnam, University of Wisconsin, Milwaukee; Deborah Bott Slaton, University of Kentucky; and M. Sherry Smith, Chicago State University. To each of you, and to the many others who have contributed to the production of this text, I extend my sincerest thanks.

Ruth Lyn Meese

FOUNDATIONS FOR INSTRUCTION

CHAPTER 1

THE LEARNERS AND THEIR TEACHERS

Focus

As you read, think about the following questions:

◆ *How do schools reflect today's society?*

◆ *What is Goals 2000 and how will it affect programs for students with special education needs?*

◆ *What special programs are currently operating to help children with low achievement become successful in school?*

◆ *What is the purpose of compensatory education programs such as Chapter 1?*

◆ *What is the Individuals with Disabilities Education Act?*

◆ *Who are "Section 504 students" and how do these children differ from those in special education?*

For some students, learning is relatively easy and exciting. Yet, for many youngsters who are performing below grade level, learning is a difficult process and school is a constant struggle. Some children who are having problems are enrolled in special education programs for students with disabilities. Most of these students spend a portion of their school day in the regular classroom. Those who do not qualify for special education services receive instruction chiefly from the classroom teacher. Whether in a special education program or in the regular classroom, children who struggle to learn challenge the skills of their teachers.

This book is primarily about students with mild disabilities. The term *mild disabilities* is often used to describe students with learning disabilities, emotional/behavioral disorders, and mild mental retardation. These youngsters share certain characteristics and have similar instructional needs (Hallahan & Kauffman, 1977; Henley, Ramsey, & Algozzine, 1996). Despite the term *mild*, however, they all have significant problems with learning and behavior that interfere with their progress in school, and they all require special assistance from their teachers.

Although this text is intended for teachers of students with mild disabilities, I believe that other children who are low achieving but who are not in special education programs can also benefit from the instructional strategies described in this book. As you read, please bear this in mind, along with the following additional beliefs that guide my thinking:

- ◆ All children and youth can learn when appropriate goals are set for them and when effective teaching methods are used.
- ◆ All children and youth deserve the best instruction their schools can offer.
- ◆ Effective teaching strategies for students with mild disabilities are similar to those for other at-risk students.
- ◆ Effective teaching strategies for students must match the unique needs of the learner, regardless of a categorical label.
- ◆ Effective teaching strategies for students with mild disabilities include those in published research studies as well as those observed by professionals to work in actual practice in specific school settings.
- ◆ Special education and regular classroom teachers should collaborate to improve instruction for all students who struggle to learn.

This text is arranged in three parts. In Part One, "Foundations for Instruction," the three chapters include an introduction to today's schools, to learners with mild disabilities, and to teaching approaches designed for these learners. Part Two, "Organizing for Instruction," includes four chapters examining methods used by teachers to enhance communication, manage the classroom environment, assess student progress, and plan instruction. In Part Three, "Providing Instruction," the focus shifts to effective teacher behaviors, strategies to enhance student-mediated learning, improving oral language skills, reading and written language instruction, mathematics instruction, methods for teaching social studies and science in the regular classroom, and techniques to develop social skills and independent living skills.

In the balance of this introductory chapter, let's take a look at what's happening in our schools as we enter the twenty-first century. Then, following a brief overview of the special programs currently underway in the public schools, some very special learners and their teachers will be introduced.

Schools, Society, and Achievement

During the 1980s, several national reports emphasized problems in America's schools (Carnegie Council on Adolescent Development, 1989; National Commission on Excellence in Education, 1983; National Governor's Association, 1986). Chief among the concerns listed in these reports were poor school achievement, substandard schools, lack of adequately trained teachers, and the unmet needs of students at risk for dropping out of school. These concerns continued throughout the 1990s (Rose & Gallup, 1998), along with additional public outcries to improve school safety (Dwyer, Osher, & Warger, 1998).

In 1985, for example, almost 25% of 17-year-olds still in school did not have the skills necessary to read simple magazines, and only 50% had the skills to read popular novels and newspaper stories (National Assessment of Educational Progress, 1985). According to a more recent assessment, only 42% of America's 17-year-olds were able to read at the highest levels, and very few students were proficient in writing, mathematics, or science (National Center for Education Statistics, 1990). As a matter of fact, the National Center for Education Statistics (1998) reported little change in the reading proficiency of 9-, 13-, and 17-year-olds since 1971. Although the Center reported stable scores in writing proficiency between 1984 and 1996 for students in grades 4 and 8, students in grade 11 scored slightly lower in 1996 than in 1984. In mathematics proficiency, however, 9-, 13-, and 17-year-old students all demonstrated improvement from 1976 through 1996 with 9-year-olds achieving the greatest gains.

Moreover, in 1990, according to the National Center for Education Statistics (1991), 4.1% of the 15- to 21-year-olds in grades 10 through 12 dropped out of school. In addition, 12.1% of all individuals aged 16 to 24 (an astonishing 3.8 million people) had failed to complete high school and were not enrolled in school. By 1996, 5% of students in grades 10 through 12 failed to return to school (National Center for Education Statistics, 1998). These figures were even higher for youth living in poverty and for young people of Hispanic background. Apparently, for many youngsters, school is not a successful, satisfying venture.

Demographics, too, continue to change the face of education. In 1976, only 24% of students in grades 1 through 12 were from culturally or racially diverse backgrounds; however, by 1995, 35% of the children and youth attending public schools were African-, Hispanic-, Asian-, or Native-American. According to the National Center for Education Statistics (1998), the largest population growth occurred in the number of Hispanic students enrolled in grades 1 through 12 and in the number of individuals in the United States with limited English proficiency. As we enter the twenty-first century, we can expect children from increasingly diverse cultural and ethnic backgrounds to be attending public schools in the United States.

Today's teachers believe that societal problems hamper school performance. For example, 14.4% of public school teachers viewed absenteeism as a serious problem in the 1993–94 school year, and 24% of teachers reported student apathy to be a serious problem (National Center for Education Statistics, 1998). In addition, 28% of public school teachers viewed lack of parental involvement as a serious problem, up from 25% in the 1990–91 school year. A startling 76% of all teachers believed many children attending their school to be "latchkey kids," youngsters left alone after school hours (Harris & Associates, 1989). In fact, Eitzen (1992) reported approximately three million children aged five to thirteen to be without adult supervision after school. Moreover, in 1994, approximately 25% of all children were born to unmarried mothers, and fewer than 49% of all children in the United States lived with both of their biological parents in 1995 (National Center for Education Statistics, 1998).

Furthermore, reports of drug use among youth are once again on the rise after a period of decline during the 1980s (National Center for Education Statistics, 1998). Among seniors in public high schools in 1997, 6% reported using cocaine and 39% reported using marijuana, up 3% and 17%, respectively, since 1992. Moreover, 75% of the seniors reported that they had consumed alcohol in the previous year, and 53% stated that they had used alcohol in the previous 30 days.

Absenteeism, alcohol and drug use, and the latchkey phenomenon are all related to a changing economy and changing family structures. According to the National Center for Children in Poverty (1998), over 14 million children in the United States are living in poverty (e.g., an annual income of under $10,504 for a single parent with one child). Of all the children under the age of six in the United States, 23.2% (over 5 million) live in homes below the poverty level. Less fortunate youngsters are homeless. The National Coalition for the Homeless (1998) reports that families constitute the fastest-growing homeless group. Families with children, for example, comprised approximately 40% of homeless people in 1997, and 25% of the urban homeless were children under the age of 18.

Poverty and poor adult supervision are related to low achievement and high drop-out rates (Eitzen, 1992). Even more alarming, however, is the increasing level of violence in today's schools. In one recent survey, 47% of teachers reported disruptive student behaviors during class to be a significant problem (U.S. Centers for Disease Control and Prevention, 1997). For example, 14.5% of students surveyed in 1997 reported that they had been in at least one fistfight on school property during the previous 12 months, and 16.2% said they had carried a weapon to school within the last 30 days. The National Center for Education Statistics (1998) also reported increases in fear for personal safety at school expressed by students between 1985 and 1995. In 1995, 15% of all 12- to 19-year-olds reported being victims of crimes at school, while during the 1993–94 school year, 12% of all elementary and secondary school teachers were threatened with injury. Of the teachers surveyed, 4% stated they had been attacked by their students. Because of these concerns, as well as national coverage by the media of violent events such as the shootings at Columbine High School and at other schools, many school districts have now developed "zero tolerance" policies for weapons, illegal substances, and disruptive behavior at school.

Schools, after all, are social institutions, and problems in our society are reflected in our schools through student behavior and academic performance.

To address these societal changes and their impact on the schools, Congress passed the Goals 2000: Educate America Act in 1994. These goals state that by the year 2000:

1. All children in America will start school ready to learn.
2. The high school graduation rate will increase to at least 90%.
3. American students will leave grades 4, 8, and 12 having demonstrated competency in challenging subject matter including English, mathematics, science, foreign languages, civics and government, economics, arts, history, and geography; and every school in America will ensure that all students learn to use their minds well, so they may be prepared for responsible citizenship, further learning, and productive employment in our modern economy.
4. U.S. students will be first in the world in science and mathematics achievement.
5. Every adult American will be literate and will possess the knowledge and skills necessary to compete in a global economy and exercise the rights and responsibilities of citizenship.
6. Every school in America will be free of drugs, violence, and the unauthorized presence of firearms and alcohol, and will offer a disciplined environment conducive to learning.
7. Members of the nation's teaching force will have access to programs for the continued improvement of their skills and the opportunity to acquire the knowledge and skills needed to instruct and prepare all American students for the next century.
8. Every school will promote partnerships that will increase parental involvement and participation in promoting the social, emotional, and academic growth of children.

Interestingly, children with special education needs are specifically included in Goals 2000. The legislation defines "all students" and "all children" as: ". . . American Indians, Alaskan Natives, Native Hawaiians, students or children with disabilities, students or children with limited English proficiency, school-aged students or children who have dropped out of school, migratory students or children, and academically talented students and children." Obviously, Goals 2000 is designed to encompass a wide range of students.

Certainly, the Goals 2000 objectives are admirable in their intent, but the impact they will have on special education programs is as yet unclear. An expert committee convened by the National Academy of Sciences recommended that all students, including children with disabilities, have access to challenging standards and that educators and policy makers be held accountable for the performance of every student (McDonnell, McLaughlin, & Morison, 1997). To that end, the Individuals with Disabilities Education Act Amendment (IDEA) (Public Law 105-17), legislation reauthorized by Congress in 1997, holds schools accountable for helping students with disabilities attain performance goals and standards. To the maximum extent appropriate for each child, students with disabilities are to be educated in the general education curriculum and expected to meet rigorous academic standards. Most states are developing standards by which students and schools will be assessed, and national professional organizations have already set standards in disciplines such as mathematics and science (e.g., the National Council of Teachers of Mathematics, and the National Science Education Standards Project).

Such standards will pose a tremendous challenge for students who struggle to learn and for the men and women who teach them. Most states now have or are developing statewide measures to assess the performance of students (U.S. Department of Education, 1997). These assessments are often "high stakes" tests, because students must achieve, a minimum score in order to be promoted to the next grade, to receive credit for a particular course, or to graduate. Teachers, schools, and school districts may also be evaluated based on the performance of their students. The student with a mild disability will most likely be expected to participate in statewide testing programs, albeit with certain modifications to accommodate for his or her disability, and test scores for students with disabilities are to be included in accountability data reported by the states (IDEA, 1997).

Special educators must understand the demands placed on classroom teachers and work with the teachers to provide a sound and successful education for all children. I firmly believe that all children can learn when appropriate goals are set for them, when effective instruction is provided, and when special educators and regular classroom teachers collaborate in order to assist all students experiencing difficulty in school. Given proper instruction, most children will develop important skills necessary for success in school and in later life. Fortunately, those instructional techniques that are effective for students with mild disabilities can be equally effective for other children with learning or behavioral problems who are in regular classrooms or in compensatory education programs (Slavin, Karweit, & Madden, 1989; Ysseldyke & Algozzine, 1982). Indeed, for this reason, children with learning problems who are not in special education programs are also included in discussions throughout this text. In addition, the reader may find helpful resources regarding societal problems, Goals 2000, and special programs by visiting the World Wide Web sites listed in Box 1.1.

Special Programs

Some children having difficulty in school may receive part or all of their education through special programs. These programs, which receive federal funding, include compensatory education programs, special education programs, and Section 504 services.

Compensatory Education Programs

Compensatory education programs are federal efforts designed to help youngsters from low socioeconomic backgrounds who are performing below the level of their peers. Chapter 1, previously known as Title 1, is the largest of these programs, serving children who are struggling in the areas of reading, language arts, and mathematics. Schools receive Chapter 1 funds based on the number of low income students they serve, and they must use these funds to assist students to achieve the same high standards set for all children within each state according to Goals 2000 (McDonnell, et al., 1997).

Box 1.1

Web Watch

Americans with Disabilities Act: http://www.usdoj.gov/crt/ada/adahom1.htm

Home page created by the U.S. Department of Justice for information on the ADA; information for students, families, and employers of people with disabilities.

American Federation of Teachers: http://www.aft.org

Surveys of teachers and administrators; policies and trends in the schools.

Centers for Disease Control and Prevention: http://www.cdc.gov/

Statistics and information regarding health and safety issues as well as violence prevention.

Children's Defense Fund: http://www.childrensdefense.org

Statistics and information regarding the status of children; poverty, violence, and homeless children.

Council for Exceptional Children: http://www.cec.sped.org/

Home page for CEC; information on publications and divisions for children and youth with various disabilities; links to related sites.

Ideapractices: http://www.ideapractices.org

Information on IDEA, resources, links to other sites, and tips regarding how schools are implementing IDEA mandates.

National Center for Education Statistics: http://nces.ed.gov

Home page for NCES; links to sites such as The Condition of Education reports (68 indicators important to Goals 2000 covering progress in America's schools) and the National Assessment of Educational Progress, a report describing the achievement of students in public schools.

National Dropout Prevention Center: http://www.dropoutprevention.org

Information and statistics regarding dropouts and dropout prevention programs.

National Education Association: http://www.nea.org

National association for teachers; statistics, surveys, and information regarding policies, programs, and practices in the schools.

National Information Center for Children and Youth with Disabilities (NICHCY):
http://www.nichy.org

Publications and information regarding various disabilities; information on IDEA, Section 504, and ADA.

Office of Special Education and Rehabilitative Services:
http://www.ed.gov/offices/OSERS/OSEP/index.html
An office within the U.S. Department of Education overseeing IDEA; access to reports to Congress and statistics on the implementation of IDEA.

U.S. Department of Education: http://www.ed.gov

Information on America's schools; links to major programs and national reports.

Most Chapter 1 students are in elementary schools and receive remedial instruction in reading and/or mathematics. Prior to 1981, Chapter 1 instruction occurred primarily in a "pull-out" setting, necessitating that participating children leave the regular classroom for periods of remedial help. In 1981, however, when Chapter 1 was reauthorized, legislation mandated that schools develop school-wide programs designed to link funded services to the regular curriculum. Schools, for example, might use Chapter 1 funds to implement an early, intensive, tutoring program in each classroom to improve the reading performance of all children in kindergarten through third grade. To date, research indicates that students receiving Chapter 1 services experience only limited academic gains, and that the intervention is not sufficient to raise achievement levels of participating students in high-poverty schools to those of children in low-poverty schools (Puma, Karweit, Price, Ricciuti, Thompson, & Vaden-Kiernan, 1997).

Students receiving Chapter 1 services are not specifically prohibited under federal law from also receiving special education services. Thus children in special education may also benefit from the school-wide programs being implemented. As a matter of fact, the federal law governing special education now encourages coordination of services across federally funded programs.

Special Education Programs

Special education programs are designed to serve children with disabilities that impair their performance in school. Since the passage in 1975 of Public Law 94-142, the Education for All Handicapped Children Act, public schools have served millions of youngsters in special education programs. Now renamed the Individuals with Disabilities Education Act Amendments of 1997 (Public Law 105-17), this legislation guarantees a free, appropriate public education (FAPE) to all children with disabilities from birth through age 21. Part B of the Act specifically benefits children aged 3 through 21 who have disabilities that adversely affect their ability to learn in the general education program. Disabilities covered under IDEA, Part B, include specific learning disabilities, emotional disturbance, mental retardation, autism, other health impairments, orthopedic impairments, traumatic brain injury, speech or language impairments, hearing impairments, and visual impairments. In addition, IDEA (1997) provided a new category, developmental delay, to assist children aged three to nine experiencing delays in physical, cognitive, communication, adaptive, or social/emotional development.

According to the most recent figures reported to Congress on the implementation of IDEA, students between the ages of 6 and 17 with disabilities made up 10.6% of all children enrolled in schools during the 1995–96 school year (U.S. Department of Education, 1997). Just over five million children aged 6 to 21 were enrolled in special education programs, with children aged 6 to 11 making up almost 46% of the total enrollment. In addition, the vast majority of these children were enrolled in programs for students with mild disabilities.

For example, of those children aged 6 to 21 in special education, most (51.2%) were in programs for students with learning disabilities. Another 11.5% were in programs for children with mental retardation, and 8.6% were in programs for youngsters with emotional disturbances (U.S. Department of Education, 1997). During the 1994–95 school year, an overwhelming majority of students with disabilities (95%) received their special education in regular public school buildings (U.S. Department of Education, 1997). Of these youngsters, almost half (44.5%) were in regular classroom placements, spending at least 80% of the school day in the regular classroom. (For a more detailed discussion of special education services, see Chapter 3.)

Although the majority of students in special education are in the regular classroom setting, some spend at least a portion of the school day in special education classes. For example, 28.7% of students in special education receive resource room services, spending at least 21% but no more than 60% of the school day outside of the regular classroom in special education or related services (U.S. Department of Education, 1997). Only 22.5% of all children aged 6 to 21 receiving special education services spent over 60% of their school day in separate special education classrooms, and very few (4.35%) were in separate facilities, homebound, or in residential programs (U.S. Department of Education, 1997).

Unfortunately, students from racial and ethnic minorities are disproportionately represented in special education programs. African-American children, for example, are overrepresented in programs for students with mental retardation, emotional disturbance, and learning disabilities (U.S. Department of Education, 1997). Moreover, students of Hispanic or Native American background are underrepresented in special education programs. Students in special education programs are also more likely to drop out of school or to come from homes below the poverty level than are their peers without disabilities.

Section 504 Services

Many other students with disabilities qualify for special services, yet they may not be in special education programs. That is, some students may not be eligible for special education services according to the specific definitions set forth in IDEA (1997) although these children and youth may still have disabilities prohibiting their full participation in schools. Two federal laws protect students with disabilities from discrimination: Section 504 of the Vocational Rehabilitation Act Amendments of 1975 (Public Law 93-112) and the Americans with Disabilities Act (ADA) of 1990 (Public Law 101-336). Because both pieces of legislation deal with discrimination, they fall under the auspices of the Office of Civil Rights.

The ADA is broader in scope than is Section 504, protecting individuals with disabilities across the life span from discrimination in private employment, transportation, public accommodations, state and local government activities and programs, or telecommunications. Section 504 of the Vocational Rehabilitation Act, on the other hand, applies only to programs receiving federal financial assistance. Because schools are agencies of state and local governments and because they receive federal funding, they may not discriminate against persons with disabilities. A school, for example, may not refuse to hire an otherwise qualified teacher simply because he or she has a disability. Similarly, schools cannot prevent a child who uses a wheelchair from participating in physical education activities when other children without disabilities have access to such activities.

Both the Rehabilitation Act and ADA prohibit discrimination against "otherwise qualified" people with disabilities, and both use the same broad definition of "disability." Both acts define a person with a disability as one who: (1) has a physical or mental impairment that substantially limits one or more major life activity (e.g., breathing, walking, learning); (2) has a record of such an impairment (e.g., a child with cancer that is in remission); or (3) is regarded as having such an impairment (e.g., a child with disfiguring facial scars). If a child is of school age, he or she is "otherwise qualified." Some children, however, may not have disabilities adversely impacting their performance in the general education classroom as defined specifically under IDEA (e.g., a learning disability or mental retardation), but may nonetheless have a physical (e.g., a missing hand) or mental (e.g., attention deficit/hyperactivity disorder) impairment limiting their access to school programs or activities as broadly defined under the Rehabilitation Act. These students qualify for services under Section 504, and to prevent discrimination they receive accommodations or modifications to their educational program (e.g., taped textbooks or extended time on tests) through a document given titles such as a "Section 504 Plan," an "Accommodation Plan," a "Service Plan," or an "Access Plan."

Students qualifying for special services under Section 504, then, are not in special education programs under IDEA (1997). In fact, IDEA funds cannot be used to assist students qualifying only under Section 504 (Reid & Katsiyannis, 1995). Nevertheless, Section 504 mandates that students with disabilities have adjustments made on their behalf within the classroom and school setting whenever necessary. To that end, when a student is having continuing difficulty in the classroom, school personnel often first evaluate the child's eligibility for special education under IDEA (1997). If the child is determined to be ineligible for special education services, professionals usually consider whether or not the child qualifies under Section 504. Classroom and special education teachers are frequently participants in both decision-making processes.

Special Programs Summary ◆

Children who are struggling in schools may receive assistance through compensatory education, special education, or Section 504 services. Children in special education and those having Section 504 plans may benefit from school-wide programs offered under Chapter 1. Similarly, IDEA (1997) does not prohibit children in regular classrooms, with or without disabilities, from benefiting as appropriate supplementary aids and services are provided to a child receiving a special education program. For example, a special education teacher may work full-time within a fourth-grade classroom containing two children with learning disabilities and one child with a behavior disorder. As the special education teacher modifies activities to meet the specific needs of the special education children, nothing prevents other students in that classroom from benefiting as well. Although the student having a Section 504 plan is not in special education, his or her classroom teacher may adjust instruction and class activities in accordance with the Accommodation Plan in such a way that others may benefit too. Special education and classroom teachers, as well as those providing compensatory education programs, must work together whenever possible to coordinate activities in order to maximize educational opportunities for all students.

Now that we have briefly reviewed some of the special programs in today's schools, let's turn our attention to some special students and their teachers. ◆

Special Students: Their Schools and Teachers

The students, schools, and teachers described in this section are entirely fictitious. Yet they are representative of actual students, teachers, and schools throughout the United States. Please acquaint yourself with these special students and their teachers. They will appear throughout this text in vignettes used to illustrate teaching strategies and in application exercises at the end of each chapter. Although only basic information about each youngster is given here, details are included in Appendix A for the students who receive special education programs.

Oak Hill Elementary School

Oak Hill Elementary School is located in the northern section of Byrd County, which is a large, primarily suburban, public school district near a large city of approximately 500,000 people. The school system is growing rapidly and presently serves just over 40,000 youngsters in its 60 schools. Some low-income families live in the southern and eastern portions of the county; however, the northern and western ends of the county are home primarily to middle- to upper-income professional people. Approximately 60% of the children attending school in Byrd County are Caucasian, 18% are African-American, 15% are Hispanic-American, and 7% are Asian-American. Approximately 9% of the students attending Byrd County schools are bilingual.

Oak Hill Elementary is an attractive, modern school facility serving over 600 students in kindergarten through grade 5. The school has full-time art, music, and physical education teachers and a staffed, "state-of-the-art" computer lab and library. Housed within the school is a program for students with developmental delays as well as a classroom for children with severe/profound mental retardation. The school also serves 41 children with learning disabilities and 12 children with emotional disturbances/behavior disorders in resource room and regular classroom combinations.

Ms. Lopez is a special education teacher at Oak Hill Elementary. She is in her fifth year of teaching, serving as an LD/ED teacher in a cross-categorical program for children with mild disabilities. Ms. Lopez's classroom is housed in the fourth-grade wing of the building, although she works closely with members of the third-, fourth-, and fifth-grade–level teams. Most of her students are included in the regular classroom for at least 80% of the school day; therefore, Ms. Lopez often teaches in the regular classroom alongside her general education colleagues, particularly for science and social studies. For some of her students, however, she provides direct instruction in the resource room in reading, mathematics, and social skills.

Ms. Kirk, with 12 years of classroom experience, is the fourth-grade lead teacher at Oak Hill Elementary School. This year she has 27 students in her class. The walls within and immediately outside of Ms. Kirk's classroom are decorated with student work samples and projects, and the student desks and chairs are arranged in clusters of five or six. Although Ms. Kirk proudly speaks of all of her students as individuals with unique needs and abilities, four children in her class are of special concern to her.

Travis. Travis is a 9-year-old who was identified last year as a student with a learning disability. He lives with his mother (a registered nurse) and two older sisters in a comfortable, modest home about one mile from Oak Hill Elementary. Travis is of above-average intelligence, yet he reads at only the beginning second-grade level. He has difficulty decoding unknown words and reads with little comprehension. His manuscript and cursive writing are almost illegible. Although Travis can readily recall the basic addition and subtraction facts through the tens, he has problems with place value and with copying and aligning numbers. He has not yet mastered the principles of multiplication. Travis has never been retained in a grade, but according to his previous teachers, Travis seems to have trouble paying attention, and he often "tunes out" during lessons and seatwork. They state that he knows something one day and "forgets" it the next, but quickly add that he is a very polite, well-behaved child. Travis enjoys science activities and hopes someday to become a geologist. Ms. Lopez works with Travis in the resource room for approximately two hours daily to improve his reading and math skills. In addition, Ms. Lopez assists Ms. Kirk to include Travis in the regular classroom for science, social studies, health, and all other activities.

Joey. Joey is a 10-year-old boy who was retained one year in kindergarten because of poor social skills. While in the first grade, Joey continued to experience significant interpersonal problems with his peers and teachers. Following a comprehensive evaluation, Joey began to receive special education services for children with emotional disturbance/behavior disorders. Joey is constantly "on the move," out of his seat, and disrupting others. When corrected by his teachers or confronted by his peers, Joey lashes out, alternately fighting, crying, and calling them names. He is not well liked by his classmates. His papers, desk, and "personal space" are messy, and he frequently forgets or misplaces his books, homework, pencils, and other important items, which he then must "borrow" from those nearby. Joey also has difficulty with his schoolwork. Although he is of average intelligence, he functions approximately two years below grade level in all academic skills. When Joey was three years old, his twin brother died in an automobile accident. Now Joey is the only child in the family. His mother works at a local convenience store and his father works the evening shift at a factory across town. Both parents express frustration at their inability to control Joey and his temper tantrums at home. Joey sees Ms. Lopez daily in the resource room for help with reading, math, and social skills.

Celie. Celie is a new 9-year-old at Oak Hill Elementary. Her parents recently relocated to a large apartment complex in Byrd County. Celie has one younger sister and one younger brother at home. She cares for her brother and sister after school while her mother goes to a part-time job. Celie is a well-mannered child. She is of average intelligence, but there are wide gaps in her learning. Her father is a migrant laborer in the construction industry; therefore, the family has moved frequently to be near his work. Celie reads at the third-grade level, with some difficulty with fluency and comprehension, but math is particularly troublesome for her. She uses her fingers for basic addition, and she is confused by place value. Regrouping is therefore difficult for her. Her written sentences are marked by many misspelled words and by faulty punctuation. Celie dislikes reading and math; however, she enjoys art, an area in which she shows a strong talent. Celie is not in a special education program.

Kevin. Kevin is a 10-year-old boy. Like Joey, he was retained one year in kindergarten. Kevin, however, is of below-average intelligence, and he functions about two years below grade level in all academic areas. Kevin is easily frustrated with his schoolwork. He sometimes cries when he can't do his assignments or when the other children tease him. He is the "main target" for Joey, who tries to provoke Kevin's tears. Kevin's second-grade teacher referred him for testing to determine if he was eligible to receive special education services. The eligibility committee decided, however, that he did not qualify for special education or Section 504 services. Kevin lives with his mother, a beautician. His grandmother also lives with them. He does not know where his father lives, nor has he seen him for several years.

Apple County Middle School and Apple County High School

The Apple County Public School District serves approximately 2,700 children in Kindergarten through grade 12. Within the school system are three elementary schools, one middle school, and one high school. Apple County is primarily a rural, agricultural community, although some light industries (furniture and porcelain manufacture) have recently located there. Apple County Middle School enrolls about 650 children in grades 6 through 8. Apple County High School serves almost 600 students in grades 9 through 12. In both schools, the student body is approximately 60% African-American, 35% Caucasian, and 5% Hispanic-, Asian-, and Native-American.

Mr. Abel is an itinerant special education teacher who serves students at both Apple County Middle School and Apple County High School. Although he is one of seven special educators employed by the county to teach at the middle and high schools, he is the only itinerant teacher at that level. Mr. Abel grew up in Apple County and attended a nearby college to become licensed as a teacher of children with mild mental retardation. After teaching in a self-contained special education classroom for seven years, he returned to the college to earn his Master's degree, adding licensure for mild disabilities to his teaching credentials. He now divides his time between the middle school and the high school, which are in close proximity, serving a total of 18 students in a cross-categorical, special education program. Although most of his students experience learning disabilities, his caseload also includes three students with mild mental retardation.

Mr. Abel considers his position to be demanding, but he knows his students, their parents, and the community well. In addition, he works closely with several teachers at the middle school, including Ms. Booker, the sixth-grade English teacher, and Mr. Mathis, a mathematics teacher. Mr. Abel is also extremely proud of his working relationship with several teachers at the high school, including the ninth-grade earth science teacher, Ms. Stone, and the geography teacher, Mr. McNally. These teachers work hard to help all their students succeed. For five of their students, however, they have "gone the extra mile."

Susan. Susan is a 13-year-old sixth-grader with mild mental retardation. Her appearance is often unkempt. She lives in an old farmhouse with her grandmother, her 29-year-old mother, an uncle, his wife, and their three young children. Susan is performing three to four years below grade level in all academic areas. She lacks confidence in her ability to complete her assignments, often asking her teachers, "Is that right?" after each item. When she makes errors, she becomes frustrated and cries. Susan is shy and soft-spoken and she rarely interacts with her peers. At Apple County Middle School, Mr. Abel helps Susan in her mainstreamed classes, particularly in language arts with Ms. Booker and in general math with Mr. Mathis.

Leon. Leon is an 11-year-old sixth-grader attending Apple County Middle School in Ms. Booker's language arts class and in Mr. Mathis' general math class. Although Leon is of average intelligence, he is failing both classes. He is not eligible for special education or Section 504 services, however. Leon constantly "tests" his teachers. He is late to class; rarely prepared with books, homework, or other necessities; and disrespectful when addressing his teachers. Attempts to contact Leon's parents are usually unsuccessful because his mother works the evening shift at a local plant, sleeping during the day, and his father works from 7AM to 3PM at the plant before going to a second part-time job. Leon returns to an empty home after school each day.

Taylor. Taylor is an 11-year-old sixth-grader attending Apple County Middle School. She is of average intelligence; but according to her teachers, she has always had great difficulty "paying attention." She is easily distracted by noises in the classroom or hallway, and consequently takes longer than other students to complete her assignments. Although her third-grade teacher referred Taylor for testing for special education, she was not eligible for services under IDEA. When she was in the fourth grade, however, her physician diagnosed her with an attention deficit/hyperactivity disorder. Currently, Taylor takes medication to help her pay attention in school, but she is also the recipient of a Section 504 plan. Taylor's access plan specifies that she be given preferential seating to limit distractions in her classes as well as extended time to complete assignments and take all tests. Taylor has Ms. Booker for language arts and general math with Mr. Mathis.

Robert. Robert is a 15-year-old ninth-grader at Apple County High School. He has been in a program for students with learning disabilities since the third grade. Robert reads at about the fifth-grade level and performs mathematics at approximately the sixth-grade level. He has trouble with the language and organizational structure of his textbooks. Robert's spelling and handwriting are poor; consequently, he often cannot read the notes he takes in his classes. His written paragraphs are short and poorly organized, and he is a poor test-taker. Robert is earning D's and low C's in most subject areas. He sees Mr. Abel in a resource room for assistance with study skills and learning strategies. In addition, Mr. Abel helps Ms. Stone, Robert's earth science teacher, and Mr. McNally, Robert's geography teacher, to adapt tests, lectures, and assignments to meet Robert's needs. Robert is hoping to enter the program for heating and refrigeration at the local technical school. Although he is often frustrated with his schoolwork, he is a young man with a good sense of humor and supportive parents. His mother is a teacher at one of the county's elementary schools and his father owns a large orchard in the county.

Marcus. Marcus is a 14-year-old ninth-grader at Apple County High School. He receives Chapter 1 reading services from the school division, but he is failing most of his classes and is often absent from school. When he is in attendance, Marcus frequently puts his head down on his desk during class discussions and rarely participates. Marcus does not complete his homework; he cannot read the assigned textbooks. When asked what he would like to do after graduation, he responds, "I'm gonna get outta this place and work at my uncle's garage." Marcus lives with his grandmother; his parents are divorced. His father, a truck driver, is often away from home for weeks at a time. Marcus is of low to average intelligence. He has earth science with Ms. Stone and geography with Mr. McNally.

Summary

According to several national reports, America's schools fail to help many students attain adequate achievement levels. Today's schools reflect societal problems including poverty, drug use, and violence. Educational reforms such as Goals 2000 are directed at eliminating these problems and enhancing school achievement.

Some children who are struggling in school receive help in the form of special education programs for students with mild disabilities. Others receive compensatory education programs or federal assistance under Section 504. Still others receive only the assistance provided by teachers in regular classrooms.

Given proper instruction and appropriate goals, all children can learn. Instructional techniques likely to be effective with students with mild disabilities are also likely to assist children who are poor achievers but who have not been assigned to a special education program.

At Oak Hill Elementary School, Travis, Joey, Celie, and Kevin are students in Ms. Kirk's fourth-grade class. Travis and Joey receive special education services under IDEA (1997) from Ms. Lopez, their special education teacher. Celie and Kevin remain in the regular classroom and receive no special services, although the adjustments Ms. Lopez makes in Ms. Kirk's classroom on behalf of Travis and Joey often benefit Celie and Kevin as well.

In Apple County, Mr. Abel is an itinerant special education teacher serving the middle school and the high school. At Apple County Middle School, he works closely with the English teacher, Ms. Booker, and the mathematics teacher, Mr. Mathis. Susan, Leon, and Taylor, sixth-graders, are in the same English and general math classes, but only Susan reports to Mr. Abel for special education. Taylor receives assistance from Ms. Booker and Mr. Mathis in the regular classroom according to her Section 504 plan. Ms. Stone is an earth science teacher, and Mr. McNally is a geography teacher at Apple County High School. Both have Robert, a student with learning disabilities, and Marcus, a student with learning problems, in their classes. However, only Robert receives special education services from Mr. Abel, although Marcus participates in a school-wide compensatory education program funded under Chapter 1.

Application Exercises

1. Interview a classroom teacher at either the elementary or secondary level. Find out if this teacher perceives absenteeism, the drop-out rate, substance abuse, or low achievement to be a problem at his or her school. Next, interview a special education teacher at the same grade level. What similarities or differences are there in the problems perceived by these teachers?

2. Arrange to spend a day observing in an elementary- or secondary-level classroom. Count the number of boys and the number of girls in the class and compute the percentage of each. Also compute the percentage of children from various cultural, ethnic, or racial groups in the class. Next, spend a day observing in a special education class for children with mild disabilities. Compute the percentage of boys, girls, and culturally diverse students for this class. Are there differences in the student populations of these two classrooms?

3. For the elementary and secondary schools used in Questions 1 and 2, determine how many teachers, administrators, and other staff members (e.g., custodians, bus drivers, cafeteria helpers, and office staff) are from culturally or racially diverse backgrounds. What is the ratio of males to females? How might the gender or cultural/racial background of teachers, administrators, and staff affect how these individuals interact with students? Are any students in the school you observed receiving Section 504 plans or attending Chapter 1 programs? Describe the special services provided in the school.

4. Consult the resources on the World Wide Web listed in Box 1.1. What information would be important for you to include in a workshop to be presented to classroom teachers? Why?
5. Using InfoTrac, an online service provided by Wadsworth, locate one article regarding each of the following pieces of legislation: IDEA (1997), Section 504, ADA, or Goals 2000. Give a short summary of the article and a carefully considered reaction to its contents. What new information did you learn?

LEARNERS WITH MILD DISABILITIES

Focus

As you read, think about the following questions:

◆ *Do children with mild disabilities differ from their low-achieving peers?*

◆ *What are the major cognitive, academic, and social-emotional characteristics shared by children with mild disabilities?*

◆ *How does knowledge of the characteristics of children with mild disabilities help teachers make decisions about curriculum or instruction?*

◆ *What information must be included on the student's Individualized Education Program?*

Learners with mild disabilities exhibit a wide variety of characteristics. Accordingly, the reader should keep in mind that not all of the characteristics discussed in this chapter will apply to every child having difficulty in school. Moreover, each characteristic may affect a child's performance to varying degrees. Nevertheless, when planning instruction, the teacher may find it helpful to keep in mind those characteristics representative of many children who have mild disabilities, as well as those children with low achievement who are not so labeled. Consider, for example, the following conversation between Ms. Kirk and Ms. Lopez:

Ms. Kirk: I am concerned about Travis, particularly his inability to pay attention. He takes such a long time to get started and to finish his work. I'm afraid he might fall even further behind the other children in my classroom. I do have other children, though, who have at least as much difficulty keeping up as Travis does.

Ms. Lopez: I noticed that the desks in your classroom are arranged in groups. Is there another child in the group who could be paired with Travis to help get him started and to answer his questions?

Ms. Kirk: That's not a bad idea. I have another child who has trouble staying on task, and a buddy system helped him. You know, that student isn't in any type of special education program; yet, he's a lot like Travis in several ways. Often, I don't see the difference between a child like Travis and my other boy. Anyway, the same teaching methods seem to help them both. So, what's the difference?

Special education teachers often hear similar comments and questions from the regular classroom teacher: "She does better than several of the other children not in special education. What's the difference?" Let's examine the issues surrounding this situation.

Services, Labels, and Children with Mild Disabilities

Although IDEA (1997) entitles students with various disabilities such as visual or hearing impairments, autism, and traumatic brain injury to a free appropriate public education, the vast majority of children in special education programs are considered to have mild disabilities and are placed for most of the school day in either the regular classroom or a combination of the regular classroom and the special education resource room (U.S. Department of Education, 1997). Typically, these are children with learning disabilities, mild mental retardation, or emotional/behavioral disorders as defined under IDEA (1997). (See Box 2.1 for the current IDEA definitions for each of these categories.)

Approximately 44% of all students aged 6-21 with learning disabilities are in the regular classroom for at least 80% of the school day, and another 39.5% are in a combination of the regular classroom and the resource room (U.S. Department of Education, 1997). Only 18.4% of all students with learning disabilities are in separate special education classes. Students with emotional disturbance/behavioral disorders are also likely to be in the regular classroom or in the resource room (22% and 25%, respectively, of children aged 6-21 with E/BD). Children and youth with mental retardation, however, are still served more

Box 2.1

Current Definitions

The most widely accepted definitions for mental retardation, learning disabilities, and emotional disturbance are those set forth in IDEA, 1997 (Public Law 105-17). Although each has been criticized for various reasons, these are the definitions currently governing most services and programs for children with mild disabilities.

Mental Retardation

"Mental retardation refers to significantly subaverage general intellectual functioning existing concurrently with deficits in adaptive behavior and manifested during the developmental period" (Grossman, 1983, p.11.). In order to define mental retardation as a disability specially affecting a child's progress in school, IDEA (1997) adds to the end of the Grossman definition the phrase "that adversely affects a child's educational performance." Although IDEA relies on the Grossman definition, the American Association on Mental Retardation published a new definition in 1992 that places greater emphasis on behavioral competence than Grossman's definition did: "Mental retardation refers to substantial limitations in present functioning. It is characterized by significantly subaverage intellectual functioning, existing concurrently with related limitations in two or more of the following applicable adaptive skill areas: communication, self-care, home living, social skills, community use, self-direction, health and safety, functional academics, leisure, and work. Mental retardation manifests before age 18" (Luckasson et al., 1992, p.1).

Learning Disabilities

"Specific learning disability means a disorder in one or more of the basic psychological processes involved in understanding or in using language, spoken or written, which disorder may manifest itself in an imperfect ability to listen, think, speak, read, write, spell, or do mathematical calculations. Such term includes such conditions as perceptual disabilities, brain injury, minimal brain dysfunction, dyslexia, and developmental aphasia. Such term does not include a learning problem that is primarily the result of visual, hearing, or motor disabilities, of mental retardation, of emotional disturbance, or of environmental, cultural, or economic disadvantage" (IDEA, 1997, SEC.602.26).

(The interested reader is referred also to Hammill, 1990, and to Hammill, Leigh, McNutt, & Larsen, 1981, for discussion of issues surrounding the federal definition of learning disabilities and for an alternative definition proposed by the National Joint Committee on Learning Disabilities.)

Emotionally Disturbed

I. The term means a condition exhibiting one or more of the following characteristics over a long period of time and to a marked degree that adversely affects a student's educational performance:

A. An inability to learn that cannot be explained by intellectual, sensory, or health factors;

B. An inability to build or maintain satisfactory interpersonal relationships with peers and teachers;

C. Inappropriate types of behavior or feelings under normal circumstances;

D. A general pervasive mood of unhappiness or depression; or

E. A tendency to develop physical symptoms or fears associated with personal or school problems.

II. The term includes children who are schizophrenic. The term does not include children who are socially maladjusted unless it is determined that they are seriously emotionally disturbed (IDEA, 1997).

(The interested reader is referred also to Kauffman, 1997, for a discussion of the issues surrounding the federal definition of emotional disturbance and its origin. In addition, the reader may wish to consult the Council for Children With Behavior Disorders Newsletter, February, 1991, available from the Council for Exceptional Children in Reston, Virginia, for a new definition of emotional disturbance/behavioral disorders proposed by the National Mental Health and Special Education Coalition.)

often in separate special education classrooms (55.26%) than in the regular classroom or the resource room (a total of approximately 37%).

The *regular classroom, resource room,* or *separate special education classroom* are terms used to describe the primary setting in which instruction takes place for students with mild disabilities. Consequently, the terms are also often used to refer to the role assumed by the special education teacher (e.g., a resource room teacher, a collaborative teacher, or a self-contained teacher). (See Table 2.1 for a description of special education services and teacher roles.) Teachers should not automatically assume, however, that the regular classroom, the resource room, or the self-contained special education classroom are the only services appropriate for students with mild disabilities. For some students, "mild" disabilities represent significant impairments requiring special schools or even residential facilities (U.S. Department of Education, 1997). The Individuals with Disabilities Education Act Amendments (1997) require that a continuum of service options be available to meet the unique needs of individual students in special education programs. That is, students with disabilities are to be educated in the Least Restrictive Environment (LRE): the setting in which the child can receive an appropriate education that is, to the maximum extent possible, alongside peers without disabilities.

Labeling a child, however, may not accomplish very much. In fact, it may do little more than grant that child access to special education services. Labels and terms used to describe special education services tell the teacher little about a child's instructional needs. For example, a child with a learning disability may have difficulty in certain academic areas, but no attendant behavioral problems. Another child with a learning disability may exhibit severe attentional and behavioral problems in addition to academic deficits, necessitating more intensive educational programming (McKinney, 1987). Children within a categorical area of special education may differ from one another as much as they differ from those youngsters in other categories.

In fact, the categories of learning disabilities, mild mental retardation, and emotional disturbance overlap considerably (Hallahan & Kauffman, 1977;

Table 2.1   Special Education Services and Teacher Roles

Service	Description	Role of Special Educator
Regular Class	Student is in the regular classroom at least 80% of the school day.	Consult with regular teacher to adapt material or instruction. May engage in coteaching or collaborative teaching with regular teacher.
Resource Room	Student is in the regular classroom most of the day (less than 80% but more than 60%) but spends some time with the special educator daily or weekly, depending upon individual student needs.	Provides instruction in basic academic/social skills or learning strategies. Consults with regular teacher to adapt materials and/or instruction. May also engage in coteaching or collaborative teaching with regular teacher for part of the school day.
Self-Contained Classroom (part-time & full-time classes in the regular school)	Part-time: Student is in a special education class more than 60% of the day for one or more academic areas but may be in regular classrooms for art, music, P.E., etc. Full-time: Student receives all instruction in the special education classroom.	Provides instruction in all academic subject areas. May consult with regular teacher to adapt materials and/or instruction in regular classroom. Integrates learning through community-based instruction.
Special Day School	Student attends a special school for more than 50% of the school day.	Provides instruction in all areas, integrating community-based learning experiences.

Henley, Ramsey, & Algozzine, 1996). Some authorities argue that children within these three groups cannot be reliably distinguished from one another using the present federal definitions and psychometric testing practices (Gresham, MacMillan, & Bocian, 1996; Halgren & Clarizio, 1993; MacMillan, Gresham, Bocian, & Lambros, 1998; Reynolds & Heistad, 1997; Ysseldyke, 1987). For example, young children eventually identified by the schools as having emotional/behavioral disorders may first have been identified as children with learning disabilities (Duncan, Forness, & Hartsough, 1995; Forness et al., 1998). Moreover, 53% of students with emotional/behavioral disorders meet at least one of the definitions of learning disability commonly used by the schools (Glassberg, Hooper, & Mattison, 1999). Furthermore, assigning a child to a particular category of special education does not mean that the youngster will receive instruction that is vastly different from that received by children bearing other diagnostic labels.

This may be particularly true for those students receiving the bulk of their education in the regular classroom (Espin, Deno, & Albayrak-Kaymak, 1998; Smith, 1990; Zigmond & Baker, 1995). Despite many years of study, researchers are unable to prescribe teaching approaches that differ substantially from one another based solely on the labels assigned to students in different special education categories (Allington & McGill-Franzen, 1989; Bender, Scott, & McLaughlin, 1993; Lloyd, 1984; Ysseldyke, O'Sullivan, Thurlow, & Christenson, 1989).

Although they have been the focus of considerable research, children with mild disabilities are also difficult to distinguish from other low-achieving children not placed in special education programs (Algozzine & Korinek, 1985; Reynolds & Heistad, 1997). For example, students with *borderline intelligence* (those with IQ's between 70 and 85) often are not eligible for special education services as students with mild mental retardation or learning disabilities, yet they present significant learning and behavioral problems in the classroom (MacMillan, Gresham, Bocian, & Lambros, 1998). Also, students with learning disabilities are not reliably distinguished from other students with low achievement, sharing approximately a 37% degree of overlap (Kavale, Fuchs, & Scruggs, 1994). Such findings have led some researchers to call students with learning disabilities the "lowest of the low achievers" (Algozzine, Ysseldyke, & McGue, 1995), although others suggest that these students might have qualitative differences in learning or behavior distinguishing them from their low-achieving counterparts (Kavale, 1995).

Regardless of how students are labeled, effective teaching methods for children with mild disabilities do not differ substantially from those likely to help youngsters who are having difficulty in school but who are not placed in special education (Christenson, Ysseldyke, & Thurlow, 1989; Fister & Kemp, 1993; Slavin, Karweit, & Madden, 1989). This statement must not be misinterpreted as meaning that all students will succeed given identical instruction, identical goals, or placement in the regular classroom. Some authorities rightfully argue that the curriculum or the intensity of instruction may need to be altered for many students with mild disabilities, even though the teaching methods may not differ (Beirne-Smith, Ittenbach, & Patton, 1998; Fuchs & Fuchs, 1995). For some students the "mild disability" represents a significant problem affecting all aspects of the child's life. Such difficulties may require a more functional orientation to the curriculum (e.g., teaching daily living skills or social skills) or a greater degree of intensity and specificity during instruction than that typically found in the regular classroom (Baker & Zigmond, 1995).

Nevertheless, for most students with mild disabilities, instruction takes place primarily in the regular classroom, within the general education curriculum (IDEA, 1997). As school reform continues and performance standards increase, the special and regular education teachers must work together to provide the most powerful teaching techniques available to assist all students having difficulty. Knowledge of shared characteristics, then, may enable teachers to make better instructional decisions for students with mild disabilities as well as for other children who are having difficulty. Let's now consider the nature of those cognitive, academic, and social-emotional characteristics that youngsters with mild disabilities and others struggling to learn have in common.

Cognitive Characteristics

Cognition generally refers to processes involved in thinking. Students with mild disabilities may have below-average intellectual ability, and they may have difficulty maintaining or focusing attention, and/or organizing and retrieving information from memory. Although each of these problems may affect the child to varying degrees, all may result in less efficient learning for the youngster with learning disabilities, emotional/behavioral disorders, or mild mental retardation.

Intellectual Ability

Children with mild disabilities may vary widely with respect to intellectual ability. By definition, children with mental retardation are substantially below average in general intellectual functioning and have difficulty adapting their behavior in order to function competently in their environment (Grossman, 1983). More specifically, in addition to limitations in adaptive behaviors, these youngsters usually score near or below 70-75 IQ points on a standardized test of intelligence. Students with learning disabilities, on the other hand, are generally thought to have intellectual ability within the average, or even above-average, range (i.e., an IQ score of 85 or above on a standardized test of intelligence). But despite adequate intelligence, youngsters with learning disabilities do not do well in many academic areas. Authorities debate how, or even whether or not, to measure this discrepancy between IQ and achievement as a defining characteristic of learning disabilities (Bateman, 1992; Fletcher et al., 1998). Others refute the notion that learning disabilities and mental retardation cannot occur concomitantly (Hammill, 1990; Hammill, Leigh, McNutt, & Larsen, 1981; National Joint Committee on Learning Disabilities, 1988). Finally, children with emotional disturbance/behavior disorders demonstrate an inability to learn that cannot be explained by intellectual factors (Bower, 1981; IDEA, 1997). Thus, for children having "mild" behavior disorders, adequate intellectual ability is implied within the definition.

In practice, however, there is considerable overlap in intellectual ability across these three special education categories. For example, children with IQ scores in the below-average range may sometimes be considered for identification as learning disabled if they exhibit no impairments in their adaptive behavior, but show a discrepancy between their ability and their actual achievement (Frankenberger & Fronzaglio, 1991; MacMillan, Gresham, Bocian, & Lambros, 1998). Furthermore, children with mild to moderate emotional disturbances score anywhere from the range of mental retardation to giftedness on intelligence tests, with the majority having tested IQs in the slightly below-average range (Kauffman, 1997).

More recently, the construct of "intelligence" has been broadened. Gardner and Hatch (1989), for example, argue that there are at least seven different types of intelligence—logical-mathematical, linguistic, musical, spatial, bodily-kinesthetic, interpersonal, and intrapersonal—not all of which are tapped by traditional IQ tests. Sternberg (1997), too, asserts that students may demonstrate analytical, practical, or creative intelligence. These authorities suggest that all students may show distinctive patterns of strengths and weaknesses across several areas of intellectual ability. New definitions of intelligence like these increase the importance over tested IQ of a child's actual performance and ability to function in the regular classroom environment. The American Association on Mental Retardation's latest definition of mental retardation (Luckasson et al., 1992), as well as recent performance models for identifying learning disabilities (Fuchs & Fuchs, 1998; Torgesen & Wagner, 1998), emphasize this shift toward deemphasizing traditional intelligence tests when determining children eligible for special education. As a matter of fact, some authorities suggest that IQ is inconsequential, or even irrelevant, in the "real world" of special education students in the classroom (Forness, Keogh, MacMillan, Kavale, & Gresham, 1998; MacMillan & Forness, 1998).

Knowledge of the categorical label, then, gives the teacher little information about either the child's intellectual ability or actual performance in the classroom. In addition, the teacher must be careful not to limit the child who has a relatively low IQ score by automatically assuming that the child has a reduced capacity to learn. Simply knowing an IQ score tells the teacher very little about how or what a child may learn. Nevertheless, because IQ tests are correlated with academic achievement, children scoring in the below-average range of intelligence often experience more academic failure than those scoring higher.

Attentional Deficits

Children with mild disabilities often exhibit attentional deficits that affect their progress in the classroom. For example, many youngsters who have attentional problems are hyperactive, impulsive, or inattentive. These behaviors are detrimental to classroom adjustment and to school achievement (American Psychiatric Association, 1994). The American Psychiatric Association (1994) lists the following major criteria for Attention Deficit/Hyperactivity Disorder (ADHD):

◆ Severity: The child's attention deficit/hyperactivity symptoms must be more severe and frequent than those of other children at the same developmental level;
◆ Some of the child's symptoms must have been evident before age seven; and,
◆ The child's behaviors must have persisted for at least six months before the diagnosis of ADHD.

In addition, the APA (1994) suggests that children may exhibit an attention deficit/hyperactivity disorder that is of two types: a) the Predominantly Inattentive Type (e.g., the child makes careless mistakes, doesn't appear to listen when directly spoken to, has difficulty organizing and completing activities, has problems sustaining attention, is easily distracted, etc.); or b) the Predominantly Hyperactive-Impulsive Type (e.g., the child fidgets, leaves his/her seat, runs or climbs about excessively, is constantly "on the go," has difficulty waiting his/her turn, or frequently interrupts others). Most children with attention deficit/hyperactivity disorder, however, are of the Combined Type, evidencing at least six of the listed behavioral symptoms for both the Inattentive and Hyperactive-Impulsive types of disorders.

According to the APA (1994), between three and five percent of the school-aged population may have an attention deficit/hyperactivity disorder. Some of these students are eligible for special education services under IDEA (1997), often as children with learning disabilities or emotional/behavioral disorders. Authorities estimate that 20% to 30% of students with learning disabilities also have attention deficit/hyperactivity disorder (Riccio, Gonzalez, & Hynd, 1994). Moreover, as many as 52% of the school-identified children with emotional/behavioral disorders also have ADHD (Reid, Maag, Vasa, & Wright, 1994). Other children with attention deficit/hyperactivity disorder may not meet the eligibility criteria under IDEA, Part B (1997); however, they may still qualify for assistance according to Section 504 of the Rehabilitation Act Amendments of 1975 if their learning is substantially limited. Children identified as ADHD alone, though, may have less severe impairments than those identified with both attention deficit/hyperactivity disorder and a learning disability or emotional disturbance (Bussing, Zima, Belin, & Forness, 1998).

Some children with mild disabilities may experience difficulty coming to attention and focusing on the task at hand. Others may respond impulsively, not considering all the alternatives to a problem, or they may have trouble paying attention long enough to complete a task. (See Box 2.2.) Consequently, children with mild disabilities may make errors on assignments, or find themselves in troublesome situations in the classroom more frequently than their peers. Finally, some youngsters with mild disabilities, particularly those with mild mental retardation, may have difficulty attending to more than one part of a task at a time (Brooks & McCauley, 1984). For example, the student who is devoting a considerable amount of attention to decoding words on a page may have little attention left to remember and comprehend what was read. Therefore, teachers must construct tasks so that relevant features are emphasized, and they must reward their students for paying attention.

Memory and Thinking Skills

Paying attention is only the first step in learning. Students must also organize information in meaningful ways so that it can be stored in memory and used to solve problems. Children with mild disabilities often have considerable difficulty organizing and retrieving information from memory in a purposeful manner. Some children cannot retain information in short-term memory immediately after hearing or seeing it. Others have difficulty using their working memory to hold something in mind while simultaneously receiving additional information (e.g., a child may have trouble keeping the first event in a story in mind while hearing the second and third events) (Ashbaker & Swanson, 1996; Swanson, 1994).

One reason for this difficulty is that many youngsters with mild disabilities are not aware of those strategies their peers often use to help themselves organize and remember important information (Forness & Kavale, 1993; Reid, Hresko, & Swanson, 1996; Scruggs & Laufenberg, 1986; Torgesen & Kail, 1980). For example, they do not spontaneously use such techniques as verbal rehearsal

Box 2.2

According to his teachers, Travis often has difficulty paying attention. He "tunes out" during lessons and has trouble maintaining his attention when completing seatwork. Let's observe Travis while he is working on a math assignment in his fourth-grade class:

Ms. Kirk: Let's do the first problem on the practice sheet together. Now, 1/7 + 3/7 = _____. What's the first thing to do, Tammy? Right! Check the denominators. They are both seven. So, what do I do next, Travis? (Noticing Travis has been rubbing his pencil eraser with his finger and examining the pieces of rubber) Travis, please put your pencil down. Now, look at the problem. (Pointing) The denominators are both the same, seven. So, what do I do next?

Travis: You add the top numbers together and leave the bottom the same.

Ms. Kirk: Good job. One plus three equals four. So the answer is four sevenths (Writing 4/7). Now, you do the rest. You have ten minutes before we get ready for lunch.

Travis: (Looks at his paper and fills in all of the denominators across the first row of five problems. When Peter at Travis's cluster of tables begins to erase a problem, Travis watches him. He then examines his own eraser and begins to erase marks off the top of his desk.)

Ms. Kirk: (Noticing Travis playing with his eraser again, Ms. Kirk moves to Travis's table and touches his paper.) Travis, you need to finish the practice sheet before lunch. Look at the second problem (Pointing). You have the correct denominator. Now, what is the numerator? (Travis writes the correct answer.) Good job, Travis! Now, do the next problem and keep on working. Let's see if you can do the first two rows before I come back. (Ms. Kirk moves on to another student.)

Travis: (Writes answers quickly to the next five problems. However, when he lays his pencil down to get a tissue from his pocket, the pencil rolls off his desk. He crawls under his chair to get the pencil, finds the point broken, and is off to the pencil sharpener . . .)

(i.e., repeating to oneself, aloud or silently, something to be remembered) or clustering (i.e., organizing material into small chunks containing similar items). When taught to use such strategies, however, the memory performance of many children with mild disabilities improves significantly (Hallahan, Kauffman, & Lloyd, 1985; Beirne-Smith, Ittenbach, & Patton, 1998).

A related factor contributing to the memory deficits of youngsters with mild disabilities is metacognition (Flavell, 1979). *Metacognition* means knowledge about one's own thought processes and learning. It involves not only an awareness of the strategies and skills necessary to accomplish a task effectively, but also the ability to monitor one's performance while completing the task. For example, as you read a paragraph, you may monitor your own comprehension and reread certain sentences when you encounter new words or difficult concepts, or you might construct a first-letter acronym (e.g., HOMES) to help you remember the names of the Great Lakes for a geography test. Although many children with mild disabilities do not spontaneously use metacognitive processes to direct and monitor their learning, they can be taught to employ these skills. Teachers must model effective problem-solving and/or memory strategies during lessons, explicitly show students how and where to use these strategies, and reward students for using them appropriately (Deshler & Schumaker, 1988). (See Box 2.3.)

Academic Characteristics

The most widely shared characteristic of students with mild disabilities is academic difficulty. Although some children have deficits in only one or two specific academic areas, other youngsters have significant and pervasive difficulty in all areas of academic endeavor, particularly in reading, the language arts, and mathematics.

Reading

Without a doubt, the academic area in which children with mild disabilities most often encounter failure is reading. Their reading difficulties include phonological, syntactic, and semantic problems that hinder their ability to become fluent readers. For example, students with underlying phonological deficits, which involve the inability to detect and remember sounds in spoken language, may later exhibit weak segmentation and sound-blending skills when attempting to decode new words (Samuels, 1988). Phonological awareness, then, is a strong, albeit not the only, predictor of average to superior reading achievement (Committee on the Prevention of Reading Difficulties in Young Children, 1998; Scarborough, 1998).

Other youngsters have syntactic deficits, involving an inability to cluster words into meaningful phrases on the basis of sentence structure (Wiig, 1990). For other children, semantic problems, such as not being able to remember new vocabulary or to understand the use of figurative language, reduce comprehension of what is read. In addition, some students experience difficulty when asked to identify relationships among sentences and/or paragraphs, especially when this information must be inferred. They are hard-pressed, for example, to distinguish between main ideas and supporting details. Moreover, these deficits in reading affect performance in all other academic areas, particularly as students in the secondary grades are expected to read expository text for content (Stanovich, 1986).

Special educators must provide systematic and repeated practice in the basic phonological, decoding, and comprehension skills, coordinated with instruction in the regular classroom, if their students are to be successful and independent readers. In addition, teachers must take care not to penalize students with poor reading skills by basing content-area instruction primarily on textbook reading assignments.

Language Arts

In addition to reading, the language arts encompass listening, speaking, spelling, handwriting, and composing skills. Children with mild disabilities experience more difficulty with oral expression and listening comprehension than do nondisabled peers (Wiig, 1990). They are also likely to have numerous problems with written expression. Illegible handwriting and/or a slow writing speed hinder the process of composing, as well as assignment completion and note taking in the regular classroom (Berninger & Stage, 1996; Graham, 1990; Isaacson & Gleason, 1997; Weintraub & Graham, 1998). In addition, students with mild disabilities may have difficulty remembering the written equivalents for letter sounds or using phonetic rules to spell words correctly (Carpenter, 1983), and they may make frequent punctuation, capitalization, and word-usage errors (Deno, Marston, & Mirkin, 1982). Mechanical errors such as these influence how acceptable written products are to teachers (Graham, 1992). Finally, students with mild disabilities may have difficulty grasping the purpose for writing or understanding the needs of the reader (Englert, Raphael, Fear, & Anderson, 1988), or they may have trouble generating content, planning written products, and producing and revising written text (Graham, Harris, & Sawyer, 1987; Isaacson, 1987).

Children with mild disabilities need frequent, real-life writing experiences with many opportunities to plan, revise, and edit their work. They also need direct instruction in specific writing skills and strategies. Teachers must nevertheless provide alternatives to written assignments when the goal of instruction is not writing skill, but rather the demonstration of content-area knowledge.

Mathematics

Many students with mild disabilities also have trouble with mathematics. Among the difficulties these youngsters experience are problems remembering basic arithmetic facts and the meaning of mathematical symbols, understanding place value, performing operations using fractions and decimals, and following the steps in complicated mathematical tasks like long division (Cawley, Parmar, Yan, & Miller, 1996; Wallace & McLoughlin, 1988). In addition, children with mild disabilities are likely to experience difficulty solving arithmetic word problems and understanding concepts of time and money (Cawley & Parmar, 1992; Horton, Lovitt, & White, 1992; Jitendra & Xin, 1997). Teachers must provide sequenced instruction, frequent practice opportunities, feedback, and explicit strategies for problem-solving if their special education students are to master mathematical skills (Mastropieri, Scruggs, & Shiah, 1991). Teachers must also show their students where and when to apply mathematical skills, monitor student progress, and reward youngsters for using new skills appropriately (Lloyd & Keller, 1989; Mercer & Miller, 1992).

Social-Emotional Characteristics

Children with mild disabilities may not be able to interact appropriately with their peers and teachers. For example, some youngsters with mild mental retardation may not share play or work materials with others (Siperstein & Leffert, 1999), or they may evidence behaviors associated with loneliness and depression (Heiman & Margalit, 1998). Although students with learning disabilities may not exhibit depression more often than their peers (Maag & Reid, 1994), they may misinterpret social cues and the feelings of others (Weiss, 1984). They may also choose less effective solutions to social problems than do their peers (Tur-Kaspa & Bryan, 1994). Consequently, they may violate social norms or respond inappropriately to those around them, further isolating themselves from their classmates. Children with behavioral disorders also have difficulty building and maintaining interpersonal relationships, and can exhibit extreme behavioral excesses and deficiencies when compared with their peers (Kauffman, 1997).

In addition, some children with mild disabilities tend to be less task-oriented, more distractable, and less independent than their nondisabled counterparts (McKinney, 1989). Such "off-task" behaviors are problematic in the classroom and are often considered disruptive and intolerable by the regular classroom teacher (Ysseldyke, Algozzine, & Thurlow, 1992). Moreover, some students may exhibit disruptive behavior in order to escape or avoid academic demands they believe they cannot meet (Shores, Gunter, Denny, & Jack, 1993). In fact, studies

Box 2.4

Susan lacks confidence in her ability. She is very dependent on others for help, even when she is capable of performing a task on her own. In general math class, with Mr. Mathis, Susan is afraid she will make errors:

Mr. Mathis: (Pointing to the overhead projector he has been using during his lesson) Okay, everyone, you've done a good job helping me fill out these checks. Now, it's your turn to fill out a check. Look at the first check on your worksheet. What goes on the first line, Bob? Yes, today's date. Write in the date, everybody.

Susan: (Raising her hand) I don't understand.

Mr. Mathis: (Pointing) We write today's date on this line. What is today's date?

Susan: October 25, 2000.

Mr. Mathis: That's right. It's written on the board. Now, you write it on your check.

Susan: (Copies the date from the board and raises her hand) Is this right?

Mr. Mathis: (Looks at Susan and nods his head) Now, everyone, let's make this check out to the Surprise Shop (Writes it on the board). Write "Surprise Shop" next to "Pay to the order of" on your check.

Susan: (Looking around at the others and then at the board, she begins to copy "Surprise Shop" on her check. Halfway through her copying, she looks up, looks around at the others, and then raises her hand.) Is this right?

show that teachers often avoid instructional interactions with students demonstrating undesirable behaviors and pay more attention to inappropriate conduct than to appropriate behavior (Gunter & Coutinho, 1997). Special educators must prepare students to handle not only the academic expectations of the regular classroom but also the social expectations if their mainstreaming efforts are to be successful (Downing, Simpson, & Myles, 1990).

Youngsters with mild disabilities may also hold maladaptive beliefs about themselves and their abilities. Many students in special education programs suffer from low self-esteem or a poor academic self-concept (Stanovich, Jordan, & Perot, 1998). They question their academic competence and depend on others for help with tasks that they are capable of performing independently (Bryan, 1986). (See Box 2.4.) Some children with mild disabilities have an external locus of control, believing situations in their lives to be the result of such uncontrollable forces as chance. Children who have an external locus of control do not take responsibility for their successes, but often ascribe their failures to low ability (Bryan, 1986). Such youngsters exhibit "learned helplessness" (Abramson, Seligman, & Teasdale, 1978), giving up easily in the face of even small difficulties because of their belief that no amount of effort will prevent their failure. Many students with mild disabilities are at risk of entering a vicious cycle of failure: doubt regarding their ability to succeed, lack of effort when faced with a task perceived to be difficult, subsequent failure "confirming" their lack of ability, and increased expectancy of failure in the future (Licht, 1984). Therefore, teachers must construct tasks to demonstrate that success is attainable, and they must reward students for accomplishments resulting from appropriate effort.

Individualizing Instruction

The teacher must remember that each student, including the student with mild disabilities, is a unique individual. As mentioned earlier in this chapter, knowledge of a student's special education label gives the teacher very little information regarding how best to teach that child. However, a basic understanding of the major cognitive, academic, and social-emotional characteristics often displayed by problem learners can provide a starting point for anticipating the kind of instruction they might require. (In addition to the web sites listed in Chapter 1, see Box 2.5 for other web sites offering information on specific characteristics of students with mild disabilities.) The teacher must then consider the skills, abilities, and behaviors demonstrated by the individual child and design instruction tailored to that youngster's unique characteristics and needs. For some students with mild disabilities, the curriculum and instruction received in the regular classroom will suffice if some adjustments are made by the teacher. For those who are experiencing significant behavioral, motivational, or academic difficulties, however, the curriculum must be altered to emphasize daily living and social skills. For each student, joint planning and instruction by the regular and special educator will be necessary to keep the child in the regular classroom as much as possible. Such individualized instruction is essential for mainstreamed students with mild disabilities, and is equally helpful for other youngsters with low achievement who are not placed in any special education program.

This does not mean, however, that every child in the regular or special education classroom must be provided with one-on-one instruction. For example, children at similar skill levels may be grouped for instruction in a particular area of need, regardless of a categorical label. Similarly, the student with a mild disability, or the learner with no disability but other special needs, may be paired with another child for assistance or placed in a cooperative learning group in which all students share responsibility for helping one another to succeed (Slavin, Karweit, & Madden, 1989). Teachers can also adapt instruction to the unique needs of their students with mild disabilities or low achievement. For example, the teacher may give students a photocopied outline of a lesson for them to fill in while he or she completes an identical outline on the overhead projector. Or the teacher can modify assignments, perhaps by altering the number of problems for practice in mathematics. Teachers must begin by using those instructional techniques likely to be successful with most students with mild disabilities, and then adjust the type and intensity of instruction to suit the individual child.

Teachers must realize, however, that intensive, individualized instruction appropriate to the unique needs of some children with mild disabilities may be

Box 2.5

Web Watch

American Association on Mental Retardation

http://www.aamr.org
Major organization for professionals interested in mental retardation; links to other related sites.

American Psychological Association

http://www.psych.org
The homepage for the major professional association for psychology; information on behavior disorders and attention deficit/hyperactivity disorders; links to other related sites and resources.

Children and Adults with Attention Deficit Disorders

http://www.chadd.org
Information on legislation and resources related to attention deficit/hyperactivity disorders.

Learning Disabilities Association

http://www.ldanatl.org
Information on characteristics of students with learning disabilities; publications and resources; links to other sites related to learning disabilities.

LD Online: The Learning Disabilities Project

http://www.ldonline.org
Information for parents, teachers, and children regarding learning disabilities and attention deficit/hyperactivity disorder.

Pacer Center

http://www.pacer.org
Information for parents, teachers, and other professionals serving children with emotional and/or behavioral disorders.

The ARC

http://www.thearc.org
Originally called the Association for Retarded Citizens, the ARC is a major association for parents and volunteers interested in mental retardation; information on mental retardation, legislation, and programs; links to related sites.

quite difficult to achieve in the regular classroom. In fact, Baker and Zigmond (1995) observed very little "specific, directed, individualized, intensive, remedial instruction of students who were clearly deficient academically and struggling with the schoolwork they were being given" (p.178) in inclusive, regular classroom settings. Similarly, other researchers suggest that students in resource room settings may receive instruction more closely tailored to their needs than those in regular class placements (Espin, Deno, & Albayrak-Kaymak, 1998). Clearly, if students continue to fail within the general education program, teachers must examine not only the appropriateness of the classroom environment but also the nature of the instruction being provided.

The Individualized Education Program

Under IDEA (1997), the primary vehicle for implementing an appropriate education for students with mild disabilities is the Individualized Education Program, or IEP. When a child is determined to be eligible for special education services, a multidisciplinary team that includes the child's parents, a classroom teacher, a special educator, and, whenever possible, the child, must develop the IEP before special education services can begin. The IEP is a written document negotiated by members of the IEP team detailing the special education and related services to be provided. (See Appendix B for sample IEPs.)

According to IDEA (1997), the IEP must contain the following information:

- ◆ A statement of the child's present levels of educational performance including how the child's disability affects his/her involvement and progress in the general curriculum.
- ◆ A statement of measurable annual goals and short-term objectives to meet the child's needs.
- ◆ A statement of the special education and related services and supplementary aids and services to be provided to the child, or on behalf of the child.
- ◆ A statement of program modifications or supports that will be provided to help the child to advance appropriately toward attaining the annual goals and to be involved in the general curriculum or extracurricular activities with other children with and without disabilities.
- ◆ An explanation of the extent, if any, to which the child will not participate with nondisabled children in the regular class.
- ◆ A statement of whether or not the child will participate in state- or district-wide assessment of student achievement and either a justification of why the assessment is not appropriate for the child or an explanation of any individual modifications that will be necessary in order for the child to participate.
- ◆ The projected date for the beginning of the services and the anticipated frequency, location, and duration of those services.
- ◆ A statement of how the child's progress toward the annual goals will be measured and of how the child's parents will be regularly informed at least as often as parents of children without disabilities are informed of their child's progress.

Classroom teachers, special educators, and parents must work together to design an individualized program based on the unique characteristics and needs of the child in special education. The IEP is intended to be an essential tool for ensuring that each student who has a mild disability will receive an appropriate education alongside his or her nondisabled peers. Services, curriculum, and effective instruction are three critical variables to be considered by the IEP team in order to ensure that the child is receiving quality instruction and making reasonable progress toward appropriate goals and objectives.

Summary

Children with mild disabilities exhibit numerous cognitive, academic, and social-emotional characteristics. Some students with mild disabilities have below-average intellectual ability, while others have average or above-average intelligence. Many children with learning disabilities, emotional disturbances, or mild mental retardation exhibit memory deficits or attentional problems. These students may not focus on the task at hand, or they may fail to make use of problem-solving strategies that come naturally to their peers. Almost all students with mild disabilities have academic deficits in reading, the language arts, and/or mathematics. Such difficulties range from only minor problems in one academic area to significant and pervasive deficiencies in all academic areas, often in combination with attentional or behavioral troubles. Many youngsters with mild disabilities suffer from low self-esteem. They may find it difficult to build and maintain satisfying interpersonal relationships with peers and teachers.

Knowledge of shared characteristics among children with mild disabilities represents only a starting point for instructional planning. Students in special education programs differ from one another as much as they differ from their nondisabled peers. The IEP is the means for determining an appropriate and individualized education for each child in special education. Teachers, however, must design instruction to meet the individual needs of each learner regardless of whether the child has a disability. In addition, teachers must consistently focus on the whole child as an individual with interests and strengths that can be used to enhance learning.

Application Exercises

1. Interview a regular classroom teacher at a chosen grade level who has at least one child with a mild disability mainstreamed in his/her class. What are the major cognitive, academic, and social-emotional needs of the special student(s)? Be certain not to use names or identifying information when presenting your answers to this question. (Note: IDEA, [1997] requires that information about children in special education programs remain confidential.) What differences, if any, does this teacher see between the student(s) with mild disabilities and other children with low achievement in the classroom?

2. What are some common characteristics shared by Travis, Joey, Celie, and Kevin? How might these shared characteristics serve as a starting point for instructional planning?

3. What are the identification criteria used by your local public school district for determining eligibility for special education services for students with learning disabilities, emotional disturbance/behavioral disorders, or mild mental retardation?

4. Browse the web sites listed in Box 2.5. What additional characteristics of students with mild disabilities did you find? How do these characteristics relate to curriculum and instruction?
5. Given the characteristics of students with mild disabilities, generate a list of instructional implications for classroom teachers. For example, if a student has attentional problems, teachers might gain the child's attention before presenting directions.

CHAPTER 3

APPROACHES TO TEACHING LEARNERS WITH MILD DISABILITIES

As you read, think about the following questions:

◆ *How are services, curriculum, and instructional methods interrelated?*

◆ *What are some of the current issues surrounding the provision of special education services and instruction to students with mild disabilities?*

◆ *Can students with mild disabilities be fully included in the regular classroom?*

◆ *Which approaches to teaching learners with mild disabilities are supported by research?*

Over the years, numerous approaches to teaching learners with mild disabilities have become popular, only to fall out of favor after a relatively short time. Although not supported by research, some approaches were intuitively appealing to teachers, who believed strongly that these methods would improve the academic performance of their students with special needs. Vestiges of these approaches are still apparent in special and regular education classrooms today, and new fads continue to come and go. Other teaching methods have survived the tests of time and research, continuing to improve the academic achievement, social acceptance, and behavior of many children with mild disabilities. Consider, for example, the following exchange between Ms. Lopez and her student, Joey:

Ms. Lopez: Joey, your first reading assignment today is on page 34 of your book. Let's turn to page 34.

Joey: (Turns to page 34 and also slips a paper out of his assignment notebook) I read this one yesterday and I bet I read it better today! I'm gonna smash my record!

Ms. Lopez: (Looking at Joey's graph on the paper in his assignment notebook) Yes, you read at a rate of 75 words per minute yesterday with only six errors. I bet you can reach your goal today! What's the goal?

Joey: Eighty-five words a minute and only five errors.

Ms. Lopez: Are you ready? (She has a stopwatch ready to time Joey and a photocopy of the reading passage in front of her. At a nod from Joey, she starts the stopwatch.) Begin!

Joey: (He reads the passage as Ms. Lopez follows along on her page. When he finishes, Ms. Lopez stops the watch.) How did I do?

Ms. Lopez: (Counting) Ninety words per minute, Joey, and four errors! Super job!

Joey: (Smiles and pulls out his pencil to plot the information on his graph) See. I told you I was gonna smash that goal today!

Procedures derived from the principles of applied behavior analysis, such as the direct, daily, repeated measurement and recording of a specific targeted behavior, as illustrated in the preceding scenario, are among the most effective techniques known to teachers of students with special educational needs. What other instructional methods are supported by the research literature? Where, what, and how should students in special education be taught?

In this chapter, we will first examine the interrelated nature of special education services, curriculum, and instruction. We will also explore some of the current issues concerning the provision of special education services and instruction to students with mild disabilities in inclusive classroom settings. Finally, we will discuss current research-supported approaches to teaching learners with mild disabilities, as well as some popular approaches for which effectiveness has not always been empirically confirmed.

Services, Curriculum, and Instruction

In Chapter 2 we discussed the settings in which students with mild disabilities are likely to receive their special education services. Teachers must make decisions, however, regarding not only the location of special education services, but also the curriculum and instructional methods to use in order to meet the unique needs of their students with mild disabilities. These three aspects of special education are interrelated and vitally important for special learners.

Services

Recall from Chapter 2 that youngsters with learning disabilities, mild mental retardation, or behavioral disorders frequently receive their special education in the regular classroom, often with the special educator providing resource room assistance to the student and/or consultation services to the regular classroom teacher. Increasingly, too, regular and special educators are sharing instructional responsibilities for students with disabilities, and for other children achieving below grade level, through collaborative or coteaching arrangements within "inclusive" classroom environments (Morsink, Thomas, & Correa, 1991). In fact, some authorities argue that the continuum of services outlined in IDEA (1997) should be abolished and that all students with disabilities should be returned full-time to the regular classroom (Gartner & Lipsky, 1987). We will return to the important issue of "inclusion" momentarily!

Curriculum

Although the question of where to educate students with mild disabilities is an important one, the related question of what the students are taught is even more important. Teachers must carefully address curricular issues in a manner consistent with the IDEA (1997) mandate that students receive an appropriate education in the least restrictive environment. The least restrictive environment is that environment in which opportunities for integration with nondisabled peers are maximized, at the same time providing the child with an appropriate education. For many students with learning disabilities or behavioral disorders, college or technical school might be a likely outcome upon graduation. These students must progress through the regular school curriculum, perhaps with additional instruction from the special education teacher in learning strategies or social skills, or accommodations by the regular classroom teacher to circumvent specific skill deficits. Students receiving the regular education curriculum are often taught in the regular classroom, and they are to be held accountable to the maximum extent appropriate for their ability to meet the performance goals and standards set for all children within a state (IDEA, 1997).

On the other hand, some students with learning disabilities, behavioral disorders, or mild mental retardation may need a modified curriculum emphasizing functional academics (e.g., learning to read in order to follow a recipe or learning to count money and make change) and social skills. Such a curriculum should provide these youngsters with the skills necessary for getting and keeping a job and for living productive, independent lives as future adults.

(See Chapter 15.) This curriculum, however, might entail placement in a self-contained classroom for most of the school day, or even placement in special school settings. Although these students may not participate in the general state or school district assessments of student learning, states must still conduct alternate assessments to determine the progress of these students toward appropriate performance goals and indicators (IDEA, 1997).

Instruction

Whereas *services* and *curriculum* refer to where and what students are taught, *instruction* refers to how teachers provide appropriate learning experiences for their students. Teachers must provide quality instruction to learners with mild disabilities, regardless of the setting or the curriculum. In fact, Slavin et al. (1989) maintain that the setting for special and remedial education is not as important as the quality of instruction received. Rather, they suggest that effective programs for students who have mild disabilities, and others who are low achievers, should include the following five elements:

1. Instruction designed to accommodate individual needs
2. Instruction based on frequent assessment of student progress
3. Immediate and intensive direct instruction to strengthen skills and prevent small deficits from becoming larger ones
4. Collaboration between the regular and special education teachers and consistency in the teaching methods used in various settings
5. Teaching behaviors that provide students with high levels of on-task time, support, and success

These essential elements of effective instruction are embodied in the teaching approaches we will consider later in this chapter. Such intensive instruction, however, may not always be possible in inclusive classroom settings. Let's examine some of the issues surrounding the inclusion of students with mild disabilities in the regular classroom.

Issues Regarding Special Education Services, Instruction, and Inclusion

During the 1980s, special education programs began to draw criticism. Although earlier self-contained classrooms for students with mild disabilities had largely been replaced with resource room and regular classroom programs, these early efforts at "mainstreaming" did not result in consistently-improved social status for children with disabilities (Sabornie, 1985). In addition, students with learning problems did not consistently demonstrate increased academic achievement as a result of their special education programs (Anderson & Pellicer, 1990; Slavin, 1988). Some authorities charged that students who were pulled out of the regular classroom for remedial help were actually spending less time on appropriate learning tasks than their counterparts in the regular classroom (Slavin, Karweit, & Madden, 1989). These critics also suggested that students in pullout programs may miss essential instruction and activities in the regular classroom and that they may become confused if the materials, methods, or expectations of their special education teachers differ from those of their regular classroom teacher.

These criticisms and others fueled arguments against pullout special education and other remedial programs. Such arguments were motivated by the desire to reform special education and return all students with disabilities to the regular classroom.

Furthermore, as the public schools implemented Public Law 94-142 it became evident that some students who were in need of support services, but who did not meet federal eligibility criteria, would not be served. For example, students who were achieving just below average, who lacked motivation, who were abused and neglected, or who were from dysfunctional families were not necessarily eligible for special education services (Reynolds, Wang, & Walberg, 1987). According to Madeleine Will, then assistant secretary for the Office of Special Education and Rehabilitative Services, PL 94-142 was designed to provide services for students already failing in their learning environment and not to provide preventative services to eliminate learning difficulties for students prior to failure (Will, 1986).

Such problems with the implementation of PL 94-142 have resulted in a call for significant changes in the delivery of services for those who experience learning problems. The Regular Education Initiative (REI) issued by Will cited the following problems with the current system of special education:

1. Special education pullout services have not proven to be effective, although this is the common method of providing support services.
2. Special education services, as well as other services for students at risk (see Chapter 1), are fragmented and segregated.
3. Special education is provided in a categorical fashion, but not all students fit into categories.
4. Services are not preventative in nature.
5. Parents are not truly active participants in the special education process.

Will (1986) suggested that regular and special educators and administrators be empowered to design and implement school-based alternative strategies and approaches for educating students who have learning problems. These approaches should focus on early intervention and prevention of learning problems in the regular classroom rather than on categorical pullout programs. She also argued that needed reforms in special education must include the integration of special and regular education resources, the provision of special services without labeling of students, and greater support in regular education. Regular educators, therefore, should be involved cooperatively throughout the process.

Reynolds et al. (1987) also strongly supported a major restructuring of special education. These authorities argued for "rights without labels," to ensure that screening, assessment, and appropriate programs would be provided for all students with special needs. Similarly Stainback, Stainback, and Bunch (1989) called for a *complete* merger of regular and special education services, and others argued that some students were often labeled to receive support services, even when their disabilities were not significant (Wilson, 1991). Taylor (1988) even charged that students with disabilities were often trapped by the system, unable to access the regular classroom and curriculum once they were determined eligible for special education and placed in a resource or self-contained classroom setting.

During the late 1980s and throughout the 1990s, the *inclusion* movement grew from arguments used by advocates of the Regular Education Initiative. Although in some schools, *inclusion* continued to mean preserving the continuum of service options appropriate to meet the educational needs of the individual student, in other schools *inclusion* came to mean placing all students with disabilities in the regular classroom full time, regardless of their level of severity. With the passage of the Individuals with Disabilities Education Act Amendment in 1997, inclusion received additional impetus in the schools as the law strengthened the connection between special education and the general education curriculum. IDEA required that students with disabilities must be provided with supplementary aids and services designed to enable the child to progress in the general education curriculum alongside his or her nondisabled peers. IDEA favored placement of students with disabilities in the regular education classroom, unless parents and teachers agreed that the student would receive no benefit, the cost of the necessary supplementary aids and services would be prohibitive, or the education of other students in the classroom would suffer.

Proponents of *full inclusion* argue that *all* students have the right to an education in the regular classroom in an environment not segregated from peers. They charge that any separation from nondisabled peers is inherently unequal and, therefore, placement in the regular classroom should not be dependent on empirical data but rather on doing the "right thing" (Jenkins et al., 1994). Furthermore, *full inclusionists* argue that the placement of the child is more important than the curriculum or quality of instruction in determining student success; therefore the continuum of services should simply be abolished (Fuchs & Fuchs, 1995).

In conjunction with the school reform movement discussed in Chapter 1, *inclusionists* call for systemic change in how schools serve all children, either with or without disabilities (McLeskey & Pugach, 1995). Schools implementing full inclusion, then, bring special education services to the child *within* the regular classroom, rather than removing the child from the class to receive the services. (See Box 3.1 for an example of full inclusion in practice.) Supplementary aids and services provided to enable the child to access the general education curriculum might include:

- Regular and special educators collaborating or coteaching to help all children within the same classroom.
- Paraprofessionals or instructional assistants assigned full-time to help an individual student who has more severe needs.
- Reduced class size in regular classrooms that include students with disabilities.
- Adaptations or modifications to curriculum, instruction, assignments, testing, or grading practices.
- Flexible groupings of students designed to promote cooperative learning or peer tutoring opportunities.

Can all students realistically be served within the regular education classroom? Should the continuum of services, mandated in IDEA (1997) and designed to ensure the least restrictive environment for all students with disabilities, be

Box 3.1

Inclusion in Action

Inclusion calls for teachers to form collaborative partnerships in which they share responsibility for planning and delivering instruction and for monitoring academic progress and student behavior. In the best inclusive arrangements, special and regular classroom teachers work so closely together that their roles are almost indistinguishable from one another. That is, students believe that more teachers are now available to help them learn (Pugach & Wesson, 1995). Collaboration, then, is an essential element of inclusive schooling.

Collaborative Teaching at the Elementary Level

Ms. Lopez and Ms. Kirk work together to plan and teach social studies collaboratively in Ms. Kirk's fourth-grade classroom. Their principal has arranged their schedules so that they have a daily planning period together and so that Ms. Lopez can be in Ms. Kirk's classroom at the same time each day for their "collaborative" students, Joey and Travis. During their joint planning time, both teachers share ideas for how instruction and materials might be adapted to meet the needs of all students in the class. Ms. Lopez suggests techniques to incorporate learning strategies and social skills into the present social studies unit, and Ms. Kirk provides expertise on the fourth-grade social studies curriculum. During the "collaborative" period, Ms. Lopez coteaches the social studies lessons with Ms. Kirk, leading discussions, answering questions, assisting students, demonstrating learning strategies, adapting tests, and checking assignments.

Inclusion at the Secondary Level

This year, Mr. Abel and Mr. McNally are piloting a collaborative teaching arrangement in the ninth-grade geography class for one period each day. In addition to planning and teaching cooperatively, Mr. Abel will monitor the academic progress and behaviors of students with mild disabilities, such as Robert, included in Mr. McNally's class. For example, on a daily basis, Mr. Abel checks to be sure that Robert is taking notes, accurately writing down assignments in his notebook, and using in-class study time wisely. In addition, he makes sure that Robert understands important concepts and makes note of those areas that will require reteaching and/or reinforcement during Robert's resource room period. Mr. Abel also helps Robert apply learning strategies taught in the resource room to remember information in Mr. McNally's geography class.

abandoned? Should paraprofessionals, often the *least* trained individuals, be responsible for teaching students who are among the hardest to teach? Can regular and special education teachers truly share roles and responsibilities effectively within the same classroom? Not all professionals would agree (see, for example, Kauffman, 1995; MacMillan, Gresham, & Forness, 1996; Mather & Roberts, 1995; Roberts & Mather, 1995).

Opponents of full inclusion argue that no empirical data currently exists to support inclusive classrooms over traditional resource room or self-contained environments. As a matter of fact, research suggests that students with learning disabilities and emotional/behavioral disorders evidence greater academic achievement gains when participating in pullout programs (Fuchs & Fuchs, 1995). Apparently, students with mild disabilities receive less individualized instruction in the regular classroom than in the resource room setting (Deno, Foegen, Robinson, & Epsin, 1996). Regular educators often find instructional adaptations suggested for students with mild disabilities to be unfeasible given the large number of students and the lack of resources typically found in the regular classroom (Houck & Rogers, 1994; Zigmond & Baker, 1995). Moreover, regular classroom teachers, teaching toward a model group of children, tend to tolerate less deviance in classroom behavior and achievement than do their special education counterparts (Gerber, 1995). In fact, teachers have fewer academic interactions than behavioral interactions with students who have mild disabilities (Bulgren, & Carta, 1993). That is, they pay more attention to special education students when they are misbehaving and direct less attention to them regarding their performance on academic tasks.

Practicing teachers also believe that traditional service-delivery systems in special education, particularly pullout programs, do serve the needs of their students (Marston, 1996). Semmel et al. (1991) found that both regular and special education teachers prefer pullout programs, yet these teachers still believe that students with mild disabilities have a basic right to education in the regular classroom. Many teachers, however, believe that a redistribution of special education resources to the regular classroom would reduce their instructional load and help them to teach all students more effectively (Minke, Bear, Deemer, & Griffin, 1996; Semmel et al., 1991). Nevertheless, many teachers hold negative views regarding inclusion and believe that inadequate resources and time, large class sizes, lack of teacher preparation, and the dubious benefit for some students presently preclude the success of inclusive classrooms (Scruggs & Mastropieri, 1996; Vaughn, Schumm, Jallad, Slusher, & Saumell, 1996).

Summary of Issues Regarding Special Education Services, Instruction, and Inclusion ◆

Powerful arguments exist on both sides of the inclusion debate. I support some of the systemic changes advocated by the proponents of inclusion, particularly cooperation, collaboration, and shared responsibility among special and regular educators in order to assist problem learners in the regular classroom and prevent unnecessary special education referrals. I do not, however, advocate acceptance of full inclusion unless extensive research demonstrating positive effects is forthcoming. In this text, inclusion will be taken to mean preserving the continuum of service options mandated by IDEA (1997) and including students with mild disabilities in the regular classroom, to the extent that the child is able to receive an education appropriate for his or her unique needs. **I believe that the quality of instruction received, not the physical setting in which it is delivered, is the most important element in determining student success.** (See Table 3.1 for a description of factors necessary for successful inclusion.) Let's turn now to an examination of the effectiveness of some popular instruc-

Table 3.1   **Factors Necessary for Successful Inclusion**

Teachers Must Have

Positive attitudes toward inclusion
Training in collaboration and accommodation strategies
Compatible "teaching" personalities
Shared roles and responsibilities
Realistic expectations
Time to train and to plan for inclusion
Ongoing support
Trained Instructional Assistants or Paraprofessionals

Administrators Must Provide

Support for inclusion
Time for all parties to become prepared
Adequate personnel and materials resources in the classroom
Adjustments to class size
Schedules designed to foster shared planning and teaching
Options to meet the needs of different teachers, parents, and students

Parents and Students Need

Accurate information about inclusion
Inclusive classrooms as one option among many
Freedom to choose

tional practices used to teach students with mild disabilities. Then we will discuss more recent approaches validated by empirical research. ◆

Popular Teaching Approaches and Fads

Despite the accumulating research evidence to support the effectiveness of certain practices in special education, some teachers cling to more traditional instructional approaches or jump to the newest fads like whole language instruction or facilitated communication for students with autism(Kauffman, 1996). Many of the traditional approaches are outgrowths of the early work of such pioneers in the field of mental retardation as Alfred Strauss, Heinz Werner, and Laura Lehtinen (Hallahan & Cruickshank, 1973; Strauss & Lehtinen, 1947). Although not all traditional approaches to instruction have been supported by current research, some are still commonly accepted and widely used by special education teachers. These include stimulus reduction procedures, multisensory approaches, modality-based instruction, and diet/drug therapies. Unfortunately, parents and teachers often "jump on the bandwagon" before the original claims of effectiveness are empirically validated.

Stimulus Reduction

Strauss and Lehtinen (1947) first recommended the use of structure and reduced environmental stimulation when teaching the "brain-injured mentally retarded child." William Cruickshank and his colleagues later took a similar approach to the education of children with attentional problems and hyperactivity, children who today are often thought to have learning disabilities or emotional disturbances (Cruickshank, Bentzen, Ratzeburg, & Tannhauser, 1961). Stimulus reduction techniques are applied in carefully structured teacher-directed programs that attempt to minimize distracting elements in the child's surroundings. All irrelevant environmental stimuli are reduced and important instructional materials are highlighted in some way. For example, study carrels or cubicles are often used as individual work areas, and unused materials are put away so that they do not distract the child from his or her work. Assignments are often presented by giving only one item at a time or by using color to enhance the stimulus value of the material to be learned.

Although these procedures are still advocated by some special education teachers today, research regarding their effectiveness is not promising. In 1975, Cruickshank reported improved attention to task, but no gains in academic achievement, for those children in his experimental program. Other studies (for

Research on the effects of stimulus reduction has yielded mixed results. These procedures may help some students pay attention, but they do not result in automatic gains in academic achievement.

example, Gorton, 1972; Jenkins, Gorrafa, & Griffiths, 1972; Rost & Charles, 1967; Shores & Haubrich, 1969; Sommervill, Warnberg, & Bost, 1973) have yielded similar findings; however, these studies have been criticized for numerous methodological flaws (Hallahan & Kauffman, 1975). Although certain stimulus reduction procedures (e.g., presenting one task or direction at a time, maintaining a structured classroom environment) may help some children with attentional deficits, teachers should not rely solely on these techniques to improve academic achievement for their students with mild disabilities.

Multisensory Approaches and Modality-Based Instruction

Many teachers believe that children learn best if multiple sensory inputs are used in the learning activity. Fernald's (1943) VAKT (i.e., visual, auditory, kinesthetic, tactile) technique exemplifies a multisensory instructional approach. For example, when learning to read new words, students first dictate a story. The teacher writes each new word on a card, and subsequently holds up the cards for the student to see. As each card is viewed, the teacher pronounces the word clearly. Students then repeat each new word while looking at it, trace the word with their fingers as they say it, and then copy the word. Throughout instruction, teachers emphasize to students that this is a new and different way to learn.

Fernald (1943) originally used this multisensory approach to motivate and instruct delinquent, disabled readers, but today, numerous programs are purportedly based on her methods (for example, Gillingham & Stillman, 1956). In addition, teachers often encourage their students to see, hear, touch, and feel words, letters, or numbers by having them trace letters made from sandpaper or write words in trays filled with sand. Although the effectiveness of these techniques is not supported by a substantial body of research, many teachers strongly believe that they help pupils who have difficulty learning to read, write, or spell. One interesting research question that remains unexplored is whether the purported effectiveness of multisensory approaches is due to the use of the senses in combination, or to the structure, repetition, and strategic practice that characterize the technique.

A related approach is to determine the child's preferred sensory channel for learning. Proponents of this approach assume that in order for special education children to learn, instruction must be adjusted to match the sensory channel that is strongest for the individual child (Carbo, 1983, 1987, 1988; Carbo, Dunn, & Dunn, 1986; Dunn, 1988). Teachers advocating such methods believe that some children, for example, may learn best through the visual modality. For others, auditory channels may be preferred. A teacher using this approach might teach the visual learner to read by presenting sight words, while teaching letter-sound associations to an auditory learner.

Matching instruction to a student's preferred learning modality, however, is another approach whose effectiveness has not been empirically confirmed (Kavale & Forness, 1987; Kavale, Hirshoren, & Forness, 1998). Although some teachers still believe that students with mild disabilities can best be taught through preferred sensory channels, no evidence exists for such an aptitude-treatment interaction (Lloyd, 1984). When teaching through learning modalities, teachers should use common sense: what they say they should also show, and what they show they should also say. That is, instruction should incorporate both oral and visual presentations by the teacher and active involvement by the student.

Modality-based instruction should not be confused with accommodation strategies. Accommodation strategies offer students alternative ways to learn new information or to complete assignments. Rather than assuming that learning-modality preferences can be identified and that instruction can be matched to these strengths, the teacher using accommodation techniques attempts to circumvent deficiencies in specific academic skills. Accommodating deficits in basic skills in order to meet individual learning needs is a time-honored tradition among both special and regular classroom teachers. For example, Robert, with severe handwriting problems, might use a laptop computer to complete written work in Mr. McNally's geography class. Similarly, Travis might use a calculator when solving mathematical word problems in order to circumvent his difficulty in remembering the addition and subtraction facts.

Finally, some *learning styles* advocates claim that students evidence individual preferences in how they approach instructional tasks (Carbo, 1987). For example, some students may like to complete their work in a quiet environment while seated at a table. Others may prefer to work sprawled on the floor or need frequent breaks and lots of movement. Still other students may work better when given the opportunity to complete tasks with a partner or small group. Teachers can certainly adjust the classroom environment to suit the needs and preferences of their learners.

Diet/Drug Therapies

Teachers often encounter children with attentional problems or hyperactivity who are taking Ritalin, Cylert, or other medications prescribed by a physician. Although these drugs can be quite effective in improving the behavior of many children, teachers must remember that drugs are not a panacea. They are only one part of a total educational program in which teachers must provide for the individual instructional needs of their students. In addition, teachers must be aware of the potential side effects of these drugs. Common side effects of psychostimulants include insomnia, reduced appetite, weight loss, nausea, skin rashes, irritability, and dizziness (Forness & Kavale, 1988; Forness, Sweeney, & Toy, 1996). Moreover, dosage levels high enough to reduce a child's hyperactivity may actually impair his or her cognitive performance (Forness, Swanson, Cantwell, Guthrie, & Sena, 1992). The child may, for example, appear sleepy or lethargic in class. Newer time-release versions of these medications may also produce peaks and valleys in performance for children, impairing consistent progress and behavior throughout the school day (Pelham, Swanson, Furman, & Schwindt, 1995).

Teachers should be prepared to monitor carefully the behavior of students taking any medication and, if necessary, report their observations to the child's parents and/or physician. Finally, teachers should refrain from suggesting to

Box 3.2

Student Medications and the Teacher's Responsibilities

Teachers today assume many responsibilities including the management of students taking medications. Taylor's teachers, for example, must ensure that she takes her medication as stated in her Section 504 plan. Just before her language arts class with Ms. Booker, Taylor reports to the school clinic where her medicine is located. The *Faculty Handbook of Policies and Procedures* developed for Apple County Middle School, consistent with that state's law, includes the following statement regarding administering prescription medicines to students:

> . . . Under no circumstances are teachers or students to keep prescription medicines in the classroom. Parents or guardians must notify the school in writing when their child must take medication during the school day. Such medication is to be taken immediately to the school clinic and secured in a locked, properly-ventilated and/or -refrigerated container.

Responsibilities of Clinic Personnel:

Clinic personnel will keep a log for all prescriptions entering the clinic including the student's name, the physician's name, the date, the type of medication, and the dosage to be given according to the physician's directions. Clinic personnel will also be authorized to administer the medication to students as prescribed and will be required to note on the medication log the following information:

___ Student Name
___ Name of Person Giving Medication
___ Date and Time Medication Given
___ Type of Medication
___ Exact Dosage
___ Unusual Student Comments, Complaints, or Behaviors

Responsibilities of Teachers:

Teachers will ensure that students have adequate time to report to the clinic for prescribed medicines without penalty. Teachers should carefully observe students taking prescription medications and document unusual behaviors. These observations should be shared immediately with parents or guardians.

---

parents or other teachers that a child might require drug therapy. (See Box 3.2 for a discussion of the teacher's responsibilities regarding medications taken by students during school hours.)

A similar approach to treatment of attentional problems and hyperactivity involves careful control of the child's diet. In the Feingold (1976) diet, for example, children are prohibited from eating foods containing additives. Rapp (1986) also suggests that some students may experience allergies to certain food groups such as wheat, corn, nuts, or milk that, in turn, affect the child's ability to pay attention in school. Sugar, too, has often been implicated as the culprit in precipitating hyperactivity. To date, however, the results of well-conducted research studies fail to support any relationship between hyperactivity and the ingestion of certain foods, additives, or sugar (Whalen, 1989). In short, teachers must evaluate their instructional methods rather than the child's diet when explaining or treating inattentive behavior.

Fads

Fads are teaching approaches popularized by the media and by those having a vested interest in a product or process. Educational innovations regularly come and go in both regular and special education classrooms; however, special educators and parents of special-needs children may be particularly vulnerable to "scams" (Kauffman, 1999). To date, little research evidence exists to support the use of controversial "therapies" such as:

- ◆ Vision Training—asking children to string beads in specific patterns in order to improve the performance of the eyes and increase reading achievement (Silver, 1995).
- ◆ Tinted Lenses—-providing lenses to children with reading problems to filter out certain light frequencies, improve depth perception, and reduce distortions in print or background (Irlen, 1983).
- ◆ Vestibular Functioning and Sensory Integration Training—-using motor activities to improve balance, eye movement, and spatial orientation in children with learning disabilities and poor reading performance (Ayres, 1978).

Summary of Popular Approaches

Not all of the popular approaches for teaching children with mild disabilities have research support. Clearly, evidence of the effectiveness of modality-based instruction and diet therapy is lacking. Stimulus reduction and drug therapy may improve a child's attention to task, but not necessarily improve his or her academic achievement. Multisensory approaches have the support of practitioners in the field but lack conclusive research support. Teachers should choose instructional methods supported by research and best practice, rather than relying on familiar techniques presumed to be helpful, or on fads that may appear and then rapidly fall from favor. ◆

Research-Based Approaches

Among the more recent approaches to teaching learners with mild disabilities are applied behavior analysis, direct instruction, cognitive strategy training, peer tutoring, cooperative learning arrangements, and authentic instruction. Each has a growing research base and increasing popularity in both regular and special education classrooms. In addition, consultation and collaboration are two strategies designed to support students with mild disabilities within the regular classroom and prevent needless referrals to special education. Although these approaches will be discussed in greater depth in the coming chapters, the following brief descriptions serve as an introduction.

Applied Behavior Analysis

Without a doubt, applied behavior analysis has been used successfully to improve the overt behaviors and academic performance of many children with mild disabilities. This approach relies on the direct, repeated measurement and recording of observable behaviors targeted for change. Environmental events preceding and following these targets are arranged to increase appropriate behaviors and decrease inappropriate behaviors. You might recall in the opening vignette, for example, how Ms. Lopez measured Joey's oral reading rate by timing him with a stopwatch, and how Joey eagerly recorded his performance on a graph. This is an example of how applied behavior analysis can make instruction not only more successful, but more enjoyable for the child as well. (For excellent reviews of applied behavior analysis with exceptional students, the interested reader may wish to consult Alberto & Troutman, 1999; Kerr & Nelson, 1998; or Zirpoli & Melloy, 1997.)

Direct Instruction

Like applied behavior analysis, direct instruction emphasizes direct measurement and careful sequencing of the component skills necessary to perform a specific task. It also focuses on the teaching process, offering special educators powerful techniques for improving the academic achievement of their students with mild disabilities (Lloyd, 1988).

Direct instruction grew from the work of Bereiter and Engelmann (1966), who advocated the use of a highly-structured, repetitive approach to teaching basic skills to disadvantaged preschoolers. Teachers using direct instruction present clear, well-sequenced, highly-focused, fast-paced lessons; systematically present many relevant examples of the new skill or concept to be learned; elicit frequent responses from students taught in small groups; and provide immediate corrective feedback. Direct instruction emphasizes mastery of critical concepts and skills. Although teachers can use direct instructional techniques when teaching within the regular curriculum (Carnine, Silbert, & Kameenui, 1990), direct instructional materials with demonstrated effectiveness are also available commercially. These include Corrective Reading (Engelmann, Johnson, Carnine, & Meyers, 1999), Reading Mastery (Engelmann & Bruner, 1995), and Corrective Mathematics (Carnine & Engelmann, 1981).

The term *direct instruction* first entered the wider educational sphere through the work of Rosenshine (1976), who used the term with reference to certain teacher behaviors correlated with the academic achievement of their students. Demonstration, guided practice, and feedback also became the hallmarks of Mastery Teaching, or the Instructional Theory Into Practice (ITIP) Model, popularized by Hunter (1982) during the 1980s in regular classrooms across the United States. According to Englert (1984), similar patterns of teacher behaviors also correlate with the academic achievement of students in special education classrooms. (See Chapter 8 for a detailed discussion of direct instruction and effective teacher behaviors in special education.)

Cognitive Strategy Instruction

Unless explicitly taught to do so, students with mild disabilities often fail to transfer the skills and behaviors learned in the classroom to new situations (Gerber, 1988; Stokes & Baer, 1977). Also, students with learning disabilities, mild mental retardation, or behavioral disorders often fail to take an active role in their own learning and fail to devise strategies that could help them accomplish tasks more efficiently (Torgesen, 1982).

Teachers want their students to become independent and self-directed. They want their students to take responsibility both for their own learning and for their own behavior. Strategy Instruction, also called Cognitive Behavior Modification (Meichenbaum, 1977), Learning Strategy Instruction (Deshler & Schumaker, 1986), and Metacognitive Strategy Instruction (Flavell, 1979), offers promise for helping students with mild disabilities to set goals, devise or select effective ways to approach a task, and monitor their own performance.

Strategy Instruction combines the powerful teaching technologies of applied behavior analysis and direct instruction with concern for cognitive processes (i.e., those thoughts and feelings children have about themselves and about their learning). To increase the effectiveness of this approach, strategy instruction and feedback must first be explicit (Kline, Schumaker, & Deshler, 1991). Later, such scaffolding built by teachers to support students early on is slowly removed and students take over the monitoring of their own strategy use (Hock, Schumaker, & Deshler, 1993). Through strategy training, students are taught how to improve important behaviors, including attending to seatwork tasks (Hallahan, Lloyd, & Stoller, 1982), comprehending reading passages (Palincsar, 1986), or memorizing content-area information (Mastropieri & Scruggs, 1989). In addition to providing teachers with important instructional methods, strategy instruction is now the focus of an entire curriculum for secondary-level students with learning disabilities (i.e., the Strategic Instruction Model developed by Donald Deshler, Jean Schumaker, and their colleagues at the University of Kansas [Deshler, Ellis, & Lenz, 1996]). An explicit curriculum of learning strategies, however, may be difficult for teachers of adolescents with mild disabilities to implement within the inclusive classroom (Scanlon, Deshler, & Schumaker, 1996).

Peer Tutoring

In an attempt to maximize the time spent on academic tasks by learners with mild disabilities, teachers at both the elementary and secondary levels have involved other students as instructional aides. Often, children without disabilities serve as tutors for their counterparts in special education programs. However, students with mild disabilities can also serve as tutors for younger peers. Class-wide peer tutoring can be an additional means to allow all students opportunities for interaction and feedback from one another (Delquardri, Greenwood, Whorton, Carta, & Hall, 1986; Mathes, Fuchs, Fuchs, Henley, & Sanders, 1994).

In order for peer-tutoring programs to be successful, the teacher must remain actively involved. Teachers must plan structured lessons for tutors to follow, train tutors to use important interpersonal behaviors that will facilitate learning, and monitor the performance of both tutors and tutees (Jenkins & Jenkins, 1988). Although peer-tutoring programs can improve the academic achievement of learners with mild disabilities, they do not necessarily improve the self-concept of these learners (Scruggs & Richter, 1985).

Cooperative Learning

In a recent effort to improve the academic achievement and social acceptance of students with mild disabilities, as well as other students with low achievement in inclusive classrooms, teachers have arranged students into cooperative learning groups. Rather than competing against one another for grades, group members share the responsibility for helping each other learn. Although groups may compete against one another, the emphasis within each group is cooperation and shared responsibility.

For example, Johnson and Johnson (1987) describe a tournament arrangement in which students from mixed-ability learning groups assist one another to learn and then compete with students of similar ability from other groups. Slavin (1990) discusses a similar arrangement, whereby students from mixed-ability teams called

Cooperative learning arrangements promote increased academic achievement for students with mild disabilities in inclusive classrooms.

STADs (i.e., Student Teams Achievement Divisions) attempt to ensure that each team member will improve previous scores on quizzes covering the material learned. Other cooperative learning groups use jigsaw arrangements in which each group member makes a specific and essential contribution toward a final group product (Aronson, Blaney, Stephan, Sikes, & Snapp, 1978). Class-wide peer tutoring also becomes cooperative learning when students work in teams to help one another learn (Maheady & Harper, 1987; Maheady, Sacca, & Harper, 1988).

Although research results on cooperative learning arrangements are mixed (Anderson, Reder, & Simon, 1996), most of the results appear promising. Johnson and Johnson (1986) report that nondisabled peers have more positive attitudes toward mainstreamed students with disabilities as a result of cooperative learning groups. Moreover, Slavin et al. (1989) suggest that some cooperative learning arrangements may also enhance the academic achievement of these students. These researchers believe, however, that to be effective cooperative learning must include both group incentives and individual accountability. All group members must participate equally in order for the group to be successful. (See Chapter 9 for a detailed discussion of cooperative learning arrangements, peer tutoring, and strategy instruction.)

Authentic Learning

To help students with mild disabilities generalize and apply what they are learning, teachers may need to construct opportunities for real-world problem solving. For example, Bottge and Hasselbring (1993) taught adolescents in remedial math classes to solve complicated mathematical problems using fractions by "anchoring" instruction to real-life situations, such as building a kite with only a limited amount of money. Other teachers make arrangements for their students to participate in service learning projects whereby children with mild disabilities read to younger children or assist older citizens in a nursing home (Yoder, Retish, & Wade, 1996). Similarly, community-based instruction affords students numerous ways to practice essential skills in an authentic context like using money to place an order in a fast-food restaurant or making a purchase in a grocery store (Beakley & Yoder, 1998; Wehman, 1996). When new skills or abstract concepts are systematically applied to solve real-world problems, students' motivation and learning improve (U.S. Department of Education, 1997).

Consultation and Collaboration

Consultation and collaboration, or collaborative team teaching, are two additional strategies designed to assist problem learners. Although both have varying definitions among professionals (see, for example, Johnson, Pugach, & Hammittee, 1988; Morsink, Thomas, & Correa, 1991; Phillips & McCullough, 1990), in this text the terms are defined in the following manner:

◆ Consultation—the sharing of information or expertise through explanation or demonstration by one person to another (Morsink, Thomas, & Correa, 1991).

♦ Collaboration—a type of consultation in which all people involved are viewed as having unique areas of expertise and who interact equally to resolve problems (Villa, Thousand, Paolucci-Whitcomb, & Nevin, 1990).

The consultant, then, is an expert who provides information and advice to others. The consultation process may involve school psychologists, special education teachers, counselors, principals, or regular education teachers (Phillips & McCullough, 1990). The consultant plays an indirect, rather than direct, role in providing services to students. For example, a school psychologist may provide suggestions to the special educator on how to handle the acting-out behavior of a young student who has recently learned that his parents are separating, or a special education teacher may give a regular classroom teacher ideas about how to reduce distractions in the general education setting for a student with attention problems.

On the other hand, collaborative team teaching, or collaboration, implies an equal partnership among all parties. Special educators, regular classroom teachers, paraprofessionals or instructional assistants, parents, and students themselves may all be members of collaborative teams. There are numerous examples of collaboration used in teaching both regular and special education students (see, for example, Affleck, Madge, Adams, & Lowenbraun, 1988; Self, Benning, Marston, & Magnusson, 1991; Wiedmeyer & Lehman, 1991). Instructional teaming, for example, may be used to adapt the regular educational environment to meet the needs of special, regular, and at-risk learners, and systematic teaching and multi-aged groupings are encouraged (Wang & Birch, 1984). A teacher trained in special education might also be assigned to a regular classroom of about 24 students, approximately one-third of whom are children with special needs. The special educator shares responsibility for planning and implementing instruction alongside the regular classroom teacher (Affleck, Madge, Adams, & Lowenbraun, 1988). In some school districts this model may be referred to as coteaching. The common factor, however, is the shared responsibility by regular and special educators for teaching students with special needs *within* the regular classroom.

Through collaboration, special educators and regular classroom teachers work cooperatively as partners to plan and provide instruction for all students in the class. For example, the special education teacher may share information regarding curriculum design or behavior management and the regular classroom teacher may contribute information and instructional methods specific to a particular content area. Because both professionals work together as a team, the pupil-to-teacher ratio is reduced and instructional resources are pooled (Thousand & Villa, 1989). Furthermore, the number of special education referrals and placements may be reduced as a result of collaborative efforts (Chalfant, Pysh, & Moultrie, 1979; Self, Benning, Marston, & Magnusson, 1991). Collaborative, coteaching arrangements are increasingly being used to foster inclusion in the regular classroom of students with mild disabilities (Villa & Thousand, 1995). (See Table 3.2 for a summary of effective approaches for teaching students with mild disabilities and Box 3.3 for some interesting web sites describing inclusion in the schools.)

Box 3.3

Web Watch

The following web sites provide the interested reader with additional information on inclusion:

Friends of Inclusion

http://www.inclusion.com/resource.html
This site provides many links to other web sites containing information on the inclusion of individuals with differing disabilities.

The Inclusion Series

http://www.comforty.com/inclusionseries.html
This site offers ways to include individuals with disabilities both at school and in the community.

Note: The reader will find additional information regarding inclusion on many of the web sites listed in the previous chapters.

Table 3.2 Effective Approaches to Teaching Children with Mild Disabilities

Special educators can improve the academic achievement of their students with mild disabilities by using teaching approaches validated by empirical research. Research-based procedures include effective instructional practices as well as grouping arrangements.

Effective Instructional Practices:

Direct, daily measurement of student progress
Explicit, well-structured lessons
Many clear examples
Tasks broken into sequenced steps
Clear feedback
Repetition of key skills and concepts for mastery
Opportunities for both supervised and independent practice
Meaningful learning tied to real-world applications
Strategies to increase retention and application of information learned
Modifications to assignments and/or activities to accommodate unique characteristics of the learner

Effective Grouping Arrangements:

Peer tutoring
Cooperative learning
Collaborative teaching
Flexible groups based on skills and needs

Summary

Students with mild disabilities are already behind their peers academically. They have many needs, but only limited time. Therefore, the teacher's ability to make appropriate decisions regarding instructional services, content, and methodology for special learners is critical. Special education teachers must base their decisions about service and curricular options on careful assessment of individual student need rather than on current availability of programs or materials. A range of service options, from inclusion in the regular classroom to segregated placement, is necessary in order to meet the needs of all students with mild disabilities. Full-time inclusion in general education may be the setting in which some, but not all, students with mild disabilities can receive an appropriate education.

Similarly, teachers must use the most powerful instructional techniques possible. Effective approaches to teaching children with mild disabilities include applied behavior analysis, direct instruction, cognitive strategy instruction, peer tutoring, cooperative learning arrangements, authentic learning opportunities, and consultation or collaboration among professionals. Research evidence suggests that these methods enhance the academic achievement of many students in special education programs, and that each holds promise for future usefulness.

The teacher must remember, however, that even approaches that have been tested and proven effective for most students may not work for all students. Teachers must carefully observe the individual child's response to a given instructional approach. If that approach is not leading to academic gains or to increased social acceptance for the youngster, the teacher must choose a different method of instruction for that child.

Teachers must begin with intensive, direct instruction of essential academic and social skills identified through daily assessment of student performance. As these skills are mastered, strategies related to specific content-area knowledge or to particular environmental or task demands can also be taught explicitly. To be most effective, strategy instruction must be integrated with direct instruction of relevant skills and content, rather than treated as a separate curricular offering (Pressley et al., 1990). As students master strategies and skills, teachers can arrange peer tutoring or cooperative learning groups to facilitate integration into the regular classroom and to enhance instructional time. Similarly, applied behavior analysis can be used to build appropriate behaviors in the special education setting and to maintain these behaviors within the regular classroom. Consultation and collaboration may enable children with mild disabilities to be included in the general education curriculum, and student learning and motivation may improve when instruction is tied to the "real world." (We will return to these critical areas repeatedly in the coming chapters.)

Although teachers may use traditional or popular methods when teaching students with mild disabilities, not all of these are supported by research. Modality-based instruction and diet therapy, for example, lack research evidence of effectiveness. On the other hand, stimulus reduction and the careful use of drug therapy appear to improve the child's attention to task, but not necessarily his or her academic achievement. Although teachers believe that modality-based and multisensory approaches have positive outcomes for many youngsters with mild disabilities, research does not fully support this claim.

Service, curriculum, and *instruction* refer to three interrelated ideas: the where, what, and how of teaching. Special education teachers must make many decisions regarding the appropriate setting and curriculum for youngsters with mild disabilities. However, it is important to remember that quality instruction must take place, regardless of the setting, if students in special education are to master the chosen curricular option. The responsibility for wise decisions and quality instruction rests squarely with the teacher.

Application Exercises

1. Contact a local school system. Describe the range of services provided to students in special education programs in that school district.
2. Ask two or three special education and regular education teachers in your local school system if inclusion is used in their school. If so, how is inclusion implemented? How do these teachers feel about inclusion? Summarize their answers in one or two paragraphs.
3. Interview two or three special education teachers at both the elementary and the secondary level from local school districts. What curricular options are available for students at each level? Which instructional methods do these teachers most often use?
4. Interview two or three regular classroom teachers at both elementary and secondary levels from local school districts. Which instructional methods do these teachers most often use? Are there differences in the approaches most often used by the regular classroom teachers and by the special education teachers you interviewed in Question 3? Why or why not?
5. Browse the web sites on inclusion listed in Box 3.3. If you had to explain inclusion to a parent of a child with a mild disability, what information from the Internet would you include in your explanation? Why?
6. Locate at least three articles on inclusion from InfoTrac. Summarize the arguments for and against inclusion presented by each of the authors. Write a paragraph stating your position regarding inclusion.

ORGANIZING FOR INSTRUCTION

COMMUNICATING FOR STUDENT SUCCESS

Focus

As you read, think about the following questions:

◆ *What skills are essential for successful consultation, collaboration, and coteaching?*

◆ *How can teachers communicate with other professionals in the school?*

◆ *How can teachers communicate with parents and guardians of students with mild disabilities?*

◆ *How can teachers coordinate the activities of paraprofessionals and volunteers?*

Recall from Chapter 2 the range of service options necessary to provide an appropriate education for students with mild disabilities. Those models involving student placement in the regular classroom for all or part of the school day (e.g., the resource room) require ongoing communication among regular and special educators if students are to be successful in their mainstreamed classes. In addition, consultation models and collaborative or coteaching arrangements depend on skilled communications and cooperative efforts among professionals. This point is illustrated by the activities of Ms. Lopez.

Ms. Lopez coteaches each afternoon in Ms. Kirk's fourth-grade social studies class. At the moment, Ms. Lopez is assisting Celie and Kevin with a group project in social studies. Although Celie and Kevin are not eligible for special education services, both are "at risk." Both are likely to experience academic failure unless they receive special help. The teachers at Oak Hill Elementary School hope to maintain Celie and Kevin in their regular class and to strengthen their academic performance through this collaborative, coteaching arrangement.

As soon as Ms. Lopez helps Kevin locate a word in the dictionary, she notices that Travis is staring out the window. He is not interacting with his group nor is he working on his contribution to the group's social studies project. Ms. Lopez moves toward Travis, and he immediately resumes his task. Ms. Lopez surveys the classroom and is pleased to see that all of the students are attending to their social studies projects. Joey is using colored pencils to decorate the cover of a booklet about colonial life that he and other members of his group wrote together.

The social studies period passes quickly. As Ms. Lopez looks at her watch, she notices that in five minutes she must attend a meeting of the Teacher Assistance Team. A third-grade teacher has asked for help in solving the academic problems of one of the children in her classroom. Ms. Lopez also remembers that she has an appointment at 3:30 with the school psychologist. This time, Ms. Lopez will be the consultee, seeking information about a behavioral intervention to help Joey generalize appropriate social skills in both his regular and special education classes. At 4:00, Ms. Lopez will attend a parent–teacher conference with Travis's mother to discuss ways to increase the time Travis spends working on his homework.

Busy teachers like Ms. Lopez must possess superb communication and human-relations skills in order to assume their many roles. In this chapter, we will first examine the communication skills required of consultants and collaborators and suggest ideas to facilitate successful consultation and collaborative teaching. Next, we will explore ways to communicate with parents and enhance their involvement in educational programming for their children with special needs. Finally, we will present methods by which to communicate with paraprofessionals and volunteers who perform many essential duties in special education classrooms.

Consulting and Collaborating

You may recall from Chapter 3 that consultation and collaboration are processes essential to facilitating the inclusion of students with mild disabilities in the regular classroom. Both require an extensive knowledge base, including curriculum design, instructional methods, cognitive and developmental theory, and behavior management. In addition, positive human relationships and effective communication skills are essential to successful consultation and collaboration.

Communication Skills

Knoff, McKenna, and Riser (1991) identify several behaviors of effective consultants. These include practicing in an ethical manner, maintaining confidentiality, respecting the consultee, and being approachable. On the other hand, behaving in an authoritative or aggressive manner, attempting to be colorful or funny, exhibiting a deferential attitude, and self-disclosing during consultation can lead to negative outcomes according to these authors. Consultants must demonstrate an enthusiastic attitude toward the consultation process and be willing to learn from others (Idol, Nevin, & Paolucci-Whitcomb, 1994).

Apparently, an essential characteristic of skilled consultants and collaborators is the ability to build and maintain an open and trusting rapport with others. Such rapport is based on mutual respect and clearly communicates that all parties are viewed as equals (Gutkin & Curtis, 1990). Trust, respect, and rapport, of course, are built through many positive communications with professionals and parents over the course of the school year. (See Figure 4.1 for an illustration of one form of ongoing positive communication.)

Gutkin and Curtis (1990, pp. 822–825) suggest that communication will be facilitated through the following behaviors:

1. Setting the Proper Tone: The consultant is sincere and respectful during interactions with others.
2. Listening and Encouraging: The consultant listens attentively and encourages others to talk.
3. Demonstrating Empathy: The consultant responds in an understanding and nonjudgmental manner.
4. Paraphrasing: The consultant rephrases to ensure that both parties clearly understand what has been said.
5. Summarizing and Previewing: The consultant sums up progress and helps to set the agenda for the next meeting.

Skillful communication, however, depends upon attention to both verbal and nonverbal behavior. Whereas verbal behavior is what we say, nonverbal behavior is how we say it. If we are not careful, our words might send one message and our actions another. For example, Ms. Lopez approaches Ms. Kirk and states, "You said Joey had a problem in class today. Do you want to talk about it?" At the same time, Ms. Lopez is looking at her watch, scowling, and tapping her foot. In this instance, Ms. Kirk would not be likely to sit down and talk about Joey!

Body posture, facial expressions, gestures, and eye contact may send messages that are either intimidating or encouraging. For example, crossed arms and a "nose-to-nose and toe-to-toe" body posture are threatening to most people. Teachers should maintain a relaxed body posture when talking with others, standing or sitting slightly off to one side with arms down and visible. Whereas eye contact in Anglo-American culture is generally seen as positive, in Native-American, Asian-American, and African-American cultures, eye contact

Teacher Feature

"First Place Winners" at Apple County High School:

Mrs. Stone:

  Mrs. Stone changes the seating arrangement of her classes every two weeks, allowing each student to have a "front row" seat sometime during the grading period. She also has discovered that if she waits for a week and then gives her students a second quiz on the same material, her student's grades improve. Mrs. Stone also offers after-school study sessions to students who need extra assistance in completing assignments, and she recently presented a mini-workshop for special education teachers in the county. Cheers for Mrs. Stone!

Mr. McNally:

  Mr. McNally gives his students a monthly planning sheet to help them note assignments, due dates, and quiz dates. He checks this sheet on a weekly basis, and he often adds positive comments on a student's sheet regarding his or her progress!

FIGURE 4.1 ◆

The newsletter above illustrates one way to improve communication and positive relationships among professionals in schools. In this newsletter, Mr. Abel wrote a "Teacher Feature" to highlight the contributions of regular classroom teachers to the success of his students included in their classes.

with authority figures is sometimes seen as a sign of disrespect (Chan, 1987; Gilliam & Van Den Berg, 1980; Simpson, 1982). Also, the tone, volume, and rhythm of the spoken message may communicate confidence and respect or distrust and fear.

  Turnbull and Turnbull (1997) suggest that teachers practice several techniques to improve communication. For example, they can ask open-ended questions that encourage elaborate responses (e.g., "What behaviors did Joey exhibit in class today?"), or they can paraphrase what the other person has said. For instance, if Ms. Kirk answers the question about Joey's behavior by saying, "Joey was constantly pushing and hitting the other children today," Ms. Lopez might respond by saying, "Joey was quite aggressive with the other children today." By paraphrasing, the teacher can check whether or not he or she has correctly understood what was said. In addition, paraphrasing allows the initial speaker to hear the message from a slightly different perspective.

  Active listening also enables teachers to check their understanding of a message and helps the speaker feel he or she has been understood and accepted (Turnbull & Turnbull, 1997). Active listening responds to the feelings behind a message as well as to the message itself. For example, suppose Ms. Kirk responded to the question about Joey's behavior by saying, "Joey was out of his seat constantly. He was pushing and hitting the other children, and I couldn't seem to get him to stop no matter what I said or did." Ms. Lopez might convey empathy by responding, "It's frightening when Joey behaves so aggressively and it's frustrating when he won't listen." When teachers use active listening, they demonstrate a sincere interest in the feelings of others, encouraging openness and honesty.

Occasionally, parents or colleagues become upset during consultative or collaborative meetings. At times of conflict, teachers must remain calm and attend to their nonverbal communications. Usually, when individuals are upset, they need to know that someone is listening to them. Active listening, paraphrasing, and open-ended questions will often de-escalate the situation as the distraught individual realizes that he or she is being heard and understood (Turnbull & Turnbull, 1997). In addition, although it is difficult, teachers must not take personally what is said during emotional outbursts. When consulting or collaborating with others, the teacher must maintain a professional manner.

Consultation

Numerous versions of consultation models exist; however, each emphasizes the role of a specialist providing indirect services to a client through problem-solving activities (Gutkin, 1996). Pugach and Johnson (1995), however, suggest that consultation is most effective when consultants shed their expert or specialist roles and become partners with teachers and parents. Effective consultants assume the role of an assistant. Ms. Lopez, for example, makes positive comments when she observes good things occurring in Ms. Kirk's classroom. She also sends positive notes to Ms. Kirk and gives her credit for successes. In addition, Ms. Lopez is constantly asking Ms. Kirk, "What can I do to help you and our students?"

At the same time, consultants must carefully structure interactions to promote success and communicate that structure to others. Most consultation models organize problem solving in a series of steps, including defining and clarifying the problem, analyzing forces impinging on the problem, brainstorming solutions, evaluating and choosing from among the alternatives, specifying responsibilities, implementing the chosen solution, and evaluating effectiveness (Gutkin, 1996). Morsink, Thomas, and Correa (1991) identify eight steps to structure the consultation process. (See Table 4.1.)

Once rapport has been established, the next step is to gather information. Sources of information include the student's parents, other teachers, the principal, the school nurse, guidance counselors, and school records. Collecting information from many different sources enables the consultant to determine the settings in which the child is likely to display problem behavior; the intensity, duration, and frequency of the behavior; and the expectations of those who are objecting to the behavior (Polsgrove & McNeil, 1989). Consultants must ensure that information on which they will base their decisions and recommendations is objective.

Table 4.1 The Consultation Process

According to Morsink, Thomas, and Correa (1991), the consultation process involves the following eight stages:

1. Establishing the relationship: Meet and establish rapport with the consultee.
2. Gathering information: Check a variety of sources to get background information about the problem.
3. Identifying the problem: Determine the history and frequency of the problem and define it in measurable terms.
4. Stating the target behavior: Consider whether the behavior must be increased or decreased and determine the criteria by which to evaluate progress.
5. Generating interventions: Discuss options to consider and select alternatives to try.
6. Implementing the interventions: Put the interventions into effect and collect data on their success or failure.
7. Evaluating the interventions: Determine whether the desired outcomes have been achieved and modify the interventions if necessary.
8. Withdrawing from the consultation relationship: End the process when the goal is reached or when an agreement has been made to discontinue.

Source: Morsink, C.V., Thomas, C.C., & Correa, V.I. (1991). *Interactive teaming: Consultation and collaboration in special programs.* New York, NY: Macmillan, p. 45. Reprinted with permission.

Next, the consultant identifies the problem. In this critical step, the problem behavior or academic skill about which the teacher is seeking help is pinpointed and clarified. For example, after speaking with Travis's mother, Ms. Lopez determines that Travis must increase the amount of time he spends on homework from fifteen minutes to one hour each evening. After identifying and clarifying the problem, the consultant and parent must analyze the forces impinging on the problem; in this case, the amount of time Travis spends watching television after school and the time he is unsupervised before his mother returns home from work. They then brainstorm alternative strategies and choose from among the alternatives. For example, they may decide to set aside a specific time and place for homework. Ms. Lopez will be responsible for giving Travis a daily homework sheet to be signed by his mother and returned the next day. Travis's mother and Ms. Lopez will then evaluate together the effectiveness of the chosen intervention (Gutkin & Curtis, 1990). Throughout the process, Ms. Lopez must be sure to specify clearly who will do what and when, and she must set aside a time and place to meet to conduct follow-up discussions in order to evaluate and readjust the agreed upon intervention. (See Box 4.1 for an illustration of the consultation process and Figure 4.2 for a useful problem-solving format.)

Although consultation can be an important role of special educators, special education teachers actually spend very little time in consultation activities (Idol-Maestas & Ritter, 1985). Johnson, Pugach, and Hammitte (1988) cite insufficient time, large numbers of students, limited resources, and lack of administrative support as barriers to effective consultation in the schools. In addition, they suggest that classroom teachers may believe that special educators do not appreciate the demands of the regular classroom. Therefore, problem-solving

Box 4.1

Mr. McNally has requested a consultation with Mr. Abel regarding Marcus's performance in geography class. Marcus has not performed well during the current grading period, and Mr. McNally is concerned that he will fail. In the following dialogue, some of the strategies for successful consultation offered by Gutkin and Curtis (1990) and by Morsink, Thomas, and Correa (1991) are shown in parentheses. Let's listen to the conversation:

Mr. Abel: Hi. How are you doing? (Establishing rapport)

Mr. McNally: Okay. You?

Mr. Abel: Fine, thanks. Did you see the game Friday night? That was a great game!

Mr. McNally: Yeah. The kids played really well.

Mr. Abel: I understand that you want to talk about Marcus. I know he's been having difficulty in class. (Reviewing the information)

Mr. McNally: Yeah. I'm afraid I need to do something fast. He just doesn't seem to be doing his work.

Mr. Abel: Tell me how he works in class. (Defining and clarifying the problem)

Mr. McNally: He doesn't. He doesn't listen. He stares out the window or he just puts his head down on the desk and sleeps.

Mr. Abel: So he doesn't pay attention or participate in class. (Paraphrasing)

Mr. McNally: No, when he's there, he doesn't participate at all.

Mr. Abel: How many assignments has he completed?

Mr. McNally: Let me look in my grade book. Let's see. He turned in five, no, six of the twelve class assignments since the grading period started the week before last, and he got an "F" on the quiz Friday.

Mr. Abel: Marcus needs to turn in his assignments. (Stating the target behavior) Do you know of anything that might be going on at home or school that could be affecting his work? (Analyzing forces impinging on the problem)

Mr. McNally: Well, a couple weeks ago, Marcus told me his mother started working the evening shift. I think he's got a younger brother or sister at home that he baby-sits.

Mr. Abel: So Marcus may not be able to get his work done if he's watching his brother or sister. Maybe he's tired from staying up later, too.

Mr. McNally: He told me about his mother when I asked him about this map project just after the grading period started. He finally turned it in, but it was late.

Mr. Abel: Let's think about what we could try to help Marcus get his assignments done. What does he need to turn in in order to pass this grading period? (Listing strategies to improve performance; determining criteria for judging success.)

Mr. McNally: I think he said his mother leaves at five o'clock. Maybe he could come back to my room after school to get his work done. I think he walks. Anyway, he'll need to have at least 75% of his work completed correctly to pass, and he has to pass the end-of-year test for geography to graduate with his class.

Mr. Abel: Okay. That means he needs to complete two more of the missing assignments correctly and then keep up with the rest. It's nice of you to accept the assignments late. How many points will you deduct for being late? (Establishing criteria for evaluation)

Mr. McNally: I usually drop the grade one letter when students are late by a week or two like he is, so Marcus will need to do "A" or "B" work on both missing assignments to get the passing grade. I'll ask Marcus tomorrow if he walks and if he'd like to stay after school to get help to get the work done. Maybe that will get him on the right track.

Mr. Abel: All right. I'll check with you tomorrow right after school to see what Marcus said. Do you need any special materials for Marcus? Or do you want me to stay after and work with him on certain days, too? (Specifying responsibilities and follow-up)

Mr. McNally: No, but thanks.

Mr. Abel: Okay. You let me know tomorrow if you need anything. I'll see you tomorrow afternoon at 3:00. (Closing the consultation contact)

Mr. McNally: Thanks. See you tomorrow.

◆

strategies offered by special education teachers who assume an expert role may not be perceived as feasible by regular educators.

Because many different types of consultation models are used, research results on the effectiveness of consultation are mixed (Idol, 1993). Nevertheless, reviews of research indicate that consultation produces positive results about 75% of the time (Sheridan, Welch, & Orme, 1996). Consultation continues to be an important and promising problem-solving process for teachers.

Collaboration

According to some authorities, the most effective form of consultation is one in which all parties are viewed as having equal expertise (Gutkin & Curtis, 1990; Pugach & Johnson, 1995). Consultation that involves contributions by all parties and that considers all parties to be experts is known as collaborative consultation, or simply collaboration (Idol et al., 1994). When collaborating, teachers, parents, and other professionals generate viable educational interventions (Donaldson & Christiansen, 1990) during interactions characterized by mutual respect, open communication, and consensual decision-making (West, 1990).

Collaboration is taking place, for example, when a special educator and a regular classroom teacher (e.g., Ms. Lopez and Ms. Kirk) work together on a social studies curriculum for students who are reading three levels below grade expectancy. Collaboration is also taking place when a teacher and the school psychologist design a behavior management plan across the entire school day for a

PEOPLE PRESENT: _____

DATE: _____

P: Problem Statement
(Define the problem in specific terms.)

A: Alternative Strategy Chosen
(List all alternatives and choose one.)

R: Responsibilities
(Specifically list who will do what and by when.)

E: Evaluate Outcomes
(Did the strategy you selected solve the problem?)

FIGURE 4.2

This format for problem solving will help teachers "PARE" a problem down to size when consulting or collaborating with others.

student, like Joey, who has been unable to follow classroom rules. When a teacher meets with a speech-language therapist and a parent to design a home-school language-intervention program, the three here are also involved in a collaborative process.

Collaboration is a problem-solving method that draws on the professional expertise of two or more individuals who work together to achieve a common goal (Villa, Thousand, Nevin, & Malgeri, 1996). However, according to Phillips and McCullough (1990), for collaboration to take place in schools, the following central tenets must be acknowledged by professionals engaging in the process.

1. Joint responsibility for problems (i.e., all professionals share responsibility and concern for students);
2. Joint accountability and recognition for problem resolution;
3. A shared belief that pooling talents and resources is mutually advantageous, with the following benefits:
   a. A wide range of solutions generated;
   b. Diversity of expertise and resources available;
   c. Superiority and originality of solutions generated;
4. A belief that teacher or student problem resolution merits expenditure of time, energy, and resources; and,

5. A belief that correlates of collaboration are important and desirable (i.e., group morale, group cohesion, increased knowledge of problem-solving processes and specific alternative classroom interventions) (p. 295).

It should be noted, however, that joint responsibility and accountability do not preclude designating one member of the collaborative group as a case manager to facilitate the group's activities. The case manager might coordinate services needed by the student and his or her family, delegate responsibilities, and ensure follow-up activities (Morsink et al., 1991).

Coordinating needed services might, for example, entail obtaining appropriate curricular materials needed to implement Individualized Educational Program (IEP) objectives for Travis, or it may mean referring Joey's family for services provided in a community mental-health center. The case manager acts as the clearinghouse for locating materials and services and for obtaining access to them. Although members of collaborative teams must function together as a group, each contributing equally to the problem-solving effort, the case manager may still choose to delegate specific responsibilities to each team member in order to facilitate the problem-solving process. Delegating responsibilities will be more easily accomplished if the case manager follows the guidelines suggested by Morsink et al. (1991) as listed in Table 4.2.

Finally, follow-up activities are critical if goals are to be met. Follow-up must be conducted in a systematic manner so that all parties involved know when and how the follow-up activities will occur. For example, the case manager should establish the next meeting date, time, and place before the group adjourns, and he or she should provide the means for regular communication in order to monitor progress. Figure 4.3 illustrates a communication form used by Mr. Abel

---

Table 4.2 **Delegating Responsibility**

Teachers may need to delegate responsibilities to members of a collaborative team. These may include other teachers and professionals, parents, and paraprofessionals. The following suggestions will help teachers ensure that delegated responsibilities are performed correctly:

1. State the task clearly and objectively.
2. Tell the person why the task is important.
3. Give "permission." Unless others know to whom authority has been delegated to accomplish the task, they may not cooperate fully.
4. Clarify the results that are expected. It is important to tell designees what to accomplish but not how to do the job.
5. Allow for interaction. Make certain that the task and its results are clear by asking the designee to restate what is to be done. Also allow time for questions or clarification.
6. Agree on follow-up. Set a time and place to meet after the task has been completed in order to evaluate the results. It is not adequate to say, "Let's get together sometime and talk about it some more."

Source: Morsink, C.V., Thomas, C.C., & Correa, V.I. (1991). *Interactive teaming: Consultation and collaboration in special programs.* New York, NY: Macmillan, p. 195. Reprinted with permission.

STUDENT: _____   TEACHER: _____

SUBJECT: _____   DATE: _____

GRADING PERIOD: _____   DUE DATE: _____

I would appreciate your response to the items below so that I may better assist you with this student. Please circle the appropriate responses and drop the completed form in my box by the due date indicated. Thank you!

I. PREPARATION

Problem   No Problem

Circle Problem Areas (if any):
Tardy to class
Unprepared with paper, pencil, and book(s)
Does not complete homework
(Please list missing homework
under "comments.")

Other: _____

_____

III. CLASS PARTICIPATION

Problem   No Problem

Circle Problem Areas (if any):
Does not complete assignments
    (Please list missing work under "comments.")
Does not follow instructions
Does not take notes in class
Does not ask questions
Does not participate in class discussions
Does not have a good attitude toward class
Other: _____

II. BEHAVIOR

Problem   No Problem

Circle Problem Areas (if any):
Does not work quietly
Distracts others
Uses inappropriate language or tone of voice
Does not pay attention
Inappropriately interacts with other students

Other: _____

_____

IV. ACHIEVEMENT

Estimated Grade_____

Do you desire a conference?
Yes_____ No_____
If yes, when is a convenient time?

_____

V. COMMENTS

Please note specific skills or concepts with which the student is having difficulty. Include names of texts, specific pages, materials, etc. Please also note upcoming work and/or missing home work and class assignments.

VI. ACTION TAKEN (Note when action was taken and by whom):

FIGURE 4.3

Mr. Abel uses a mainstreaming checklist like this one to monitor Robert's performance in his regular classes. The checklist goes to teachers once each week. Classroom teachers circle problem areas and make comments. When problems are noted, Mr. Abel documents the action he and others take.

to provide systematic follow-up to monitor Robert's progress in his main-streamed classes.

Collaboration can be an effective way to provide educational services to a variety of students within the same school or classroom. According to Thousand and Villa (1989), "School personnel who effectively collaborate will agree that each teacher, left alone, is limited in the instructional responses he or she can conceptualize or deliver. However, when a school staff pool their conceptual, material, technical, and human resources, students and staff benefit from the collective wisdom" (pp. 99–100). In order to benefit from collective wisdom, teachers must keep the child as the focal point and seek out others who have information, materials, and strategies necessary to meet the child's needs (Johnson, Pugach, & Devlin, 1990).

Johnson, Pugach, and Devlin (1990) offer several suggestions to move teachers toward collaboration:

1. Collaborative efforts must be sanctioned at the administrative level. Teachers need support and freedom to engage in mutual problem solving.
2. Teachers should be given assistance with clerical work and other noninstructional tasks to leave them more time to interact with each other. Teacher aides, parents, volunteers, or student helpers might be used to serve this purpose.
3. Teachers should be encouraged to organize meeting times for the purpose of mutual problem solving. Prearranged after-school meetings or meetings scheduled during mutual planning periods would provide a set time for teachers to discuss problems they are facing.
4. Specialist and classroom teachers should be given opportunities to coteach. This could enhance mutual understanding of the unique expertise each has to offer.
5. The use of specialized terminology should be avoided. Using jargon that others do not understand can imply an expert-to-novice relationship. Hierarchical relationships are rarely conducive to collaboration.
6. Faculty or inservice meetings could be reserved for collaborative problem solving (p. 11).

Pugach and Johnson (1988) and Voltz, Elliott, and Harris (1995) also offer some excellent ideas to provide teachers with the time they need for collaborative activities. These include the use of floating substitutes to cover classes for teachers engaged in collaborative problem solving; coordination of activities like art, music, and physical education so that collaborative teams can meet; and use of principals as substitute instructors.

Educators who have been involved in collaborative efforts have reported success in resolving instructional problems (Everson, 1990; Meyers, Gelzheiser, & Yelich, 1991; Voltz et al., 1995). Thousand and Villa (1989) urge teachers to make every effort to seek out all potential members of the collaborative team, and they call for schools to restructure to promote shared decision making and collaborative teaching in order to facilitate inclusion (Villa et al., 1996).

Collaborative Teaching to Facilitate Inclusion

Bauwens and Hourcade (1995) suggest that regular and special educators should participate in cooperative or collaborative teaching arrangements. They define cooperative teaching as ". . . a restructuring of teaching procedures in which two or more educators possessing distinct sets of skills work in a coactive and coordinated fashion to jointly teach academically and behaviorally heterogeneous groups of students in integrated settings" (p. 46). Collaborative or coteaching procedures include team teaching, complementary instruction, and supportive learning arrangements (Bauwens & Hourcade, 1995, 1997; Vaughn, Schumm, & Arguelles, 1997).

Ms. Lopez and Ms. Kirk, for example, might team teach when they take turns presenting the social studies content, providing enrichment activities, asking questions, and monitoring student progress. On the other hand, if Ms. Kirk assumes primary responsibility for teaching the social studies information while Ms. Lopez teaches helpful learning strategies and classroom behaviors, they are using complementary instruction. Finally, Ms. Kirk might teach the social studies content with Ms. Lopez engaging students in follow-up, reinforcement, and enrichment activities, such as cooperative learning groups or peer tutoring pairs, to help students practice, review, and extend learning. In this model, Ms. Lopez and Ms. Kirk are participating in a supportive learning arrangement.

Vaughn, Schumm, and Arguelles (1997) suggest some additional models to enhance coteaching and move beyond the typical procedures of "tag-team teaching" (i.e., one teacher teaches while the other watches and then the roles are reversed) and "grazing" (i.e., one teacher teaches while the other drifts around the room). They offer the following strategies:

◆ One Group with One Lead Teacher and One Teacher "Teaching on Purpose"—Ms. Kirk teaches the social studies lesson while Ms. Lopez continuously moves to individuals or small groups of students to present mini-lessons to review, reinforce, and extend learning.

◆ Two Groups with Two Teachers Teaching the Same Content—Following a large-group social studies lesson, Ms. Lopez and Ms. Kirk each work with a group of students to reinforce the lesson content, give feedback, and monitor student mastery of the information.

◆ Two Groups with One Teacher Reteaching and One Teacher Teaching Alternative Information—Ms. Lopez and Ms. Kirk place students in flexible groups based on the knowledge and skills acquired during the social studies lesson. Ms. Kirk reteaches one group the skills they are lacking and Ms. Lopez presents additional information for students in the group ready to advance.

◆ Multiple Groups with Two Teachers Monitoring and Teaching Varied Content—In this model, Ms. Kirk and Ms. Lopez arrange students into cooperative learning groups. They monitor the progress of the groups and also pull individuals or small groups of students for mini-lessons as necessary.

Regardless of the coteaching arrangement chosen, collaborative teachers must resolve many issues if they are to be successful. For example, Ms. Lopez and Ms. Kirk must negotiate clearly defined teaching roles, classroom management procedures, and grading practices they can both comfortably "own" or they may feel that they are "stepping on each other's toes" (Wood, 1998). In addition, joint planning time, adjusted student schedules, reduced caseloads, administrative support, and adequate staff development opportunities are persistent problems experienced by those who engage in collaborative teaching (Salend et al., 1997; Walther-Thomas, 1997). When difficulties such as these are resolved, however, coteaching proponents report several benefits including renewed energy and enthusiasm for teaching, instructional improvement, and added services for students (Reinhiller, 1996).

Despite the increasing use of collaborative teaching models in inclusive classrooms, not all authorities agree that these arrangements produce positive outcomes for students with mild disabilities (see, for example, Boudah, Schumaker, & Deshler, 1997; Klingner, Vaughn, Hughes, Schumm, & Elbaum, 1998; Saint-Laurent et al., 1998). Moreover, collaboration and coteaching may not succeed unless parents are enlisted as supportive partners in the process.

Parents as Partners

In the best collaborative arrangements, parents are considered to be equal participating partners (Morsink et al., 1991; Thousand & Villa, 1989). Parents, however, may have mixed views of inclusion, wanting integration for their children but fearing that the quality of the program may suffer (Hobbs, & Westling, 1998; Fisher, Pumpian, & Sax, 1998; Westling, 1996). The Individuals with Disabilities Education Act (IDEA) (1997) mandates involvement by parents in planning and decision making, and parents should be encouraged to take an active role in both processes. Moreover, research demonstrates that schools facilitating parental involvement increase overall student achievement (Thorkildsen & Stein, 1998).

All too often, however, parents are perceived by teachers as adversarial and responsible for their child's problems (Sonnenschein, 1981). Parents who are rushed for time or who believe that their opinions are not valued by professionals may feel that they are not respected by teachers and may choose to withdraw from the process (Turnbull & Turnbull, 1997). In fact, parents may not involve themselves in school activities for several reasons, including the following:

1. They made poor grades as a child.
2. They are contacted only when there is a problem.
3. They are afraid schools will say that their child is "dumb" or that they are "bad" parents.
4. They lack confidence in their ability to talk with professionals (Gonder, 1998).

Still other parents may be unable to leave their jobs or obtain childcare or transportation to attend school meetings.

In addition, some parents or guardians from culturally or linguistically diverse backgrounds may be quite interested in their child's progress in school, but the teacher may "miss" or misinterpret this interest (Linan-Thompson & Jean, 1997). Travis's mother, for example, might believe that her son is "just a little slow"; therefore, she may not push him to complete his homework or advocate for additional services at school to meet his needs. Ms. Lopez, on the other hand, might interpret this behavior to mean that Travis's mother is not concerned about her son's progress. Misunderstandings might easily result if Ms. Lopez does not clearly communicate to Travis's mother what a learning disability is and how the school can work with her to help Travis. Teachers must be sensitive to the needs of families from diverse backgrounds (Garcia & Malkin, 1993; Harry, Allen, & McLaughlin, 1995).

For whatever reason, some parents may prefer to have only limited involvement in educational programming for their children (Winton & Turnbull, 1981). Parental preference for only limited participation does not obviate the need for teachers to solicit their involvement, however. Beale and Beers (1982) identified three types of approaches used by schools when interacting with parents:

◆ Category 1: Teach them what they need to know. This approach focuses on parent education and training and emphasizes the expert role of educators. Ms. Lopez, for example, might teach Travis's mother to monitor his behavior at home when he is completing homework assignments, or she might demonstrate a specific method to help Travis rehearse material orally when studying for a test.
◆ Category 2: Bring them in and put them to work. This approach uses parents as volunteers and increases parental involvement in the school. Ms. Kirk might use parents of the children in her classroom as helpers or as chaperones on field trips.
◆ Category 3: I talk, you talk, we talk. This approach stresses honest communication and collaboration between parents and teachers and requires effective communication skills and respect for parents as equal partners in the education process.

The key element to a successful partnership with parents is regular and open communication. Too often, parents hear from the child's teacher or school only when a behavioral or learning problem surfaces. In order to establish and maintain a positive relationship with parents, communication must be ongoing and offer a non-threatening avenue for parents to express concerns and ask questions (deBettencourt, 1987). Notes sent home on a regular basis, telephone calls to discuss progress, home visits where permissible, or invitations to visit the classroom are all ways of keeping the communication lines open. Shea and Bauer (1991) suggest the following strategies to facilitate teacher–parent communication:

◆ Daily or periodic written reports on progress sent home with students
◆ Telephone calls or recorded telephone messages
◆ Praise notes or positive letters; for example, the note sent by Ms. Lopez to Joey's parents regarding his improvements in behavior (Figure 4.4)
◆ Two-way notebooks in which teachers and parents write questions and positive comments to each other
◆ Behavioral or achievement awards
◆ Monthly calendars, notices, or newsletters about class and student activities

```
                                                     October 23, 2000



Dear Mr. and Mrs. Greenhill,

    Joey has successfully completed his work contract for the week

of October 16! He completed 5/5 class assignments, kept his

assignment sheet up-to-date all week, and kept his desk neat. He

has earned a ticket to the class coke party on Friday. He is also

excited about the pizza that you promised him as a part of his reward!

    Joey's work contract for next week will be the same, but with

the addition of the following:  Joey will keep his weekly homework

notebook neat, with all of his assignments in the correct order.

    Please call me if you have any questions.

                                    Sincerely yours,

                                    Susan Lopez
                                    Ms. Lopez
```

FIGURE 4.4

A Note from Ms. Lopez to Joey's Parents

Notes, Letters, and Two-Way Notebooks

Notes and letters sent home to parents should provide good news more often than bad news. Parents are busy people; therefore, notes and letters should be concise and to the point. When requesting a school visit, teachers should express a clear reason for the request. For example, when Ms. Lopez arranges a visit by Joey's parents for his IEP meeting, she should remind them of the agreed-upon meeting place, date, and time, and ask his parents to think about goals for Joey for the school year. Marion (1979) cautions that teachers must guard against a condescending tone or use of educational jargon in letters or notes sent home. Also, a sign-off portion for parents, when appropriate, may ensure that they received the message.

Although personal notes and letters are excellent ways to maintain communication with individual parents, weekly, biweekly, or monthly class or school letters and newsletters are other important means of keeping parents informed. Many teachers send an introductory letter home to all parents at the start of each school year. These letters might welcome the child and the parents to the classroom, list supplies and materials required by the child for the school year, and emphasize the importance of the parents to the child's educational activities. Shea and Bauer (1985) suggest several additional items that might be included in letters or newsletters:

- A list of the year's scheduled subjects, activities, or special events
- An invitation to parents to visit the classroom or the school
- An invitation to parents to participate in the class as volunteers
- A list of special classroom rules and procedures
- The teacher's telephone number
- Suggestions for parents wishing to help at home

Two-way notebooks, sometimes called "passports" (Runge, Walker, & Shea, 1975), are spiral-bound notebooks that children carry with them during the school day. Teachers, bus drivers, other school personnel, and parents make comments in the notebook regarding the child's academic or behavioral progress. To encourage children to carry this notebook, teachers may assign points to be exchanged for a reward. Shea and Bauer (1991) suggest that comments written in the two-way notebook be brief, positive, honest, and responsive. That is, when parents request a meeting or assistance, teachers must be certain to follow through. It is also important to be

Parents are equal partners in the best collaborative arrangements, particularly when teachers encourage regular and open communication.

consistent in using this system of communication and to guard against the use of jargon. Furthermore, the worries and aggravations of a bad day should not be projected onto the child or his or her parents. Williams and Cartledge (1997) state that persistence and conveyance of an attitude that one's primary interest is to help the student are keys to making the two-way notebook work.

Telephone Calls

Although telephone calls from school may be threatening to some parents, teachers can help to eliminate this threat by calling parents at the start of the school year to introduce themselves and by periodically calling parents to deliver positive comments. Teachers should refrain from making numerous phone calls home regarding a child's behavior at school. Some teachers maintain a calendar or cards rotating in a file box to ensure periodic phone calls to parents. Of course, any time the teacher attempts to contact the child's parents, whether by telephone or by letter or note home, he or she should document the contact on a log sheet. The log should include the date, time, and method of contact; the name of the person contacted; and a brief summary of the conversation. (See Figure 4.5 for a sample contact log.)

Contact Log for: Travis Johnson

Date	Time	Type of Contact	Person Contacted	Content
9/9	8:05 AM	Phone call	Mrs. Johnson	Invited her to meet to talk about Travis completing homework.
9/10	4:00 AM	Conference at School	Mrs. Johnson	Planned ways to encourage Travis to do homework. Ms. Lopez to provide an assignment sheet. Mrs. Johnson to sign sheet & schedule a time/place for homework 1 hour per night before supper.
9/11	9:03 AM	Phone call	From Mrs. Johnson	Mrs. Johnson says Travis is doing his homework but needs many breaks.

FIGURE 4.5

Ms. Lopez documents all letters, notes, phone calls, and meetings with parents. Shown above is part of her contact log for Travis.

Marion (1979) points out that teachers must show courtesy and respect in their phone conversations with parents. Using a polite and respectful tone of voice and addressing parents as "Mr./Mrs." (or, when appropriate, "Ms.") may make the difference between a positive and a negative contact. In addition, teachers should call parents in the evening, rather than interrupting them at work.

Teachers who have access to home computers sometimes use web pages and e-mail to communicate with students and parents during after-school hours. In addition, some teachers use recorded telephone messages to give information on upcoming classroom events. Others use recorded messages as a "hot-line" to announce homework assignments and tips to help students complete their homework.

Communication About Homework

Regular classroom teachers, special educators, and parents voice similar concerns regarding homework (Buck et al., 1996; Epstein et al., 1997). Most of these concerns center on clear and frequent communication between parents and teachers about homework (Jayanthi, Bursuck, Epstein, & Polloway, 1997). For example, teachers may not be free to make phone calls during the school day, they may be unable to make long distance calls from school, or they may have family commitments of their own during the evenings and weekends. Parents, too, may have busy work and personal schedules, they may be unable to give assistance with homework, or they may find that their children lie to them, saying they do not have homework. Finally, special educators and regular classroom teachers may not communicate with one another about homework assignments. Such communication problems can intensify the anxiety that parents, students, and teachers may feel regarding the increased standards for achievement and stiffer homework policies used in many schools today. Some excellent suggestions to remedy these concerns about homework communication are offered by Jayanthi and colleagues (see, for example, Jayanthi, Bursuck, et al., 1997; Jayanthi, Sawyer, Nelson, Bursuck, & Epstein, 1995):

- State homework policies and long-range assignments with due dates on a newsletter at the start of the semester or every few weeks. Send newsletters and other homework announcements home on brightly colored paper.
- Use recorded telephone messages, audiotapes, and electronic mail to give homework assignments and assistance.
- Require assignment notebooks of all students. Write homework assignments on the chalkboard and check to ensure all students correctly copy the assignment. Alert parents at the start of the school year that the assignment notebook will come home every evening. (Some schools even provide these notebooks to all students and require parents to sign them daily!)
- Provide opportunities such as peer tutoring or after-school programs to help students complete homework, with assistance as needed, at school.

◆ Provide convenient and frequent times for parents and teachers to conference "face-to-face" regarding student performance.

Parent Conferences

Parents have a legal right under IDEA (1997) to be provided with all available information about their child and his or her progress; therefore, teachers will be involved in numerous parent–teacher conferences throughout the school year. Parent–teacher conferences are conducted for planning the IEP, for reporting pupil progress, and for problem solving. Although these conferences can be intimidating for both parents and educators, careful planning can help to alleviate anxiety for everyone.

DeBettencourt (1987) suggests that, prior to the conference, teachers should prepare an outline of all information they wish to share or collect. In addition, she encourages teachers to prepare an agenda for the meeting and to give parents a copy of the agenda before the meeting begins. (See Figure 4.6 for an agenda used during Ms. Lopez's conference with Travis's mother.) Other ideas for parent–teacher conferences offered by deBettencourt (p.26) include (a) stating objectives in clear terms that parents can understand, (b) holding the conference in a small room free from distractions, (c) starting on time and keeping to the scheduled time limit, (d) arranging chairs so that parents and teachers can see each other without obstacles, and (e) presenting all information clearly, using jargon-free language. Additional suggestions for successful parent–teacher conferences are presented in Table 4.3.

Shea and Bauer (1991) describe several purposes for parent–teacher conferences, including making progress reports, engaging in problem solving, and discussing the IEP. They recommend that teachers help parents to participate successfully in parent–teacher conferences by providing them with a letter or newsletter at the start of the school year offering conference tips. (See Figure 4.7.) Shea and Bauer (1985) also recommend several excellent "Do's and Don'ts" for teachers conducting parent–teacher conferences. These suggestions are presented in Table 4.4.

I. Welcome & Preview Meeting
II. Share samples of Travis' work
III. Discuss homework assignments completed.
IV. Discuss homework assignments not completed.
V. Discuss ways to increase homework completed by Travis.
VI. Summarize

Ms. Lopez gave Mrs. Johnson a copy of the agenda when she arrived. Mrs. Johnson wrote her own comments and questions on the agenda as the discussion proceeded.

FIGURE 4.6 ◆

Ms. Lopez planned an agenda for the parent-teacher conference she held with Travis's mother, Mrs. Johnson. Shown above is the agenda she used during the conference.

Table 4.3   Suggestions for Successful Parent–Teacher Conferences

1. Establish communication with parents *before* problems arise.
2. Communicate with parents in a positive manner.
3. Schedule conferences regularly and frequently to discuss student progress rather than scheduling them only for problem resolution.
4. Schedule conferences at mutually agreed-upon times and places. Consider the parents' work schedules and childcare concerns. Provide help with childcare and transportation arrangements if possible.
5. Plan your conference. Provide a written list of student achievements and progress, as well as concerns about the student.
6. Schedule the conference in an inviting environment rather than in a conference room or office if possible. If the conference must be in the classroom, arrange the table and chairs to avoid obstructions between you and the parents. Be sure parents have adult-sized chairs. Place flowers, refreshments, or other items on the table to enhance the environment and parental comfort.
7. Have student work samples available for parents to review. These samples should exhibit strengths as well as weaknesses.
8. Provide objective documentation of problems or concerns. Refrain from making negative statements or subjective comments.
9. Make positive comments about student performance and behavior, emphasizing student strengths, before discussing problem areas.
10. Listen to the parents' concerns and questions. Provide adequate time for parents to reflect on information and to ask questions.
11. Answer parents' questions clearly and honestly.
12. Monitor parental understanding of the information you provide by questioning and paraphrasing.
13. Review and summarize statements made by teachers and parents during the conference and at the end.
14. Before the meeting is concluded, be sure that all parties understand the next steps to be taken; for example, who is responsible for particular activities and how follow-up communication will take place.
15. Set a time, place, and date for the next meeting if appropriate.

Finally, Perl (1995) encourages teachers to think of problem-solving conferences as opportunities to strengthen relationships between parents and teachers. Focusing on a common goal—assisting the child—can help teachers and parents to see the possibilities, rather than just the problems. He maintains that teachers can self-monitor their level of competence in skills such as caring, building rapport, listening, empathizing, reflecting emotions, and clarifying statements. Skill in each of these critical behaviors can help teachers focus on student and parent strengths in order to empower families. (See Box 4.2 for some interesting web sites offering assistance to families of children and youth with disabilities.)

Paraprofessionals and Volunteers

Paraprofessionals and volunteers play extremely important roles in the education of students with mild disabilities. Paraprofessionals, sometimes called

Before the Conference

1. Make arrangements for your other children if necessary. Conferences are for you and your child's teacher. Small children can be distracting and take time away from the discussion.
2. Jot down any questions you may have for the teacher. For example:
   How is my child progressing in reading, math, and other subjects?
   Does he or she get along well with other students?
   Does he or she get along well with teachers?
   What do the tests say about my child?
   What are the class rules and how is misbehavior handled?
3. Talk to your child about the conference. Find out whether he or she wants you to ask any questions or voice concerns.
4. Collect any records or information that might help the teacher. Try to anticipate questions, gather materials, and prepare answers.

At the Conference

1. Please be prompt and stay only for your scheduled time. Please feel free to schedule another conference if we do not cover all the necessary information in the allotted time.
2. Discuss only the child at issue. He or she is the focus of this conference. Let's stick to the subject.
3. Ask questions about your child's education. Please advocate for your child. Know your rights and those of your child.
4. Volunteer information that may help the teacher plan programming for your child.
5. Feel free to take notes during the conference.

After the Conference

Please feel free to contact your child's teacher for further clarification or information at
_____.

FIGURE 4.7 ──◆

Shea and Bauer (1991) suggest that teachers can encourage parental participation in conferences by giving them a handout like this one at the start of the school year. Adapted from: Shea, T.M., & Bauer, A.M. (1991). *Parents and teachers of children with exceptionalities: A handbook for collaboration.* Boston, MA: Allyn & Bacon, p. 146. Reprinted with permission.

teacher aides, instructional assistants, or paraeducators, are salaried full-time or part-time members of the school's staff. According to Fimian, Fafard, and Howell (1984), paraprofessionals may or may not be licensed teachers, although they usually have designated classroom duties.

Volunteers, on the other hand, are parents, college students, senior citizens, or others who donate their time and talents in order to help out during the school day. Volunteers may, for example, help teachers make instructional materials, games, or bulletin boards at school or at home. They may listen to children read, read to children, or help as tutors. In addition, volunteers may have special skills, talents, or experiences to draw upon in providing enriching activities for students with mild disabilities and their peers. Volunteer room mothers or fathers are also invaluable sources of help for classroom parties and for special events such as field trips or field days.

The teacher can encourage volunteerism in the classroom by "advertising" his or her needs. Some teachers periodically send home letters listing classroom

Table 4.4   Suggestions for Successful Parent–teacher Conferences

Parent-teacher conferences will proceed more smoothly if teachers keep in mind several "Do's" and "Don'ts" when meeting with parents.

1. Don't make parents defensive by criticizing them, their children, or their lifestyle.
2. Don't argue. Teachers are not always right, nor do they have all the answers.
3. Don't belittle the students, the school, the administration, or the school system.
4. Don't talk or gossip about other children or parents. Maintain confidentiality.
5. Don't become overly personal. Avoid embarrassing the parents.
6. Don't assume that the parents are "problem parents" or that they need, want, or will accept your help or advice.
7. Don't dwell on negatives. Seek the positive and remain positive throughout the conference.
8. Don't promise things that are not deliverable.
9. Don't assume full responsibility for the child. Share responsibility with the parents and with other teachers.
10. Don't take yourself too seriously. Teachers are human and they do make mistakes.
11. Don't avoid difficult topics because of your own anxiety. Everyone is nervous but gets over it with success and experience.
12. Do listen to parents. They can provide you with valuable information.
13. Do listen to parents. Be friendly, relaxed, and empathetic.
14. Do listen to parents. Let them speak or think without interruption.
15. Do prepare for the conference by gathering materials and making an outline beforehand.
16. Do emphasize the positive.

Adapted from: Shea, T.M., & Bauer, A.M. (1991). *Parents and teachers of children with exceptionalities: A handbook for collaboration.* Copyright © 1991. Reprinted with permission of Allyn & Bacon.

needs and ask parents to check the duties they can comfortably assume (e.g., providing cookies for a class party or cutting out paper hearts for a bulletin board). Others use the monthly newsletter to praise volunteers for their efforts and to specify additional needs in the future.

Paraprofessionals may also assume a number of important duties in the classroom. In special education classrooms they may provide instructional support by supervising independent work, reinforcing concepts taught by the teacher, modifying or making materials, listening to students read, or reading to them. In addition, they may offer behavior-management support by praising students for appropriate behaviors, and they may offer diagnostic support by correcting and grading papers, or observing and recording academic or social behaviors (McKenzie & Houk, 1986). Paraprofessionals also prepare bulletin boards or instructional games, locate and order materials or supplies, type and

Box 4.2

Web Watch

Resources for Parents and Families

Family Village

http://www.familyvillage.wisc.org
Links to other sites on specific disabilities; discussions and chat rooms for parents; information by topical area of disability; Shopping Mall for technology assistance for parents of children with disabilities.

National Parent Information Network

http://www.npin.org
Abundant information for parents of children with disabilities and links to related sites.

Sonic Net

http://www.sonic.net/nilp/
Programs and services for families of persons with various disabilities.

Special Education Resources on the Internet (SERI)

http://www.hood.edu/seri/serihome.htm
Special education information for both parents and teachers of children and youth with various disabilities.

Special Needs Education Network

http://www.schoolnet2.carleton.ca/snel
A special needs education network of resources for both parents and teachers.

Working Woman

http://workingwoman.com/articles/zclancy.htm
Good information that parents of a child with special needs might find useful.

duplicate written materials, take attendance, record grades, and supervise students during lunch or recess.

With the passage of IDEA in 1997, more paraprofessionals than ever before are being hired by schools in order to provide children with disabilities the supplementary aids and services necessary to maintain them in the regular classroom. A paraprofessional, for example, might be assigned full-time to just one child with a disability and accompany that child throughout the school day. For example, paraprofessionals are increasingly providing one-on-one assistance for students with challenging behaviors who are included in the regular classroom (Freschi, 1999). Recent estimates range from 250,000 to 280,000 para-educators in special education classrooms alone, with approximately 500,000 instructional assistants providing some type of direct services to students through Chapter 1 or other classrooms (Council for Exceptional Children [CEC], 1997). French (1998, 1999) and French and Pickett (1997) report that paraprofessionals are now assuming many critical responsibilities of teachers such as planning and delivering instruction, managing behaviors, and testing students. In addition, paraprofessionals from culturally or linguistically diverse backgrounds may serve as essential team members, assisting teachers in communication with students and their parents (Miramontes, 1990).

Little research exists, however, to document the efficacy of paraprofessionals assuming these professional duties, or of their preparation to do so (Jones & Bender, 1993). In fact, instructional assistants may sometimes "hover" over students with disabilities, fostering dependence, limiting peer interactions, and disrupting instruction for other students (Giangreco, Edelman, Luiselli, & MacFarland, 1997). When paraeducators assume high levels of responsibility for student learning and behavior in inclusive classrooms, role confusion with general educators can result (Marks, Schrader, & Levine, 1999). Freschi (1999) suggests that one-on-one assistance by paraprofessionals in the classroom must be considered a temporary arrangement with a definite ending point in sight so that the student can become as independent as possible. Having the teacher and the paraprofessional routinely switch roles and slowly reducing the level of support provided by the aide can ease the student's transition from the paraeducator to the teacher.

Nevertheless, the benefits of using paraprofessionals or volunteers in the classroom can be numerous. Boomer (1980, 1982) and the CEC (1997) cite the following benefits of using paraprofessionals (Note that these benefits can pertain to volunteers as well):

1. The student-to-teacher ratio is decreased, thereby increasing individual attention to each child.
2. Paraprofessionals enable alternative classroom arrangements to provide small-group and one-on-one activities with supervision.
3. Paraprofessionals contribute strengths and talents that the teacher may not have.
4. Paraprofessionals help teachers form a more complete and accurate picture of a student through continuous feedback and mutual problem solving, resulting in better decision making and enhanced instructional creativity.
5. A positive relationship between the teacher and the paraprofessional facilitates emotional support and meaningful dialogue throughout the school day.
6. Paraprofessionals act as liaisons between the teacher and other staff members.
7. Paraprofessionals provide teachers partial relief from non-instructional duties, by assisting with or taking over such tasks as taking attendance or collecting lunch money.

Using paraprofessionals and volunteers to greatest advantage requires careful planning and communication (Boomer, 1981). McKenzie and Houk

(1986) suggest that paraprofessionals should be matched with teachers according to their particular skills. Ms. Lopez, for example, might require an assistant to give her instructional support by reviewing new vocabulary with Travis. She may also need help in monitoring and rewarding Joey for appropriate social skills. Mr. Abel, on the other hand, may require assistance with making and duplicating materials for his students.

Regardless of the tasks to be performed, teachers must clearly communicate responsibilities and expectations to paraprofessionals and to volunteers. Unfortunately, teachers often view paraprofessionals as peers and may not be prepared to provide them with the direction and supervision they require in order to function effectively (French, 1998; French & Pickett, 1997; Salzberg & Morgan, 1995). The teacher must monitor the performance of assistants, giving them feedback, evaluating their progress, and recognizing their efforts. The following procedures are recommended when working with paraprofessionals and volunteers:

◆ Orient assistants to the school. Orientation sessions can be conducted for a group when more than one assistant is new to the school. However, whether conducted individually or with a group, assistants will require a tour of the school; introductions to principals and other professionals, as well as to one another; and information regarding school schedules, policies, and procedures. When appropriate, they should be provided with a copy of the faculty/student handbook. In addition, assistants may be trained as a group to operate the school copier, computers, or audiovisual equipment.

◆ Orient assistants to the classroom. Provide nametags or a seating chart for identifying students. Introduce the assistant to the children and show the assistant where materials are located in the classroom. Provide a personal space for the assistant, including a table or desk, a chair, and a place to secure his or her belongings.

◆ Plan responsibilities for assistants. Although the teacher assistant may be involved in the planning process, the teacher is still responsible for all activities within the classroom.

◆ Prepare and post a written schedule of duties for all assistants. The schedule might include specific daily responsibilities in addition to ongoing duties. As the needs of the classroom change, the duties of the assistants should change as well.

◆ Clearly tell assistants what they are to do and demonstrate tasks for them whenever possible. If, for example, Ms. Lopez asks her assistant to make multiplication flash cards for Travis, she will need to specify exactly which facts are to be included. She may also want to show the assistant a sample flash card. Ask assistants specific questions to be sure they understand directions, and provide them with the opportunity to ask for clarification. (See Box 4.3.)

◆ Schedule daily conferences with assistants to plan and evaluate their responsibilities, give specific feedback, and offer praise for their accomplishments.

Box 4.3

Ms. Lopez Instructs a Paraprofessional

Ms. Lopez has the assistance of a paraprofessional, Mrs. Mau, for three hours daily. During her planning period, Ms. Lopez met with Mrs. Mau to review her assignments for the day.

Ms. Lopez: Showing Mrs. Mau an index card on which the word *where* is clearly printed, and a list of 14 other words) I need you to print the words from this list neatly onto these index cards just like I did with this first word, *where.* Use the alphabet over the chalkboard as a guide for making the letters since Travis has trouble recognizing them when they're not printed the same way he's learning to write.

Mrs. Mau: Okay. I can do that right after I copy the math sheets for Ms. London. She needs those by 11:00. Did you want me to start working on these words with Travis to day?

Ms. Lopez: Yes, these are his new words, and I'd like you to review them with him every day this week first thing when Travis comes for resource. Use the new list of words to make a check sheet for yourself like this one (showing Mrs. Mau a paper that has words listed in a column on the left side and the days of the week across the top). Put Travis's name on the top of the check sheet. Then hold up each card for Travis. Give him five seconds for each word. If he says the word within the five seconds, put a plus sign on the blank under the day for that word like this (demonstrating on the old checklist she used as a model). If Travis doesn't say the word in five seconds, tell him the word, have him repeat it, and put a minus sign on the blank. Any questions?

Mrs. Mau: Yes. What if Travis says the wrong word during the five seconds?

Ms. Lopez: Oh, yeah. If he says the wrong word, tell him the correct word, let him repeat it, and still put the minus on the blank. If he starts to say the wrong word and then corrects himself, go ahead and put the plus sign on the line and tell him good job. Okay?

Mrs. Mau: Okay.

Ms. Lopez: I'd like to see the check sheet today, so after you and Travis are done with the words, give him the sheet and let him bring it to me when I start his reading group. Put the index cards of his words in Travis's folder, then you can finish the bulletin board you started yesterday. It's gonna look good!

Mrs. Mau: All right! I'll get these copies made for Ms. London and then I'll start on the word cards.

Paraprofessionals and volunteers can assist the teacher of students with mild disabilities in several ways. Even more importantly, when the teacher carefully plans and schedules responsibilities, clearly communicates the

expectations for each task, and offers appropriate feedback and praise, paraprofessionals and volunteers can provide valuable assistance for students with mild
disabilities.

Summary

Good communication skills are an absolute necessity for teachers of students
with mild disabilities. Consultation and collaboration require teachers to communicate clearly and honestly in order to maximize success for their students
with learning and behavioral problems. Clear and honest communication requires attention to both the verbal and nonverbal behaviors exhibited by students.

Contact with parents also requires skillful and sensitive communication.
Teachers may communicate with parents through telephone calls, written notes
or letters, or parent–teacher conferences. Clear, concise, ongoing communication will help teachers enlist the support of parents as partners in the education
of their children with mild disabilities.

Paraprofessionals and volunteers provide important assistance for students
with special needs. Careful planning and clear communication of responsibilities and expectations will increase the likelihood that classroom assistants will
contribute to student success.

Application Exercises

1. Interview a practicing special education teacher in a local school system. Ask
   this teacher to suggest useful techniques for systematic communication with
   regular classroom teachers and with parents.
2. Contact teachers or administrators in a local school division. Are consultation
   and collaboration used in this school system? If so, how are these models implemented?
3. Interview a special education teacher in a local school system. What methods
   does this teacher use to plan, schedule, and conduct parent–teacher conferences?
4. Create a file for parental communication. From the professional literature
   and InfoTrac, gather sample notes, progress reports, newsletters, and so
   forth, for communicating with parents.
5. Interview a paraprofessional in a local school system. Ask this person to explain in detail his or her duties in the special education classroom. Ask also
   what assistance the paraprofessional most appreciates from the supervising
   teacher.
6. Pair up with a regular educator. List important skills that characterize regular classroom teachers and special educators. Are there similarities? What are
   some important skills that special educators can learn from regular classroom teachers?
7. Ms. Booker states, "Susan is constantly asking me for help when I know she
   can do her work. She wants my help every step of the way, and I think the
   other children resent her trying to get all my attention. She takes a lot of my

time. . . " Assume you are Mr. Abel. Paraphrase Ms. Booker's comment. Frame an active-listening response reflecting the emotion as well as the content of Ms. Booker's message.

8. Browse the web sites listed in Box 4.2 regarding communicating with families. Design a handout for parents describing web sites and organizations that they may find helpful.

CHAPTER
5

MANAGING THE CLASSROOM ENVIRONMENT

Focus

As you read, think about the following questions:

◆ *What do the terms classroom management and discipline really mean?*

◆ *What responsibilities for promoting appropriate behaviors are required of teachers under the Individuals with Disabilities Education Act (IDEA) Amendments (1997)?*

◆ *What can teachers do to create a classroom atmosphere conducive to efficient learning and appropriate behavior?*

◆ *How can teachers maintain a positive classroom environment?*

◆ *What can teachers do to maximize the amount of time used for planning and instruction?*

Whether a teacher is a novice preparing for his or her first year in the classroom, or a veteran of several years of teaching, managing the classroom environment, particularly managing the behavior of students, can be a frightening prospect. An organized and sequential approach to classroom management will reduce the stress that teachers frequently experience as they plan for the new school year.

For example, Ms. Kirk knows that there will be several students with special needs in her classroom this year. She has learned that the best way to create a positive atmosphere in her class is to begin the school year well prepared. Before the school year begins, she plans the physical arrangement of her classroom. She also considers instructional objectives and materials for her students as well as their diverse cultural backgrounds. At the beginning of the school year, she sets aside some time each day to instruct her students in the rules, routines, and procedures to be implemented in her classroom. Her students know what is expected of them regarding behavior and achievement.

Mr. Abel knows that the "general attitude" of his students can sometimes become negative. To counter this negativism, he considers several sources of reinforcement that may motivate his students. He determines which reinforcers are likely to be readily available and which will be the most helpful in terms of the age and interests of each student. Then he introduces a behavior-management program to his students.

Ms. Lopez sometimes becomes so bogged down in the mechanics of running a classroom that she finds little time for planning. Interruptions, correspondence, and record keeping are eating away at her time. An inservice course on computers, through which she learns of a software package to record data collected for each student, and a few suggestions from a more experienced teacher on how to maximize time in the classroom, keep Ms. Lopez from becoming discouraged.

In this chapter, we will examine classroom-management techniques for teachers. First, we will explore ways in which teachers can manage the physical environment and promote a positive climate in the classroom. Next, we will discuss the teacher's management of time. After introducing the reader to reinforcement, a particularly important principle for teachers to understand, we will consider what IDEA (1997) has to say about behavior and discipline of students with mild disabilities.

Classroom Management and Discipline

As described by O'Melia and Rosenberg (1989), classroom management frequently invokes "images of docile students, tyrannical teachers, and sterile settings, where academic achievement takes a back seat to compliance with rules and procedures. Rarely does the phrase invoke scenes of talented teachers and scholarly students engaged in educationally effective endeavors" (p. 23). Classroom management, however, when properly designed and implemented, can make the difference between meaningful experiences and merely putting in time for students. Successful classroom management can also be the difference between a rewarding career and utter frustration for teachers.

Classroom management has been defined as "the positive manipulation of the learning environment to promote successful behavior and skill acquisition" (O'Melia & Rosenberg, 1989, p. 23). Specifically, classroom management involves the manipulation of the physical environment, the emotional climate, the time allocated to various activities, and, of course, classroom discipline.

Discipline, too, is a commonly misunderstood term. To many, discipline means punishment. Punishment, however, is only a small part of discipline. Effective discipline involves teaching students rules and proper conduct, and then giving them the opportunity to practice these appropriate actions and to receive rewards for doing so.

Gartland (1990) and Charles (1999) identify three kinds of discipline: (a) preventive discipline (taking measures to avoid inappropriate behavior), (b) supportive discipline (assisting students when they first show signs of inappropriate behavior), and (c) corrective discipline (stopping and redirecting misbehavior when it occurs). (See Table 5.1 for some elements of each form of discipline.) Unfortunately, many teachers overuse this third type, corrective discipline. The successful teacher will integrate preventive, supportive, and corrective discipline into a well-coordinated program that is implemented consistently. Discipline that emphasizes prevention of inappropriate behaviors increases the amount of time available for instruction. According to Charles (1999), the more effort that is expended in preventive discipline, the less a teacher will need supportive or corrective discipline.

Sabatino (1987) defines *preventive discipline* as "the teacher's realization that discipline begins with a positive attitude that nurtures students' learning of personal, social, and academic skills. It is the realization that discipline is as much a teaching/learning interaction as is any academic subject matter . . ." (pp.8-9). With this definition in mind, I shall offer suggestions to the teacher that will enhance the behavior and learning of students in the special education and/or regular classroom.

The primary focus of this chapter will be on preventive discipline: proactive strategies and activities that will minimize the need for supportive or corrective discipline, both of which are essentially reactive techniques. Proactive strategies include managing the physical environment, the rules and routines, and time in a way that promotes a positive atmosphere conducive to learning and appropriate behavior. In addition, the teacher may use reinforcement or, with special care, punishment, to maintain a positive classroom atmosphere.

Promoting a Positive Atmosphere

Classroom management begins long before the students enter on the first day of school. It involves careful planning in several different areas: the physical environment, the classroom climate, the rules and operating procedures, and the use of time.

The Physical Environment. The physical structure or arrangement of the classroom contributes to learning and appropriate behavior (Minner & Prater, 1989; O'Connor, 1988; Stainback, Stainback, & Froyen, 1987). Aspects of physical

Table 5.1 Three Types of Discipline

Preventive Discipline

◆ Make your curriculum as worthwhile and enjoyable as possible.
◆ Remember that students crave fun, belonging, freedom, power, and dignity.
◆ Be pleasant and helpful. Ask your students for input and help.
◆ Reach clear understandings with your students about appropriate class conduct.
◆ Discuss and practice appropriate behaviors.
◆ Continually emphasize good manners and abidance by the "Golden Rule."
◆ Be the best model you can by showing concern, etiquette, courtesy, and helpfulness.
◆ Discuss manners frequently and call attention to student improvements.

Supportive Discipline

◆ Use signals directed to a student needing support.
◆ Learn to catch students' eyes and use headshakes, frowns, and hand signals.
◆ Use physical proximity when signals are ineffective.
◆ Show interest in student work. Ask cheerful questions or make favorable comments.
◆ Sometimes provide a light challenge such as, "Can you complete five more before we stop?"
◆ Restructure difficult work by changing the activity or providing help.
◆ Give hints, clues, or suggestions to help students get going.
◆ Inject humor into lessons that have become tiring.
◆ Remove seductive objects such as toys, comics, notes, and the like. Return them later.
◆ Acknowledge good behavior in appropriate ways.
◆ Use suggestions, hints, and "I-messages" when students begin to drift toward misbehavior.
◆ Show that you recognize students' discomfort: ask for a few minutes more work.

Corrective Discipline

◆ Stop disruptive misbehavior. It is usually best not to ignore it.
◆ Talk with the offending student or invoke a consequence appropriate to the misbehavior in accordance with class rules.
◆ Remain calm and speak in a matter-of-fact manner.
◆ Follow through consistently, the same way each day.
◆ Redirect misbehavior in positive directions.
◆ If necessary, talk with students privately about misbehavior. Ask how you can help and how they can solve the problem.
◆ Be ready to invoke an insubordination rule for students who refuse to stop misbehaving.

Source: Charles, C.M. (1999). *Building classroom discipline* (6th ed.). NY: Addison Wesley Longman, pp. 261-262.

structure include (a) teacher proximity and view, (b) separation of space, (c) traffic patterns, (d) extraneous stimuli, and (e) seating arrangements. Each can play an important role in determining behavior and academic achievement.

Teacher Proximity and View. A teacher's close proximity to students keeps youngsters on task and increases the level of instructional control in the classroom. Attention to directions, completion of assignments, and cessation of inappropriate behavior all improve when a teacher is closer to his or her students (Gunter, Shores, Jack, Rasmussen, & Flowers, 1995). For example, Ms. Kirk might place Joey and Travis near her primary work area, thereby allowing her to engage in more effective exchanges with these two students. In addition, Ms. Kirk must be aware of what is actually going on in the classroom at all times. She arranges the classroom furniture and equipment so that she can make a quick visual sweep of the room in order to detect students who may need assistance and to check student interactions (Stainback, Stainback, & Froyen, 1987).

Sometimes teachers arrange bookcases and room dividers to make quiet areas in the classroom. This makes monitoring of the classroom difficult, if not impossible. Some students may take advantage of these blind spots to engage in behaviors that are not consistent with teacher expectations. Continuously circulating about the classroom in order to bring the teacher frequently within about three feet of each student's desk and assigning a paraprofessional to monitor areas of the classroom out of the teacher's view can help to alleviate this problem.

Separation of Space. The clear demarcation of three kinds of space is important to the overall climate of the classroom. Ms. Kirk reserves one area of her classroom for group instruction, another area for individual seatwork, and a third for independent activities chosen by the children. In addition, she sets aside space for peer tutoring and team activities. In many classrooms, the desks are arranged in groups of four or five to enhance teamwork, and are left in that arrangement for large-group instruction. Work areas should be separate from traffic areas, and quiet areas should be separate from noisy areas. Specific rules and routines should apply to each of the areas in order to provide structure and to improve the teacher's instructional control (Minner & Prater, 1989; O'Connor, 1988).

Traffic Patterns. Ms. Kirk also carefully considers how students will move about in her classroom. Points that will receive a lot of traffic (e.g., the pencil sharpener, wastebasket, water fountain, and Ms. Kirk's desk) are placed to accommodate the traffic flow. Heavily-traveled routes are clear of obstacles. When traffic areas are not congested, the probability of disruptive behaviors is reduced (Stainback, Stainback, & Froyen, 1987).

Extraneous Stimuli. Ms. Kirk considers the distractibility of her students when arranging the classroom, and she attempts to reduce extraneous stimuli. Students who are easily distracted work as far as possible from high-traffic areas, doors opening into hallways, and windows (Minner & Prater, 1989). Ms. Kirk never seats students near the area designated for independent activities if they have difficulty concentrating. Sometimes she uses study carrels (i.e., stimulus reduction) as one solution to remove Travis and other easily distractible students from the extraneous stimuli that may keep them off task.

Seating Arrangements. The arrangement of seats and the assignment of students to those seats contribute to student attention and participation. Mr. Mathis is aware that the students who sit in the front and center of a classroom frequently participate more and achieve higher grades. Since all students cannot sit front and center, he carefully chooses which students will be assigned to those seats. Mr. Mathis also moves around the room while teaching, checking to see that all students are attending as they should (O'Connor, 1988). Of course, seats must be arranged to allow easy teacher access to every area of the classroom and to every student's desk.

Ms. Lopez and Mr. Abel also consider the same elements of the physical environment in their special education classrooms. They both use physical proximity, separation of space, traffic patterns, removal of extraneous stimuli, and attention to seating arrangements to promote student learning and behavior. Because one important goal of special education is to prepare children with disabilities for success in regular classrooms, Ms. Lopez and Mr. Abel arrange their classes to approximate the regular classroom environment as much as possible for those students who come to them for special education services. According to Minner and Prater (1989), "generalization of newly acquired behavior may be difficult for children who first acquire those skills in one type of environment and are expected to demonstrate them in a very different setting" (p. 95).

Classroom Climate

Within the classroom, the term climate refers to the prevailing attitudes of students and teachers toward the process of learning, and to prevailing behavioral expectations for students. A wholesome classroom climate is necessary for the growth and development of successful students and teachers.

A classroom and school climate that is nonpunitive and accepting of diversity promotes efficient learning more than does a hostile or threatening climate (Freiberg, 1998). Ms. Kirk and other competent teachers know this. They recognize the need to understand what motivates them and their students. Since the affective climate is such an important component of the learning environment, teachers must know what makes a climate wholesome, and then use that knowledge to create the best possible climate in their schools and classrooms (O'Connor, 1988).

Sabatino (1987) has suggested several ways to achieve a positive classroom climate and enhance student behavior:

1. Inform students of what is expected of them. Frequently, teachers neglect to tell students what behaviors are appropriate and expected. Teachers should always communicate classroom rules to their students and help them practice the rules to prevent discipline problems.
2. Act in a manner consistent with a positive learning climate. Students respect a teacher who is firm and decisive, but at the same time kind and patient. The application of consistent discipline teaches students that certain behaviors are or are not acceptable. Inconsistency, on the other hand, leaves students confused about the consequences for particular behaviors. Optimism, planned instruction, appropriate and realistic expectations, consistency, and human understanding are essential to a positive learning climate.
3. Provide meaningful learning experiences. Meaningfulness is important to all students, but it is especially important to students in special education programs who may not understand the value of what they are to learn, and

also to those from culturally or ethnically diverse backgrounds. Learning must relate to students' needs and concerns. When learning is drawn from family and community experiences, students are motivated to become active participants in the process (Clarke et al., 1995).

4. Avoid threats. Although students' obedience in the classroom is essential, discipline should not result from threats. Threatening a student with some form of punishment for inappropriate behavior generally will create additional discipline problems. Further, when we use such language as "If you do _____ one more time . . ." we are teaching that to do "it" once is all right, but to do "it" again is punishable.

5. Demonstrate fairness. Setting limits and dealing with misbehavior when it occurs are demonstrations of fairness. Treating all students in exactly the same way is not demonstrating fairness. Teachers must be willing to match learner needs and characteristics to the disciplinary actions. When disciplinary action must be taken, the teacher should analyze the particular offense, calmly state the reason for the action, and describe expectations for future behavior.

6. Exhibit self-confidence and build it in students. Teachers must be models of self-confidence. When teachers recognize each student as an individual and consider each student important enough to know personally, they are enhancing students' self-esteem and self-confidence (Stainback, Stainback, & Froyen, 1987).

7. Recognize positive student attributes. Sincere and specific praise creates feelings of self-worth in students. When teachers take the time to recognize appropriate behaviors and student achievements rather than dwell on failures, they promote a positive classroom climate (Stainback, Stainback, & Froyen, 1987).

8. Time the recognition of student behavior. Timing is important in administering both rewards and punishments. In both cases the teacher should respond as soon as possible after the student's behavior. Teachers need to anticipate situations before they occur, and then act in a consistent manner. Failing to affirm acceptable behavior, overreacting to minor events, or failing to fit a disciplinary action to a transgression make teachers less effective in training students to distinguish between appropriate and inappropriate behaviors.

   In addition, a professional demeanor reduces the chance that major discipline problems will develop from minor classroom infractions (Stainback, Stainback, & Froyen, 1987). Teachers demonstrate a professional demeanor by remaining calm in the face of student misbehavior, by drawing as little attention as possible to the misbehavior, by redirecting the student back on task or into appropriate behavior, by handling discipline problems in private whenever possible, and by handling classroom problems themselves rather than passing them on to other school personnel.

9. Use positive modeling. A primary goal of classroom management is to help students move from externally-controlled behavior to self-control. Teachers influence the success of this goal by the attitudes and behaviors they display. Teachers must first demonstrate positive attitudes toward the rules and regulations that govern their own behaviors. They must practice what they

preach by modeling, for example, courtesy in the face of rudeness, and respect for ideas different from their own. Gallagher (1997) urges teachers to treat all students with dignity. These attitudes will, in turn, influence students' respect for classroom and/or school rules.

10. Structure the curriculum and classroom environment. When the curriculum is too easy or too difficult, when the physical arrangement of the classroom does not facilitate student self-control and learning, and when expectations for student achievement are unrealistic, discipline problems are likely to occur. Research demonstrates that task difficulty and a boring curriculum can lead to frustration and increased levels of disruptive behavior (Clarke, et al., 1995; DePaepe, Shores, Jack, & Denny, 1996).

Teachers must foster the attitude that each student shares responsibility with the teacher for achievement of personal learning objectives. This attitude focuses student attention on learning and may reduce potential behavior problems. Such an attitude may be promoted by working with each student to select appropriate objectives that will encourage a goal orientation in the classroom (Stainback, Stainback, & Froyen, 1987).

Teachers cannot prevent all behavior problems. However, they can structure a learning climate that supports problem solving and reduces friction between the learner and the environment. Deluke and Knoblock (1987) advise teachers to show respect for each of their students, letting each one know that he or she is appreciated and valued as an individual. Teachers like Ms. Lopez respond to students' verbal and nonverbal communications by listening, by taking the time to draw them out when they seem upset, by making eye contact, and by acknowledging what is being said. In this way, she communicates the message that what the students are saying is important. (See Box 5.1.)

One indicator of teacher respect is the ability to interpret the meaning of a student's behavior. Students misbehave for a variety of reasons, some of which are not readily apparent. Teachers often must delve deeply to uncover the reasons for problem behavior (Deluke & Knoblock, 1987).

Rules and Routines

In the effectively-managed classroom, rules and routines are designed to create an orderly environment. Knowledge of what is expected of them goes a long way toward reducing students' inappropriate behavior. Although very similar in meaning, rules and routines are easily distinguished. Rules apply to classroom conduct. They are the "guiding principles" by which all in the classroom community, including the teacher, must live. Routines refer to the daily operating procedures, to the ways in which noninstructional activities are carried out (e.g., asking for help, turning in papers, getting a drink, using the restroom).

The first days of the new school year are a critical time for setting the tone for the remainder of the year and for establishing classroom order. Therefore, the teacher must give thought to selecting appropriate rules before the first day of school. By identifying the rules and routines of other teachers on her team,

Box 5.1

Ms. Lopez Listens to Joey

Joey rushes into the classroom, slams the door, hurls his books on his desk, and glares defiantly at Ms. Lopez. Ordinarily, Ms. Lopez might remind Joey of the rules for making a proper entrance into the classroom, but something in Joey's facial expression and body posture cues her that he is upset. She decides to try to get Joey to talk so that she can find out what the problem is. She squats down next to Joey's desk:

Ms. Lopez: (Softly and calmly) Looks like you're upset, Joey.

Joey: (Slumps in his seat and continues to glare)

Ms. Lopez: Want to talk about whatever happened?

Joey: She shouldn'ta told me that.

Ms. Lopez: Somebody told you to do something on your way to class today?

Joey: I was coming here.

Ms. Lopez: You were on your way to class and somebody told you something.

Joey: Yeah, that teacher, she told me to move along. I had to get the paper.

Ms. Lopez: You were coming to my classroom and you were getting a paper. Tell me about the paper.

Joey: It fell off the bulletin board in the hall and kids in her class were walking on it. I was just trying to get it, and she told me to get going. She shouldn'ta told me that.

Ms. Lopez: You were trying to help by picking up the paper that fell off the bulletin board so that it didn't get messed up, and a teacher told you to get to class? What did you do next?

Joey: I told her I was going to pick up the paper, and she couldn't stop me. She ain't my teacher to tell me to get to my room.

Ms. Lopez: Then what happened?

Joey: She said if I didn't get moving, she would get the principal to come and get me.

Ms. Lopez: So then you came on here to my class. Maybe the next time something like that happens you can try to explain that the paper fell off the bulletin board and that you were trying to pick it up. Maybe that way a teacher wouldn't get mad or think you were not being polite. I am very pleased that you shared that with me, Joey. It's hard to talk about things like that when we're angry, and especially when we're trying to be helpful. Do you feel ready to begin class now?

Joey: Yeah.

as well as those of the school and the district, Ms. Kirk may verify the appropriateness of intended classroom rules and procedures. In order to promote ownership of classroom rules, she may involve the students in generating and selecting rules. Ms. Kirk should have several rules in mind first, however, and she should guide the students as they voice their ideas to ensure that all necessary rules are included.

Whether the rules are teacher- or student-generated, they should be prioritized, with the most important rules being introduced first. Initially, three to five essential rules that clearly state what students are expected to do will be sufficient. (See Box 5.2.) Additional rules may be introduced as they are needed (Gartland, 1990). Because students do not always know what behavior is expected of them, Curwin and Mendler (1988) caution teachers to phrase rules positively so students will know what they are to do. Furthermore, they suggest that teachers must be able to give a reasonable explanation as to the importance of rules. If, for example, Mr. Abel cannot explain to his students the reason behind his rule to remove hats in the classroom, he may need to reconsider the value of the rule.

Ms. Kirk must also consider certain aspects of the classroom that, although not instructional in nature, may play a large part in determining the efficiency of learning and the appropriateness of behavior. The daily operating procedures that students must follow, the routines or "nitty gritty" of classroom management, must be determined in advance by the teacher and introduced and practiced in much the same way as classroom rules (Olson, 1989). As shown in Table 5.2,

---

Box 5.2

Ms. Kirk Establishes Classroom Rules

Ms. Kirk begins each school year with four or five essential classroom rules. She posts the rules and tells students why each rule is important. Each rule is clear, and the consequences for rule violations and rule adherence are clear as well. Ms. Kirk is always willing to listen to student concerns about her rules, however, as the school year progresses. She is willing to modify the rules as circumstances require. She does insist, though, that students practice the rules that they have agreed upon, and she enforces each rule consistently. Ms. Kirk usually posts the following rules before a new school year begins:

1. Complete assignments and activities during each class period. (Consequences: Incomplete assignments will be completed during recess or after school as homework to be signed by your parent. Free time to choose an activity or book when assignment is completed early.)
2. Ask permission to leave your seat. (Consequences: You will lose the privilege that you failed to request properly. When you request permission to leave your seat, you may do so if the reason is legitimate.)
3. Speak politely to teachers, staff, and fellow students. (Consequence: You will give a written apology to anyone you speak to in a rude manner.)
4. Ask permission to speak during group lessons or independent work time. (Consequence: Those who speak without permission will not be acknowledged and will lose a minute of recess time.)

Table 5.2   Nitty-Gritty Routines

Routines for Beginning and Ending the Day

- At the elementary level, establish a set place for each student to put his or her coat, lunch box, backpack, etc.
- Have students "sign in" as they enter the classroom or remove their name from a pegboard and place it in a designated basket.
- Allow time for students to write in a personal journal or daily log.
- Post a puzzle, riddle, or problem of the day on the board for all to solve. Allow extra credit for correctly completing this opening assignment.
- Have students evaluate their work or set new goals for the next day.
- Ensure that students copy homework assignments into an assignment notebook.
- Have students state or write one important new thing they learned during the day.
- Read a story or play a game such as "Jeopardy" using the information learned in class.
- Pass out certificates or rewards earned by students.

Routines for Distributing and Collecting Materials

- Use table, group, or row monitors to get, distribute, and collect materials.
- Rotate the job of table, group, or row monitor so that all students have the responsibility at some time.
- Reward students for swiftly and quietly distributing and collecting materials.
- Have paraprofessionals or volunteers distribute or collect materials or place completed work in folders to go home with young children.

Routines for Handing in Work

- Use an "in" basket on your desk or on a nearby table in which students may place completed papers.
- Use an "out" basket for graded work to be picked up by students at a specified time each day.
- Use individual work folders for students to place work in at the end of a set period.
- Use plastic baskets or folders in a box by the door for students to place work in as they leave.
- Place work in boxes, color-coded by subject area.
- Put work in a class folder at the end of each period using a different folder or color for each period.

Routines for the Restroom, Pencil Sharpener, and Water Fountain

- Post a sign-out sheet at the door for bathroom breaks.
- Allow only one student at a time to leave the classroom to use the restroom or get water.
- Require students to use the water fountain or restroom only at preset times during the day or only during individual work, although you must make allowances for emergencies.
- Have students turn over a card hanging near the door as they leave for the restroom and turn it back over as they reenter the classroom.
- Give students a "count to three" for speeding up water breaks.
- Require two pencils to be sharpened as students enter the room.
- Keep extra pencils in your desk that may be "purchased" with points earned or some other collateral held until the pencil's return.

Routines for Requesting Help

- Devise an age-appropriate "help sign" for students to place on their desk when they require assistance.
- Post and practice a series of steps for requesting help: ask an assigned peer buddy, raise your help sign, try the next item or assignment.
- Student takes a numbered ticket, and when the teacher finishes assisting the student the teacher places the number back on a peg and writes the next number on the board.
- Student completes work from a folder containing assignments he or she is capable of completing independently for review and maintenance of learning until help is available.

Table 5.2   Nitty-Gritty Routines—*cont'd*

Routines for Finishing Work Early

◆ Post a set of activity choices for things students may do if they finish work early, such as reading a library book or something from the class bookshelf.

◆ Use the computer when work is completed correctly.

◆ Work on homework.

◆ Complete an activity for extra credit from a prepared set of activity cards (e.g., writing an ending to a story, using the newspaper or World Wide Web to answer current events questions).

Adapted from: Meese, R.L. (1996). *Strategies for teaching students with emotional and behavioral disorders.* Pacific Grove, CA: Brooks/Cole, pp. 134-135.

Meese (1996) offers some suggestions for handling nitty-gritty questions facing teachers.

Although all classroom rules and routines should be posted using age-appropriate language and/or pictures, merely posting rules does not ensure that students will understand them. Gartland (1990) offers the following suggestions for teaching students the rules, the routines, and their consequences:

1. Follow a clear, specific plan when introducing classroom rules and routines to students.
2. Explain the rationale for each classroom rule and routine.
3. Specify consequences for both adherence to and infractions of rules and routines.
4. Model appropriate behavior in accordance with the rules and routines established.
5. Provide adequate time for students to practice appropriate behaviors.

Rules and routines generated by both the teacher and the students and determined appropriate for classroom implementation should be transmitted to parents or guardians in a classroom newsletter (see Chapter 4). Knowledge of these rules and routines may help parents solve problems with their children at home.

Time Management and Transitions

Increasing student time on task is the major goal of time management. The longer students are on task, the more they learn and the better they achieve. In addition, when students are focused on productive activities they are less likely to present discipline problems (Stainback, Stainback, & Froyen, 1987).

Time in the classroom falls into four broad categories: (a) allocated instructional time, (b) actual instructional time, (c) engaged time, and (d) academic learning time (Gartland & Rosenberg, 1987). Allocated instructional time refers to the amount of time the school or the teacher sets aside to teach a particular subject or lesson. Actual instructional time is a subset of allocated instructional time. This is the amount of time during which the instruction is actually delivered. Engaged time is the amount of time the student is attending to the teacher's lesson or to the task. Academic learning time, the most meaningful of the categories of instructional time, is the amount of time the student is actively attending to instruction at a correct level of difficulty and with a high rate of success (Berliner, 1984). During academic learning time, the student's assessed strengths and weaknesses should be accurately matched to the assignments or to the instruction.

In some schools the amount of time in a particular period is limited by bells or by changing classrooms. In these circumstances, teachers may not be able to increase allocated instructional time beyond, for example, a fifty-minute period or a ninety-minute block. They may, however, increase actual instructional time by using several methods that have proven successful for both elementary and secondary grades (Gartland & Rosenberg, 1987).

Establish Rewards for School Attendance and Punctuality. Teachers should make students aware of expectations regarding school attendance. Some school districts have mandated that students who are absent more than a certain number of school days will not be promoted to the next grade. Others hire full-time assistants or use volunteers to call home each time a student is absent. Teachers must not assume, however, that students and parents are aware of these policies. By establishing rewards for school attendance and punctuality, and by planning lessons that are meaningful and relevant for students, teachers help to ensure that students will spend more time in class. In addition, teachers should begin and end classes on time, thus becoming a model of punctuality.

Minimize Interruptions. Teachers must minimize interruptions during the presentation of instruction. In some schools, for example, announcements can only be broadcast over the intercom to everyone at certain times of the day, and visitors are restricted in their movements throughout the building. Cohen and Hart-Hester (1987) suggest several ways to reduce interruptions during instructional time, including the following:

- Arrange the room so that the teacher is not facing the door and so that eye contact cannot be made with passers-by who might be encouraged to stop.
- Use body language to indicate to would-be intruders that you are busy.
- State to the intruder that this is not a good time to talk, and indicate a more appropriate time.

Encourage Disruption-Free Transitions Between Activities. Transition time typically refers to the movement of students from one activity or place to another. Verbal and nonverbal signals may be used to eliminate confusion and to facilitate movement during transition times. Ms. Kirk, for example, might flick the lights and give her students a "three-minute warning" prior to a change in activity. In addition, she must give her students clear and specific directions regarding what they are to do next. Rather than a vague direction such as "Get ready for math," Ms. Kirk might say instead, "Put your spelling books in your

Teachers who listen to their students promote a positive classroom atmosphere that supports problem solving and shared responsibility.

desk, get out your math books, and open to page 78." Figure 5.1 gives suggestions for how teachers can facilitate transitions, thereby increasing instructional time.

Teachers at the secondary level may use their chalkboards to minimize disruptions between activities. By listing the activities on the board before class time, teachers prepare students for what is to come, thus maximizing instructional time. Frequently, teachers at the secondary level inadvertently allow students to determine when instruction will end. Students will, for example, begin packing up to go to the next class well before the bell rings. Teachers can use this time at the end of class for reviewing the day's lesson and previewing what is to come tomorrow.

Maintain an Academic Focus. By maintaining an academic focus and limiting the amount of time devoted to noninstructional activities, teachers increase the amount of actual instructional time available within the time allocated. Noninstructional activities (e.g., classroom discipline, organizational tasks, announcements, social interactions, transitions) are negatively correlated with academic achievement. Teachers must ensure that less than 15% of class time is spent on such activities (Gartland & Rosenberg, 1987). Table 5.2 offers suggestions for routines to enhance instructional time and decrease noninstructional time. Remember, increased academic learning time results in higher academic achievement.

Schedule Activities Carefully. Scheduling is another important aspect of time management and preventive discipline. Maintaining a daily schedule provides structure for students and eliminates the need for constant questioning about "what's next." Informing students in advance about changes in the daily schedule keeps confusion to a minimum when changes do occur.

In the regular classroom, the entire class has one schedule. Individual students, especially those receiving special services, will have additional schedules. The individual schedules will be a subset of the group schedule. For example, within the block of time allocated for language arts or mathematics in Ms. Kirk's classroom, Travis may go to the resource room for individualized instruction

---

Lining Up Activities

◆ Have students alphabetize themselves.
◆ Dismiss students by specific characteristics ("All students wearing the color red line up first.")
◆ Have students discuss ordinal concepts (who is first, second) and prepositions (who is before, after).
◆ Change your voice to a whisper or to a different tone.

Seated Activities

◆ Have students see how many words they can spell from a word written on the blackboard that is associated with the upcoming lesson.
◆ Challenge students to solve a story problem from an equation or to write a story starter to be used in a future writing activity. Be sure the challenges relate to the upcoming lesson.

Relocating Activities

◆ Use finger plays or nursery rhymes with young children (Open–Shut Them, Five Little Monkeys).
◆ Play "I SPY" ("Travis, I spy something in the hallway that starts with a 'D'.")
◆ Play counting games ("Silently count the number of people we pass in the hall and divide that number by 3." Count the number of classrooms we pass and estimate the number of children in the classrooms.")

Multiuse Activities

◆ Have students name two facts previously learned in a social studies or science less ("Name two facts about whales").
◆ Have each student tell one sentence of a story; however, each sentence must contain a newly learned vocabulary word.

FIGURE 5.1 _____ ◆

Suggested Transition Activities Adapted From: Myles, B.S., & Hronek, L.J. (1990). Transition activities: A classroom management tool. *LD Forum, 15*(3), pp. 20-22. Council for Learning Disabilities. Reprinted with permission.

from Ms. Lopez. The remainder of his schedule may follow that of the group. (See Box 5.3 for a sample schedule for Travis.)

Parts of the day are scheduled in advance by school administrators. Lunch, planning, and various resource periods such as art, music, physical education, or computers, are not totally under the teacher's control. Nevertheless, the teacher can plan activities around these preset times to greatest advantage by considering, for example, the students' needs for movement and variety. Gallagher (1979) offers several suggestions for scheduling classrooms and students. These suggestions may be particularly helpful early in the school year for both classroom teachers and special educators:

1. Provide each student with a daily schedule. Actively teach the schedule rather than assuming students will understand and follow it.
2. Alternate high-probability tasks with low-probability tasks. That is, abide by "Grandma's Law" and plan for activities students enjoy to follow less enjoyable ones (e.g., recess follows spelling). Also plan for quiet activities to follow noisy, active ones.
3. Schedule work that can be finished by the end of the school day.
4. Plan for some leeway time. Students may enjoy an activity and want more time, or they may finish a task more quickly than you estimated. In addition, fire drills or other building-level events may create changes in your schedule.
5. Require students to complete one task before beginning another whenever possible.
6. Provide time reminders and signals to prepare students for transitions.
7. Don't assign additional work if tasks are completed ahead of schedule, but rather structure routines to provide students with acceptable choices upon early work completion.
8. Plan ahead and anticipate students' needs.
9. Establish expectations in advance and do not introduce unexpected activities.
10. Include feedback and evaluative remarks with a student's individual daily schedule.
11. Provide positive feedback.

Use Positive Teacher Behaviors. Several teacher behaviors are also related to engaged time, and thus to academic learning time, because they increase student attention to task. For example, at least half of class time should be spent on interactive activities, including demonstrating content material, monitoring oral reading, providing opportunities for student responses, providing corrective feedback, and reinforcing correct behaviors (Gartland & Rosenberg, 1987). Moreover, teachers should display enthusiasm during academic presentations and should try to engage all students in group activities. Approximately 35% of instructional time should be spent monitoring controlled and independent practice. This practice might include teacher-directed seatwork, activities at the chalkboard, independent seatwork, or sustained silent reading. Teachers can increase the on-task rates of students during practice by giving clear instructions, by giving corrective feedback, by reinforcing correct responses, by using novel and motivating assignments, and by using study carrels (Gartland & Rosenberg, 1987). Finally, teachers can enhance the on-task rates of young

Box 5.3

Travis's Schedule

Travis reports to Ms. Lopez's classroom for reading and mathematics instruction on a daily basis. Ms. Kirk and the other members of the fourth-grade team at Oakhill Elementary School exchange students for both reading and mathematics so that students may be grouped by similar skills and needs. When reading and math time begin, therefore, Travis changes classes just like his peers, reporting to Ms. Lopez instead of to a regular fourth-grade classroom teacher. For all other subjects, Travis remains in Ms. Kirk's class. The following daily schedule is typical for Travis:

Daily Schedule for Travis

8:30-9:00	Attendance/Journals/Board Work/Announcements
9:00-10:00	Reading/Language Arts with Ms. Lopez
10:00-10:30	Music or Art
10:30-10:45	Bathroom Break/Snack
10:45-11:45	Mathematics with Ms. Lopez
11:45-12:30	Lunch/Recess/Bathroom Break
12:30-1:00	Story/Writing Time
1:00-2:00	Social Studies or Science (Ms. Lopez coteaches with Ms. Kirk.)
2:00-2:30	Health, Physical Education, or Computer Lab
2:30-3:00	Homework Assignments/Jobs/Preparation for Dismissal

children by providing a visual reminder of the expected behavior, such as a picture of children reading independently, placed on the chalkboard or worn around the neck on a string. (See Figure 5.2 for some practical techniques for making the most of instructional time.)

Using Computers to Maximize Instructional Time

Teachers of exceptional students have many demands on their time. Unfortunately, some of the most important aspects of teaching, including planning and presenting instruction, receive less attention than they deserve because of paperwork and other administrative demands on the teacher. The technology available to schools today may be used to decrease the time teachers spend managing paperwork and to increase the productivity of instructional tools for use in the classroom. Specifically, the microcomputer can be used to manage data or to assist the teaching-learning process. For example, the computer can be used to produce teaching aids, tests, or lesson plans; to compute and record grades; to maintain information and performance data on individual students; to develop and update Individualized Education Programs (IEPs); and to generate correspondence.

I am working with a small group of students while the others in my resource room are doing independent work. I have carefully explained the assignments to the other children so that I can concentrate on my group. We begin our lesson. We are interrupted not once but several times as I try to teach. I see that I am losing the attention of the students in my group. My frustrations increase. My calm answers become brusque, my patient requests to wait become irritated orders. Help! We need a better way to manage our time!

I first became aware of a need to teach time management to my students when I changed from teaching at the high school level to an elementary resource room. In high school, the class periods are defined by bells. Older students are often able to wait to ask questions until it is their turn. But it is quite a different story with younger students.

After trial and error, I discovered help right in my own kitchen. A kitchen timer became our classroom bell. Here's how it works:

I get the students settled with their independent assignments. We have a question-and-answer period for a few moments until everyone is satisfied. The timer is set for fifteen minutes (or more or less, depending on the ages of the students and our needs).

While the timer is running, I work with my group. No one may interrupt us for those fifteen minutes. "Peer tutors" who have been selected from older students will answer questions that cannot wait. I also provide foolproof seatwork that a student may turn to if he cannot proceed on his assignment until he is able to consult with me.

When the timer rings, we take a break, and I answer questions and change activities when appropriate. The benefits of this simple technique are many:

1. Students working with me get a continuity of instruction and attention that was not possible when we were frequently interrupted.
2. Students working independently learn that they can often solve their own problems if they think about them for a few minutes.
3. Students who cannot proceed with their work learn to find alternatives so they can use their time effectively instead of sitting and wasting time.
4. "Tutors" have an opportunity to assume some classroom responsibility for their fellow students. This often reinforces skills, and it certainly builds egos.
5. Students improve their concept of time.

Another kitchen item that has helped my young students with time management is the three-minute egg timer. I use this small hourglass to motivate my students. I indicate a small section of the assignment to be completed, put the egg timer on the desk, and whisper, "Beat the clock!" It is amazing to see how the children sit up, grab their pencils, and get to work as the sand slips through the glass. My young students are learning the concept of using every minute productively.

Finally, another kitchen staple, the paper plate, has been useful as a private clock for those students who cannot yet tell time. In our class, students come in and out on different schedules. The younger children would always ask me, "When do I leave?" Now we set their individual clocks made of a paper plate with cardboard hands to their departure time (or any other time they made need to remember). When their clock matches the wall clock, they know it is time to go. I also write the time in words and numbers on the clock, and they quickly learn their own schedule.

FIGURE 5.2 ◆

Time Management From the Kitchen Adapted from: Hoffman, E. (1988). Time management from the kitchen. *Academic Therapy*, 23(3), pp. 275-277. Copyright © by Pro-Ed, Inc. Reprinted with permission.

The computer can also help students complete tasks, or it can become a teaching device. In fact, IDEA (1997) requires that "assistive" technology devices and services be provided to children with disabilities whenever necessary. IDEA defines assistive technology as any item, piece of equipment, or product system, whether acquired commercially off the shelf, modified, or customized, that is used to increase, maintain, or improve functional capabilities of a child with a disability. The key idea behind using the microcomputer as assistive technology, then, is that the teacher is not simply saving time, but rather is finding ways to enhance the education of students.

Salpeter (1997) reports that school preference for either DOS/Windows-compatible computers or Apple and Macintosh systems is split 50-50. Either way, these computers are used instructionally to provide drill and practice activities for students who need reinforcement of particular skills. They are also used to motivate and reward students. Hannaford (1993) suggests that computers help students learn material in less time and increase student attention and time on task. Teachers, too, can save time by using the word-processing, database, and spreadsheet applications of computers.

Word-processing applications enable educators and students to edit, move, copy, and print text in various formats, and merge print with pictures or information from databases. The use of templates is a valuable time-saving feature of word processors that enables teachers to create letters, newsletters, forms, lesson-plan formats, student worksheets and assignments, and IEP objectives. This type of application saves time for the teacher when one format may be needed on several occasions (Blackhurst, 1989).

The benefits of word processors are not limited to teachers, however. Students in special education programs, especially those with poor spelling or handwriting, can use word processors to improve their writing. Editing capabilities and spelling and grammar checkers work together to improve the readability and acceptability of a student's written work. Moreover, with desktop publishing programs now available, teachers and students can create posters, signs, banners, cards, and calendars of professional quality.

Database management also offers the educator the capabilities of organization, storage, and retrieval of large bodies of information. In the classroom, Mr. McNally may choose to use a database in geography so that his students can sort countries by climate or by the types of products exported. Then his students can use a wide array of formats for displaying the information in the database to create a variety of different reports. For example, the countries can be grouped alphabetically by product or by climate in a table-style report.

The spreadsheet application enables the educator to store and manipulate numerical data. Data are arranged in rows and columns, and formulas are entered to perform a variety of calculations, such as averages, percentages, and ranges of test scores. Spreadsheets are versatile because all of the totals can change whenever new data are added. Teachers can use spreadsheets to compute student grades and to score standardized tests.

Newer applications of computer technology are increasingly enlivening classrooms today. The CD-ROM provides simulations that allow Ms. Stone's students to explore the solar system or to browse multimedia encyclopedia for information on the planets, including graphics, video, and sound effects. Ms. Kirk's students can use the CD-ROM to practice letter-sound associations, vocabulary, or mathematics skills through games containing motivating animation and sound, and they can enjoy children's literature through interactive talking storybooks. Electronic mail (e-mail) enables teachers and students to communicate with others around the world via the Internet, and the World Wide Web (WWW) provides information in text, graphic, audio, and video format on every conceivable topic. Students can get "as-it-happens" reports on current events, search the WWW for data on any subject, take a virtual tour of a museum, or participate in on-line "chats" with children from other states or countries. Teachers can browse the web for lesson plans, locate resources, access large databases, or join on-line discussion groups with other teachers. Both teachers and students can even order materials or take on-line classes over the Internet.

The Internet and the World Wide Web are valuable learning tools for students and teachers; however, teachers must help students learn to use these resources with caution. Teachers must help students evaluate the credibility of information obtained over the "information superhighway," and they must monitor student activities on the Internet. For example, schools should develop clear policies for teachers and students using the Internet, and they can use filtering software such as Cyber Patrol (**http://www.cyberpatrol.com**) or Net Nanny (**http://www.netnanny.com**) to screen out inappropriate web sites. Most importantly, however, Bakken and Aloia (1998) urge teachers to give students several rules for using the Internet, including the following:

◆ Don't give out personal information such as your first or last name, address, telephone number, social security number, or where you go to school.
◆ Don't give out your password, if you have one.
◆ Don't send a picture of yourself over the Internet.
◆ Tell a teacher or parent about any new friends you make over the Internet.
◆ Don't arrange a face-to-face meeting alone with any new friends you make on the Internet.
◆ If someone on the Internet makes you feel bad, tell a parent or teacher about it.
◆ Don't believe everything you read on-line.

The use of the microcomputer in education offers some teachers an exciting challenge, although it may be a source of stress for those who have not yet mastered it. Whether the computer is used as an instructional tool with students or as a management tool to handle a large volume of paperwork, it has the potential to be a valuable time-management asset for every teacher.

Maintaining a Positive Classroom Environment

Recall that Gartland (1990) and Charles (1999) defined the three types of discipline as preventive, supportive, and corrective. So far we have focused attention on the preventive type, in which the teacher organizes the environment and prepares for students to learn and behave appropriately within the structure provided. However, the teacher cannot always prevent misbehavior. The other forms of discipline, supportive and corrective, may need to be implemented for particular students in specific instances. The effective use of reinforcement and punishment are necessary skills for the maintenance of a wholesome classroom environment.

Reinforcement may be defined as any consequence of a behavior that increases the likelihood of that behavioral response occurring again. When Joey brings his homework to class and receives Ms. Kirk's praise, and when that praise encourages him to bring his homework to school every day, Ms. Kirk's praise is considered to be reinforcement. If Ms. Kirk's praise does not result in

Joey's turning in homework each day, that praise is not considered to be reinforcement. Students will repeat a response pattern in order to gain a particular desired reinforcer.

Two kinds of reinforcement exist: positive reinforcement and negative reinforcement. *Positive reinforcement* involves the delivery of a reward following a behavior, increasing the likelihood of the behavior in the future. When Ms. Kirk gives students stickers for turning in their homework, and, in turn, the rate of homework completion increases, she is using positive reinforcement. *Negative reinforcement* also increases the likelihood of a behavior; however, negative reinforcement involves the removal of an aversive (i.e., unpleasant) stimulus as a consequence of the behavior. For example, if Ms. Kirk tells her students, "Those who complete their daily math worksheet and receive a grade of 'A' will not have homework," she is using negative reinforcement, assuming, of course, that having homework is "unpleasant" and that "A-getting" increases.

Punishment, which is frequently confused with negative reinforcement, is designed to reduce the likelihood that a particular behavioral response will recur. Punishment carries with it unpleasant connotations and may occur in the form of an aversive consequence, such as scolding, following an inappropriate behavior. Punishment may also involve the removal of a privilege or the loss of points. For example, punishment might occur when Ms. Kirk states, "Kevin you have been talking rather than working on your math problems, so you will finish your math during your free time this afternoon." The important idea behind punishment, however, is that the behavior of interest *decreases* when the consequence is applied.

Reinforcement

Alberto and Troutman (1999) describe two forms of positive reinforcers: primary and secondary. *Primary* reinforcers are those that have biological significance to an individual, including reinforcers such as food and drink. Although the use of snacks in the classroom on a regular basis may not be feasible, teachers who use such primary reinforcers (e.g., candy, popcorn, or soft drinks) as rewards for good behavior have found them to be very effective.

Secondary reinforcers, on the other hand, receive their strength through frequent association with primary reinforcers. Parents, for example, often pair a secondary, social reinforcer (e.g., verbal praise) with a primary reinforcer (e.g., a treat) for their young children. By the time the child enters school, many types of secondary reinforcers are well established. Teachers also may pair the primary reinforcer with a secondary reinforcer to which the child responds. For example, Ms. Lopez may pair a candy bar at the end of class (a primary reinforcer) with a sticker or verbal praise (secondary reinforcers). A transfer from the primary to the secondary reinforcer occurs when students are reinforced by the sticker or verbal praise without the presence of the candy bar.

Secondary reinforcers may include praise, grades, tokens, stars, stickers, and permission to engage in preferred activities. These frequently are more appropriate in the school setting than food or soft drinks. More naturally occurring secondary reinforcers include nonverbal expressions (e.g.,smiles) and teacher proximity. Should there be a student for whom secondary reinforcement has no value, the teacher must first establish an association between a primary reinforcer and a secondary reinforcer. Cohen and Hearn (1988) suggest two things for teachers to keep in mind: first, never present a primary reinforcer without pairing it with a secondary reinforcer and, second, once the association has been made, gradually remove the primary reinforcer.

A number of reinforcers that teachers might use with students are presented in Figure 5.3. Some may be appropriate for any age or grade level, whereas others are likely to lose potency for older students. For example, verbal praise, lunch with the teacher, or working at the teacher's desk may be reinforcing for younger students, while older students like Robert may not wish to be singled out for such attention. Thus, Mr. Abel, who teaches in the middle and high school, must be careful to select age-appropriate reinforcers that are based on student preferences and that are practical and available in the school setting (Reynolds, Salend, & Beahan, 1989). In each instance, teachers must know their students and observe what is reinforcing for them.

One way to ensure that effective reinforcers will be selected is to observe students' activities to determine which reinforcers they choose on their own. In addition, teachers might allow students to sample the available reinforcers or have them select desired reinforcers through a reinforcement survey (See Figure 5.4). For students who will not respond in detail to an open-ended survey, teachers may use interviews or provide a menu of possible reinforcers on which the student circles choices or provides answers by specific categories, such as this:

Favorite snacks: _____type of candy bar
_____type of soft drink
_____type of snack food

Reynolds, Salend, and Beahan (1989) identify five types of positive reinforcers commonly used in school settings: edible, tangible, activity, social and academic. Edible reinforcers are the lowest level in the hierarchy of reinforcement because they are highly intrusive. Tangible reinforcers, such as pins, stickers, and posters, have a constantly-changing value. Teachers must be prepared to adjust these reinforcers in order to keep up with the latest fad. Activity reinforcers are highly motivating alternatives to both edible and tangible reinforcers. They allow students to engage in a task that often serves as a learning experience as well as a reinforcer. Carefully-structured free time, probably the most highly desired activity reinforcer, can be used to play an instructional game, visit the library or gymnasium, or make an art project. Extra computer time, or time allotted to listen to music or to watch a video, are also motivating reinforcers, especially for many secondary-level students.

Social reinforcers are the least intrusive of the secondary reinforcers available because they closely match the environment and do not require the teacher to make or do anything special. Teacher comments, especially those in writing, free time with the teacher, and positive body language such as smiling are teacher behaviors that may reinforce student behavior.

Academic reinforcers are, perhaps, the most appropriate form of reinforcement that can be offered to secondary-level students. Academic reinforcers are logical consequences for appropriate school behavior. Such reinforcers might include school-wide announcements of achievement or effort,

Receiving smiles, winks, etc.
Using the gym or library during unassigned times
Getting stamps or stickers
Making a phone call home
Eating lunch with the teacher
Writing notes to a classmate
Being line leader
Getting a chance to solve codes or puzzles
Getting time to spend in a student lounge
Working with a volunteer
Getting peer recognition
Getting good grades
Being hall monitor
Getting a photo in the newspaper
Getting free time
Watching videos
Selecting time for completing assignments
Videotaping
Assisting the custodian, secretary, or librarian
Getting a snack or soda
Choosing a special work spot
Using the computer
Working at the teacher's desk
Displaying progress
Getting no homework
Assisting in another room or grade
Getting permission to skip a test
Participating in a special project
Taking class roll
Using a tape recorder or calculator
Creating a bulletin board
Having a class dance or party
Purchasing something from the class store
Receiving tickets to a school event

FIGURE 5.3

Classroom Reinforcers Adapted From: Cohen, S.B., & Hearn, D. (1988).
Reinforcement. In R. McNergney (Ed.), *Guide to Classroom Teaching*, Boston, MA:
Allyn & Bacon.

recognition of excellent work by displaying it in a hallway or display case, or mid-semester progress reports (Reynolds et al., 1989).

Another effective reinforcer for many secondary-level students is the removal of a certain amount of work. This is considered a negative reinforcer in that an aversive stimulus is removed with the goal of increasing the desired behavioral response. Appropriate behavior may be reinforced, for example, by eliminating a homework assignment or by waiving an upcoming test (Reynolds et al., 1989).

Group reinforcers, which can be delivered to the class contingent upon the behavior of either the entire group or of individuals, are highly motivating to many students. Groups may be rewarded with structured free time, the opportunity to rent an educational video, a party for the entire class, or a special game the class enjoys. Although many students have access to videos or games, such activities often offer broadening experiences for

1. The thing I like best about school is _____

_____.

2. I feel really good when someone tells me that I _____.

_____.

3. The school subject I like best is _____.

4. My favorite snack is _____.

5. If I could do anything in school that I wanted, I would _____

_____.

6. If I could do anything at all that I wanted, I would _____

_____.

7. The thing that makes me enjoy school the most is _____

_____.

8. In my free time I like to _____

_____.

FIGURE 5.4 ◆

Reinforcement Survey. From: Cohen S.B., & Hearn, D. (1988). Reinforcement. In R. McNergney (Ed.), *Guide to Classroom Teaching*. Boston, MA: Allyn & Bacon. Reprinted with permission.

students who do not have such access. Educational trips and outings also can provide both reinforcement for class behavior as well as new learning experiences (Reynolds et al., 1989).

If reinforcement is to be used effectively, the reinforcer must be contingent upon demonstration of the appropriate behavior. Students who receive their rewards regardless of their behavior learn that they do not have to perform in order to get what they want.

Sometimes the teacher finds it necessary to implement a contingency contract with a student. A *contingency contract* is a document specifying the terms of an agreement in which the pupil and teacher jointly determine a task to be performed in a certain time period and an expected reward for the student upon completion of the task (see Figure 5.5). When the agreement involves several tasks or additional people, the contract may be more detailed and may be written and signed by all parties involved.

Some students seemingly defy reinforcement. That is, the things that we typically rely on as reinforcers may not be reinforcing to all students. Furthermore,

I, _____ , will _____

_____ by _____ _____ .

After successfully completing this, I may _____

_____ .

Student Signature: _____

Teacher Signature: _____

Date Signed: _____ Date Completed: _____

FIGURE 5.5 ◆

Sample Contingency Contract

scolding, a consequence most teachers believe to be unpleasant and punishing, may actually be reinforcing for some students. In such cases, teachers must determine exactly what is reinforcing the inappropriate behavior and seek to remove it.

Punishment

A consequence that is presented following a particular behavior may only be considered punishment provided it has the effect of eliminating or reducing the probability that the behavior will be repeated. Alberto and Troutman (1999) encourage teachers to focus on positive behavior reduction strategies that build and reward appropriate behaviors rather than simply using punishment to eliminate inappropriate ones. Nevertheless, extinction, response cost, and time out are often used in educational settings to reduce inappropriate behavior.

Extinction. Extinction refers to the process of eliminating an inappropriate behavior by withdrawing whatever reinforces it. Many times the reinforcer is teacher attention. When that attention is withheld, the behavior is reduced. For example, whenever Joey calls out in class without waiting to be called on, Ms. Kirk reprimands him. Joey, however, might be calling out to get his teacher's attention. The reprimand, while Ms. Kirk intends it to be aversive, actually functions as a reinforcer to maintain and increase Joey's behavior. If Ms. Kirk ignores Joey's call-outs consistently over time, they will gradually decrease and eventually disappear. When such a plan is implemented, Ms. Kirk must prepare for an initial increase in Joey's "call-out" behavior because he is accustomed to receiving attention for his behavior. This "pre-extinction burst" is the point at which many teachers state that planned ignoring does not work or that it only makes matters worse. In fact, if Ms. Kirk gives up in exasperation and scolds Joey for his call-outs, she has made matters worse by reinforcing Joey's behavior and making it even more resistant to change. Eventually, however, if Ms. Kirk continues to withhold her attention, the call-outs will decrease.

Cohen and Hearn (1988) add a note of warning concerning the use of extinction procedures: "Be sure you have pinpointed what is reinforcing the behavior" (p. 64). If the teacher has applied extinction techniques consistently over time and the inappropriate behavior has not decreased, something unaccounted for could be reinforcing the behavior. Joey's classmates might laugh and giggle when he calls out so that he continues to receive the attention he is seeking. Extinction should not be used unless the teacher can ensure that the student is not receiving reinforcement. In addition, the teacher must consistently reward an appropriate behavior to replace the inappropriate one. Ms. Kirk, for example, might reinforce Joey each time he raises his hand to speak while consistently ignoring the call-outs.

Response Cost. Response cost is another form of punishment involving the removal of certain amounts of a positive reinforcer each time a student demonstrates a specific inappropriate behavior. For example, in a token system where students are earning points for good behavior or academic accomplishments, a specified number of points are deducted each time an inappropriate behaviors occurs. Reducing the minutes of recess or free time are additional examples of the response cost procedure following inappropriate behaviors.

When using response cost, teachers must take care to remove only privileges and not activities, such as music, art, physical education, or lunch, to which students are entitled. In addition, teachers must ensure students are earning rewards for good behaviors more rapidly than they lose points or privileges for inappropriate ones. For example, if Joey loses all of his recess time in the first hour of the day, he will probably choose to misbehave even more because he has nothing else to lose! As a rule of thumb, positive reinforcement and response cost should occur in a four to one ratio. That is, each time Joey loses a minute of recess, Ms. Kirk should quickly find four opportunities to reward Joey for appropriate behavior in order to keep him in the "plus column."

Time Out. *Time out* is the abbreviation for a procedure known as *time out from positive reinforcement*. Time out is a punishment because the opportunity to earn rewards is removed from the child for a period of time in order to decrease an inappropriate behavior. Thus, if time out is to be successful, the teacher's classroom and learning activities must be highly positive and rewarding so that the child will not want to be removed from them. In addition, children lose academic learning time and are not being taught more appropriate behaviors while in time out. Thus, teachers should use time out infrequently and with caution, and only in conjunction with a plan to teach and reward appropriate behaviors as alternatives to the inappropriate ones.

The least restrictive form of time out is nonseclusionary time out. In this procedure, Ms. Lopez might simply remove from Joey the opportunity to earn points or minutes of free time. For example, she might prepare a card with a green side and a red side and place these near Joey's desk. While Joey is behaving appropriately, the green side is showing and he is earning his points. However, if Joey behaves inappropriately, Ms. Lopez calmly turns the card to the red side for three minutes, during which time Joey cannot earn any points.

Exclusionary time out is somewhat more restrictive because in this case the child is removed from the ongoing activity for a specified period of time. Ms. Lopez might, for example, ask Joey to sit for five minutes in a time-out chair contingent upon his inappropriate behavior, or she might have him sit and watch the T-ball game from the edge of the blacktop during recess. Sometimes Ms. Kirk simply asks her students to take a "think break" behind a screened off area in order to "stop and cool down." The strength of an exclusionary time out, then, is that children will see others engaging in a highly reinforcing activity and receiving rewards for doing so.

Exclusionary time outs will not work, however, if teachers cannot keep the child in question in the time out area. Moreover, if the child becomes the focal point of attention during the time out by engaging in loud, rude, or silly behaviors, exclusionary time out will not be effective. Finally, sending the student into the hallway or to the office as a form of exclusionary time out is rarely effective. The student often obtains many forms of positive reinforcement from peers while in the hallway or office, and he or she cannot be supervised while in the halls.

Seclusionary time out is also known as *isolation* time out because the student is removed to a specially designed time out room. In-school suspension, for example, is a seclusionary time out procedure commonly used in secondary schools. Stage (1997) suggests, however, that in-school suspensions may not be effective if students seek to avoid difficult academic tasks and teacher disapproval during class time.

Gast and Nelson (1977a & 1977b) recommend that the time-out period should be no more than five minutes in length and that the time-out room should be (a) at least six-by-six feet in size, (b) properly ventilated and lighted, (c) free from objects and fixtures, (d) not locked, and (e) monitored carefully. In addition, they suggest that teachers calmly inform students of the behavior resulting in the time out, the length of the time out, and the behaviors the child must demonstrate to be released. Furthermore, teachers should not interact with students during the time out period, and students should be returned to the activity they were engaged in before the time out, whenever possible, in order to avoid negatively reinforcing the child's inappropriate behavior.

Yell (1994) makes the following recommendations for teachers using time out procedures:

1. Know and adhere to local and/or state policies regarding time out.

2. Develop written procedures for using time out. Give copies of these to all teachers and inform parents and students of the possible use of time out and the behavior that could result in its use.
3. Obtain written parental consent for the use of time out.
4. Involve the IEP committee in determining the use of any behavior reduction procedure such as time out.
5. Use time out only to reduce dangerous or highly disruptive behaviors and only in conjunction with the simultaneous teaching of more appropriate behaviors.
6. Keep the time out period proportionate to the inappropriate behavior and to the age and physical condition of the child.
7. Keep thorough and accurate records of each time out that include (a) the student's name, (b) the date, (c) the time in and out of time out, (d) the behavior resulting in the time out, (e) the total length of the time out, (f) the name of the person implementing and monitoring the time out, (g) unusual occurrences during time out, (h) the student's behavior following the time out, and (i) the names of witnesses present.
8. Collect data to monitor the effects of the time out and verify that the time out procedure is decreasing the behavior.

Presenting an aversive consequence after misbehavior is the most intrusive form of punishment. For example, parents often use scolding as a common child-rearing practice. This form of punishment, however, does not motivate learning and can backfire on teachers by creating a negative classroom climate and by drawing attention to inappropriate student behavior. Other forms of punishment in which an aversive stimulus follows an inappropriate behavior include after-school or Saturday detention.

An aversive stimulus should be used only as a last resort for undesirable behaviors. If a teacher finds it necessary to use this form of punishment, the most effective practice is to pair the punishment of an inappropriate behavior with the reinforcement of an alternative appropriate behavior. In this way, the student is learning what to do as well as what not to do (Cohen & Hearn, 1988). In addition, teachers are advised first to check school policy regarding punishment and to obtain parental permission regarding the punishment to be used and the behaviors that might result in that punishment. Teachers must also make every effort to document the effectiveness of the form of punishment in question and to switch to a less aversive form of punishment such as response cost as soon as possible.

All teachers must have a clear understanding of how to structure the classroom environment to prevent behavior problems and how to manage behavior problems when they occur. "When things get out of hand" is a bad time to implement a classroom-management program. The effective teacher plans the environment very carefully and begins to teach and reinforce desirable behavior on the first day of school. The effective teacher also learns quickly what motivates appropriate and inappropriate behaviors in each student. Finally, the effective teacher recognizes that no instruction and, certainly, no learning can take place in a classroom that does not have a positive management system established as soon as possible.

Special Considerations: IDEA and Behavior

IDEA (1997) adds important new responsibilities for teachers when managing the behavior of students with mild disabilities. For example, when a child's behavior impedes his or her learning or that of others, teachers must include positive behavioral interventions, strategies, and supports to address that behavior on the child's Individualized Education Program (IEP). A positive behavior intervention plan is a proactive strategy based on a functional assessment of a child's behavior (see Chapter 6). Armstrong and Kauffman (1999) describe a functional assessment as having two goals: (a) finding the consequences maintaining a particular behavior (i.e., its function), and (b) replacing the behavior achieving that function with a more acceptable one.

For example, Ms. Lopez might count the number of times Joey makes inappropriate comments to his peers during thirty-minute blocks of time. She might also consider the nature and difficulty of the work and observe the responses of Joey's peers. If Ms. Lopez determines that the function of Joey's behavior is simply to gain the attention of his peers, she might devise a behavior intervention plan to replace his inappropriate word choices with more appropriate ones that allow Joey peer attention. On the other hand, Joey's behavior might occur most often when the work is difficult. In this case, Ms. Lopez might examine the requirements of the assignment, break the task into smaller steps, and provide more frequent rewards as Joey completes each step. As Ms. Lopez implements the plan, she must continue to count Joey's comments to determine if the plan is effective, and she must make adjustments as needed.

Positive behavior intervention plans must set reasonable goals for students. For example, Ms. Lopez cannot expect Joey to go from twenty inappropriate comments during a thirty-minute period to zero in just one step. In addition, she must be sure to teach Joey appropriate comments to replace the inappropriate ones and reward him for using these alternatives. Involving Ms. Kirk and Joey's parents in developing the plan and focusing on rewarding desired behavior rather than punishing undesirable behavior are keys to success.

IDEA (1997) also requires careful consideration of any disciplinary measures used for children and youth with mild disabilities (See, for example, Johns, Guetzloe, & Yell, 1997 and Katsiyannis & Maag, 1998). Specifically, if Joey's behavior violates the student code of conduct, and suspension or expulsion would be the normal disciplinary procedure, the law sets forth the following provisions:

◆ The school must conduct a Manifestation Determination Review: Within ten school days of the disciplinary action, Ms. Lopez, Joey, Ms. Kirk, the principal, Joey's parents, and other qualified individuals must determine if the misbehavior was a manifestation of Joey's disability. In doing so, the IEP team must consider whether or not the special education, supplementary aids and services, and behavior intervention strategies were consistent with Joey's IEP and educational placement. In addition, the team must determine if Joey's disability impaired his ability to understand the consequences of his actions or to control the behavior subject to the disciplinary proceedings.

Box 5.4

Web Watch

Violence Prevention and Safe Schools Web Sites

Blueprints for Violence Prevention: http://www.Colorado.EDU/cspv/blueprints
Model programs, resources, and assistance for preventing violence in schools and communities.

Center for Effective Collaboration and Practice
http://www.air-dc.org/cecp/default.htm
Recommendations for improving services for children with behavioral disorders; emphasis on families and systems change to reduce behavioral disorders among children and youth at risk; links to sites on school safety and violence prevention.

Center for the Prevention of School Violence: http://www.ncsu.edu/cpsv
A clearinghouse for violence prevention information and resources for schools; links to related sites.

Early Warning Timely Response: A Guide to Safe Schools
http://www.ed.gov/offices/OSERS/OSEP/earlywrn.html
Full text of a report supported by several national organizations including the Council for Exceptional Children; describes early warning signs for school violence, characteristics of safe schools, and plans for violence prevention and responses to violence.

Keep Schools Safe: http://www.KEEPSCHOOLSSAFE.ORG
School security, crisis management, concise discipline codes, law enforcement participation, and other topics related to school safety.

National School Safety Center: http://www.nsscl.org/home.htm
School safety studies; promotes safe schools week; publications, training, and links to related sites.

National Youth Gang Center: http://www.iir.com/nvgc/
Gang-related legislation, publications, and programs for gang prevention.

Oregon Social Learning Center: http://www.oslc.org/
Projects and information on antisocial behavior and effective parenting; information regarding prevention of antisocial behavior in children.

Safe and Drug Free Schools Program: http://www.ed.gov/offices/OESE/SEFS
U.S. Department of Education site giving initiatives to meet Goals 2000; news updates, model programs, and links to related sites.

- If, after considering all relevant information, the team determines that his behavior was not related to his disability, Joey may be suspended, expelled, or disciplined congruent with the disciplinary procedures that apply to students without disabilities. There can be no cessation of Joey's special educational services, however.
- On the other hand, if the IEP team determines that Joey's behavior was related to his disability, then his IEP must be revised so that he can be provided with an appropriate special education program. The team should conduct a functional assessment of his behavior and plan the positive behavior interventions and supports necessary for Joey to be integrated with his peers to the maximum extent possible.
- During the Manifestation Determination Review, Joey may remain in his current educational placement. School personnel, however, may place Joey in an appropriate Interim Alternative Educational Setting (IAES) during the review process with parental agreement. In addition, a hearing officer may place Joey in an IAES for no more than 45 days if he or she has evidence that maintaining Joey in his current placement is likely to result in injury to Joey or to others. The school may also order Joey's placement in this IAES for up to 45 days if he carries a weapon to school or to a school function. They may do so as well if Joey knowingly possesses or uses illegal drugs or sells or solicits the sale of a controlled substance while at school or at a school function.
- School personnel are not prohibited from reporting a crime committed by a child with a disability to appropriate state law enforcement and judicial authorities so that they may exercise their responsibilities. The school must also ensure that copies of all special education and disciplinary records are sent to the appropriate authorities.

Consistent with the school reforms reviewed in Chapter 1, then, IDEA clearly is designed to promote safer schools (See Box 5.4). The responsibility to promote safety in school, however, obligates teachers to provide for a reasonable standard of care for all students. Yell (1997) urges all school personnel to develop written policies in accordance with state law and to keep thorough records whenever behavioral incidents occur. Such records can be critical if student behavior or misconduct results in injury and potential liability. (See Figure 5.6 for a sample Behavior Incident Report.)

Summary

The goal of classroom management is to increase the amount of time available for instruction. Teachers must minimize the amount of time spent on behavior management and noninstructional activities and maximize the amount of time spent in demonstration and practice of academic tasks. Preventive discipline may eliminate many of the management crises that occur in the classroom. While teachers cannot prevent all discipline problems,

```
Student: _____     Date: _____

Teacher: _____     Time: _____

Student behavior prior to the incident:

Description of incident:

Did behavior endanger the safety of students or disrupt the learning environment?  If yes,
how?

Description of teacher action to correct the misbehavior:

Results of action:

Remarks:

Parents/Guardian notified:   Yes _____   No _____

Signatures

Teacher: _____

Principal: _____

Witness: _____

Parents/Guardian: _____
```

FIGURE 5.6 ————————————————————————————————————◆

A Sample Behavior Incident Report. From: Yell, M.L. (1997). Teacher liability for student injury and misconduct. *Beyond Behavior,* 8(1), 4-9.

they can plan an environment in which students are engaged in appropriate and meaningful academic tasks to the maximum extent. The skillful use of reinforcement and punishment also helps teachers to maintain a positive classroom climate.

Teachers must ensure that each student's IEP contains positive behavioral supports and strategies whenever necessary. For those students with mild disabilities who violate the school code of conduct, a Manifestation Determination Review must occur to consider the relationship between the child's disability and his or her misconduct and to evaluate the appropriateness of the special education being provided.

Application Exercises

1. Interview a classroom teacher and a special educator. Ask them how the rules for their classes are determined. Ask them how they teach their students to follow the rules and routines.

2. Observe in an elementary/secondary and a special education classroom. Watch for uses of primary and secondary reinforcers, group reinforcers, extinction, response cost, and time out. Which reinforcers do the teacher's think work best? Do certain students respond better to one form of reinforcement than to another? Do students respond better to reinforcement than to punishment?

3. Browse the web sites listed in Box 5.4. Which of the recommendations for creating safe schools have you seen implemented locally? Ask a classroom teacher and a special educator what "safe schools" practices are in place where they teach. How effective do these teachers believe the policies to be?

4. Use InfoTrac to locate three articles offering teachers tips for classroom management. Then browse the Internet for three additional classroom-management tips. Which of the six tips do you believe classroom teachers would find acceptable? Why?

ASSESSING STUDENT PROGRESS

Focus

As you read, think about the following questions:

◆ *Why do teachers use various types of assessment methods, including both informal and formal assessment?*

◆ *How can teachers assess student progress in a specific curriculum?*

◆ *How are assessment data used to plan and modify instruction?*

◆ *What can the teacher do when assessment reveals that a student is not progressing as expected?*

◆ *What is meant by referral, screening, and eligibility?*

◆ *What modifications can be made when students with mild disabilities participate in state- or district-wide assessments or need adjustments to local policies and practices regarding grades?*

◆ *What special considerations are important for assessing students from culturally, ethnically, or linguistically diverse backgrounds?*

Assessment refers to the process of gathering information that will enable teachers to make informed decisions about students and their performance. Assessment, then, is more than merely testing students. Rather, it involves collecting data to form a holistic picture of a student so that the teacher can plan instruction and promote student progress. If accurate objectives for students are to be maintained, assessment must become a daily strategy within the classroom.

Teachers use several types of assessment everyday. Many of these methods are common in both regular and special education classrooms. Most methods of assessment help the teacher gain information about academic progress. Others provide clarification about social-emotional needs or behavioral problems. In addition, some assessment methods give the teacher information about the classroom environment, curricular materials, or teaching strategies. In combination, these various forms of assessment give the teacher the needed documentation by which to make informed educational decisions to promote student achievement. The following conversation between Ms. Kirk and Ms. Lopez illustrates how these two teachers use assessment to make instructional decisions:

Ms. Kirk: Good morning.

Ms. Lopez: Hi, how are you!

Ms. Kirk: I'm glad I happened to see you this morning. I want to ask you a question about Travis.

Ms. Lopez: Sure. What is it?

Ms. Kirk: Travis is having difficulty writing in his journal in the morning. He's writing only one or two simple sentences but I know he has a lot more to say than that. I'm wondering if he doesn't say too much in his writing because he has trouble spelling the words.

Ms. Lopez: Can you think of an example?

Ms. Kirk: Let's see . . . I know! He visited some family over the weekend and was writing about that in his journal on Monday, but all he said was something like, "We went to see my aunt. We had fun." I'll show you the journal when we meet later today. He went to Washington, and he never even said that.

Ms. Lopez: Hmmm . . . He does have difficulty spelling even simple words. Have you tried giving him a list of terms to use? That seems to help him in his other subjects.

Ms. Kirk: I've done that in the past, but we've been rushed on the journals lately. The students are going to have to identify a topic from their journals this week, though, to expand as a piece for their portfolio.

Ms. Lopez: Great. I'll look at Travis's journal this afternoon, and then tomorrow morning I'll help him choose a piece to expand. I'll also help him make a list of terms related to that topic during his resource period tomorrow if that's okay with you. We can talk some more about it when I see you this afternoon.

Ms. Kirk: Okay, see you after school.

Teachers use many types of assessment to gather data and make informed instructional decisions. Instructional decisions must be based on empirical data, not on opinion, or teachers will waste valuable student time and effort. In this chapter, we will examine several assessment methods. First, we will explore informal assessment in the classroom, including curriculum-based assessment, authentic performance and portfolio assessment, criterion-referenced testing, observational recording procedures, and checklists and rating scales. Next, we will explore options for modifying state- or district-wide assessments of student progress as well as options for grading students with mild disabilities. Finally, following a discussion of formal assessments used in the referral, screening, and eligibility process, we will identify some issues related to the assessment of students from culturally, ethnically, or linguistically diverse backgrounds.

Informal Assessment in the Classroom

Informal assessment procedures make use of any data the teacher collects to monitor the progress of students and make instructional decisions. These data may be collected through teacher-made or commercially-prepared curriculum-based assessments, through error analysis using permanent products or work samples and probes, through authentic, performance-based assessments and portfolios, through criterion-referenced testing, through observational recording, or through checklists and rating scales. Informal assessment methods often employ the specific curricular materials used when teaching students.

Curriculum-Based Assessment

When assessment involves the actual curricular materials that students are using, the procedure is called curriculum-based assessment (Blankenship, 1985) or curriculum-based measurement (Deno, 1985; Shinn, 1989). Curriculum-based measurement grew from the work of Stanley Deno and his colleagues at the University of Minnesota who sought to align testing more closely with teaching. Curriculum-based assessments may be teacher-made, or teachers may be provided with commercially-prepared curricular materials. Some examples of common curriculum-based assessments in the elementary classroom follow:

- ◆ Daily spelling tests that include words from the student's spelling book
- ◆ Comprehension questions following a story in a basal reader
- ◆ Addition facts taken from an exercise in the student's mathematics workbook
- ◆ Timed reading of passages from a reading series
- ◆ Timed reading of a list of sight words or specific letter-sound associations

Teachers often design their own curriculum-based tests to assess progress. In many cases, commercially-prepared assessment instruments encompass a large body of information, such as an entire chapter or a whole topical unit. Students who are not monitored on a continual basis may struggle with a unit or chapter before the teacher realizes that they are not progressing through the curriculum as expected. For this reason, teachers should measure progress frequently. Frequent and direct assessment, when used to evaluate student objectives, helps teachers determine the effectiveness of instruction (Fuchs, 1993) and results in more frequent teacher modification of that instruction as well as more specific goals for students (Fuchs, 1986; Fuchs, Fuchs, & Stecker, 1989). Curriculum-based assessment also provides measurement that is sensitive to changes in student performance throughout the school year (Shinn, 1988). Moreover, teachers who use curriculum-based assessment tend to set more ambitious goals for their students (Fuchs, Fuchs, & Hamlett, 1989).

Curriculum-based assessment may be used in any subject taught in school, and it may be particularly useful in inclusive settings such as elementary and secondary content-area classes (King-Sears, Burgess, & Lawson, 1999; Marston & Tindall, 1995). To assess student progress in social studies, for example, Ms. Kirk might survey the information in the text, consider the learning activities in the classroom, and select representative questions or projects to determine whether or not her students have attained the key concepts and skills to be learned. According to Fuchs and Deno (1994), curriculum-based assessments do not have to be drawn just from the actual instructional material used in the classroom. They suggest that controlled materials mirroring the actual curricular materials or materials representing more generalized outcomes or goals of the curriculum can also be used as long as three essential features occur. These features include (a) repeated testing on material of comparable difficulty over time, (b) an assessment incorporating valid indicators of the critical outcomes for instruction, and (c) data allowing teachers to know when and how to adapt instruction. Sufficient planning time to construct curriculum-based assessments and to interpret their results is also essential if students are to make academic gains (Allinder, 1996).

Bennett (1982) suggests the following guidelines for teachers developing their own informal curriculum-based assessments:

1. Specify the purpose for the assessment. Teachers must clearly state an objective specifying what skill or behavior is to be measured. Ms. Lopez, for example, may wish to assess whether Travis can write words using the "ay" spelling pattern when she dictates such words to him.
2. Construct or select procedures that are relevant to the purpose for assessment. In order to assess Travis's performance when writing words with the "ay" spelling pattern, Ms. Lopez must compile a list of words with this pattern (e.g., hay, play), and she must ask Travis to write the selected words.
3. Select assessment tasks that are representative of the objective of interest. Ms. Lopez must give Travis words using the "ay" pattern to write if she is to assess his performance on this objective. Asking Travis to read or point to words having the "ay" pattern requires a different behavioral response. To assess whether Travis can spell words using the "ay" pattern, Ms. Lopez must dictate such words and then observe whether or not Travis spells them correctly.
4. Specify dimensions on which performance will be judged and criteria for determining what will be considered a correct response. Ms. Lopez considers a correct response in spelling to be all letters present and in the correct sequence. She must decide, however, whether or not Travis's performance should be judged on the basis of legibility as well. Because handwriting must be legible for others to be able to read it, Ms. Lopez decides that Travis must also write his letters clearly before his performance will be judged correct.
5. Specify criteria for evaluating overall performance and the rationale for selecting these criteria. Ms. Lopez determines that Travis must spell words

having the "ay" pattern with 100% accuracy. She sets this criterion because using common spelling patterns without error must become automatic with Travis if he is to progress in his writing skills.

6. Use as comprehensive an assessment as possible. Ms. Lopez must gather a representative sample of work in order to assess Travis's ability to spell words having the "ay" pattern. If she gives Travis only two or three words with this pattern, she will not know whether he can spell "ay" words or whether he has simply memorized two or three particular words. Ms. Lopez may also wish to present Travis with some "non-examples" of "ay" words (e.g., "cake" and "lake") to be sure that Travis knows when to use the "ay" spelling pattern.

According to Choate, Enright, Miller, Poteet, and Rakes (1992), curriculum-based assessment offers an "authentic" picture of student performance. Moreover, Deno (1985) and Fuchs and Deno (1994) maintain that it can provide teachers with numerous advantages. For example, curriculum-based assessment:

◆ helps the teacher determine what to teach;
◆ facilitates evaluation of student progress and program effectiveness;
◆ provides an efficient, valid, and reliable means of evaluation;
◆ increases student achievement by assessing what is taught;
◆ helps with decision making in referring, screening, and evaluating students for special education eligibility; and
◆ complies with the requirements of the Individuals with Disabilities Education Act (IDEA) (1997) that a student's present level of educational performance be specified, that goals and objectives be written to address individual student needs, and that objective procedures be used for evaluating student progress toward instructional objectives.

Finally, King-Sears, Burgess, and Lawson (1999) suggest that classroom teachers in inclusive settings can use curriculum-based assessment to improve learning outcomes for their students. They offer specific steps in the APPLY strategy to guide this process:

A = Analyze the curriculum. Determine the foundational skills, important competencies and principles, and ultimate outcomes for students.

P = Prepare items to meet curriculum objectives. Devise a probe containing many examples of the critical skills students must master, such as the math probe shown in Figure 6.1.

P = Probe frequently. Give the CBA several times across days in order to make decisions about student learning.

L = Load data on a graph. Use a graph format to plot daily performance data as shown in Figure 6.2.

Y = Yield to results. Make decisions regarding student progress and revise instruction accordingly.

Using Student Work Samples and Probes. In addition to teacher-made or commercially-prepared tests, using the actual work products of the student is yet another form of curriculum-based assessment. Assessment based on a student's daily work is called direct measurement. Student worksheets, workbook pages, book reports, answers to the questions at the end of a chapter, and problems assigned for practice from the text can all be used in direct measurement.

Work samples are permanent products representing a student's performance at a given point in time. Permanent products may also include library records of books checked out, attendance records, or sign-up sheets for time to work on projects (Fagley, 1984). Permanent products provide a lasting picture of a student's strengths, interests, or weaknesses that can be used to guide instructional decisions.

Probe sheets offer one of the best ways for teachers to gather permanent information about a student's performance. Probes are detailed assessments administered in a specified, usually brief period of time, such as one to three minutes, and they are used to assess a student's fluency with a particular skill. Correct and incorrect student responses per minute (i.e., rate) and percentage of correct responses are two measures that teachers may obtain by using probes (see Figure 6.1). Probes can be excellent measures of student learning when academic outputs such as the number of words or digits correctly written or the number of words correctly read are recorded.

Date: _____   Skill: 2-digit + 2-digit no regrouping _____
Teacher: _____   Student: _____
                             Text: _____

									(digits)
11 +48	20 +44	72 +15	13 +25	23 +26	21 +66	11 +16	82 +14	10 +29	35 +22
									(20)
10 +38	29 +60	35 +53	40 +18	34 +23	24 +35	40 +59	23 +51	20 +12	87 +12
									(40)
32 +62	41 +26	50 +22	34 +44	41 +12	30 +28	26 +63	50 +21	50 +15	75 +12
									(60)
60 +37	32 +34	34 +14	20 +63	10 +16	23 +76	62 +27	11 +67	48 +31	35 +44
									(80)
57 +41	10 +35	51 +16	33 +62	20 +63	19 +80	45 +21	11 +51	23 +72	22 +76
									(100)
41 +26	50 +22	19 +80	45 +21	87 +12	20 +12	11 +67	10 +16	13 +25	11 +48
									(120)

FIGURE 6.1

Example of an Arithmetic Probe From: Salvia, J., & Hughes, C. (1990). *Curriculum-based assessment: Testing what is taught.* New York, NY: Macmillan, p. 98. Reprinted with permission.

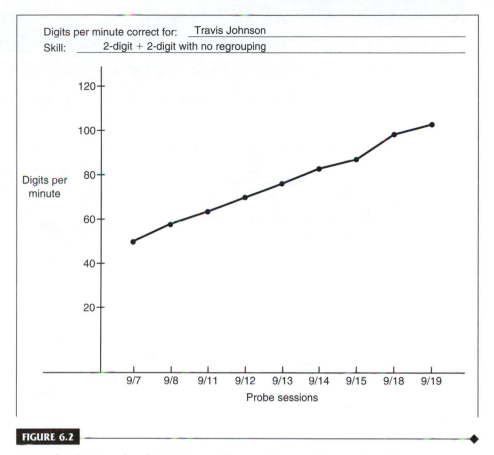

Digits per minute correct for: ___Travis Johnson___
Skill: ___2-digit + 2-digit with no regrouping___

FIGURE 6.2

A Student's Graph of Digits per Minute Correct Determined by an Arithmetic Probe

To construct a probe, teachers first specify an instructional objective and then select items by which to measure achievement of the objective. In the example provided in Figure 6.1, the objective is skill acquisition in solving two-digit plus two-digit addition problems with no regrouping. Only addition problems of this type are included as probe items. Of interest is the number of digits written correctly each minute. In order to assess the degree to which the student has mastered this particular skill, the probe must include more items than the student can complete in the allotted time. Salvia and Hughes (1990) suggest that teachers reduce student anxiety when using probes by informing students that there are more problems on the probe than any student can complete in the given time period.

Following assessment through a probe, the teacher may prepare a chart or graph to display pupil progress (see Figure 6.2). For example, Ms. Lopez might graph the digits written correctly per minute after Travis completes an addition probe. Or, she might also construct a record sheet, such as the one for Travis's performance on arithmetic work samples shown in Figure 6.3.

Student	_Travis Johnson_		Skill	_Addition with regrouping_	

Objective _Given 2-digit plus 2-digit addition problems with regroupings_
Travis will write the sums with 100% accuracy over 3 consecutive days.

Date	# of problems	# correct	# wrong	% correct	Comments
9/18	25–best ever math series, p. 39	18	7	72	no regrouping
9/19	25–best ever math series, p. 40	21	4	84	no regrouping– careless errors
9/20	25–b.e.m.s. p. 43	25	0	100	no regrouping
9/21	25–b.e.m.s. p. 44	25	0	100	no regrouping
9/22	30–b.e.m.s. p. 45 (review)	30	0	100	no regrouping
9/25	20–b.e.m.s. p. 49	10	10	50	Regrouping from ones to tens

FIGURE 6.3 ◆

Sample Record Sheet from Travis's Work Samples From: Salvia, J., & Hughes, C. (1990). *Curriculum-based assessment: Testing what is taught.* New York, NY: Macmillan, p. 104. Reprinted with Permission.

Analyzing Student Errors. Once the teacher completes a curriculum-based assessment, he or she must analyze student errors in order to make instructional decisions. In error analysis, the teacher examines the student's responses to determine whether there is a pattern of errors that indicates that the student has not yet mastered the specified task. For example, Ms. Kirk might discern that a student is using a faulty algorithm in mathematics after observing the following errors on an arithmetic test:

705	217	342	438	814
-381	-123	-204	-269	-782
484	114	142	231	172

In this case, the student is subtracting the larger digit from the smaller digit without an understanding of place value and the need to regroup.

Through error analysis, the teacher can determine the reason for errors. For example, the student may not have understood the directions for the task, or the error may have been the result of carelessness. In other cases, errors are due to lack of understanding of the skill or concept. If the reason for the error is not clear, the teacher may ask the student to explain how he or she arrived at a particular answer (Howell, 1986). (See Box 6.1 for an example of an error analysis.)

In Box 6.1, Ms. Lopez discovers that Travis has forgotten part of the rule for spelling words that have the "ay" pattern, but that he has mastered the "ee" words. Therefore, she decides to provide additional practice activities for Travis using the "ay" pattern and to probe his mastery of that pattern before testing him again on the complete spelling list.

Box 6.1

Ms. Lopez Conducts an Error Analysis

Teachers often use curriculum-based assessment and student work samples to analyze student errors and plan for instruction. Let's listen to a conversation in Ms. Lopez's room during a spelling lesson with Travis:

Ms. Lopez: Travis, let's look at the work you completed yesterday in spelling.

Travis: Okay.

Ms. Lopez: It looks like you had some trouble with the new vowel pattern we've been working on this week. What is your new vowel pattern?

Travis: Uh . . . the "ay?"

Ms. Lopez: That's right. Tell me the rule for the "ay" pattern.

Travis: Um . . . a long /a/ sound is spelled A-Y.

Ms. Lopez: Travis, a long /a/ sound *at the end of a one-syllable word* is spelled A-Y.

Travis: Oh yeah!

Ms. Lopez: Tell me some words on the list that have the "ay" pattern.

Travis: Um . . . "hay" and "play."

Ms. Lopez: Good. Those are some of the words with the "ay" pattern. Let's look through your spelling list again. The "ay" words are the only words that gave you trouble. I think you've figured out the "ee" words pretty well. We'll do a practice activity tomorrow on just the "ay" words, and I'll test you on just those words before we do the whole spelling list again. Okay, now let's take another look at those tricky "ay" words. . . .

Dickinson (1980) recommends the following steps to help teachers with error analysis:

1. Pinpoint the problem. The problem must be defined in ways that are observable and measurable. For example, Ms. Kirk may find that Celie does not give complete information when asked, "What is your address?" Celie gives the correct apartment number, city, and state, but she does not give the correct street name and zip code.
2. Determine if the task or behavior is in the student's repertoire. For example, Ms. Lopez may note that Joey knows how to get her attention appropriately in the resource room; however, he is not using this skill when necessary in his mainstreamed classroom with Ms. Kirk.
3. Determine what sets the occasion for the response. The teacher must determine exactly which stimuli set the occasion for an incorrect response. If Ms.

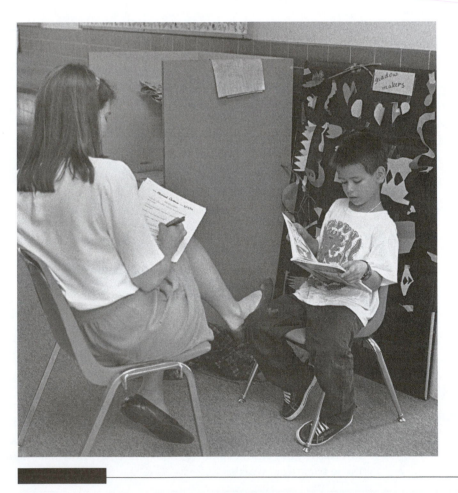

Teachers use informal assessments like curriculum-based measurement daily to help determine what to teach.

Kirk were to observe, for example, that Joey was using the proper steps to get her attention during math, but not during social studies, she might examine the stimuli to which Joey was exposed during math and social studies classes. She may note, for example, that several of Joey's friends sit near him during social studies, but not during math. Joey appears to enjoy attention from these friends.

4. Perform a task analysis. When a task is not in a student's repertoire, the teacher performs a task analysis to determine the lowest skill not mastered that is essential to the task.

Using Task Analysis. Task analysis is used to break down a task into its smallest steps or substeps, thus enabling teachers to determine exactly where a student's mastery of a particular skill begins and ends. According to Howell (1985), a student who is missing a substep of a task is missing one of the essential building blocks of the complete task. Constructing a task analysis requires at least four steps:

1. Identify an instructional objective (e.g., the student will say the letters of the alphabet in the correct order within a 30-second time limit).
2. Break down the desired skill into its component parts by watching someone else perform the skill, by performing it yourself, by logically analyzing the skill, or by using a normal developmental sequence such as that provided in a basal reading series (e.g., the student might first be required to say the letters "A-F" in correct sequence, then "A-P", then "A-Z").
3. Sequence the steps for teaching purposes, using either the temporal order for tasks or increasing levels of difficulty.
4. Specify any necessary prerequisite behaviors. For example, some prerequisite skills for long division include the ability to write the numerals, to recall the subtraction, multiplication, and division facts, and to line up numbers on a page.

Error analysis and task analysis are integral components of effective instruction. A teacher may, for example, analyze a student's errors on a work sample involving long division. Upon examining the work sample, the teacher may determine that the student knows the subtraction, multiplication, and division facts and that he or she is performing the operations in the correct sequence. However, the student is lining up numbers incorrectly following the multiplication step. The teacher now knows that the entry-level behavior for instruction with this student is the step of placing the multiplied number in the correct position prior to the subtraction step.

Task analyses may be conducted for any curricular area. Performing a task analysis prior to teaching a skill and analyzing student errors during instruction will provide the teacher with information necessary for sound educational decision making.

Authentic, Performance-Based Assessment and Portfolios

Authentic assessment and performance assessment are two terms often used interchangeably to refer to testing a student's ability to produce an answer or product that demonstrates his or her knowledge or skills (Coutinho & Malouf, 1992). Authentic, performance-based assessments are alternatives to traditional measures in which students simply select or give correct responses. To the contrary, performance assessment relies on student-generated responses and products that relate to "real-world" problems and outcomes of interest to students (Elliott, 1998). In fact, many states are now using performance assessments to measure student progress in subject matter at all grade levels.

Although teachers of art and music have relied on performance measures for many years, classroom and special education teachers are only now applying such assessments to academic tasks. For example, Ms. Kirk might ask Travis to construct a diagram or model of the solar system during science class rather than having him take a test on which he must label the planets, or she might have students create and present a project on the American colonial period. Simulations, presentations, experiments, videotapes, and written products are all possible means of authentic, performance-based assessment.

Portfolios are another form of performance assessment. With teacher guidance, students select various items to place in their portfolio to document their learning and progress across curricular areas. For example, Travis might choose the following items to place in his language arts portfolio: a graph of his oral reading rate, a simple storybook he wrote and illustrated, a tape recording made while he was reading his story to a kindergarten child, and a selection from his daily journal which he considers to be his best work.

According to Salend (1998), a portfolio helps the student assume more control over his or her learning. It can also serve as a vehicle for measuring a child's current level of functioning and his or her progress toward annual goals and objectives on the Individualized Education Program (IEP). The portfolio, then, is an excellent tool to facilitate communication between parents and teachers about student progress. Salend (1998) and Pike and Salend (1995) offer the following guidelines to teachers when using portfolios:

- ◆ Identify the goals of the portfolio. Will the portfolio be used to make instructional decisions, to identify and share information about students, or to demonstrate mastery of IEP goals?
- ◆ Determine the type of portfolio to be used. A showcase portfolio presents the students' best work. A reflective portfolio helps students and teachers think about effort, attitudes, use of learning strategies, and achievement. The cumulative portfolio demonstrates changes in learning over time, and the goal-based portfolio presents items to verify mastery of IEP objectives.
- ◆ Establish procedures for organizing the portfolio. Portfolios can be stored in three-ring binders, expandable accordion-type files, or boxes. They can be organized by IEP goals and objectives, by subject areas such as reading or mathematics, or in chronological order. Student work can also be scanned and saved on a computer diskette, and multimedia computer programs can be used to create electronic portfolios that integrate graphics, video, and sound.
- ◆ Choose a range of authentic classroom products that relate to the objectives of the portfolio. (See Table 6.1.)

Table 6.1 A List of Possible Portfolio Products

◆ Student artwork
◆ Written language samples
◆ Tests
◆ Audiotapes or videotapes of a student's work or a presentation
◆ An entry from the student's journal
◆ A list of books read
◆ Work the student considers his or her best
◆ Photographs of models or projects created by the student
◆ Probes
◆ Graphs of student progress
◆ Written reports

◆ Record the significance of items included in students' portfolios. Students should create concise, written captions for each item included in the portfolio. Captions should state how the item was developed or why the student chose to include the item. Students might, for example, describe what they learned or what they can now do as a result of the project chosen for inclusion in the portfolio.

◆ Review and evaluate portfolios periodically. Students can present their portfolio to peers, parents, and teachers. The information in the portfolio can be used to evaluate student outcomes and to provide new teachers with valuable data about the student's performance as he or she moves up the grades.

Performance assessments and portfolios may assist students who have mild disabilities, as well as other students who are at risk, such as those with limited English proficiency, to demonstrate learning better than traditional paper-and-pencil tests would (Dalton, Tivnan, Riley, Rawson, & Dias, 1995). Portfolios also give teachers instructionally relevant data that allow them to make better decisions about students who are culturally or linguistically diverse (Rueda & Garcia, 1997). In addition, portfolios may be an alternative means through which student performance outcomes can be measured when students are unable to participate in state- or district-wide assessments mandated by IDEA (1997) (Ysseldyke & Olsen, 1999). Finally, performance assessments can be used in combination with curriculum-based assessments to improve instructional planning by teachers (Fuchs & Fuchs, 1996).

Criterion-Referenced Assessment

In addition to deciding which work samples to analyze for errors or which items to examine from a student's portfolio, the teacher must decide the level of acceptable performance. In other words, how will the teacher determine that a student has mastered an objective? A test that has a preset level for mastery is called a criterion-referenced test. A criterion-referenced test compares a student's performance to a preset criterion rather than to the performance of other students.

The criterion is often an objective that states that a student can perform a particular task to a specified level. (See Chapter 7 for a discussion of writing educational objectives.) For example, an objective for Joey might state, "Given a probe sheet of two-digit minus two-digit numbers without regrouping, Joey will write the correct answers at a rate of 50 digits per minute with three or fewer errors." In order to meet the specified criterion, Joey must correctly write answers to the subtraction problems on the probe at the given rate and accuracy level.

Criterion-referenced assessments are informal measurements that are either teacher-made or commercially available. One commercially-prepared criterion-referenced test often used by teachers is the Brigance Comprehensive Inventory of Basic Skills, Revised (Brigance, 1999). The Brigance, available through Curriculum Associates, assesses numerous skills and subskills from the early childhood level through grade nine. The objectives with criterion levels for mastery provided by the Brigance are helpful to teachers when evaluating student performance toward educational goals on IEPs.

Some students will struggle in the classroom despite the teacher's best efforts to modify instruction. For these students, the multidisciplinary team collects both formal and informal assessment data to determine the child's eligibility for special education.

Observational Recording Procedures

Another common method used for informal assessment of both academic and behavioral performance is direct observation. For example, the teacher may ask a student to solve a mathematical calculation on the chalkboard or on paper and listen as the student explains the steps. The teacher may also listen to a student read from a basal reader or observe a student as he or she presents an oral book report. Observational data may include, for example, the number of times Susan asks for help during a thirty-minute period, the length of time Joey remains seated during social studies, or the percentage of time that Travis is on task during mathematics lessons. In order to gain an accurate picture of academic and behavioral performance through direct observation, the teacher may use anecdotal recording, event recording, duration recording, or time-sampling procedures.

Anecdotal Recording. An anecdotal record is a written description of a student's behavior in a particular setting or instructional time period (Alberto & Troutman, 1999). When completing an anecdotal record, the teacher may wish to use a format such as that shown in Figure 6.4. Using this form, the teacher writes the time of the observation; the antecedents, or events that occurred before the child's behavior; the observed behavior of the child; and any consequences following the child's behavior. The teacher must be careful to record only what the child and others actually say or do rather than to interpret motivations or feelings.

Event Recording. Event recording, sometimes called frequency counting, is a simple method involving direct observation of student behavior. In event recording, the teacher simply tallies the number of times a particular behavior occurs over a specific period of time. This method is useful for behaviors that are discrete; that is, those behaviors having a distinct beginning and ending, such as using an inappropriate word, hitting a peer, or turning assignments in on time.

Time	Antecedent	Behavior	Consequence
9:30	Ms. Kirk says "Group I may line up."	Joey walks to the line.	Ms. Kirk says "Nice job for Group I. Now Group 3 line up."
	Celie runs to line.	Joey says "You ran. You can't run to line up."	Celie talks to her friend.
9:35	Kevin drops a ball and runs to get it.	Joey kicks ball away from Kevin.	Ms. Kirk says "Go get the ball, Joey."

FIGURE 6.4 ◆

A Sample Anecdotal Recording Form

In order to observe changes in behavior over time, the teacher may display the data on a chart or graph. If the amount of time during an observational session stays constant, the teacher can use the actual number of behaviors counted. If, however, the observational time varies from session to session, the teacher must convert frequency to rate (i.e., the number of times the behavior occurred divided by the amount of time observed gives the teacher the number of behaviors per unit of time) before graphing or charting the data.

As an example of event recording, Mr. Mathis might be concerned that Leon talks out inappropriately in his afternoon classes. He asks Mr. Abel to collect data on Leon's "talk-outs" over a period of three days. The event recording might look like this:

Student name: Leon		Week of: October 9–13
Day	Time	Number of Talk Outs
Tues.	12:30–1:30	‖‖‖‖ ‖‖‖‖
Weds.	1:30–2:30	‖‖‖ ‖‖‖‖ ‖‖
Thurs.	2:30–3:30	‖‖‖‖ ‖‖‖‖ ‖‖‖‖

The data gathered may suggest to Mr. Abel that Leon becomes more talkative in the late afternoon, or perhaps he becomes more talkative as the week progresses. More data could be gathered to determine the validity of each hypothesis. This information would be particularly helpful to Mr. Abel when planning a positive behavior-intervention strategy for Mr. Mathis and Leon's other teachers.

Duration Recording. Duration recording is used to determine the length of time that a behavior lasts. For example, Ms. Lopez might record the amount of time Joey remains in his seat during reading or the length of time Celie sucks her thumb during observation periods. If Ms. Lopez records the number of seconds or minutes for each occurrence of the observed behavior separately, she will also know the number of times the behavior occurred. Again, if the length of the observation periods remains constant, Ms. Lopez may simply record the total amount of time for the behavior (e.g., 35 minutes in seat for Joey). If the observation times vary, however, Ms. Lopez must convert her data to a percentage of time before graphing (e.g., Celie spent 27% of the time observed sucking her thumb). The percentage would be the number of minutes engaged in thumb sucking divided by the total number of minutes in the observation period, times 100.

Time Sampling. Time-sampling procedures enable the teacher to estimate the frequency and duration of behaviors without having to time or count every occurrence. To use momentary time sampling, the teacher divides a period of time into equal intervals. For example, Ms. Kirk divides the language arts period of one hour into twenty three-minute intervals. She sets a small kitchen timer or the "beeper" on her watch to sound after three minutes and, at the sound, she looks to see if Travis is or is not on task at that exact moment. (For Ms. Kirk, "on task" means that Travis is looking at his language arts book, writing on his paper, or looking at her when she is speaking.) If Travis is on task at that moment, Ms. Kirk places a plus mark (+) next to the observed interval on her observation sheet. If Travis is not on task, she places a minus mark (−) on her form (See Figure 6.5). At the end of the observation period, Ms. Kirk computes the percentage of time that Travis was on task by dividing the number of observed occurrences (the plus intervals) by the total number of intervals observed and multiplying by 100. (In this case, the total was only 17 intervals because Travis was excused to use the restroom for a few minutes.)

Checklists and Rating Scales

Additional measures of behavior and academic performance include checklists and teacher rating scales. Checklists are sequential lists of skills that the teacher completes for a particular student. The checklist for reading, for example, may be taken from the scope and sequence chart included in the teacher's guide accompanying the basal reading series. Other examples of checklists include a sequential list of fine-motor skills necessary prior to beginning instruction in manuscript writing, a list of punctuation or capitalization skills for acceptable written work, or a sequence of mathematics skills necessary for a specific vocational education program such as auto mechanics. A portion of a mathematics checklist, listing the skills for multiplication and division, is presented in Figure 6.6.

Rating scales are instruments by which the teacher judges a student's performance or behavior. The rating is often completed using a Likert scale measure, such as a rating of 1 to 5 on a social skills list, with a 1 indicating that the student has mastered the skill in the teacher's estimation, and a 5 indicating that the student has not mastered the skill. Students receiving high scores on this instrument would be in need of social skills training. Conversely, those with lower scores would need relatively less training.

Commercially-prepared rating scales are available to measure specific behavioral or social-emotional skills as well as academic competence. For example, the Social Skills Rating System (Gresham & Elliott, 1990), available from American Guidance Service, contains rating scales for parents and teachers of children aged three through eighteen across both social and academic domains. Similarly, The Walker-McConnell Scale of Social Competence and School Adjustment, available from Pro-Ed, also includes a simple teacher rating scale for kindergarten through sixth grade (Walker & McConnell, 1988).

A Summary of Informal Assessment

Many forms of informal assessment provide valuable information on which to base instructional decisions. These include curriculum-based assessment, performance and portfolio assessment, criterion-referenced testing, observational

| Student | Travis Johnson | | Date | 10/21 |

Student _Travis Johnson_   Date _10/21_

Time _9:30 – 10:30 AM (Lang arts)_   Interval length _3 minutes_

Behavior observed _On-task—Writing, reading L.A. book, looking at teacher, speaking when recognized by teacher_

Interval #	+	−
1	+	
2	+	
3	+	
4	— N/O	
5	— N/O	
6		—
7		—
8	+	
9	+	
10	+	
11	+	
12	+	
13	+	
14		—
15		—
16	+	
17	+	
18	— N/O	
19		—
20		—

Intervals observed _17_

Intervals on task _11_

% Intervals on task _65%_

FIGURE 6.5

Time-Sampling Data for Travis's On-Task Behavior

Skill Area	Above Average	Average	Below Average
Multiplication			
Tables 1-5	____	____	____
Tables 6-10	____	____	____
One-place	____	____	____
Two-place	____	____	____
Three or more places	____	____	____
Uses zero as a place-holder	____	____	____
Multiplying by 10, 100, 1,000	____	____	____
Decimals	____	____	____
Division			
Tables 1-5	____	____	____
Tables 6-10	____	____	____
Short division	____	____	____
Long division/ subtractive method	____	____	____
Long division/ regular notation	____	____	____
Use of zero as a place-holder	____	____	____
Dividing by 10, 100, 1,000	____	____	____
Decimals	____	____	____
Conversion of fractions to decimals	____	____	____

FIGURE 6.6 ◆

A Sample Checklist of Arithmetic Skills. From: Guerin, G., & Maier, A. (1983). *Informal assessment in education.* Mountain View, CA: Mayfield Publishing Co. Reprinted with permission.

recording, checklists, and rating scales. Although some authorities caution teachers to use informal assessment techniques carefully (Bennett, 1982), others argue that these procedures offer viable alternatives to formal, standardized testing (Deno, 1985; Marston & Magnusson, 1985; Shinn, Tindal, & Stein, 1988). ◆

Standards Assessment and Grading

Special educators often equate assessment with identifying students for special education programs or with monitoring student progress on the IEP. Classroom teachers, on the other hand, use assessment to monitor the progress of students in the regular curriculum. Two recent assessment issues of critical concern to all teachers, however, are the participation of students with mild disabilities in state- or district-wide testing programs and equitable grading of students with disabilities who are included in the regular classroom.

Standards Assessment. Recall from Chapter 1 that most states now have mandated "high stakes" testing to measure student performance toward specified outcomes. Such testing is more than assessment of student progress, however, because schools are also held accountable for that progress. Schools and school districts not making progress at a preset level may be placed on probation by the state, receive a warning or loss of accreditation, be taken over by the state education agency, or lose funding (Erickson, Ysseldyke, Thurlow, & Elliott, 1998). The performance of schools and school districts on these assessments is made available to the public and frequently published in local newspapers. Similarly, students performing below a specified level on these tests may be retained a grade, receive a failing grade in a class, or not be permitted to graduate from high school.

In the past, students with disabilities were often excluded from state- or district-wide assessments because schools believed that (a) testing for special education provided sufficient data regarding how these students were progressing in school; (b) such tests were too difficult for these students, causing them unnecessary frustration and poor self-esteem; (c) these students were learning a different curriculum than that taught in the regular classroom; and (d) including the scores of students with disabilities along with those of other students would lower the overall scores for the state or district (Elliott, Ysseldyke, Thurlow, & Erickson, 1998; Erickson et al., 1998; U.S. Department of Education, 1997). Such fears are unfounded, however. Unless students with disabilities participate in large-scale testing programs, the achievement of these students will not be considered in evaluating a school's performance and schools will have no incentive for improving the education of those students for whom scores "don't count" (Thurlow, 1998).

IDEA (1997), the Americans with Disabilities Act, and Section 504 of the Rehabilitation Act Amendments now all mandate that students with disabilities be included in state- or district-wide assessments whenever possible. For students in special education, the IEP team must decide whether or not it is appropriate for the student to participate in the assessment program, and if so, they must specify on the IEP any accommodations necessary to facilitate his or her participation. In addition, states are now developing alternative assessments to measure a student's progress toward specific performance indicators for those students who have a different curriculum than that of the regular classroom and for whom the IEP team decides the current assessment program is inappropriate.

Most students with mild disabilities are included in the regular classroom for the majority of the school day. Therefore, most of these students will be expected to participate in the state- and district-wide assessments. Common accommodations to allow their participation include alterations to the time, setting, presentation format, or response mode (Erickson et al., 1998; Thurlow, Ysseldyke, & Silverstein, 1995). Robert, for example, may need extended time to take the test, frequent rest breaks, permission to take the test in the morning rather than in the afternoon, and testing over several days or several sessions. Travis might do better if the test is given in a small-group rather than large-group setting, or if he can take the test in a study carrel or separate room free from distractions. In addition, Travis may perform better if he can dictate his answers to a scribe or use a computer, have his answers recorded for him, or have an assistant transfer his answers from his test booklet to an answer sheet. Other students may require the test to be presented in large print or in Braille, with magnification, or via sign language, and some may require the test to be read orally. Finally, according to Elliott, Kratochwill, and Schulte (1998), some children with disabilities may also need instruction in test-taking skills prior to the test or verbal encouragement throughout the test to maintain motivation.

As more students with disabilities participate in "high stakes" testing, states will face several challenging issues. States must, for example, maintain student confidentiality, yet at the same time they must report test data for students with disabilities along with that of students without disabilities. In small school districts that have few students with disabilities, it might be relatively easy to match the test scores to the child with a disability (U.S. Department of Education, 1997). Moreover, states are not yet sure exactly how to report the data for students with disabilities. An important and unresolved issue is whether or not the scores of students with disabilities who have accommodations to take the test can be compared to the scores of those who did not have such accommodations. Finally, concerns remain regarding "gray-area students," those who are in the classroom and regular curriculum but who are having difficulty demonstrating what they know. These students may not be able to succeed on the "high stakes" tests even with accommodations, yet the alternative assessment program may be inappropriate for them as well. Professionals are rightly concerned that many students with mild disabilities may simply fall through the cracks and drop out of school (Elliott, Ysseldyke, et al., 1998).

Grading. As students with mild disabilities are increasingly included in the regular classroom, both classroom teachers and special educators are worried about policies and practices that ensure fair grades for all students. Grades are used not only to communicate to parents a student's progress, but also to compute the student's academic rank or class standing for graduation and to report pupil performance on applications for college or for scholarships. Teachers, then, may view grades as a reflection of the quality of a student's work as compared with others.

Students with disabilities, however, often have lower grade-point averages than do their peers without disabilities, and one third of these students have at least one failing grade in a class (Valdes, Williamson, & Wagner, 1990). According to research, elementary, middle, and high schools most frequently give letter grades or number grades and use a percentage cutoff as the grading system (see, for example, Bursuck, Polloway, Plante, Epstein, Jayanthi, & McConeghy, 1996, and Polloway, Epstein, Bursuck, Roderique, McConeghy, & Jayanthi, 1994). In addition, grades are most often based on tests, homework, and projects, with attendance, behavior, extra credit, or other variables accounting less frequently for a portion of the grade. Most school districts do have a policy that allows modifications to grading for students with disabilities. Many schools, for example, permit students with mild disabilities to be graded according to their accomplishment of goals and objectives on the IEP; however, students may not necessarily receive a standard high school diploma for doing so.

If students with mild disabilities are to be graded fairly in the classroom, teachers must believe that modifications to grades are reasonable and feasible.

According to Schumm and Vaughn (1991), though, teachers rate adaptation of grading or scoring criteria as the least desirable accommodation to be made in the classroom. Similarly, students must believe that alterations in grading practices are fair. Research indicates, however, that students with and without learning disabilities differ in their perceptions of grading adaptations (Bursuck, Munk, & Olson, 1999). Because most students hold negative perceptions regarding adaptations to grading policies, teachers will experience resistance and pressure from students and may be hesitant to modify their practices. Christiansen and Vogel (1998) suggest that classroom teachers and special educators must share responsibility for grading students with disabilities by:

- Developing policies consistent with district, state, and federal policies and guidelines;
- Identifying their own and their colleagues' theoretical approaches to grading (for example, assessing student progress against a standard of mastery versus comparing the progress of one student to that of others); and
- Cooperatively determining the grading practices for individual students.

As teachers work to develop grading practices for individual students, they might consider curriculum-based assessments as well as portfolios to document the progress of students toward goals and objectives on the IEP or toward the mastery of subject-area knowledge and skills. Bradley and Calvin (1998) offer several suggestions for changes in grading practices to "level the playing field" for all students in the classroom:

- Use points and percentages, rather than letter grades, to grade differentiated assignments. For example, if Travis has only 10 words on his spelling list and other students have 20, Travis will score 100% if he gets 10 out of 10 words on his spelling test correct.
- Change the grading scale consistently for all students rather than using a traditional grading scale for most students in the classroom while using a different scale for those students who have disabilities.
- Match grading criteria for some students with the goals and objectives of the IEP. For example, Robert shouldn't have his grade lowered for incorrect spelling on written work in science if his IEP states that he is working on spelling goals and objectives.
- Develop rubrics for scoring each assignment and for computing grades that consider the unique needs of all the learners in the classroom. Ms. Stone, for example, might specify that a written report in earth science is to be worth a total of 100 points (15% of the total grade for the marking period) and that the report will be graded according to the following criteria:

Technical Adequacy (50 points)
Follows format given: 10 points
Typewritten: 5 points
Correct spelling: 5 points
Correct capitalization: 5 points
Correct punctuation: 5 points
Correct grammar: 5 points

Neat and well-organized: 5 points
Uses at least 10 references: 10 points

Content (50 points)
Introduction: 10 points
Accuracy of Information: 15 points
Thorough Coverage of Topic: 15 points
Summary: 10 points

Ms. Stone can then adapt her grades to accommodate for the needs of each learner. For example, she would not penalize Robert for spelling errors, although she might require him to correct the errors before the final grade is computed for the report.

- ◆ Use a variety of options for computing grades. Options might include portfolios, contracts, work samples, and credit for effort. Do refrain from grading solely on effort, though.

Summary of Standards Assessment and Grading ◆

Students with mild disabilities are included in the regular classroom and must be assessed and graded in a fair and equitable manner. IDEA (1997) mandates appropriate accommodations in "high stakes" state- or district-wide testing programs whenever appropriate. Moreover, IDEA (1997) requires that an appropriate education be given to students with disabilities and that supplementary aids and services necessary for maintaining the student in the regular curriculum to the maximum extent possible be provided. This requirement implies that special educators and classroom teachers must collaborate in order to ensure that students with mild disabilities are graded in accordance with the IEP. ◆

Referral, Screening, and Eligibility for Special Education

From time to time, the classroom teacher may have students who continue to exhibit academic or behavioral problems despite the teacher's best efforts. By using curriculum-based assessment, performance assessment, criterion-referenced assessment, observation, and rating scales, the teacher may determine that a student is not making progress at an acceptable rate. Informally, the teacher may ask another professional for advice. Classroom teachers, special education teachers, guidance counselors, principals, or school psychologists may be able to suggest intervention strategies that can be implemented in the classroom. In some cases, the teacher may be able to solve the problem without a referral for an evaluation to determine eligibility for special education.

Prereferral Teams. Recall from Chapter 3 that in some school systems professionals work together in structured problem-solving teams. These might be called Teacher Assistance Teams (Chalfant, Pysh, & Moultrie, 1979), Student Support Teams (Glickman, 1990; Ramey & Robbins, 1989), Mainstream Assistance Teams (Fuchs, Fuchs, & Bahr, 1990), or Prereferral Intervention Teams (Graden,

Casey, & Bonstrom, 1985; Safran & Safran, 1996). Professionals on these teams help one another formulate instructional or behavioral interventions that enable students to make progress in the regular classroom. Interventions are implemented before the classroom teacher makes a referral for formal evaluation to determine a child's eligibility for special education services.

Special educators and classroom teachers agree that the prereferral activities of these teams should focus on clarifying student problems, on designing general curriculum interventions, and on reviewing student records (Simpson, Ormsbee, & Myles, 1997). They disagree, however, on the composition of the teams. General educators view referring teachers, school administrators, and school psychologists as essential team members. On the other hand, special educators believe referring teachers, special education teachers, and school administrators are more essential members than are school psychologists.

According to Graden, Casey, and Bonstrom (1985), in schools that use prereferral intervention strategies, the number of students who are referred, tested, and subsequently placed in special education programs decreases, preventing needless assessment and placement in special education by solving students' learning or behavioral problems within their regular classrooms. Safran and Safran (1996) and Welch, Brownell, and Sheridan (1999), however, caution that the research results on school-based prereferral intervention or problem-solving teams are mixed. Referrals to special education do not always decrease when schools use prereferral intervention teams, and these teams do not always result in documented improvements in student learning and behavior.

Nevertheless, prereferral intervention strategies suggested by a Teacher Assistance Team or Mainstream Assistance Team may include a change in the curriculum for a particular student for whom the pace may be too rapid. An objective observer might also visit the classroom to determine whether such environmental factors as glare on the chalkboard or a distracting seating arrangement may be creating difficulty for the student who is not making progress. In addition, changes in the teacher's instructional strategies may make the difference for a student with learning problems. The team might suggest, for example, that a teacher try posting an outline of his or her lesson on the overhead projector or chalkboard. Or, the teacher assistance team members might help one another adjust instructional or classroom management strategies to suit the needs of learners from culturally, ethnically, or linguistically different backgrounds (Craig, Hull, Haggart, & Perez-Selles, 2000). Each activity conducted by the team gives team members additional information about the student and his or her responses to chosen interventions.

Referral, Screening, and Evaluation for Special Education Eligibility

The teacher who has documented the failure of a substantial number of intervention efforts made on behalf of a struggling student may soon conclude that additional help is needed. The teacher then makes a referral for assessment by the school or school system's child-study or multidisciplinary team. Although the exact procedures vary for each state and/or school district, this referral usually includes any supporting documentation gathered by the teacher through informal assessments such as student work samples, direct observation in the classroom, or skills checklists. Documentation should also include a description of the modifications attempted with the student, as well as data regarding the student's response to each intervention.

A referral by the classroom teacher usually begins the process to determine whether or not a child should be evaluated for possible placement in special education. Because special education resources are limited, the procedures used to determine eligibility for special education programs are rigorous. IDEA (1997) requires that, for initial evaluations, the parents must give their informed consent. In addition, the law now requires professionals first to examine existing data, including evaluations and information provided by parents and curriculum-based assessments and observational data provided by classroom teachers. The multidisciplinary team may include parents, a classroom teacher, a special educator, the school principal, guidance counselors, the school psychologist, a school social worker or "visiting teacher," a physical or occupational therapist, speech-language therapists, or any other qualified professionals. The task of this team is to determine (a) if any additional information is necessary to make a decision about the child's eligibility for special education, (b) if the child has a particular category of disability as defined under IDEA (1997), and (c) the child's present levels of educational performance and his or her educational needs. The use of existing data, including that provided by parents, should help in preventing unnecessary and costly evaluations of students and assist professionals in making informed decisions regarding an appropriate education for each child.

If upon examination of the student's records and all available data the team decides additional information is needed, parents must be informed of the types of evaluation procedures to be used and the purposes for each. Parental consent for evaluation is not the same as consent for placement in a special education program. When conducting an evaluation, IDEA (1997) mandates school districts to do the following:

♦ Ensure that the child is assessed in all areas of suspected disability.
♦ Use a variety of assessment tools and strategies in order to gather relevant functional and developmental information, including information provided by the parent, that may assist in determining whether the child has a disability and the content of the child's IEP, and also including information related to enabling the child to be involved in and progress in the general curriculum.
♦ Refrain from using any single procedure as the sole criterion for determining whether a child has a disability or for determining an appropriate educational program for the child.
♦ Use technically sound instruments that may assess the relative contribution of cognitive and behavioral factors, in addition to physical or developmental factors.
♦ Select and administer tests so as not to be discriminatory on a racial or cultural basis, including giving tests in the child's native language or other mode of communication unless it is clearly not feasible to do so.
♦ Ensure that any standardized tests given to the child have been validated for the specific purpose for which they are used, are administered only

by trained personnel, and are given in accordance with any instructions provided by the producer of such tests.

Although the evaluation must assist professionals in determining the educational needs of the child, the types of tests used by the multidisciplinary team may differ from those used by the classroom teacher. Many of the tests used by the team are called norm-referenced tests. Such tests have been administered to a large sample population to determine academic or intellectual performance of the typical student at a certain grade level or from a particular group. The score of the individual being tested is compared to the mean or average score of the sample group. Norm-referenced achievement testing enables the team to determine, for example, if a fourth-grade student who is having difficulty reading is significantly behind his or her peers. If norm-referenced tests indicate that the student is significantly behind peers, further diagnostic tests may be given to determine the specific reading skills that are presenting difficulty for the student. Examples of norm-referenced tests are given in Table 6.2 and web sites containing information about such tests are listed in Box 6.2.

Table 6.2 Examples of Norm-Referenced Tests

Tests of Intelligence and Cognitive Ability:
Kaufman Assessment Battery for Children: K-ABC. (Kaufman & Kaufman, 1983). An individually-administered test of intelligence and achievement for children aged two through twelve. Sixteen separate subtests to measure sequential processing, simultaneous processing, and achievement in reading and arithmetic. American Guidance Service.

Stanford-Binet Intelligence Scale, Fourth Edition. (Hagen, Satler, & Thorndike, 1986). An individually-administered test for people aged two through adult assessing cognitive functioning in four domains: Verbal Reasoning, Quantitative Reasoning, Abstract/Visual Reasoning, and Short-Term Memory. Riverside Publishing Company.

Wechsler Intelligence Scale for Children, Third Edition. (Wechsler, 1991). This test is a measure of general intellectual ability. The test provides IQ scores and indexes. Psychological Corporation.

Tests of Academic Achievement:
Kaufman Test of Educational Achievement, Comprehensive and Brief Forms/NU. (Kaufman & Kaufman, 1997). An individually-administered battery that measures academic achievement in grades one through twelve across reading, mathematics, and spelling. NU norms are a 1997 update of a national sampling of more than 3,000 individuals. ASSIST program available for computerized scoring. American Guidance Service.

Peabody Individual Achievement Test, Revised: PIAT-R/NU. (Markwardt, 1997). An individually-administered achievement test for ages 5 to 22 comprised of six subtests: General Information, Reading Recognition, Reading Comprehension, Written Expression, Mathematics, and Spelling. NU norms are based on a 1997 sampling of over 3,000 individuals. ASSIST program available for computerized scoring. American Guidance Service.

Wechsler Individual Achievement Test (WIAT). (Wechsler, 1991). An individually administered achievement test. Correlates well to the Wechsler Intelligence scale for children. Includes tests of reading recognition, reading comprehension, spelling, written language, math calculation, and math reasoning. Psychological Corporation.

Table 6.2 **Examples of Norm-Referenced Tests—*continued***

Wide Range Achievement Test, Third Edition. (Wilkinson, 1994). An individually-administered test for reading, spelling, and arithmetic for individuals aged 5 through 75. Pro-Ed.

Woodcock–Johnson Psychoeducational Battery. (Woodcock & Johnson, 1989). A battery of four achievement tests, including reading, mathematics, written language, and knowledge, and a test of eight cognitive abilities. For ages 2–90+, the test is available in Engish and Spanish versions. Computerized scoring is also available. Riverside Publishing.

Diagnostic Tests:
Key Math, Revised/NU: A Diagnostic Inventory of Essential Mathematics. (Connolly, 1997). A diagnostic math assessment for ages 5 to 22. NU normative information is based on a 1997 sampling of over 3,000 individuals. Measures skills in basic concepts, operations, and applications. ASSIST program available for computerized scoring. Appropriate for kindergarten through ninth grade. American Guidance Service.

Test of Adolescent and Adult Language, Third Edition. (Hammill, Brown, Larsen, & Wiederhold, 1994). Assesses spoken and written language skills for individuals aged 12 to 24. Available with a computerized scoring system. Pro-Ed.

Test of Language Development—Primary Level, Third Edition. (Newcomer & Hammill, 1997). Assesses understanding and use of spoken language in children aged four to eight. Consists of nine subtests and is available with a computerized scoring system. Pro-Ed.

Test of Language Development—Intermediate Level, Third Edition. (Hammill & Newcomer, 1997). Assesses understanding and use of spoken language and grammar for children aged eight to twelve. Consists of five subtests and is available with a computerized scoring system. Pro-Ed.

Test of Written Language, Third Edition. (Hammill & Larsen, 1996). Eight subtests measuring spelling, punctuation, capitalization, grammar, vocabulary, and story construction in both contrived and spontaneous formats. Appropriate for individuals aged seven to seventeen. Computerized scoring system available. Pro-Ed.

Woodcock Reading Mastery Tests, Revised/NU. (Woodcock, 1997). A battery of tests assessing reading skills from initial letter identification to reading comprehension for individuals from kindergarten to adulthood. Updated 1997 norms are based on a sampling of over 3,000 individuals. ASSIST program available for computerized scoring. American Guidance Service.

Behavior Rating Scales:
AAMR Adaptive Behavior Scales—School, Second Edition. (Lambert, Nihira, & Leland, 1993). Assesses social and daily living skills of children aged three to eighteen. Computerized scoring system available. American Association on Mental Retardation. Pro-Ed.

Behavior Rating Profile, Second Edition. (Brown & Hammill, 1991). Teacher, parent, and student rating scales for behavior of students aged six to eighteen at home, in school, and with peers. Pro-Ed.

Vineland Adaptive Behavior Scales. (Sparrow, Balla, & Cichetti, 1984). Assesses communication, daily living, motor, and socialization skills for individuals from birth through adulthood. ASSIST program available for computerized scoring. American Guidance Service.

Although norm-referenced tests may indicate whether a student's performance is different from his or her peers, these tests have limitations (Marston & Magnusson, 1988). Salvia and Hughes (1990) report that the small number of items included in norm-referenced tests of achievement often do not match what the student is taught in the specific curriculum. Moreover, a limited number of items will not allow for the detection of small improvements over time (Good & Salvia, 1988). In addition, Salvia and Ysseldyke (1998) state that students with mild disabilities often are not included in significant numbers in the population samples used in creating many norm-referenced tests. Some researchers also question whether or not subtests on specific revised measures of achievement and intelligence are correlated closely enough for professionals to be confident of their validity (See, for example, Daub & Colarusso, 1996, and Slate, Jones, Graham, & Bower, 1994). Others question the ability of such tests to determine consistently whether or not a child has the significant discrepancy between ability and achievement necessary to identify a learning disability (Slate, 1996). Norm-referenced tests of intelligence or ability are also criticized for cultural bias (Chinn & Hughes, 1987; Reschly, 1987) and for bias against the attentional problems and deficient strategic behaviors often exhibited by students with mild disabilities (Telzrow, 1988). Despite their limitations, norm-referenced tests are frequently used to determine if a student differs greatly from his or her peers.

In addition to tests of achievement, the student who has been referred for academic difficulties may be administered a test of intellectual or cognitive ability by the school psychologist. Behavior rating scales, social skills checklists or rating scales, and direct observation of behavior in various settings may be completed for students presenting behavioral or social-emotional difficulties, and a medical evaluation may help to determine if a student has health problems that interfere with learning or behavior. The purpose for gathering such extensive information is, of course, to make the best possible decision regarding whether or not a child requires special education services as well as to determine the educational needs of the child.

For those students already in a special education program, IDEA (1997) provides a "stream-lined" process. At least every three years, students must be reevaluated to determine whether or not they are still eligible for special education and related services. The IEP team is responsible for deciding if additional information is necessary for making this decision. Team members, including the parents, might review existing data and decide that they have sufficient information to determine that the child continues to be a child with a disability. On the other hand, the parents or other team members might decide that additional information is necessary in order to make an informed decision. IDEA now requires that parents must give informed consent before a reevaluation, as well as an initial evaluation, for special education eligibility. Therefore, additional assessment may take place for the triennial review, but only with the parents' permission.

Eligibility

Typically, when members of the multidisciplinary team have completed their assessment, a meeting is scheduled for the parents and other team members. At this meeting, team members discuss test results and other information gathered from the comprehensive evaluation (see Appendix A for sample multidisciplinary evaluations for Travis and Joey). It is at this point that the team, including the parents, must decide if the student is eligible for special education services according to the specific criteria for eligibility in use by the particular state and school system. If it is determined that the student is not eligible for special education services, the team will, it is hoped, make additional recommendations for the teacher in order to alleviate the child's learning or behavioral difficulty. Frequently, it is at this point that teams will use the data collected to determine whether or not the child might qualify for accommodations under Section 504. If so, an accommodation or Section 504 plan is created for the child.

If the student is determined eligible for special education, a copy of the evaluation report and the documentation determining the child's eligibility must be given to the parents. At this point, the IEP team that includes the parents, the child's classroom and special education teacher, other members of the multidisciplinary team, and the student, whenever appropriate, will meet to negotiate an IEP detailing the individualized education program to be provided for the child. The child is not placed in special education until the IEP is developed because it is the IEP that details the special education and related services to be provided. (See Chapters 2 and 7 for additional discussion of the IEP. See also Appendix A for sample IEPs.)

According to IDEA (1997), parents have a legal right to be informed, in a language and manner they can understand, of the types of tests to be given to their child and the purpose for each test. Parents must give their consent before the tests may be administered, and they have the right to be informed fully of the results of each of the tests. Parents must understand that their input is necessary and valued. Research indicates that parents tend to be passive during the eligibility and IEP process (Barnett, Zins, & Wise, 1984; Vaughn, Bos, Harrell, & Lasky, 1988). Moreover, some parents who have low incomes or who are from culturally, racially, or ethnically diverse groups may not be fully informed or may not understand the process of eligibility concerning their children (Brantlinger, 1987; Harry, Allen, & McLaughlin, 1995; Linan-Thompson & Jean, 1997). The teacher is encouraged to review the ideas suggested in Chapter 4 for increasing communication with parents.

At any point during the evaluation or reevaluation for eligibility or during the IEP process, parents and school districts have the right to disagree. IDEA (1997) mandates the "right to due process" or certain procedural safeguards that must be provided. When disagreements occur, states have an obligation to offer voluntary mediation to help the parties resolve their disputes, although parents do not have to participate in such mediation. They may choose to present their complaint before a local- or state-level impartial hearing officer; however, mediation may help parents and school professionals resolve disputes without the adversarial relationships fostered by hearings, appeals, and court proceedings (Hodge & Shriner, 1997).

Assessment of Culturally, Ethnically, and Linguistically Diverse Learners

One issue of critical concern to parents and teachers is the misidentification of students from culturally, racially, ethnically, or linguistically diverse populations. When students are misidentified and placed in special education, or conversely, when students who should be in special education are not so identified, serious consequences can result. Children inappropriately identified may be stigmatized when given a label such as "mentally retarded" or "emotionally disturbed," and students removed from the classroom may not have access to a quality education in the regular curriculum (U.S. Department of Education, 1997).

Recall from Chapter 1 that although African-Americans comprise about 16% of the total student population, they are overrepresented in special education programs. African-American children make up about 32% of the students with mild mental retardation, 24% of the students with serious emotional disturbance, and 18% of students with learning disabilities (U.S. Department of Education, 1997). They are 2.5 times more likely to be identified as students with mild mental retardation and 1.5 times more likely to be identified as having a serious emotional disturbance than are their non-African-American counterparts (Oswald, Coutinho, Best, & Singh, 1999). Moreover, African-American students living below the poverty level are more likely to be identified as having mild mental retardation, while those from wealthier homes are more likely to be identified as seriously emotionally disturbed.

Students from homes where English is not the primary language are also at risk of identification for special education placement. Teachers may not be prepared to teach students with limited English proficiency, or they may not understand cultural differences affecting learning. Thus, teachers may over-refer language-minority students for special education placement (Bos & Reyes, 1996). On the other hand, in some large, urban school districts that have a large population of students from linguistically diverse backgrounds, teachers may not refer children who really do need assistance. They may fail to do so because they are unsure how to identify these students properly and because they fear litigation arising from misclassification (Gersten & Woodward, 1994).

Several reasons have been suggested for the misrepresentation in special education programs of students from diverse backgrounds. For example, the majority of teachers are white females who may not understand the needs of students from backgrounds different from their own. In addition, many standardized assessment instruments used to identify children for special education programs lack validity with children from linguistically and culturally diverse populations. Using translators to interpret tests may further skew the test results, and although a few tests have been translated to Spanish, some words and phrases may not translate exactly (Council for Exceptional Children [CEC], 1997). Moreover, any given language may have several different dialects, complicating the accuracy of test translations. Finally, students from culturally different backgrounds may lack experiences with concepts included on some assessment instruments; therefore, they will be more likely to miss these items even if their primary language is English.

IDEA (1997) mandates that students cannot be placed in special education if the determinant factor is limited English proficiency. IDEA also requires that students must be tested for special education in a manner that does not discriminate on the basis of language or cultural or racial background and that all standardized tests have been validated for the specific purposes for which they are to be used. In order to make the most accurate decision possible, the CEC (1997) and Leung (1996) recommend teachers use the following assessment procedures for students from linguistically diverse backgrounds:

♦ Refrain from referring a child for special education evaluation until the child has had approximately two years to learn English and to adjust to a new culture, unless, of course, the child is of school age and has no obvious language skills.

♦ Obtain the services of an expert in the second language to help adapt the curriculum and instruction to accommodate the language difference.

♦ Observe for other signs of a disability not dependent on language, such as difficulty with gross or fine motor skills or self-help skills.

♦ Select evaluation techniques that are as unbiased as possible and use a certified bilingual professional, rather than an interpreter, to administer the tests.

♦ Document that a specific test was given in a nonstandard manner and, therefore, the results are "invalid."

♦ Realize that although a student may score "below grade level" on a standardized test, the test results may still indicate that the student has learned a great deal of information in a limited amount of time, reflecting positively on the student's ability.

♦ Use only trained interpreters or bilingual professionals to interview parents who do not speak English, and spend time developing rapport and seeking clarification when interacting with the parents.

♦ Use multiple sources of information including observations of behavior, portfolio assessments, and interviews.

Summary

Teachers use many forms of informal assessment on a daily basis. Curriculum-based measurement, criterion-referenced tests, observations, checklists, and rating scales all may be used to help teachers evaluate student progress. By carefully analyzing the data obtained by these means as well as from performance assessments and portfolios, teachers can make better instructional decisions.

Teachers occasionally have students who do not make progress at the expected level or rate. These students may require changes in the curriculum or in the classroom environment. The teacher may consult a Teacher Assistance Team or Mainstream Assistance Team for intervention strategies to help such children succeed in the regular classroom. Careful implementation and documentation of these intervention strategies, however, may not be enough support for some students. For these youngsters, the teacher may make a formal referral to a multidisciplinary team to screen and, perhaps, evaluate the child to determine his or her eligibility for special education services. Norm-referenced tests are formal, standardized measures used by the multidisciplinary team to determine whether a child's abilities are sufficiently discrepant from those of his or her peers to warrant special education services.

IDEA (1997) requires that parents be involved as members of the multidisciplinary team deciding a student's eligibility for special education. In addition, the law mandates that all existing data must be used for decision making and that assessment must focus on determining the child's educational needs. A student cannot be placed in special education if his or her difficulty is the result of a lack of instruction in reading or mathematics or if he or she is of limited English proficiency. In addition, students with mild disabilities are to be included in state- or district-wide assessments, with appropriate accommodations determined by the IEP team, and their teachers must make every effort to use equitable grading practices.

Application Exercises

1. Review a teacher's guide to a reading or mathematics series at a chosen grade level. Does the guide include a scope and sequence chart? Does the guide contain information that could be used to design a criterion-referenced test? Locate and describe the types of tests included with the curricular materials.

2. Examine a teacher's guide for a reading, language arts, mathematics, science, or social studies series. Choose a skill for a given grade level. Then, perform a task analysis for your chosen skill.

3. Examine the psychoeducational evaluation for Travis shown in Appendix A. What additional information will the teacher need for instructional planning? If you found out that Travis would be entering your classroom next week, what informal assessments might you give him?

4. Visit a school or school system and ask to see information about parents' rights in special education. Was the information readily available? Describe the information. Was it easy to read and understand? Why or why not?

5. Kevin makes the following mistakes on his arithmetic paper:

$$
\begin{array}{cccc}
22 & 73 & 24 & 45 \\
\times 7 & \times 4 & \times 4 & \times 2 \\
\hline
214 & 712 & 216 & 410
\end{array}
$$

Explain Kevin's error. List the preskills and perform a task analysis for this multiplication skill. Where will you begin instruction with Kevin in order to correct his error?

6. Interview a special education teacher and a classroom teacher at a chosen grade level. What forms of assessment do these teachers routinely use? How do these teachers use the information they gather through assessment? Include both informal and formal assessments in your discussion.

7. Ask a special education teacher from a local school district to describe to you the types of accommodations offered for students with disabilities taking the state- or district-wide tests given at a particular grade level.

8. Find out from a local school whether or not prereferral intervention teams are used. Describe the membership on these teams. How do these teams function? What opinions do classroom and special education teachers hold regarding these teams and their effectiveness?

9. Ask a special education and a classroom teacher to describe their policies and procedures for grading students with mild disabilities included in the regular classroom. Describe the similarities and differences in their practices. What are the written policies for grading for the school or school district? Do you believe these practices to be fair? Why or why not?

10. Search InfoTrac for current articles on evaluating students from culturally, racially, and linguistically diverse backgrounds. Make a list of at least five relevant issues for discussion in your class.

11. Browse the web sites listed in Box 6.2. Request a catalogue from the publishers and organize these into a file for future use.

PLANNING FOR SUCCESSFUL INSTRUCTION

Focus

As you read, think about the following questions:

◆ *How do teachers plan for both group and individual activities?*

◆ *What are the elements of well-written educational objectives?*

◆ *How do student stages of learning influence the teacher's planning?*

◆ *How is the IEP related to planning and instruction in the classroom?*

◆ *How can teachers plan for effective collaborative teaching in inclusive classroom settings?*

A smoothly running classroom, where students are actively engaged in appropriate academic tasks to achieve preset objectives, is the goal of the effective teacher. But students do not successfully reach their academic potential by accident! A carefully planned, finely tuned, active classroom in which students achieve success is the result of considerable time, effort, and organization on the part of the teacher. Let's observe Joey as he works in Ms. Kirk's fourth-grade classroom and then goes to Ms. Lopez's resource room for his reading instruction:

Joey moves to the computer with a CD-ROM of the encyclopedia he has selected from the materials in Ms. Kirk's room. He inserts the CD-ROM into the computer and can't quite remember what he was to do. He knows that Ms. Kirk color codes her subjects: the green folder is for social studies, blue is for health, and red is for science. He takes the red folder out and turns to the weekly assignment page. Today is Wednesday and on his assignment page are these words:

WEDNESDAY: Group I. Look up the geologic time scale. Write down the life forms of the Paleozoic era. Have a list of the life forms ready to report to your other group members tomorrow.

Joey looks up the geologic time scale on the computer and begins to write down the names of life forms. He completes his assignment and places the paper inside the pocket of his red folder. Tomorrow he will meet with his group and they will exchange information about the eras of the geologic time scale. Joey knows that the groups will begin giving their reports to the class on Monday. He plans to help his group decide how to present the material when they meet on Friday. He wants to suggest drawing some pictures of the different life forms. Because he is interested in geology, Joey has some books and pictures at home. He will offer to bring some pictures on Monday, if his group thinks it is a good idea. Joey also thinks some of the pictures on the CD-ROM could be used, too.

Ms. Kirk walks by Joey and smiles as she looks over his work. She moves around the room to survey students in the other groups. Other students are writing down information for their science reports. Group II students are using a special-materials science kit on the back table. Joey's group used the kit on Tuesday. Group III students are constructing their portion of the geologic time line. Group I completed that task on Monday. By Friday, all three groups will be ready to plan their presentations for this science unit.

Ms. Kirk informs the students of the time and Joey puts his folders away. He returns the CD-ROM to the materials shelf. He picks up a small piece of paper on the floor by his desk and exits the room, saying, "Bye, Ms. Kirk."

"Bye, Joey!" responds Ms. Kirk. "Thanks for cleaning up. See you later."

Joey walks down the hall to Ms. Lopez's room. He enters, saying, "Hi, Ms. Lopez."

Ms. Lopez smiles and replies, "Hi, Joey. I like that shirt. Is it new?"

"Yeah, I got it for my birthday." He grins. "Are we starting the new story today?"

"Yes, we are!" says Ms. Lopez. "Look on your assignment sheet for the page number."

Joey takes his folder from the mailbox by the door. Inside, he sees the assignment for the day: "Winter Surprise," page 67. Joey takes the card out of the pocket in his folder. Ms. Lopez has written the new vocabulary words for the story on one side of the card as well as a short outline of the story. Joey looks at the words, listens to a recording of Ms. Lopez pronouncing them on a cassette tape she has placed in his folder, and tries to pronounce them silently himself. He skims the outline and then turns the card over to read his study strategy:

1. Read your new words. (Remember to review the words on the cassette tape if you have trouble.)
2. Read the story silently.
3. Reread the first sentence of each paragraph.
4. Write down the main events of the story.
5. Read the story aloud with your partner.
6. Answer the story questions. Check your answers.
7. Group discussion.

Joey places his folder on his desk and walks to the bookcase. He finds his reading book and returns to his seat. He quietly pronounces each of his new words. Then he turns to his story and reads silently.

Ms. Lopez scans the room and notices that Joey is reading. She sits down at the group table with five students. Travis and two other students are also reading "Winter Surprise" silently. Ms. Lopez directs the spelling instruction for the five students who are on the same spelling unit. As the spelling instruction continues, she notices as Joey quietly walks to the box of answer keys to check his comprehension questions. He proudly marches to the wall chart and colors in a box by his name with a blue marker. Blue means that he has answered the questions with 100% accuracy. Joey then moves to the reading partner table with Travis. They take turns reading the new story aloud.

Ms. Kirk organizes learning in her classroom by using thematic units, small groups, large groups, individual work, weekly assignment sheets, and color-coded folders. Ms. Lopez employs small groups, partners, individual work, study strategies, academic self-monitoring, and daily assignment sheets based on her students' Individualized Educational Programs (IEPs). Both teachers know the exact performance level of each student in their classes and assign work that will help the students achieve preset objectives.

Both teachers also use a variety of instructional methods and curricular materials to meet the needs of individual students. Each student in Ms. Lopez's class uses an individual assignment sheet that consists of assignments designed to meet objectives written on his or her IEP. Whenever possible, Ms. Lopez groups students with similar needs for direct instruction. Ms. Kirk's students are working to meet the mastery levels set forth in the state curriculum guidelines for science in the fourth grade. Her students must pass a state-level test demonstrating mastery of key science concepts at the end of the year.

In this chapter, we will examine how teachers go about the tasks of planning and of writing educational objectives. We will also examine how student stages of learning influence the teacher's planning, and we will discuss the information to be included on the student's IEP, an essential component of the planning process for youngsters in special education programs. Finally, we will explore how classroom and special education teachers can collaborate to plan instruction for inclusive classrooms.

How Teachers Plan

Planning instruction for a classroom of students can be a complex and time-consuming task. It can also be an interesting and exciting challenge that will result in successful teaching and maximum learning. Good planning enables the teacher to use curricular materials and teaching methods effectively to help students reach educational goals.

Several factors influence teachers as they plan. According to Brown (1988), for example, plans made by middle school teachers are influenced by textbook content, weaknesses of the curricular materials used in the school district, students' interests and abilities, availability of materials, knowledge of what worked in previous years, and time allocated to the class or subject. The middle school teachers in Brown's study felt that they were often restrained by school policies, such as curriculum guides and school schedules. Vaughn and Schumm (1994) found that middle school teachers most often consider content coverage, classroom management, and student interest and motivation when planning. Vaughn and Schumm contend that the pressure to "cover the content" may increase as states implement high-stakes, accountability testing programs, forcing students with mild disabilities to "get it [knowledge or skills] the first time."

Schumm and Vaughn (1992) also report that teachers of mainstreamed students with mild disabilities view budget constraints, accountability, lack of equipment and materials, substandard physical environment of the classroom or school, large class size, and limited instructional time as barriers to planning. The teachers in this study were not likely to develop individualized lesson plans for students or to use the IEP as a resource for planning. Although these teachers expressed willingness to adapt lessons, assignments, or tests in response to student progress (a process called interactive planning), they were less likely to preplan these adaptations or to set new objectives for learning based on student performance (a process called postplanning). Nevertheless, preplanning, postplanning, and interactive planning are essential responsibilities of teachers at all grade levels.

In a related research study, Jeanne Schumm, Sharon Vaughn, and their colleagues found that elementary school teachers planned more for the individual needs of all their students than did secondary-level teachers (Schumm, Vaughn, Haager, et al., 1995). When preplanning, elementary teachers considered the needs of particular students within the plans they created for the class as a whole. Both elementary and middle school teachers believed it to be their responsibility to provide a strong support system for students with mild disabilities included in the classroom. On the other hand, teachers in secondary schools saw their classrooms as preparation for success in the "real world." These teachers tended to focus on the group and the student's responsibility for seeking any help he or she might need.

Fuchs, Fuchs, and Bishop (1992) maintain that general and special educators may view the planning process somewhat differently. They suggest that general educators are more likely than special educators to focus on instructional activities as they plan. At the elementary level, for example, teachers often integrate learning around a central theme in a unit plan. Special educators, on the other hand, focus more on specific procedures, such as direct instruction or metacognitive strategies, and their planning is often guided by a student's IEP. In addition, both general and special educators who use curriculum-based assessment may be more likely to use data to monitor student performance and adjust instruction than to yield to curricular pressures.

Teachers may also differ regarding their perceptions of the nature of curriculum in special education. Many teachers believe the IEP constitutes the curriculum for students with disabilities (Sands, Adams, & Stout, 1995). Most special education teachers, for example, focus on a student's IEP goals and objectives in lesson planning (Searcy & Maroney, 1996). For some teachers, though, the purpose of the IEP is to document instructional and curricular adaptations or modifications to meet students' needs within the standard curriculum. This viewpoint will become increasingly important as students with mild disabilities are expected to participate in state- and district-wide assessments and inclusive classrooms.

Backward Planning and Thematic Units

Apparently, then, different teachers approach planning in different ways. Long-range goals are a common starting place, however, for all teachers to begin planning for instruction (Brown, 1988; Slavin, 1991). The process of beginning with long-range plans and moving to monthly, weekly, and daily plans is called the backward planning process (Slavin, 1991). This process enables the teacher to keep the final outcome or long-term goal in mind as the students progress through the daily curriculum. The teacher begins by examining curriculum scope and sequence charts, state curriculum guidelines and standards, current levels of performance, and annual IEP goals for students who receive special education services. Having determined the goals for instruction, the teacher can then break down the curriculum into smaller units for learning. Once this general blueprint has been designed, the teacher may begin planning for daily instruction.

Ms. Kirk, for example, reviews the curriculum at the beginning of the school year and determines that there are twelve topical units to cover in the science curriculum. She decides to cover each topic in a three-to-four-week period. With this in mind, she carefully builds thematic units around each of the major science topics. This format allows her to integrate learning across reading, writing, mathematics, science, and social studies on a daily basis. She examines each curricular area to determine how particular skills within each area can be used to support learning in the others.

For example, in a unit on the solar system, Ms. Kirk uses the textbook, gives homework, assigns various group projects and experiments, requires introductory-level library research reports, uses the computer and other instructional technology, and has weekly and unit tests. She uses the library visits and the computer to teach research skills within the context of her science unit. Her students go on-line, connecting with NASA, for example, for up-to-the-minute data on space travel. She also incorporates the science unit topics into independent and class reading activities, choosing stories and books for reading that are related to the solar system. Vocabulary and spelling words are drawn from these stories, and students use these words to write stories of their own about space travel. During math, Ms. Kirk's students use their mathematics skills to construct a scale model of the solar system and to calculate the quantity and weight of items needed for a space station. Her students also explore the history and politics of space exploration during social studies as they learn about the persecution of various early astronomers and the "rush to space" following Sputnik.

Throughout her units, Ms. Kirk varies the projects and group arrangements. She encourages peers to pair up and help one another in research and study activities. Whenever possible, Ms. Kirk arranges to take the class on field trips related to the current science unit. Her class has visited the local science museum to see a presentation in its planetarium, and they have been to a geological dig being conducted by a nearby university. This year she is also arranging for the mother of one of her students, a space scientist at the university, to speak to the class.

Ms. Kirk follows essentially the same format for each topic in the science curriculum, but she creatively varies teaching methods and group projects as she integrates instruction in her thematic units. She manages to keep her instruction on target because she has carefully planned the year by units, weeks, and days. She has organized her classroom so students know what to expect and can independently move from one assignment to the next. This allows her the freedom to work with the whole class, with small groups, or with individual students as needed.

On the other hand, Ms. Lopez takes the approach of basing her planning on the IEPs developed for each of her students. On each IEP, the student's current level of performance is specified for every area in which the student is having difficulty. Based on the child's current level of performance, Ms. Lopez and the other members of the student's IEP team plan annual goals. These annual goals are simply the "best estimate" of what a student with mild disabilities might accomplish by the end of the school year, given the special education services provided. For example, if assessment data indicates that Travis does not know the multiplication facts, then a reasonable goal for Travis for the current school year might be written like this: "Travis will write the product for multiplication facts through the nines by the end of May." Notice that this annual goal states an observable student behavior (i.e., write the product) as an outcome of instruction. To enable Travis to accomplish this goal, Ms. Lopez breaks down the long-term goal into specific short-term objectives that she uses to plan and monitor her daily instruction.

Writing Educational Objectives

Successful teachers prepare and plan for each day. Daily instruction is most effective when educational objectives are written for each class lesson or for an individual student when he or she is receiving special education services. Objectives help the teacher to articulate the purpose for instruction, the ways in which instruction will take place, and the criteria by which to judge when students have successfully mastered the material.

One of the most frequently used models for writing educational objectives, shown in Table 7.1, is Bloom's taxonomy (Bloom, Englehart, Furst, Hill, & Krathwohl, 1956). This system attempts to categorize objectives across cognitive, affective, and psychomotor domains of learning. According to Slavin (1991),

---

Table 7.1 Bloom's Taxonomy: Sample Behaviors for Each Level Across Three Domains

Level	Domain		
	Cognitive	Affective	Psychomotor
	The student will:		
1. Knowledge— Recalling facts.	Identify the state capitals of the states in the region.	Choose the most appealing architecture for a capitol building.	Construct a model of a capitol building.
2. Comprehension— Emphasizing meaning.	Answer chapter questions about the history of each capital city.	Describe an interesting tourist area he/she would like to visit.	Draw a city map of a specific capital city.
3. Application— Using rules and generalizing.	Write a set of rules for the class similar to those of the city.	Describe the advantages of the city rule he or she feels is the most important.	Construct a mock town meeting to debate and vote on the city rules.
4. Analysis— Breaking information into parts.	Identify the parts of city government.	Describe the qualities necessary for an effective city leader.	Draw a chart to illustrate positions in the city government.
5. Synthesis—Putting elements together into a whole.	Compile a list of state and city rules affecting the city school.	Create a brochure to inform new residents of favorite local attractions.	Make a model of the city to depict land forms and tourist areas.
6. Evaluation— Judging against a criterion.	Compare and contrast the rules in the city with those of another city in the state of about the same size.	Select the most important rule for a city in the state.	Write an editorial for a local newspaper to justify the importance of the rule chosen.

Bloom's taxonomy is not meant to imply a sequence from simple to more complex behavior, but rather is meant to remind teachers to use a variety of objectives from each of the three domains and on differing levels. The behavioral matrix show in Table 7.2 provides examples of objectives at different levels for the cognitive domain.

Teachers of students in special education programs often write behavioral objectives. That is, the short-term objective on the student's IEP is written to specify a measurable and observable student behavior (e.g., write, point to, state) that will move the student toward an annual goal. The objective also clearly delineates the conditions under which the student is expected to perform (e.g., the rate of presentation, the quantity or level of the material) and the criterion by which mastery of the objective will be determined (e.g., a percentage correct, a time duration). For example, to help Travis accomplish his annual goal of being able to write the products for the multiplication facts through the nines, Ms. Lopez might write the following short-term objective: "Given the multiplication facts from the ones through the fives presented in random order on a daily probe sheet, Travis will write the products with 100% accuracy within 3 minutes." The phrase "Given . . . on a daily probe sheet," specifies the conditions under which Travis will perform. The measurable student behavior is "write," and the criteria for mastery are "with 100% accuracy" and "within 3 minutes." Ms. Lopez uses this short-term objective to guide her lesson planning in mathematics for Travis.

The Individuals with Disabilities Education Act (IDEA) (1997) requires that the IEP must include a statement of how the child's progress toward annual goals will be measured. In addition, the student's parents must be regularly informed—at least as often as parents of students without disabilities—of their child's progress toward the goals and the extent to which the progress is sufficient to allow the child to meet the goal by the end of the year. By specifying in the short-term objective a condition of daily probes, Ms. Lopez has set a schedule for measuring progress. With Ms. Lopez's assistance, Travis can graph his rate of progress toward the objective and share this information with his parents at the end of each week. When Travis completes this objective, Ms. Lopez can move to the next objective in the sequence: "Given the multiplication facts from the sixes through the nines presented in random order on a daily probe sheet, Travis will write the products with 100% accuracy within 3 minutes."

Wolery, Bailey, and Sugai (1988, pp. 49-55) offer several excellent suggestions for the teacher when writing behavioral objectives for students:

1. Keep the objective as brief as possible, omitting unnecessary words such as "will be able to" (e.g., "Travis will write . . ." rather than "Travis will be able to write . . .").
2. Be sure to include the exact conditions under which the student will perform the targeted behavior, and the criteria for determining student mastery.
3. Phrase the objective in positive terms. State what the student will do rather than what he or she will not do.
4. State the desired learning outcomes in observable and measurable terms. Refrain from using terms such as *understands, knows,* or *comprehends;* use instead such terms as *reads orally, prints,* or *sorts.*

Table 7.2 Sample Behaviors for the Cognitive Domain

Level of Objective	Example I	Example II
	Main Idea of a Story	*Colonization of Africa*
1. Knowledge	Define "main idea."	Make a timeline to illustrate how Africa was split into colonies.
2. Comprehension	Identify the main idea of the story.	Interpret a map of Africa showing its colonization by European nations.
3. Application	Identify the main idea of a newspaper article.	Locate articles in the newspaper that illustrate the influence of colonization on Africa today.
4. Analysis	Give ways to find the main idea in stories.	Contrast the goals and methods used by different European nations in colonizing Africa.
5. Synthesis	Write a new story based on the main idea of a story you've read.	Write an essay on the European colonization of Africa from the perspective of a Bantu chief.
6. Evaluation	Judge the author's effectiveness on presenting the main idea of the story.	Debate the positive versus negative impact of colonization on African countries today.

Adapted From: Slavin, R.E. (1991). *Educational psychology* (3rd ed.). Upper Saddle River, NJ: Prentice Hall, p. 215. Reprinted with permission.

5. Choose objectives for students that are functional; that is, they should have immediate usefulness or lead students to more advanced skills. They should also be realistic—neither too hard nor too easy for the student.
6. Write the objectives to reflect not only the acquisition of knowledge or skills, but also to demonstrate the ability to apply the skill to solve new problems or to use it in the natural environment.

Teachers must think carefully about the student behaviors, conditions, and criteria for success specified in short-term objectives. Each of these must lead the student toward attainment of the annual goals, and, therefore, must be based on the student's current level of performance. Each portion of the short-term objective must also make sense. For example, teachers should use only one student behavior in each short-term objective. If Ms. Lopez wrote an objective stating, "Travis will identify and write the products for the multiplication facts through the nines," she will have difficulty evaluating Travis's performance. Travis may be able to identify the correct product for a particular multiplication fact when he is given two or three choices; however, he may not be able to write the product on his own.

Similarly, teachers sometimes fall into a pattern of phrasing the criterion for success as a percentage of accuracy. Although a percentage of accuracy often does make sense, it is not appropriate for all skills. For example, how would the teacher measure that the letter "H" is formed with at least 90% accuracy? What portion of the letter "H" constitutes 90%? A better criterion for this skill might be "using the correct strokes and staying within the lines." Moreover, would the teacher wish a student to cross the street with 90% accuracy? One would certainly worry about that one error within ten!

Effective teachers carefully consider the objectives written for each daily lesson plan and vary the conditions, student behaviors, and domains and levels of learning to promote student achievement. As lessons are planned, the teacher also considers the current mastery level of the students. In some school systems, students will not advance to more difficult skills or to new topics unless the teacher has determined that sufficient mastery has occurred. For example, if most of the students in Ms. Kirk's class fail a unit test in math or achieve a mastery level below that specified in the preset objective, it is important that Ms. Kirk revise her plans to reteach the troublesome skill before progressing to the next instructional unit. For children in special education programs, mastery of objectives is essential before students progress to new skills or concepts. Special education teachers must document the progress of their students toward the goals and objectives specified on the IEP. Therefore, Ms. Lopez's planning is based on student performance data she gathers through ongoing assessment procedures such as those described in Chapter 6.

Objectives are only one part of a daily lesson plan, but they are probably the most important element of the teacher's planning process. Daily lessons and activities should flow from the chosen educational objectives, and the objectives should be chosen based on student need and performance, in addition to curricular requirements for the specific grade level. A comprehensive lesson plan includes an objective, a lesson opening, a demonstration or presentation of new material, guided practice with the new skill or concept, independent practice, a lesson closing, and an evaluation to determine whether or not students have met the given objective. Each of these components of a lesson will be discussed in detail in Chapter 8. For now, however, the reader is reminded that without a carefully written educational objective, even the time spent pursuing the most exciting classroom activities may be time wasted.

Instructional Options and Grouping

Teachers may choose from a variety of instructional options when designing lesson plans for their students. The teacher may choose, for example, to modify the curriculum (see Chapters 14 and 15), to use specific teaching methods, to structure the classroom in a special way, or to give students organizational guides. As shown in Table 7.3, teaching methods that are effective for students in special

---

Table 7.3   Some Common Instructional Methods and Implications for Learners with Mild Disabilities

Level of Objective	Example I	Example II
Direct Instruction	Teacher actively involved with students. Demonstrates information and uses guided practice to check understanding.	Demands student attention. Uses learning time efficiently. May be used for rehearsal of facts and may promote automatic behavior. Provides opportunities to respond and receive feedback on accuracy.
Modeling	Teacher or peer demonstrates correct method or strategy to be used.	Improves learning when strategies or behaviors are clearly labeled and rehearsed or when peers receive awards for their use.
Computer Technology	Students use software in pairs or individually for simulations, drill and practice, communication, and information.	Improves learning and retention skills. Improves motivation to learn and increases opportunities for links to the real world.
Cooperative Learning Groups and Peer Tutoring	Students share responsibility for helping each other learn in small, structured groups or in pairs monitored by the teacher.	Increases academic learning time and student responsibility for learning. Provides opportunities for feedback and development of social skills. Roles and responsibilities must be clearly explained and student accountability must be planned.

education programs include direct instruction with extensive guided practice (Lloyd, 1988; Rosenshine, 1986), modeling (Englert, 1984), computer technology (Blackhurst, 1997), and cooperative learning groups or peer tutoring (Slavin, 1990). (see also Forness, Kavale, Blum, & Lloyd, 1997). Teachers must also choose instructional options sensitive to the cultural diversity within the classroom. Sensitivity to the selection of reading materials (Taylor, 2000) or games (de la Cruz, Cage, & Lian, 2000) accurately reflecting a diverse population can enhance student motivation and success. Classroom structure refers to how students are arranged for their instruction. Students may, for example, receive instruction in large or small groups, through one-on-one instruction with the teacher or a paraprofessional, through peer tutoring, or in cooperative learning arrangements. Organizational guides help students understand the daily schedule, lessons, or activities. These may include advanced topical outlining of lessons written on the chalkboard, projected on a screen, or photocopied on sheets of paper for individual use.

In considering instructional options, teachers decide which will best help students achieve preset objectives. Ms. Kirk, for example, may choose to use small-group instruction for the reading groups in her classroom and large-group instruction for the presentation of new information in her health lessons. Class-wide peer tutoring (Maheady, Sacca, & Harper, 1988) may be an appropriate instructional choice for Ms. Kirk's fourth graders who are practicing newly learned social studies content. On the other hand, direct instruction may be Ms. Kirk's preferred method for introducing new social studies skills and concepts to her students. Instructional decisions are always made with student objectives and needs in mind.

A teacher may select a particular option for a specific reason, such as to use time most efficiently or to allow for incidental learning to occur. (Incidental learning is non-targeted learning as a result of interaction during a lesson.) For example, large-group instruction may be an efficient use of teacher time, but small-group instruction increases the acquisition of information through observational and incidental learning for students with mild learning problems (Keel & Gast, 1992; Stinson, Gast, Wolery, & Collins, 1991). To help a student catch up with peers, however, intensive one-on-one instruction is more effective than group instruction (Baker, Young, & Martin, 1990). A teacher might use large-group instruction with students who are able to acquire information at approximately the same level or rate, one-on-one instruction with a student who is far behind the others, and small-group instruction with students who are likely to acquire additional information through observational or incidental learning. A one-week rough outline of the science activities to be completed by groups in Ms. Kirk's class is presented in Figure 7.1.

Planning for effective instruction becomes easier as teachers gain experience. In fact, Searcy and Maroney (1996) report that special education teachers most often use a commercially prepared lesson-plan book in which they write out their plans for independent practice, materials, and evaluation of student objectives. These teachers use "conscious mental planning" for most elements of their lessons, preferring to use a short, plan-book format for jotting down only what they perceive to be the essential components such as prerequisite skills, page numbers, or student objectives. Slavin and Madden (1989) offer the

Group I	Group II	Group III	Individual
11-6-00 Review terms (teacher directed)	Group project; (individual assignments)	Research with science kit at back table	Provide advanced organizers to Celie, Kevin, Joey, and Travis
11-7-00 Group project (individual assignments)	Research with science kit at back table	Review terms (teacher- directed)	Check contract for Joey
11-8-00 Research with science kit at back table	Review terms (teacher- directed)	Group project (individual assignments)	Check contract for Joey

11-9-00
Whole-Group Instruction: Explain presentations for next week; check homework and collect homework notebooks

11-10-00
Work on presentations by groups for Monday

FIGURE 7.1

Ms. Kirk's One-Week Outline for Science Activities

following general planning tips, which beginning teachers may find particularly useful:

- Use the backward planning process. Look at the whole unit you will cover and break it down into manageable parts. Look at the student's current level of performance, annual goals, and short-term objectives. Break these down into small learning steps.
- Always monitor the progress of each student. Know whether students have mastered objectives and plan instruction accordingly.
- Plan more than you can cover in a period. It is much easier to move the activities or concepts to the next day than to be caught with 30 minutes of unprepared time!
- Have extra content-related activities ready. Always provide enrichment activities or additional games for drill and practice for students who finish work early. Never use this additional work as punishment for inappropriate behavior, however.
- Have a substitute folder ready with several days' worth of lessons. The substitute folder might include the names of students listed on a seating chart, specific comments about individual student needs, information about classroom rules and routines, and detailed daily lesson plans. Substitute folders will, of course, require frequent updating.
- Arrange instructional groups for various subjects and use the groups in your planning process. Once students learn the classroom routines, alternate teacher-directed lessons with independent work, peer tutoring, or cooperative learning. Alternating the classroom structure will allow you to give direct instruction to one small group while other children are

engaged in appropriate learning activities with one another or under the supervision of a paraprofessional.

◆ Alternate group membership. Teachers should place students in small, flexible groupings based on their performance and interests.

Stages of Learning

In addition to grouping and curricular considerations, teachers should keep learning stages in mind when planning lessons for their students. As students progress from limited or no knowledge of a skill or concept to using the skill appropriately in differing contexts, they pass through four stages in their learning. These stages are acquisition, proficiency, maintenance, and generalization.

Teachers cannot assume that students will pass through these stages on their own. Helping students acquire and become proficient with new skills requires careful planning. Ensuring that students maintain their newly acquired skills over time and that they use these skills appropriately when necessary entails even more systematic and detailed planning. Objectives and instructional methods chosen by teachers must reflect student performance at each stage of learning and must change as students progress from one stage to the next.

The Acquisition Stage

The acquisition stage is the initial stage of learning when the student is thought to have only limited knowledge or no knowledge of a skill or concept. This stage

Students may receive instruction in large or small groups depending on the lesson objectives. Here the teacher uses group instruction for students who are performing at approximately the same level and rate.

is considered to be the entry level of learning. Students may vary somewhat at this beginning stage of learning; some may have a little knowledge of the skill and others may have no knowledge at all. All students at this stage, however, are unable to perform the skill without teacher assistance.

In order to help students acquire a new skill or concept as rapidly as possible, teachers use direct instruction. That is, they tell students what is to be learned, explain why the skill or concept is important, clearly demonstrate the new skill or concept, and provide guided practice so that students receive immediate feedback about how well they are doing. At the acquisition stage, learning is highly teacher-directed and interactive, with the teacher posing questions and offering all students many opportunities to respond correctly.

Earlier in this chapter we mentioned Travis's long-term goal of being able to write the products for the multiplication facts through the nines. At this point, Travis may know some, but not all, of the multiplication facts. He is at the acquisition stage of learning. To help Travis acquire the multiplication facts through the nines, Ms. Lopez will determine which facts Travis does and does not know, and she will plan direct instructional lessons focused on the short-term objectives for multiplication written on Travis's IEP. Ms. Lopez will also use manipulatives to help Travis acquire the concept that multiplication is a fast way to add equal-sized groups (e.g., that $3 \times 4 = 12$ means three groups of four each).

The Proficiency Stage

Once students have acquired a new skill or concept, they must become automatic or fluent in its use. Students in the proficiency stage of learning require drill and practice activities until they have demonstrated mastery of the new material. At the proficiency stage, instruction is still highly interactive, although students may now work with a peer tutor, paraprofessional, or computer, rather than with the teacher, in order to receive corrective feedback. In fact, paraprofessionals are increasingly assuming instructional roles in order to maintain students with mild disabilities in inclusive classrooms. French (1990a and 1990b), for example, reports that paraeducators are often viewed by teachers, parents, and students as "real teachers" because they assist students with assignments, projects, and group work. Such instructional duties can indeed enhance the success of students at the proficiency stage of learning.

Students at the proficiency stage of learning now "know" the new material, but they may make numerous errors or respond hesitantly. For example, when Travis "understands" the concept of multiplication and has had practice using manipulatives to illustrate the multiplication facts through the fives, he is entering the proficiency stage of learning. Now Travis must learn, for example, to respond automatically that $3 \times 4 = 12$. Recall the short-term objective Ms. Lopez wrote for Travis: "Given the multiplication facts from the ones through the fives presented in random order on a daily probe sheet, Travis will write the products with 100% accuracy within 3 minutes." This objective is written for the proficiency stage of learning to ensure that Travis recalls the given multiplication facts accurately and rapidly. Travis will have daily, supervised drill and practice activities with a paraprofessional, and probes to determine when he has mastered this objective.

The Maintenance Stage

As students become proficient with a new skill or concept, teachers must help them retain the material over time. At the maintenance stage, students receive periodic review or practice with the skill so that they will maintain their accuracy and speed. Practice activities at the maintenance stage are more independent than are those at the acquisition and proficiency stages of learning. Students at this stage may, for example, complete homework assignments and independent seatwork activities that are not immediately checked for accuracy by the teacher or the paraprofessional. Students also may play instructional games or use computer programs that have built-in self-checking features.

To ensure that Travis retains the multiplication facts through the fives even though he is now entering the proficiency stage with the "six" and "seven" facts, Ms. Lopez plans periodic review activities, games, and probes using the "one through five" facts. She also adds a maintenance criterion to Travis's objective: "Given the multiplication facts through the fives presented in random order on a daily probe sheet, Travis will write the products with 100% accuracy within 3 minutes on four consecutive probes conducted at one week intervals." By adding the maintenance criterion, Ms. Lopez plans systematically to provide and check for Travis's retention of the targeted multiplication facts.

The Generalization Stage

During the generalization stage, students begin to use skills or concepts appropriately in new situations. For example, Travis may now apply the multiplication facts to solving word problems in mathematics or in science in his regular classroom, or he may use these facts when assisting his grandmother to compute totals for purchases of several identical items at the supermarket.

Generalization of skills is problematic for many learners with mild disabilities. Teachers cannot assume that generalization, or skill transfer, will take place naturally; hence, they must plan systematically for it to occur (Stokes & Baer, 1977). Unfortunately, IEP objectives written by teachers often do not address generalization of skills (Billingsley, 1984).

Wolery, Bailey, and Sugai (1988) suggest that teachers include a generalization objective for each acquisition objective written. These authors argue that for an objective to be considered mastered, the behavior must be performed fluently with someone other than the person who taught it to the child, in different settings, with different directions and/or materials, and in naturally occurring situations in which it is appropriate and necessary. To accomplish generalization, then, teachers must begin during the acquisition stage to vary systematically the people, settings, materials, and directions in teaching a new skill or concept. In addition, teachers may ask students, or tell them, where a new skill or concept may be useful at school, at home, or in the community. Teachers may also enlist the help of parents, other teachers, and peers to prompt or reward appropriate demonstration of a skill in the natural setting.

Stages of Learning and Planning

In planning, teachers set objectives appropriate for the level of performance and stage of learning of their students. They also plan instructional activities to reflect the degree of teacher assistance required by students at each learning stage.

Planning will be most accurate if the teacher knows exactly how well students are performing in the curriculum. If there are two students with learning problems who need instruction in specific areas, for example, the teacher may plan time for one-on-one instruction with these youngsters. At the same time, other students in the classroom may be engaged in independent tasks at the maintenance stage of learning, or they may be working with a paraprofessional or peer tutor on tasks designed to promote proficiency. Teachers who know student performance levels and who adjust instructional arrangements and activities accordingly are able to plan for a group diverse in abilities and interests (Bennett & Desforges, 1988).

Inaccurate planning may result if student progress is not monitored closely. According to Bennett and Desforges (1988), teachers may underestimate the progress of high achievers and overestimate the progress of low achievers when performance has not been monitored. Moreover, inaccurate assessment of student progress results in lack of adequate instructional time for students who are struggling, or wasted instructional time for students who have already mastered skills or content.

Cohen and deBettencourt (1991) suggest pretesting students to determine academic needs and skill levels in order to prevent wasted instructional time and to increase academic engaged time (recall that academic engaged time is the time in which students are actively engaged in appropriate tasks with a high rate of success). These authors state that a high level of academic engaged time may actually lower the probability of at-risk students dropping out of school. In addition to knowing the skill level of students, Kameenui and Simmons (1990) suggest that teachers identify the skills that may present problems for students and preteach those skills to at-risk learners before introducing lessons that require use of the skill. These preteaching lessons may be brief, but they should ensure that students have mastered prerequisite skills or tasks.

Rappaport (1991) advocates the holistic assessment of students with reading disabilities in order to provide accurate instruction. Holistic assessment takes into account student interests, skill levels, strengths, and weaknesses. Airasian (1991) argues that teachers must consider pupil characteristics along with instructional factors in order for successful planning to occur. (See Table 7.4.)

Accurate assessment of student skill levels is attained through direct daily measurement and curriculum-based assessment. Student performance data, obtained through the measurement procedures described in Chapter 6, are used to write educational objectives, plan instructional activities, and monitor student progress. For students receiving special education services, these objectives are included on the Individualized Education Program.

Table 7.4	**Factors to Consider When Planning for Instruction**

Pupil Characteristics:	*Instructional Resources:*
◆ Ability	◆ State curriculum mandates
◆ Work habits/socialization	◆ Time
◆ Special learning needs	◆ Textbook/instructional packages
◆ Prerequisite skills	◆ Other resources (space, aides, equipment, etc.)

From: Airasian, P.W. (1991). *Classroom assessment.* New York, NY: McGraw-Hill, p. 83. Reprinted with permission.

Planning and the IEP

Recall from Chapter 2 that when it has been determined that a student is eligible for special education services, a multidisciplinary team must develop an Individualized Education Program, or IEP, for that student before special education services can begin. IDEA (1997) requires that the student's parents or guardians, the special education teacher, the classroom teacher, other professionals as necessary, and, whenever appropriate, the student himself or herself be included as members of the IEP team. Including the student in this process may help him or her to develop a sense of ownership of the IEP (Kroeger, Leibold, & Ryan, 1999). The IEP details the exact special education services to be provided to the student; therefore, it may be no older than one calendar year. Every year, or more frequently if required, the team meets to negotiate the IEP.

In addition to a description of the special education and related services to be provided to the student, the IEP must specify the student's current levels of performance and the annual goals and short-term objectives planned for the student. IDEA (1997) also requires a statement regarding the extent to which the student will and will not participate in the regular curriculum, as well as a description of the supplementary aids and services necessary for such participation. In addition, the IEP team must decide whether or not the student will take any state- or district-wide assessments and they must list all necessary accommodations if it is determined that the student will take these tests. Furthermore, IDEA mandates that by age fourteen a statement of the student's transition needs must be included on the IEP (see Chapter 15). Goals and objectives designed for maximum successful employment and other post-school outcomes, such as participation in advanced placement or vocational education courses, are common transition needs for students with mild disabilities. Finally, at least one year before the student reaches the age of majority under state law, the IEP must contain a statement that the student has been informed of his or her rights and that these will transfer to the child on reaching the age of majority.

The IEP, then, is the link between curriculum and instruction for students in special education programs. Thus, IDEA (1997) implies that the core curriculum in the classroom will be the "curriculum of choice" for most students with mild disabilities. Goals, objectives, supplementary aids and services, and modifications or accommodations are to be provided in order to enable the child to be educated in the general education curriculum alongside his or her nondisabled peers to the maximum extent possible. A partial IEP for Travis is shown in Figure 7.2 and an example of one annual goal with objectives for Joey is presented in Figure 7.3. In addition, sample IEPs for Travis, Joey, Susan, and Robert are included in Appendix A.

INDIVIDUALIZED EDUCATION PROGRAM

CONFIDENTIAL

Name: Travis Johnson
Teacher: Ms. Kirk
Services Begin: 9/7/00

Current Grade/Year: 4th, 2000-01
Eligibility: Specific learning disabilities
Services End: 9/6/01

Special Education Services	Person Responsible	Time
Resource Room for reading and mathematics to provide intensive instruction not available in regular class	Ms. Lopez	2 hours per day
Regular classroom for all other instruction with collaborative teaching by 4th grade teacher and special education teacher for science and social studies	Ms. Kirk and Ms. Lopez	4 1/2 hours per day

Related Services	Person Responsible	Time
None		

Signatures:		Date:
Susan Lopez	LD Teacher	9-7-2000
Ms. Kirk	4th-grade Teacher	9-7-2000
Mr. Grier	Principal	9/7/2000
Mrs. L. Johnson, Mother		9-7-2000

FIGURE 7.2

Part of an IEP for Travis

Will <u>Travis Johnson</u> participate in the state-wide testing program scheduled in May for the 4th grade?

Yes <u> X </u> No <u>   </u>

If yes, list all accommodations that will be necessary:

<u>   Testing in a separate room   </u>

<u>   Testing administered and monitored by Ms. Lopez   </u>

<u>   Extended time for testing   </u>

<u>   Frequent rest breaks   </u>

NOT CONFIDENTIAL

Annual Goal: Travis will write the sum for two-digit plus two-digit addition problems with regrouping by May.

Short Term Objective	Evaluative Schedule/ Strategies/Materials	Teacher	Date Met
Given a probe with 50 two-digit plus two-digit addition problems with no regouping, Travis will write the sums with 100% accuracy within 3 minutes.	Teacher-made probe sheets; Best Ever Math Series; Manipulatives; flash cards; daily probes	Ms. Lopez	9/22
Given base ten blocks and any two-digit plus two-digit addition problem requiring regrouping from the ones to the tens, Travis will exchange ten ones blocks for one tens block correctly within 30 seconds.	Base ten blocks; Best Ever Math Series; Teacher-made daily probes	Ms. Lopez	10/3
Given a probe sheet with 50 two-digit plus two-digit addition problems with regouping only from the ones to the tens, Travis will write the sums with 100% accuracy within 3 minutes daily for one week.	Teacher-made probe sheets; Best Ever Math Series	Ms. Lopez	10/9
Given a probe sheet with any two-digit plus two-digit addition problem, Travis will write the sums with at least 90% accuracy within 3 minutes daily for two consecutive weeks.	Teacher-made probe sheets; Best Ever Math Series; base ten blocks	Ms. Lopez	

FIGURE 7.2—continued ◆

Part of an IEP for Travis

The concept of backward planning is often used in the development of the IEP. That is, the IEP team uses the information regarding the student's current level of performance first to determine the degree to which the student will participate in the regular curriculum and, next, to write annual goals. The annual goals are then broken down into short-term objectives. Later, the teacher may

Name: Joey Greenhill		Academic Year: 2000-01
Teacher: Ms. Lopez		Date: September 7, 2000

Annual Goal: Joey will complete the third grade reader by the end of the
academic year.

Objective:	Evaluation:	Date of Completion:
Given 100 new vocabulary words from the first 3rd grade reader shown randomly in written phrases, Joey will verbally decode the words with at least 90% accuracy by January.	Individually administered list of phrases from the Best Ever Third Grade Reader Number 1. (Untimed)	1/16/01
Given 5 comprehension questions following each story in the first 3rd grade reader, Joey will verbally answer the comprehension questions with at least 80% accuracy by January.	Comprehension questions following each story in the first reader at the 3rd grade level in the Best Ever Reading Series. Untimed unit tests given orally to Joey.	

FIGURE 7.3 ◆

A Sample Annual Goal with Objectives from Joey's IEP

break these short-term objectives down into even smaller steps for daily lesson planning and instruction. For most individuals with mild disabilities, the goals, objectives, and lessons will be designed to increase the student's current levels of performance and his or her success in the core curriculum.

Short-term objectives are stated in behavioral terms and are monitored frequently. Recall that well-phrased objectives specify conditions, observable student behaviors, the criteria for measuring success, and evaluation schedules for monitoring performance. In other words, a short-term objective on the IEP would not be phrased, "Travis will know his multiplication facts," or, "Travis will increase his reading comprehension." Rather, the objective might read, "Given any 200-word passage from the third-grade basal reader, selected at random by the teacher, Travis will read the passage aloud at a rate of 150 words per minute with fewer than three oral reading errors." When stated in this manner, the objective conveys to the teacher the precise behavior expected of Travis (read a passage aloud), the conditions under which he must perform (a timed reading of a 200-word passage randomly selected from the third-grade reader), and the level of performance required for mastery (an oral reading rate of 150 words per minute with no more than two errors). This objective is not only based on Travis's current reading performance, but it is also designed to increase his success in Ms. Kirk's classroom. The well-written instructional objective guides teacher planning and enables the teacher to determine student progress toward the annual goal.

In turn, frequent measurement of student performance toward goals helps the teacher make informed instructional decisions. The teacher sets a criterion level for mastery under a specified set of conditions for a targeted student behavior, and then changes the conditions, behavior, or required level of performance when data indicate that the initial objective has been met. Giek (1992) recommends considering the student's learning rate and past retention rate as guidelines for setting the criterion for mastery.

In addition, the teacher must write objectives that will promote generalization of skills or concepts to new environments. Billingsley, Burgess, Lynch, and Matlock (1991) provide guidelines for writing objectives with generalization in mind (see Table 7.5).

To save teacher time and promote generalization as well as student independence and ownership of learning, students may log their own progress on a chart or graph. Such self-monitoring increases student motivation (Giek, 1992) and improves classroom management (McConnell, 1999). Ms. Lopez, for example, uses a self-monitoring wall chart for reading. Her students color in the appropriate box for the story they read, selecting the color that is coded for the degree of accuracy they have attained upon self-checking their

---

Table 7.5 A Checklist for Instructional Objectives With Generalized Outcomes

Components of Generalization Objectives:

1. Is the learner specified?
2. Is the behavior specified (and functional)?
3. Are the performance conditions specified?
4. Are the criteria specified?
5. Are persons responsible for reporting success named?
6. Is a target date set?
7. Is this a realistic objective?

Dimensions of Generalization:

1. Do the conditions indicate the need for the behavior among people in general?
2. Do the conditions indicate the need for the behavior with respect to various objects/materials?
3. Do the conditions indicate the need for the behavior across settings/time?
4. Do the conditions indicate the need for the behavior on a "spontaneous" basis, on an "as needed" basis, or on an "as appropriate" basis?

Adapted from: Billingsley, F.F., Burgess, D., Lynch, V., & Matlock, B.L. (1991). Toward generalized outcomes: Considerations and guidelines for writing instructional objectives. *Education and Training in Mental Retardation*, 26, 357. Reprinted by permission.

story-comprehension questions. By looking at the wall chart, Ms. Lopez and the student both know the last story read, as well as how accurately the comprehension questions were answered. Travis and Joey can use similar self-monitoring procedures on an individual basis to promote the generalization of new reading skills and strategies to Ms. Kirk's fourth-grade classroom.

Writing behavioral objectives and measuring student progress toward these objectives directly and frequently is at the heart of the IEP. The most important outcome of well-written objectives is accurate measurement of how well students are learning. This information, in turn, guides the teacher in planning daily instruction and providing appropriate special education services.

Planning for Collaborative Teaching in Inclusive Classrooms

An appropriate education for students with mild disabilities often takes place within the regular classroom and curriculum. Because these students are included in general education for the majority of the school day, special educators and classroom teachers must collaborate to plan meaningful instruction for their "inclusion students." The classroom teacher knows the curriculum for his or her particular grade, and many teachers at the elementary and middle school levels are experts at integrating learning through thematic units. The special educator, on the other hand, understands how to break larger chunks of information into smaller sequential steps for learning, and he or she is an expert at modifying and adapting instruction according to the IEP to meet the needs of students with mild disabilities. Together, regular and special education teachers can pool their skills across grade levels to form a strong action-planning team (Shure, Morocco, Di Gisi, & Yenkin, 1999).

One factor often impacting collaborative planning at the high school level is the building schedule. In an attempt to provide Carnegie units for graduation credit and still maintain some student choice, many schools have adopted *block scheduling*. That is, students may spend 90 minutes in class periods each day rather than the typical 30-50 minutes. They meet in these classes every day for one semester (often called 4/4 blocks because students take 4 classes/semester) or every other day or week on alternate schedules (often called A/B blocks because students rotate through the same classes across the full school year). Such schedules may reduce the number of classes, teachers, and homework assignments students must deal with on a daily basis and provide teachers with time for instructional methods other than lecture. Special educators report that, with careful planning, block scheduling can provide more time for collaboration and more flexibility in using the resource room to teach the skills and strategies students need to be successful in their content classes (Santos & Rettig, 1999).

As a starting point for collaborative planning, Schumm, Vaughn, and Harris (1997) suggest teachers ask three critical questions: (a) What do we want all students to learn? (b) What do we want most, but not all, students to learn?(c) What will only a few students learn? Such questions are not meant to remove opportunities for learning from any students, but rather are intended to differentiate key concepts and skills that all students should know from enrichment and extension of the basic concepts and facts appropriate for only a few students. Teachers can determine the critical skills and concepts by carefully scrutinizing state or school-district guidelines and standards or the curricular materials used in the classroom.

After teachers have determined the degree of student learning, they must consider instructional strategies and adaptations that will be necessary in order for students with mild disabilities to learn the essential skills and concepts. According to Schumm, Vaughn, and Harris (1997), teachers must discuss adaptations for (a) grouping students (e.g., cooperative learning groups or peer pairs); (b) presenting critical concepts (e.g., using advance organizers or modifying the pace of instruction); (c) teaching specific learning strategies (e.g., note-taking or reading comprehension strategies); and (d) modifying both in-class or homework assignments and tests as necessary. Once teachers have specified the adaptations that will be required, they can sequence learning activities and instructional procedures to coteach thematic units and daily lesson plans. Box 7.1 provides an example of collaborative planning efforts between Ms. Stone and Mr. Abel, and Box 7.2 lists Web sites offering suggestions to enhance planning.

Box 7.1

Ms. Stone and Mr. Abel Engage in Collaborative Planning

Ms. Stone: I want all of the students in this class to define the terms *igneous, metamorphic,* and *sedimentary*. I also want all of the students to be able to tell me the processes that result in rocks of each of these types.

Mr. Abel: Okay, I've got that. (Writing on a lesson plan form.) Is there anything that some, but not all, of the students should know?

Ms. Stone: Yes, I think most of the students should be able to classify rocks by the correct category, if I give them some specific examples. I'm including Robert in this group. Then, my top students need to be able to tell me the properties for various rocks that lead to specific industrial uses.

Mr. Abel: For Robert and our other students with learning disabilities, I don't think this information will be a problem. I think we could present definitions in a large-group format using the overhead projector and then use the video you mentioned yesterday to illustrate the processes forming the rocks. During the video, we can have students list the steps in each process on a note-taking guide. What do you think?

Ms. Stone: Okay. Then we can break out into small groups for classifying the rocks.

Mr. Abel: I'll check the video out of the library after school today. Will you present the definitions on the overhead or do you want me to do it?

Ms. Stone: I'll do that if you'll make up the note-taking guide to use during the video.

Mr. Abel:	Okay with me. I'll make a copy of the guide on a transparency, too, so I can fill in key steps in each process on the overhead projector during the video. That should help Robert and some others be more successful.
Ms. Stone:	Good idea. After the video, can you summarize the definitions and processes? Then I'll give them the directions for the small-group work and walk them through an example. I've already got all the materials for this work so don't worry about that! After we get them started, I can float to help all the groups and you can reteach the definitions and processes if some students are still having trouble, but I don't think that's going to be necessary the way we have this structured. If it's not, we can both help the small groups.
Mr. Abel:	Okay. I'll be in right after school today to see what rocks you have for the classification activity.
Ms. Stone:	I have a bunch of them!
Mr. Abel:	What homework should we plan for the first night . . . ?

Similarly, Dyck, Sundbye, and Pemberton (1997) encourage teachers to differentiate the learning objectives, activities, and assessments that will be appropriate for "nearly all," "most," or "some" of the students in the classroom. Teachers can fine-tune their planning by determining which students will be included in each group or activity, the activities that will be used to keep all students motivated, and the teacher primarily responsible for each activity and assessment. This information can be recorded on a collaborative lesson-planning form such as that shown in Figure 7.4.

Box 7.2

Web Watch

Web Resources to Enhance Planning

The National Center to Improve Practice

http://www.edc.org/FSC/NCIP

A web site designed to promote the use of technology to advance educational outcomes for students with disabilities. Discussion groups.

Special Education Resources Internet

http://www.edc.org/FSC/NCIP

A web site providing information and resources to improve instruction in special education. Links to related sites on the World Wide Web.

Date:_____ Class Period/Subject:_____

Unit/Topic:_____

Lesson Objective(s):_____

_____

_____

Key Skills/Concepts/Terms:

List key skills/concepts/terms for some students:

List key skills/concepts/terms for a few students:

List key skills/concepts/terms for a few students:

Materials/Resources:

Materials/resources   Person responsible   Date needed

Evaluation Procedures:

Describe:

Modifications needed (Give student name and necessary accommodations):

Person responsible:

In-Class Assignments:

Describe:

Modifications needed (Give student name and necessary accommodations):

FIGURE 7.4 ◆

A Form for Collaborative Lesson Planning

Person responsible:

Homework Assignments:

Describe:

Modifications needed (Give student name and necessary accommodations):

Person Responsible:

Lesson Activities:

Students/group:

Sequence of activities:

Person responsible:

All:

_____
Some:
(List)

_____
Few:
(List)

FIGURE 7.4—continued ─────────────────────────────────────── ◆

A Form for Collaborative Lesson Planning Adapted from: J.S. Schumm,
S. Vaughn, & J. Harris (1997). Pyramid power for collaborative planning. *Teaching
Exceptional Children*, 29(6), p. 65. Copyright ©1997 by the Council for Exceptional
Children. Reprinted by permission.

Summary

Accurate planning is necessary for maximum educational achievement.
However, special and regular education teachers may use different methods to

plan and organize for instruction. Classroom teachers often plan learning around thematic units or content to be covered. Special educators most often plan based on the IEPs of their students.

Teachers must write educational objectives to guide the planning and provision of appropriate instructional activities for their students. Well-written behavioral objectives include conditions under which a student will perform, observable student behaviors, and criteria for determining success. Objectives also must reflect the levels and stages of learning. If students are to progress from the acquisition of new material to the generalization of skills, teachers must plan for this learning to occur.

Students receiving special education services must have up-to-date Individualized Education Programs developed by an IEP team. The IEP consists of annual goals and short-term objectives written in behavioral terms. Frequent and direct measurement of student progress will enable the teacher to determine when the student has mastered an objective. New objectives may then be written so that valuable academic time is not wasted.

Classroom and special education teachers must collaboratively plan for the success of students with mild disabilities who are included in the regular classroom. Supplementary aids and services, annual goals, and short-term objectives on the IEP must be designed with the student's successful participation in the classroom, to the greatest extent possible, firmly in mind.

Application Exercises

1. Interview a special education teacher in a local school system. What strategies does this teacher use when developing daily lesson plans? What factors influence his or her planning decisions?

2. Interview a classroom teacher in a local school system. Gather the same information as in Exercise 1. Are there similarities in the planning strategies used by classroom teachers and special educators? Are there any differences? Compare and contrast the strategies used by these teachers and the factors that influence their planning.

3. An annual goal in geography for Robert reads, "Robert will label the states of the United States on a blank map by May." Write a short-term objective for this goal. Be sure to include conditions, behavior, and criteria for mastery. How will you measure Robert's progress toward this goal?

4. Using Bloom's taxonomy, write an objective in the cognitive, the affective, and the psychomotor domain for the annual goal given for Robert in Exercise 3. If you can, write a goal at each level for the cognitive domain.

5. Assume Robert is at the acquisition stage of learning for the short-term objective you wrote in Exercise 3. What activities might you plan at this stage of learning? What activities will you plan to help Robert become proficient with the skill? How will you ensure that Robert maintains the skill over time? How will you plan for generalization to occur?

6. Arrange, if possible, to examine an IEP for a student receiving special education services in a local school system. Remember to keep the information on the IEP confidential as required by IDEA. Can you locate each required component on the IEP?

7. Browse InfoTrac for at least three articles containing tips regarding how classroom and special education teachers can collaboratively plan for students with mild disabilities included in the regular classroom. If you were in charge of a workshop on collaborative planning for "inclusion" teachers in your school, which tips would you share with these teachers and why?

8. Browse the web sites featured in Box 7.2 for information on constructing IEPs. Browse these sites as well for information related to collaborative planning for inclusion. Make a file of at least ten "good ideas" to share with your colleagues.

PART

THREE

PROVIDING INSTRUCTION

EFFECTIVE TEACHER BEHAVIORS

Focus

As you read, think about the following questions:

◆ *How do constructivist teaching approaches differ from empiricist approaches?*

◆ *Why should teachers of children with special needs consider the allocation of time, the management of transitions, and the provision of academic learning time important instructional variables?*

◆ *What specific behaviors indicate that a teacher is teaching effectively?*

◆ *How do teaching behaviors differ from one phase of a lesson to another and from one stage of learning to another in the direct instructional model?*

◆ *How can teachers integrate elements from both the empiricist and constructivist teaching philosophies to teach effectively in today's classroom?*

Teachers sometimes attribute the failure of students to lack of ability or poor home environment. Such statements as, "His parents aren't very supportive," or, "She's really a slow learner," reflect a belief that the final responsibility for academic achievement rests with the child and his or her family rather than with the school and the teacher. Effective teachers, however, assume full responsibility for the performance of all children in their classrooms, and they focus on those variables over which they have control. Let's listen to a conversation in the faculty lunchroom at Apple County Middle School:

Mr. Mathis: What's this "Success" project supposed to be about? I got a flyer in my box this morning for the meeting tomorrow afternoon.

Ms. Booker: I think it's to help us figure out more ways to reach our difficult students. I heard that some of the special education children would be involved, along with other kids the guidance counselors think might drop out of school.

Mr. Abel: I think you're right. I heard in the office yesterday that we were going to brainstorm ways to motivate and teach our at-risk kids to help keep them in school. I think it's supposed to be a school-wide effort to improve the performance of kids who are having trouble.

Mr. Mathis: The project sounds good. Some of my kids are hard to teach, like Leon, for example. I'm worried we could lose him, and I'm open for any suggestions I can get to help him and the other kids stay in school and like learning.

Teachers can and do make a tremendous difference in how much and how well students learn. Effective teachers, therefore, focus on their own skills and behaviors rather than on variables over which they have no control.

In this chapter, we will focus on variables controlled largely by teachers. First, we will review two contemporary and seemingly incompatible philosophies regarding effective teaching: the empiricist and the constructivist models. Next, we will review the teacher's use of time and some specific teaching behaviors affecting the academic achievement of students with mild disabilities. Following a discussion of the critical elements of the direct instructional model (a well-researched, empiricist teaching philosophy) we will discuss how the empiricist and constructivist paradigms can be integrated to help students with mild disabilities achieve success in the classroom.

Empiricist and Constructivist Teaching Philosophies

Teaching philosophies are models, or paradigms, used to explain beliefs about how students learn, and therefore, how teachers should teach. Various instructional philosophies exist; however, most fit within either the empiricist or the constructivist paradigms. Both have useful suggestions for teachers to improve the academic achievement of children in special education programs.

Empiricist Philosophies

Empiricist models of teaching are based on notions of scientific inquiry. That is, teachers and researchers using this paradigmatic frame of reference seek instructional methods that will result in predictable and verifiable learning by the students. Effective instruction in this model is seen as a linear, sequenced set of teaching activities leading to student mastery of preset outcomes, or mastery learning.

Direct instruction and mastery learning typify the empiricist teaching philosophies. Direct instruction grew from the work of Bereiter and Engelmann (1966), who developed highly-sequenced teaching techniques and curricular materials for reading and mathematics skills. Later, Rosenshine (1986) and Stallings (1987) broadened the direct instructional model to describe features of teacher-directed instruction, such as time on task, that correlate with student achievement. Hunter (1982) popularized direct instruction through her mastery learning model, describing lesson-planning formats and teaching procedures applicable to the regular classroom.

Both direct instruction and mastery learning emphasize highly teacher-directed, explicit lessons. The teacher selects the learning activities, carefully sequences discrete skills, and leads students through lessons focused on student attainment of specific objectives. According to Adams and Engelmann (1996), if the student doesn't learn the material, the teacher hasn't taught it. Research has consistently demonstrated that direct instruction leads to increased academic achievement for students. (See, for example, Adams & Engelmann; Forness, Kavale, Blum, & Lloyd, 1997; and White, 1988.)

Constructivist Philosophies

Constructivist teachers view teaching and learning as holistic, student-driven processes (Harris & Graham, 1994, 1996a; Heshusius, 1989; Poplin, 1988; Resnick, 1987; Skrtic, 1995). These authorities believe that children must be active participants in the learning process rather than passive recipients of information imparted by teachers. Teachers, then, do not teach a sequence of discrete skills that must be mastered before students can move to the next higher level of thinking and learning. Instead, they begin with the knowledge and experiences of their learners and engage them in authentic activities designed to lead to a deep and full understanding of information. All learning occurs within a social context, and all learning is activity-based, real-life, hands-on, discovery-oriented, and centered on helping students solve interesting and meaningful problems.

Contemporary examples of the constructivist paradigm include *whole language* or *literature-based* classrooms in which authentic children's literature and writing activities are integrated to form the basis for all other instruction (Goodman, 1989; Graham & Harris, 1994). (See Chapter 11 for a description of the Whole Language philosophy.) In addition, teachers using a constructivist philosophy make frequent use of thematic units and consciously make connections between what students know and what they need to know. To create such connections they build "scaffolds," or a framework, to give students just enough support to be successful, while simultaneously challenging them in their zone of proximal development (Vygotsky, 1978). Teachers build scaffolds through the questions they pose, by overt modeling of their inner thought processes, and by teaching students to use cognitive learning strategies (Palincsar, 1986). Constructivist teachers, then, view learners as cognitive apprentices (Rojewski & Schell, 1994) and believe that learning takes place only through ongoing, interactive dialogues between experts (i.e., teachers) and novices (i.e., students) (Englert & Mariage, 1996; Englert, Raphael, Anderson, Anthony, & Stevens, 1991). The effectiveness of constructivist approaches with children in special education has not yet been demonstrated as well as direct instruction has; therefore, teachers should use these methods carefully. Nevertheless, constructivist philosophies hold promise for helping students with mild disabilities succeed in the classroom (U.S. Department of Education, 1997). (See Table 8.1 for a comparison of the empiricist and constructivist teaching paradigms.)

Table 8.1 Comparison of Empiricist and Constructivist Teaching Philosophies

Empiricist Philosophy	Constructivist Philosophy
Effective instruction is teacher-directed and sequential.	Effective instruction is student-centered and holistic.
Instruction is explicit to reduce confusion.	Learning occurs as the result of confusion and a need to know.
Careful feedback on errors promotes student learning.	Errors promote student learning.
Teachers select and organize learning activities to achieve preset goals and objectives.	Students select and organize learning activities to achieve their own goals.
Knowledge must be meaningful to motivate students to learn.	Students create their own meaning of knowledge.
Teaching begins with what students know.	Teaching begins with what students know.
Students must be active learners.	Students must be active learners.
Authentic tasks improve learning.	Authentic tasks improve learning.

We will return to the use of constructivist teaching approaches later in this and other chapters. For now, however, let's examine research on the teacher's use of time, as well as research on effective teaching behaviors that have been linked to student achievement within the traditional, empiricist model in special education.

Research on the Use of Time

During the 1970s, research efforts focused on those variables linked to the academic achievement of students, particularly in reading and mathematics, over which teachers could exert control. Berliner (1984), for example, stressed the importance of the teacher's use of time. Teachers must first allocate time for instruction, both across and within given content areas, if their students are to achieve in those subjects.

Simply allocating time for instruction, however, is not enough to effect positive student outcomes. Students must be *on task* and *engaged* in an instructional activity if learning is to occur. Although teachers in different classrooms may schedule similar amounts of time for instruction in an academic area, the actual time children spend involved in learning tasks varies greatly from classroom to classroom. Haynes and Jenkins (1986), for example, reported that students in resource rooms spend only 44% of their allocated time engaged in instructional activities. Yet engaged time is more closely related to student academic achievement than is allocated time.

Clearly, how teachers organize and use instructional time influences student performance. This means that teachers must plan ways to convene instructional groups quickly. Materials must be prepared in advance and placed in accessible locations, and directions must be given so that they are easily understood. Clear rules, routines, and signals must be established to ensure smooth movement from one activity to another. Unless teachers plan organized transitions from one activity or place to the next over the course of the school day, the time used for transitions will considerably decrease the amount of time available for instruction.

What students actually do during instruction, however, is the most critical factor influencing their achievement. Students must be actively engaged in an appropriate task with a high rate of success. Berliner (1984) calls this important variable *academic learning time* (see Chapter 5). Thus, it is not enough for students with low achievement to be simply on task. The task must be an appropriate one, chosen because it relates directly to the content for which they will later be held accountable. Moreover, the students must be active participants, experiencing a high level of success with that task. Rosenshine (1983) suggests that children must achieve success rates as high as 90% to 100% before teachers can assume that their students have mastered a particular task. It is extremely important, then, that teachers carefully plan how to maximize academic learning time for their students. (See Box 8.1.)

Research on Teacher Effectiveness

Teachers must do more than just manage their instructional time wisely. Certain teaching behaviors are more closely related to increased academic

Box 8.1

Maximizing Academic Learning Time

During the 1970s and 1980s, the educational research literature reflected an increased knowledge of how teachers affect student academic achievement. According to research syntheses produced by the Northwest Regional Educational Laboratory (1990), effective teachers plan for the optimal use of student time. The following recommendations are based on the practices of effective teachers:

1. Use a preplanned curriculum in which learning goals and objectives are sequenced to facilitate student learning. Maintain a brisk pace during instruction, introducing new learning objectives as rapidly as possible (Englert, 1984; Good, Grouws, & Backerman, 1978).

2. Form instructional groups within the classroom to be sure all students thoroughly learn the material. These groups should be formed according to student achievement levels for specific academic skills. Group membership should be reviewed and adjusted frequently as skill levels change.

3. Keep noninstructional time to a minimum, using classroom-management strategies that minimize disruptive behaviors. Effective teachers continue to be aware of all students in the classroom while working with individuals or small groups, and they communicate that awareness to other students. Effective teachers also establish classroom rules and routines and prepare activities and materials before students arrive.

4. Set challenging but attainable standards for all learners. All students should be held accountable for appropriate behavior and achievement and be given help immediately and intensively when they experience difficulty.

5. Provide additional learning time and activities on priority objectives for at-risk students. Effective teachers continue to communicate the expectation that all students will be held accountable for meeting classroom performance standards. Comparisons are made, however, only to the student's own past performance rather than to that of other children.

Adapted from: Northwest Regional Educational Laboratory (1990). *Effective schooling practices: A research synthesis 1990 update.* Portland, OR: Northwest Regional Educational Laboratory. Reprinted by permission.

learning time and achievement of students than are others. According to Rosenshine (1983), effective educators exhibit six specific teacher behaviors:

1. Reviewing and reteaching previous work
2. Clearly presenting new concepts and skills
3. Providing supervised student practice in order to check understanding
4. Giving immediate positive and corrective feedback during practice sessions and reteaching if necessary
5. Providing structured independent practice opportunities to promote mastery
6. Using periodic reviews to ensure maintenance of concepts and skills learned

Effective teachers assume an active role in directing the learning of all students. They orient students to lesson goals and objectives, present key skills and concepts clearly and concisely, and use questions to check student understanding and focus attention on important elements of the lesson (Brophy & Good, 1986; Stallings, 1985). Effective teachers also pace their instruction appropriately, introducing new objectives and learning activities as rapidly as possible while still ensuring thorough mastery of content by students (Good, Grouws, & Backerman, 1978). Appropriate yet brisk pacing keeps students alert and interested and reduces student error.

These indicators of effective instruction are particularly applicable when teaching academic skills to students with mild disabilities. Stevens and Rosenshine (1981) maintain that, for students with academic deficits, effective instruction takes place in teacher-directed groups that are academically focused. In these groups, students receive more teacher demonstration and feedback and spend more time engaged in learning tasks than when they work alone. Moreover, effective instruction is also individualized for members within each group (Stevens & Rosenshine). This does not mean, however, that individual students are given additional workbook or worksheet practice pages to complete on their own during time allocated to special education. Students are instead given many opportunities to respond correctly to questions posed by their teachers during interactive teaching sessions. Extensive content coverage, task engagement, feedback, and success are critical to the academic achievement of children with learning difficulties (Englert, 1983, 1984; Sindelar, Smith, Harriman, Hale, & Wilson, 1986).

Direct Instructional Strategies

Direct instruction is an effective teaching model within the empiricist paradigm that emphasizes fast-paced, well-sequenced, highly-focused lessons (Gersten & Keating, 1987; White, 1988). These lessons are delivered to small groups of students who are given many opportunities to respond and receive feedback about the accuracy of their responses (Lloyd, 1988). Teachers provide repetition of key lesson elements and enthusiastically engage all students equally in active practice. At the acquisition stage of learning, the quality of all instruction is essential (Slavin, Karweit, & Madden, 1989). For students who are already behind their same-age peers, students with mild disabilities, and students facing possible school failure, the *quality, intensity,* and *clarity* of instruction are of vital importance. Therefore, direct instruction appears particularly well suited to meet their needs (Englert, 1984).

Teachers who use direct instruction plan lessons that are congruent with a necessary student outcome. That is, if students must later demonstrate on a test or by other means that they can add decimal numbers to the hundredths place, correctly placing the decimal points in the answers, then the teacher writes an appropriate instructional objective and focuses all teaching and practice on that objective (Box 8.2). Typically, such lessons follow a predictable pattern. The teacher opens the lesson, clearly demonstrates the skill or concept to be learned, guides the student through practice using the new skill, and closes the lesson. The teacher also provides ample opportunity for every student to become proficient with the new skill and to use the skill independently (Hunter, 1982). The teacher continuously monitors student progress toward the learning objective and uses feedback on student performance to adjust lessons as needed.

Box 8.2

Mr. Mathis Uses Direct Instruction

Mr. Mathis, a teacher at Apple County Middle School, is about to begin a lesson with his sixth-grade general math class. Susan is a student with mild mental retardation who has been mainstreamed into the class of approximately 19 children. Leon, also in the class, is a young man "at risk" for school failure. Mr. Mathis maintains that all of the students in this class have academic and behavioral difficulties and are children with special needs; therefore, his lessons are highly interactive and follow the direct instructional model. He plans his lessons in such a way as to motivate students and help them make connections to their daily lives.

Mr. Mathis plans to teach a lesson on adding decimal numerals. His lesson plan states the following objective:

"Given ten addition problems with no regrouping, using decimal numerals to the hundredths place, the students will write the correct sum with at least 90% accuracy and with a correctly-placed decimal point." Mr. Mathis has decided to present the lesson in the form of a rule for adding decimals. On the board, he has written the objective and the steps to follow:

1. Line up the decimal points;
2. Bring the decimal point down; and
3. Add the numbers.

In addition, Mr. Mathis has items of interest to the children, with accompanying price tags, hidden in a box on his desk.

After the children are seated, he begins his lesson. (Note key elements of the direct instructional method enclosed in brackets.)

Mr. Mathis: We've been working hard writing decimal numerals, like money. Let's review. Help me write the price for this notebook from the school store. (He pulls the notebook from the box, keeping the price tag hidden from his pupils.) Let's see. This notebook costs three dollars and forty-five cents. Write that cost on your paper, everybody. (He waits about five seconds.) Now, tell me how to write that number . . . Anna? [Lesson opening and review of preskills]

Anna: You write the three, then a decimal point, and then you write the four and the five.

Mr. Mathis: (He writes according to Anna's instructions) Super! Is this correct? (He points to the number on the board.) Yep. That's right: three dollars and forty-five cents. Remember the word "and" stands for that decimal point in the number.

	Let's try another one. (Mr. Mathis pulls a school banner from the box, repeating the process to review this skill with the children.) Now, suppose I wanted to buy both this school notebook and this school banner. How would I know how much money that would cost? John?
John:	You'd have to add the two things together.
Mr. Mathis:	Good. I'd have to add together the prices of the notebook and the banner. Today, we are going to learn how to add decimal numerals together. [Statement of purpose] Watch me. On the board are three steps I must follow to add decimal numerals together. [Demonstration] I must line up the decimal points, bring a decimal point down into my answer, and add like I always do. (He points and reads aloud.) This notebook costs $3.45, and this banner costs $1.12. (He points to the prices written on the board.) The first thing I must do is write the numbers so that I line up the decimal points. (He writes the numbers on the board and points to the decimal points one over the other.) Now, I must bring a decimal point down into my answer and make sure it's lined up with the other decimal points. (He places a decimal point in the answer.) Now, all I have to do is add as I always do. (He fills in the sum as he speaks.) Five plus two is seven. Four plus one is five. Three plus one is four. The cost of the notebook and the banner together is $4.57. Let's do another one. [Guided practice] (He pulls a school hat from the box and puts it on his head so that the children laugh as the price tag, clearly visible, dangles down.) How much does this cost, Susan?
Susan:	Two dollars and fifty-five cents.
Mr. Mathis:	Come up and write that price on the board, Juan. Good. $2.55. Stay here, Juan, and let's get the others to help us find out how much it would cost to get ready for the game Friday night if I wanted to buy a school hat to wear and a school banner to carry. (He points to the first step on the board.) What's the first thing Juan must do, Leon? [Focused questions]
Leon:	He's gotta write the numbers so the decimal points line up.
Mr. Mathis:	Yep. Okay Juan, you've written the price of the hat, $2.55, and the price of the banner is $1.12. (He points to the price written on the board earlier in the lesson.) Leon says the first step is to line up the decimal points. Watch and be sure he's correct, everyone. (Juan writes $1.12 correctly under the $2.55.) Is he correct, Leon?
Leon:	Yeah.
Mr. Mathis:	Sure is. [Feedback and involving others] Now, what's the next step, Pete?
Pete:	Bring a decimal point down to the answer.
Mr. Mathis:	Exactly. Bring a decimal point down to the answer. (Juan does this as Mr. Mathis talks.) Good job, Juan. Now, what's the last step, Shanda?
Shanda:	Add the numbers.
Mr. Mathis:	Yes, add the numbers as we always do. Now, while Juan is working the problem on the board, check to be sure his addition is correct, everyone. (Juan writes $3.67 as the answer.) Is he correct, Susan?
Susan:	Yes.

Mr. Mathis:	That's correct. Good job! Thank you, Juan. Now, let's work the next one together. You do it at your seat, and I'll do the problem up here at the board. Let's see. (Mr. Mathis pulls from the box a small calculator tagged with the price $6.24.) Suppose I want to buy this calculator and a notebook. How much does the calculator cost, Marvin?
Marvin:	Six dollars and twenty-four cents.
Mr. Mathis:	Yes. And the notebook, Leon?
Leon:	Uh . . . (Mr. Mathis holds up the notebook with the price tag so that Leon can see it.) . . . yeah. It costs three dollars and forty-five cents.
Mr. Mathis:	Good. Now, what is the first thing we must do, Taylor?
Taylor:	Write the numbers and line up the decimal points.
Mr. Mathis:	Super! Do that on your own paper, everyone. (As the children write, Mr. Mathis puts the problem on the board and then quickly moves to check student work.) Excellent! Now, what must we do next, Sam?
Sam:	Bring the decimal point down into the answer.
Mr. Mathis:	Yes, bring a decimal point down into the answer. Do that on your paper, and I'll put one in my problem up here. Okay, check and be sure your problem looks just like mine. (He quickly scans the room to be sure all decimal points are lined up correctly.) Now, what is the last step, Juan?
Juan:	Add.
Mr. Mathis:	Okay. Add on your papers, everyone. Be sure to check my answer to see if it's right. (He writes the sum, $9.69, on the board after the students begin to work.) What's the correct answer, Mike?
Mike:	You're right. It's nine dollars and sixty-nine cents.
Mr. Mathis:	Good job. It's easy to add decimal numerals like money together. All we have to remember is to write the numbers so that the decimal points all line up. Then, we bring a decimal point down into our answer and add as we always do. [Reviewing important concepts to close the lesson] Now, it's your turn to practice. (He pulls several more items from the box, each with a clearly visible price tag, and places them along the chalk tray with the notebook, banner, hat, and calculator.) On this worksheet are ten prices to find. You will need to write the cost for the two items in each problem so that the decimal points line up. Then, you will bring a decimal point down into the answer and add just as we always do. [Providing independent practice] When you get your practice sheet, we'll do the sample problem at the top together. (He passes out the worksheets.) What are the items to buy in the sample problem, Susan?
Susan:	The hat and the calculator.
Mr. Mathis:	Yes. So what will we write first, Marvin?
Marvin:	The $2.55 for the hat and the $6.24 for the calculator.
Mr. Mathis:	Yep. And how will I write these numbers, Marvin? (He points to the steps still on the board as a reminder.)
Marvin:	Oh. Write them so the decimal points line up.
Mr. Mathis:	Good. Do that on your paper, everyone. (He writes this on the board as well.) Now, what do we do, Josh?

Josh:	Put the decimal point down in the answer and add the numbers up.
Mr. Mathis:	Okay. You gave us the two last steps to do. (He places a decimal point in his problem on the board.) We put the decimal point down in the answer and we add as usual. Do that, everyone. (He walks around checking papers to be sure all decimals are properly lined up.) What did you get, Sarah?
Sarah:	Eight dollars and seventy-nine cents.
Mr. Mathis:	Is she right, Pete? (Pete nods "yes.") Good. (He writes the correct answer on the board for his sample problem.) Now, we have fifteen minutes to finish the ten problems on the page . . . Work quietly and raise your hand if you need my help. [Giving directions for what to do next]

Opening the Lesson

At the beginning of the lesson, teachers must gain student attention and orient them to the purpose for the lesson. Students learn best when teachers use advance organizers (Lenz, Alley, & Schumaker, 1987); therefore, teachers must tell students (orally or in writing) what will be learned, why the information is important, and how new learning relates to what they already know (Englert, 1983, 1984). During this phase, teachers must quickly set the pace for the coming lesson and motivate students to learn the material. To open a lesson, teachers might choose to do any combination of the following:

1. Gain student attention. Begin the lesson on time and with enthusiasm. Give a clear signal that the lesson is about to start (e.g., "Look," "Let's begin," "Eyes on me,").
2. Review or summarize previous learning. Provide a few quick practice trials using important preskills learned previously. Relate the new lesson to past learning or to future needs.
3. If appropriate, remind students of important rules to follow during the lesson (e.g., "Remember, we don't criticize each others' suggestions during brainstorming.").
4. Succinctly state the purpose for the lesson. Some teachers like to write the lesson objective on the chalkboard in an abbreviated form as well. This, of course, must be done before students enter the classroom. Main points to be emphasized can also be written on the board in advance and referred to during the lesson. This outline and statement of purpose, whether written or oral, is called an *advance organizer* and is designed to help students see the relationship among key lesson elements.
5. State why the skill or concept should be learned. For example, relate it to the students' daily lives or to something they already know. Help them see the usefulness or relevance of the skill and help them to set a performance goal, such as number correct on a mathematics practice sheet or quiz.

Once students have been oriented to the lesson and know the purpose and importance of the information to follow, the teacher can introduce the new skill or concept to be learned. This next phase of the lesson is often referred to as a *teacher demonstration.*

Demonstrating the New Skill or Concept

For low-achieving students, a short demonstration that is *explicit, repetitive,* and *focused* on the lesson objective is vital (Ysseldyke, Christenson, & Thurlow, 1987). This means that teachers must devise concise, well-organized, step-by-step explanations using language the students will understand, explaining all new vocabulary terms, and repeating essential lesson elements. Teachers must analyze tasks, breaking the new skill or concept into carefully-sequenced, manageable steps. Examples must be carefully chosen for the demonstration, and teachers must constantly focus student attention on the key features of these items.

For example, if Ms. Lopez presents a lesson on the Consonant-Vowel-Consonant-e (CVCe) rule, she might begin with the words *made, dime, Pete,* and *cube* on the chalkboard. She would state the rule, "When words follow the CVCe pattern, we say this (pointing to the initial vowel) letter name and the /e/ is silent," and then allow students to practice reading the words under her guidance (Carnine, Silbert, & Kameenui, 1990). Later, she might include words such as *cap, tub,* and *hid* in her word list to check student understanding and ensure that students can identify the relevant feature of the task (i.e., the CVCe pattern).

Once the teacher has clearly demonstrated the new skill or concept, he or she must immediately move students to numerous, controlled practice trials with close teacher supervision. This interactive teaching phase of the lesson is often called *prompted-practice* or *guided practice.*

Giving Guided Practice

Although a clear demonstration is critical for the academic success of students with mild disabilities, even more important is the opportunity to practice the new skill or concept under direct teacher supervision (Ysseldyke et al., 1987). Teachers ask questions during guided practice sessions, providing all students with numerous opportunities to respond successfully and to receive immediate feedback on their answers (Hunter, 1982). Thus, asking questions and giving feedback are related and critical skills for special education teachers.

Asking Questions. Effective questions allow the teacher to verify that students understand information presented. They also elicit accurate, substantive responses. That is, good questions lead students to the correct answer, focus attention on important features of the learning task, and require active participation by all students. Some authorities maintain that students must respond correctly to a teacher's questions at least 80% of the time for learning to occur (Wittrock, 1986). This means that questions should be planned in advance so that both the meaning of the question and the type of response called for are clear.

At the acquisition stage of learning, particularly for instruction in basic skills, questions posed by teachers should be narrowly focused and rapidly paced. They should have only one correct answer and involve recall of literal or factual knowledge. At the initial stage of learning, questions that require such lower levels of thinking enable students to respond successfully until they become firm or automatic with the new information (Englert, 1984; Mastropieri & Scruggs, 1987). Later, as students apply their newly-acquired skills in different situations, the teachers' questions should become more open-ended, challenging students to use higher-level thought processes and to make slower, more carefully considered responses.

Regardless of the level of questioning, teachers must ensure active participation by all students throughout the lesson. To do this, teachers should ask a question first, then call on particular students to answer. In addition, teachers might ask questions that require only a one- or two-word answer and then signal all students to respond together in what is known as *choral responding.* For example, the teacher might say "Everyone" or use a preestablished hand signal to ensure that all students answer simultaneously. Alternatively, the teacher might ask a question, direct all students to think about the answer for a moment, then ask for all students to respond. Children can use response cards during choral responding to increase their rate of active participation; this also allows the teacher to check easily for understanding (Heward et al., 1996). (See Figure 8.1.)

Response cards allow all students to make more frequent answers to questions posed by teachers. They can be preprinted with answer choices, or students can write their own answers on small chalkboards or on laminated boards using dry-erase markers. In response to a question from Mr. Mathis, for example, students could select and hold up a preprinted response card containing the words *No/False* or one containing the words *Yes/True.* Similarly, when asked by Ms. Stone to classify a particular rock, students might hold up one of three cards having the words *metamorphic, sedimentary,* or *igneous* preprinted on them. Or students in Ms. Lopez's math class could place brightly-colored, plastic clothespins on one of several choices preprinted on a response card, such as a penny, nickel, dime, or quarter, when she asks them to identify various coins.

According to Heward, Gardner, Cavanaugh, Courson, Grossi, and Barbetta (1996), both preprinted and write-on response cards have several advantages. Preprinted response cards produce high rates of active student responding, promote errorless learning, and are easy for the teacher to see. Instruction is limited, however, to simple recognition tasks, and they are not useful for lessons that have a large number of different answers. Although write-on response cards enable students to give creative and elaborate responses in lessons having multiple correct answers, they are more difficult for teachers to read. In addition, because it takes time for students to write and erase responses, overall active student response rates may be lower and error rates higher than when using preprinted cards. Heward (1996) and his colleagues offer the following guidelines to teachers using response cards:

- ◆ Use cards to give many active responses during a 15 to 20 minute period rather than for single responses given sporadically during the period.
- ◆ Model several question-and-answer trials to give students practice using the cards.
- ◆ Maintain a lively pace.
- ◆ Provide clear cues when students are to hold up or put down their cards (e.g., "Cards up" or "Cards down").
- ◆ Provide feedback based on the majority response.
- ◆ When one-fourth or more of the class displays the incorrect answer, state or display the correct answer and repeat the same question again immediately.
- ◆ Remember that students can learn from seeing the responses of others, so don't let them think it's cheating to look at the response cards their classmates hold up.

FIGURE 8.1 ◆

Using Response Cards to Increase Student Learning Adapted from: Heward, W.L., Gardner, R., Cavanaugh, R.A., Courson, F.H., Grossi, T.A., & Barbetta, P.M. (1996). Everyone participates in this class: Using response cards to increase active student response. *Teaching Exceptional Children, 28*(2), 4-10. Copyright ©1997 by the Council for Exceptional Children. Reprinted with permission.

Whether the teacher chooses individual or choral responses, students must know the type of response that is expected, and they must have adequate time to think and answer. Teachers should allow at least three seconds of "wait time" for lower-level questions and additional time for higher-level questions before signaling students to respond (Northwest Regional Education Laboratory, 1990). Moreover, if a student gives an incorrect or incomplete response, the teacher must "stay with" the same child, allowing more "wait time," asking additional questions, or giving specific feedback until an accurate answer has been given.

Giving Feedback. Students must know whether their answers are correct or incorrect. In addition, teachers must help students correct inaccurate answers as quickly as possible. Giving feedback, then, is another skill critical for special education teachers to master (Box 8.3).

When students respond to questions correctly , the teacher must immediately acknowledge the accuracy of the answer. Failure to do so may produce uncertainty and confusion for children in special education programs. If students

Box 8.3

Examples of Questions and Feedback During Guided Practice

Question	Example	Feedback	Example
Fact/Recall	What's the word?	Restate correct answers	"Yes! The word is *rope.*"
Focus student attention	Does the suffix begin with a vowel?	Acknowledge correct answers overtly	Smile & give a "thumbs-up" sign
Lead to right answer/ensure high accuracy	Are the decimal points lined up?	Give specific praise quickly	"Good, your decimal points are lined up."
Check student understanding	What is the second step?	Reinforce by confirming correct part of answer and rephrase the question	"Yes, add is the 3rd step. But what do we do *before* we add?"
Ask question then give a clear signal to respond	Is the word a proper noun? (pause) Susan? or Everybody?	Prompt	"Joe is the name of a person."

are hesitant or not yet firm with the answers they give, the teacher should provide an immediate and explicit statement indicating to everyone that the answer was correct. Often, this can be accomplished by simply restating the answer given by the child (e.g., "Yes, the word is 'hope'."). In this way, all students have one more opportunity to hear the correct response. Teachers can also follow correct answers with instructive feedback to extend learning beyond that contained in the initial question (Werts, Wolery, Gast, & Holcombe, 1996). For example, when Travis correctly decodes a word during social studies, Ms. Kirk can use instructive feedback by responding, "Yes, the word is *vehicle. A* vehicle is a form of transportation like a car or truck."

Teachers must take care, however, not to interrupt the pace of a lesson with an overabundance of artificial, nonspecific praise. If students are answering questions quickly and accurately, the teacher may choose to acknowledge correctness simply with a nod, a "yes," a thumb's-up sign, or some other overt signal that indicates acceptance of the answer given. If praise is used, it should be delivered quickly, sincerely, and specifically, so students know what was correct about the given answer.

When students give an inaccurate answer, the teacher should immediately and specifically indicate any portion of the response that was correct. Then the teacher should rephrase the question, redirecting the child's attention to important features of the task and leading the child to the correct answer. If students are still unable to answer the question, prompts may assist them to respond correctly (see Box 8.4). Teachers should not, however, continue to probe students when they obviously do not know the answer to a question asked of them. In this instance the best course of action would usually be to state the correct answer without embarrassing the student and move on without interrupting the pace of the lesson. The teacher should, of course, give the student the same question again later in the lesson in order to check for understanding. Teachers must provide numerous opportunities for all students to respond with high levels of success (Greenwood, Delquadri, & Hall, 1984).

Kline, Schumaker, and Deshler (1991) offer an excellent sequence for giving individual feedback in order to correct errors made by students with mild disabilities. These authors maintain that feedback conferences can be conducted with individual students and that these feedback conferences should include the following elements:

1. The teacher should make at least three positive statements about the student's work.
2. The teacher should give a description of the student's error and specific examples of the error should be identified.
3. The teacher should model the correct answer and provide supervised practice for the student of ways to correct the error.
4. The teacher should make summary statements about what was learned in the feedback conference to be rephrased by the student later as written goals.

Through the interactive teaching process used during guided practice, asking questions, and giving feedback, teachers are able to monitor student performance and adjust instruction immediately. If students are unable to respond, teachers should rephrase questions, provide prompts, or reteach the skill or

Box 8.4

Giving Feedback Using Prompts

Prompts help students to achieve a high rate of successful responding during guided practice sessions. To be most effective, prompts should be planned *before* a lesson begins. In this way, teachers can give students only that level of assistance necessary to reach accuracy levels of 80% to 90% or better during the initial stages of learning. For most students with mild disabilities, prompts will fall loosely on a hierarchy from the least amount of assistance to the greatest amount of assistance. (See Wolery, Bailey, and Sugai, 1988, for an excellent description of the system of least prompts.) For example, when a student makes an error, the teacher might begin prompting at the "top" of the hierarchy, cueing the student to respond. If the cue fails to produce a correct answer, the teacher might then move down the hierarchy, systematically giving increasing levels of assistance.

Type of Prompt	Description	Example
Cue	Ask again; student may not have attended to the question	"Read the word."
Visual	Highlight correct response audibly or visually	*Feet* (Teacher underlines the double-vowel pattern)
Verbal	Partially supply or describe the answer	"The *smallest* coin." "Line up the _____."
Model	Show or tell the correct answer	"The word is *rope*. What's the word?"
Manual	Give physical assistance	Place hand over the child's to write his or her name

concept using different examples and smaller teaching steps. When students are responding to the teacher's questions confidently and with at least 80% accuracy, they are ready to practice the new material independently.

Providing Independent Practice

Once students achieve a high level of correct responding during guided practice, the teacher must provide them with opportunities to practice new skills and concepts independently. Independent practice allows the student to become proficient with new information. The teacher also may plan independent practice activities to help students maintain or apply previously learned information. Moreover, student performance during independent practice helps the teacher evaluate accomplishment of lesson objectives and adjust additional instruction accordingly.

Often, independent practice takes the form of a seatwork task. To be effective at the initial stages of learning, however, it is essential that seatwork be directly related to the lesson objective and require a response similar to that demonstrated and practiced under teacher guidance. For example, if the demonstration and guided practice involve children stating the time to the hour as the teacher moves the hands on a large clock, the independent practice activity must follow a similar oral format. If students in special education programs are suddenly asked during independent practice to draw the hands on a clock in order to illustrate a given hour, their performance will likely deteriorate. "Stating" time to the hour and "drawing" the hands on a clock are two different behavioral responses, and students with special educational needs do not readily generalize across new skills or situations unless they are explicitly taught to do so (Stokes & Baer, 1977). Unfortunately, the teacher might be left with the mistaken impression that "these students never pay attention or retain what they learn," when, in fact, the teacher has set up the conditions for student failure.

In addition, teachers sometimes wrongly use independent practice activities to fill class time and to keep students busy. Seatwork should never be used merely to fill time in any classroom. Independent seatwork should be used only when it will enable students to become proficient with new information, or when it will help them to maintain and/or apply previously learned skills. If the seatwork task is not related to lesson objectives, teachers should choose another activity.

As students complete independent practice activities, the teacher must still actively monitor their performance. Teachers should walk students through the first few problems or examples and then circulate among the students to check understanding and accuracy, to provide clarification or assistance, and to reteach when necessary. Often, however, the teacher of special education or other at-risk children must give direct instruction to another small group of students after the first group has begun to work independently. This means that teachers must communicate to children the expectation that all seatwork will be accurately completed during a specified time period. In addition, if independent practice is to flow smoothly, teachers must establish rules regarding appropriate ways to get help or acceptable activities to choose upon completion of seatwork.

Independent practice does not have to be conducted solely as individual paper-and-pencil tasks. A paraprofessional, parent volunteer, or peer tutor can be enlisted to continue teacher-directed practice, providing additional opportunities for children in special education programs to answer questions and receive immediate feedback. Similarly, students may participate in cooperative learning arrangements, with both group incentives and individual accountability, to help one another master new skills and concepts. Computer drill and practice programs may also be useful as independent activities to provide immediate feedback if they are directly related to the lesson objective and to the guided practice given by the teacher.

Closing the Lesson

As teachers come to the end of a direct instructional sequence, they either follow guided practice with independent practice or move students into a new lesson. Regardless of the next instructional activity, teachers must indicate to students that the lesson has ended.

To bring closure to a lesson the teacher may choose to review or summarize the main points learned. For example, students could read a list of new vocabulary words in a final "firm-up" trial. The teacher may also remind students about the importance or usefulness of the new information, reestablishing the relevance of what was learned. Students could also be asked to summarize for one another the new information and its relevance. Finally, the teacher may give specific directions regarding what students are to do next (see Box 8.5). These directions could refer to either the independent practice or to a totally new instructional activity. When giving directions, though, teachers must always remember to be specific (e.g., "Now, please put your reading books on the shelf, get out your math book, and open it to page 63."). In addition, they should check student understanding by observing what students do or by asking one child to restate the directions given.

Evaluating Instruction

Following each lesson, teachers must systematically evaluate whether or not students have accomplished the instructional objective(s). This ongoing process of

---

Box 8.5

Giving Directions for Independent Practice

In special education classrooms, directions must be clear, concise, and specific. The following suggestions may help teachers provide proper directions for independent practice activities:

1. Obtain everyone's attention *before* giving directions.
2. As you give the directions, watch each student. Look for signs of confusion or inattention as you speak.
3. Ask students to repeat or rephrase the instructions when you finish. You may wish to ask students who are likely to have difficulty to repeat the directions after you.
4. Ask the students specific, step-by-step questions to be sure that they understand what they are to do.
5. Work through one or two items with the group, following the directions given, before allowing students to begin independent work.
6. Place a clear reminder of the directions and/or a sample work item on the board for all students to see.
7. Circulate around the room as students work independently.
8. If you cannot circulate, be sure to remind students of the rules for obtaining help (e.g., check with an assigned peer) and for acceptable behavior upon work completion.

reflecting on student performance is known as *formative evaluation.* (By contrast, *summative evaluation* is done through tests following a period of instruction.) Formative evaluation allows for immediate corrective action by the teacher. Gathering information regarding student performance daily, or even moment-to-moment, permits teachers to adjust instruction immediately to suit the needs of students.

Suppose, for example, students were achieving accuracy levels of 80% to 90% or better during practice sessions. In this case, the teacher would probably maintain or increase the pace of instruction. However, if students were making frequent errors, the teacher would critically examine all instructional variables, with the following questions in mind:

1. Is the lesson objective appropriate? Is the objective stated appropriately for the stage of learning (i.e., acquisition, proficiency, maintenance, or generalization)? Is the criterion level set too high or too low?
2. Are students properly motivated to learn the lesson? Do they see the relevance and usefulness of the lesson content? Are student goals realistic?
3. Do students have the necessary preskills for this lesson? Is the pace of instruction on target?
4. Is the demonstration clear? Is the demonstration task properly sequenced? Do the examples clarify the skill? Are important parts of the task clear to students and are they repeated numerous times?
5. Are questions clear and designed to lead students to correct responses? Do all students have sufficient opportunity to respond? Do they have adequate "wait time" to think and answer?
6. Are students given immediate and specific feedback for each answer? Do students know when answers are correct? Are questions and prompts designed to focus student attention on the correct answer?
7. Does the guided practice match the lesson objective and the demonstration? Do students need additional guided practice?
8. Does the independent practice activity match the instructional objective? Does the independent practice activity require the same behavioral response as the demonstration and guided practice? Do students understand the directions and know what they are to do? Do students need additional independent practice opportunities before evaluation of their performance?
9. Does the evaluation procedure, whether an independent practice activity or an oral or written test, match the instructional objective and require the same behavioral response as was required during guided practice?

Integrating Empiricist and Constructivist Philosophies

The empiricist teaching philosophy, exemplified by direct instruction, has been the dominant model in special education for many years. Clearly, direct instruction does improve the academic achievement of students with mild disabilities. Some authors suggest, however, that direct instruction only teaches rote, lower-level skills in a manner that does not help students think, and that does not motivate them or help them make connections between what is learned and the real world (Resnick, 1987). On the other hand, others maintain that direct instruction is not necessarily incompatible with teaching approaches derived from the constructivist paradigm. (See, for example, Adams & Engelmann, 1996; Anderson & Barrera, 1995; Harris & Graham, 1996b; Kronick, 1990; Mercer, Jordan, & Miller, 1996; Pressley, Hogan, Wharton-McDonald, Mistretta, & Ettenberger, 1996.) Rather than polarize in camps arguing for competing philosophies, they maintain that teachers must integrate techniques from the two philosophies in order to meet the needs of the diverse population of learners in today's classrooms (see Box 8.6 for web sites containing ideas for lessons).

Some approaches, such as direct instruction, do have a higher probability than others of increasing the academic achievement of students with mild disabilities; however, no single approach will always result in better learning for every student. Students with limited English proficiency and bilingual students with learning disabilities, for example, may learn well when instruction is embedded in a meaningful context and takes place through interactive dialogues (Echevarria & McDonough, 1995; Fueyo, 1997). Teachers can integrate direct instruction and constructivist strategies by first directly teaching students the essential skill or concept they need to know and then engaging students in tasks designed to help them use the skill to solve real-world problems (Gersten, 1998). The following guidelines for integration are suggested.

Box 8.6

Web Watch

Web Sites Containing Ideas for Lessons

AskERIC

http://ericir.syr.edu
Links to teacher-developed lessons in many different content areas.

Association for Direct Instruction

http://www.adihome.org
Information and resources on the direct instructional teaching method and teaching resources using direct instruction.

National Center to Improve the Tools of Educators

http://www.darkwing.uoregon.edu/~ncite/index.html
A site promoting the use of principles of effective instructional design, particularly through the use of textbook and computer technology.

Teacher's Network

http://www.teachnet.org
A searchable database of classroom projects and ideas for teachers.

- Determine what students already know and use this knowledge as a starting point for instruction.
- Activate what students know through questions and short discussions during lesson openings. Provide background experiences when necessary information is lacking.
- Situate learning in real-life, authentic contexts whenever possible. Community-based, real-life, hands-on, concrete tasks may ultimately improve student motivation and generalization of skills.
- Provide direct instruction of skills and concepts whenever needed. Don't be afraid to TEACH!
- Provide scaffolds through clear explanations, leading questions, prompts, and carefully-chosen examples during the acquisition stage of learning.
- As students acquire proficiency with skills, reduce the level of support. Use questions such as "What do you mean by . . . ?" "What would happen if . . . ?" or "How did you know that . . . ?" to extend thinking and enable students to construct their own explanations.
- Systematically overlap learning and provide repetition for maintenance by pointing out connections across subject areas or within thematic units.
- Model the inner thought processes used during complex problem solving by "thinking aloud" for students. Provide a graphic, visible reminder of these thought processes as a cognitive framework that students can refer to later.
- Teach cognitive learning strategies to help students support their own learning.

Summary

Teachers are responsible for the academic performance of children in special education programs. Teachers who allocate sufficient time to instruction and then provide lessons designed to maximize academic learning time for all pupils increase the achievement levels of their students. Effective teachers, then, focus on their own teaching behaviors, examining how they plan lessons and deliver instruction.

Direct instruction is one particularly effective method for teaching children with mild disabilities. It allows for instruction that is intensive, highly-structured, repetitive, and interactive. Teachers focus lessons on appropriate instructional objectives and orient students to the lesson purpose. Teachers give clear demonstrations, ask many questions to elicit correct answers from all students equally, and offer students immediate corrective feedback. After the demonstration and guided practice, teachers afford students numerous opportunities to practice new skills and concepts independently. They also close lessons clearly by reviewing key lesson elements, summarizing the purpose and usefulness of the lesson, or issuing clear directions regarding what students are to do next. Throughout the lesson, student performance is monitored closely by the teacher, and instruction is adjusted immediately to increase the success rate for all students. Structure, repetition, and high rates of successful responding are necessary elements for effective instruction in special education classrooms.

Constructivist teaching approaches center learning on meaningful and authentic experiences for children. Teachers model inner thought processes, pose questions, and engage students in dialogues to solve interesting problems. Techniques from the constructivist paradigm can be integrated with empiricist methods such as direct instruction to improve learning for students in the classroom.

Application Exercises

1. In Box 8.2, Mr. Mathis is delivering a lesson on adding decimal numbers. Does he state the lesson objective or purpose? How does he make the material relevant for the students and motivate them to learn? Does Mr. Mathis give students a clear demonstration of the new skill? What questions does he use consistently to focus student attention on the important features of the task? Are all students responding actively and successfully? Are they receiving immediate feedback regarding the accuracy of their answers?

2. On page 206, Ms. Lopez is conducting a lesson on the CVCe rule. Use the format that follows to write a lesson plan for Ms. Lopez. (Be specific and write exactly what you will say and do.)

   ◆ Objective: Be sure to include a condition, measurable student behavior, and the criteria for determining success.
   ◆ Opening: What will you say or do to establish interest in the topic and relate the forthcoming new information to what is already know by the students? Will you review preskills or state the lesson purpose? What rules will you establish to structure the lesson?
   ◆ Demonstration: How will you present the new skill or concept? What examples will you use? How will you focus student attention on the important features of the task?
   ◆ Guided Practice: What examples will you use? What questions will you ask to structure this practice, check student understanding, focus student attention, and keep all students actively engaged in the learning task? What prompts might you plan to ensure successful student responding?
   ◆ Closing: What will you say or do to close the lesson? Will you restate the relevance or review and/or summarize the material? Will you give specific directions for what students are to do next?
   ◆ Independent Practice: What task will students complete independently? Are you sure that this activity directly matches the lesson objective and corresponds to both the demonstration and the guided practice?
   ◆ Evaluation: How will you evaluate whether students did or did not accomplish the objective? Are you sure that your evaluation procedure matches the objective, the demonstration, and the practice activities?

3. Browse the web sites listed in Box 8.6. Locate a lesson plan in the area of mathematics. Does this lesson appear to be constructivist or empiricist in nature? What are the likely trouble spots for students with mild disabilities par-

ticipating in this lesson? Modify the lesson to fit the direct instructional lesson-planning model given in Exercise 2.

4. Use Infotrac to locate two articles on the direct instructional teaching model and two articles on the constructivist philosophy. What arguments do the authors of these articles use to justify their approaches to teaching? Compare and contrast the approaches suggested in each set of articles.

STUDENT-MEDIATED LEARNING

Focus

As you read, think about the following questions:

◆ *How can teachers use cooperative learning groups to individualize instruction?*

◆ *How can peer tutoring work to the advantage of both tutors and tutees?*

◆ *How can teachers help students with disabilities learn to work independently using cognitive behavior modification and learning strategies?*

Because each student with a disability must have an Individualized Education Program (IEP) to receive services, according to the Individuals with Disabilities Education Act of 1997, and because that IEP must specify specially-designed instruction unique to the needs of the student, many teachers have misconstrued IDEA to mean that students with disabilities must have one-on-one instruction from a special educator at all times. Although some students with disabilities may require instruction in a one-on-one teacher-student mode, most do not need it. Many of the needs of students with mild disabilities may be met through small, cooperative learning groups, peer tutoring, and learning strategies.

For example, in Mr. McNally's geography class, the students have differing ability levels. In order to accommodate these varying levels, Mr. McNally knows that he must provide a variety of reading materials and activities for his students. He plans to use cooperative learning groups, recognizing that they can help him to accomplish several goals. Activities that involve all students in the learning process not only improve achievement but also facilitate the social integration of students with disabilities.

Ms. Kirk has students both with disabilities and with exceptional abilities in her classroom. She has considered several methods by which to give each student the instruction he or she needs to achieve academically. Grouping by ability seems to be the most commonly used technique, but Ms. Kirk recognizes that this may not be the best method. By investigating the current educational journals and talking with teachers in other schools, she has become aware of several peer-tutoring strategies that are being used successfully to meet the academic needs of many diverse students. When she implements peer tutoring in her classroom, Ms. Kirk realizes many benefits, not the least of which is improved academic performance by her pupils.

Mr. Abel has twenty students who visit his classroom daily. These students are all assigned to general education classrooms where they receive the majority of their instruction. In the resource room, Mr. Abel knows that he must maximize time by training his students in strategies that will enhance their performance in the regular classroom rather than simply by tutoring them in content areas. He has chosen to teach learning strategies and use cognitive behavior modification techniques to improve his students' academic and behavioral performance in the regular classroom.

In each of the preceding examples, the teacher is striving to meet the unique needs of students by using the most appropriate methods. With careful teacher planning and supervision, these methods will enable the students to assume greater responsibility for their own learning, as well as that of others. Such student-mediated methods as cooperative learning, peer tutoring, and strategy training may increase academic learning time for students with mild disabilities by providing more opportunities for active engagement with appropriate tasks when the teacher is involved in direct instruction with others. These methods are also extremely valuable to teachers seeking to provide appropriate learning experiences to learners from culturally diverse backgrounds.

Cooperative Learning

Placing students with mild disabilities in the regular classroom deeply influences their lives. It allows for the development of constructive relationships between them and their nondisabled peers. However, the risk of making things worse, as well as the potential for making things better, is a possibility that cannot be overlooked (Johnson & Johnson, 1986). Friendships and other positive relationships may result for students both with and without disabilities when inclusion is successful. But if inclusion is unsuccessful, students with disabilities may experience rejection, stereotyping, or ill treatment from their peers. According to Johnson and Johnson, simply placing students with mild disabilities in the general education classroom does not ensure that mainstreaming will go well. Successful integration of students with mild disabilities into the general education classroom depends on how well the teacher structures relationships among students.

Teachers may structure academic lessons in any of three basic ways: (a) in a competitive struggle to determine who's "best"; (b) along individual lines without peer interaction; and (c) in a cooperative manner, in which students help each other master the assigned material (Johnson & Johnson, 1986). The first two options tend to isolate students from one another. Each student is concerned only for himself or herself. By contrast, the third option allows teachers to structure lessons around shared goals toward which students work together, encouraging, discussing, and helping one another to understand the material. Thus, Johnson and Johnson suggest that teachers use cooperative learning whenever they want students "to learn more, like school better, like each other better, have higher self-esteem, and learn more effective social skills" (p. 554). Cooperative learning may be used both in general education classrooms that include students with mild disabilities and in special education classrooms that contain students with varying levels of achievement.

Cooperative learning can be used, for example, to improve social skills among young children. Fad, Ross, and Boston (1995) describe numerous cooperative learning activities to enhance social skills among very young children in three-member groups, such as coloring the beginning, middle, and ending of a story or making a book with three pages. Before children engage in these activities, though, teachers must first describe to them the exact behaviors expected. Teachers can accomplish this by using pictures or by writing and stating what behaviors "look like" and "sound like" on a T-chart (Fad, Ross, & Bostin, 1995). (See Figure 9.1.) According to Prater, Bruhl, and Serna (1998), students with mild disabilities may need direct instruction in particular social skills necessary for success before placement in the cooperative learning group occurs.

The basic elements that must be present for cooperative learning to take place are positive interdependence, individual accountability, collaborative skills, and group processing (Johnson & Johnson, 1986). Cooperative learning is also characterized by heterogeneity and teacher intervention when appropriate (Center for Special Education Technology, 1990). (See Box 9.1 for a listing of cooperative learning elements.) *Positive interdependence* refers to the perception that each individual is linked with the other individuals in the group, and that the success of one is dependent upon the success of all. (See Box 9.2.) *Individual accountability* refers to the assessment of each group member's performance to determine who needs additional help in mastering the material or completing the assignment. In this process, group points may be assigned for improvement in individual scores. *Collaborative skills* include leadership, decision making, trust building, communication, and conflict management. Because groups

Looks Like	Sounds Like
One friend holding, one friend waiting her turn.	"Here, you can have it now."
Handing a toy to your friend.	"Thanks for sharing."
Friends playing together.	"I like taking turns."
Happy children.	"You're nice."
I have a turn, then you have a turn.	"Let's play dress-up now."

FIGURE 9.1

Written Statements for Ways We Share From: Fad, K.S., Ross, M., & Boston, J. (1995). We're better together: Using cooperative learning to teach social skills to young children. *Teaching Exceptional Children*, 27(4), 28–34.

Box 9.1

Elements of Cooperative Learning

Cooperative learning is more than just putting students together in groups. It is a teaching strategy characterized by

◆ Positive goal interdependence of group members. This may consist of having a common goal, sharing materials, or assigning members different parts of the task.
◆ Individual accountability. Each group member is asked to be responsible for his or her own learning, as well as being responsible for helping others learn.
◆ Heterogeneous groups. The composition of the class should be reflected in each of the groups. The teacher assigns students who differ in ability, culture, race, and gender to work together. These differences enable students to make unique contributions toward the group goal.
◆ Teacher observation and intervention (when appropriate). While students are working, the role of the teacher ideally should be to monitor the groups. When problems in understanding the content or in interactions occur, the teacher may help focus the group on the problem. Rather than solving the problem, the teacher should try to help the group discuss possible solutions.
◆ Instruction in collaborative skills. Emphasis is on building skills that help students to work together. Role playing and examples of the skill are used to depict the expected behavior. *How to actively listen* or *how to disagree in an agreeable way* are two skills that may be modeled.
◆ Group processing/debriefing at the conclusion of the lesson. There needs to be discussion of the content, as well as how the group functioned while working together. The observations of the teacher, as well as student input, should be used to create a plan for the next time the group meets.

From: Center for Special Education Technology (September, 1990). Contract No. 300-87-0115 with the Office of Special Education Programs, U.S. Department of Education. Reprinted by permission.

Box 9.2

Positive Interdependence

The perception that one is linked with others such that one's success is dependent upon the success of others and, therefore, that each member equally contributes to and partakes of the group's success is referred to as *positive interdependence.* It is a sense of fate and mutual causation. The ways in which a teacher may structure positive interdependence include the following:

1. Positive goal interdependence exists when students perceive that the goal of the group is to ensure the learning of all group members. This may be done by giving each student an individual test and taking a group average for each member's grade or by requiring one product from the group.
2. Positive reward interdependence exists when all group members receive a reward based on their overall achievement. Giving a single grade for the group's efforts, adding bonus points to each member's individual score when every member achieves the criteria, or giving nonacademic rewards such as free-time or food when all group members reach criteria are examples.
3. Positive resource interdependence exists when resources are distributed so that coordination among members is required if the goal is to be achieved. Two examples are jigsawing materials so that each member has part of a set of materials or information, and limiting the resources given to the group (e.g., only one pencil, book, or dictionary).
4. Positive role interdependence exists when members are given specific complementary roles to play in the group, such as leader, recorder, or time keeper.
5. Positive task interdependence exists when a division of labor is structured so that the actions of one member have to be completed if the next group member is to complete his or her responsibilities.

From: Johnson, D.W., & Johnson, R.T. (1986). Mainstreaming and cooperative learning strategies. *Exceptional Children, 52*(6), p. 555. Council for Exceptional Children. Reprinted by permission.

cannot function without collaborative skills, they must be taught in the same way that academic skills are taught. For example, during a cooperative group activity in which students "map" the main elements of a story—such as the characters, setting, problem, events, and outcome—students can be taught a "leader" routine and given a prompt card listing cues for each step of the routine (Mathes, Fuchs, & Fuchs, 1997). (See Figure 9.2.) *Group processing* refers to discussions on how the group is functioning. This discussion should focus on whether or not members are achieving their goals and whether or not the actions of members are helpful. Such discussions provide the feedback necessary for students to determine the success of their participation (Johnson & Johnson, 1986).

Although cooperative learning may take many different forms, all are characterized by students working in small groups to help one another master academic material (Slavin, 1991). Student Team Learning (STL), developed at Johns Hopkins University, is a collection of cooperative methods in which attainment

```
                        Main Characters

Tell:     I think the Main Characters are _____

          because _____.

Ask:      Who do you think the Main Characters are?
          What is your evidence?

Discuss:  Let's discuss the answers and decide on the group's answer.

Record:   I'm going to write _____ in the Main Characters
          section of the Story Map.

Report:   Our group said the Main Characters were............
```

FIGURE 9.2 ── ◆

A Prompt Card For the Leader Routine From: Mathes, P.G., Fuchs, D., & Fuchs, L.S. (1997). Cooperative Story Mapping. *Remedial and Special Education*, 18(1), 20–27. Copyright ©1997 by PRO-ED, Inc. Reprinted by permission.

of team goals depends on all team members learning the objectives. "The students' tasks are not to **do** something as a team but to **learn** something as a team" (Slavin, p. 73). Team rewards, individual accountability, and equal opportunities for success are concepts that are central to STL methods. As described by Slavin,

> using STL techniques, teams earn certificates or other team rewards if they achieve above a designated criterion. The teams are not in competition to earn scarce rewards; all (or none) of the teams may achieve the criterion in a given week. Individual accountability means that the team's success depends on the individual learning of all team members. This focuses the activity of the team members on explaining concepts to one another and making sure that everyone on the team is ready for a quiz or other assessment that they will take without teammate help. Equal opportunity for success means that students contribute to their teams by improving over their own past performances. This ensures that high, average, and low achievers are equally challenged to do their best and that the contributions of all team members will be valued (p. 73).

Slavin (1991) identifies four STL methods: Student Teams-Achievement Divisions (STAD) and Teams-Games-Tournaments (TGT), both of which are adaptable to many subjects and grade levels; Team Assisted Individualization (TAI) for mathematics in grades three through six; and Cooperative Integrated Reading and Composition (CIRC) for reading and writing instruction in grades three through five. Another cooperative learning technique that has received attention in the literature is called Numbered Heads Together (Kagan, 1990).

Student Teams-Achievement Divisions (STAD)

In the STAD approach, a heterogeneous group of students is divided into four-member teams. For example, after Ms. Stone presents a lesson, her students work within their teams to ensure that all have mastered the material. Then her students take individual quizzes independently. Students' quiz grades are compared to their own past grades and each student is awarded points based on the amount of improvement over earlier performances. The points of all team members are then combined to determine the team score. Teams reaching a predetermined criterion receive certificates or some other reinforcer.

STAD has been used for many subject areas at many grade levels. Slavin (1991), however, suggests that it works best with fact-oriented material, such as math computations, language usage, geography and map skills, and science facts.

Teams-Games-Tournaments (TGT)

The TGT approach is structured around teams working together also, but weekly tournaments take the place of the quizzes of STAD. In the tournaments, students compete with members of the other teams to provide points for their team. In Mr. McNally's class, the tournaments take place at tournament tables, each with three to four students of comparable abilities. The winner of each table contributes the same number of points to his or her team, regardless of which table played. This method ensures equal opportunity for success for low achievers who compete against low achievers and high achievers who compete against high achievers. High-performing teams earn the rewards (Slavin, 1991).

Team Assisted Individualization (TAI)

TAI also uses learning teams with members of mixed ability. The high-performing teams, as in TGT and STAD, receive certificates. However, the approach combines cooperative learning with individualized instruction and is designed to teach mathematics to students in grades three through six. Students are placed in an individualized mathematics sequence based on their scores on a placement test. Team members work on different units, help each other with problems, then check each other's work. The unit tests are taken independently, and team rewards are determined by points assigned for passing scores and perfect papers. Using this method, the amount of materials management that teachers must do is reduced. Teachers are able to spend time giving instruction to small groups of students who are working on the same objectives (Slavin, 1991).

TAI uses the same motivational factors as STAD and TGT, with students encouraging and helping one another so that the team can succeed. The individualization of TAI, however, is what distinguishes it from STAD and TGT. Because most concepts in mathematics are built on prerequisite concepts, students must master the prerequisites before later skills can be mastered. In TAI, since students are working at their own levels, they have the opportunity to master the prerequisites before moving on to higher-level concepts. TAI depends on a specific set of instructional materials that cover skills and concepts from addition to algebra. The materials include lesson guides with suggested methods for introducing mathematics with manipulatives, demonstrations, and examples (Slavin, 1987).

Cooperative Integrated Reading and Composition (CIRC)

Cooperative Integrated Reading and Composition is a program for teaching reading and writing in upper elementary school. The teacher uses a basal or literature-based reading series and traditional reading groups (see Chapter 11). For example, while Ms. Kirk is meeting with the "Blue Jays," pairs of students from the "Cardinals" and the "Orioles" are working together on other activities, such as reading to one another, making predictions, practicing spelling and vocabulary, or completing other comprehension activities. The sequence is generally teacher instruction; team practice; team pre-assessments, during which team members determine who is ready for the quiz; and quizzes. Teams receive certificates based on the average performance of team members on all of the activities (Slavin, 1991).

Numbered Heads Together

According to Kagan (1990), Numbered Heads Together is a cooperative learning structure that can be used with almost any subject matter at almost any grade level. It has been described as a "teacher questioning strategy designed to actively engage all students during adult-led instruction and discussion" (Maheady, Mallette, Harper, & Sacca, 1991, p. 25). In most teacher-questioning situations, the students are forced to compete for teacher attention and praise. As one student is called on to respond, the others lose their turn; moreover, should a student give an incorrect response, there may be additional loss of teacher attention and praise (Kagan, 1990). Numbered Heads Together provides a way to increase the participation of students with lower achievement, at the same time maintaining the participation of those with higher achievement. As described by Maheady, Mallett, Harper, & Sacca, Numbered Heads Together works in the following way:

> First, students are placed into small (four-member) heterogeneous learning teams consisting of one high achieving, two average achieving, and one low achieving pupil(s). Students number themselves 1 to 4 and sit together during teacher-directed lessons. After the teacher directs a question to the entire class, pupils are instructed to "put their heads together, come up with their best answer, and make sure that everyone on the team knows the answer." The teacher then asks, "How many Number ____ (1, 2, 3, or 4,) know the answer?" After one randomly selected student responds, the teacher can ask, "How many other Number ____ agree with that answer?" or, "Can any Number ____ expand upon the answer?" Teachers then recognize and/or reward all students who provide or agree with correct answers, as well as those who offer meaningful expansions. Since students are given time to discuss possible answers prior to responding, it is more likely that everyone, including low achievers, will know the correct responses. Moreover, since teams cannot predict which group member will be called upon to respond, they are more likely to ensure that everyone knows the answer.

Forming Cooperative Teams

Kagan (1990) identifies four major types of team structure for cooperative learning groups: (a) heterogeneous teams, (b) random groups, (c) interest groups, and

(d) homogeneous/heterogeneous language-ability groups. Each type has its advantages and disadvantages. For example, if heterogeneous grouping is the only formation, then high achievers never have the opportunity for the academic stimulation of interaction with each other, and low achievers are likely to miss leadership opportunities since they are never on the same team. Conversely, according to Kagan, the exclusive use of homogeneous grouping eliminates the opportunity for peer tutoring and support.

Heterogeneous groups may be formed by placing one high achiever, two average achievers, and one low achiever on each team. The teacher assigns the teams, ensuring heterogeneity of ability, gender, and ethnicity. Nonheterogeneous teams may be formed by allowing students to group themselves according to their own friendships or interests, or by random selection in which students draw a number for team assignments. Each of these team formation methods, however, may pose problems. Self-selection runs the risk of promoting cliques of students, with some being the "in" groups and others being the "out" groups. Random selection may produce "loser" groups, with those students having the lowest achievement being assigned to the same team. For these reasons, teacher-selected, heterogeneous groups are generally preferred. Sometimes, however, the teacher may find that other team formations will meet the needs of the class (Kagan, 1990). Figure 9.3 presents Kagan's approach for forming heterogeneous teams.

To facilitate the formation of cooperative learning groups, teachers may choose to use a classroom sociogram (Peck 1989). (See Figure 9.4 for the Sociometric Grid.) Students with high group status are identified by the sociogram. These students will have demonstrated the ability to influence their peers. The teacher then can strategically place students with high ratings in cooperative learning groups to maximize positive peer pressure.

When the teacher chooses to use random teams, a simple method for assigning team members is to have students draw numbers from a hat. The Puzzled People method uses a picture torn into four parts, four sentences in a content-related statement, or four lines of a proverb or poem (Kagan, 1990). The steps for Puzzled People using torn pictures are as follows:

1. Have students tear pictures into four parts.
2. Have them mill around the room and trade pieces—each with one other person. (They keep their hand raised until they have made a trade, so those who have not yet traded can see who to trade with.)
3. Then, let them solve the puzzle by grouping with the others who hold pieces of the same picture.

Random teams offer variety, a perception of fairness, and the opportunity to transfer skills to a new group. As stated previously, however, this method might lead to the four lowest achievers in the class being in the same group. Generally, random groups cannot stay together for as long a period of time as heterogeneous teams can (Kagan, 1990).

Occasionally, teachers find it useful to allow students to form their own teams. For certain projects, allowing students with similar interests to explore a topic in depth results in learning opportunities not otherwise possible. Sometimes permitting best friends to work together brings new energy into learning (Kagan, 1990).

Step 1: Rank Order Students. Produce a numbered list of students, from highest to lowest achiever. The list does not have to be perfect. To produce the list, use one of the following (in order of preference): pretest, recent past test, past grades, or best guess.

Step 2: Select Team 1. Choose top, bottom, and two middle achievers. Assign them to Team 1, unless a) they are all of one sex; b) they do not mirror the ethnic composition of the class; c) they are worst enemies or best friends; d) they are unfavored choices on the Sociometric Grid (See Figure 9.4). In these cases, you move up or down one student from the middle to readjust.

Step 3: Select Remaining Teams. To produce Team 2, repeat Step 2 with the reduced list. Then use the even further reduced list to assign to Teams 3, 4, and so on. If you end up with one or two students left over, distribute them to other teams so that you have one or two five-member teams (pick teams with a frequently absent student); with three left over, have a team of three.

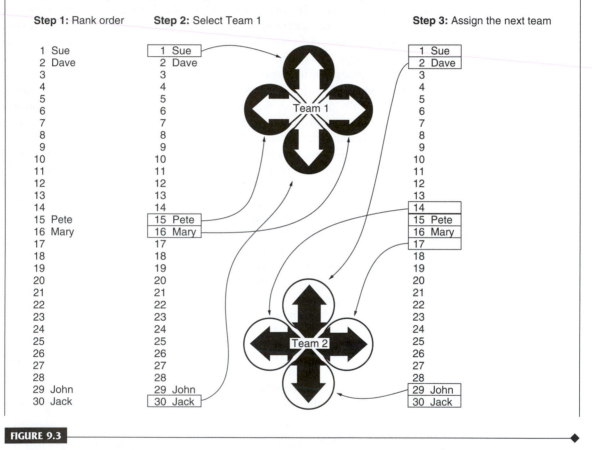

Step 1: Rank order   **Step 2:** Select Team 1   **Step 3:** Assign the next team

---

FIGURE 9.3

How to Form Heterogeneous Teams: Teacher Assignments Using the Ranked-List Approach From: Kagan, S. (1990). *Cooperative learning: Resources for teachers.* San Juan Capistrano, CA: Resources for Teachers.

A fourth basis of team formation is homogeneous grouping by language abilities or needs. At certain times in the instructional cycle (for example, when teachers have students with limited English proficiency), teams formed by homogeneous English language ability are necessary. However, as Kagan (1990)

This approach was developed by Susan Masters and Lucille Tambara (Maple Hill Elementary School, Diamond Bar, CA). It allows consideration of the relations among students. To use the Sociometric Grid, first present students with a list of their classmates and have them place a plus by the names of the three persons they would most like on their team and a minus or check mark by the names of the three persons they would least like to be on their team. For instructions consider:

> "We are forming new teams and to form the best teams possible I would like to know your preferences. Here is a list of your classmates. Please put a plus by the names of the three classmates you would most like to have on a team for the next six weeks, and a check mark by three people you would prefer not to be on a team with this time. You may want to make new friends, so you might place a check mark by the names of your best friends. I cannot promise you will be on a team with someone you have given a plus, or that you will not be on a team with someone you have given a check, but I will consider your preferences when I make the new team assignments."

Next, make a grid which contains all of that information, like so:

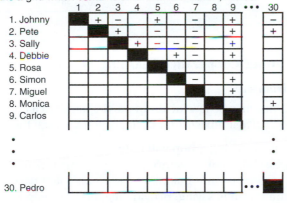

In the sociometric grid above, the choices of each student toward each other are indicated by a +, −, or blank. The black squares are filled in to indicate that students cannot nominate themselves. Thus, Johnny indicated he would like to have as teammates students 2 (Pete), 5 (Rosa), and 9 (Carlos), and that he would prefer not to have as teammates students 3 (Sally), 7 (Miguel), and 30 (Pedro). Note, the chart is filled out with the choices for only the first four students. Carlos is very popular; Miguel is very unpopular.

For teacher's use: Write in the three pluses and three minuses following the name of each student, indicating their preferences. While assigning teams you may wish to avoid pairing students if a minus occurs. Although some students may not be a favorite of anyone, and may have quite a number of students who do not want to be on their team, it is almost always possible to find at least three others for whom the unpopular student is not a least favored alternative. You may want also to avoid certain pluses as they represent "best friends" who can pair, minimizing interaction along many lines within teams.

FIGURE 9.4　◆

The Sociometric Grid From: Kagan, S. (1990). *Cooperative learning: Resources for teachers*. San Juan Capistrano, CA: Resources for Teachers, p. 64.

points out, "while homogeneous by language, an attempt is still made to make the team heterogeneous on other dimensions such as content ability, sex, and, if possible, ethnic background. Thus the team is really a homogeneous language/heterogeneous ability team" (p. 69).

Integrating Students with Disabilities into Cooperative Learning Groups

When students with mild disabilities are in general education classes, teachers may need to make special efforts so that the cooperative learning process can be as effective as possible. For example, Johnson and Johnson (1986) point out that (a) students with disabilities may be fearful and anxious about participating in groups, (b) students without disabilities may be afraid that their grades will be affected by having students with disabilities in their groups, and (c) students with disabilities may be passive and withdrawn in the group. Box 9.3 offers some suggestions for dealing with these issues.

Box 9.3

Overcoming Concerns about Cooperative Learning Groups

Anxious Students with Disabilities

Many students with disabilities may be fearful about participating in a cooperative learning group with nondisabled peers. Their anxiety may be alleviated through the following actions:

1. Explain the procedures the learning group will follow.
2. Give the students with disabilities a structured role so that they understand their responsibilities. Even if a student cannot read, he or she can listen carefully and summarize what everyone in the group is saying, provide leadership, help to keep the group's work organized, and so forth. There is always some way to facilitate group work, no matter what disability a student may have.
3. Enlist the aid of a special education teacher to coach the students with disabilities on the behaviors and collaborative skills needed within the cooperative group. Pretraining in collaborative skills and periodic sessions to monitor how well the skills are being implemented will increase the confidence of the students with disabilities.
4. Enlist the aid of a special education teacher to pretrain the students with disabilities in the academic skills needed to complete the group's work. Try to give the students with disabilities a source of expertise the group will need.

Anxious Nondisabled Students

Many nondisabled students may be concerned that the students with disabilities will lower the overall performance of their group. The three major ways of alleviating their concerns are as follows:

1. Train nondisabled students in helping, tutoring, teaching, and sharing skills. The special education teacher may wish to explain to the group how best to teach the group member. Many teaching skills, such as the use of praise and prompting, are easily taught to students.
2. Make the academic requirements for the students with disabilities reasonable. Ways in which lessons can be adapted so the students at different achievement levels can participate in the same cooperative group follow:
   a. Use different criteria for success for each group member.
   b. Vary the amount each group member is expected to master.

c. Give group members different assignments, lists, work, or problems and then use the average percentage worked correctly as the group's score.

d. Use improvement scores for the students with disabilities. If it is unclear how to implement these procedures, consult with the special education teacher to decide what is appropriate for the specific student.

3. Give bonus points to the groups that have students with disabilities. This will create a situation in which nondisabled students want to work with their classmates with disabilities to receive the bonus points.

Passively Uninvolved Students with Disabilities

When students with disabilities are turning away from the group, not participating, not paying attention to the group's work, saying little or nothing, showing no enthusiasm, or not bringing their work or materials, the teacher may wish to try the following:

1. Jigsawing materials so that each group member has information the others need. If the passively uninvolved student does not voluntarily contribute his or her information, the other group members will actively involve the student.

2. Divide roles and assign the passively uninvolved student one that is essential to the group's success.

3. Reward the group on the basis of average performance. This will encourage other group members to derive strategies for increasing the problem member's involvement.

From: Johnson, D.W., & Johnson, R.T. (1986). Mainstreaming and cooperative learning strategies. *Exceptional Children*, 52(6), 555-560. Council for Exceptional Children. Reprinted by permission.

◆

According to Cohen (1998), teachers can make cooperative learning groups equitable for students with disabilities or those with limited English proficiency by creating a set of mixed expectations for everyone. Teachers must tell students that the cooperative tasks will require many different types of abilities and that no one will have all of these abilities. Ms. Kirk, for example, might explain to her students that some of them will be good at observing what happens during a science experiment and others will be good at constructing a model to explain the scientific principle involved. Still others will be good at writing an explanation in a report. All of these abilities will be needed for the group to do the best possible job. Cohen also encourages teachers to make the competence of all group members, particularly those of low status, known through specific, truthful, and public statements.

Although cooperative learning arrangements provide students with extra support and encouragement, they are not a panacea, nor are they always appropriate for all students with mild disabilities. Students with behavioral disorders or mild mental retardation, for example, may negatively affect the participation and listening of group members (Pomplun, 1997). In addition, cooperative learning groups are not the only means by which students can help one another. Peer tutoring offers teachers yet another promising effective technique to increase instructional time and academic achievement in the classroom (Forness, Kavale, Blum & Lloyd, 1997).

Peer Tutoring

Within every classroom the potential exists for additional instructional assistance for teachers pressed for time and resources. Students who have reached a higher level of achievement can be trained to tutor classmates who are not achieving as well. Peer tutoring provides teachers with a way of ensuring that every student will receive additional instruction and/or practice that may be needed in acquiring particular skills. Peer tutoring may take the form of same-age tutors, cross-age tutors, regular class students tutoring students with mild disabilities, students with mild disabilities tutoring other students with disabilities, students with mild disabilities tutoring students without disabilities, and class-wide peer tutoring arrangements.

Peer tutoring offers a number of advantages to both tutors and tutees. Peer tutoring promotes interaction between two students by allowing them to work with and help each other. Moreover, some children learn better from other students than from an adult, perhaps because the communication is more direct and straightforward, or perhaps because the tutors remember what the problems were when they were learning the material, and thus can explain it better. Both tutors and tutees tend to sharpen their academic skills as a result of reviewing the material. For example, peer tutoring has been shown to improve the reading skills of students with disabilities, particularly when they serve in the role of tutor (Mathes & Fuchs, 1994). Students who act as tutors also gain confidence (Eiserman, 1988). According to Yasutake, Bryan, and Dohrn (1996), when tutors are trained in tutoring procedures, as well as in making positive attribution statements such as, "You're really putting a lot of effort into this work," both tutors and tutees improve their perceived competence.

Same-Age Tutorial Programs

Same-age or same-grade tutorial programs may be implemented from preschool to college. Using students to tutor their classmates is probably the most prevalent form of peer tutoring because teachers do not have to be involved in a specific program with other teachers in order to initiate the process. In the classroom, teachers can use peers to drill each other, check each other's work, and reinforce teacher instruction.

Same-age peer tutoring between students with and without disabilities helps those with mild disabilities to improve academically and stimulates others to be creative in their approaches to learning. The opportunity to interact and to learn about one another that peer tutoring affords all students is, however, the most important aspect of the program. "Students are able to interact on a regular basis and to grow in their knowledge that all people are more alike—and special—than they are different" (Henrico County Public Schools, 1989, p. iv).

In one middle school in Virginia, talented and gifted students designed a peer-tutoring program for students with learning disabilities, mild mental retardation, and behavioral disorders, as well as for those for whom English is a second language (ESL) (Henrico County Public Schools, 1989). To participate in the tutoring program, students in the talented and gifted program must complete an application, conduct research to learn about educational, social, physical, and psychological needs of special education students, and take an examination. Once accepted into the peer tutoring program and trained in methods for tutoring, student tutors work under the supervision of an experienced tutor. Sometimes a group of tutors will work with an entire special education class, but most tutoring is done on a one-on-one basis. Tutoring sessions usually take place once or twice a week, but some tutors schedule more sessions. All tutors work under the supervision of a faculty member.

The tutoring manual, *Tutoring: Lending a helping hand*, was written by a group of students in the talented and gifted program under the guidance of their teacher (Henrico County Public Schools, 1989). The students have included such topics as "Lesson Plans," "Confidentiality," and "Rewards" in their manual, as well as observation forms, the tutoring calendar, lesson-plan forms, a tutoring record, and the tutor's pledge. The manual gives background information on each of the types of disabilities and tips and techniques for tutoring students with disabilities. (See Table 9.1 for the tips that these students recommend.)

Class-Wide Peer Tutoring

Class-Wide Peer Tutoring (CWPT) is one version of same-age tutoring that has been researched extensively (Greenwood, 1991; Greenwood, Delquadri, & Hall, 1989). The procedure is a variation on cooperative learning because students within the same classroom work with one another to help each other learn and to earn points for their team. To conduct CWPT, the teacher divides the class into two teams. Within each team are heterogeneous tutoring pairs. Sometimes the tutoring pairs are of similar ability, and sometimes they contain one student with high achievement and another with low achievement. Students in each tutoring pair take turns teaching each other the skills. One student serves as the tutor, teaching and monitoring the skill of his or her partner and assigning points based on the partner's performance. Then the two students reverse roles.

CWPT usually takes place in approximately thirty-minute sessions two to four days per week. During tutoring sessions, each partner spends approximately ten minutes as the tutor and ten minutes as the tutee, with the remaining ten minutes used for assigning, tallying, and reporting points. Following the tutoring session, the teacher obtains the scores from every student in the class and also assigns bonus points for students who exhibited particularly noteworthy cooperative or work-related behaviors. The points for each tutoring pair are then totaled to obtain scores for the two teams.

CWPT has been used to improve the academic performance of students in basic skills such as spelling, recognition of sight words, and math facts at both the elementary and secondary levels (Maheady & Harper, 1987; Maheady, Sacca, & Harper, 1988). Allsopp (1997) also reports that CWPT can be used to improve higher-level thinking skills such as algebraic problem solving. Similarly, others suggest that CWPT can be used to improve skills in areas such as health and safety or social studies (Reddy et al., 1999).

Several variations of CWPT exist. For example, in Peabody Class-Wide Peer Tutoring, or Peabody Peer-Assisted Learning (PALS), all tutoring pairs contain both a higher- and a lower-performing student (Fuchs, Fuchs, Mathes, & Simmons, 1997; Mathes, Fuchs, Fuchs, Henley, & Sanders, 1994). Both students

Table 9.1 Tips and Techniques for Tutoring Students with Mild Disabilities

1. Make a calendar showing when you are to tutor and keep it handy. Never skip a tutoring session.
2. Schedule frequent talks with the teacher to understand the individual needs of each student and to discuss problems and progress.
3. Know beforehand what you are going to be tutoring so that you can plan ahead. Ask to borrow copies of textbooks and workbooks.
4. Always keep a record of whom you tutored, when you tutored, and what subjects you taught. You need these records to help monitor your students' progress.
5. Be a good role model. Always use good manners and be considerate.
6. Be patient. Remember that the student needs a lot of time to learn something new.
7. Keep the student on task. Ask questions to get him to pay attention.
8. Never do the student's work for him. When he gets stuck, ask questions that lead him to find the answer for himself.
9. When working on reading, read aloud with the student. Ask her to read the first paragraph. Then you read the next one. Continue alternating until the assignment is finished. Remember to ask questions at the end of each paragraph to be sure that the student understands what has been read before starting a new paragraph.
10. When the student stumbles over a hard word in a reading assignment, use a folded piece of paper to cover up all but the first part of the word. Have the student sound out the first part, then move the paper to the right just enough to show the second part of the word. Continue gradually moving the paper to the right until the student has sounded out the whole word. Have the student repeat the word until he is comfortable with it. Come back to the same word a few more times as you continue reading to be sure that the student really knows it.
11. Make flashcards to teach new vocabulary words. Use the set of cards several times to be sure that the student knows the words. Also use flashcards to review basic mathematics skills.
12. When working on written assignments, do not allow the student to settle for phrases and incomplete sentences. Encourage her to write a complete sentence by asking questions (who, what, when, where, how, why).
13. When working on math problems involving more than one column of numbers, have the student use a folded sheet of paper to cover one column while he works out the other one.
14. Use pictures and objects to illustrate concepts. They make learning interesting and fun and help students understand abstract concepts. For example, use concrete objects to illustrate fractions or concepts from geometry. Use maps in history to show where specific events took place.
15. Be positive and give lots of praise. Try to avoid using words like *wrong* or *incorrect*. If the student gives a wrong answer, say something like, "Let's try that again," and be ready to ask questions to lead the student in the right direction.
16. Review, review, and review even more. Students often learn best when something is repeated many times.
17. Be a good friend. Listen to the student and ask questions about her interests. Be friendly whenever you see her at school.
18. At the beginning of each session, ask the student to tell you what the assignment for the day is. Ask him why it is important to know what he is studying.
19. If you have access to a computer, find or write some educational games to use as rewards. Help the students learn to use word-processing programs.
20. If the student says something negative to you during the tutoring session, do not get upset. Remain calm and ask, "Do you really mean what you said or are you just frustrated?" Most of the time the student will admit that he was frustrated. Take time to talk about his feelings and then get him back on task by asking questions.

21. Use your knowledge about the student's personal interests when making up practice problems and exercises. For example, when studying grammar and composition, create sentences about favorite topics.
22. Make pictures and diagrams to illustrate lessons that require reading and comprehension. Playing games like Win, Lose, or Draw, Pictionary, Trivial Pursuit, or Jeopardy can be helpful.
23. Help students develop a system of highlighting in their notes. For example, in history notes, all dates could be highlighted in one color and the names of people in another color.
24. After passages have been read or concepts have been taught, ask the student to explain orally what she has learned. Do not ask questions like, "Do you understand?" or accept the answer, "Yes, I do." Be sure to have the student demonstrate that understanding has occurred.
25. Be careful never to talk about tutoring when other students are around.

Adapted From: Henrico County Public Schools, (1989). *Tutoring: Lending a helping hand.* Richmond, VA: Henrico County Public Schools, Programs for Gifted and Talented, pp. 6-14.

in the pair still serve as tutor and tutee; however, the higher performing student serves as the tutor first. In addition, points are kept by the pairs on a weekly card and assigned to the team at the end of the week. After four weeks, new pairs are formed and new team assignments made.

In another variation of CWPT, Peer-Assisted Learning Strategies for First-Grade Readers (First-Grade PALS), strong and weak first-grade readers are paired (Mathes, Grek, Howard, Babyak, & Allen, 1999). The stronger partner tutors first, and then the two reverse roles. Again, the teacher assigns each pair to a team and computes the points for each team. In this approach, however, tutoring focuses on phonological awareness as well as on making predictions, reading, and summarizing stories.

Cross-Age Peer Tutoring

Peer tutoring benefits both the tutor and the tutee, especially when the tutors are students with mild disabilities. The use of students with mild disabilities as tutors for younger children with lower-level skills offers promise for reinforcing concepts that students in special education programs have learned. Robert, for example, might benefit from helping a younger child like Travis practice reading or math skills. Schrader and Valus (1990) describe a tutoring program that uses high school students with severe learning disabilities in a cross-age tutoring project. These students provide reading instruction to primary-grade students who are having difficulty with reading. The tutors are trained in such teacher behaviors as "giving clear directions, giving positive and corrective feedback, and avoiding over prompting. [They] are also trained in the use of established techniques for teaching reading" (pp. 590-591). The tutors spend one class period per day for a nine-week period in this project.

Peer-tutoring activities, when carefully structured and supervised by teachers, can be an effective technique for increasing the academic learning time of students in both regular and special education classrooms. Sometimes, however, students must engage in independent learning activities. In these instances, teachers need to help students take greater responsibility for their own learning.

Cognitive Behavior Modification Strategies

Education involves more than just providing students with a body of knowledge or a set of skills. Teachers are also concerned with training students to know how to learn and how to assume responsibility for themselves. Cognitive Behavior Modification (CBM) offers the teacher effective procedures for helping students take charge of their own learning and control their own behaviors (Forness et al., 1997; Meichenbaum, 1981).

Teachers cannot be expected to keep a classroom full of students actively involved in the education process all the time. However, students with learning or behavior problems frequently become passive learners. They depend on teachers to direct their learning, control their behavior, and reward their performance. Teachers cannot be expected to monitor every student's actions and reinforce every response. Students must be taught to take responsibility for their own performance. For teacher and student well-being, students must learn to act independently so that reliance on teacher direction is reduced. Students, however, may not know how to take responsibility for their own learning and behavior. CBM may be used to teach students learning strategies and to improve their academic performance and behavior in the classroom (Williams & Rooney, 1986).

Cognitive behavior modification procedures may be adapted to fit numerous classroom tasks that students must perform. These procedures include self-management strategies such as self-monitoring and self-recording, self-reinforcement, and self-instruction. In addition, instructional models based on cognitive behavior modification procedures are available. The most well-known and best researched of these are the Strategic Instruction Model developed by researchers at the University of Kansas Institute for Research on Learning Disabilities (Deshler & Schumaker, 1988), and the mnemonic strategies developed by Mastropieri and Scruggs (1991, 2000).

Self-Management Strategies

Whenever we try to regulate our own behaviors to accomplish specific tasks we are using self-management strategies. For example, you might set a goal for yourself to read a certain number of pages in the textbook each day for a class you are taking. Then you might monitor your progress and give yourself a small daily reward for meeting your goal. If students with mild disabilities are to become more on-task, academically productive, and independent in the classroom, they must learn to self-monitor, self-instruct, and self-reinforce.

Self-monitoring and self-recording. Self-monitoring is a simple self-management technique that can be used for a variety of academic or social behaviors. If you are trying to lose weight, for example, you might be aware of the number of calories you consume at each meal or your daily weight from the bathroom scale. In order to self-monitor, students must first observe their own behavior and then evaluate whether or not they have accomplished a specific goal. Self-assessment is an important component of any self-monitoring procedure (Sainato, Strain, Lefebvre, & Rapp, 1990).

Following self-assessment, students can self-record their behaviors. Self-recording is a simple and effective way for students to monitor their behavior (McDougall, 1998). To construct a visible and permanent reminder of behavior, students can place a mark on a checklist or self-monitoring form each time they demonstrate a particular targeted behavior (see Figure 9.5). For example, you might record your daily weight or keep a written account of the calories you consume. Merely counting the behavior makes the student more aware of behaviors that are present or absent, and thus the behavior improves. In addition, students can construct a graph in conjunction with any self-recording system. Joey can self-monitor and graph his oral reading rate, the number of "talk-outs" occurring during class time, or the number of "polite" words such as *please* and *thank you* that he uses during one-hour periods. Similarly, Travis can graph the number of arithmetic problems he correctly completes during three-minute timed probes, and Robert can graph the amount of time he spends studying each day. Plotting recorded information on a graph provides students with a visual display of behavior and can serve as a form of self-reinforcement.

Self-monitoring and self-recording have been used to help children change numerous behaviors in both special and general education classrooms. Teachers have helped students reduce their disruptive outbursts (Hogan & Prater, 1993), increased the time that students with attention deficits spent on task (Hallahan, Lloyd, Kosiewicz, Kauffman, & Graves, 1979; Mathes & Bender,

	Yes	No
Am I working?		
Did I stay in my seat?		
Did I complete my work?		

FIGURE 9.5 ◆

A Sample Self-Recording Form From: Johnson, L.R., & Johnson, C.E. (1999). Teaching students to regulate their own behavior. *Teaching Exceptional Children, 31*(4), 6–10. Reprinted by permission.

1997), and improved math fluency (McDougall & Brady, 1998) through the use of self-monitoring. In addition, self-monitoring procedures have helped students match their teacher's expectations for appropriate class behaviors (e.g., being on time, completing homework and class assignments, bringing materials to class) (Clees, 1995) and engage in creative story writing (Glomb & West, 1990; Martin & Manno, 1995).

According to Maag, Reid, and DiGangi (1993), self-monitoring of academic productivity and accuracy is more effective than self-monitoring of on-task behavior alone. Moreover, structured teaching methods such as the following are needed to ensure that students with mild disabilities will self-monitor and self-record properly (Dunlap, Dunlap, Koegel, & Keogel, 1991; Graham, Harris, & Reid, 1992; Hallahan, Lloyd, & Stoller, 1982; O'Leary & Dubey, 1979):

◆ Define the behavior in observable terms. Demonstrate the behavior for the student and be sure he or she can identify examples and nonexamples of the targeted behavior. Elicit the student's involvement and ensure the behavior is one that he or she perceives is important to change.

◆ Identify reinforcers and allow the student to deliver these to himself or herself whenever possible.

◆ Design a self-monitoring device. Use sticker charts, checklists, or graphs. Be sure the system is age appropriate and as inconspicuous as possible.

◆ Teach the child to use the self-monitoring device. Be explicit in demonstrating both the self-monitoring and self-recording procedures. Give the child many opportunities to practice with specific feedback regarding his or her performance.

◆ Don't worry if the student is not completely accurate when self-monitoring. Research suggests that self-assessment and self-monitoring need not be totally accurate for the procedure to be effective in changing the behavior. Of course, if the self-monitoring does not result in a positive behavioral change, the teacher may need to train and reward accuracy before the student self-monitors.

◆ Systematically reduce the cues to self-monitor by fading, for example, the self-recording sheet.

Self-reinforcement. After students self-monitor and self-record, they must reward themselves for engaging in appropriate behavior rather than wait for the teacher to do so. When you are studying for a class, for example, you might reward yourself for a period of "good studying" by watching your favorite television program or talking to a friend. Similarly, Travis might be taught to tell himself, "I'm doing a good job at paying attention!" as he is working at his desk. According to DiGangi and Maag (1992), self-reinforcement is most effective when it is used with an explicit self-monitoring procedure.

In the classroom, students select reasonable reinforcers they wish to earn and assist teachers in determining the standard of performance necessary for earning the chosen rewards. Research suggests that teacher-determined and student-determined reinforcement demonstrate equal effectiveness, so allow students to determine and administer their own rewards whenever possible (Hayes et al., 1985). The following guidelines may help teachers use self-reinforcement with their students:

- ◆ Be sure students are proficient with the self-monitoring procedure before using self-reinforcement.
- ◆ Obtain the student's help in determining the targeted behavior, the reinforcement, and the behavior-to-reinforcement ratio.
- ◆ Precede student self-reinforcement with teacher delivery of reinforcement.
- ◆ Slowly turn responsibility for reinforcement over to the student by having both the student and the teacher decide whether or not reinforcement should take place. Reward the student's accuracy in matching the teacher's decision.
- ◆ Gradually fade the teacher's reinforcement, but check periodically and reward the student's accuracy.

Self-instruction. Self-instructional strategies teach students to "talk themselves through" many academic and behavioral tasks. Donald Meichenbaum (1977), one of the originators of self-instructional training, based his work on the research of Luria (1961) and Vygotsky (1962), who investigated the role of language in guiding the behavior of children. They noticed, for example, that a child's behavior seemed to be under the control of an adult's overt language first. Later, the child's overt language controls his or her own behavior, and finally, behavior is regulated through the child's covert speech, that is, his or her private thoughts. Our overt language and covert self-talk both appear to mediate, or guide, our behaviors.

You might remember, for example, first learning how to do a particular dance. Someone probably told you how to do the steps and said them out loud as you attempted the dance. Later, as you practiced, you might have said the steps aloud, "Right foot, left foot . . . ," to guide yourself through the dance. Finally, these instructions became internalized and you simply thought about the steps as you danced.

Meichenbaum (1977) suggests the following general steps be used when conducting self-instructional training:

1. The teacher performs the task while talking aloud (cognitive modeling). The demonstration of one's thought processes should include
   a. a problem definition ("What is it I have to do? I have to get these 15 math problems finished before the bell."),
   b. a statement to focus attention and guide the response ("I need to work slowly and carefully."),
   c. a statement of self-reinforcement ("I'm doing a good job."), and
   d. a statement modeling coping skills or ways to handle errors ("It's okay. I can erase that mistake and start again.").
2. The child performs the task under the direction of the teacher (i.e., overt, external guidance).

3. The child performs the task while instructing himself or herself aloud (i.e., overt self-guidance).
4. The child whispers the instructions while performing the task (i.e., faded, overt self-guidance).
5. The child performs the task while guiding himself or herself via private speech (i.e., covert self-instruction).

Meichenbaum (1981) urges teachers to permit students to use their own verbalizations for self-instruction whenever possible. Furthermore, he suggests that not all students will need to follow all of the steps in self-instructional training, particularly Step 4, whispering to guide oneself through the task. Meichenbaum offers the following additional guidelines for teachers using self-instructional training:

1. Analyze the target behavior including all requirements for successful performance.
2. Listen for ineffective strategies the child currently is using.
3. Select training tasks that approximate the target behavior.
4. Involve the child in devising the self-instructions.
5. Make sure the child has the necessary component skills before beginning self-instructional training.
6. Tell the child how the self-instructions will be useful for his or her academic or social performance.
7. Point out specific tasks and settings where the self-instructions can be used.
8. Use many different trainers, tasks, and settings to promote generalization.
9. Include specific coping skills to help the student manage failure.
10. Practice until a specific criterion level is reached, then systematically provide follow-up maintenance sessions.

Teaching Learning Strategies

Because most students are never taught how to learn, many students with and without mild disabilities struggle with the learning process. They often need direct instruction in learning how to learn, or learning strategies. For example, in the inclusion classroom, especially in the content areas such as science and social studies, students like Robert are expected to read the text, participate in class discussions, take notes, study, and take tests in the same manner as students without disabilities. Yet, students with learning problems frequently have difficulty with those skills. A common complaint that teachers have about students with mild disabilities is their lack of preparation for classes, that is, their failure to have pencil, paper, homework, books, or assignments with them. Thus, if students with mild disabilities are to survive in the mainstream, they must be taught how to organize themselves, participate in class, and study efficiently.

Using Cognitive Behavior Modification and self-instructional training as a foundation, researchers have developed numerous learning strategies to help students become organized, correctly complete their work, and remember information they need to know (Scruggs & Mastropieri, 1989; Deshler & Schumaker, 1988). The Strategic Instruction Model and mnemonic strategy instruction are two well-researched approaches for teaching learning strategies to students with mild disabilities.

The Strategic Instruction Model. The ultimate purpose of cognitive behavior modification and strategy training is independence. With the emphasis that CBM places on the self, the student is learning not to depend solely on the teacher or anyone else for control, instruction, or reinforcement. The student is also enhancing self-confidence and self-esteem by knowing that he or she has the ability to gain self-control. In order to promote this independence, researchers at the University of Kansas devised the Strategic Instruction Model (Deshler & Schumaker, 1988; Ellis, Deshler, Lenz, Schumaker, & Clark, 1991). The model consists of two major parts: a learning strategies curriculum to teach students strategies for acquiring, storing, and expressing information learned in content classrooms (See Table 9.2 for examples of strategies from this curriculum); and content-enhancement routines to help teachers organize units and lessons so that students with mild disabilities can understand and recall difficult content (Boudah, Lenz, Bulgren, Schumaker, & Deshler, 2000; Tralli, Colombo, Deshler, & Schumaker, 1996). (See Chapter 14 for content enhancement routines and additional learning strategies.)

The learning strategies in the Strategic Instruction Model are taught using first-letter acronyms. That is, a keyword is constructed from the letters beginning each sequential step in the strategy. For example, one representative learning strategy described by Alley and Deshler (1979) is SCORER, a test-taking strategy designed to improve student performance on objective tests. The SCORER

Table 9.2 **Sample Learning Strategies from the Strategic Instruction Model**

The Learning Strategies Curriculum offers several strategies in three different strands: acquiring, storing, and expressing information.

Acquiring Information	Storing Information	Expressing Information and Demonstrating Competence
Interpreting	First-letter	Assignment completion
Visuals	Mnemonic	Error monitoring
Multipass	Listening and	Paragraph writing
Paraphrasing	note taking	Sentence writing
Self-questioning	Paired associates	Test taking
Visual imagery		Theme writing
Word idenfication		

(Note to Reader: Information about the Strategic Instruction Model may be obtained by writing to Coordinator, The Center for Research on Learning, 3061 Dole Center, University of Kansas, Lawrence, KS 66045-2342. Please note that you must receive training in the Strategic Instruction Model in order to obtain most of the materials from the CRL.)

strategy is taught using the procedures listed in Box 9.4, and the letters in the acronym, SCORER, stand for the following steps in the strategy:

S = Schedule your time. Allot more time for the harder questions and those with a greater point value.

C = Clue words. Look for tip-off words. For example, *all, always, none,* and *never* frequently indicate false answers. *Usually* and *sometimes* frequently indicate true answers.

O = Omit the difficult questions on the first pass. Mark the questions you skip with a light check mark in the margin.

R = Read your answers. Look for clues in other test items to help you answer questions you are uncertain about. Eliminate alternatives you are certain are incorrect, then make your best guess. When you have answered the easy questions, go back to the checked questions. If you are still uncertain about the answer, add another light check mark in the margin.

E = Estimate your answers. On test items that require calculations, roughly estimate the answer to help prevent careless errors.

R = Review your work. Read through all the questions as time permits. Don't be eager to change answers. Change only those you have a good reason for changing. Start with the questions with two check marks, then those with one check mark, then the unmarked questions. If there is no penalty for guessing, be sure to take your best guess and do not leave any questions blank.

Although not a part of the Strategic Instruction Model, the FORCE strategy that is described in Box 9.4 is a similar step-by-step procedure designed to assist students in preparing for tests. The FORCE strategy is also consistent with the guidelines for teaching learning strategies suggested by Deshler, Schumaker and their colleagues at the University of Kansas Institute for Research on Learning Disabilities (Deshler, Alley, Warner, & Schumaker, 1981).

For strategy training to be effective, however, the teacher should keep in mind several guidelines. The required task, the strategies currently in use by the student, the setting in which the task must be performed, the student's level of motivation, and the materials which the student must use are all important considerations in choosing the learning strategies to teach a particular student (Deshler & Schumaker, 1988). Teachers of students with mild disabilities should also follow the essential steps described in Box 9.4 when teaching learning strategies (Ellis et al., 1991). In addition, given the demands on teachers to cover subject matter, content-area teachers may not readily teach and reinforce learning strategies, even in the most cooperative and inclusive classrooms (Scanlon, Deshler, & Schumaker, 1996).

Mnemonic strategies. Students with mild disabilities may better remember content from subject area classes when their teachers use memory-enhancing devices, or *mnemonics*, during instruction (Mastropieri & Scruggs, 1991; Mastropieri, Scruggs, Whittaker, & Bakken, 1994). According to Scruggs and Mastropieri (1989), mnemonics involving *reconstructive elaborations* may assist students in the memorization of difficult vocabulary or complex information. To

Box 9.4

The Steps of FORCE

F = Find Out   Your teacher announces a test. If you don't receive all of the information that you need, ask questions. For example, "What will the test cover?", "What types of questions will be used?"

O = Organize   Collect all necessary materials for taking the test, such as notes, old tests, or books.

R = Review   Do the general review necessary to study for the test; for example, skim chapters, charts, maps, summaries, questions, or vocabulary from the text; highlight notes; review old tests and assignments.

C = Concentrate   Make a study sheet (cue sheet) by putting important information in question/answer form.

E = Early Exam   Practice the test by pretesting. For example, take turns asking questions with a partner or study buddy. Have your parents or other adults help you drill from your study sheet. Take your own test from your study sheet. Then review weak spots until you are certain of what you know. There may be a few items you want to review right before the test.

When teaching learning strategies, include the following important steps:

1. *Measure preskills, current study habits, and current attitudes* toward the learning strategy. A preskill and attitude questionnaire (developed by the teacher) can easily be presented in a true/false format. Example questions include the following: "I can take notes easily from the board"; "I keep most of my old tests, notes, and so forth"; "I do not feel frustrated when I take tests"; "I don't mind asking a teacher for help"; and "I have an obligation to ask questions when I need help." Results from this questionnaire and other student data, as well as teacher observation, help to establish whether a student is ready for instruction in the FORCE strategy. Preskills include knowledge of parts of a book, organizational skills, note taking, outlining, and knowledge of various test formats (e.g., objective, essay, matching). Approximately 75% mastery of preskills is needed prior to implementation of the strategy.

2. *Describe the new strategy* and how the previously-learned preskills relate to its effectiveness. Present a rationale for using the strategy. Why should a student bother to use it? A teacher might pose the following question to the class: "If I could show you a way to study for a test that would improve your grades in most cases, would you be interested?"

3. *Offer specific and isolated instruction of the strategy.* If the strategy is supposed to be important to the students, then it must be important to you, their teacher, to provide specific class time for instruction and implementation.

4. *Model each component of the strategy* using role play whenever possible. The teacher might say, for example, "F stands for FIND OUT. If the teacher announces a test, but doesn't fill you in on sufficient details about it, ask the appropriate questions at an appropriate time and in an appropriate manner. The keyword here seems to be 'appropriate'. Let's role play some appropriate and inappropriate questions and times."

5. *Rehearse verbally* with students often. There are always times of the day when one might say, "Which part of FORCE is that?" or "Which component of FORCE could you use to improve your grade?" Sometimes, one of the questions on a quiz could be, "What does the F stand for in FORCE?"

6. *Practice on controlled materials.* Begin implementation with high-interest materials that are at a comfortable reading level for the students. The primary concern at this point is for the students to learn the strategy.

7. *Practice on actual classroom materials.* It is important to use the strategy in a relevant situation as soon as possible. A pretest checklist can be given to students to assist them in monitoring their use of the strategy. Examples of items on the checklist are
   a. "What will the test cover? Notes, maps, old tests, chapter questions, handouts, homework assignments, text, worksheets?"
   b. "What pages in the text will be covered, if any?"

8. *Reinforce the use of the strategy* after the test with a post-test evaluation sheet (developed by the teacher). This questionnaire will help determine the extent to which the student used the strategy. Sample questions include, "Did you prepare a study sheet in a question/answer format from materials that were covered on the test?" and "Did you test yourself either alone or with another person by asking questions from a study sheet?" Also teach students to provide reinforcement for one another and for themselves. A conversation with Robert, who did not do as well on a test as he had a few weeks before, went something like this: "I usually study with Joe, but I didn't this week. Next week, I'll work with him. It seems to help—studying with him right before the test." At this point Mr. Abel may ask, "That's great you realize that, Robert. What part of FORCE is that?"

9. *Provide frequent opportunities to use the strategy.* It might be helpful to test frequently, at least once a week, in order to give the students plenty of chances to put the strategy into action.

10. *Chart the test scores and post-test evaluation sheets.* Evaluate the results and discuss with the students the relationships between the two graphs (test scores and information gained from post-test evaluation sheets). It is important to point out any pattern that establishes a correlation between test scores and strategy use.

11. *Explicitly suggest the use of FORCE in other classes.* If the teacher offers assistance to the students in self-monitoring and self-evaluation, students learn to depend on themselves to organize and study materials for tests. Frequent reminders help. This is an area in which parents can become powerful allies. They can remind students to use the strategy when studying other subjects and find ways in which the strategy can be used in the home setting.

From: Wehrung-Schaffner, L., & Sapona, R.H. (1990). May the FORCE be with you: A test preparation strategy for learning disabled adolescents. *Academic Therapy, 25*(3), pp. 293-296. Copyright ©1990 by PRO-ED, Inc. Reprinted by permission.

construct these mnemonic devices, teachers first list the terms to be learned that are unfamiliar to students. These are then "reconstructed" to acoustically similar, yet familiar, keywords. Finally, the familiar words are "elaborated" by creating a visual image of the familiar term connected to or interacting in some way with the information to be remembered.

For example, if Robert must remember that the Earth's mantle is made of solid rock, Ms. Stone might use a reconstructive elaboration. She might reconstruct the word *mantle* to the familiar keyword *man* and then elaborate by having Robert picture a man made from solid rock (Mastropieri, Scruggs, Whittaker, & Bakken, 1994). (See Figure 9.6.) Similarly, Mr. McNally might help students like Robert remember states and their capitals by using keywords in mnemonics such as those suggested by Mastropieri and Scruggs (1991, 2000):

Mantle
(Man)

Made of solid rock

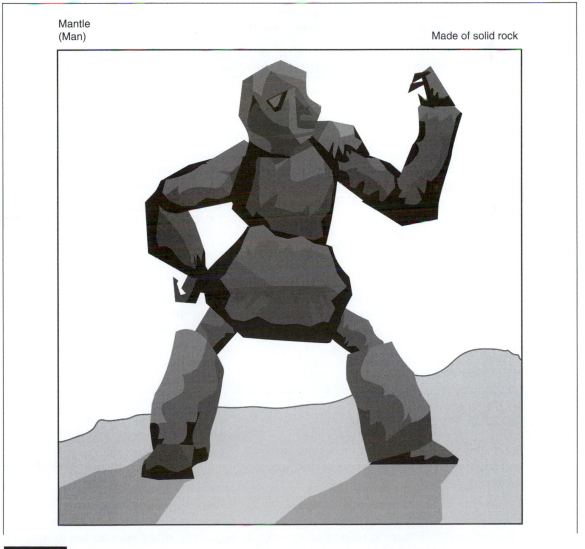

FIGURE 9.6

Using a Mnemonic in Earth Science From: Mastropieri, M.A., Scruggs, T.E., Whittaker, M.E.S., & Bakken, J.P. (1994). Applications of mnemonic strategies with students with mild mental disabilities. *Remedial and Special Education, 15*(1), 34–43. Copyright ©1994 by PRO-ED, Inc. Adapted with permission.

- ◆ Arkansas (Ark) and Little Rock—picture an ark stuck on a little rock.
- ◆ Louisiana (Louise & Anna) and Baton Rouge—picture Louise and Anna twirling batons and wearing rouge.
- ◆ Minnesota (Mini-soda) and St. Paul—picture St. Paul ordering a mini-soda.

Mnemonic strategy instruction has been used successfully to help students with mild disabilities remember English and foreign language vocabulary words (Mastropieri, Scruggs, Levin, Gaffney, & McLoone, 1985) as well as science content (Veit, Scruggs, & Mastropieri, 1986). In addition, students with mild mental retardation improved their memory for vocabulary words and social studies facts when these were presented through mnemonic strategies (Mastropieri, Scruggs, Whittaker, & Bakken, 1994).

A Summary of Cognitive Behavior Modification Procedures ◆

Although cognitive behavior modification procedures such as self-management, learning strategies, and mnemonics hold promise for improving the academic and behavioral skills of students with mild disabilities, the generalization of these procedures from the special classroom to the regular classroom remains problematic (Mastropieri & Scruggs, 1998; Rooney & Hallahan, 1985; Scanlon et al., 1996). If teachers are to maximize the probability that their students will use these strategies appropriately, they must teach only those strategies that relate to their students' needs and carefully follow the procedures described in this chapter. (See also Box 9.5 for web sites containing information on teaching learning strategies.) ◆

Summary

Both classroom teachers and special educators encounter students with widely varying ability levels and needs. Such diversity may challenge the teacher when providing individualized instruction for students with mild disabilities. Through

---

Box 9.5

Web Watch

Information on teaching learning strategies may be obtained by contacting the following web sites:

Center for New Discoveries in Learning
http://www. howtolearn.com#join
Products and information related to learning strategies and other approaches to teaching.

Center for Research on Learning
http://www.ku-crl.org/htmfiles/corc.html
Information on the Strategic Instruction Model. Products and training dates.

cooperative learning groups and peer-tutoring arrangements, students with disabilities and other students with low achievement can receive additional instruction and reinforcement of skills. Students with and without mild disabilities will also benefit from instruction in cognitive behavior modification procedures that may enhance their ability to study and guide them in monitoring and controlling their own behaviors. Mnemonic strategies and learning strategies also enable students with mild disabilities to help themselves to learn.

Application Exercises

1. Observe cooperative learning groups in a general education classroom. Ask the teacher how the team members were selected and what the responsibilities of each team member are.
2. Interview a student with a learning disability in a secondary school to determine the types of tasks required of him or her in general education classes. Inquire as to what kind of activities best facilitate the student's learning process (e.g., cooperative learning groups; peer tutoring, either as tutor or tutee; learning strategies).
3. Observe in a classroom using peer tutoring. Ask the teacher how peer tutors are selected, trained, and monitored. Ask some of the tutor-tutee pairs to express the things they like most about peer tutoring.
4. Browse InfoTrac for five articles containing self-management strategies such as self-monitoring, self-recording, or self-reinforcement. Share these with your colleagues. Construct a file of tips and information on self-management strategies to use in your classroom.
5. Browse the web sites listed in Box 9.5. If you were Mr. Abel, which learning strategies would you teach to Robert to improve his performance in the classroom? Why?
6. List three specific mnemonic strategies you've used when studying for a test (e.g., a particular first-letter acronym, a keyword). Share these in a discussion with your colleagues.
7. List terms to be remembered for a class you are taking. Create a reconstructive elaboration to help yourself remember each of these terms. Share your mnemonic creations with your classmates.

ORAL LANGUAGE INSTRUCTION

Focus

As you read, think about the following questions:

◆ *What is meant by* language *and by* the language arts?

◆ *What are the components of language?*

◆ *What difficulties with oral language do students with mild disabilities exhibit?*

◆ *How is phonemic awareness related to success in reading?*

◆ *How can teachers help students improve phonologic, syntactic, and semantic skills?*

◆ *How can teachers help students who are culturally or linguistically diverse develop English language skills?*

Because of the importance of language skills, the language arts curriculum often comprises a significant portion of each school day, particularly at the elementary level. The *language arts* are a set of interrelated skills that include listening, speaking, reading, and writing. Although these skills are related, listening and speaking are usually considered to be oral language skills while reading and writing are considered written language skills. Reading will be addressed in Chapter 11 and the written language skills will be discussed in Chapter 12. In this chapter, we will explore the importance of oral language skills for later success in school. However, you are encouraged to keep the interrelated nature of these four areas in mind as you read this and the subsequent two chapters. Let's listen, now, to Ms. Kirk and Ms. Booker at a national convention as they begin a workshop that they are both attending regarding oral language skills :

Mediator:	Okay, to get this workshop started, let's share some of the concerns you have with your students, and I'll make a list of them here.
Ms. Booker:	(Referring to Susan) I have a student with mild mental retardation in my sixth-grade language arts class. I'm trying to include her in as many activities as possible, but she's thirteen and her oral language skills are so delayed. She speaks in only five- or six-word sentences, and her vocabulary is quite limited. She's also very shy, so it's hard to get her to participate in class. I'm looking for suggestions to help my inclusion students with oral language development.
Ms. Kirk:	I'm looking for suggestions for my inclusion students, too. I have several of them in my fourth-grade class. One of them (thinking of Travis) has attention deficit hyperactivity disorder, and he also has trouble with both reading and writing. He can't seem to tell the sounds in words to decode them or to spell them. Lately, I've been seeing on the World Wide Web and reading in one of my journals that phonemic awareness is important for reading. I want some more information on that. (She looks around as other teachers in the discussion group nod in agreement, then she continues.) I also have a student in my class who has limited English proficiency (referring to Celie), and a young man (thinking of Joey) with a behavior disorder who never seems to be able to say the right thing at the right time. He always antagonizes the others with what he says. I think social uses of language are also important to develop in my classroom.
Ms. Booker:	So do I. (Others nod agreement.) I'm also interested in helping my students with cultural differences and those with English as a second language to increase their oral language skills.
Mediator:	Okay, we've got a number of great topics listed for our discussion. We'll be talking about these during the workshop, and they are also covered in other sessions during the convention. Are there any other topics of concern we haven't listed?
Ms. Kirk:	Oh! One more. My student who has trouble reading and writing also seems to have problems finding words. He'll sometimes tell me a definition as though he's forgotten the word itself. He'll say

something like, "We went to the, the place where there's sand and water," instead of saying, "We went to the beach."

Mediator: Okay, I've got it.

These teachers, like all teachers, have children in their classrooms with diverse languages and varying ability in language arts skills. Nevertheless, helping children communicate through spoken language is an important goal of the language arts program for most teachers. In this chapter we will first explore the nature of oral language and language development. Next, we will address the difficulties children with mild disabilities may have with oral language, particularly in developing phonemic awareness. Following a discussion of activities for developing oral language skills in students with mild disabilities, we will take a look at some curricular materials and computer software programs available to help teachers foster the oral language skills of their students. Finally, we will examine instruction for children who have cultural differences or limited English proficiency.

The Nature of Language and Language Development

Language is the means by which we communicate our ideas. Thus, language involves the use of an arbitrary system of symbols, or codes, to represent ideas, objects, and relationships (Bloom & Lahey, 1978). Language also requires a set of rules to ensure that these arbitrary symbols are used in an organized and predictable way. This system of symbols and rules governs both oral and written language.

Oral language, then, involves the child's ability to understand and use the symbols and rules of spoken communications. Listening, or comprehending the oral communication of other people, is considered to be a *receptive language* skill. On the other hand, speaking, or the production and encoding of one's own ideas, is an *expressive language* skill. Both are necessary if students are to communicate effectively with peers and teachers. Moreover, if students are to communicate competently, they must understand the components of spoken language, including its *form, content,* and *social function* (Bloom & Lahey, 1978). (See Table 10.1.)

Form

Language form consists of *phonology, morphology,* and *syntax.* Phonology refers to the system of sounds and rules for combining these sounds in a language. A *phoneme* is the smallest unit of sound; however, phonemes convey no meaning of their own. For example, the word map contains three different phonemes (i.e., /m/ /a/ /p/), but these have no meaning unless they are sequenced and pronounced together as a word. The English language consists of about 44 different phonemes, including both consonant and vowel sounds and their combinations.

The smallest unit of meaning in a language is the *morpheme;* thus, *morphology* refers to the system of rules governing the structure of words. Root

Table 10.1 Components of Oral Language

The teacher must consider many components of oral language when providing instruction to children with mild disabilities. According to Bloom and Lahey (1978), the following are critical elements of any program for oral language development:

Component	Definition
Form	
Phonology	The smallest unit of sound produced by speakers in a language (e.g., /ch/); The rules governing the order of sounds to produce words and the intonations used to give meaning.
Morphology	The smallest unit of language that has meaning. *Free morphemes* have meaning and can be used alone (e.g., the word *big*). *Bound morphemes* are attached to the root word and change its meaning (e.g., *est* added to *big* to make *biggest*).
Syntax	The word order in sentences and the rules used to govern the order of words in the language.
Content	
Semantics	Vocabulary for labeling objects and concepts; the relationships among ideas and concepts expressed.
Function	
Pragmatics	The use of language for social functions and communicative purposes.

words are *free morphemes* that can be used alone to convey meaning (e.g., map, run, and fast). On the other hand, affixes such as suffixes and prefixes are *bound morphemes*. Although these have meaning (e.g., *re* means "to do again"), in order to be used they must be attached to a root word to change its meaning (e.g., *rerun, maps, fastest).*

Finally, *syntax* refers to the rules we use for combining words into sentences and understanding the relationships among various sentence elements. Loosely defined, *syntax* is the set of rules of grammar for a language. For example, in English we would say "the tall tree" rather than "the tree tall." A subject, a verb, and an object (e.g., Susan loves baseball) comprise the basic syntactic structure in English. Knowledge of syntax, then, is necessary for students to produce and comprehend complete sentences, including statements, questions, negations, and passive constructions (Wiig & Semel, 1984).

Content

Content refers to *semantics*, or the meaning attached to words and their combinations. Children, for example, must develop vocabulary related to objects (e.g., shoes, apple, Daddy) and actions (e.g., jumping, eating) so that they can accurately label items and events. In addition, semantic knowledge is necessary to categorize concepts and ideas according to various classes or properties. For example, one might categorize *shoes* under the general class of *items of clothing*. One might also categorize them by their properties (e.g., leather, lug soles, man-made materials, high heels) or by specific examples (e.g., dress shoes, sandals, sneakers). Semantics involves more than merely developing vocabulary, though, because children also must understand the relationships among objects and events (e.g., Travis and his cat; going to a restaurant and eating). Furthermore, children must understand that word meaning can change depending on the context of a sentence (e.g., "She will *run* for office"; "He can *run* fast") or when words are used figuratively (e.g., in idioms such as *"Run* that by me again!")

Social Functions

Pragmatics refers to the study of language in social interactions. According to McLaughlin (1998), we use language to accomplish specific social functions such as carrying on a conversation about a particular topic in order to obtain information or convey our point of view. We also use language to control another person's actions (e.g., "Stop that!") or to give hints and make requests. As children grow, they progress from using language simply to satisfy their own needs (e.g., "Want juice") to exchanging jokes and using social pleasantries (e.g., "Hi. How are you?" "Fine thank you. And you?"). In addition, interpreting the intent or needs of others and adjusting one's language accordingly is a critical skill for communicative competence. Communicative competence, then, is dependent on one's knowledge of socially appropriate communicative behaviors and conventions, both of which are critical pragmatic language skills (Wilcox, 1986).

Form, content, and function are three interrelated components of language that influence one another as children develop language skills. Although there is great variability in when children develop various language skills, most achieve language milestones at about the same age. Let's take a brief look at how these skills usually develop in children.

Language Development

According to McCormick and Schiefelbusch (1990), children develop a remarkable number of language skills from birth to age five. In fact, most of the research on language development has focused on children too young for school. In the first weeks of life, infants gaze at their mothers or caregivers and receive feedback, such as, "I see you." By the end of the second or third month of life, infants are cooing, laughing, and differentially responding to sounds and people. Between six and twelve months of age, children typically understand their own name and basic words such as *No*, respond to simple directions like, "Come to Daddy," recognize the names of everyday objects and familiar people, and wave "bye-bye." By this age, children are also babbling, or producing common speech sounds and then engaging in vocal play, and putting together sounds of the language with intonations such as "da, la, da, da."

Somewhere around 12 to 18 months, children say their first words, and they begin to use speech to interact with others. Typically, at this age, children use one word to convey an entire sentence (e.g., "Juice" for "More juice please"). Vocabulary expands from 5 to 50 words at 12 to 18 months to 200 to 300 words between 18 and 24 months. At this age, children are often using plurals as well as simple verbs, adverbs, and adjectives. They may also understand possessives and put two or more words together into simple sentences.

Between the ages of 2 and 5, children expand their vocabularies to approximately 2,500 words. Their sentences become longer; they ask questions using *who, what, when, where, why* and *how;* they use prepositions such as *on, in,* or *under;* they use the past tense; and they begin to understand and use conjunctions and compound and complex sentences. By the time most children enter school, they have mastered the basic elements of the language, and they are using language socially to tell stories, explain events, and engage peers and others in play activities.

As children progress through school, however, they continue to develop their language skills. According to research (see, for example, Bashir & Scavuzzo, 1992; Owens, 1995; Scott & Stokes, 1995; and Wiig & Secord, 1994), school-age children:

- Expand their speaking vocabulary from 2,500 to over 50,000 words.
- Increase the breadth of definitions and uses for various words.
- Understand and use figurative language.
- Increase sentence length from an average of about 9 words per sentence at age nine to 10 to 12 words per sentence during high school.
- Understand and use passive sentence construction as well as more complex sentence structures.
- Understand and use inflectional endings, suffixes, prefixes, and irregular verbs.

Children also begin to develop competence in using language for social functions. For example, they are able to use words to express their positive or negative feelings, and they are able to "see from the eyes of another." As children grow to adolescence, they use sarcasm and social conventions, and they adjust their communications to suit the needs of the listener or the situation.

Teenagers skilled in the social uses of language, for example, might adjust their voice tone, intonations, and facial expressions to convey sympathy when a peer has lost a boyfriend. Or they will, hopefully, use a more respectful tone of voice than they might ordinarily use with peers when speaking with the principal or with a police officer!

Teachers can take advantage of the many opportunities in their own classrooms for youngsters with or without mild disabilities to practice oral language skills. Rather than breaking down oral communication into isolated receptive and expressive language skills for drill and practice, the teacher can use the natural environment to enhance oral language development. Children can talk about the numerous activities that take place in the classroom. Classroom events provide opportunities for instruction and practice of language in context throughout the school day. The following suggestions can easily be incorporated into ongoing programs in most classrooms:

1. Model good listening skills.

   ◆ Allow children to finish what they have to say rather than interrupting or finishing statements for them.
   ◆ Give a child your attention when he or she is speaking.
   ◆ Focus on what a child has to say rather than on whether or not the child is using proper grammar and sentence structure.

2. Model good speaking skills throughout the day.

   ◆ Use proper grammar yourself.
   ◆ Use "self-talk" to think aloud and to model "expert" use of particular language structures. For example, when modeling verb tenses or syntax for Celie, Ms. Kirk models, "The storm *blew* the ship off course," to validate and also to correct Celie's statement, "The ship *blowed* off course."
   ◆ Expand on what children say, modeling longer and more complex sentence structures to express the same ideas. For example, when Kevin says, "I like to make kites. Mine didn't go up," Ms. Kirk might reply, "You enjoy making kites, but yours didn't go up."
   ◆ Elaborate on what children say, providing for them, or eliciting from them, additional details or ideas regarding the topic at hand. For example, in science class, when Kevin answers that the habitat for a giraffe is a grassland, Ms. Kirk might say, "Yes, the habitat for a giraffe is a grassland. That's also the habitat for some types of elephants and for zebra. A grassland is a habitat for grazing animals."
   ◆ Describe for children what they are doing to link language use with their actions and environment. Say, for example, "When you mixed the red and yellow paints together, you made orange."

3. Consistently reinforce children for good listening and for good speaking with peers and teachers.
4. Use concrete activities and experiences for language development.

   ◆ Provide pictures to illustrate new vocabulary or sentence structures.
   ◆ Ask children to act out new sentence forms and structures.

- ◆ Use simple language forms and vocabulary when teaching new concepts, tying unknown words and structures to familiar ones.
- ◆ Allow children to give and follow directions to help each other make something, play a game, or engage in some other activity together.
- ◆ Have children role play making telephone calls, interviewing for a job, greeting someone, ordering from a menu, and so forth, to practice pragmatic language skills in realistic social contexts.

5. Use subject areas for language instruction and language practice throughout the day.

- ◆ Have students retell stories to one another or summarize the main idea or sequence of events after listening to a speaker or reader.
- ◆ Have students generate questions before reading or listening to a lesson.
- ◆ Follow reading and writing activities with discussion to clarify and expand on ideas.

Language and Children with Mild Disabilities

Oral language skills, both receptive and expressive, play a vital role in a student's progress through school. Therefore, teachers must help their students understand and use spoken language effectively. Teachers can capitalize on the language-rich nature of classrooms (e.g., giving and following directions, listening to stories) to provide meaningful activities for language development and practice. In this way, most students with mild disabilities can experience oral language as a functional tool for communicating with peers and teachers.

For those youngsters requiring more intensive intervention, the teacher must work collaboratively with a speech and language specialist. Special educators and classroom teachers will undoubtedly have in their classrooms children like Celie, Travis, and Susan. In fact, students with mild disabilities, particularly learning disabilities, often have language-based learning difficulties (Wiig & Secord, 1994).

They may have, for example, difficulty with the form, content, or use of language that inhibits their progress in school. Generally, students with mild disabilities have less well-developed vocabularies than their peers (Wiig & Secord, 1994), and they tend to use concrete definitions for words. They also have more difficulty than do their peers with words that have more than one meaning, and complex syntactic structures (e.g., passive sentences, conjunctions such as if . . . then . . .) develop at a slower pace when compared with peers. Moreover, according to German (1992), students with mild disabilities may have considerable difficulty storing and retrieving words. That is, they may have a word "on the tip of the tongue," but be unable to retrieve it for use in a sentence, resorting instead to a description (e.g., "The things you put on your feet").

Children with mild disabilities also may have difficulty with both receptive and expressive language. For example, youngsters who have difficulty comprehending spoken language may have problems following a sequence of directions or understanding multiple-meaning words, figurative language, and complex sentence structures (Wiig & Semel, 1984). Similarly, those students who experience production difficulty because of expressive language problems may use incorrect grammar and only simple sentence structures, or they may find it difficult to retrieve the proper word to communicate a concept. Expressive and receptive language, as well as form, content, and use, influence one another. Thus, if Susan has a limited vocabulary (i.e., semantic-content), she may be behind peers in adding suffixes, prefixes, and inflectional endings to words (i.e., morphological skills that are a component of form). In addition, she may not use language in interactions with peers because she lacks content vocabulary.

Finally, many children with mild disabilities exhibit pragmatic language deficits. That is, like Joey, they have difficulty understanding and effectively using language in social contexts. These youngsters may fail to adapt their communicative style to suit the needs of the listener, and they may be unable to maintain conversations or repair communication breakdowns (Bryan, Donahue, & Pearl, 1981; McDonough, 1989). Often, teachers and principals believe these students to be disrespectful. Similarly, peers may view them negatively or as "troublemakers." (See Chapter 15 for additional discussion of pragmatic language and social skills.)

Of particular concern to teachers, however, is the relationship between language development and reading disabilities. Although the exact nature of this relationship is unclear, difficulty with semantics, syntax, and phonology all may hinder reading ability at various points during a child's school career (Snyder & Downey, 1997). For example, expressive vocabulary, naming skills, and letter identification are each associated with a child's future reading ability. During the early grades, however, phonological awareness appears to be most closely related to later reading skill (Liberman, Shankweiler, Fischer, & Carter, 1974; Wagner, Torgesen, & Rashotte, 1994).

Phonological Awareness Skills and Reading Problems

Over the past two decades, research has consistently indicated the importance of *phonological awareness* to skillful reading (Adams, 1990; Snow, Burns, & Griffin, 1998). Phonological awareness refers to a child's ability to attend to the sound structure of a language, as distinct from its meaning. Phonological awareness includes both phonemic awareness and phonics.

Phonemic awareness is the ability to attend to, identify, and manipulate the sounds of spoken language. More specifically, the term refers to an awareness that spoken words or syllables can be thought of as a sequence of phonemes, or sounds. On the other hand, *phonics* most often means learning the sounds for letters and letter combinations. Whereas phonics maps letters to their sounds, phonemic awareness emphasizes the sounds themselves. Only when students are proficient with manipulating the sounds of spoken language are they ready to match the sounds to the written symbols. Phonemic awareness, then, precedes phonics instruction and includes the oral ability to:

◆ Recognize and produce rhyming words.
◆ Detect separate words in sentences.

◆ Recognize similarities and differences in words or word parts.
◆ Count, segment, blend, and delete word parts such as compound words (e.g., "Put together the words *snow* and *man*. What word do you get?") or syllables (e.g., "Listen to the word *turkey*. What is left if you take *tur* away from *turkey?*").
◆ Count, segment, blend, substitute, and delete phonemes (e.g., "What sounds do you hear in cat?" or "If you put the sound /m/ in place of /c/, what would you have?").

By kindergarten, children vary widely in their phonological awareness. According to Snow, Burns, and Griffin (1998), some children enter kindergarten aware of syllables and even some phonemes within words. Others enter kindergarten unable to detect any sound units within words. Those children with good phonological awareness skills in kindergarten almost always progress to become good readers; however, those with weak phonological awareness may still go on to become normal readers. Thus, phonemic awareness is an inaccurate predictor of poor reading ability, but a good predictor of superior reading ability (Scarborough, 1998).

Adams (1990) also reports that phonemic awareness is both a predictor of reading ability and a consequence of learning to read. That is, as children begin to learn basic letters and letter-sound associations, they may also develop keener phonological awareness. Writing, too, can help children refine their phonological skills in kindergarten or first grade if they are encouraged to analyze words in order to "figure out" their spellings. Nevertheless, numerous researchers (see, for example, Adams, 1990; Liberman & Shankweiler, 1985; and Torgesen, 1995) suggest that early, intensive, and explicit instruction in phonological awareness is necessary for all young children if they are to learn to read, particularly those youngsters at risk for reading problems.

Students with dyslexia, for example, most often have phonologically-based reading disabilities (Shaywitz, Escobar, Shaywitz, Fletcher, & Makuch, 1992). According to Adams, Foorman, Lundberg, and Beeler (1998), phonemic awareness training can prevent, or remediate, specific reading disabilities for many of these children. Moreover, Adams (1990) suggests that early intervention in phonemic awareness is essential because phonics instruction is not likely to be successful unless children first have training in phonological awareness (Juel, Griffith, & Gough, 1986).

All children, then, will profit from activities designed to promote phonological awareness. Children with mild disabilities, however, may require explicit and prolonged instruction in this skill, as well as activities to address semantic and syntactic language deficits.

Activities to Develop Semantic, Syntactic, and Phonological Ability

Special educators and classroom teachers can take advantage of many ongoing activities in the classroom to promote oral language skills. As suggested earlier in this chapter, much language instruction can occur within the context of interesting and meaningful activities, rather than during isolated drill and practice.

Content

When teaching content (semantics), Ms. Kirk, for example, might label objects verbally (e.g., "This picture shows a pond."), emphasize the salient features of new concepts being taught (e.g., "A pond is a small body of water. A lake is larger."), use new vocabulary in sentences throughout the day, and illustrate relationships among old and new vocabulary by categorizing (e.g., "Lakes and ponds are bodies of water.") or by using semantic maps (See Figure 10.1). For students like Susan, teachers will need to use more frequent repetitions of new vocabulary and systematically present examples, as well as nonexamples, of the new concept (e.g., showing pictures of ponds, lakes, and oceans as examples of bodies of water and pictures of deserts and forests as nonexamples).

Form

Teachers can help students learn language form through naturally-occurring activities in the classroom. Ms. Lopez might begin instruction on new morphological skills with concrete examples and familiar vocabulary. For example, when teaching possessives, she might begin with items belonging to children in the classroom and immediately link the owner and item to the written form (e.g., Celie's desk). Or, to teach comparisons using *er* and *est*, Ms. Lopez might have three students line up according to their height (e.g., Celie is tall. Kevin is taller. Travis is tallest.).

Similarly, teachers can use concrete examples, familiar vocabulary, and simplified sentences to teach more difficult syntactic structures. Ms. Lopez might emphasize the subject and verb by having students engage in actions which she then verbalizes (e.g., "Kevin jumps." "Travis runs."). Later, sentences such as these can be reenacted and placed in past tense, expanded to a subject, verb, and object (e.g., "Celie pushed Travis."), or transformed into passive constructions (e.g., "Travis was pushed by Celie.").

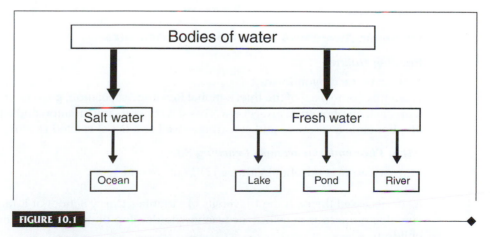

FIGURE 10.1

A Simple Semantic Map to Illustrate the Concept of Bodies of Water

Recall, too, the importance of activities for teaching phonemic awareness, particularly in the early grades. (See the web sites listed in Box 10.1 for information on phonemic awareness and activities to promote its development.) For students who have difficulty detecting separate sounds in spoken language, teachers can use Elkonin boxes (See Figure 10.2) (Elkonin, 1973). That is, teachers can prepare pictures of familiar items and place below the picture a matrix containing the same number of boxes as there are phonemes in the pictured item. Then, the teacher can model placing a chip or a block onto each box as he or she slowly says the name of the item, stressing each phoneme in turn. In addition, teachers can use the following suggestions to develop critical phonemic awareness skills:

- Have children clap, snap, or tap for each word in a sentence. Start with simple sentences and gradually increase the length. Ms. Lopez might say, "Watch me clap for each word in this sentence. I can fly a kite (clapping once for each word). Now you try it with me, I can fly a kite. (The children clap and say the words with her.) Your turn. Listen to this sentence. My dog is big. Say it and clap." If children have difficulty with this activity, Ms. Lopez can construct Elkonin boxes, modeling and then having students move a block into a box for each word in the sentence.

- Play games with rhyming words. Match objects or pictures of things that rhyme (e.g., box, fox). Play "Go fish" or "Memory" with picture cards of rhyming pairs. Read or say nursery rhymes stressing rhyming pairs. Then, have students state the rhyming words. Children can often recognize rhyming pairs before they are able to produce these on their own. Therefore, start with recognition-level games, and then move to activities in which children must complete a sentence that you say that contains a

---

Box 10.1

Web Watch

Phonemic Awareness Information and Activities

Reading Online

http://www.readingonline.org
From this home page of the International Reading Association, go to their critical issues site, then click on phonemic awareness. This site contains information and a position statement on phonemic awareness and research as well as a list of related readings.

PALS: Phonemic Awareness Learning Site

http://www.curry.edschool.Virginia.EDU/curry/cente
rs/pals/
A site accessed through the University of Virginia's Curry School of Education. This center contains numerous activities for teachers to develop phonemic awareness skills in young children.

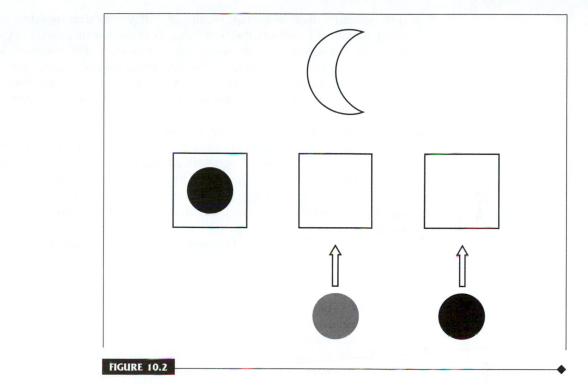

FIGURE 10.2

*Sample Elkonin Boxes: To help children hear the three phonemes in
moon, the teacher would say, "This is a moon." Then, moving each disk
in turn, the teacher would say, "/m/ /oo/ /n/, moon." Notice that no letters
are needed for this task. Children are not yet learning the letter sounds,
but rather to hear the sounds within words.*

pair of rhyming words, such as, "The big red fox (stressed) jumped over the
_____." Use two or three pictures as clues initially if these are necessary.

◆ Have children clap, snap, or tap for parts of words. For example, demonstrate clapping for each part of a compound word such as popcorn. If
students have difficulty, use pictures to illustrate each part of a compound word (e.g., snow and man) and tap each picture as you say each
part. Or, make Elkonin boxes. Prepare a sheet of paper with a picture of
the compound word and two squares side by side. Place one block into
each square as you say each part of the compound word.

◆ Blend and segment compound words, first with pictures, then orally.
Ms. Lopez might show Travis pictures of a foot and a ball, saying, "This
is a foot. This is a ball (touching each in turn). If I put foot and ball
together (moving the pictures closer), I get football." Later, Ms. Lopez
might say, "Listen. Birdhouse. Now, I'll say it again, but I won't say
bird. (Pausing) House. Listen, again. Bedtime. Say it with me. Bedtime.
Now say it again, but don't say bed." If Travis has difficulty with this
activity, Ms. Lopez can use pictures of a bird and a house or a bed
and a clock as visual clues.

- Have students clap, snap, tap, stomp, or jump with each syllable in a word. Simply tell students they are going to break words apart. They do not need to know syllable division rules at this stage! For example, Ms. Kirk can say words slowly at first, placing a block into an Elkonin box for each syllable she says (e.g., "/ta/ /ble/"). She can start with simple words that have only one or two syllables and then progress to words of three or more syllables.
- Have students blend and segment syllables in a word. Say, for example, "Listen. /pump/ /kin/ (Pausing between each syllable). I said the word pumpkin. Listen, again. /ti/ /ger/. What word did I say?" Start with two-syllable words, moving gradually to words that have three or more syllables. Similarly, you might say, "Listen. *Picnic.* Now I'm going to say it again, but I won't say /nic/. *Pic.* Listen again. Say picture. Now say it again, but don't say /ture/. Now say *picture* again, but don't say /pic/." First have students delete the initial and ending syllables. Later, have them delete the initial, ending, and then middle syllables of longer words.
- Have students listen for the beginning and ending sounds in words. For example, Ms. Lopez might ask Travis to listen for the first sound in cat /c/. When he is proficient with identifying the initial sounds in words, she might have him identify the last sound. As she does, she might use different color blocks and Elkonin boxes to represent sounds while orally stressing the sound of interest. It is not necessary for Travis to know that *c* makes /c/ or *t* makes /t/. The goal at this level is to detect different phonemes in spoken words. Later, Ms. Lopez can ask Travis to tell her the sound he hears in the middle of a word such as cat. She might place a block in each square on a sheet of paper as she says, "Listen. /c/ /a/ /t/. What sound was in the middle (pointing to the middle block)?"
- Have students blend phonemes into words. Say, for example, "Listen, I'm going to put together /u/ /p/ (pausing between each). Up. Listen again and put them together, /a/ /t/. (Students respond, "at.") Good, at. Move from words that contain two phonemes to those composed of three (e.g., sit, read) or four phonemes (e.g., desk, truck). Again, Elkonin boxes can be used if students have difficulty with this task.
- Have students delete initial, final, then medial phonemes from words. Have students state, for example, a word such as *pig*. Then, tell them to say the word again, but don't say /p/ or don't say /g/.
- Have students substitute one phoneme for another in a word. For example, use different color blocks and Elkonin boxes to represent each phoneme and demonstrate saying, "Here is sit. (Placing blocks as you say each phoneme, /s/ /i/ /t/) Now I'm going to change *sit* to *bit*." (Represent the /b/ with a different color block.) Have students change from one word to another, beginning with initial and then ending phonemes. Later, have students change medial phonemes (e.g., Change sit to sat.). Gradually eliminate the blocks as students become proficient at manipulating the phonemes.
- When students become proficient with some of these phonemic awareness skills, the teacher may begin to introduce simple letter-sound

associations (i.e., phonics). For example, Ms. Lopez might teach her younger students that the sound /m/ is represented by a written symbol, the grapheme *m*.

Sample Commercial Materials, Tests, and Computer Software

Teachers can also use the many materials and computer software programs that are available to help students develop oral language skills. In addition, many tests exist to help teachers assess receptive and expressive language skills (see Table 10.2).

Phonemic Awareness in Young Children. Marilyn Adams and her colleagues have compiled a collection of wonderful phonemic awareness activities in a classroom curriculum entitled *Phonemic Awareness in Young Children* (Adams et al., 1998). In addition to the activities, the book contains an informal assessment of phonemic awareness skills, reproducible materials, and poems, fingerplays, and chants. (The book is available from Paul H. Brookes Publishing Company, P.O. Box 10624, Baltimore, MD 21285-0624.)

The Phonological Awareness Kits and The Phonological Awareness Test. Robertson and Salter (1995) have a collection of phonemic awareness activities and materials in *The Phonological Awareness Kit* for children aged 4 through 8. The boxed set contains cubes and picture cards using the Elkonin method, as well as numerous ideas for developing skills such as rhyming or segmenting, blending, and isolating and deleting word parts and phonemes. An intermediate-level kit is also available for students aged 9 through 14. This kit contains similar activities and materials, but the pictures and format are more appropriate for older children.

In addition, Robertson and Salter's phonological awareness kit is keyed to a standardized test of phonological awareness called *The Phonological Awareness Test* (Robertson & Salter, 1997). The test is appropriate for children aged 5 through 9. It contains nine subtests (Rhyming, Segmentation, Isolation, Deletion, Substitution, Blending, Graphemes, Decoding, and Invented Spelling) and yields both standard scores and percentiles. (Both the phonological awareness kits and test, as well as other materials and tests for semantic and syntactic learning, are available from LinguiSystems, Inc., 3100 Fourth Avenue, East Moline, IL 61244-9700.)

The Peabody Language Development Kits. Also of help to teachers are the Peabody Language Development Kits (Dunn, Smith, Dunn, & Horton, 1981). Available in two levels, preschool and 1, these kits are for children aged 4 to 6, or older youngsters with learning difficulties. The kits contain colorful puppets, pictures, and posters, as well as audiocassettes, hands-on materials, and teacher's guides. The kits focus on key oral language skills such as describing, labeling, following directions, and sequencing. (The Peabody Language Development Kits are available from American Guidance Service, 4201 Woodland Rd., P.O. Box 99, Circle Pines, MN 55014-1796.)

Table 10.2 Tests of Language Skills

Clinical Evaluation of Language Fundamentals—Revised (Semel, Wiig, & Secord, 1987). San Antonio, TX: The Psychological Corp.	A test of syntax and semantics for ages 5 through 16. Contains 11 subtests.
Comprehensive Receptive & Expressive Vocabulary Test (Wallace & Hammill, 1994). Austin, TX: Pro-Ed.	School version for ages 4 through 17 and adult version for ages 18 through 89. Receptive test contains photo sets; student selects picture of word. In expressive test, student tells meaning. Also available in computer version.
Kindergarten Language Screening Test—2 (Gauthier & Madison, 1998). Austin, TX: Pro-Ed.	Quick screening for ages 4 through 6 in following commands, understanding directions, repeating sentences, comparing and contrasting common items, and using spontaneous speech.
Peabody Picture Vocabulary Test—3 (Dunn & Dunn, 1998). Circle Pines, MN: American Guidance Service.	Assesses receptive vocabulary and verbal ability for ages 2 through 90. Computerized scoring available.
Test of Adolescent Language—3 (Hammill, Brown, Larsen, & Wiederholt, 1994). Austin, TX: Pro-Ed.	For ages 12 through 24. Tests receptive and expressive language, reading, writing, vocabulary, grammar, and spoken and written language skills.
Test of Early Language Development—2 (Hreskso, Reid, & Hammill, 1991). Austin, TX: Pro-Ed.	Tests both receptive and expressive language skills, semantics, and syntax for ages 2 through 7.
Test of Language Development—3, Primary (Newcomer & Hammill, 1997). Austin, TX: Pro-Ed.	For ages 4 through 8. Contains nine subtests assessing understanding and meaning of spoken words, grammatic understanding and completion, and phonemic analysis.
Test of Language Development—3, Intermediate (Hammill, & Newcomer, 1997). Austin, TX: Pro-Ed.	Assesses understanding and meaning of spoken words, sentence combining, word order, and grammar. For ages 8 through 12. Six subtests.

DISTAR Language Program. The DISTAR language kits, developed by Engelmann and Osborne, are available through Science Research Associates. These kits are designed for students in preschool through fourth grade and focus on both receptive and expressive language. The program uses a scripted, highly structured, direct instructional format. Skills included are using complete sentences, asking and answering questions, and following directions. In the more advanced levels, complex syntactic structures and parts of speech are also taught.

Computer Software. Many publishers of educational software now offer programs for language development. For example, Laureate Learning Systems, available through Edmark, has several programs on CD-ROM to develop syntax and vocabulary. *Simple Sentence Structure* teaches subject-verb-object word order. The program, in both Mac and PC versions, allows teachers to set varying amounts of on-screen instruction, cueing, and feedback to help individual students. *Swim, Swam, Swum: Mastering Irregular Verbs* enables students with language disabilities or English as a second language in grades K through 5 to master over 200 irregular verbs. Teachers can group verbs with similar forms, view the automatic records of student progress, and set the program to give voice assistance and animation for children who have difficulty. *The Language Activities of Daily Living Series: My House, My Town, and My School* facilitates language development in students with more severe language impairments Pre-K and up. The program teaches names and functions of common objects, as well as words to describe them. Teachers can control the lessons by selecting which objects will be used in each group.

Bright Start, Incorporated, also offers a new program entitled *Leap Into Phonics.* The program, for children in Pre-K through first grade, emphasizes detecting environmental sounds; rhymes; sounds and syllables in words; beginning, middle, and ending sounds; phoneme substitution; and blending. Printable student progress reports and a teacher's manual with reproducible activity sheets are included in the program.

A Summary of Language Activities

Explicit and intensive instruction in phonemic awareness is essential if some children are to become proficient readers. Teachers can promote language by harnessing ongoing activities in the classroom. For example, they can use concrete examples, familiar people and objects, and simple sentences in order to introduce new vocabulary or more complex syntactical structures. In addition, numerous tests, materials, and computer software programs are available to help students develop or refine their language skills. ◆

Students with Cultural Differences or English as a Second Language

You probably recall from Chapter 1 that school populations today are becoming increasingly diverse. Many children come to their classrooms from cultures that have values, beliefs, or behaviors that differ from those of their teachers. For many of these culturally different students, the language spoken in the home is also at variance with that of the school. These children may be bilingual, or they may enter school with little or no English proficiency. Other children, such as those adopted from abroad at age 3 or older, may also enter school with limited English language skills. According to reports, over 8 million children with limited English proficiency currently live in the United States (Correa & Heward, 1996).

Although other factors such as socioeconomic status or school quality also affect achievement in school, students coming from homes in which English is not the primary language may be at risk for problems in learning to read. According to August and Hakuta (1997), this may be particularly true if the child has not yet attained proficiency with spoken English prior to beginning reading instruction. In fact, for students entering school with no English proficiency,

Snow, Burns, and Griffin (1998) urge teachers to begin initial reading instruction in the first language and not introduce literacy instruction in English until some level of oral proficiency in the language has been attained.

Many problems can arise during instruction with linguistically diverse children when words, concepts, or sounds cannot be translated from one language to another. For example, the prepositions *in* and *on* indicate a distinct position in English. Yet, in Spanish, *en* conveys the meaning of both prepositions. Similarly, McLaughlin (1998) offers the following examples of difficulties with translating from one language to another:

- In English, /ng/ can only end, but never begin, a syllable. In several African languages, however, /ng/ can begin a syllable.
- In *Ja govorila*, the Russian phrase for *I said*, the verb *govorila* conveys much more information than the English verb. It implies that the speaker is female, has already spoken, and will continue to speak more.
- Intonations affect languages differently. Thus, in English we might inflect a statement to make it a question by raising the intonation at the end as in, "I look okay?" On the other hand, a change in intonation changes the meaning of phonemes in Chinese. The word *chyan* might mean *thousand, money, shallow* or *owe* depending on whether the speaker uses a rising, falling, level, or dipping intonation.
- Concepts themselves may be difficult to translate. In English, we use only the word *snow*. Eskimo languages, however, use a number of different words to convey this concept—drifting snow, blowing snow, wet snow, falling snow, and so forth.

Other culturally diverse children may not be bilingual or linguistically different. They may come from homes in which English is the only language spoken. However, these children might use an English dialect rather than standard American English. A dialect is a unique, consistent, and recognizable variation within a primary language (McLaughlin, 1998), such as a Southern accent or African-American Vernacular English, also called *Black English* or *Ebonics* (Gollnick & Chinn, 1998). Because dialects have their own set of sounds and rules, children may become confused when letters, words, or sentences sound different in the classroom than they do in the home (Snow et al., 1998). For example, pin and pen might sound the same to children speaking with a Southern dialect. Or, children in New England might drink a "soda," while those in the Midwest might drink "pop" (McLaughlin, 1998). Similarly, the child who says, "He be driving to work," versus, "He driving to work," is conveying a subtle change of meaning: "He drives to work," versus, "He is driving to work today." Thus, children speaking English dialects different from that of the majority in the school may be at risk for later difficulty in learning to read.

Authorities differ in their approaches to teaching students from linguistically diverse backgrounds. Proponents of bilingual education argue that content knowledge and skills must be taught in the student's native language and that these will transfer after he or she becomes proficient in English (August & Hakuta, 1997). In this model, as students begin to learn English through English as a Second Language (ESL) programs, they also receive "sheltered content instruction" or "structured immersion." That is, teachers might simplify or adjust their English for instruction, or they might use a child's native language to clarify a point or to answer a question (Gersten, 1999). On the other hand, many educators today favor English Language Development (ELD) as the primary approach. These teachers believe that students need instruction in basic conversational English and academic language as well as systematic instruction in the conventions of English and grammar.

Nevertheless, through multicultural education, teachers can help students with cultural or linguistic diversity to develop English skills and to learn and participate in the classroom. Multicultural education respects cultural pluralism and assumes that cultural differences have value (Gollnick & Chinn, 1998). Teachers can use the following suggestions from several authorities (see, for example, Chamot & O'Malley, 1994; Cummins, 1989, 1994; Fueyo, 1997; Ruiz, 1989; Salends, Dorney, & Mazo, 1997; Sileo & Prater, 1998) to enhance instruction and language skills for children from culturally and linguistically diverse backgrounds:

◆ Keep in mind the developmental sequence of language.
◆ Learn about different cultures and languages yourself. (See the web sites listed in Box 10.2.)
◆ Create opportunities for children to share their cultures and languages with one another.

Box 10.2

Web Watch 2

Selected Web Sites on Cultural and Linguistic Diversity

American Studies Web: Race and Ethnicity

http://www.georgetown.edu/crossroads/asw/race.html
Sponsored by Georgetown University and the American Studies Crossroads Project, this site contains many links to sites on various cultures and groups, including African-American, Asian-American, Native-American, and Latino/Hispanic-American.

National Association for Bilingual Education (NABE)

http://www.nabe.urg
A site containing information, resources, and links for those interested in bilingual education.

National Clearinghouse for Bilingual Education (NCBE)

http://www.ncbe.gwu.edu/
This site is funded through the Office of Bilingual Education in the U.S. Department of Education. Based at George Washington University, this site offers links to numerous other sites and resources on bilingual education, English as a Second Language, multicultural education, and specific languages and cultures.

- Create classroom or school newsletters for parents and children using various languages.
- Ensure that communication with parents is achieved by providing an interpreter or giving them written information in their native language.
- Choose curricular materials, including books, videos, software, and bulletin board displays, that represent diverse cultures in ways that are not stereotyping.
- Use curriculum in a meaningful context so that the communicative purpose is clear.
- Make connections between the student's personal experiences and the curriculum.
- Use collaborative learning arrangements when possible.
- Pair new students from linguistically or culturally diverse backgrounds with "buddies" of similar backgrounds who have been at the school longer.
- Permit students to use their first language at school and provide tutors who can speak the language.
- Pose questions to clarify directions and understanding of content, rather than assuming students understand and know what to do.
- Give the child "wait time" before giving assistance.
- Simplify your language during instruction, and repeat key points or new vocabulary.
- Use familiar, concrete examples, and "hands-on" learning materials.

Box 10.3

Suggestions for English Language Development in Content Instruction

Gersten (1999) offers the following suggestions gleaned from research for teachers interested in merging English language development with content area learning:

- Avoid oversimplifying information with contrived, intellectually insulting material when teaching academic content in English. In science and math, all students are learning a new technical vocabulary and there is great potential to use concrete objects.
- Use visuals to reinforce verbal content.
- Use both oral and written modalities frequently.
- Strategically use synonyms. Word choice and sentence structure need to be consistent and concise. Pay attention to the use of metaphors and similes and other highly culture-specific phrases and expressions.
- Focus on approximately five to eight core vocabulary words in each lesson. Do this by carefully selecting words (e.g., key words for understanding a story), linking words or concepts to words known in the native language, showing new words in print, and using visuals such as concept maps to demonstrate new concepts or word meanings.
- During the early phases of language learning, modulate and be sensitive when providing feedback and correcting language usage; however, during later stages, identify errors and provide specific feedback to individual students.

Adapted from: Gersten, R. (1999). The changing face of bilingual education. *Educational Leadership, 56*(7), 41-45.

◆ Respond to what children say rather than to *how* they say it. You can extend language skills by modeling the correct English in your response (e.g., when Kevin says "He brung the present to his dad," Ms. Kirk might respond with, "Yes, he brought the present to his dad.").

Teachers must be sensitive to the needs of students from culturally and linguistically diverse backgrounds. They must also recognize that all children are individuals, rather than assuming that all children in one cultural or linguistic group are the same. When teachers respect individual students and help children to become comfortable in the classroom, they will enhance language development. (See Box 10.3 for additional suggestions for developing language skills during content instruction with students who have limited English proficiency. Also, see Table 10.3 for a list of attributes that African-American students value in their teachers.)

Table 10.3   Attributes of Good Teachers

According to McIntyre and Battle (1998), African-American students with emotional and behavioral disorders identify "good" teachers as having the following attributes:

Most Important Attributes

Personality Traits

◆ Likes kids.
◆ Is a nice person.
◆ Is friendly.
◆ Is fun to be around.
◆ Has a good sense of humor.
◆ Likes you even if you act up.
◆ Is relaxed and easygoing.

Respectful Treatment of Students

◆ Cares about you.
◆ Listens to you.
◆ Respects your opinion.
◆ Keeps your secrets private.
◆ Talks with you when you have problems.
◆ Gives you a chance and doesn't judge you right away.
◆ Stays calm and doesn't yell at you for little things.
◆ Tells the truth and doesn't lie to you.
◆ Tells the truth when telling other people about you.
◆ Doesn't treat you like you are stupid and doesn't underestimate you.

Less Important Attributes

Behavior Management Practices

◆ Is consistent so you know what to expect and how he or she will act.
◆ Can't be "conned" or fooled by lies that kids tell.
◆ Lets you know what he or she expects you to do.
◆ Notices when you do good work or try your best.

Table 10.3	**Attributes of Good Teachers—***continued*

Instructional Skills

◆ Acts like he or she knows what he or she is doing.
◆ Does a good job of explaining things.
◆ Helps you understand why it is important to know what you are learning.
◆ Makes sure you know everything you need to know before teaching new stuff.
◆ Tells you how what you already know will help you in life.
◆ Gives you information you can use in real life outside of school.
◆ Gives interesting lessons.
◆ Makes you try hard and demands your best effort.
◆ Doesn't embarrass you when you make mistakes.
◆ Is patient and doesn't rush you. Goes over things again without getting upset.

From: McIntyre, T., & Battle, J. (1998). The traits of "Good Teachers" as identified by African-American and white students with emotional and/or behavioral disorders. *Behavioral Disorders, 23*(2), 134-142.

Summary

Children must become proficient with the form, content, and function of language. *Form* includes phonologic, morphologic, and syntactic skill. *Content* refers to semantics, or vocabulary and the relationship among words. *Function* means a child's ability to use language for pragmatic, social purposes.

Although there is variation in when children acquire different language skills, most achieve language milestones within an approximate age range. Children with mild disabilities, however, may be delayed in both receptive and expressive language skills. They may have a limited vocabulary, difficulty understanding figures of speech or words that have multiple meanings, deficits in pragmatic language, or problems understanding and using complex sentence structures. In addition, they may lack phonological awareness, a skill critical for success in learning to read.

Many tests are available to help teachers assess language skills. In addition, teachers can choose from various materials and computer software programs now on the market to enhance their students' language development. Sensitivity to multicultural education and utilization of the opportunities presented by ongoing activities in the classroom are two ways in which teachers can promote language growth in culturally and linguistically diverse learners.

Application Exercises

1. Examine two different curricular materials used at a chosen grade level. What evidence do you find that individuals from various cultural and linguistic communities are included without stereotyping in these materials?
2. Browse the web sites listed in Box 10.2. Pick a culture about which you know very little. If you were to present a workshop to your peers on this culture, what information would you include?

3. Browse the web sites listed in Box 10.1. Find at least three activities for developing phonemic awareness. Demonstrate these to your colleagues in class.
4. Locate at least three articles regarding the relationship between phonemic awareness and reading achievement from the professional literature on InfoTrac. Then, assume you must convince your principal that you need funding for a phonemic awareness program in your classroom. Develop a position statement to justify your point of view.
5. Complete the following statement: The difference between phonemic awareness and phonics is . . .
6. Interview an individual who learned English as a second language. What difficulties, if any, did he or she experience in school? Are there words, phrases, or concepts from his or her native language that do not translate easily to English?

CHAPTER 11

READING INSTRUCTION

Focus

As you read, think about the following questions:

◆ *What is meant by a "Whole Language" approach to reading and the language arts?*

◆ *How do authorities differ in their ideas about the nature of reading and reading instruction?*

◆ *What role does direct instruction of phonics skills play within a whole language curriculum?*

◆ *Which approaches to initial reading instruction are supported by research for use with children with mild disabilities?*

◆ *What are some effective methods for helping children with mild disabilities comprehend materials they read?*

Children and youth with mild disabilities have numerous deficits in the language arts. Reading is, without a doubt, the area in which most of these youngsters experience the greatest difficulty; however, listening, speaking, spelling, handwriting, and written expression are related language arts that also present significant hurdles (Fessler, Rosenberg, & Rosenberg, 1991; Scruggs & Mastropieri, 1986). Recall that in Chapter 10 we explored oral language skills, such as listening, speaking, and phonemic awareness, that are critical for success during reading instruction. Specific methods for teaching spelling, handwriting, and written expression will be discussed in Chapter 12. In this chapter, we will focus primarily on reading instruction, an area crucial to school success; however, we will also explore within this chapter the interrelated nature of reading and the other language arts. Keep these relationships in mind as you read both Chapters 11 and 12.

As children move up the grade levels, they are expected to use reading and writing skills more and more to obtain and demonstrate knowledge. Youngsters lacking these basic skills face a serious disadvantage across the entire curriculum when compared with their average-achieving peers. Consider, for example, the case of Robert in his earth science class with Ms. Stone:

Ms. Stone: (Having completed her introduction of igneous, metamorphic, and sedimentary rocks, she is passing out a study guide and assigning homework.) Tonight, please read Section 5.2 in your text, pages 314 to 320, and answer the five questions on your study guide. You have ten minutes left in the class period to go ahead and start your homework with your lab team. (She writes the page numbers on the board as students begin working.)

Robert: (Opening his textbook to the proper page, he reads quietly.) Scientists have id, i-den, identified three ba, basi, basic pro, pro, processes by which rocks are formed. These pro, processes are used, useful class, classi, classifying . . . These processes are used by geo, geo, geologists when class, classifying rocks for study. I-ge-neous, Ig-e-neous, Ig-ne-ous rocks are formed when . . . (He looks up as he becomes aware that the other three students on his lab team have located the answer to the first question on the study guide: "How do geologists classify rocks?" He writes on his paper: "Geolugists clasify rocks by igneus, metamorfic, and saidamentery.")

Students like Robert, who must struggle to read the textbook or to write coherent answers to questions, fall further behind their classmates every day (Coutinho, 1986). How can teachers help youngsters with mild disabilities learn to read and write more effectively? This question will serve as the central theme for both Chapters 11 and 12.

Let us turn first to a discussion of the reading process, a summary of the difficulties encountered by students with mild disabilities when learning to read, and an examination of the interrelated nature of reading and the other language arts. Then we will present effective methods for teaching children with mild disabilities to read.

The Nature of Reading and Reading Problems

Researchers use many models to explain how children learn to read. For example, authorities may consider reading to be a "top-down," a "bottom-up," or an "interactive" process. In addition, some researchers emphasize developmental or information-processing models when explaining the nature of reading. All models, however, emphasize two major elements: decoding or recognizing words and comprehending the meaning of written text.

Goodman (1970) and Smith (1971) were among the first to describe reading as a top-down process. According to these authorities, the reader brings to the reading task past experiences and background knowledge about language and about the world. Rather than relying on individual words or parts of words to obtain meaning, the reader predicts meaning as reading occurs, advancing hypotheses about what is read based on prior knowledge and reading to confirm these predictions. Thus, the reader is an active participant in constructing his or her own meaning from the text. Proponents of a bottom-up model, on the other hand, view reading as a process of decoding individual letters and words and of putting words and sentences together to achieve meaning (Liberman & Shankweiler, 1985). Rather than bringing meaning to the text, the skillful reader extracts the meaning by fluently decoding or recognizing words.

Today, however, many authorities accept an interactive position (Spiro & Myers, 1984; Stanovich, 1980). This view holds that the reading task is composed of alternating or simultaneous use of both top-down and bottom-up processes. The mature reader brings to the printed page background knowledge and experience, using these to predict and construct meaning from the text. When unknown words are encountered, though, the reader may switch to a bottom-up strategy. Thus, background knowledge and decoding skill interact during the reading process.

Similarly, Chall (1983) proposes a developmental model of reading in which children progress through a sequence of stages. In stage I, children learn the alphabet and the sounds of letters. During stage II, youngsters practice the basic decoding and word-recognition skills learned in stage I in order to achieve fluency and speed and to gain meaning from text. By stage III (grades 4 to 8), children must learn from reading so that in high school, stage IV, they can read substantial amounts of text with differing points of view. Although this model emphasizes the mastery of component reading skills, particularly in stages I and II, Chall (1983) believes that the child's prior experience and knowledge influence how rapidly the youngster will progress. Moreover, when faced with difficult text or unknown words, children will revert to stage I or II skills.

Gunning (1996), too, describes a series of stages through which children pass as they learn to read. In the first stage, emergent literacy, from birth to age five, children learn important concepts about print and its functions. During the second stage , beginning reading, youngsters in kindergarten and first grade learn basic alphabetic principles, letter-sound associations, and easy, high-frequency words. Stage three, growing independence, takes place in grades 2 and 3. At this stage, children become proficient with the basic decoding and word recognition skills and begin to read longer, more complex sentences. In stage four, reading to learn, students in grades 4 to 6 are expected to refine their reading skills and apply them to obtain information from various types of text. Finally, in grades 7 and beyond, children in stage five, abstract reading, must read for information and pleasure, as well as to evaluate the merit of what they read.

LaBerge and Samuels (1974) also hold that children progress through a hierarchy of reading skills, from decoding to comprehension. In their information-processing model, however, attention is a critical element. Children must become automatic and fluent with lower-level reading skills, recognizing letters and remembering letter-sound correspondences, in order to free a limited attentional capacity for higher-level, comprehension skills. Therefore, according to this model, the goal of initial reading instruction is fluent decoding.

Each of these models helps to explain the difficulty children with mild disabilities may have when learning to read. For example, Stanovich (1986a) maintains that much of the variance in reading ability among children and youth may be due to differing levels of decoding ability. Because poor readers are deficient in decoding skills, they may be too dependent on top-down processes, guessing at words based on the first letters and on the context. On the other hand, Samuels (1987) holds that poor readers rely on bottom-up processes more than do mature readers. Poor readers often use the single letter as the unit of recognition, placing heavy demands on short-term memory and hindering comprehension. Most authorities now agree, though, that poor readers have deficits in phonological processes, the skills necessary for segmenting, blending, and manipulating phonemes (i.e., units of sound), more often than they have deficits in visual processes (e.g., letter reversals) (Foorman & Liberman, 1989; Lenchner, Gerber, & Routh, 1990; Mann, Cowin, & Schoenheimer, 1989). (See Chapter 10 for a discussion of these phonological skills.)

Although poor readers may have problems with reading comprehension that cannot be explained solely by deficient decoding ability, there is evidence to suggest that the primary difficulty for most poor readers originates with inadequate decoding skill (Spear & Sternberg, 1986). Deficits in decoding ability limit the child's future interaction with text, thus limiting the knowledge and experience the child may gain from reading (Stanovich, 1986b). Unfortunately, children in the bottom reading groups may not receive the intense instruction in decoding skills, coupled with exposure to extended text, necessary to accelerate their progress and allow them to access school knowledge (McGill-Franzen & Allington, 1991).

Because children with mild disabilities often encounter difficulty with decoding and word recognition, special educators must emphasize these essential skills during initial reading instruction. Teachers must remember, however, that students with mild disabilities also need instruction and practice with connected text (i.e., rich examples of quality literature) if they are to learn to comprehend what they read. Finally, rather than endless drill and practice of isolated skills on workbook pages, youngsters with mild disabilities must have opportunities to integrate reading and writing activities.

Whole Language and Reading Instruction

Recently, literature-based approaches to teaching reading have become increasingly popular. Criticism of skills-oriented reading materials and instruction, in such national reports as Becoming a Nation of Readers (Anderson, Hiebert, Scott, & Wilkinson, 1985), at least partly account for the popularity of a "whole language" philosophy regarding reading and the language arts. Advocates of a whole language perspective believe that children must learn to read and to write in a natural context, and that reading and writing skills are inherently connected (Goodman, 1986). Rather than breaking reading and writing into separate component skills, whole language proponents maintain that all skill instruction must be integrated with the literature being read. Therefore, as described by Butler (1987), teachers using a whole language philosophy typically:

1. Read quality literature to children;
2. Read and reread rhymes, songs, poems, and stories, particularly those with predictable or repetitive lines (e.g., "I'll huff, and I'll puff, and . . .");
3. Set aside time each day for sustained silent reading for everyone, including the teacher;
4. Provide guided reading for small groups of children using books selected to suit the interests and abilities of group members;
5. Provide individualized reading opportunities;
6. Organize language experience activities so that children may talk and write about what they do;
7. Afford children numerous opportunities to write about topics of interest, focusing initially on the content rather than on the form;
8. Model "expert" writing for children;
9. Provide opportunities for children to share or publish finished writing; and
10. Demonstrate reading and writing with content-area text.

Although whole language advocates realize that some time must be spent on decoding skills, they maintain that this instruction must always be integrated with quality literature. They criticize the skill-building drill-and-practice activities of traditional classrooms as boring exercises bearing little resemblance to authentic reading and writing experiences. They suggest instead that teachers use repetitive lines within stories and poems to help children figure out the code on their own (Cullinan, 1987). Moreover, whole language proponents argue that the books often used with poor readers are so controlled in vocabulary and style that most children find them stilted and unappealing. According to whole language advocates, poor readers do not understand why they are completing drill-and-practice activities; moreover, they are frustrated with the dull stories they are expected to read (Routman, 1988).

Whole language proponents properly remind us that all children need exposure to quality literature and that reading and writing are related activities. Nevertheless, the reader must remember that children with mild disabilities do not learn well from indirect instruction. Although whole language may increase a student's motivation to read, the teacher must provide systematic instruction in decoding and comprehension skills if youngsters with mild disabilities are to learn *how* to read (Chall, 1989; Gersten & Dimino, 1990; Stahl & Miller, 1989). We will return to this discussion later in the chapter; however, for now, let's examine the major approaches used during initial, or developmental, reading instruction.

Developmental Reading

Developmental reading refers to a sequence of daily activities designed to teach children to read for the first time. Many children with mild disabilities fail in their developmental reading programs. Others may participate in these programs, to some extent, in their mainstreamed classrooms. For these reasons, special education teachers must understand the developmental reading programs used in their schools. Let's turn to an examination of two important concerns regarding the developmental reading program: basal reading series and research on initial reading instruction.

Basal Reading Series

A series of books, the basal readers, still forms the core of the developmental reading program in most classrooms today (Reutzel & Cooter, 1996; Snow, Burns, & Griffin, 1998). Historically, these books increased gradually in difficulty from preprimers, primers, and the first reader through about the eighth-grade level, with the difficulty, or readability, of each level achieved by controlling the decoding skills, vocabulary, and sentence complexity presented. The teacher's edition of the basal reading series typically contains a scope and sequence chart detailing the skills to be taught and the order in which they are to be presented. The teacher's manual also includes a version of the student's text and lesson plans for the teacher to follow. In addition, the basal reading series provides the teacher with supplementary activities and skill-building workbooks and worksheets to guide instruction. For an additional cost, charts, posters, big books, classroom book sets, CDs, computer software, videos, puppets, and other related materials may also be obtained. (See Table 11.1 for a list of web sites for publishers of reading series.)

Table 11.1 **Some Selected Publishers of Basal Reading Series**

Harcourt-Brace-Jovanovich	Scholastic
http://www.harcourt.com/	**http://www.scholastic.com/**
Houghton-Mifflin	Scott Foresman
http://www.hmco.com/	**http://www.scottforesman.com/**
Macmillan-McGraw Hill	Silver Burdett and Ginn
http://www.macmillan.com/	**http://www.sbgschool.com**
Open Court	
http://www.opencourt.com/	

Within the teacher's manuals are suggestions for specific instructional procedures. Most basal reading series use either a *directed reading activity* or a *directed reading-thinking activity* as a guide for reading lessons. In the directed reading activity, the teacher begins by motivating students to learn the material. Next, the teacher presents new vocabulary or concepts and actively guides students while they read the story by asking specific questions to set a purpose for reading and check for comprehension. Finally, the teacher develops related skills using drill, workbook pages, and independent assignments, and evaluates the effectiveness of the lesson. By contrast, in the directed reading-thinking activity the teacher serves to facilitate, rather than guide, lessons. With teacher assistance, children set their own purposes for reading and formulate their own questions. The teacher then challenges them to think about the validity of the answers they propose or the conclusions they draw (e.g., "What evidence is there in the story to support your statement?").

Although basal reading series are comprehensive instructional programs, they usually emphasize one of two major approaches to initial reading instruction: a code-emphasis approach (i.e., a bottom-up philosophy of the reading process) or a meaning-emphasis approach (i.e., a top-down theory). All basals include activities designed to increase both decoding and comprehension skills; however, the relative emphasis each receives within the series defines the approach used.

Code-emphasis basals begin with letters and/or letter sounds. Children learn consistent letter-sound associations and other essential phonics skills to help them unlock the code and become independent readers. Comprehension skills are included within these series, but the primary focus, initially, is on decoding.

Although all code-emphasis basals begin with decoding skills, they differ in how these skills are presented. Direct-synthetic phonics programs present letter-sound (i.e., grapheme-phoneme) correspondences and sound blending explicitly. For example, children learn the sounds /m/, /a/, and /n/ individually, and then learn to move from one sound to another to blend the word *man*. Indirect, or analytic, phonics programs, on the other hand, present letter sounds only within the context of whole words. Children learn the sound /d/ as in *daddy* or, in the special case of linguistic approaches, the sounds within word families (e.g., an, can, Dan, fan, man, Nan, pan, ran, tan, van).

Meaning-emphasis basals, however, begin with words children often use. Because these frequently-occurring words are familiar to most children, they are presumably easier for children to recognize. Youngsters learn to read words by sight, as whole units having meaning, and to use context clues to identify unknown words. Throughout reading instruction, the focus is on comprehension and the meaning of words within connected text. The whole language movement represents a recent resurgence of interest in the meaning-emphasis approach.

To that end, today's basal reading series contain anthologies or collections of children's literature more often than carefully controlled text. McCarthey and Hoffman (1995) assert, for example, that contemporary basal reading series contain stories that have reduced vocabulary control, increased decoding demands, few adaptations, greater variation in genre, predictable text, and more engaging literary quality. Anderson (1995) also reports that the proportion of literature-based stories in basal readers increased from only 17% in 1987 to 87% in 1993. Similarly, Hoffman and McCarthey and their colleagues report a number of changes in current basal reading series and resultant classroom practices, including (a) diversity in format (e.g., big books, tradebooks, and anthologies), (b) greater predictability and use of patterned text, (c) less control of vocabulary (e.g., a reduced number of words but an increased number of unique words), and (d) a decreased focus on phonics and isolated skills instruction (see, for example, Hoffman et al., 1994, 1998 and McCarthey et al., 1994).

Such changes, however, are not without criticism. Shannon (1992) and Shannon and Crawford (1997), for example, suggest that basal reading series, regardless of whether or not they are literature-based, "deskill" teachers and contribute to failure and a prescribed classroom culture. Moreover, Reutzel and Larsen (1995) report that current literature-based basals omit or change key illustrations such that important story elements are lost; change the ethnicity, gender, or roles of main characters; or print only excerpts from the complete story. These authors assert that anthologies of literature are *still* textbooks that differ from the original, "real" stories. Similarly, Noll and Goodman (1995) maintain that the repetitive structure teachers are encouraged to use with each story in the basal overwhelms the actual literature, much like "using a howitzer to kill a butterfly" (p. 243).

On the other hand, Baumann, Heubach and their colleagues refute the notion that teacher's editions accompanying the basal readers control and "deskill" the teacher (see, for example, Baumann & Heubach, 1994, 1996; and Hoffman et al., 1995). These authorities suggest that teachers make decisions about what skills to teach and what methods to use regardless of suggestions made in the teacher's manuals. Unfortunately, few teacher's manuals provide adequate suggestions for teachers regarding how to adjust lessons to suit the needs of students with mild disabilities included in the classroom (Schumm, Vaughn, Haager, Klingner, 1994).

Of particular concern is research suggesting that many current basal reading series do not emphasize reading fluency or explicit instruction in sound-symbol relationships, critical skills for students to master if they are to learn to read (Stein, 1993). According to Stein, the student readers accompanying most basals used in kindergarten and first-grade classrooms contain less than 15% of wholly decodable words. That is, there is little relationship between any decoding skills or sight words taught to students during reading lessons suggested in the teacher's manuals and the actual words children must read in subsequent stories. In fact, Stein, Hohnson, and Gutlohn (1999) determined that students are unable to decode 32 percent to 57 percent of the words they encounter in six of seven popular basal reading series. Because basal readers are such an important component of the developmental reading program, teachers are encouraged to consider the advantages and limitations of basals (see Table 11.2). Teachers must also be prepared to augment lessons in basal reading series with systematic practice in phonics so that students can better transfer decoding skills to literature-based basal readers (Snider, 1997).

Table 11.2	**Suggested Advantages and Limitations of Basal Reading Series**

Advantages

- ◆ A sequenced curriculum of skill instruction is provided. Skills instruction is arranged to provide for both initial instruction and a systematic review of skills taught.
- ◆ A continuous arrangement of instruction from grade to grade is supplied.
- ◆ To save teachers' time, a completely prepared set of stories, instructional directions and activities, instructional practice materials, and assessment and management devices is available.
- ◆ Stories are arranged in a sequence of ascending difficulty.
- ◆ Reading skills are gradually introduced.
- ◆ Teachers are provided structured lesson plans.
- ◆ Students are exposed to a variety of literary genres in basals.
- ◆ Organization and structure of basals are helpful to beginning teachers just learning about the reading curriculum.
- ◆ Organization and structure are reassuring to administrators and school patrons that important reading skills are being taught.

Limitations

- ◆ Vocabulary control renders story content dull and repetitious.
- ◆ Cropping pictures removes supportive scaffolding for younger readers.
- ◆ Skill instruction is rarely applied in or related to comprehending the story content.
- ◆ The basal lesson design in teacher's editions very often fails to relate one part of the lesson (e.g., vocabulary introduction) to subsequent parts of the reading lesson (e.g., discussion of story for comprehension).
- ◆ Stories often do not relate to students' interests.
- ◆ The format of basals is often less appealing than the format of trade books.
- ◆ Special interest group censorship leads to the selection of stories that contain little real subject matter content, that deal with few real-life applications, or that present societal or ethical content for right-living.
- ◆ The application of readability formulas to text selections results in stories and text features that are void of content and inconsiderate of the reader's need to understand.
- ◆ Teacher's editions seldom contain useful directions on how to teach reading comprehension.
- ◆ A rigid adherence to the basal leaves little room for teacher creativity and decision making.
- ◆ The grading or leveling of basal readers promotes the use of traditional ability or achievement groups in classrooms.

From: Reutzel, D.R. (1991). Understanding and using basal readers effectively. In B. Hayes (Ed.), *Effective strategies for teaching reading* (p. 259). New York: Allyn & Bacon.

Research on Developmental Reading Approaches

Over the years, debate has raged regarding the "best" approach for initial reading instruction. In a classic review of both experimental and correlational research on reading instruction, *Learning to Read: The Great Debate*, Chall (1967) drew the following conclusions:

1. A code-emphasis approach produces better reading achievement by the third grade than a meaning-emphasis approach.
2. Children of average and below-average intelligence and children of lower socioeconomic backgrounds learn to read better with a code-emphasis approach.

3. Both code-emphasis and meaning-emphasis approaches produce reading failures, but failures are more serious within the meaning-emphasis approach.

Later, in an updated version of this classic, Chall (1983) states that, although phonics instruction has become widely accepted and taught early in the grades, authorities are now debating the "best" method for phonics instruction. She adds, however, that experimental and correlational evidence favors a direct-synthetic phonics approach, particularly for children with mild disabilities.

In response to a congressional request for a reevaluation of phonics instruction and a renewed interest in meaning-emphasis approaches, Adams (1990) reviewed a substantial body of research on the teaching of reading. Although very little research in her review involved special education populations, Adams drew these conclusions:

1. Programs using systematic phonics instruction in addition to connected reading are superior to those that use either alone.
2. A child's knowledge of the letters of the alphabet and his or her ability to discriminate phonemes are the two best predictors of first-grade reading achievement.
3. Teaching explicit (i.e., direct-synthetic) phonics is more effective than teaching indirect phonics.
4. The most important outcome of phonics instruction is not the ability to sound out words, but rather the ability to recognize letters, letter patterns, and words automatically.

More recently, the Committee on the Prevention of Reading Difficulties in Young Children released a synthesis of research findings regarding initial reading instruction (Snow et al., 1998). This project was conducted by the National Academy of Sciences, and was jointly sponsored by the U.S. Department of Education, Office of Special Education Programs, and the U.S. Department of Health and Human Services. According to this report, adequate reading instruction demands that children:

◆ Use reading to obtain meaning from print,
◆ Be exposed to frequent and regular spelling-sound relationships,
◆ Understand the structure of spoken words,
◆ Learn the alphabetic equivalents of spoken sounds—the letters and their sequences in words,
◆ Have sufficient practice with reading to achieve fluency with various types of text,
◆ Possess sufficient background knowledge and vocabulary for texts to be meaningful and interesting,
◆ Gain control over procedures for monitoring comprehension and repairing misunderstandings, and
◆ Experience continued interest and motivation to read.

Ideally, with intensive decoding instruction early in the grades, only a very few children would fail to learn to read. Unfortunately, though, most children with mild disabilities are referred to special education programs because of reading problems. Reid Lyon and his colleagues at the National Institute of Child

Health and Development (NICHD) maintain that for children to learn to read, the teacher must (a) teach phonemic awareness directly and at an early age; (b) systematically teach frequent, highly regular sound-spelling relationships; (c) show children how to sound out words; (d) use connected text that children can decode to practice the sound-symbol relationships they learn; (e) read aloud interesting, authentic stories to develop language comprehension; and (f) separate decoding instruction from comprehension of interesting text in a balanced approach (see, for example, Fletcher & Lyon, 1998). Initial reading instruction for children with mild disabilities, then, must be explicit, direct, and focused on essential phonics skills (Snow et al., 1998). As children become automatic and fluent with decoding and word recognition, their teachers may emphasize direct instruction of comprehension skills and comprehension strategies. Although initial reading instruction should be structured and highly focused, teachers can still read quality literature to children with mild disabilities and provide them with opportunities to talk and write about what they read. The consensus today is that most children need a balance between phonics and meaning to become good readers (Learning First Alliance, 1998). (See Box 11.1 for web sites containing information on reading and reading research.) Let's turn now to a discussion of remedial reading instruction for youngsters with reading disabilities.

Box 11.1

Web Watch

Web Sites for Reading Research, Information, and Children's Literature

Center for the Improvement of Early Reading Achievement (CIERA)

http://www.ciera.org

Information on reading and literacy. Publications, tool kits for tutors, and links to many sites containing research and tips for reading instruction.

Cyber Guide for Literature

http://www.sdcoe.k12.ca.us/score/cyberguide.html

A wonderful resource for children's literature, including related lesson plans and activities, as well as links to other literature web sites.

Multicultural Resources

http://www.falcon.jmu.edu/~ramseyil/mutipub.htm

Numerous articles and suggestions for multicultural children's literature organized by cultural groups.

Reading Online

http://www.readingonline.org

Homepage for the International Reading Association, this site contains research on reading and reading instruction, critical issues, phonemic awareness, an electronic classroom, professional materials, and an international forum.

The Center for the Future of Teaching and Learning

http://www.cftl.org

Contains research on reading, from the National Institute of Child Health and Human Development, including the report, *30 Years of Research: What We Now Know about How Children Learn to Read.*

The Children's Literature Web Guide

http://www.ucalgary.ca/~dkbrown/index.html

A central web site for finding children's literature. Many links to other sites regarding literature for children.

The International Dyslexia Association

http://www.interdys.org

Homepage for International Dyslexia Association. The site contains reports, information exchanges, and resources.

Remedial Reading Approaches

For many children with mild disabilities, the typical reading lesson in the regular classroom is inadequate (Simmons, Fuchs, & Fuchs, 1991). Words are not repeated frequently enough in the basal readers for children with learning disabilities, emotional disturbance, or mild mental retardation to master them (Chall, 1983). In addition, many familiar first words introduced in meaning-emphasis or whole language preprimers and primers (e.g., *you* or *the*) are difficult to decode because they contain irregularities or letters representing other than their most common sounds (Kameenui & Simmons, 1990).

Repetition and explicit teaching are hallmarks of special education classrooms. Successful remedial reading instruction, therefore, adheres to these principles of effective teaching and includes an early emphasis on phonics skills and sight word recognition. In addition, teachers maintain that, for some children, a specialized multisensory approach or the language experience approach (LEA) may be useful. Moreover, as children in special education classrooms become fluent with decoding and word recognition, their teachers must provide direct instruction in comprehension skills and strategies.

Phonics Instruction and Phonics Programs

Children with mild disabilities must be directly taught the phonics skills necessary to "unlock" the code. (See Table 11.3 for some essential phonics skills.) Initially, students learn the most common letter-sound associations for the consonants and the short vowels. Carnine, Silbert, and Kameenui (1997) suggest that teachers begin with "more useful" letter sounds (i.e., the short vowels and the consonants *b, c, d, f, g, h, k, l, m, n, p, r, s,* and *t,* although not necessarily in that order) and that they separate aurally or visually similar letters by at least three dissimilar ones. As students become automatic with five or six

Table 11.3 Essential Phonics Skills

Consonants:
Voiced Sounds (b, d, g, j, l, m, n, r, v, w, x, y, z)
Unvoiced Sounds (c, f, h, k, p, q, s, x, t)
Continuous Sounds (c, f, l, m, n, r, s, v, w, x, y, z)
Stop Sounds (b, c, d, g, h, j, k, p, q, t, x)

Single Consonants with One Sound:

b	bear	l	lake	t	turtle
d	dog	m	money	v	vase
f	face	n	nose	w	wagon
h	hen	p	pear	y	yellow
j	jug	q	queen	z	zebra

Single Consonants with Two or More Sounds:

c	cat	g	goat	s	six	x	xylophone
c	city	g	germ	s	is	x	exist
				s	sure	x	box

Qu usually has the sound of *kw*; however, in some words, such as *bouquet,* it has the sound of *k*.

Beginning Consonant Blends

bl	blue	pr	pretty	tw	twin
br	brown	sc	score	wr	wrench
cl	clown	sk	skill	sch	school
cr	crown	sl	slow	scr	screen
dr	dress	sm	small	shr	shrink
dw	dwell	sn	snail	spl	splash
fl	flower	sp	spin	spr	spring
fr	from	st	story	squ	squash
gl	glue	sw	swan	str	string
gr	grape	tr	tree	thr	throw
pl	plate				

Ending Consonant Blends

ld	wild	rk	work
mp	lamp	sk	risk
nd	wind	st	fast
nt	went		

Consonant Digraphs

ch	chute	sh	ship
ch	choral	th	three
ch	church	th	that
gh	cough	wh	which
ph	graph	wh	who

Vowels

Continuous and Voiced Sounds:
a, e, i, o, u
y is usually a consonant at the beginning of a word and a vowel in any other position.

Table 11.3 Essential Phonics Skills—*continued*

Short Vowel Sounds	Long Vowel Sounds
a bat	a rake
e bed	e jeep
i pig	i kite
o lock	o rope
u duck	u mule
	y my
	y baby

Controlled Vowels

Three consonants usually affect or control the sounds of some, or all, of the vowels when they follow these vowels within a syllable. They are r, w, and l (sometimes known as <u>R</u>eally <u>W</u>eird <u>L</u>etters).

r	w	l
car	law	all
her	few	bell
dirt	now	
word		
fur		

Vowel Digraphs (Most common phonemes only)

ai	pain
ay	hay
ea	each or weather (Other phonemes are common.)
ee	meet
ei	weight or either (Other phonemes are common.)
ie	piece (Other phonemes are common.)
oa	oats
oo	book or moon
ou	tough
ow	low

You can teach the mnemonic, "When two vowels go a-walking, the first one does the talking, and the second one is silent," but there are many exceptions.

Diphthongs (Pronounced dif' thongs.)

au	haul*	oi	soil
aw	hawk*	ou	trout
ew	few	ow	cow
ey	they*	oy	boy

*In a diphthong, both of the vowel letters are heard and they make a gliding sound, which is heard most easily in words like cow and boy. Some speakers may hear the examples of au, aw, and ey given here as digraphs (one sound) rather than diphthongs.
Adapted from: *Locating and correcting reading difficulties (7th ed.)* (pp. 233-235), by J.L. Shanker & E. E. Ekwall, 1998, Upper Saddle River, NJ: Merrill/Prentice Hall.

grapheme-phoneme relationships, sound blending may be introduced using regular consonant-vowel (CV) or consonant-vowel-consonant (CVC) words (e.g., *at, map*). For example, once students master the sounds of the letters *a, m, t, s, i,* and *d,* they can blend many one-syllable words. The sequence described in Table 11.4 is recommended for teaching blending with regular one-syllable words with short vowels.

When students master basic letter-sound correspondences and are successfully sound blending, they must learn useful letter combinations and phonics rules. Letter combinations include the following:

- ◆ The vowel and consonant digraphs: two vowels or two consonants that together make one sound, such as *oa* in *boat* or *sh* in *ship*;
- ◆ The diphthongs: two vowels, each modifying one another and both contributing to the sound produced, such as *oy* in *boy*;
- ◆ The "r-controlled" vowels: a vowel followed by the letter *r*, such as *ar* in *smart*; and
- ◆ The "l-controlled" vowels, such as *ol* in *cold*.

Teaching these letter combinations permits the child to attack words generally considered to be "irregular" as if they were "regular." That is, once students have mastered the basic letter combinations, they can be prompted to "look in the middle of the word" for spelling patterns whenever pronunciation errors occur (Schworm, 1988). Moreover, students can be told to try the most common sound for letters and letter combinations first when they are decoding unknown words. If these do not make sense in a sentence, then they can try the less common sounds. In addition, useful phonics rules that may be taught include:

- ◆ the CVCe pattern (e.g., *made, hope*)
- ◆ *kn* at the start of a word is pronounced like *n* (e.g., *knife*)
- ◆ *wr* at the start of a word is pronounced like *r* (e.g., *wrong*)
- ◆ *ck* at the end of a word has the sound of *k* (e.g., *check*)

Table 11.4 A Teaching Sequence for Blending Regular One-Syllable Words with Short Vowels

Carnine, Silbert, and Kameenui (1997) recommend the following sequence when teaching blending:

1. VC and CVC words beginning with continuous sounds (i.e., sounds that may be prolonged and stretched such as /m/ or the vowel sounds, as in *me* or *man*);
2. CVCC words beginning with continuous sounds (e.g., *fill, mist*);
3. CVC words that begin with stop sounds (i.e., sounds that can't be prolonged, such as /p/ in *pat*);
4. CVCC words that begin with stop sounds (e.g., *band* or *past*);
5. CCVC words that begin with two continuous consonant sounds (i.e., the two-letter consonant blends such as in *slam* or *flat*);
6. CCVC words beginning with one continuous and one stop sound (e.g., *stop* or *skip*); and
7. CCVCC words (e.g., *blast* or *crust*) and CCCVCC words (e.g., *struck* or *splint*).

- *ght* together are pronounced like *t* (e.g., *light*)
- *c* followed by *e, i,* or *y* makes the *s* sound (e.g., *cent*)
- *c* followed by *o, a,* or *u* makes the *k* sound (e.g., *cotton*)
- *g* followed by *e, i,* or *y* makes the *j* sound (e.g., *gem*)
- *y* sounds like *i* at the end of a one-syllable word (e.g., *my, by*) and like *e* at the end of longer words (e.g., *baby, daddy, grocery*) (Carnine, Silbert, & Kameenui, 1997).

More advanced decoding skills involve the structural, or morphemic, analysis of words. That is, children learn to break words into meaningful parts. These may include compound words or a base word plus frequently occurring prefixes, such as *un-*; suffixes, such as *-ness*; or inflectional endings, such as *-ing*, *-ed*, or *-s*. Again, teaching useful rules may assist youngsters with mild disabilities with recognizing or spelling unknown words. Examples of useful rules include the following:

- The "doubling rule": When suffixes beginning with a vowel are added to a CVC word, the final consonant in the word is doubled (e.g., *fat* becomes *fatter* but *sing* stays the same in *singing* and *sad* stays the same in *sadness*).
- The "y" rule: When a consonant comes before a *y* in a base word, the *y* changes to *i* before an ending is added (e.g., *happy* changes to *happiness* or *happiest*, but *play* remains the same, as in *played*).
- The "e" rule: When a suffix beginning with a vowel is added to a word that ends with an e, drop the e and add the ending (e.g., *hope* becomes *hoping*). (Note that *hop* becomes *hopping* because the doubling rule, not the "e" rule, applies!)

Special education teachers often supplement the basal reading series with direct instruction of phonics skills. In order to provide explicit and comprehensive instruction with enough repetition to ensure proficient decoding, teachers may wish to choose one of several code-based programs available commercially as the core for reading lessons. Many of these programs are total reading curricula that could also be considered developmental; however, they are most often used for remedial reading, and therefore will be included here in our discussion. Teachers may also wish to consult as resources several older phonics programs, including The Writing Road to Reading (Spalding & Spalding, 1962), Phonetic Keys to Reading (Harris, Creekmore, & Greenman, 1967), and the Phonovisual Method (Schoolfield & Timberlake, 1974).

The Reading Mastery Series and Corrective Reading.

Reading Mastery is a highly-structured and rapidly-paced reading program (Engelmann & Bruner, 1995), with Levels I, II, III, and the Fast Cycle designed for children in kindergarten through third grade. Reading Mastery IV, V, and VI are for children reading from the fourth- through the sixth-grade levels. The program uses a direct-synthetic phonics approach and provides teachers with scripted 30-minute lessons, detailed hand signals to guide student responding, and specific error-correction procedures (see Box 11.2). Because the authors believe letter sounds to be the most useful association to learn (Engelman & Bruner), students are initially taught to recognize the sounds of letters rather than the letter names. In addition to letter-sound correspondence, sound blending, and letter

Box 11.2

Direct Synthetic Phonics Instruction

When using a direct-synthetic phonics approach, letter-sound correspondence and sound blending are taught explicitly. The following example from Reading Mastery is illustrative of this approach. The teacher is given the following instructions:

Say, "Everybody look at the book," and offer praise to children who look.

Say, "mmm. This is mmm." while pointing to the *m*.

Say, "Say mmm." Pause and say, "Good."

(The teacher continues this procedure pointing to *m* and to a picture as a distracter. Notice that the *m* is introduced by its sound rather than by its name.)

Later, sound blending is introduced through a "sound-sliding" game. Children are taught to hold sounds and to slide slowly from one sound to another using an arrow from left to right under the letters as a directional clue. Next, youngsters "say it fast" to produce a word as in the following example:

a. "Let's follow the arrow and say the sounds." Point to *a*. "Aaaa. Keep it going. Louder."

b. Have the children hold /a/ until you point to *m*. Do not pause. Point to *m* and say, "mmmm."

c. Return to the beginning of the arrow. "Let's do it again." Move rapidly from *a* to *m* saying "aaammm." Pause, then say, "Again." Repeat three times. Then say, "Say it fast!" Pause and say, "Yes, *am*."

d. "Let's follow the arrow and see what word this is: aaammm. Say it fast!" Pause and say, "Yes, *am*. *Am*. I am happy."

Adapted from: *Reading Mastery: Levels I, II, Fast Cycle*, by S. Engelmann & E. C. Bruner, 1995, Blacklick, OH: Science Research Associates.

combinations, Reading Mastery gives the student practice in both literal and inferential comprehension skills.

The Corrective Reading program (Engelmann, Johnson, & Carnine, 1999; Engelmann, Haddox, Hanner, & Osborn, 1999) follows an instructional sequence similar to that of Reading Mastery; however, the format is more appropriate for older children and adults. Designed for remedial or non-reading students in fourth grade and above, Corrective Reading provides lessons in two strands: Decoding and Comprehension. Again, lessons for teachers to follow are scripted, but real-life applications and a group-reward system provide motivation for older children with reading problems.

Both Reading Mastery and Corrective Reading have an extensive research base (Adams & Engelmann, 1996). Although most studies report favorable results for low-achieving children (Carnine & Silbert, 1979; Stallings, 1974) and for students with learning disabilities, mild mental retardation, or emotional disturbance (Polloway, Epstein, Polloway, Patton, & Ball, 1986), some suggest only mixed effectiveness (Kuder, 1990, 1991). In addition, some teachers object to the scripted nature of the materials, maintaining that these programs inhibit "teaching creatively." One must remember, however, that the progress of children, not the whims of the teacher, should dictate program selection. Both Reading Mastery and Corrective Reading are available from Science Research Associates.

Reading Horizons. *Horizons: Learning to Read* (Engelmann, Engelmann, & Davis, 1997, 1998; Engalmann & Hanner, 1998) offers highly sequenced, scripted lessons integrating reading and spelling. Level A, for average or below-average first graders or second grade non-readers, introduces 700 words in 155 lessons. Letter combinations are underlined and silent letters are printed in blue to prompt students to pay attention to these salient word elements critical for decoding. Similarly, phonetically irregular words are highlighted with a wavy underline. Phonetically decodable stories accompany lessons, and real children's literature (e.g., Margaret Wise Brown's *Goodnight Moon*) is included for practicing skills such as rhyming. Reading Horizons is also available in two Fast Track versions: A–B (for students up to grade 2) and C–D (for students in third grade and up). Horizons: *Learning to Read* is available through Science Research Associates.

Gillingham-Stillman Method. Although originally said to be a multisensory procedure using the Visual-Auditory-Kinesthetic-Tactile (VAKT) approach, the Gillingham-Stillman method (Gillingham & Stillman, 1973) consists of direct-synthetic phonics instruction. This program emphasizes how letters and words look, how they sound, and how the speech organs or the hands feel when producing the letter or the word. In addition, the history of the English language is included as a fundamental part of the program in order to enable the child to understand inconsistencies in pronunciation and spelling and to attack unknown words more effectively. Originally designed for pupils at the high school level, the method is successful with older and younger individuals as well (Guyer & Sabatino, 1989).

Within the teacher's manual are explicit guidelines for the instructor to follow. For example, the program requires a minimum of 2 years of lessons for approximately 45 minutes to 1 hour each day. Moreover, teachers and parents are requested not to permit the child access to any materials that do not conform to the method until new habits and skills are acquired. Parents and teachers may, of course, read content textbooks or other literature aloud to the child so that he or she may keep up with classwork.

Instruction begins with the introduction of letters on letter cards, starting with the consonants *b, f, h, j, k, m, p, t,* and the short vowel sounds. White cards are used for the consonants; salmon-colored cards are used for the vowels. Later, buff-colored cards introduce additional phonemes for reading and spelling. Each letter is shown initially with a keyword, which is always repeated first before the child states the letter name or sound. Letter names and sounds are introduced using the following procedures:

1. Show the letter card, say the letter name, and have the child repeat it.
2. Show the letter card, say the letter sound, and have the child repeat it.
3. While saying the letter sound, have the child feel your throat and his or her own throat for vibrations or have the child feel the breath flow from your mouth and his or her own mouth against the hand.

4. Write the letter in cursive, pointing out the strokes and any identifying visual clues for the letters, and have the child trace the letter while saying first the letter name and then the letter sound until he or she can write the letter correctly from memory.
5. Say the letter name and have the child say the sound.
6. Say the letter sound and have the child say the name.
7. Say the letter sound and have the child write the letter from memory.
8. Use the first six letters introduced for practice in sound blending.
9. Progress to Simultaneous Oral Spelling (SOS), during which the child repeats a word dictated by you, names the letters in the word, writes the word while again naming each letter, and reads the word he or she has written.
10. Teach additional phonograms (e.g., digraphs *ch* or *sh*) and word attack/spelling rules (e.g., for a one-syllable word ending in *f, l,* or *s* following only one vowel, double the *f, l,* or *s,* as in *puff, tell,* or *kiss*).

Children keep new words in word boxes and progress to reading controlled stories containing mostly CVC words and a few irregular sight words. Teachers give students any sight words necessary for story reading, and students silently prepare to read each sentence, asking for assistance only if necessary. When students finally read orally, they are expected to read fluently and with expression. Later, teachers dictate the same stories for pupils to write. Timed readings and graphs are also used to enhance pupil motivation and record progress.

In some variations of the Gillingham-Stillman approach (e.g., the Wilson Reading System), students are also taught the origin of English words. Yoshimoto (1997), for example, reports that about 50% of English words are derived from Latin roots. Moreover, Greek-root words are often evident in the sciences and medicine. Understanding these roots, as well as the meanings of suffixes and prefixes, enables students to achieve a higher-level understanding of the language.

The Gillingham-Stillman Method (Gillingham & Stillman, 1973) is a highly structured and repetitive approach to teaching synthetic phonics skills. Critics suggest, however, that students with mild disabilities may become confused when asked to learn both the letter name and the letter sound, and Stahl, Duffy-Hester, and Stahl (1998) report that only a "disappointing amount of research" has actually been conducted on the method and its variations. In addition, the contrived stories may be boring, particularly to older students. Finally, school districts may be unable to allocate the extended time necessary for the program when faced with standards for learning objectives at each grade level and content requirements for graduation credits. (For information on this approach write to the Orton Dyslexia Society, Inc., 724 York Road, Towson, MD 21204. Materials may also be obtained through Educator's Publishing Service listed in Appendix B.)

The Herman Method for Reversing Reading Failure. Like Reading Mastery, the Herman reading program (Romar Publications) (1975), developed by Rene Herman, is a highly structured, direct-synthetic phonics approach requiring a minimum of 2 years of daily lessons. Similar to the Gillingham-Stillman method, the Herman program was developed to be multisensory in nature. The materials are designed for children in grades 3 through 12 who are below the 25th percentile in reading achievement. Detailed lesson plans and objectives are included in the teacher's manual, and skills are presented using a multimedia format. Computer software programs have recently been added to the original 20 instructional filmstrips. In Set A, children progress from basic consonant and short vowel sounds associated with keywords, to digraphs, beginning blends, sight words, and phrase reading. In Set B, more difficult letter combinations, prefixes, suffixes, and syllable-division rules are introduced. In addition, handwriting and spelling are integral parts of the total package. Although little research evidence exists in the literature to support the program itself, the heavy emphasis on intensive, structured phonics makes the Herman reading program attractive to many special education teachers. (For information on this program, write to Romar Publications, 4700 Tyrone Ave., Sherman Oaks, CA 91423.)

Recipe for Reading. Nina Traub, the originator of Recipe for Reading (Traub & Bloom, 1990), was a student of Anna Gillingham. Therefore, Recipe for Reading follows the multisensory notions of the Gillingham-Stillman approach and uses similar sound cards (red printing for vowels and vowel digraphs and black for consonants). Traub and Bloom (1990), however, group the letters to be learned according to their kinesthetic feel. That is, the first letters learned in the sequence (i.e., hard *c*, short *o*, short *a*, *d*, hard *g*) are made by turning the hand in a circle to the left. The child learns to pronounce each letter sound when shown the sound card and then to name and write the letter when the teacher makes its sound. Children also learn to write and spell words before they are asked to read them, segmenting words by listening first for the initial sound, then the medial vowel, and finally the ending sound (e.g., /b/ /a/ /t/). Later, students write sentences dictated by the teacher, read from phonetic storybooks, and play phonetic word games. Recipe for Reading is appropriate for elementary-age children; however, it can be adapted for the middle school grades. The program is available from Educator's Publishing Service.

Wilson Reading System. Also based on the work of Gillingham and Stillman, The Wilson Reading System (Wilson, 1996) is most appropriate for secondary-level students and adult nonreaders with dyslexia. Parts 1 through 5 emphasize decoding and Parts 6 through 8 focus on encoding. Parts 9 and 10 stress comprehension skills. The Wilson Reading System teaches students letter-sound associations as well as syllable division rules (e.g., open syllables, those ending in a vowel, usually have the long vowel sound, as in *bro*/ken, and the closed syllable takes the short vowel sound), prefixes, suffixes, and a history of the English language. Reading, spelling, and writing are integrated, and stories have adult content. Each lesson uses the following representative sequence: Warm-up reviewing with sound cards, teach and review concepts, word cards, word lists, sentence reading, quick drills of sounds, review concepts for spelling, dictation, passage reading, and listening comprehension. (Materials and training for the program can be obtained by contacting Barbara A. Wilson, Wilson Language Training Corporation, 175 West Main Street, Millbury, MA 01527-1441. Phone number: (508) 865-5699.)

Merrill Linguistic Reading Program. The Merrill Linguistic Reading Program (1986) is a popular indirect, analytic phonics program available from Science Research Associates. Rather than direct teaching of letter-sound correspondence and sound blending, children learn sounds through the presentation of consistent word families following the CVC pattern and having only minimal differences (see Box 11.3). Later, additional spelling patterns (e.g., CVCe words) and irregular sight words are introduced. Although the program follows a whole-word orientation, consistent letter-sound combinations are stressed. Because words are grouped in families, the stories are often contrived and stilted, making comprehension difficult for many students with mild disabilities (Adams, 1990). Thus, the primary strength of the program, the controlled vocabulary, is also its greatest weakness.

Box 11.3

Indirect Analytic Phonics through a Linguistic Approach

In an indirect, or analytic, phonics approach, children learn the letter-sound associations through an examination of sounds within whole words. Some indirect analytic phonics programs present new words in word families so that children can spot consistent letter-sound patterns. The following example from the Merrill Linguistic Reading Program (1986) is representative of this approach. Teachers introduce new words using the following procedure:

1. Write the word on the chalkboard.
2. Pronounce the word.
3. Spell it, pointing to each letter.
4. Pronounce the word again.
5. Give a sentence using the word in context.
6. Have pupils offer sentences using the word.
7. Have pupils read the word and spell it as you point to each letter. (Be sure pupils look at the word.)

Then, when introducing new words, teachers present the word in *minimum contrast* with familiar words:

1. Write the familiar word on the chalkboard.
2. Write the new word directly beneath it. For example,

   cat
   can

3. Have pupils read the familiar word.
4. Pronounce the new word and spell it.
5. Ask pupils how the two words differ.
6. Use steps 5, 6, and 7 described in the preceding procedure.
7. After the minimum contrast with a familiar word has been established, present subsequent words in the new pattern together. For example,

   can
   man

8. Ask pupils how the words differ.

The following is an example of a story from the *Merrill Linguistic Reading Program* (1986). As you read the story, note the consistent word pattern:

A Man in a Van
Look at the van, Jan.
A man is in the van.
Jan ran to the van.
Dan ran to the van.
The man ran the van.
Dan is not in the van.
Jan is not in the van.

Adapted from: *I can, teacher's edition: Level A: Merrill linguistic reading program*, (pp. 6 & 46), by M.K. Rudolph & R.G. Wilson, 1986, Columbus, OH: S.R.A./Merrill. Adapted with permission.

Phonic Remedial Reading Lessons. The Phonic Remedial Reading Lessons (Kirk, Kirk, & Minskoff, 1985) consist of 77 analytic phonics lessons providing repeated practice in sound blending through whole words. In each lesson, children first sound out the phonetic elements and then blend them into the given words. The lessons are designed for children reading below the third-grade level who require structure and repetition to learn to read. The Phonic Remedial Reading Lessons are also a valuable resource material for teachers, providing them with excellent word lists for constructing drill-and-practice activities. (These lessons are available through Academic Therapy Publications, 20 Commercial Blvd., Novato, CA 94949.)

Computer Software Programs for Phonics Practice. In order to make phonics and decoding fluency practice more enjoyable for children with mild disabilities, many teachers are turning to computer software programs. Numerous programs with colorful graphics and sound are now available on CD-ROM from several publishers. Some favorites include:

- *The Learning to Read Bundle* (designed by Software for Success) available from Sunburst (i.e., *A to Zap!* for PreK-1, *First Phonics* for K-2, and *Reading Who? Reading You* for K-2);
- *Reading Blaster Jr.* (created by Davidson) available from Edmark for grades K-3;
- *The Reader Rabbit* series (designed by The Learning Company) available from Edmark or Sunburst for Preschool through grade 4;
- *JumpStart Kindergarten* and *JumpStart First Grade Reading* (designed by Knowledge Adventure) available from Edmark; and
- *Kid Phonics 1* and *2* (created by Davidson) for PreK-4 also available from Edmark.

Each of these software packages comes in both Mac and PC versions. Most come with a teacher's manual containing additional suggestions for lessons or integration with the curriculum. Contemporary software programs such as these also permit teachers to set learning levels for individual children, challenge individual students by automatically increasing the difficulty level depending on his or her performance, and enable teachers to print reports to monitor student progress.

Summary of Decoding-Skills Instruction ◆

Without a doubt, fluent decoding skills are necessary if children with mild disabilities are to become independent readers. Single-consonant and short vowel sounds, sound blending with CVC words, the most frequent sounds of common letter combinations, and high utility rules are the basic ingredients for structured practice with phonics skills. These are also the elements of many direct-synthetic phonics programs. Although each of the programs we have explored has both its proponents and its critics, the choice of a particular program is probably less important than a basic commitment to *systematic* and *intensive* instruction in the essential decoding skills.

Many words in the English language, however, are not phonetically regular. These words must be taught and practiced as sight words, words to be recognized immediately as whole units. In addition, if students are to become fluent readers, they must progress from letter-by-letter decoding strategies to rapid and automatic recognition of whole words and phrases (Ehri & McCormick, 1998). Let's turn now to a discussion of sight word instruction and sight word programs used in special education classrooms. ◆

Sight Word Instruction and Sight Word Programs

Students who understand the phonemic code and the morphemic rules of our language are able to attack most unknown words. As children become more skillful readers, they may also use the context of the sentence (i.e., semantic and syntactic structures), in addition to phonic and morphemic analysis, to determine word possibilities.

Stanovich and Stanovich (1995) caution, however, that rapid, automatic eye movements enable good readers to see every single letter on a page and that only poor readers guess at words in context. According to these authorities, using context clues to predict upcoming words is not an efficient approach to reading because naturalistic text is not very predictable. Similarly, Ehri and McCormick (1998) suggest that good readers simultaneously use many different processes to read words: decoding skills, a sight word vocabulary, and reading unknown words by analogy to known words (e.g., decoding *greet* by drawing an analogy with the known word *feet*). In good readers, these processes develop together and reinforce one another because decoding skills are necessary to retain sight words in memory. Sight words are necessary to form analogies with unknown words, and forming analogies enables children to learn new spelling patterns and more advanced decoding skills. Thus, to develop proficient sight word recognition, students need a solid foundation in decoding skills (Ehri, 1995).

Nevertheless, some children with mild disabilities are unable to master the many phonics skills necessary to become fluent decoders. These students need to develop a functional sight word vocabulary consisting of necessary survival words (e.g., *women*, *exit*, *danger*) or vocational words (e.g., words necessary for completing job applications and other forms). Teachers of adolescents often must curtail decoding practice in order to focus on words essential for independent living or content-course completion. Teachers at the elementary or middle school may choose to supplement phonics instruction with sight words from the basal reader or from a list of high-frequency words such as the Dolch words (Johnson, 1971) or the Fry New Instant Word List (Fry, 1980). (See Table 11.5.) These words must be sufficiently practiced and then applied to phrases from text, however, if students with mild disabilities are to recognize the words in context (Levy, Abello, & Lysynchuk, 1997). In addition, teachers can use com-

---

Table 11.5 Fry's New Instant Word List

According to Fry (1980), the first 10 words on this list make up about 24% of all written material. The first 100 words make up about 50% of all reading material, and the 300 words listed comprise about 65%.

1. the	28. had	55. out	82. than	109. place	136. means	163. turned
2. of	29. by	56. many	83. first	110. years	137. old	164. here
3. and	30. words	57. then	84. water	111. live	138. any	165. why
4. a	31. but	58. them	85. been	112. me	139. same	166. asked
5. to	32. not	59. these	86. called	113. back	140. tell	167. went
6. in	33. what	60. so	87. who	114. give	141. boy	168. men
7. is	34. all	61. some	88. oil	115. most	142. following	169. read
8. you	35. were	62. her	89. its	116. very	143. came	170. need
9. that	36. we	63. would	90. now	117. after	144. want	171. land
10. it	37. when	64. make	91. find	118. things	145. show	172. different
11. he	38. your	65. like	92. long	119. our	146. also	173. home
12. was	39. can	66. him	93. down	120. just	147. around	174. us
13. for	40. said	67. into	94. day	121. name	148. form	175. move
14. on	41. there	68. time	95. did	122. good	149. three	176. try
15. are	42. use	69. has	96. get	123. sentence	150. small	177. kind
16. as	43. an	70. look	97. come	124. man	151. set	178. hand
17. with	44. each	71. two	98. made	125. think	152. put	179. picture
18. his	45. which	72. more	99. may	126. say	153. end	180. again
19. they	46. she	73. write	100. part	127. great	154. does	181. change
20. I	47. do	74. go	101. over	128. where	155. another	182. off
21. at	48. how	75. see	102. new	129. help	156. well	183. play
22. be	49. their	76. number	103. sound	130. through	157. large	184. spell
23. this	50. if	77. no	104. take	131. much	158. must	185. air
24. have	51. will	78. way	105. only	132. before	159. big	186. away
25. from	52. up	79. could	106. little	133. line	160. even	187. animals
26. or	53. other	80. people	107. work	134. right	161. such	188. house
27. one	54. about	81. my	108. know	135. too	162. because	189. point

Table 11.5   Fry's New Instant Word List—*continued*

190. page	209. country	228. don't	247. got	266. four	285. almost
191. letters	210. plants	229. few	248. group	267. carry	286. let
192. mother	211. last	230. while	249. often	268. state	287. above
193. answer	212. school	231. along	250. run	269. once	288. girl
194. found	213. father	232. might	251. important	270. book	289. sometimes
195. study	214. keep	233. close	252. until	271. hear	290. mountains
196. still	215. trees	234. something	253. children	272. stop	291. cut
197. learn	216. never	235. seemed	254. slide	273. without	292. young
198. should	217. started	236. next	255. feet	274. second	293. talk
199. American	218. city	237. hard	256. car	275. later	294. soon
200. world	219. earth	238. open	257. miles	276. miss	295. list
201. high	220. eyes	239. example	258. night	277. idea	296. song
202. every	221. light	240. beginning	259. walked	278. enough	297. being
203. near	222. thought	241. life	260. white	279. eat	298. leave
204. add	223. head	242. always	261. sea	280. face	299. family
205. food	224. under	243. those	262. began	281. watch	300. it's
206. between	225. story	244. both	263. grow	282. far	
207. own	226. saw	245. paper	264. took	283. Indians	
208. below	227. left	246. together	265. river	284. really	

From: Fry, E. (1980). The new instant word list. *The Reading Teacher*, December, pp. 284-289. The International Reading Association. Reprinted with permission of publisher and author.

mercial materials and effective teaching strtegies designed to promote mastery of sight words.

Edmark. The Edmark Reading Program (1972) is appropriate for children with mental retardation, learning disabilities, or emotional disturbance, as well as for low-achieving students who are having difficulty with traditional reading materials. Edmark is a highly repetitive reading system originally designed for institutionalized individuals with mental retardation. In Level 1 of the program, 150 sight words, capital letters, punctuation, and the endings *s*, *ing*, and *ed* are introduced. Level 2 introduces 200 additional sight words and includes stories about adolescents in true-to-life situations. Both levels are also available in software versions. At completion of the program, students are reading at approximately the third-grade level.

The Edmark Functional Word Series contains 4 modules, each introducing 100 words. The four modules teach students aged nine through adult nonreaders essential words for understanding signs, placing orders in fast food chains or restaurants, finding items in grocery stores, and getting and keeping a job. Like the Edmark Reading Program, the Functional Word Series is available in both hard copy and software versions. Both programs in the Edmark series are quite effective in teaching students with mild disabilities a basic sight-word vocabulary.

(For literature on the Edmark Reading Program and Edmark Functional Word Series, write to Edmark Corporation, P.O. Box 97021, Redmond, WA 98073-9721, or visit their web site at **www.edmark.com**).

Reading Milestones. Originally designed for students with hearing impairments, Reading Milestones (Quigley, McAnally, King, & Rose, 1991) is also appropriate for children with mild disabilities or limited English proficiency. The program comes in five levels and emphasizes frequently-used words and regular spelling patterns. Initially, the program "chunks" words into phrases, uses picture cues, and carefully controls vocabulary and syntax so that each word has only one meaning (see Figure 11.1). Upon completion of the program, students are reading at approximately the fourth-grade level and are ready for two additional levels, Reading Bridges Level I and II, to move them into a standard sixth-grade reading curriculum. (Reading Milestones can be obtained through Pro-Ed in Austin, Texas.)

Input Organization. Simms and Falcon (1987) suggest that teachers rearrange lists of sight words into more meaningful groupings than grade-level categories. For example, through direct instructional procedures, teachers may introduce children with mild disabilities to "action" words (e.g., put, pull, open), "when" words (e.g., *before, after, soon*), "no" words (*don't, never, no, not*) or "color" or "number" words. Drill-and-practice activities are then planned to ensure mastery of each semantic category before moving on to a new one. Again, teachers must remember to present words in meaningful phrases rather than as isolated list items during demonstration and practice activities.

Another method by which "input" might be organized is by words that are known (i.e., immediately recognized) and words that are unknown. In order to enhance motivation during drill-and-practice activities, teachers can mix in a few "known" words with those the student has not yet mastered. Use of this technique also provides a review of words learned previously, and thus helps to ensure that they are maintained.

Time Delay. When providing drill and practice with sight words, teachers may use time-delay procedures to enhance student responding (Touchette, 1971). Time delay is a data-based procedure designed to minimize student error and maximize reinforcement for correct answers by providing consistent prompts when children are unable to respond independently (Stevens & Schuster, 1988). However, rather than providing an immediate prompt, the teacher might delay prompting for a few seconds in order to allow the child an opportunity to respond. The delay may be constant or progressive (Kleinert & Gast, 1982).

Using a zero-second time delay, for example, the teacher might present the sight word *put* along with three other words on a flash card, cue the student to point to *put*, and immediately prompt by pointing to the word *put*. Later, the teacher might begin to fade the prompt by increasing the time delay to five seconds. That is, after presenting the words on a flash card and cueing the student to point to *put*, the teacher would wait for five seconds before prompting

The cat   jumps.

FIGURE 11.1 ──◆

A Sample Page from Reading Milestones From: Quigley, S.P., King, C.M., McAnally, P.L., & Rose, S. (1991). *Reading Milestones, Level I, Red Book 1.* Austin, TX: Pro-Ed. p. 50. Adapted with permission.

(Touchette & Howard, 1984). The student could also be told to wait if he or she is unsure of the correct response, and a prompt is delivered only if it becomes necessary. The student could *begin* to read the word at any time before the end of the five-second interval without prompting, receiving reinforcement for successful reading or teacher assistance to correct errors.

The time-delay procedure is useful for teaching sight words to individual students with mild disabilities (Browder, Hines, McCarthy, & Fees, 1984) or to children in small groups (Keel & Gast, 1992). When using a time delay with groups of children, however, the teacher should first obtain and reinforce the attention of all members of the group (e.g., "Everyone look") and then call for choral or individual responding to the cue, "Read the word," or "What word?" (Gast, Wolery, Morris, Doyle, & Meyer, 1990; Wolery, Ault, Gast, Doyle, & Mills, 1990). Again, in the initial trials, the teacher may use a zero-second time delay. When students respond individually or collectively at a criterion of 100% under a zero-second time delay, the teacher may increase the delay. Under each time-delay condition, the teacher must take care to collect data. Knowing the percentage of unprompted correct responses, prompted correct responses, unprompted errors (i.e., errors made before delivery of the prompt), and prompted errors (i.e., errors made within a specified number of seconds following delivery of the prompt) enables the teacher to adjust instruction accordingly to improve learning and decrease errors.

Imagery and Paired Association. High-imagery words (Hargis, 1982) are typically nouns or verbs that bring to mind an immediate picture (e.g., *horse* for children in a rural community or *bus* for those in an urban environment). To use these visual associations for instructional purposes, the teacher places the sight word on one flashcard and a picture to illustrate it on another card (Bos & Vaughn, 1998). Instruction begins by presenting both cards simultaneously, pronouncing the word, and asking students to read the word. Gradually, the picture cards may be removed, using them for prompts only if necessary. In addition, students may point to a word, given two or three choices for one picture, in a word-recognition rather than a recall task. Or, they may choose the correct word to "fill in the blank" when the teacher reads a sentence to the child.

An alternative association for some children with mild disabilities is the word-configuration clue. Again, the teacher places the sight word on a flash card, but this time draws an outline around the word to illustrate the overall shape of the word. Gradually, the outline would be faded as the child successfully reads the word.

Word Identification Strategy. The Word Identification Strategy (Lenz, Schumaker, Deshler, & Beals, 1984) is useful for decreasing the oral reading errors and, to a lesser extent, increasing the reading comprehension of older students needing assistance in content courses, such as science or social studies. The procedure harnesses what these students may know about phonics, structural analysis, and context clues to give them a systematic strategy for attacking unknown words. The seven steps of the strategy can be remembered using the mnemonic illustrated in Box 11.4.

Using the procedures for teaching learning strategies developed by researchers at the University of Kansas (Deshler, Alley, Warner, & Schumaker, 1981; Ellis, Deshler, Lenz, Schumaker, & Clark, 1991), students with learning disabilities can successfully learn the word-identification method to determine unknown words in content-area classes. The teacher must remember, however, that improved word identification (i.e., fewer oral reading errors) does not necessarily lead to improved reading comprehension (Lenz & Hughes, 1990). (See Chapter 9 for additional information on Learning Strategies.)

Computer Software Programs for Sight Word Practice. Several software packages provide optional activities for student practice with sight words.

Box 11.4

The DISSECT Strategy

According to Lenz, Schumaker, Deshler, and Beals (1984), students with mild disabilities can learn strategies to identify words. DISSECT gives students a seven-step process:

D = Discover the context by skipping the unknown word and reading to the end of the sentence to see if the word can be determined by the meaning of the sentence.

I = Isolate the prefix and box it off.

S = Separate the suffix and box it off.

S = Say the stem and then say the stem along with any prefixes or suffixes.

E = Examine the stem, if it cannot be named easily, by using one of three rules:

1. If the stem or a part of the stem begins with a vowel, separate the first two letters. If the stem or a part of the stem begins with a consonant, separate the first three letters.
2. If rule number one does not work, isolate the first letter of the stem and then try to apply rule one.
3. When two different vowels are together in the stem, pronounce both vowel sounds. If that does not "sound right," try again, saying each vowel sound in turn until the word is identified.

C = Check with someone else if the word is still unknown.

T = Try the dictionary if no help is available.

From: "A word strategy for adolescents with learning disabilities," by B.K. Lenz & C.A. Hughes, 1990, *Journal of Learning Disabilities, 23*, pp. 149-158. Reprinted with permission.

For example, *Words Around Me*, available from Edmark, teaches students 280 vocabulary words grouped in seven categories: Personal, Kitchen, Home, Outdoors, School, Community, and Colors/Shapes/Verbs. Teachers can switch between English and Spanish on both Mac and PC versions of this entertaining program. Similarly, *First Thousand Words* (Usborne's) comes in both PC and Mac formats with built-in English and Spanish versions. In this program, children aged 5 to 7 can play several games with delightful animation and sound effects in each of 35 different "Places to Go" (e.g., Kitchen, Party, Hospital, Circus, Families, Country). *Bubble Land Word Discovery* (designed by Ednovation, Inc., and available from Sunburst) is a multimedia dictionary package for children PreK through grade 2. In this program, on both PC and Mac formats, children match common objects in their environment (e.g., a pet store, the playground) to words. In addition, teachers may wish to obtain one of many other multimedia dictionaries now available on CD-ROM. Several of these require no reading and include wonderful graphics and sound, including two from Edmark: *The Picture Cue Dictionary* (Attainment) for teaching life-skill sequences to older individuals with mild disabilities (e.g., shopping, keeping house) and *My First*

Amazing Words and Pictures (DK Multimedia) for students in PreK through grade 2.

Summary of Sight Word Instruction and Programs ◆

Students with mild disabilities must practice irregular commonly-used words as "sight words." Automatic recognition of these words as whole units is necessary if children are to progress beyond laborious letter-by-letter decoding to fluent, independent reading with comprehension (Levy et al., 1997).

Many materials and techniques are available to help students master essential sight words. The teacher may also wish to use more "specialized" methods for teaching reading skills through a whole-word approach. Let's first examine these "special" techniques before turning our attention to reading comprehension. ◆

Specialized Remedial Reading Approaches

A few remedial reading methods follow the meaning- emphasis philosophy, connecting whole words and sentences directly with their meaning in context. Although phonics skills may be woven into reading programs using these methods, decoding is not a core element of instruction. Therefore, teachers might choose one of these special methods for students who are not motivated to practice reading or for those unable to master decoding skills even after extensive instruction. These specialized methods include the multisensory approach and the language-experience approach. Two other specialized methods, Reading Recovery and Book Buddies, are school-wide attempts to prevent reading failure among children who have difficulty learning to read. Data-based instruction is yet another specialized approach useful for teaching either decoding or sight word skills.

Fernald's Multisensory Approach. Grace Fernald worked initially with adolescents with behavioral problems who were having difficulty reading. Her multisensory VAKT (i.e., Visual-Auditory-Kinesthetic-Tactile) approach represented a "new way" for these unmotivated students to learn to read and spell (Fernald, 1943). A teacher using the VAKT method allows the child to select words he or she wants to learn. The teacher then prints or writes one of these words in crayon on a card, models the strategy for the child, and asks the child to practice the word by:

1. Saying the word, tracing the word with a finger while saying each part of the word, and then saying the whole word again;
2. Writing the word without looking at the card and then comparing this effort with the original on the card; and
3. Continuing to trace the word until he or she can write it correctly from memory at least three consecutive times.

Fernald (1943) stresses the importance of always writing the word as a total unit. That is, if the child makes an error while writing a word, he or she must begin the word all over again rather than erasing and starting from the middle of the word. In addition, Fernald recommends that children begin writing stories on topics they choose after they have learned to read and write several words. Any additional words the child requires for the story are supplied by the teacher and practiced by the child using the steps described. As children complete their stories, they file all new words in a word bank or word box and then read their stories to the teacher and/or the group from a typewritten copy provided by the teacher.

Essentially, this approach emphasizes the meaning of words in a context determined by the student. In addition, the method fosters student reliance on repetition and the visual configuration of words as useful strategies for practicing and mastering unknown words. Fernald (1943) maintains that students will soon progress from the tracing stage to looking at a printed word, saying it, and writing it from memory. Later, the student will no longer need to write words in order to remember them. Although teachers believe that multisensory approaches such as Fernald's help students with mild disabilities learn to read new words, supportive research evidence is lacking. Teachers who want to try multisensory methods should use them only to supplement direct instruction with repetitive, systematic practice activities and not as a primary instructional method.

The Language Experience Approach. The Language Experience Approach (LEA) stems from the philosophy that what a child experiences he or she can talk about, and that what a child can talk about he or she can write about and then read (Stauffer, 1970). The LEA, therefore, integrates oral language, reading, and writing through activities that are meaningful for an individual child or for a small group. To implement the LEA, the teacher selects a topic or provides an activity of interest for the children. The teacher then discusses the activity with the children, helping them to organize their thoughts and plan what they want to say.

Following the discussion, the students dictate a story to the teacher, or to a paraprofessional or volunteer, who records it exactly as told by the children (see Box 11.5). For an individual pupil, the teacher may wish to sit next to the young-

---

Box 11.5

A Language Experience Story

The following story was written by Joey with assistance from Ms. Lopez:

In art class we made these kites. We had to take some sticks and put them together across. Then we cut some paper and drew whatever we wanted. I made mine look like a shark. It was cool with these big teeth. We had to wrap the paper around the sticks and staple it on. And we put a tail on the kite out of string and tied these knots around some paper. The best part was when we got to take the kites outside and fly them. Mine was awesome. It was the best. Nobody could get their kites to fly very good.

ster so that he or she can see the page as dictation occurs. For small groups of students, the teacher may use large chart paper, the chalkboard, or the overhead projector, having each child contribute to the story. After dictation, the teacher rereads the story to the children, asking them whether they want to make any changes or additions. Next, the children read the story, individually or chorally, as the teacher points to each word. Finally, the teacher provides each child with a typed copy of the story, and the children practice reading the story to one another. New words are put on word cards, practiced, and filed in individual student word banks. Teachers can also cut the sentences from the story apart for students to practice reading them or to provide activities focused on sequencing events.

The LEA is a highly motivating approach for reluctant readers and a useful introduction to the meaningfulness of reading and writing for beginning readers. Through the LEA, students can begin to make associations between letters and sounds, and between spoken and written words. Alone, however, the LEA is insufficient as an initial reading method for most children with mild disabilities. For these youngsters, beginning reading instruction must emphasize phonics and structural analysis skills.

Reading Recovery. Reading Recovery is an early intervention program for "high-risk" first graders that was originally developed by researchers in New Zealand (Boehnlein, 1987; Clay, 1993). The method offers one-on-one, intensive, tutorial assistance for 30 minutes each day to children having difficulty during their first year of learning to read. The program is intended to supplement the ongoing reading and writing instruction in the regular classroom with literacy strategies used naturally by good readers. At the heart of Reading Recovery is interaction with a caring, supportive teacher trained to use the following sequence of activities during each lesson (Clay; Pinnell, 1990):

1. Familiar rereading. The child rereads favorite books he or she has read previously. These books may be selected by the child or by the teacher and are read for enjoyment and fluency.
2. Rereading new books and obtaining a running record analysis. The child reads the new book from the previous day's lesson. The teacher may assist the child when he or she is "stuck"; however, the primary goal here is for the child to read as independently as possible while the teacher records the types of word identification, comprehension, and other strategies the child is using.
3. Writing a message. The child composes a message or story over one or more days. The story is written with teacher assistance so that the child can predict, when possible, letters to represent the sounds. The child reads the message or story aloud and reassembles the story from sentence strips made and cut apart by the teacher.
4. Reading a new book. The teacher or child selects a new book to explore, looking at pictures, making predictions, and identifying one or two keywords after examining the initial letter. Finally, the child reads the new book with teacher assistance.

Books selected for reading are at the correct level if the child can recognize the words with 90% to 95% accuracy. In addition, many familiar books are "patterned" stories or poems containing predictable, repetitive lines. Children often delight in repeating these known words alone or with the teacher, and patterned books are well-suited to the prediction of letter-sound associations. In addition, teachers help children to "make and break" words using magnetic letters (Clay, 1993). This activity adds a phonological component to Reading Recovery and helps children practice phonetically regular words. According to Stahl and his colleagues (1998), these types of activities enable teachers to embed phonics instruction within the context of real-life reading and writing activities.

Reading Recovery is receiving acclaim and some empirical research support (Center, Wheldall, Freeman, Outhred, & McNaught, 1995). Little evidence exists, however, to suggest its effectiveness with children already in special education programs (Pinnell, 1990; Slavin, Karweit, & Madden, 1989). Critics argue, too, that the method demands more highly-trained personnel than many school districts can presently afford. Moreover, children will not profit from such intensive remedial instruction if they are merely returned to regular classrooms not designed to support the gains made during the special program (Snow et al., 1998).

Book Buddies. Book Buddies is a program in which community volunteers are trained to tutor children in one-on-one sessions twice a week (Invernizzi, Juel, & Rosemary, 1997). The four-part lesson plan used in each tutorial includes repeated reading of familiar text, word study, writing for sounds, and reading a new book. During word study, children progress from learning beginning consonant sounds, to ending consonants, and to CVC words. Writing for sounds encourages children to "invent" spellings for unknown sounds in words, but still holds them accountable for correctly encoding the sounds they do know. For example, a child might spell like or bike as lik and bik, once he or she learns basic letter-sound associations. Although the teacher might acknowledge the "correctness" of the spellings according to the sounds heard in the word, he or she must then begin instruction with the CVCe rule. According to Snow, Burns, and Griffin (1998), the tutors in Book Buddies must be thoroughly trained and carefully supervised for the program to be successful.

Data-based Instruction. Data-based teaching of reading skills is rooted in applied behavior analysis and direct instruction. This approach focuses on establishing precise instructional objectives and then directly measuring student progress toward those objectives. This data analysis enables teachers to make informed decisions about pupil performance, materials, and instructional procedures (see Chapter 6).

Using curricular materials at the appropriate level, the teacher might time and record a student's oral reading rate, compute the percentage of words read correctly or incorrectly from a passage or from a sight word list, or administer a probe to determine whether the student decodes CVC or CVCe words correctly. Reading errors made by students are directly recorded and analyzed by the teacher to determine instructional needs. For example, Ms. Lopez might present Travis with a list of regular CVC and CVCe words including *hat, can, bake,* and *hope.* As Travis reads the words on the list, Ms. Lopez could follow along with an identical list, placing a plus sign (+) next to the words that Travis reads correctly and a minus sign (−) and approximate pronunciation next to the words that he reads incorrectly (e.g., *bake* read as *back* and *hope* read as *hop*). Ms. Lopez would then use this information to plan additional instruction for Travis using the CVCe pattern.

According to Tindall and Marston (1996), oral reading fluency and reading with expression are two performance assessments that can be used by teachers to obtain data useful for guiding instruction. In addition, the Informal Reading Inventory (IRI) can yield data regarding a child's instructional reading level (i.e., the level of reading material a student can read with teacher assistance) and oral reading errors. Although a number of commercially-prepared IRI's exist, teachers can construct their own IRI's using actual reading materials in the classroom. To construct an IRI, teachers should use the suggestions in Box 11.6 adapted from Gunning (1996) and Taylor, Harris, Pearson, and Garcia (1995).

Box 11.6

Constructing and Using an Informal Reading Inventory

To construct an IRI:

1. Pull 100-word passages from every nth story. (For 4th through 6th grade use 200- to 250-word passages—beginning, middle, and end with no unusual words.)
2. Prepare two clear copies of each passage—one for the child and one for you to mark on.
3. Time the child's reading of the passage (oral reading rate). Before reading, tell the child to say a word again if she makes an error and wants to correct it.

   a. If the child hesitates on a word more than 5 seconds, tell the child the word and say, "continue."
   b. If the child misses word and doesn't self-correct, let the child continue without correction.
   c. If the child misses word and tries to self-correct, allow 5 seconds, then supply word and say, "continue."
   d. Stop the child if there are numerous errors and laborious reading.

4. As the child reads, mark errors on your copy of the passage.

   a. Omissions
   b. Insertions
   c. Substitutions
   d. Mispronunciations
   e. Inversions or reversals
   f. Repetitions
   g. Disregards punctuation
   h. Aided by teacher

5. If the student reads below 95% accuracy rate (six or more errors), stop the child and move to next lower passage. Continue down until the student reads with fewer than six errors. If the student reads first passage with better than 95% accuracy, fewer than six errors, move up to the next passage.

6. Prepare five to ten comprehension questions for each passage before reading. For immature readers, ask primarily literal questions. For older students, use more inferential questions.
7. Use IRI's to form instructional groups:

Level	Word Recognition	Comprehension
Independent	99% or better	90% or better
Instructional	95% or better	75% or better
Frustration	Below 90%	Below 50%
Capacity	Read aloud and check listening comprehension	75% or better

Tips and Cautions for IRI's:

1. When uncertain regarding level, begin IRI about two grades below estimated level.
2. Repetitions, self-corrections, and reading through punctuation marks may be signs of comprehension. Use caution in considering these errors. Also, analyze substitution errors. Children may substitute a word that makes sense in the sentence (e.g., sofa for couch), indicating comprehension. Or they may substitute a word that "looks" like the word (e.g., house for horse) but that doesn't make sense and demonstrates lack of comprehension.
3. Use caution with dialect-motivated "mispronunciations."
4. If you are unsure regarding a student's instructional level after completing the IRI, place the student at the lower level. It's motivating to move up—not down!

A Summary of Specialized Remedial Reading Approaches

Teachers believe that specialized remedial reading approaches motivate reluctant learners to read. In addition, The Language Experience Approach, Reading Recovery, and Book Buddies may help at-risk youngsters associate meaning with the printed word and provide enjoyable, successful experiences with books. Such approaches are dependent on embedding phonics instruction within the context of authentic reading and writing activities.

However, these approaches do not provide the intensive, systematic, direct phonics instruction required by students with mild disabilities. Very few teachers have the expertise to integrate the necessary instruction in decoding skills when one of these techniques is used as a primary approach to initial reading instruction. Special education teachers may wish, therefore, to focus intervention first on decoding skills, supplementing lessons with whole-word approaches such as the LEA or multisensory practice of new words. Data-based instruction, on the other hand, ensures student progress with essential decoding and sight word skills. A focus on decoding does not mean, however, that teachers should neglect comprehension. We will now turn to a discussion of this important goal of remedial reading instruction. ◆

Teaching Comprehension Skills

The ultimate goal of reading instruction is for students to obtain meaning from what they read. As they advance up the grades, students are expected to read both for pleasure and for content. These expectations require the student to understand different types of text, to read for different purposes, and to bring to the printed page background knowledge or experience from which meaning may be constructed (Carnine et al., 1997). Good readers, then, read fluently and with expression; moreover, they comprehend what they read.

Recent theories of comprehension emphasize the schema theory (Rumelhart, 1984). That is, based upon their background experiences, children organize the knowledge they possess about various topics. For example, if Travis has visited the beach several times, he might hold a fairly sophisticated schema of *beach*, including its appearance (e.g., sand, water, waves), plants and animals (e.g., seaweed, pelicans, fish, dolphins), and activities (e.g., swimming, surfing, flying a kite, skating or bicycling on the boardwalk). As he reads a story about the beach, Travis is able to activate his broad schema of *beach* as well as the smaller schemata he holds regarding birds or activities at the beach. His schema provides a framework, or network, of related ideas that will help him fully comprehend the story and organize the information to be retained.

On the other hand, if Joey has only seen videos of the beach but has never actually been there, he may not have a well-developed schema around which he can organize story events. According to McNamara, Miller, and Bransford (1991) though, readers can still comprehend novel text through the construction of *mental models*. Joey can activate his limited schema of *beach* to create a mental model of what a character at the beach might face. In addition, Joey might construct two different types of mental models. For example, he might form a *working mental model* to understand the events presently occurring in the story, and a *passage mental model* to explain how the current events relate to previous events and to the story as a whole. Thus, readers use both schema and the construction of mental models to comprehend new text.

The comprehension skills found in most basal reading series include those in Table 11.6. Typically, teachers in regular classrooms teach comprehension skills indirectly through the directed reading activity or the directed reading-thinking activity. That is, the teacher sets the purpose for reading, or elicits a purpose from student predictions, and then follows reading with questions designed to monitor comprehension or to evaluate conclusions. Most questions asked by teachers during reading lessons are at the literal comprehension level (Guszak, 1972). Newer basal reading series, however, offer fewer questions for teachers to ask, although they encourage teachers to use inferential-level questioning (Hoffman et al., 1994). Furthermore, teachers provide very little systematic demonstration or explanation of *how* to comprehend what is read (Jenkins, Stein, & Osborn, 1981).

For students with mild disabilities, comprehension skills may be difficult to master, even at the level of recognition or recall of facts and main ideas explicitly stated in the text, particularly if instruction is not systematic (Carnine et al., 1997). For example, youngsters with mild disabilities may lack fluent decoding and word recognition skills, hampering their reading comprehension. Moreover, many children with mild disabilities may not have the vocabulary or background knowledge, the schemata built from experiences both in the real world and with text, to enable them to understand the language of instruction or to comprehend what they read (Samuels, 1981).

Table 11.6	**Comprehension Skills**

Comprehension Level	Typical Skills Included
Literal	Understand word meanings in context; recognize or recall details, main ideas, sequence of events, cause-and-effect statements, and comparisons when directly stated in the text.
Inferential	Infer details, main ideas, sequence of events, cause-and-effect, and comparisons when not directly stated in the text; predict outcomes; use figurative language.
Evaluative	Judge fact versus opinion and reality versus fantasy; judge adequacy, validity, or worth of arguments, conclusions or sources.
Appreciative	Respond emotionally to plot and theme; identify with characters or plot; react to author's use of language or imagery.

Similarly, students with cultural differences may hold schema differing from those of the text author; therefore their comprehension may suffer. Other students lack knowledge of different text structures and of comprehension strategies (Dyck & Sundbye, 1988; Laughton & Morris, 1989; Seidenberg, 1989). Activating background knowledge, building fluency, teaching vocabulary, and direct instruction of comprehension skills and strategies, then, are important features of initial or remedial reading instruction for youngsters with mild disabilities.

Activating Background Knowledge

If students are to comprehend what they read, they must possess some background knowledge of the topic. Teachers can activate schema prior to reading a story by providing experiences, real or vicarious, about the upcoming topic. For example, Ms. Kirk might show pictures or a video about the beach before her students read a story. In addition, she might lead her students in a discussion about their trips to the beach as she writes their comments on chart paper, in a list or web format, by categories such as activities, sounds, and smells. Moreover, Ms. Kirk can introduce new vocabulary from the story, and she can help her students preview the story and make predictions about what they will read. According to Mastropieri and Scruggs (1997), strategies such as these that are designed to activate prior knowledge enhance student comprehension of novel text.

Ogle (1986) suggests a strategy called K-W-L for activating background knowledge. In this strategy, the teacher places the following three-column framework on the chalkboard, the overhead projector, or a piece of chart paper:

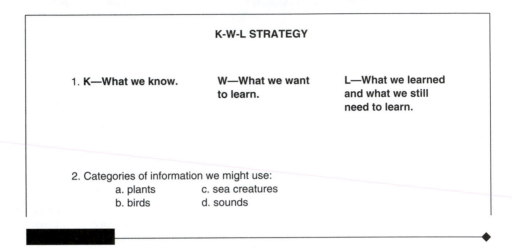

K-W-L STRATEGY

1. **K—What we know.**   **W—What we want to learn.**   **L—What we learned and what we still need to learn.**

2. Categories of information we might use:
   - a. plants   c. sea creatures
   - b. birds   d. sounds

Using the K-W-L strategy, Ms. Kirk might ask her students to brainstorm things they already know about the beach. She could then write their answers to this question under the "K" column. Following the brainstorming, Ms. Kirk might suggest some categories of information she can find from the known information, such as plants, birds, and sea creatures at the beach. She might also elicit additional categories from her students. Immediately prior to reading the story, Ms. Kirk might ask her students to generate questions to be placed under the "W" column, and she might challenge individuals to choose specific questions to guide their reading. Finally, after students have read the story, Ms. Kirk might lead them in a discussion of what they learned (i.e., the "L" column). Finally, Ms. Kirk might help students identify the questions that are still unanswered (the *K-W-L* + strategy).

Although some children may have well-developed schemata regarding particular topics, they still may be unable to comprehend text if they read slowly and laboriously with many errors. These children need activities designed to build fluency.

Building Fluency

LaBerge and Samuels (1974) suggest that students have only a limited attentional capacity to allocate to the simultaneous tasks of decoding and comprehension. Those students who, because of deficient word attack skills, must allocate an excessive amount of attention to the task of decoding have very little remaining attentional capacity to remember and comprehend what was read. According to Ashbaker and Swanson (1996), short-term memory (e.g., decoding and recognizing words) and working memory (e.g., listening to a sequence of events and trying to understand what a story is about) interact to determine reading comprehension. Thus, although fluency alone is insufficient for reading comprehension, it is an important initial goal of reading instruction for students with mild disabilities. Teachers can help students build fluency through such activities as repeated reading and previewing of text.

Repeated Readings. Repeated reading is an effective technique designed to facilitate active student practice with reading materials (Samuels, 1979). The technique is based on the theory of limited attentional capacity offered by LaBerge and Samuels (1974). Instead of expecting students with mild disabilities to read stories or passages fluently with only one reading and to progress through the basal reading series at the "normal" rate, repeated reading provides the student with additional opportunities to read each passage or story until a criterion level has been attained. The basic idea is that students with mild disabilities must master reading material before moving to a new reading selection, and that mastery is rarely achieved from a single reading experience.

Repeated reading is a relatively simple procedure. Students read and reread passages to a specified criterion for reading rate (e.g., 85 words per minute) and/or for reading accuracy (e.g., fewer than 5 word-recognition errors). Students begin with timed readings of short passages containing from 50 to 200 words at a specified reading level. Gradually, longer and more difficult passages are introduced, and the student records his or her progress on a chart or graph (Samuels, 1979). As fluency improves, comprehension is cued by prompting students to think about and remember what is read. Rather than finding the procedure boring or repetitive, teachers report that children enjoy trying to beat their own records in successive reading trials.

Variations on the technique of repeated reading include tape recording, choral and paired readings, and repeated reading of language-experience stories. Tape recording the repeated reading session affords the student an opportunity to hear himself or herself reading. Tape recording also gives the teacher the freedom to work with other children by producing a permanent product for later review (Henk, Helfeldt, & Platt, 1986). Moreover, when students read together as a group or with a partner, the time they spend engaged in actual reading increases (Stahl, Heubach, & Cramond, 1997).

Bos (1982) suggests that students listen as the teacher reads a passage or story at the appropriate instructional level and then read the story aloud along with the teacher. The student would then read the passage or story independently and record his or her word-recognition and reading rate on a chart. Bos and Vaughn (1998) recommend that this practice of choral or paired reading begin with predictable, patterned books and that the method be combined with discussion of the reading selection to set purposes and to make predictions. Additional variations offered by these authors include making cards for practicing words that students have consistent difficulty recognizing and using repeated readings with tape-recorded stories or books.

In still another variation of repeated reading, children read language-experience stories for one-minute timed trials (Peterson, Scott, & Sroka, 1990). At the end of the minute, the teacher points to each word the child has missed, clearly pronounces the word, and requests that the child repeat the word. The teacher then uses the word in its context, with the child repeating the phrase, and then the child reads the remainder of the passage untimed. Both reading rate and error rate, graphed on a standard behavior chart, can improve through this technique.

Mastropieri and Scruggs (1997) caution that although three or four readings can improve fluency and comprehension, the effect is decreased with additional readings. In addition, they suggest that repeated readings may be more effective when combined with instruction in specific comprehension strategies. Finally, Rashotte and Torgesen (1985) report that new passages must share many words with previously-read text in order for the effects of repeated readings to transfer to the new material.

Previewing. Another simple but effective method for improving fluency is previewing. Previewing helps children activate schema prior to reading text. During previewing, children look at the title, pictures, headings, and sub-headings and generate predictions regarding what they might read. In addition, the child might be given the opportunity to read silently (silent pre-viewing) or listen to a passage or story (listening previewing) before attempting oral reading. In studies comparing silent and listening previewing (Rose, 1984; Rose & Sherry, 1984), listening previewing resulted in improved reading rates for children with learning disabilities, as well as for those with behavior disorders.

Another form of previewing involves a structured overview of passage topics and subtopics, including prompts for self-questioning (Billingsley & Wildman, 1988). Using this procedure, the teacher arranges cards to illustrate the relationships among the major topics, subtopics, and details for each passage read. In addition, the teacher prompts students to generate as many *Who, What, When, Where, and How* questions as possible before actual reading begins. Billingsley and Wildman suggest that this prereading activity can increase student involvement with the text during actual reading, and thus improve comprehension.

Summary of Fluency-Building Activities ◆

Students can improve their oral reading rate and decrease word-recognition errors through such fluency-building activities as repeated readings and previewing. These activities alone, however, are not enough for some children with mild disabilities to comprehend what they read. Other deficits, such as poor vocabulary, also may hinder reading comprehension. ◆

Vocabulary

Students with mild disabilities often lack the necessary vocabulary to fully comprehend text (Carlisle, 1993; Carnine et al., 1997). In addition, vocabulary, word recognition, and decoding difficulty may, in turn, prohibit these youngsters from reading material which would help them build additional vocabulary (Stanovich, 1986b). Moreover, children with mild disabilities may have particular difficulty with words that have several meanings (e.g., *run*), which are often used in basal readers (Paul & O'Rourke, 1988), or with specific tasks they are asked to perform during vocabulary instruction and assessment (Simmons & Kameenui, 1990). Although the exact relationship between vocabulary development and reading comprehension is unknown, teachers must help students to develop a deep understanding of vocabulary through both direct instruction and multiple uses of words in context (Shake, Allington, Gaskins, & Marr, 1989).

Preteaching Vocabulary in Phrases Using Hypothesis-testing. When preteaching vocabulary, teachers must remember to teach words in meaningful phrases from the text rather than in isolation. For example, the teacher can make sentence or phrase strips using words from the reading passage and then underline the new vocabulary word or omit the new word, or all but the first letter of the new word. Using the context and/or the letter clue, students are asked to hypothesize the word choice or meaning (e.g., "What could this word be?" or "What could this word mean?") and then read on to test their hypothesis (Sindelar, 1982). Dixon (1987) suggests that teachers should "think aloud" to demonstrate this hypothesis-testing approach using unknown words encountered in text, and then guide students as they practice the procedure. According to Stahl and Fairbanks (1986), giving children information about a word's definition, as well as examples of the word used in context, improves vocabulary and reading comprehension more than drill and practice with word definitions alone.

Keywords. Mastropieri and Scruggs (1991) describe a strategy in which teachers help students to associate a visual image of the meaning with a word to be remembered. The visual image can be constructed to represent the word itself or a sound-alike or synonym for the word. For example, if the student must remember that the word *persuade* means "to convince," he or she might construct a visual image of one woman convincing another to buy a suede *purse* (i.e., a word similar in sound). Of course, if the student is unfamiliar with the word, the teacher must use direct instructional procedures to teach that *persuade* means "to convince" before using the mnemonic device (Mastropieri & Scruggs).

Rooney (1988) describes a similar technique. In her technique, children place the new vocabulary word on one side of a card and a brief version of the most common definition on the back. Under the definition, the student draws a picture to illustrate the meaning and associate the definition with the word. For example, if the student must learn that *belligerent* means "argumentative," he or she might draw a picture of two bells fighting about the rent under the word *argumentative* on the back of the card. Children may use the cards for drill-and-practice activities and file mastered words in a word box. Although the keyword strategies described previously may help students associate words with their meanings, there is no evidence to support the transfer of this strategy to comprehending passages when the words are used in context (Carnine et al., 1997).

Word Webbing. Paul and O'Rourke (1988) suggest that teachers can help students activate prior knowledge of topics and vocabulary by word webbing. Teachers can take phrases from the text containing new vocabulary (e.g., "along the river bank") and ask students questions such as, "What does the word *bank* mean?" or "What else is called a *bank*?" (e.g., a pile of snow, an inclined curve on a road, a place where money is stored) using pictures as clues if necessary. Interrelationships among these definitions can then be illustrated visually by using lines branching out to each from the word *bank*. In a similar activity, teachers can web synonyms or sentences around the central word (Paul & O'Rourke). (See Figure 11.2 for an illustration of webbing with synonyms.)

Summary of Vocabulary Instruction

Students with mild disabilities need many opportunities to read and use words in context. Preteaching vocabulary words in phrases, hypothesis testing, keywords, and word webbing may help many children expand their vocabulary (Mastropieri & Scruggs, 1997). Nevertheless, most youngsters with mild disabilities also require direct instruction in comprehension skills, such as finding the main idea. ◆

Direct Instruction of Main Idea

Although not the only necessary comprehension skill, one early and important comprehension task children are expected to master is that of finding the main idea. Frequently, basal reading materials begin this instruction by asking children to choose the "best" title for a story or the main idea of a passage when given a series of four or five choices. This level of difficulty, however, is often above that of many students with mild disabilities who may not understand the concept of "main idea" or how the main idea relates to other elements of the text.

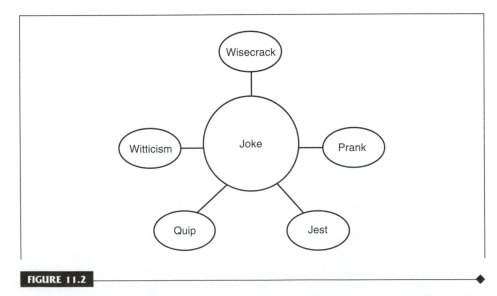

FIGURE 11.2 ◆

A Synonym Web for Joke: Ms. Kirk and the students in her fourth-grade class produced the following web to illustrate synonyms for a word overused in her student's writing—Joke.

Graves (1987) outlines a sequence for direct instruction in finding the main idea. According to this sequence, students first generate a main idea when presented with a series of pictures that clearly illustrates an activity or tells a story. For example, a picture of Susan swinging a bat, a picture of Susan running the bases, and a picture of Susan catching a ball with a glove can be used to generate the idea that Susan plays baseball. Next, students must generate the main idea for three or four sentences that contain similar elements, such as these: "Dogs need oxygen to live. Cats need oxygen to live. Horses need oxygen to live." The main idea here is that "animals need oxygen to live." The student is then ready to progress to short passages, picking out the main idea from three or four choices presented.

Teachers should begin instruction at the literal level, helping children find the main idea and details when they are explicitly stated in the text. To do this, teachers might point out the most common positions within paragraphs for the main-idea sentence (i.e., the first sentence, the last sentence, then a sentence in the middle). Using exact wording from the paragraph, the teacher can illustrate the relationship between the main idea sentence and the supporting detail sentences by likening the paragraph to a table. The main idea is represented by the broad tabletop and the details are represented by the table legs that offer support. In addition, the teacher can make sentence strips that have one color for the main idea and a different color for the supporting details. The teacher and children can then manipulate the strips to demonstrate the various positions for the main idea and detail sentences within paragraphs. Gradually, the paragraphs can be lengthened and the wording can be changed, making the choices for the main idea less and less like the actual wording in the text.

Similarly, Hanau (1974) used the illustration of Statement-PIE to represent the relationship of main ideas and details in paragraphs (see Figure 11.3). The "statement" is the main idea and the "PIE" is all the *Proof, Information,* and *Examples* offered by the author in support of the main idea. Again, the teacher might begin instruction with short paragraphs containing the statement in the first sentence and the PIE in subsequent sentences. Later, the order of sentences can be rearranged so that students can practice identifying the statement and the PIE.

Summary of Main-Idea Instruction

◆

Children with mild disabilities may need explicit and sequenced direct instruction of comprehension skills, such as finding the main idea. In addition, students in special education programs may need extensive practice if they are to master these skills even at the literal level. Finally, direct teaching of comprehension strategies, in combination with direct instruction, may help youngsters with mild disabilities to comprehend and remember what they read more effectively than either procedure used alone (Graves, 1986). Some authorities caution, however, that reducing instruction in comprehension skills to discrete steps may focus on student deficits rather than on the whole child and his or her background experiences and reasons for reading, factors considered critical for comprehension (McGill-Franzen & Allington, 1991; Poplin, 1988). ◆

Teachers can use a concrete and visual example such as Statement-PIE (Hanau, 1974) to illustrate the relationship among main idea and detail statements at the literal level. By means of the graphic pictured below, teachers can demonstrate that the main-idea statement tells what a passage is all about and that the PIE statements are all the proof, information, and examples that support the statement.

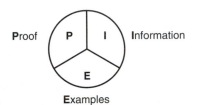

Statement—This is a super pair of shoes!

PIE—They don't cost a whole lot.

PIE—They have fluorescent shoelaces and designs on them.

PIE—They are really comfortable to wear.

FIGURE 11.3 ◆

Statement-PIE Adapted from: "Using statement-PIE to teach reading and writing skills," by C.S. Englert & A. Lichter, 1982, *Teaching Exceptional Children, 14,* p.165. Reprinted with permission.

Comprehension Strategies

Students with mild disabilities may possess adequate skill in decoding, recognizing words, and determining the main idea; however, they may still fail to comprehend what they read. Good readers engage in summarization or retelling, answering questions, and other strategic behaviors to improve comprehension or to address comprehension difficulties. Poor readers, on the other hand, do not spontaneously use these strategies to improve or monitor their comprehension. These youngsters need explicit instruction in comprehension strategies including self-questioning, paraphrasing or story retelling, using text structures, and surveying and reviewing (Mastropieri & Scruggs, 1997; Pressley, Brown, El-Dinary, & Afflerbach, 1995).

Self-questioning Strategies. In a 1982 study, Wong and Jones demonstrated that some students with mild disabilities do not engage in self-questioning while reading. Even when students are able to identify main ideas, they may not ask questions to help themselves find and remember the main idea when reading a passage. The self-questioning strategy developed by Wong and Jones lists five important steps and questions for students to follow while reading to improve their reading comprehension:

1. Ask, "Why am I studying this passage?"
2. Find the main idea or ideas and underline it/them.
3. Think of a good question about the main idea(s).

High-imagery sight words, like nouns and verbs, may be paired with a visual prompt to increase student success during initial instruction.

4. Read to learn the answer to the question.
5. Remember to look back to see how each question and answer gives you more information.

Similarly, researchers at the University of Kansas used a self-questioning strategy in combination with visual imagery to help students with learning disabilities comprehend written material (Clark, Deshler, Schumaker, Alley, & Warner, 1984). Students were taught the RIDER strategy for visual imagery and the RAM self-questioning strategy. During RIDER, students *R*ead the first sentence, *I*magine a picture, *D*escribe the image, *E*valuate the image for completeness, and *R*epeat the steps with each subsequent sentence. When students can generate common "WH" questions (i.e., *Who, What, When, Where, Why*) and recognize cue symbols for each type of question (e.g., a clock face for "when" questions), they can use the RAM strategy by *R*eading a passage and asking "WH" questions, *A*nswering the questions while reading, and *M*arking the answers with the appropriate symbols. According to these researchers, the use of both strategies resulted in greater comprehension for students in the study.

Paraphrasing and Story Retelling. Several strategies help students to summarize paragraphs or to retell stories in their own words. For example, Jean Schumaker and her colleagues at the University of Kansas taught students with learning disabilities to use a paraphrasing strategy for remembering the main idea and details in written materials (Schumaker, Denton, & Deshler, 1984). Using the acronym RAP, students *R*ead a paragraph, *A*sk themselves what the main ideas and details are, and <u>P</u>ut the main ideas and details into their own words. In addition, students are instructed both to look in the first sentence and to look for words that are repeated in order to find the main ideas.

In a procedure known as *reciprocal teaching*, Palincsar and Brown (1984) taught students summarizing, questioning, clarifying, and predicting strategies during interactive teaching sessions. Using reciprocal teaching procedures, students slowly assume, with teacher assistance, the role of "co-instructor" during reading lessons. After modeling the four strategies, the teacher prompts and gives feedback until students are able to lead discussions about stories themselves. That is, students take turns retelling stories, asking questions, clarifying information, and making predictions (see Box 11.7).

During reciprocal teaching, teachers begin reading selections by having students make predictions based on story titles, headings, or other appropriate passage features. In this way, students are encouraged to activate background knowledge and information and to set a purpose for reading. Teachers then foster practice of good questioning strategies by requiring students to ask "teacher-like" questions rather than fill-in-the-blank questions. In addition, if students are unable to ask a question, the teacher might provide an appropriate question word as a prompt. Summarizing strategies for students include finding the main idea and supporting details and stating this information in their own words without looking at the text. Students are told to look for a topic sentence or to give a name to a list of items as ways to identify main ideas. Finally, students point out information that is unclear or unknown as they clarify new vocabulary, unfamiliar expressions, or ambiguous information.

The essential element of reciprocal teaching is an interactive dialogue between the students and the teacher. Rosenshine and Meister (1994) report, however, that reciprocal teaching is most effective when it is combined with direct teaching and practice of comprehension strategies.

Using Text Structures and Story Grammars. When retelling stories, children typically rely on certain structures they have come to understand (e.g., a character in a particular setting encounters some type of conflict, which is finally resolved). These essential elements, called *story grammar*, are familiar organizational devices for narratives in many cultures. Understanding story grammar, then, may enhance the reader's comprehension of narrative passages (Stein & Trabasso, 1982).

In a study by Griffey, Zigmond, and Leinhardt (1988), story-grammar training and self-questioning strategies were combined to improve the reading comprehension of elementary-level poor readers. First, the teacher provided lessons on the story elements using the acronym CAPS (<u>C</u>haracter, <u>A</u>im, <u>P</u>roblem, <u>S</u>olution). Next, the teacher initiated training with self-questioning related to each of these story elements. For example, during reading, the teacher interjected the following questions at appropriate points in the story:

1. Who are the characters?
2. What is the aim of the story?
3. What problem occurs?
4. How is the problem solved?

Box 11.7

Ms. Kirk Uses Reciprocal Teaching Strategies

The following conversation takes place between Ms. Kirk and the fourth-graders in one of her reading groups:

Celie: My question I want to answer is what the man buy with all his money?

Kevin: Probably a big car and a new house.

Sarabeth: Maybe a boat.

Holden: I think presents for everybody.

Ms. Kirk: Interesting answers. My question, though, is since the man can only buy one thing with all that money, how can he buy all these things that he wants?

Sarabeth: I'm not sure, but I wish I had all that money!

Celie: My summary is someone this man didn't even know give him a bunch of money, but told the man he could buy only one thing with it. The man have to decide how to spend it.

Ms. Kirk: Good summary, Celie. It says in the story that because the man doesn't know who gave him all the money or why, he "ponders" who the mystery man might be. What do you suppose "ponders" means here?

Holden: Wonders.

Sarabeth: He thinks about it.

Ms. Kirk: Yes. Well, who do you predict gave him all that money?

Kevin: Maybe his uncle.

Mark: No, it was probably someone who didn't want to get caught because it was stolen money.

Celie: Someone to teach the man a lesson.

Ms. Kirk: Great answers! Let's read on to see if our predictions are accurate. Who would like to be the next teacher? Holden?

The teacher then summarized by retelling the story, providing answers to each of the questions, and writing these on the chalkboard. Later, students were reminded to use the CAPS questions when reading stories on their own.

Idol (1987) used the concept of story grammar along with story mapping to improve the reading comprehension of third- and fourth-graders with reading disabilities. During instruction, the teacher modeled how to locate the story components and write them on a story map. Students first copied information generated by the group onto their own story maps. Later, however, the children completed individual story maps while reading independently. According to Idol, ten key questions were used to generate information for story mapping and comprehension:

1. Where did the story take place?
2. When did the story take place?

3. Who were the main characters in the story?
4. Were there any other important characters in the story? Who?
5. What was the problem in the story?
6. How did _____ try to solve the problem?
7. Was it hard to solve the problem? Explain.
8. Was the problem solved? Explain.
9. What did you learn from reading this story? Explain.
10. Can you think of a different ending?

Using more sophisticated language and story-map formats (e.g., protagonist, conflict, theme), students with mild disabilities can also comprehend high school literature (Gurney, Gersten, Dimino, & Carnine, 1990) and expository text structures (Englert & Mariage, 1991). For example, graphic aids can be constructed to represent a sequence of events or cause-and-effect statements. Visual aids can also represent several attributes along which items can be compared (Carnine et al., 1997). With teacher assistance, students can complete these "story maps" and then use the map structure to facilitate comprehension of similar material in the future (see Figures 11.4 and 11.5).

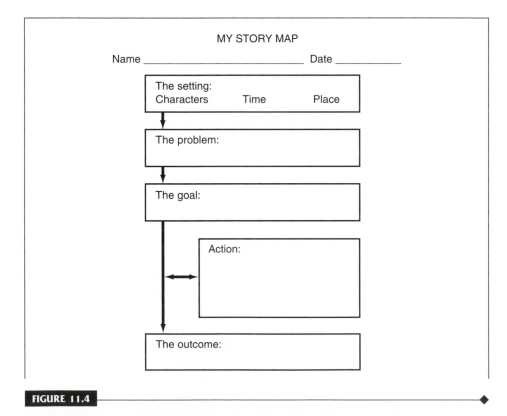

FIGURE 11.4

Using Graphic Aids to Improve Student Comprehension of Differing Text Structures: The Story Map From: Idol, L. (1987). Group story mapping: A comprehension strategy for both skilled and unskilled readers. *Journal of Learning Disabilities, 20,* page 199. Reprinted with permission from PRO-ED, Inc.

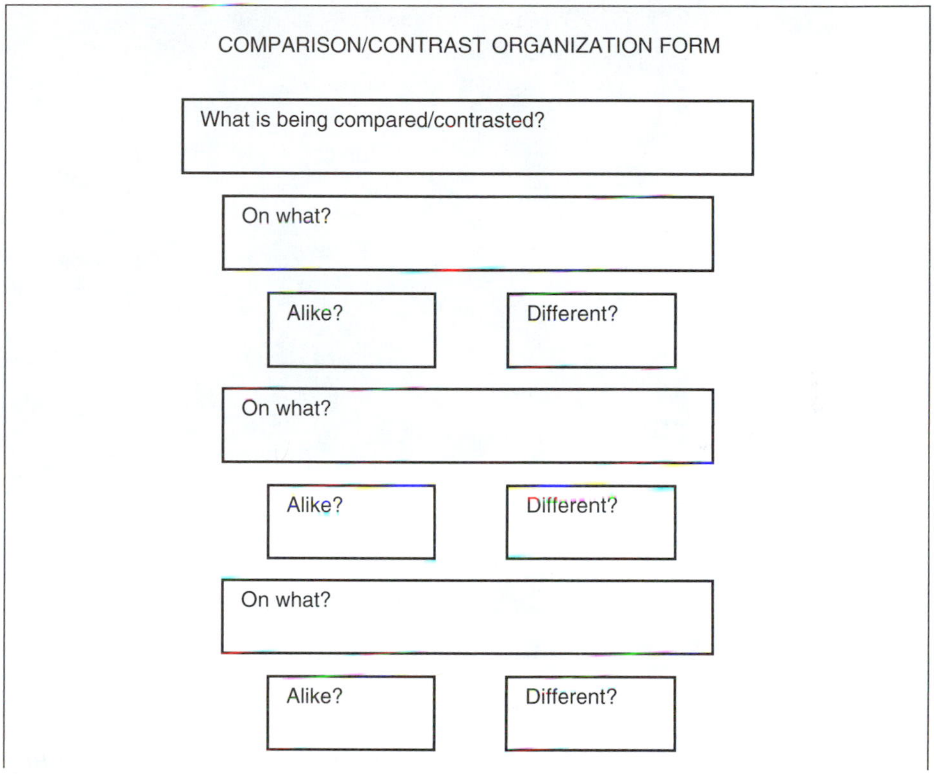

COMPARISON/CONTRAST ORGANIZATION FORM

What is being compared/contrasted?

On what?

Alike? | Different?

On what?

Alike? | Different?

On what?

Alike? | Different?

FIGURE 11.5 ◆

Using Graphic Aids to Improve Student Comprehension of Differing Text Structures: Comparison/Contrast From: "Developing successful writers through cognitive strategy instruction," by C.S. Englert & T.E. Raphael, 1990. In J. Brophy, (Ed), *Advances in research on teaching,* Greenwich, CT: JAI Press. Reprinted with permission.

Surveying and Reviewing Strategies. One study skill often emphasized for reading content-area textbooks is SQ3R (Survey, Question, Read, Recite, Review), originally developed by Robinson (1941). Good readers preview reading materials before actual reading occurs, noting chapter headings and subheadings, introductory and summary paragraphs, focusing and final questions, pictures, graphs, and new words. In this way, they get a general idea of the content, the organizational structure of the material, and a set of questions and/or purposes for reading by turning headings and subheadings into questions. While reading, and immediately following reading, students are encouraged to recite new information and to review or summarize what was learned. Children with mild disabilities, however, may not have the skills or background knowledge to survey, question, read, recite, and review without explicit instruction from the teacher.

Archer and Gleason (1989) adapted the SQ3R procedure to include a teacher-directed "Warm-up" and an "Active Reading" strategy for children in grades 3 through 6. During "Warm-up," the teacher guides students through a

Elements of a whole language approach, such as having children drama-tize or retell favorite stories, may supplement direct instruction in read-ing skills for students with mild disabilities by providing them meaningful experiences with connected text.

survey of the material to be read. Later, students are given a written reminder of the five warm-up steps and follow them independently:

Step 1: Read the title of the chapter and the introduction. (Ask, "What is the title? What will this chapter be about?")

Step 2: Read the headings and subheadings. (Ask, "What will this section be about?")

Step 3: Read the chapter summary. (Ask, "What are some important ideas from this chapter?")

Step 4: Read the questions at the end of the chapter. (Teachers should stress that the questions are very important because they indi-cate what students are expected to learn as they read the chap-ter.)

Step 5: Say to yourself, "This chapter will talk about . . ."

Following "Warm-up," students learn a strategy to become actively involved during actual reading. Called active reading, the strategy emphasizes recitation of topics and details after each paragraph has been completed. Archer and Gleason (1989) used the acronym RCRC to guide active reading:

R = *Read*
Read a paragraph.
Think about the topic.
Think about the important details.

C = *Cover*
Cover the material with your hand.

R = *Recite*
Tell yourself what you have read.
Say the topic.
Say the important details.
Say it in your own words.

C = *Check*
Lift your hand and check.
If you forgot something important, begin again.

In a more complex and sophisticated strategy designed for adolescents with mild disabilities, students are taught to make three systematic passes through content-area reading materials (Schumaker, Deshler, Alley, Warner, & Denton, 1982). The strategy, called *multipass,* consists of three sub-strategies to help students comprehend textbook reading selections: a survey pass, a size-up pass, and a sort-out pass. Each pass is taught separately using textbook materials that students can read with speed and accuracy (Schumaker, et al.):

1. Survey Pass

   To get the main ideas and a feeling for the structure of the chapter, students (a) read the chapter title and the introductory paragraph, (b) review the chapter's relationship to other chapters by looking at the table of contents, (c) read the subtitles of the chapter and think about how the chapter is organized, (d) look at the pictures and read their captions, (e) read the summary paragraph, and (f) paraphrase everything learned during the pass.

2. Size-Up Pass

   To get specific information and details without reading the entire chapter, students (a) read the questions at the end of the chapter to see what is important to learn, (b) put a check mark beside each question that can be answered from the survey pass, (c) go through the chapter page by page looking for clues like bold-faced or italicized type and subheadings, (d) turn each clue into a question and skim through the surrounding text to answer the question, (e) put the answer to the question into their own words, and (f) paraphrase all facts and ideas they can remember from the chapter.

3. Sort-Out Pass

   To self-test comprehension of the chapter, students again read and answer the questions at the end of the chapter. If they can answer a question based on the size-up pass, they place a check mark next to the question. If not, they think of a section where the answer might be located and skim for the answer. If the answer is not there, they try another section, repeating this procedure until the answer is found.

A Summary of Comprehension Strategies ◆

Teachers must provide youngsters with mild disabilities explicit instruction and practice using comprehension strategies. Successful strategies are those that activate student background knowledge and information, focus student attention on the organizational structure of the material, help students set purposes for reading, and involve students actively throughout the reading process (Mastropieri & Scruggs, 1997). ◆

Computer Software for Building Comprehension Skills

Many computer software programs are now available to provide enjoyable activities to build comprehension skills in children with mild disabilities (Lundberg, 1995; Torgesen & Barker, 1995). For example, Broderbund offers numerous titles in their *Living Books Series*. Available on CD-ROM in both Mac and PC versions, students can listen to, read, and play games with such stories as *The Tortoise and the Hare* and Dr. Seuss's *Green Eggs and Ham*. Similarly, *Magic Tales*, from Edmark, enables readers to interact with characters in folk tales from many countries and cultures, including Native American, Japanese, and Russian. *Wiggleworks* (Scholastic) has the added feature of allowing students to record themselves reading featured stories. Most computer software programs include both English and Spanish versions so that the teacher can easily switch between languages, and many allow students to highlight unknown words for computerized help with pronunciation.

A Summary of Comprehension Instruction ◆

As students master phonics and word-recognition skills, teachers must emphasize that the goal of reading instruction is not decoding text, but rather comprehension. Comprehension involves both the knowledge a student brings to a reading selection and his or her understanding of the varied types of text and purposes for reading. Comprehension instruction for children with mild disabilities must be systematic and must help students engage actively with materials before, during, and after the reading task. Fluency- and vocabulary-building activities and direct teaching of comprehension skills and strategies are components of comprehension instruction for students with mild disabilities.

Integrating Reading Instruction and the Language Arts

At the beginning of this chapter we discussed the whole language philosophy of reading instruction. Recall that proponents of whole language advocate the use of quality children's literature as a vehicle through which children can learn to read and to write. By reading, rereading, and writing about favorite stories, poems, and topics, children discover the phonetic code and connect reading with meaning. Reading and writing are interrelated skills that are not easily separated in real life; therefore, the integration of reading and writing activities intuitively makes sense to teachers.

For children with mild disabilities, however, indirect teaching methods are rarely effective. These youngsters need explicit instruction and practice in decoding skills and comprehension strategies if they are to learn to read. Nevertheless, certain elements of a whole language approach can play a vital role in reading and language arts instruction for children with mild disabilities. For example, teachers can do the following:

1. Read quality children's literature to youngsters with mild disabilities.
2. Choose reading selections based on student interest or useful content-area topics under study.
3. Have students read repetitive lines of poems or stories individually or chorally.
4. Follow up reading selections with activities such as a dramatization, retelling, or illustration of the story or poem.
5. Engage children in writing activities such as changing the ending of a story or writing a letter to the main character after reading a selection.
6. Model skillful reading and writing strategies by "thinking aloud" during both reading and writing activities.

Whole language approaches, at present, lack sufficient research support for use as a primary method of instruction for youngsters with mild disabilities. Whole language can, however, supplement direct instruction in essential reading and language arts skills for these children, providing them with motivating and meaningful experiences with connected text.

Summary

Authorities debate whether reading is a top-down, a bottom-up, or an interactive process. Today, however, most professionals do agree that mature readers draw on their background knowledge and experience, their knowledge of different text structures, and their knowledge of phonics and word-recognition skills to derive meaning from the printed page. Poor readers, on the other hand, have deficient decoding skills and more limited background information. They must depend on either a top-down or a bottom-up strategy to gain meaning from written materials.

Children in special education programs often have significant reading problems that hinder their performance in other academic areas as well. Research supports the use of systematic, direct-synthetic phonics instruction for most students with mild disabilities. In addition, these youngsters require explicit instruction in and extensive practice with sight word recognition and comprehension skills and strategies. For those students who still fail to master decoding and comprehension skills after intensive and quality instruction, building a functional sight word vocabulary or using a specialized remedial reading technique, such as Fernald's VAKT method, might become the approach of choice.

An integrated approach to reading and the language arts, the whole language philosophy, is receiving attention in both regular and special education classrooms. A whole language approach will provide children with mild disabilities experience with well-written, connected text and with meaningful reading and writing activities. These activities can motivate children and help them enjoy reading. If these youngsters are to learn to read, however, whole language programs must supplement, rather than replace, explicit instruction in decoding and comprehension skills.

Application Exercises

1. Examine two different basal reading series used in local school districts. Would you classify these as primarily meaning-emphasis or code-emphasis approaches? Justify your answer by explaining how phonics instruction is treated within each series. Examine a whole language basal reading program. How does this series differ from the other two you examined?

2. Examine two phonics-based reading programs (e.g., Reading Mastery, Corrective Reading, Reading Horizons, Recipe for Reading, the Wilson Reading System, or the Merrill Linguistic Reading Program). Compare and contrast the sequence of phonics skills and the recommended instructional techniques.

3. Robert has difficulty comprehending the language and organizational structure of his textbooks. Plan a program to help him build more fluent decoding and word-recognition skills. In addition, select a strategy to help Robert comprehend his science and social studies textbooks. If you were Mr. Abel, how would you justify the program and strategy selected?

4. Travis's school district uses a whole language approach to the reading program, indirectly teaching phonics skills through literature and writing activities. If you were Ms. Lopez, what suggestions would you make to the IEP team regarding phonics instruction for Travis? Design an instructional plan to help Travis master decoding skills.

5. Assume the role of Mr. Abel at an IEP meeting. Defend the choice of a reading program to build a functional sight word vocabulary for Susan, rather than continued instruction in decoding skills. Describe how time-delay procedures and input organization techniques might be used when teaching functional sight words to Susan.

6. Select a representative passage of 100 to 300 words from a basal reading series used in a local school system. Ask a child at the series grade level to read the passage orally for you. Record words the child reads incorrectly or repeats and any words the child substitutes for words in the passage. Time the child during reading. Compute the number of words read per minute. Do you see any pattern in words missed by the child (e.g., words substituted that do or do not make sense in the story)?

7. Design a probe to assess the following objective for Joey: "Given a probe of CCVC words beginning with two continuous consonant sounds, randomly presented in list form, Joey will verbally decode the words with 100% accuracy at a rate of at least 60 words per minute." Now assume that Ms. Lopez notes that Joey consistently omits the second consonant sound in the consonant blend. How might you correct Joey's error?

8. Browse the web sites on reading research and instruction listed in Box 11.1. Make a list of all the elements of effective reading instruction you find on these sites. Share this information in class by designing a brochure for parents illustrating effective approaches to reading instruction.

9. Locate five articles from InfoTrac regarding effective reading instruction for students with mild disabilities. Compare the information from these articles with your list of effective approaches to reading instruction compiled in Exercise 8. If you were to persuade a school board to adopt a particular curricular material for your students with mild disabilities, what research information would you include to justify your position?

10. Examine a "skills" lesson in a fourth-grade level basal reading series used in a local school district. What are likely to be the problem areas in the lesson for students with mild disabilities? Assume the role of Ms. Lopez and modify the lesson to help students like Travis achieve success.

WRITTEN LANGUAGE INSTRUCTION

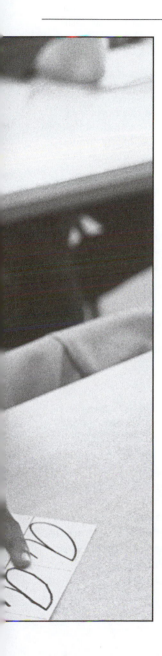

Focus

As you read, think about the following questions:

◆ *What difficulties do students with mild disabilities experience with written language?*

◆ *What are some effective methods for teaching spelling and hand-writing skills to children with mild disabilities?*

◆ *How can teachers help their students with mild disabilities compose well-written sentences and paragraphs?*

◆ *How can reading, oral language, and written language instruction be integrated for learners with mild disabilities?*

You may recall from Chapter 10 that several interrelated skills are collectively known as the "language arts." In addition to oral language and reading skills, discussed in Chapters 10 and 11 respectively, spelling, handwriting, and written expression are all considered to be language arts. Unfortunately, most students in special programs experience difficulty in one or more of these areas. Let's listen to a conversation between Ms. Kirk and Ms. Lopez regarding some of Ms. Kirk's fourth graders:

Ms. Kirk: I'm trying to provide more opportunities for my students to talk with one another and to write and share what they've written. I like the idea of a writing process. I've paired up Travis and two other students who have difficulty, Kevin and Celie, with stronger students, but I'm still concerned about their progress in writing stories.

Ms. Lopez: Can you tell me some of the things that you're concerned about?

Ms. Kirk: Well, Travis is always polite and helpful, and he wants to do well, but his handwriting and spelling skills are so weak. He can't even read what he's just written when he's done. Kevin can write only simple sentences that are very concrete, and Celie is one of my limited English proficient students. She understands more language than she's able to write right now.

Ms. Lopez: I agree that it's important to have students interact with one another during the writing process—to write and share and talk about what they're writing. Pairing those three up with stronger students is a good idea. Perhaps we might also try a story map as a framework during the prewriting stage so the students can get their characters, settings, and main events organized before they write the first draft. That way, their partners can help them with some of the spelling and ideas before they write. Also, Travis might do better if he could use the computer to draft his story. Then it would be easier for him to read to revise and edit it.

Ms. Kirk: I like the notion of story maps. I've used them before and I think that might help everyone in class.

Ms. Lopez: Do you need a sample of some I've used?

Ms. Kirk: No, I have one I like that I think might help. Do you have any recommendations on computer software for writing, though? I don't like the program I've got in my classroom.

Helping all students to write effectively is an important goal for most teachers like Ms. Kirk. Providing all students with appropriate language arts instruction, therefore, merits careful consideration and planning. In this chapter, we will briefly examine the difficulties children with mild disabilities may experience with spelling and handwriting, and we will explore effective methods for teaching these two written language skills to students in special education programs. Then we will return to our discussion of the interrelated nature of reading and the other language arts as we discuss written expression and the needs of children with mild disabilities.

Spelling, Handwriting, and Students with Mild Disabilities

Written language is a complex area within the language arts. To communicate through writing, students must apply both oral language skills (e.g., knowledge of syntax and semantics) and reading skills (e.g., sounds of letters in words). In addition, students must be able to think about and organize a topic, spell words, and legibly produce letters in manuscript or cursive form. Although in this section we will examine spelling and handwriting as separate written language skills, the reader must remember that spelling and handwriting, as well as oral language and reading, are interrelated skills used simultaneously to achieve the final goal of written language instruction: written expression.

Spelling

Spelling is a difficult skill for many students to master. Rather than recognizing letter patterns and combinations and their corresponding sounds, as when decoding words while reading, the student must recall and encode the correct sequence of letters when spelling. The task is made more difficult when we consider that even though there are only 26 letters in the alphabet, there are approximately 256 different spelling patterns to represent the more than 40 sounds in the English language. Inconsistent letter-sound correspondence and words borrowed from other languages create difficulty for students in both regular and special education classrooms. Many of the most frequently used words in children's literature and writing, for example, are irregularly spelled "spelling demons" (Graham, Loynachan, & Harris, 1993).

Gentry (1982) describes five stages through which children typically pass as they learn to spell. At each developmental stage, children use different strategies to "invent" spellings for unknown words:

◆ Precommunicative Spelling: The 3- to 5-year-old child uses scribbles and a few letters to write. However, he or she has no understanding of letter-sound correspondences.
◆ Semiphonetic Spelling: The child of 5 or 6 often spells by representing some of the major phonemes with graphemes. For example, he or she might spell "book" as *bk.*
◆ Phonetic Spelling: By age 6 or 7, many students are phonetic spellers. That is, they represent all of the phonemes in the word with an appropriate, but not necessarily correct, grapheme. The phonetic speller might spell the word *cup* as "kup."
◆ Transitional or Conventional Spelling: Children of age 7 or 8 know the letter-sound associations and also may know many spelling rules. However, these children may have difficulty with words that have irregular spellings, or they may overgeneralize the spelling rules they do know, spelling, for example, *eating* as "eatting."
◆ Correct Spelling: Typically, by age 8 or 9, children know how to spell many different words and they understand the basic rules of spelling.

These children usually recognize incorrect spellings and can think of alternative ways to spell words.

Although some students who are not in special education programs may still have difficulty with spelling, most children with mild disabilities experience problems in this area, particularly if they are poor readers. Authorities suggest that students who have trouble learning to read also have trouble learning to spell (Carpenter & Miller, 1982). Shanker and Ekwall (1998), for example, state that most good readers are good spellers and most poor readers are poor spellers. They estimate that only about 2% of all good readers are poor spellers.

According to Roberts and Mather (1997), some students with dyslexia have orthographic deficits. That is, they have difficulty storing mental representations of letters and whole words and this hinders their ability to read and to spell. However, most authorities today believe that poor readers most often exhibit deficits in phonological skills such as detecting and remembering sounds in words (Mann & Liberman, 1984). These phonological skills must be mastered in order to spell words, as well as to read them aloud. Moreover, difficulty learning to read and to spell may also affect phonological awareness (Ehri, 1989). Thus, reading and spelling are interrelated skills that have a reciprocal effect on one another and on the development of phonological ability (Snow, Burns, & Griffin, 1998).

Ekwall (1989) suggests that children may make similar errors in both reading and spelling. For example, "phonetic readers" may also be "phonetic spellers." In addition, most students are consistent in the types of spelling errors they make (DeMaster, Crossland, & Hasselbring, 1986), with the majority of errors resulting in phonetically acceptable incorrect spellings (Tovey, 1978). Children with mild disabilities, then, may be using limited information and strategies in a "best attempt" to spell unknown words (Gerber, 1984). The 9-year-old child like Travis, for example, might be performing only at the semiphonetic or phonetic spelling stage much like younger peers. Teachers, therefore, must engage in systematic analysis of errors made by students and tailor spelling instruction accordingly (Fuchs, Allinder, Hamlett, & Fuchs, 1990; Fuchs, Fuchs, Hamlett, & Allinder, 1991).

Spelling requires the student to apply knowledge of phonics and structural analysis, to visualize a word, and to write properly formed letters in the correct sequence. Because there usually is only one correct way to spell any given word, some authorities suggest that repetition and meaningful practice in spelling frequently used whole words (i.e., learning by rote) are more useful than teaching spelling rules and phonics generalizations (Shanker & Ekwall, 1998). Others argue that teaching highly generalizable phonics rules or morphemic rules may enable students to spell, and also to read, a greater number of words than rote memorization alone (Dixon, 1991). Some suggest that a combination of high-frequency words and instruction in spelling patterns must be taught in order for spelling programs to be effective (Graham, Harris, & Loynachan, 1996). Most professionals agree, however, that the approach used in the typical basal spelling series (e.g., assigning on Monday a "weekly list" of spelling words for practice throughout the week with a test on Friday) is inadequate for children with mild disabilities. (See Table 12.1 for a summary of recommendations for spelling instruction based on the research literature.)

Table 12.1   Recommendations for Effective Spelling Instruction

Templeton (1986) and Fulk (1999) offer the following recommendations in planning spelling instruction for children with mild disabilities:

1. Teach spelling with enthusiasm!
2. Stress the value and relevance of spelling across content areas and in real-world contexts.
3. Use short word lists of 6 to 12 words only.
4. Present spelling words in list form rather than in sentences or paragraphs.
5. Give students a pretest. Allow students to practice only those words missed on the pretest.
6. Have students self-correct spelling tests. This is an extremely effective procedure for children at all grade levels.
7. Use the test-study-test method, which is superior to the study-test method for most learners.
8. Rather than present words in syllable form and teach syllable-division rules, teach and have students practice whole words.
9. Give students frequent opportunities to use spelling words in context through purposeful writing activities such as journals.
10. Give students specific strategies for studying their spelling words. Writing words in the air, repeatedly copying a word, and oral spelling are not effective ways to practice spelling words. Some children do, however, use oral spelling as a support strategy to prompt or cue correct spelling when writing a word.
11. Focus most spelling practice on the word as a whole unit. Teaching highly generalizable phonemic and morphemic rules, however, can supplement rote memory.
12. Teach students to spell unknown words by analogy to other words. For example, they can spell *mast* by analogy to *fast*.
13. Reward students for good spelling across the content areas.
14. Vary practice activities. Use chaining, puzzles, games, and computer software.

Youngsters in special education programs require explicit instruction and extensive practice if they are to retain spelling words and use them correctly in written work. The suggestions offered by Dixon (1991) promise more powerful spelling instruction for most children with mild disabilities than those used in most spelling programs:

1. Focus instruction for younger spellers on true phonemic generalizations (e.g., a *k* sound at the end of a word is spelled *ck*) and important spelling patterns (e.g., cat, rat, sat).
2. As students become proficient phonemic spellers, begin to emphasize generalizable morphemic rules to prevent overgeneralization of phonemic spelling.
3. Provide rote memory practice for words that do not conform to any rules.

Teachers can link phonics and structural analysis practice in reading with spelling instruction while still providing numerous opportunities for rote memory drill. For example, after reading the word *bake* in a story, the teacher might pause and challenge students to spell the word *baking,* requiring pupils to apply the newly acquired spelling skill of adding suffixes beginning with vowels to words ending in *e.* In addition, teachers must create ways for students with mild disabilities to use spelling words in context, such as using them in journals or stories, if these children are to transfer the spelling skills they learn (Fulk, 1997). Beyond these two major suggestions, teachers might find the practices recommended in the following pages to be helpful during spelling instruction. In addition, teachers may wish to obtain one of the programs for spelling instruction listed in Table 12.2.

Use Short "Flow" Word Lists, Test-Study-Test, and Self-Correction.
Poor spellers are more likely to succeed with relatively short word lists. Rather than the weekly list of 15 to 25 words, authorities suggest that between 6 and 12 words per list is a sufficient number for poor spellers (Bryant, Drabin, & Gettinger, 1981; Graham et al., 1996). The lists should contain high-frequency words, misspelled words from a child's writing, or words clearly illustrating a particular phonemic pattern.

Table 12.2 Spelling Programs for Students with Mild Disabilities

Programs	Uses and Publishers
Corrective Spelling through Morphographs	A program for students in grades 4 and up. Intensive instruction in generalizable morphemic rules. 12,000 words in 140 lessons. Requires 1 year and follows a direct instructional format. Science Research Associates.
Instant Spelling Words for Writing	A spelling series across eight different levels. Teaches high-frequency words. Emphasizes test-study-test method, self-checking, visual imagery, and applying words in context. For grades 1 through adult. Curriculum Associates.
Speed Spelling 1 and Advanced Speed Spelling	Speed spelling teaches phonetic regularities to children in grades 1 through 3. Also for children grades 1 through 6 who haven't mastered spelling skills. Advanced Speed Spelling addresses irregularly spelled words for students in grades 7 through 12. Pro-Ed.
Spelling Mastery	Six levels for students in grades 1 and up. Teaches phonemic, whole word, and morphemic strategies for spelling. Follows an intensive direct instructional format. Science Research Associates.
Stetson Spelling Program	Teaches the 3,000 words most frequently used in writing and presents words in that order. Contains 15 levels in 230 lessons of 10 to 12 words each. Uses pretesting, self-checking, and visual imagery. Pro-Ed.
The Quick-Word Handbooks for Everyday Writers	Words frequently used in writing arranged alphabetically. Three levels: Purple (Grades 1 & 2, ESL), Yellow (Grades 2 to 8, ESL), and Aqua (Practical writing words for grade 7 through adult and ESL). Also in a Spanish version. Curriculum Associates.

Moreover, "flow" word lists may be more effective than "fixed" word lists for youngsters with spelling difficulty (Mercer, 1997). On a flow word list, new words are added to replace mastered words, while those words not yet learned to a specified criterion level remain on the list. By contrast, all words are practiced on the more typical fixed word list, even if the child has mastered some of them. Moreover, an entire fixed word list is replaced with a new one, even if the child has not yet mastered words on the old list.

Another procedure that can be used effectively with the flow word list is the "test-study-test" method. Rather than assigning words to be studied all week and then tested on Friday (i.e., a "study-test" method), the teacher gives a pretest first. Those words spelled incorrectly on the pretest then become targets for practice. Both flow word lists and the "test-study-test" method allow children with mild disabilities to focus attention on words they need to practice. Moreover, flow lists can be constructed for individual children or for the entire group. For example, words missed by the majority of children on a weekly spelling test might be retained on the list for the following week.

Self-correction immediately after a spelling test or pretest also may focus student attention on troublesome words or parts of words (Graham & Miller, 1979; Wirtz, Gardner, Weber, & Bullara, 1996). That is, the child should correct his or her own spelling paper, with teacher assistance and feedback. In addition, with words that do not follow regular phonetic rules, imitation plus modeling may be an effective error-correction procedure (Kauffman, Hallahan, Haas, Brame, & Boren, 1978). Using this technique, the teacher first writes the spelling word including the same error made by the child. Then the teacher immediately provides the correct spelling beside the incorrectly-spelled word. For example, Mr. Abel might tell Susan, "Here's how you spelled *field*," while he writes *feeld*. Next, he says, "Now, here's how to spell *field*," while he writes the word correctly.

Use Direct Instruction to Teach Phonics Rules and Spelling Patterns.

Teachers can link reading and spelling words during direct instructional lessons. If Ms. Lopez knows that her students will need to decode words following the "doubling rule" in an upcoming story, she can focus them on the rule for reading and spelling words of this type. For example, she might say, "To add an ending starting with a vowel to words having a consonant-vowel-consonant pattern (while pointing to the letters in *ing* and *run*), we double the final consonant (pointing to *n*) and add the ending (writing *running* on the board). The word is *running*." After her demonstration of some examples (e.g., *running* and *batted*) and nonexamples (e.g., *staying* and *sadly*), Ms. Lopez might use words from the story, such as *hopping* or *bigger*, on the weekly spelling list.

Graham, Harris, and Loynachan (1996) recommend a directed spelling-thinking activity with high-frequency words, much like the directed reading-thinking activity in Chapter 11. In their approach, words are grouped by important spelling patterns (e.g., the long sound of /a/ in *ay, ai*, and CVCe words) and children learn to categorize them by these patterns. Later, children are challenged to spell by analogy, spelling *lair*, for example, by thinking of a similar-sounding word (e.g., *fair* or *pair*) and its spelling pattern. The Basic Spelling Vocabulary List developed by Graham, Harris, and Loynachan (1996) contains the 850 words students most commonly use when they write, grouped by spelling patterns such as *at* or *ss*.

Provide Drill-and-Practice Activities for Retention.
Teachers can use numerous games, such as "Hangman," to motivate spelling practice, or variations on traditional "Tic-tac-toe" and board games in which students must correctly spell words to move a game piece or to place an "X" or "O." Drill activities to ensure memorization of spelling words, particularly those not conforming to phonemic rules, may also be necessary.

Time-delay procedures such as those used with sight word drills (see Chapter 11) can be used to provide nearly errorless practice. For example, using a zero-second time delay, the teacher can cue a student to "Spell _____" and then follow the cue with an immediate presentation of the word correctly written on a card (Stevens & Schuster, 1987). Later, the teacher may increase the time delay to five or more seconds before providing the prompt. Using time-delay procedures with a small group to practice writing and spelling words also improves sight word recognition (Winterling, 1990).

In order to increase motivation during spelling practice, the teacher can intersperse words the child knows among those he or she still needs to learn. Again, as with sight word drills, this procedure allows for repetition of previously mastered words to ensure that they are retained. As an additional incentive for spelling practice, students may earn rewards for correctly spelled words on spelling tests. For example, students can receive reinforcement either for individual improvement over past performance or as a member of a cooperative learning team. Moreover, self-graphing of mastered spelling words may be a motivating activity for older students with mild disabilities.

Finally, several computer programs also provide motivating drill and practice. *Spell It Deluxe* (Davidson) contains over 4,000 words at six different levels of difficulty. Children learn proofreading, commonly misspelled words, and spelling rules. In addition, new word lists are available on the Internet. In *Spellavator Plus* (MECC), children participate in motivating games. The program provides teachers with records of student progress and charts spelling patterns and errors for diagnostic use. *Stickybears Spelling* (Optimum Resource) is a version of the popular Stickybears series. Three different game activities are included at each of four levels. Children learn more than 2,000 words and teachers can modify word lists for individual children.

Some programs enable teachers to produce spelling lists for individuals or for the entire class. For example, the *Spelling Test Generator* (Optimum Resource) helps teachers to produce word lists by spelling patterns or difficulty level. In addition, teachers can produce word searches, crossword puzzles, or jumbled spellings for each word list generated. Similarly, in the *Spelling Toolkit Plus* (MECC), teachers can build word lists and create puzzles, tests, and practice activities.

Give Students Strategies for Practicing Spelling Words.
Children with mild disabilities also need direct instruction and practice in appropriate ways of studying their spelling words. Unfortunately, many methods used for spelling practice are based more on tradition than on research (Gordon, Vaughn, &

Schumm, 1993). For example, research does not support having children copy their spelling words repeatedly for practice. In addition, the typical practice activity of placing words in alphabetical order is not closely related to the ability to spell the words. Neither does research support having children practice spelling words in the air or orally as in a "spelling bee" (Templeton, 1986).

On the other hand, specific strategies that focus students on the sequence of letters or the patterns in a word are essential for effective study. Many authorities advocate a "See it, Say it, Cover it, Write it, Check it, Repeat" cycle as an effective spelling-practice strategy (Graham & Miller, 1979). Rooney (1988), however, offers a slightly different spelling strategy to help older students study unknown spelling or content-area words. In her field-tested strategy, the students are taught to follow seven steps:

1. Write the correct spelling of the word on a card.
2. Spell the word aloud.
3. Say the word and write the word, breaking it into parts.
4. Look for and mark visual clues like little words within the word.
5. With the card turned over, write the word from memory.
6. Again, mark all the visual clues.
7. Spell the word again.

Similarly, Dangel (1987) used a sequential strategy to help students aged 9 to 14 improve spelling study. The Coach's Spelling Approach uses a trace-cover-write sequence in which spelling practice is analogous to coaching a football team. The strategy involves several steps across three "coaching" phases:

1. During scouting, the student must
   a. Know the opposition by reading each word correctly;
   b. Identify the tendencies of opponents by sorting spelling words written on cards into groups that are phonetically regular or irregular; and
   c. Identify the opponent's strengths and weaknesses by arranging cards into stacks of easy and hard words.
2. During practice, the student must
   a. Practice phonetically regular words by looking at a word and saying it, tracing the word while saying it and listening to the sounds, covering the word and writing it from memory while saying it, and checking for errors;
   b. Practice phonetically irregular words by looking at a word and saying it, tracing the word and naming the letters, covering the word and writing it from memory while saying the letters, and checking for errors.
3. During the "post-game" period, the student must
   a. Compile statistics, keeping a record of spelling performance during practice and testing sessions; and
   b. Adjust practice based on the statistics.

Teachers can also help youngsters create mnemonics for remembering spelling words. First-letter acronyms, such as a rat in the house might eat the ice cream to spell *arithmetic*, are time-honored mnemonics. Or "I want a piece of pie" can help children remember the spelling of *piece*. Many children have also learned the difference in spelling between *principal* and *principle* with the mnemonic, "a principal is a pal and a principle is a rule."

Greene (1994) demonstrates a visual mnemonic strategy to aid practice and retention of spelling words. In this strategy, the correct spelling is placed on one side of a card and a visual image embedded within the word itself on the other side. For example, to remember the word look, the *oo* pattern can be drawn as eyes with eyelashes to represent the word:

Emphasize Functional Words and Whole Word Practice. Some students with mild disabilities may be unable to master phonemic and morphemic rules even with intensive and quality instruction. For these children, it is useful to construct an individualized and functional word list. For example, Marcus may need to spell number words, the months of the year, and words pertaining to personal information (e.g., place of birth, occupation, address) in order to write a check or complete a job or credit application. Similarly, Robert may need these words written on "wallet-sized" cards so that they will be available to him when needed after leaving school.

In addition, multisensory techniques may provide focused, repetitive practice of whole words (See Chapter 11). Although these approaches lack research evidence of their effectiveness, teachers report that multisensory practice helps some students with mild disabilities spell new words. Using the Fernald (1943) method, for example, the teacher:

1. Writes the word and pronounces it;
2. Asks the child to repeat the word;
3. Has the child trace the word while saying it and then copy the word while saying it;
4. Asks the child to write the word from memory; and
5. Files mastered words for later use in stories.

In the Gillingham-Stillman method (1973), the teacher uses a technique called *Simultaneous Oral Spelling*. Following dictation of a word by the teacher, the child repeats the word and names the letters in the word. Next, the child writes the word while naming each letter and reads the word he or she has written. Whereas the Fernald (1943) method emphasizes the whole word as a unit through visual, auditory, kinesthetic, and tactile stimulation, the child must rely more on letter-sound correspondences when using the Gillingham-Stillman approach.

The Johnson and Myklebust (1967) procedure is an alternative practice method that moves the student from recognition, to partial recall, to total recall of letter sequences within whole words. To practice the word *said*, for example, the teacher might present a sequence like the following while pronouncing the word slowly and distinctly:

said
s_id
sa_d

Students like Robert, Marcus, and Taylor may benefit from using technological aids such as spell-checkers that are built into most word-processing programs today. Moreover, hand-held computers such as the Franklin Spellmaster, available through most school-supply catalogues or local electronics stores, enable students to obtain the correct spelling for many frequently used words by entering the word as it sounds. Ashton (1999) suggests a strategy students with mild disabilities can use when they are uncertain about the accuracy of spelling checkers:

C = Check the beginning sound of the word and think of other letters that could make that sound

H = Hunt for the correct consonants and decide if all consonants are included in the rest of the word

E = Examine the vowels and think of other vowels that might make the same sound

C = Changes in suggested words might give a hint (e.g., if Robert types "ribid," the spelling checker might suggest "rabid." By altering this to "rapid," Robert might obtain the correct word.

K = Keep repeating the previous four steps. Then try consulting a dictionary or asking someone for assistance (p. 24)

Spelling checkers can, of course, be helpful, but they also have important limitations. According to MacArthur, Graham, Haynes, and DeLaPaz (1996), spell-checkers fail to identify incorrect words that are correctly spelled, such as *there* in place of *their*. Moreover, students are not always able to select the correct spelling from among several choices that may be offered by spell checkers.

A Summary of Spelling Instruction
◆

Children with mild disabilities require direct instruction of useful, high frequency spelling words and highly generalizable phonemic/morphemic rules. Providing words in short lists that "flow" and helping students self-correct spelling words are two other procedures that are effective with children in special education classrooms. Drill-and-practice activities and specific strategies for studying spelling words are also necessary components of effective spelling instruction for youngsters with mild disabilities. ◆

Handwriting

The goal of handwriting instruction is for students to produce written communications both fluently and legibly. To do so, they must maintain proper posture, pencil grip, and paper slant; produce letters of the correct size and shape; align letters evenly on the baseline; and properly space letters in words. They must accomplish each of these tasks automatically and recall letter shapes immediately so that they may write with ease and speed.

Although some students may claim that they do not need to write frequently, they must have legible handwriting to successfully perform such tasks as completing an order form for themselves or for a customer, filling out a job or credit application, or taking messages over the phone. Graham (1992) describes poor handwriting as an "instructional time thief" because students with handwriting problems have difficulty taking notes, take longer to complete assignments, and rob teachers of time when they must try to "decipher" illegible papers. Unfortunately, many students balk when faced with laborious handwriting practice, and many others develop poor handwriting habits as they get older.

Handwriting instruction usually begins in either kindergarten or the first grade. Children first learn the proper posture (e.g., tummy to the table and feet on the floor) and three-point pencil grip, as well as upper case and lower case manuscript letters composed of simple sticks and circles. Those letters composed solely of vertical and horizontal lines (e.g., *E, F, H, L, T*) are easier to produce and are usually taught before those made up of both straight and curved lines (e.g., *b, f, p*). Typically, the teacher demonstrates the correct letter formation, emphasizing correct starting points and verbalizing directions for letter strokes (e.g., "Start at the top. Go down. Start at the top. Go around."). Children are then provided with guided practice, first tracing the whole letter and then tracing a faded model of the letter containing only dashed lines. Later, students copy letters, from near point and then far point, and finally produce them independently.

Although teachers once believed that children in kindergarten and first grade needed large pencils and wide-lined paper for initial writing instruction, many disagree with this notion today. Graham (1992), for example, argues that research results are mixed with regard to both beginner's pencils and wide-lined paper. He suggests that young children need a mix of writing implements (e.g., crayons, markers, regular pencils) and types of paper when first learning how to write. According to Graham, however, children clearly do need systematic and direct instruction from their teachers in proper letter formation.

Cursive writing instruction usually begins in the second or third grade following an instructional sequence similar to that used with manuscript. Cursive handwriting programs often group letters in families for instruction according to the types of strokes used (Hanover, 1983). For example, cursive letters may be looped (e.g., *e* and *l*), humped (e.g., *n* and *m*), or members of the "c" or "two o'clock" family (e.g., *c, a, d*). During cursive writing instruction, the teacher also must emphasize both letter formation and connective strokes. For example, some letters end swinging up, such as *a* and *c*; others end swinging out to form a "bridge," such as *b, o, v,* and *w*. See Table 12.3 for a list of programs for handwriting instruction.

Whether it is best to begin handwriting instruction with cursive writing or with manuscript writing is debated among professionals, particularly when in reference to youngsters with mild disabilities. Those advocating manuscript maintain that it is similar to the print children are just learning to read and that the letters are easier for young children to produce (Barbe, Milone, & Wasylyk, 1983). Others claim that cursive writing has a natural flow and rhythm that tends

Table 12.3 Handwriting Programs

Programs	Uses and Publishers
Better Handwriting for You	A basal handwriting series of eight workbooks for both manuscript and cursive. Noble and Noble Publishers.
D'Nealian Handwriting Program (Thurber, 1993)	Workbooks, teacher's editions, and alphabet strips in a basal program for teaching manuscript and cursive. A "transitional" program. Scott-Foresman.
The Cursive Writing Program	Direct instructional lessons to improve speed and accuracy with cursive letters in grades 3 and 4. Uses simplified orthography, slant arrows for paper placement, and slant bars for letter formation. Emphasis on high-frequency words and letter combinations. Science Research Associates.
The Palmer Method	A handwriting series for both manuscript and cursive. A.N. Palmer Co.
SRA Lunchbox Handwriting	Individual practice activities for children in grades K through 4 in both manuscript and cursive. Uses reusable plastic overlays and directional arrows. Science Research Associates.
Tactile-Kinesthetic Writing Program	Uses 26 write-on-wipe-off cards to teach cursive letter formation. Comes with special writing paper to cue letter formation and spacing. Pro-Ed.
Zaner-Bloser Handwriting (Hackney & Lucas, 1993)	A basal workbook series for handwriting instruction and scales for evaluation of handwriting performance in grades K through 8. Also available in a traceable dot-to-dot format helpful for students with writing difficulties. Manuscript and cursive alphabet. Zaner-Bloser.

to prevent reversals, and that beginning with cursive saves instructional time by eliminating the confusing transition from manuscript to a different form of writing (Thurber, 1995; Strauss & Lehtinen, 1947). Most authorities would agree, though, that children with mild disabilities want to be like their peers; therefore, the teacher must help the child learn the form of handwriting used in the regular classroom. In addition, teachers must always remember that handwriting becomes a personal and idiosyncratic tool with time. If a student is producing legible work at an adequate speed, with writing that does not detract from communication or bias teacher and/or employer judgments about the quality of the student's performance, small irregularities in handwriting should not be of concern to teachers.

Today, in an attempt to ease the transition from manuscript to cursive handwriting, many school districts are adopting a "transitional" handwriting approach. For example, D'Nealian handwriting (Thurber, 1993, 1995) looks much like a simplified version of cursive. To produce the cursive alphabet, simple connective strokes are added (see Figure 12.1). Despite the claims made by

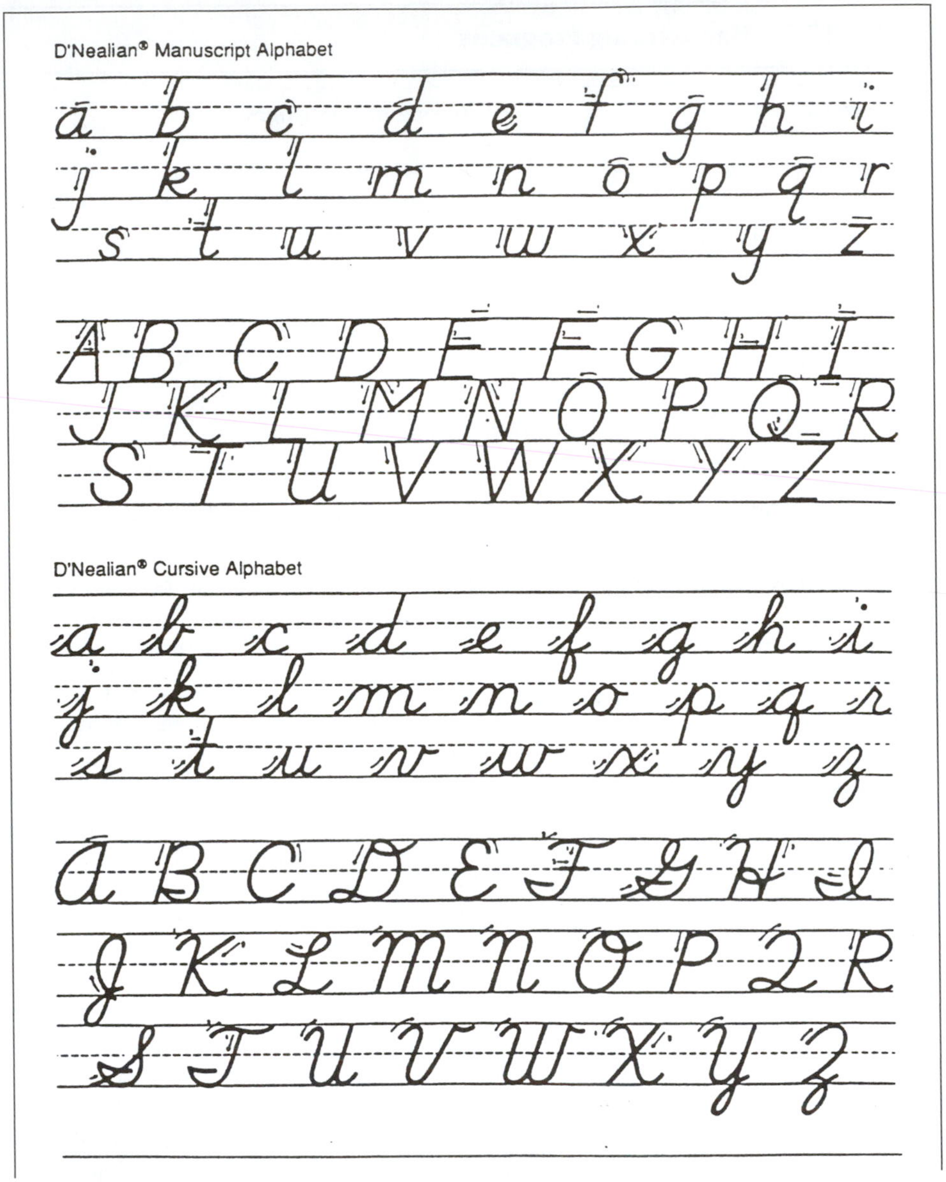

D'Nealian® Manuscript Alphabet

D'Nealian® Cursive Alphabet

FIGURE 12.1

D'Nealian Manuscript and Cursive Alphabets From: Thurber, D.N. (1993). *D'Nealian handwriting.* Glenview, IL: Scott-Foresman Company. Published by Good Year Books, an imprint of Pearson Learning. Used by permission.

producers of transitional alphabets such as D'Nealian, research does not support their superiority or use. In fact, according to Graham (1992, 1993/94), research regarding transitional alphabets suggests that:

◆ These do not save instructional time or enhance the legibility of cursive writing;

- Claims that slanted alphabets result in greater speed and fewer reversals have not been validated;
- Parents often worry that the "new" letters don't look like print;
- Teachers have to relearn how to write in order to teach the slanted alphabet; and
- Many children come to school already knowing how to print some letters, resulting in a confusing transition to the new alphabet upon school entry.

Regardless of the style of writing taught, youngsters with mild disabilities may have numerous difficulties with both manuscript and cursive handwriting. Some students have considerable difficulty producing clearly-formed letters, and others are unable to adjust legibility to meet the demands of the task, producing a final copy of a paper, for example, in the same manner as a draft (Weintraub & Graham, 1998). Illegibilities in only four letters (i.e., *a*, *e*, *r*, and *t*) account for half of all improperly shaped cursive letters across the grade levels (Newland, 1932). However, students with learning disabilities may have particular difficulty producing letters that require diagonal lines, and they also have trouble with letter closure, relative size, staying on the lines, and using correct spacing between letters and words (Johnson & Carlisle, 1996). Moreover, illegible, sloppy handwriting may potentially prejudice teachers and employers against the student with a mild disability, creating a lasting, negative first impression (Greenland & Polloway, 1994).

Improper letter formation may be due to carelessness, misunderstanding of letter strokes, improper pencil grip, or improper paper position. If the last two factors are contributing to illegible handwriting, the teacher can tape the paper to the desk or provide the child with a special pencil grip. For example, rubber grips, available from most office or teaching supply stores, or masking tape wrapped around the pencil, tend to produce the correct three-point grip. Teachers must also reinforce children for properly formed letters and provide clear directions and motivating activities for handwriting instruction and practice.

In addition, students with mild disabilities may have difficulty aligning letters on the paper and properly positioning them on the baseline. To address this problem, teachers may wish to use Right-Line Paper available through Pro-Ed (See Appendix B). This paper has raised lines so that the child can feel when he or she brings a stroke to the baseline. Alternatively, the teacher can draw color-coded horizontal lines on the child's paper or place a sheet of paper containing bold lines produced in black marker under the child's writing paper. In fact, a version of the Right-Line Paper, called Stop-Go Right-Line Paper, uses a raised red line to enable the writer both to see and feel the base and top lines.

Finally, fluency development may be a difficulty experienced by many children in special programs. Some youngsters with mild disabilities may not have an appropriate handwriting speed. They may rush to form letters, producing many illegibilities and an unreadable product, or they may produce each letter slowly and laboriously. Students who are unable to adjust their handwriting speed may have difficulty "keeping up" when taking notes or making rough drafts of assignments—tasks requiring fluency rather than neatness or legibility (Weintraub & Graham, 1998). Again, teachers can reinforce legibly written, rather than perfectly formed, letters, and they can engage children in such activities as self-checking and graphing legible letters written within a given period of time.

Sometimes parents and teachers become concerned about children who reverse letters or numbers when writing. Children younger than age 5 make frequent reversals, and those aged 5 to 7 often will reverse letters or numbers when first learning to write. Young children often reverse the letters *n*, *b*, *d*, *p*, *q*, *s*, and *y* (Lewis & Lewis, 1965). Although teachers should correct reversal errors, they should not become overly concerned that the child may have a learning disability. Research is still unclear regarding which reversals and handwriting errors will be useful for predicting later difficulty in school (Dobbie & Askov, 1995).

If children persist in making reversal errors at a frequent rate, teachers may wish to emphasize the correct starting point and strokes by using color-coded start-stop cues and directional arrows. For example, a green dot might be placed on the line as a starting point, and a red dot placed as a stopping point, during practice forming manuscript letters. In addition, the following suggestions may be helpful when assisting children to overcome reversal errors:

1. Have the child name the letter before writing it. Then, have the child self-verbalize the strokes used to form the letter as he or she is writing it. Gradually fade the self-verbalizations so as not to hinder writing speed.
2. Give the child mnemonic clues for remembering the letter. For example, have the child make a fist with each hand, extending the thumbs straight up. Then, ask the child to place his or her knuckles together. The child should see a *b* and a *d* and should be reminded that *b* comes before *d* in the alphabet. In this way, the child will know which letter faces to the right and which to the left.
3. Post a manuscript alphabet at the child's desk and require the child to refer to the alphabet before writing the letter and then to self-check against the alphabet after writing the letter.
4. Separate instruction with frequently reversed letters. For example, rather than progressing through the alphabet with letters in order, separate practice with *b* and *d* by three or four other letters rather than just with *c*.
5. For children who have severe difficulty with letter reversals, build a visual clue into the letter as a prompt and then slowly fade the clue. For example, superimpose an uppercase *B* over the lower case *b*, then fade the upper, curved portion of the capital letter.

Today, many students, both with and without mild disabilities, use the word processor or computer to assist them in producing legible written products. Isaacson and Gleason (1997) report that although computer-assisted writing does not necessary improve the quality of what is written, it may improve the appearance and acceptability of the final product. Moreover, using the computer has strong motivational appeal to students frustrated by poor handwriting. To that end, students must become proficient with keyboarding skills. Several computer software programs are now available to help students learn keyboarding and touch-typing. These include: *Key Words* (Humanities Software) for grades 3 through 12, *Kid Keys* (Davidson) in grades PreK through 3, *Type to Learn* (Sunburst) for grades 2 to adult, and *Type to Learn, Jr.* (Sunburst) in grades K through 2, *Type!* (Broderbund), and *Stickybear Typing* (Optimum Resource).

Hoffmeister (1981) and Graham (1992) offer several excellent suggestions for providing instruction and practice in handwriting. According to these authorities, the teacher should:

1. Use systematic, explicit, direct instruction during initial handwriting practice and also capitalize on "teachable moments" that occur during the context of meaningful writing activities.
2. Use supervised practice while handwriting skills are being formed. In this way, students will receive immediate reinforcement or corrective feedback to minimize the chance that errors will be practiced and habituated. Limit practice sessions to about fifteen minutes and focus on only one aspect of handwriting at a time (i.e., emphasize posture, grip, slant, size, or shape, but not all simultaneously).
3. Emphasize student self-checking of letters. Children can make individual checklists for troublesome letters so that they can concentrate on those creating the most difficulty for them.
4. Provide close-range models of correct letter formation (e.g., an alphabet strip or chart taped to the student's desk). Be sure the student receives the appropriate right- or left-handed model.
5. Avoid repeated drill of correct letter formation. Students may rush to finish this work and practice poor habits.
6. Post good handwriting on the bulletin board and reinforce handwriting performance with points, stars, or privileges of value to the student. Build legibility criteria for handwriting into all assignments when appropriate.
7. Stress legibility rather than perfection.
8. Use creative writing assignments or content-area study as opportunities for handwriting practice. For example, children can write invitations, letters, stories, poems, announcements, book reports, journals, or news articles to practice handwriting throughout the day.

A Summary of Handwriting Instruction

Children with mild disabilities need supervised practice with immediate reinforcement and correction during handwriting instruction. Generally, methods for teaching manuscript or cursive handwriting skills to youngsters in special education programs are similar to those used in regular classrooms. Special paper, pencil grips, or mnemonics also may be used to assist some students when learning to form letters. In addition, children require practice and reinforcement to produce well-formed letters at an appropriate speed. Legibility and fluency are two major interrelated components of handwriting instruction for children with special needs. ◆

Written Expression

The final goal of written language instruction is written expression. Adequate written expression requires a solid foundation in oral language, reading, and written language skills such as spelling and handwriting. In fact, because written expression is the most complex of all the language arts, special education teachers may overlook instruction in this area. They may concentrate instead on handwriting and spelling as "prerequisite skills," or focus instruction on the mechanical aspects of writing, such as punctuation, capitalization, or word usage. Although oral language, reading, spelling, and handwriting are associated with written expression, they are not sufficient to produce it (Isaacson, 1988a). Each must be taught, and all must be combined when composing written communications.

To be sure, children with mild disabilities must master mechanical or functional aspects of writing if they are to complete written assignments successfully in content-area classrooms. Furthermore, knowledge of the mechanics of writing is necessary to produce a proper business or personal letter or to fill out an application for a job. An overemphasis on mechanical skills, however, frequently makes all writing activities distasteful for youngsters. The typical drill-and-practice exercises found in grammar textbooks (e.g., correcting punctuation, capitalization, or word-usage errors in sentences or identifying the parts of speech) bear little resemblance to the actual processes used by good writers (Hayes & Flower, 1986). Moreover, many children fail to transfer to their own spontaneous writing the skills practiced during these exercises.

Teachers are rightfully concerned about fluency (i.e., the number of words and sentences children write); syntax (i.e., using more complex sentence structures such as subordinate clauses and appositives); vocabulary (i.e., varying word choice and increasingly using more "mature" words); and the aforementioned mechanical conventions of writing. Youngsters with mild disabilities require direct instruction and practice in these areas (Isaacson, 1992). This practice, however, should complement rather than replace experience with real writing tasks (Graham & Harris, 1988). That is, if youngsters with mild disabilities are to learn *how* to write for varying purposes, they must receive instruction and practice with writing *as a process.*

Students in special education classrooms have numerous difficulties with written expression. According to Isaacson and Gleason (1997), students with learning problems have difficulty with both the *author* and *secretary* roles of writing. That is, as authors they are not as likely as peers to organize their thoughts or to consider the needs of the reader and the purpose for writing. Many students lack an understanding of varying text structures and of the communicative purpose of writing (Englert et al., 1988; Newcomer & Barenbaum, 1991). Moreover, in the secretary role they make more mechanical errors than their peers do. For example, most youngsters with mild disabilities produce written work that contains a greater number of handwriting, punctuation, capitalization, grammar, or spelling errors than that produced by peers (Thomas, Englert, & Gregg, 1987) (see Figure 12.2).

Graham (1992) suggests that the author and secretary roles are interrelated. Some children may focus so much attention on the "lower level" mechanical processes that they fail to generate sufficient ideas about the topic chosen. Their written reports, then, tend to be short, containing fewer words and sentences in comparison with those of their peers (Englert et al., 1988). Others may have no difficulty producing elaborate and well-organized stories, but mechanical elements of writing such as illegible handwriting or many misspelled words may make the story virtually unreadable. Teachers must determine the writing difficulties of

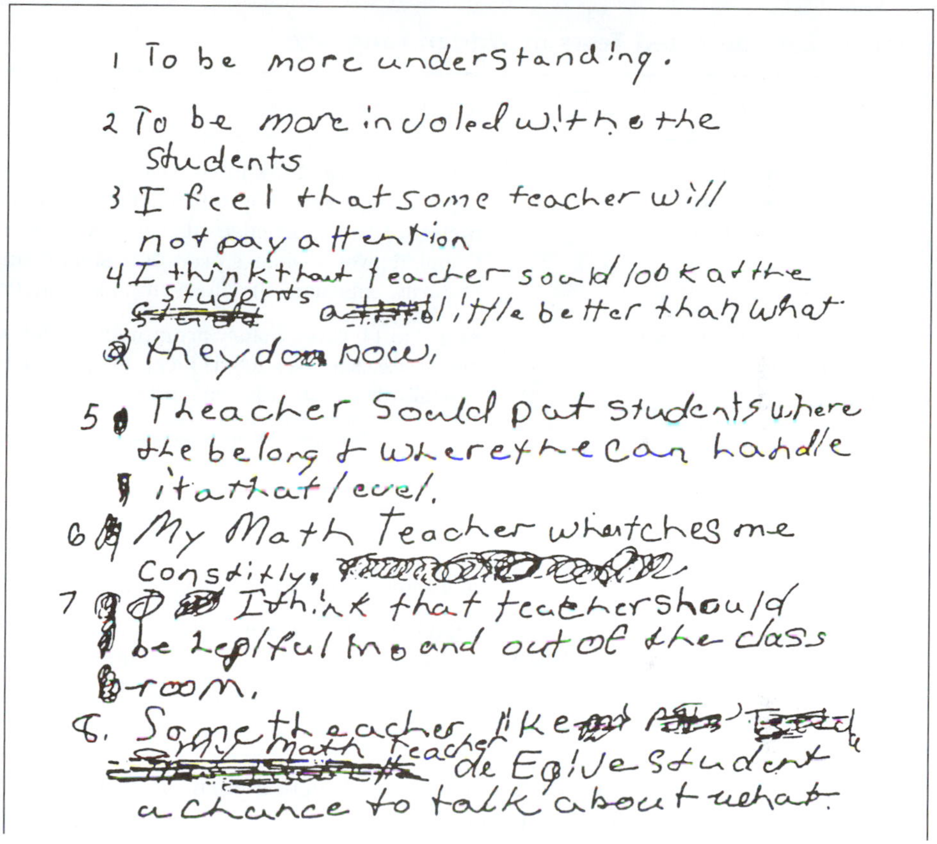

1 To be more understanding.

2 To be more involed with the the
   students
3 I feel that some teacher will
   not pay attention
4 I think that teacher sould look at the
   students   a little better than what
   they do now,

5 Theacher Sould put students where
   the belong & where the can handle
   it at that level.
6 My Math Teacher whatches me
   Constitly,
7   I think that teacher should
   be heplful in and out of the class
   room,
8. Some teacher like
               de Egive student
   a chance to talk about what.

FIGURE 12.2

A Writing Sample from a Student with a Learning Disability: This writing sample, a list of those things believed to contribute to "good teaching," was produced by a student with a learning disability. Difficulties with spelling, letter size, spacing, and alignment are apparent. From: Gallegos, A.Y., & Gallegos, M.L. (1990). A student's perspective on good teaching: Michael. *Intervention in School and Clinic, 26,* pages 14-15. Copyright © 1990 by PRO-ED, Inc. Reprinted with permission.

particular students and adjust instruction accordingly (Berninger, Abbott, Whitaker, Sylvester, & Nolen, 1995; Berninger & Stage, 1996). A writing program for students with mild disabilities, therefore, must include instruction regarding how to plan, organize, draft, and revise written work to meet the needs of various readers, as well as instruction in mechanical skills to improve fluency.

To assess written expression and determine the skills with which individual students are having difficulty, teachers may use standardized tests such as those listed in Table 12.4. Most of these formal measures contain assessments of spelling, handwriting, and grammar, as well as an estimate of the student's ability to compose well-organized sentences, paragraphs, or stories. In addition, teachers may use a number of informal assessments after obtaining a writing sample from the student on a topic of interest or

Table 12.4 Selected Tests of Written Language

Test	Description
Test of Early Written Language— 2 (Hresko, Herron, & Peak, 1996).	Ages 4 to 10; Yields a Global Writing Quotient for spelling, capitalization, sentence construction, punctuation, and metacognitive knowledge. Also gives a Contextual Writing Quotient given a picture prompt in story format, thematic maturity, cohesion, structure, and ideation. Pro-Ed.
Test of Written Expression (McGhee, Bryant, Larsen, & Rivera, 1995).	Ages 6 to 14; Gives a story prompt for students to complete and assesses areas such as ideation, grammar, vocabulary capitalization, punctuation, and spelling. Pro-Ed.
Test of Written Language—3 (Hammill & Larsen, 1996).	Ages 7 to 17; Uses a spontaneous format (i.e., a story starter) to assess story construction (e.g., plot, character); spelling, capitalization, and punctuation; and vocabulary, syntax, and grammar, as well as a contrived format for vocabulary, spelling, style (i.e., punctuation and capitalization), logical sentences, and sentence combining (i.e., syntax).
Test of Written Spelling— 3 (Larsen & Hammill, 1994)	Grades 1 to 12; Measures ability to spell phonetically predictable words, "spelling demons," and both types of words combined.

examining work placed in a student's portfolio. Informal assessments of writing skill include measures of:

- ◆ Fluency—The average number of words per sentence can be computed by counting the number of words written and dividing by the number of sentences written (Isaacson, 1988b). For example, if Travis writes 4 sentences that have 5, 7, 6, and 4 words respectively, his estimate of fluency is 22 divided by 4, or 5.5 words per sentence. Students who write more words are also generating more ideas. Moreover, as average sentence length increases, students may be writing more complex sentences and using more advanced syntactic structures.

- ◆ Syntax—To determine the types of sentence construction students are using, teachers can devise checklists. They can count, for example, the number of simple, compound, complex, incomplete, or run-on sentences a student produces in his or her writing. The percentage of each type of sentence from a writing sample can be recorded and used to measure progress over time. As Robert increases the percentage of complex sentences written, the syntactic maturity of his writing is likely to improve. In addition, incorrect verb or pronoun usage, as well as other grammatical errors, may be recorded on a checklist.

- ◆ Vocabulary—Measures of vocabulary assess the originality and breadth of a student's choice of words. Teachers may wish to measure the number of unusual words (i.e., those not included on a list of high-frequency words or not typically used by students at a particular grade level) that students write. Or teachers can compute a Type-Token Ratio (TTR), the ratio of different words used (i.e., the type) to the total number of words written (i.e., the token). For example, if Taylor wrote, "The dawn broke over the darkened sky like a candle placed before a mirror," her Type-Token Ratio would be 12 divided by 14, or about .85. (Notice that Taylor repeated the high frequency words *the* and *a*.) The highest possible value for the TTR is, of course, 1, obtained when students do not repeat any words at all in their writing. Teachers must take care to use the same number of words from the same relative location in writing samples if comparisons from different samples are to be made over time.

◆ Structure—Informal evaluations of structure examine the punctuation, capitalization, spelling, or grammatical errors made by students. One measure of structure is the Grammatical Correctness Ratio (GCR). The GCR is computed by counting the number of grammatical errors in a student's writing sample, subtracting this number from the total number of words written, dividing by the total number of words written, and multiplying by 100 to convert to a percentage. A GCR can also be computed for one or more particular types of grammatical errors. For example, Ms. Lopez might count three subject-verb agreement errors and five spelling errors in Travis's paragraph of 30 words. The overall GCR = 30-8/30 × 100 or 73%. The GCR for Travis's subject-verb agreement errors is 27/30 × 100 or 90%, and for spelling the GCR is 25/30 × 100 or 83%. As the percentage approaches 100, students are producing work containing fewer and fewer grammatical errors.

The Writing Process

Most authorities today view written expression as a recursive process. That is, good writers think about the topic and audience before they write, planning and organizing ideas accordingly. As the expert writes, he or she keeps the audience and purpose in mind while producing the initial draft. Then, good writers make revisions, eliminating ideas that are not connected to the central thesis, clarifying ambiguous statements, or inserting connectives where needed to ensure cohesive text. Finally, the expert writer edits his or her end product, proofreading for mechanical errors or for inconsistencies, before sharing the text with the intended audience (Bos, 1988). Prewriting, drafting, revising, and editing, then, are the major components of the recursive writing process. Teachers must build instructional activities and strategies around these components to help their students produce good written work. (See Table 12.5 for a description of the writing processes and products of skilled and unskilled writers. Also see Box 12.1 for some sites on the World Wide Web promoting the recursive writing process.)

Prewriting Activities

Students must consider the intended audience and plan and organize a topic during the first stage of the writing process—the prewriting stage. Some students find it difficult to generate topical ideas. For these youngsters, teachers must provide

Table 12.5   A Comparison of Skilled and Unskilled Writers

Process Dimension	Skilled	Unskilled
Prewriting	Jots notes and makes diagrams. Discusses and explores topics. Considers both purpose and intended audience.	Does not sketch out ideas or plans. Does not participate in prewriting discussion. Does not consider either purpose or intended audience.
Drafting	Writes in style appropriate for audience. Stops frequently to reread and think.	Writes in an informal style. Stops infrequently to reread and think. Overemphasizes spelling and the mechanics of writing.
Revising and Editing	Makes corrections for all errors. Keeps audience in mind while revising and editing.	Does not review or make content changes. Looks only for surface errors. Recopies only to make a neat version in ink.
Fluency	Writes many words in allotted time. Writes complete sentences.	Writes few words in allotted time. Writes incomplete sentences.
Syntax	Writes complex sentences using clauses or phrases.	Writes only simple S-V or S-V-O sentences.
Vocabulary	Uses mature words; avoids favorite words.	Repeats favorite words; uses high-frequency words.
Content	Uses appropriate style for topic and audience. Sticks to topic. Develops topic logically and organizes material well.	Disregards audience and includes irrelevant information. Does not organize or structure material coherently.
Conventions	Makes few or no errors; writes neatly.	Makes many errors; writes illegibly.

Adapted from: Isaacson, S.L. (1988). Effective instruction in written language. In E.L. Meyen, G.A. Vergason, & R.J. Whelan (Eds.), *Effective instructional strategies for exceptional children*, (p. 291 & 294), Denver, CO: Love. Reprinted with permission.

stimulation to write. Viewing videos, reading stories, or discussing activities or areas of interest could provide needed stimulation; however, Bos and Vaughn (1998) caution that students must be helped to choose their own topics about which to write. For example, youngsters may keep a list of ideas, generated with peer or teacher assistance, in a folder to serve as future topics for writing. Or students may add favorite topics to a classroom list posted on the bulletin board so that others may draw from these ideas when they can not think of topics themselves.

Additionally, teachers find it helpful to read quality literature to students or to have children share their writing with one another, modeling fresh ideas and different writing styles. Some teachers encourage students to explore ideas in

Web Watch

Sites to Promote the Writing Process

Amazon.com

http://www.amazon.com
Students may go to this popular book site to publish a review of a book they have read.

Inkspot for Young Writers

http://www.inkspot.com/young/
A great site for students to receive advice from authors and editors. Also contains links to other sites for writing activities and assistance as well as a forum for exchanging ideas.

Keypals

http://www.keypals.com/p/wwwsites.html
A site to connect to other classrooms at various grade levels for revision conferences. Students can send drafts of their work and have students in another classroom give feedback to improve writing efforts.

KidPub

http://www.kidpub.org
A site publishing all work children submit. Encourages children to write for a real audience and receive feedback on how many have read their works.

The National Council of Teachers of English

http://www.ncte.org/
The web site of the major professional organization for English teachers. Helpful site for all teachers, containing discussion groups, lesson ideas, information on the writing process, and more.

The Quill Society

http://www.quill.net
A wonderful site for students aged 12 to 24 to publish their works as well as receive helpful suggestions to improve their writing.

personal journals or give children opportunities to write poetry (See Box 12.2). Selected entries from journals can be expanded later into stories or poems for placement in a writing portfolio. Focusing on idea generation rather than on mechanics and providing students with a real audience and a meaningful purpose for writing are critical elements of all prewriting activities. Children can be given such tasks as writing a letter to request information, writing a letter to be mailed to a family member, writing an article for the school newspaper, or writing a story to be placed in the school or classroom library.

Many children with mild disabilities also need help in generating vocabulary to use when writing about a selected topic. They are likely to use only

Box 12.2

Using Personal Journals and Poetry in Writing Instruction

The following is a journal entry and poetry sample written by the author and her students during writing time in a ninth-grade English class composed of six boys with learning disabilities and emotional/behavioral disorders.

Journal Entry

Spring is coming! I can sense its approach in the change of wind and the changes in people. There is something about spring that always speaks to my heart and renews my spirit. I stood atop a building yesterday, caressed by sun and warm fresh breezes. Later, I could smell the soil, rich and moist after a gentle spring shower. I watched a rainbow appear in a darkened sky and felt the poetry of spring.

Resulting Poems

Wind
Scintillating touch!
Lifting strands from my shoulders
And strings from my heart.

Rainbow
Cascading color,
The blue sky smiles a rainbow
Caressing green Earth.

simple high-frequency words in their writing if they can not think of different words or do not know how to spell them. To address this need, the teacher and students can list words or phrases to describe an object before writing a descriptive paragraph. Similarly, teachers can elicit content-area vocabulary from students, posting this information on the chalkboard or bulletin board so that they may refer to it when writing.

In addition, most youngsters in special education classrooms require assistance with organizing topics and using varying text structures (Vallecorsa & Garriss, 1990). Numerous research studies now point to the importance of teaching students with mild disabilities strategies to help themselves plan and organize what they write (see, for example, DeLaPaz & Graham, 1997; Englert, Raphael, Anderson, Anthony, & Stevens, 1991; Sexton, Harris, & Graham, 1998; Troia, Graham, & Harris, 1999). For example, when writing simple paragraphs about a topic, special education teachers can provide children with formats, such as those illustrated in Figure 12.3 or Statement-PIE discussed in Chapter 11 (Wallace & Bott, 1989). Welch and Jensen (1990) also offer a strategy for generating and organizing ideas in simple paragraph form. Their strategy, Write PLEASE, consists of six steps prompted by the mnemonic PLEASE:

P = Pick a topic.
L = List ideas about the topic.
E = Evaluate your list of ideas.
A = Activate with a topic sentence to introduce the paragraph.
S = Supply supporting sentences.
E = End with a clincher sentence to summarize the paragraph and hold the ideas together.

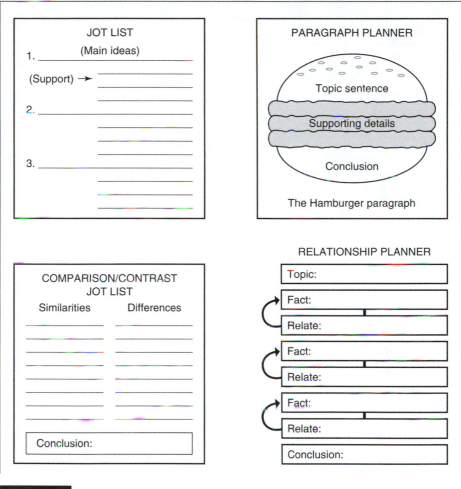

JOT LIST

(Main ideas)

1. _____

(Support) → _____
_____
_____

2. _____
_____
_____
_____

3. _____
_____
_____
_____

PARAGRAPH PLANNER

Topic sentence

Supporting details

Conclusion

The Hamburger paragraph

COMPARISON/CONTRAST
JOT LIST

Similarities   Differences

Conclusion:

RELATIONSHIP PLANNER

Topic:

Fact:

Relate:

Fact:

Relate:

Fact:

Relate:

Conclusion:

FIGURE 12.3 ◆

Formats for Organizing Writing From: Vallecorsa, A.L., Ledford, R.R., & Parnell, G.G. (1991). Strategies for teaching composition skills to students with learning disabilities. *Teaching Exceptional Children*, 23, p. 53. Copyright © 1991 by the Council for Exceptional Children. Reprinted with permission.

For more sophisticated text structures, "mapping" may be a useful prewriting activity. For example, a story map, such as that offered by Idol (1987), may improve not only a child's reading comprehension, but also the child's production of narratives or stories (see Chapter 11). A story web can help students brainstorm and integrate ideas for writing (Zipprich, 1995) (see Figure 12.4). Hagood (1997) and Montague and Leavell (1994) recommend the following instructional strategies when using story maps to improve writing skills:

◆ Discuss the elements of the story map to be used and model how to complete the story map using a story starter, such as, "One day, my friend and I saw the funniest thing."

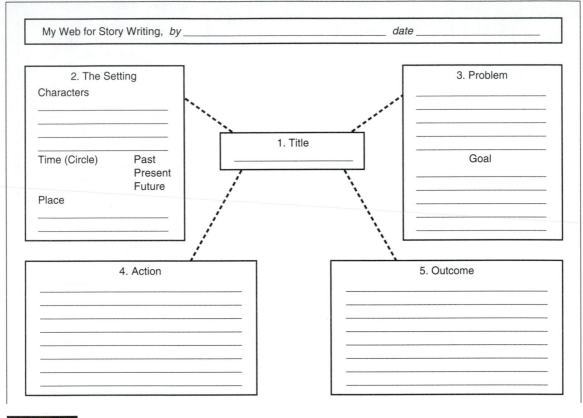

My Web for Story Writing, *by* _____ *date* _____

2. The Setting

Characters
_____
_____
_____

Time (Circle)   Past
                       Present
                       Future

Place
_____
_____

1. Title
_____

3. Problem
_____
_____
_____
_____

Goal
_____
_____
_____

4. Action
_____
_____
_____
_____
_____
_____

5. Outcome
_____
_____
_____
_____
_____
_____
_____

FIGURE 12.4

◆

A Sample Story Web for Writing From: Zipprich, M.A. (1995). Teaching web making as a guided planning tool to improve student narrative writing. *Remedial and Special Education, 16*(1), 3-15, 52. (p.6). Copyright © 1995 by PRO-ED, Inc. Reprinted by permission.

◆ After completing the story map, demonstrate how to incorporate each story element into the actual story, checking off each element on a check sheet as it is included:

Check Off Parts in the Story

_____ Characters: _____ Setting:
(Do they tell their thoughts, feelings   _____ Problem:
and reasons for doing what they do?   _____ Events:
                                       _____ Solution:

◆ Group students and use dramatization to help them incorporate all of the elements of the story map into a group story.

◆ Have students use the story map to manipulate and change elements of the story grammar using a familiar story. For example, students could change the setting or the characters in familiar stories such as *Sleeping Beauty* or *The Most Dangerous Game.*

Carnine and Kinder (1985) also taught elementary-aged children to ask themselves a series of "story-grammar" questions to generate narrative text: "Who is the story about?"; "What are they trying to do?"; "What happens when they try to do it?"; and "What happens in the end?" Similarly, Graham, Harris, and Sawyer (1987) suggest a mnemonic to help students remember essential questions they should ask themselves to make sure they include all the necessary elements when writing stories:

W-W-W; What = 2; How = 2

Who is the main character? Who else is in the story?
When does the story take place?
Where does the story take place?
What does the main character do?
What happens when he/she tries to do it?
How does the story end?
How does the main character feel?

Additionally, these authorities offer a self-instructional strategy for expository writing: think, 'who will read this and why am I writing this?', then plan what to say using TREE (i.e., a mnemonic for "note *Topic* sentence, note *Reasons*, *Examine* reasons, note *Ending*"), then write and say more (Graham, Harris, & Sawyer, 1987).

Similarly, in several studies, the written products of children were improved by providing them with formats for organizing explanatory and other text structures (see Figure 12.5). Englert and Raphael (1990) modeled an "expert" format for text structure while thinking aloud and then gave students ample practice in its use for actual writing. Wong, Butler, Ficzere, and Kuperis (1997) taught students to write compare-and-contrast essays by demonstrating how to use a planning sheet called HELPERS in Writing. On this sheet, students were to formulate an introduction by saying, "In this essay, I am going to compare and contrast _____ and _____. I have chosen to write on three different features:

1.)_____,
2.)_____, and
3.)_____."

Following the writing, students wrote concluding paragraphs containing two elements: a summary of the features and an expression of their own opinion or a statement of which feature they liked better. Hallenbeck (1996) also modeled the use of a Think-Sheet to organize explanatory paragraphs including the following questions:

What is being explained?
Who or what is needed?
Setting?
What are the steps?
   First,
   Next,
   Third,
   Then,

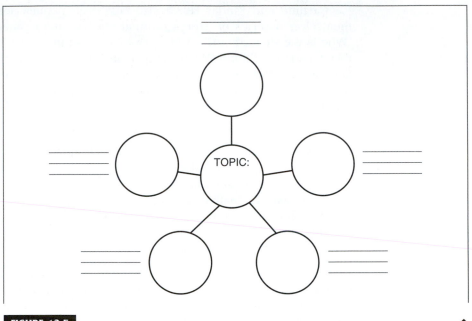

FIGURE 12.5

Expert Writing Organization Format From: Englert, C.S. & Raphael, T.E. (1990). Developing successful writers through cognitive strategy instruction. In J. Brophy (Ed.). *Advances in research on teaching,* Greenwich, CT: JAI Press. Reprinted with permission.

Fifth,

Finally,

Finally, Korinek and Bulls (1996) taught students a step-by-step strategy for writing research papers. Called SCORE A, this first-letter acronym combines the use of graphic aids and mnemonics to help secondary-level students write longer and more complicated written products:

S = Select a subject.

C = Create categories. Use a graphic aid to organize the categories. (See Figure 12.6.)

O = Obtain sources.

R = Read and take notes on notecards. Include the source's title, page number, category title, and one important fact on each card.

E = Evenly organize the information. Make a heading card for each category. Lay the remaining cards evenly under each heading.

A = Apply the process writing steps (i.e., prewriting, drafting, revising, and editing).

Summary of Prewriting Activities

Self-instructional strategies such as these may help children with mild disabilities to generate ideas and then organize them coherently before actual writing

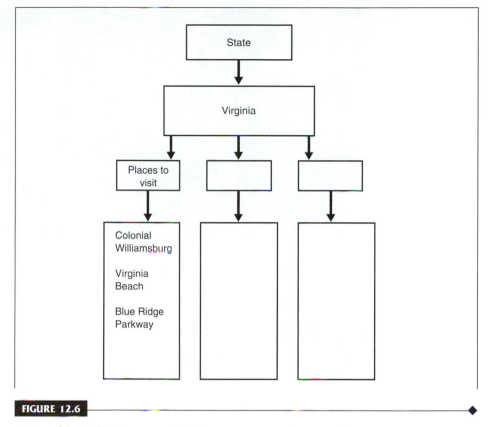

A Graphic Aid to Improve Writing From: Korinek, L., & Bulls, J.A. (1996). SCORE A: A student research paper writing strategy. Teaching *Exceptional Children, 28*(4), 60-63. (p. 61). Copyright © 1996 by the Council for Exceptional Children. Reprinted with permission.

takes place (Graham & Harris, 1989a, 1989b). Direct instruction of narrative and expository text structures can help students both comprehend and compose written work and provides an avenue for integrating reading and writing skills (Gleason, 1995). In addition, pre-cued spelling and vocabulary as well as brainstorming topical lists of ideas can improve students' writing. ◆

Drafting Activities

After children have the opportunity to generate ideas and plan what they want to say, they must write their stories or essays. During this stage of the writing process, the teacher must help students focus on their ideas rather than on the mechanical aspects of written expression. Teachers may tell students not to worry about punctuation, capitalization, grammar, or spelling while producing the first draft (Clarke, 1988). In addition, teachers might permit students to dictate their stories or provide them with a word book or word list to help them spell unknown words. Some teachers, particularly in the early grades, encourage students to "invent" spellings for words they can not yet spell. A.S.

Students who use computers may spend more time writing and revising. Consequently, they may produce a more readable written product.

Brown (1988) cautions, however, that invented spellings may hinder later spelling accuracy with older students. According to Isaacson and Gleason (1997), invented spellings may improve writing fluency (i.e., the actual number of words students write), but may hinder the acceptability and readability of the final product unless combined with a strong spelling program. (See Table 12.6 for an analysis of methods used by teachers to overcome the mechanical obstacles of writing during the drafting process.)

In addition, dialogue among students or between students and the teacher may enhance the clarity and depth of written communications. For example, children may be paired with partners and given ample time to share their writing attempts with one another as they compose their drafts. Of course, teachers will need to supervise this activity carefully to be sure students ask appropriate questions and give appropriate feedback to their peers.

Some teachers like to use a different color paper for the "sloppy copy" so that students can easily tell which version is the draft and which version is the final product (Englert et al., 1988). Also, teachers should require students to write the first draft on every other line so that revision will be easier.

Revising Activities

Revision is a difficult process even for experienced writers. During the revision stage, writers judge and improve the content and clarity of their initial writing efforts. Although mechanical errors may be detected and corrected during this stage as well, the primary focus when revising is on *what* is said.

Often children are reluctant to revise their written work; therefore, teachers must model and reward appropriate revision skills. While reading a draft version of a written product aloud, the teacher might pause to ask for clarification at certain points and help the student formulate a better way to phrase what is being said (Wong, Wong, Darlington, & Jones, 1991). In addition, the teacher will need to "think aloud," modeling evaluative and directive thoughts used by expert writers (e.g., "People may not understand what I mean

---

Table 12.6 Comparison of Methods to Overcome the Mechanical Obstacles to Writing

	Evaluative Questions		
First Draft	*Final Draft*		
Does it enable focus on ideas?	Does it improve readability?		
Method	*(Author Role)*	*(Secretary Role)*	*Notes*
Dictation	Yes	Yes	Student doesn't learn to integrate mechanics and composition.
Precued Spelling	Slightly	Slightly	Effects not significantly different from other methods.
Word Book	No	Yes	Use only for final draft.
Asking the Teacher	Inconsistently	Somewhat	Students may not be willing to ask or be aware of misspelled words. Waiting can detract from writing time.
Invented Spelling	Yes	No	Supplement with strong spelling program.
Peer Collaboration	Potentially	Potentially	Depends on how well students are prepared to work with each other.
Self-Checking	Not for first	Yes draft	Editing must be separated from drafting.
Computer-Assisted Writing	Inconsistently	Partially	Improves the appearance but not necessarily the quality of writing. Strong motivational appeal.

From: Isaacson, S., & Gleason, M.M. (1997). Mechanical obstacles to writing: What can teachers do to help students with learning problems? *Learning Disabilities Research & Practice, 12*(3), 188-194. (p. 189)

here." ; "This doesn't sound quite right." ; "I'd better move this sentence." ; "I'd better support what I'm saying here.") (Bereiter & Scardamalia, 1982).

As in drafting activities, teachers must provide numerous opportunities for children to interact when revising. Children can share their drafts with one another and use questions designed to accompany each specific text structure to evaluate their own writing or that of peers (e.g., "Did I explain what was happening?"; "Did I include a main character?"; "Did I use keywords to show the order?"). Englert and her colleagues (1988) require children to rate themselves or others on "Did I . . ." type questions using a three-choice scale (i.e., "Yes," "Sort of," or "No"). In addition, they encourage children to place question marks next to parts of their drafts that they think may be unclear.

Finally, computer software may make it easier for children with mild disabilities to revise their compositions. Vacc (1987) maintains that when children with mild disabilities use word processors, they spend more time writing and revising, and consequently produce better writing samples, than when they complete written work by hand. Others agree that computers help students with writing difficulty by making revising and editing easier, by increasing the quantity of each writing effort, by providing spell-checkers, and by allowing for ease of error correction and thus neater final copies (MacArthur, Graham, Schwartz, & Schafer, 1995). On the other hand, Isaacson and Gleason (1997) suggest that word processors improve the appearance, but not necessarily the actual quality of a student's writing. Still others suggest that using the keyboard may not be any more effective than handwriting in improving writing speed or student attitude toward writing (Lewis, Graves, Ashton, & Kieley, 1998). Nevertheless, computer applications such as talking word processors (i.e., speech synthesis and pronunciation editing), spell-checking by visually highlighting words, word cueing or word prediction, and grammar correction and tutoring may provide benefits beyond legibility for students with learning difficulties (Hunt-Berg, Rankin, & Beukelman, 1994). In fact, many computer software programs are now available to assist students in the production of quality writing, including the following:

- ◆ *Dr. Peet's Talk/Writer* (Hartley/Dr. Peet's Software)— appropriate for all age levels. Uses talking, singing, and beautiful graphics.
- ◆ *The Amazing Writing Machine* (Broderbund)—for children grades 1 through 5. Includes clip art, painting tools, and rebus symbols to enable students to transform ideas into words they can't yet spell.
- ◆ *Kid Works Deluxe/Kid Works 2* (Davidson)—a popular program that enables students in grades PreK through 4 to create and edit stories, add graphics, animation, sound, or music, and listen to their stories read back to them.
- ◆ *Student Writing Center* (The Learning Company)—used in grades 5 to 12 as a desktop publishing tool for reports, stories, letters, and so forth. Contains a spell-checker, thesaurus, writing and grammar tips, and personal journal for organizing thoughts.
- ◆ *Write On! Plus* (Humanities Software/Sunburst)—a series of writing tools for grades K through 12, including beginning writing skills, writing with picture books, elementary writing skills, steps to better writing, middle school writing skills, high school writing skills, and writing with literature.

Teachers can also help students use revision activities similar to those described previously as they use word processing programs. Graham and MacArthur (1988), for example, helped students with learning disabilities use both a self-instructional revision strategy and a word processor to improve the length and quality of written work. Youngsters learned the following six-step strategy for revising essays produced on the word processor:

1. Read your essay.
2. Find the sentence that tells what you believe. Is it clear?
3. Add two reasons why you believe it.
4. SCAN each sentence.
   Does it make sense?
   Is it connected to your belief?
   Can you add more?
   Note errors.
5. Make changes on the computer.
6. Reread your essay and make final changes.

Editing Activities

The last stage of the writing process involves editing and rewriting the final copy to be shared with an audience. The emphasis during editing is on correcting mechanical errors of punctuation, capitalization, spelling, or grammar; however, students may also make any additional changes necessary to improve the clarity and content of their compositions. When helping students edit written work, teachers should concentrate on only one or two key elements at a time, and not overwhelm students with papers covered with editing marks. By focusing direct instruction on a limited number of mechanical skills needed to complete a final written product, the teacher can provide the student, or a small group of students making similar errors, with mini-lessons designed to give meaningful practice with essential skills in context (Dowis & Schloss, 1992).

Englert and her colleagues (1988) point out that students can serve as "editors" for themselves or others, placing question marks next to unclear information, stars next to passages that seem particularly appealing or well-written, and standard editing symbols near errors (see Figure 12.7). Students with mild disabilities will require explicit instruction and practice using specific procedures to detect errors in written work, however. One helpful strategy for error monitoring combines drafting, revision, and editing activities and uses the mnemonic WRITER within a "policing" theme (Ellis & Lenz, 1987; Schumaker, Nolan, & Deshler, 1985):

W = Write on every other line.
R = Read the paper for meaning.
I = Interrogate yourself using the "COPS" questions.
   C = Have I capitalized the first word and all proper nouns?
   O = How is the overall appearance of the paper?
   P = Have I used end punctuation and commas correctly?
   S = Are the words spelled correctly?
T = Take the paper to someone else to proofread again.

Mark	Explanation	Example
◯	Circle words that are spelled incorrectly.	My (freind) and I went to the zoo last Sunday.
/	Change a capital letter to a small letter.	Mary and Jim watched /Television for one hour.
≡	Change a small letter to a capital letter.	bob loves the way I play horn.
∧	Add letters, words, or sentences.	My friend lives in the ∧house next door. (brick)
⊙	Add a period.	My dog, Frisky, and I are private detectives⊙
⌀	Take out letters, words, or punctuation.	Last summer Bob (went and) flew an airplane in Alaska.
∧,	Add a comma.	Bob visited Alaska∧Ohio∧and Florida.

FIGURE 12.7

Commonly-Used Editing Symbols From: Whitt, J., Paul, P.V., & Reynolds, C.J. (1988). Motivate reluctant learning disabled writers. *Teaching Exceptional Children, 20,* p. 38. Copyright © 1988 by the Council for Exceptional Children. Reprinted with permission.

E = Execute a final copy.
R = Reread your paper a final time.

Promoting a Classroom Atmosphere Conducive to Writing

Many children with mild disabilities dislike writing. At first, teachers may need to disregard mechanical errors in an effort to make these children feel more comfortable with writing. Teachers must promote a classroom atmosphere in which everyone writes about topics of interest without fear of being penalized for mistakes. According to Englert (1992), writing is best taught as the children and the teacher engage in dialogues about real writing (see Box 12.3).

Promoting an atmosphere conducive to writing may involve teachers sharing their own writing with students. In addition, students need many opportunities to sit in the "author's chair" and share their finished products with their peers (Graves & Hansen, 1983). Furthermore, when teachers select quality books, poems, and stories to read in class, students may discover new styles or topics for their own writing. Conferences about writing between teachers and students or among students should focus on prewriting, drafting, revising, and editing activities that are likely to result in clear written communications. Finally, Graves (1985) offers several suggestions to help teachers engage their students in writing:

1. Allow students to choose their own topics.
2. Provide time for children to write. Children must write daily, preferably for about 30 minutes.
3. Permit children to own a "topical turf," a topic about which they are the "expert" and on which they can expand over time as they write.

4. Collect all writing samples for each child and keep these in a portfolio or folder. Periodically "publish" the best works for each child or for the class in "hardcover" form.

5. Provide a predictable pattern for writing. Try to write at about the same time each day, and share your own writing with children. Move about during

---

Box 12.3

Writing Time in Ms. Booker's Sixth-Grade Language Arts Class

Ms. Booker integrates reading and writing activities in her classroom. This year, her students have a daily writing period of about 20 minutes. During this time, they jot down ideas for writing in a personal folder and work on their creations.

Ms. Booker has organized the class into six cooperative groups of four members each. During writing time, the students in each group may talk quietly with one another, sharing their writing, making suggestions, and asking questions. In addition, each group elects a weekly "editor" to review manuscripts before recopying. Twice a month, Ms. Booker plans time for children from each group to share their "best work" with the rest of the class. Periodically, she types stories and poems selected by the students for "publication" in a classroom literary magazine, a copy of which is placed in the library. The magazine is also sent home to parents. During daily writing time, Ms. Booker is constantly on the move, chatting with students and supervising groups. Although she is pressed for time, she tries to hold a 5-minute "conference" with each child at least once every two weeks.

Let's listen to a conference between Ms. Booker and Leon. Ms. Booker is very pleased that Leon has read a book, which the librarian helped him select. Although the reading was somewhat difficult for Leon, he did enjoy the book, reacting to the plight of the main character, Jimmy. Ms. Booker believes that Leon, an extremely reluctant writer, may be motivated to write about this book:

Ms. Booker: Okay, so you're saying that if you had been Jimmy you wouldn't have let them treat you the same way.

Leon: No, man!

Ms. Booker: Do you think Jimmy had a choice? I mean, what might have happened to him if he had tried to fight?

Leon: I don't know.

Ms. Booker: Would they have hurt him?

Leon: Maybe, but you don't stand for that stuff!

Ms. Booker: Do you think Jimmy had courage?

Leon: No, he didn't fight them guys!

Ms. Booker: Okay, so you believe Jimmy should have stood up to those guys right away. But didn't he finally trick them?

Leon: Yeah, Jimmy, he got 'em in the end.

Ms. Booker: So, he used his brains to get the men arrested. What would you have done if you had been Jimmy? Can you change the story to say what you would have done differently?

Leon:	Maybe.
Ms. Booker:	That might make a good thing to write about, if you want to put that on your list . . .

The next day, Ms. Booker checks back with Leon as she moves about the classroom. Leon has decided to change the story to reflect what he would have done had he been Jimmy. Ms. Booker reads Leon's unfinished version: "Jimmy wait until they guys go buy. He know they crazy. Them guy they shoodn do Jimmy what they done but he can't fight them by his self. He come done from up there."

Ms. Booker:	Hmmm, here, I'm not real sure what is meant by this part, " . . . they shouldn't do Jimmy what they done."
Leon:	You know, how they took his stuff from him and said they was gonna hurt him.
Ms. Booker:	You may need to tell your reader what these men did or they won't understand Jimmy's motive.
Leon:	Okay, I can fix that.
Ms. Booker:	Great! I just have one more question. When you write, "He came down from up there," who do you mean? Jimmy or one of the men?
Leon:	(Crossing out "He" and writing "Jimmy") Yeah.
Ms. Booker:	Super! Okay, I'll check back with you later to see your progress. (Ms. Booker moves on to another student . . .)

writing time, conferring with children and asking leading questions to help them improve their own writing. Provide direct instruction on the mechanical skills necessary for completing a piece of written work, but focus on the composing process rather than on specific skills.

6. Let children listen to and revise their own writing.
7. Have children share their writing with one another during every writing period. Encourage children to ask questions to help one another improve writing.

Summary of Written Expression

Written expression is the most complex area of all the language arts. To write, children must combine their knowledge of oral language, reading, spelling, and handwriting. In order to communicate through writing, children also must understand the differing purposes for writing, as well as various text structures. Teachers can help students learn to write by providing them with numerous opportunities to engage in purposeful writing. Prewriting, drafting, revising, and editing activities, focused on the content rather than on the structural aspects of writing, are important ways to improve a child's written expression. ◆

Summary

The language arts include both oral and written language. Listening, speaking, reading, and writing are considered interrelated language arts skills that cannot be artificially separated for instructional purposes.

In order to teach the written language skills of spelling and handwriting, however, teachers must provide children with direct instruction and supervised practice. Highly generalizable phonemic patterns and morphemic rules, repetition for rote memory, a limited number of words on a flow list, test-study-test, self-correction, and specific strategies for study and practice are useful techniques by which to improve the spelling performance of children with mild disabilities. The goal of handwriting instruction is legible, fluent written communication. Students with mild disabilities must receive explicit instruction and supervised practice during handwriting instruction.

Children must use all of the language arts skills in combination when expressing themselves in writing. In addition, written expression requires children to plan and organize ideas, to write for differing purposes, and to use varying text structures. Teachers must promote a classroom atmosphere conducive to writing in which children engage daily in interactive conferences and dialogues about their writing. The teacher can plan prewriting, drafting, revising, and editing activities designed to help children write about self-selected topics for a real audience.

Application Exercises

1. Obtain two writing samples from a child with a mild disability in a local school district. Taking care not to use any identifying information, analyze the writing samples for spelling errors. Compare the samples to a same-grade-level handwriting standard from one of the handwriting programs listed in Table 12.3. List any errors that you see.

2. Choose one of the text-structure formats presented in this chapter (e.g., explanatory organization, paragraph planner). Design a direct instructional lesson for Ms. Booker's sixth-grade language arts class using this text structure. Recall that Susan, Leon, and Taylor are members of this class.

3. Choose a revision strategy presented in the chapter. Again, design a lesson to teach this strategy to the children in Ms. Booker's sixth-grade language arts class.

4. Browse the web sites listed in Box 12.1. Help a child whom you know publish a story or poem on one of these sites. Monitor the feedback received by the child and help the child revise the submitted work accordingly.

5. Browse InfoTrac. Locate one article on each of the following topics: effective spelling instruction, teaching handwriting, and teaching writing as a recursive process to students with mild disabilities. Share the information you find with a group of three or four colleagues. Compile a list of helpful suggestions your group might include in a workshop for teachers who have students with mild disabilities in their classes.

6. Preview several of the spelling and handwriting programs mentioned in Tables 12.2 and 12.3. Also preview two or three computer software programs for teaching spelling, handwriting, and written expression. Which of these programs and software packages would you recommend to other teachers? Why?

MATHEMATICS INSTRUCTION

As you read, think about the following questions:

◆ *What are some factors likely to impair the mathematics performance of students with mild disabilities?*

◆ *How do math standards and issues in mathematics education impact students in special education programs?*

◆ *If children with mild disabilities are to function successfully as adults, which mathematics skills are essential for them to master?*

◆ *What are some generalizable teaching procedures that special education teachers can apply across the mathematics curriculum?*

◆ *What are some effective methods for teaching basic math facts and operations to youngsters with mild disabilities?*

◆ *What are some effective teaching methods and strategies for enabling students in special education programs to problem solve?*

Many children with mild disabilities experience significant difficulty with mathematics (Epstein, Kinder, & Bursuck, 1989; McLeod & Armstrong, 1982). If these students are to function independently as adults, however, they must be able to apply mathematics skills. Despite the importance of mathematics skills in everyday life, not until recently has research focused on effective methods for teaching mathematics to youngsters in special education programs. Consider, for example, the following class session in Ms. Lopez's resource room:

Ms. Lopez: (Placing on the table several base-10 blocks) "We've been dividing our blocks into equal groups, and you can do that very well. Today, we're going to divide and have remainders left. Watch me. I have one 10-stick and seven 1-units. I have seventeen units all together. I want to divide seventeen into equal groups of 3." (She writes $17 \div 3 =$ _____.) "Let's see. Can I divide these blocks into equal groups now, Travis?"

Travis: "No, `cause you got one ten-stick and seven singles."

Ms. Lopez: "Good answer! So, what must I do, Joey?"

Joey: "Trade the 10-stick in for ten 1's."

Ms. Lopez: "Excellent! If I trade the 10-stick in for ten 1's, I have seventeen 1's; I still have seventeen. Now, can I divide the seventeen 1's into equal groups of three? Let's see . . . " (She puts three 1 blocks in a pile on the table and then continues making groups of three until she has five piles of three blocks each.) "Now I have five stacks of three blocks each, and I have two 1-blocks left over. Since 2 is less than 3, I can't divide these blocks any further without making my five piles unequal. So, 17 divided by 3 equals 5 with a remainder of 2." (She writes the answer as she says it.)

Using concrete manipulatives is one effective instructional method for developing an understanding of mathematical concepts in students with mild disabilities (Peterson, Mercer, & O'Shea, 1988). In this chapter, we will explore this and other techniques to improve the math performance of children with mild disabilities. First, however, let's examine some of the factors that affect the achievement of these youngsters in mathematics, including both student and curricular difficulties.

Factors Affecting Math Performance

Many of us, as adults, have said, "I'm just not good at math." With this statement we seem to rationalize the difficulties we have experienced in learning mathematics and in applying math to our daily lives. Yet mathematics affects all of us every day. The National Research Council (1989) maintains that math affects us from many different perspectives:

◆ Practical—Making purchases, computing interest on a loan, understanding paychecks or salary increases.
◆ Civic—Understanding and computing taxes, making decisions regarding city or county budgets, understanding health statistics.

- ◆ Professional—Having the ability to make change, graphing, computing, engineering a building or roadway.
- ◆ Recreational—Keeping score in football or baseball, understanding probability in sports.
- ◆ Cultural—Making predictions and solving problems.

According to the National Assessment of Educational Progress (1992), despite the increasing importance of math in today's technological society, only 13% to 16% of 12th graders are actually proficient in mathematics. Of particular concern to teachers is the difficulty many young people experience when they must figure out how to solve mathematical problems. Although many students have problems with mathematics, those with mild disabilities typically have greater difficulty than do their peers.

Math Deficits and Students with Mild Disabilities

Students in the primary grades with learning disabilities, mild mental retardation, and/or behavioral disorders typically score below their same-age peers on static tests of math achievement (Scruggs & Mastropieri, 1986). Adolescents with behavioral disorders appear to exhibit greater difficulty in arithmetic than with reading, experiencing problems with basic skills and with time estimation (Epstein et al., 1989; Nelson, Smith, Dodd, & Gilbert, 1991). On the other hand, students with phonologically-based learning disabilities that affect their progress in reading often have difficulty in math as well. Light and DeFries (1995) suggest that 60% of students with learning disabilities also have significant deficits in math. As students with mild disabilities exit school, they may have attained, at best, only a fifth- to sixth-grade level of mathematics skill (Cawley, Kahn, & Tedesco, 1989).

Numerous factors may account for the problems in mathematics experienced by children with mild disabilities. For example, deficits in reading or handwriting may impair math performance. The child may not be able to read directions and word problems in a math textbook or copy numbers legibly and align them properly. Similarly, if the youngster has difficulty attending to instruction or remembering number sequences, basic facts, or the steps in complex operations like long division, math performance will suffer. In addition, language deficits may create difficulty for some youngsters in special education if teachers or textbooks use terms interchangeably (e.g., *subtract, less than, take away, minus*) without first clearly defining these. Moreover, as children get older, they may have a reduced motivation to practice basic mathematics skills because they believe themselves to be low in math ability and math achievement (Montague, Bos, & Doucette, 1991).

Research on the mathematics performance of students with mild disabilities indicates that these students may have both *procedural* and *representational* difficulty (Geary, 1993). Students with procedural deficits may experience difficulty when performing complex addition, subtraction, multiplication, and division problems. Representational deficits, on the other hand, refer to problems representing or coding numerical information into mathematical equations or algorithms. Although students with mild disabilities may overcome procedural difficulties, their representational deficits are more likely to persist. Youngsters with mild disabilities, then, may experience various problems in mathematics, including:

- Computation—They make slower progress than peers when learning basic addition, subtraction, multiplication, and division, and they make frequent computational errors or use faulty algorithms when these operations become more complex (Cawley, Miller, & School, 1987; Cawley, Parmar, Yan, & Miller, 1996, 1998; Cawley & Reines, 1996; Woodward & Howard, 1994).

- Automaticity—Students with mild disabilities may not automatically and efficiently execute arithmetic operations (Hasselbring, Goin, & Bransford, 1988; Kirby & Becker, 1988; Pellegrino & Goldman, 1987).

- Word Problems—Students with mild disabilities have difficulty solving even simple word problems (Parmar, Cawley, & Frazita, 1996), and problems containing irrelevant linguistic or numerical information are particularly troublesome (Englert, Culatta, & Horn, 1987). They also have great difficulty applying procedural knowledge to solve novel problems (Woodward & Baxter, 1997).

- Strategies—They may not be able to devise and apply effective "backup" strategies when they are unable to retrieve math facts (Geary, 1993; Jordan & Montani, 1997; Siegler, 1988; Swanson & Rhine, 1985), and they have great difficulty choosing appropriate strategies for problem representation (Montague & Applegate, 1993; Montague et al., 1991).

- Motivation and Attitude—Students with mild disabilities may have a poor self-perception of their performance in math and low motivation to persist at problem solving (Montague, 1996, 1997).

One intriguing recent explanation of some of the difficulties students with mild disabilities experience in mathematics draws a parallel between the phonological awareness necessary for building reading skills and the *number sense* needed for math performance. According to Gersten and Chard (1999), number sense refers to a child's ability to look at the world and draw comparisons, perform mental mathematics, fluidly and flexibly deal with numbers, and have a "feel" for what numbers mean. Most children learn these concepts and skills informally through observation and interaction with parents, siblings, and the world around them prior to school entry (Jordan, 1995). For example, many children come to school with a sense of which of two sets of items contains more than the other, or that only one number word is used to tag each item when counting a series of objects. This information is learned through informal experiences in the home such as counting the number of places to set at the table or comparing two bunches of bananas of different sizes. Students lacking these experiences that build number sense may have underlying deficits that lead to difficulty understanding the algorithms and strategies encountered during formal mathematics instruction (McCloskey & Macaruso, 1995). Because students with mild disabilities do not learn well through indirect, informal approaches, these students also "lack experiences" and may need explicit instruction to develop a number sense.

Siegler (1991) asserts that procedural knowledge and conceptual knowledge reciprocally affect one another as children learn math strategies and skills. Thus, Gersten and Chard (1991) suggest that instruction in number sense should take place at the same time students are learning computational skills. They state that "simultaneously integrating number sense activities with increased number fact automaticity rather than teaching these skills sequentially [as] advocated by earlier special education mathematics researchers appears to be important for . . . instruction of students with learning disabilities. It is also likely that some students who are drilled on number facts and then taught various algorithms for computations may never develop much number sense, just as some special education students, despite some phonics instruction and work on repeated readings/fluency and accuracy, fail to develop good phonemic awareness or any sense of the purpose or pleasure of reading" (p. 20). Apparently number sense, automatic retrieval of number facts, knowledge of effective back-up strategies, and strategies for problem representation are interrelated and essential ingredients of effective math instruction for students with mild disabilities.

Mathematics Standards and Curriculum

A significant factor contributing to the poor math performance of youngsters with mild disabilities may be the mathematics curriculum itself. According to Porter (1989), regular classroom teachers vary greatly with respect to the amount of time they devote to teaching mathematics; moreover, they devote more time to instruction in computational skills than to concept development and problem solving. In the 1980s, of the topics covered by mathematics textbooks, 70% received under 30 minutes of instructional time (Porter). This observation led the National Council of Teachers of Mathematics (NCTM) (1989) to assert that the "spiral curriculum" contained in most mathematics series, in which concepts like fractional quantities are introduced in kindergarten or the first grade and repeated with increasing difficulty at each successive grade level, allows for only superficial coverage of most topics across the grades. Thus, students do not have the opportunity to master skills before moving on to new concepts. Moreover, according to the NCTM, students should focus on problem solving and seeing connections in math.

Cawley and Parmar (1992) agree with the NCTM that students with mild disabilities require opportunities to reason, problem solve, and make connections within and among areas of mathematics, not just to practice isolated arithmetic skills, if they are to be able to use these skills when they leave school. Similarly, Woodward (1991) argues that the mathematics curriculum for children with mild disabilities must be characterized by a full range of correct and incorrect examples of a given math concept, explicit instruction, and a "parsimonious" approach in which seemingly unrelated concepts and skills are tightly linked. He maintains that the traditional spiral curriculum creates confusion in students with mild disabilities and communicates a subtle message that concepts come and go, and thus need not be remembered. Engelmann, Carnine, and Steely (1991) also describe six deficiencies in frequently used basal mathematics series from the 1980s:

1. Few provisions to ensure students will recall relevant prior knowledge.
2. Too rapid a rate to introduce new concepts.
3. Lack of coherence and explanation in the presentation of general strategies.
4. Lack of clear, concise instructional language.
5. Inadequate guided practice to serve as a transition between initial teaching and independent student performance.
6. Inadequate review to ensure retention of what is learned.

Mathematics textbooks and curricula of the 1990s have drawn criticism as well. For example, Carnine, Jitendra, and Silbert (1997) state that traditional math basals rarely identify, introduce, and provide sufficient practice with the "big ideas," the major organizing principles that have explanatory and predictive power and that are applicable in many different situations. According to these researchers, these "big ideas" must be taught before being connected with other important concepts or principles. In addition, they are critical of math textbooks for introducing content too rapidly, for not providing teachers with clear and unambiguous demonstrations, for using open-ended and ineffective manipulative activities and confusing examples, and for providing inadequate opportunities for review.

In 1989, the National Council of Teachers of Mathematics recommended a new set of standards and a new curriculum for teaching mathematics in the schools. The National Science Foundation also funded a number of standards-based curriculum projects for implementing and assessing the new standards across the grade levels. (See Box 13.1 for Web sites regarding the standards and curriculum.) Rather than an emphasis on paper-and-pencil tasks and rote math drills, important changes in the new curriculum include (a) increased attention to mathematics reasoning and problem solving, (b) analyzing and making sense of facts, (c) constructing and justifying mathematical ideas, (d) understanding statistics and probabilities, and (e) using computational devices such as calculators and computers as tools for analyzing data. According to the NCTM, the twelve essential components of a math curriculum are:

1. Problem solving,
2. Communication of mathematical ideas,
3. Mathematical reasoning,
4. Application of mathematics to everyday situations,
5. Alertness to the reasonableness of results,
6. Estimation,
7. Appropriate computational skills,
8. Algebraic thinking,
9. Measurement,
10. Geometry,
11. Statistics,
12. Probability.

In the new curriculum, then, students are to be given interesting and meaningful problems for which they are to construct and justify possible solutions

Box 13.1

Web Watch

Mathematics Standards and Standards-Based Curricula

ARC Center

http://www.arccenter.comap.com
Suggested activities and sample lessons for elementary-aged students of diverse abilities, including those with linguistic diversity. Curriculum funded by the National Science Foundation.

Curricular Options in Mathematics Programs for All Secondary Students (COMPASS)

http://www.ithaca.edu/compass
Links to secondary curricula, lessons, and suggested activities for implementing the NCTM standards at the secondary level. Includes information on National Science Foundation-funded math projects such as the Math Connections Project, the Core-Plus Math Project, and the Interactive Math Project.

K-12 Mathematics Curriculum Center

http://www.edc.org/mcc
Comprehensive site including links to the new standards-based K-12 curricula funded by the National Science Foundation, including Math Trailblazers, Connected Math, Everyday Math, and more. From this site you can download and print summaries of the 13 funded curricula.

Show-Me Center

http://www.showmecenter.missouri.edu
Numerous curriculum projects funded by the National Science Foundation for the middle school grades, including Math Thematics, Middle School Math through Application Project (MMAP), Connected Math Project, Math in Context, and MathScape 6 to 8. Site contains sample lessons and activities to implement the standards.

The Math Learning Center

http://www.mlc.pdy.edu/
Programs and workshops for implementing the NCTM standards.

The National Council of Teachers of Mathematics (NCTM)

http://www.NCTM.org
The home page for the major professional organization of mathematics teachers. Includes copies of the standards and suggestions and activities for implementing these in the classroom.

individually or as a group. For example, rather than memorizing a formula, students might construct ways to solve a problem, such as, "What if all 26 students in this class had to shake hands with everybody else? How many handshakes would that take?" (Ratnesar, 1997). Similarly, students with a deep understanding of mathematics are expected to be able to illustrate why 3 1/2 divided by 1/4 equals 14.

Although just beginning to be implemented in classrooms across the United States, such a nontraditional approach to mathematics instruction is engendering a "math war" much like the great phonics debate in the area of reading instruction. Proponents argue that the standards are based on research about how students learn mathematical ideas, and that students do not learn to think and problem solve in traditional "parrot math" classrooms (see, for example, Battista, 1999; Cossey, 1999; O'Brien, 1999; Reys, Robinson, Sconiers, & Mark, 1999; Schoen, Fey, Hirsch, & Coxford, 1999). Others suggest that students with mild disabilities can and do learn mathematics through a problem-solving process, although it may take them longer than their peers to learn concepts in the inclusive classroom setting (Woodward & Baxter, 1997). Opponents, on the other hand, assert that children cannot use mathematical concepts without some memorization and drill of facts (Bishop, 1999). Moreover, others (see, for example, Hofmeister, 1993; Hutchinson, 1993; Mercer, Harris, & Miller, 1993; Rivera, 1993) criticize the new standards for:

◆ Making little reference to students with disabilities,
◆ Not considering empirically validated instructional approaches for students with disabilities, and
◆ Promoting a "one-size-fits-all" constructivist approach to learning that fails to account for student diversity.

The debate between empiricist (i.e., traditional drill-and-practice) and constructivist (i.e., discovery-oriented) approaches to instruction (see Chapter 8) is ongoing in the area of mathematics education, much like the debate between whole language and phonics in reading (see Chapter 11). Mercer and his colleagues call for professionals to discuss what are known to be effective instructional practices for students with mild disabilities, regardless of whether or not these practices come from competing paradigms (Mercer, Jordan, & Miller, 1994, 1996; Miller & Mercer, 1997). That is, they suggest that traditional constructivist approaches to instruction call for minimal teacher support and self-directed discovery learning by students. Yet, students with mild disabilities often need extended teacher support and explicit instruction. Thus, they suggest that teachers might build mathematical understandings through authentic experiences, explicit modeling of strategies, multiple examples, and scaffolding, then proceed to mastery learning before returning to more indirect approaches to help students make use of learning in context. This explicit to implicit continuum, they argue, is not inconsistent with the constructivist paradigm, but rather is a specific application of the paradigm that is appropriate for students with mild disabilities. This call for a compromise in the "middle ground" is much like the blend of whole language and phonics now advocated by many professionals as a balanced approach to reading instruction.

Nevertheless, given the mismatch between the instruction offered by the typical mathematics curriculum and the needs of learners with mild disabilities, it is not surprising that many of these youngsters exhibit deficits in math achievement. In the following section we will present an overview of mathematics programs designed for students with mild disabilities. In addition, we will describe those skills that are critical for special education students to master if they are to function successfully and independently as adults.

Mathematics Programs for Children with Mild Disabilities

Although some students with mild disabilities will successfully complete the college preparatory mathematics curriculum, many of these youngsters require a math program that emphasizes functional skills necessary for adulthood. This means that teachers must provide systematic direct instruction not only in basic computational skills, but also in simple problem solving. Moreover, concepts of measurement, money, and time are also important in the lives of competent adults. Adults must use these skills not only on the job, but also in routine tasks of daily life, including leisure-time activities. (See Table 13.1 for a list of essential concepts and skills for a mathematics curriculum.)

Table 13.1 Some Essential Skills in a Mathematics Curriculum for Students with Mild Disabilities

---

Numeration

Counts

By ones to 100.
Cardinal and ordinal numbers.
In sequence by twos through tens.
By ones from a number through 999.
By ones from a number through 1,000,000.

Number Symbols and Place Value

Reads and writes numerals through 100.
Writes the number of objects in a set.
Aligns columns with one-, two-, and three-digit numbers.
Uses expanded place value notation.
Identifies equal, greater, and lesser numbers and sets.
Expresses numbers using decimal notation to thousandths.

Fractions

States fractions represented by pictures/manipulatives.
Illustrates fractions given orally or in written form.
Identifies fractions equal to, greater than, and less than one.
Identifies equivalent fractions.
Reads and writes simple and mixed fractional numbers.

Computation

Addition

Adds using counting-on and counting-on-from-larger strategies.
Basic addition facts in column and horizontal form.
Addition of two- by one-digit, two- by two-digit, two- by three-digit, and three- by three-digit numbers with no renaming.

Addition of 3 and 4 one-digit numbers.
Addition with renaming in the tens place.
Addition with renaming in the hundreds place.
Addition of multidigit problems with 3 or more digits.
Addition of fractions with like and unlike denominators.
Addition of mixed-number fractions.

Subtraction

Basic subtraction facts in column and horizontal form.
Subtraction of a one- or two-digit number from a two-digit number without and with renaming.
Subtraction of a one-, two-, or three-digit number from a three-digit number with renaming in the ones and tens columns.
Subtraction of one-, two-, or three-digit numbers from a three-digit number with zeroes in the ones and/or tens place.
Subtraction of single and multidigit numbers from 1,000 or larger with or without renaming and with or without zeroes.
Subtraction of fractions with like and unlike denominators.
Subtraction of mixed-number fractions.

Multiplication

Multiplication facts in column and horizontal form.
Multiplies fractions with like and unlike denominators.
Multiplies one-digit by two- or three-digit numbers with and without carrying.
Multiplies one-digit numbers by two-, three-, or four-digit numbers with zeroes in the ones, tens, or hundreds place.
Multiplies two- by two-digit, two- by three-digit, or three- by three-digit numbers.
Multiplies multidigit numbers by multidigit numbers with or without zeroes in the ones, tens, or hundreds place.

Division

Basic division facts using both division symbols.
Divides two- or three-digit dividends by one-digit divisors with or without remainders.
Division of multidigit dividends by multidigit divisors with or without remainders.
Rewrites improper fractions to whole or mixed numbers.
Converts remainders to fractional numbers.
Divides carrying quotient out to decimal value.
Converts fractions to decimal values.

Math for Daily Living

Story Problems

Expresses story problems as mathematical sentences.
Solves simple, direct story problems.
Solves indirect story problems.
Solves story problems containing extraneous information.

Table 13.1 Some Essential Skills in a Mathematics Curriculum for Students with Mild Disabilities—*continued*

Tools

Uses calculator to solve problems.
Uses simple computer programs to solve problems.

Time

Tells time to the minute using a standard clock.
Tells time to the minute using a digital clock.
Writes time to the minute from a standard or digital clock.
Computes time taken and uses time clock.
Reads time schedules (e.g., TV, plane).
Uses the calendar.

Money

Identifies all coins and bills.
States value of all coins and bills.
Writes dollar and cent amounts using decimal notation.
Adds money to make a purchase.
Makes/counts correct change.
Maintains bank records.
Computes percentages to determine discounts and price.
Computes payroll deductions and taxes.

Geometry and Measurement

Uses linear measurement (e.g., inches, feet, yards, miles) as whole and fractional/mixed amounts.
Converts from one unit of linear measurement to another.
Uses liquid measurement (e.g., cups, pints, quarts, gallons) and expresses equivalent and mixed amounts.
Uses measurement of weight (e.g., ounces, pounds, tons) and expresses equivalent and mixed amounts.
Identifies basic geometric shapes.
Computes perimeter and area of basic geometric shapes.
Computes volume.
Reads thermometer.
Uses scales and other measuring devices.

Adapted from: Silbert, J., Carnine, D., & Stein, M. (1990). *Direct instruction math (2nd ed.).* Columbus, OH: Merrill, pp.49-52.

According to the National Longitudinal Transition Studies, only about 18% of young people with learning disabilities go on to college (Wagner & Blackorby, 1996). Moreover, many students with learning disabilities, behavioral disorders, and mild mental retardation continue to need assistance as adults in areas such as workplace math (e.g., understanding paychecks and deductions), home math (e.g., budgeting, shopping, purchasing and maintaining a home), and leisure math (e.g., the economics of dating) (Dunn & Rabren, 1996; Patton, Cronin, Bassett, & Koppel, 1997). As schools implement new math standards, special educators must ensure that students are learning the functional skills they will need for life (see Chapter 15).

Today's children and youth also must master the use of calculators and computers if they are to meet the challenges of an increasingly technological world. Both are valuable tools that enable students to perform complex operations correctly and solve problems efficiently. In fact, the NCTM (1989) standards call for students to learn how to use calculators and computers to analyze data and make decisions. Unfortunately, many teachers still believe that using calculators interferes with learning basic skills and that children will become overly dependent on calculators. According to Hembree (1986), however, calculator use can increase basic skill acquisition and result in higher achievement test scores. More importantly, for students with mild disabilities, calculators can also improve a child's attitude toward mathematics and provide a means by which to problem solve when he or she understands the necessary operations but makes computational errors (Horton, Lovitt, & White, 1992). Similarly, the computer can become an instructional aid for group problem solving rather than merely a reinforcer for appropriate behavior or a means by which to gain independent drill and practice with basic skills (Malouf, Jamison, Kercher, & Carlucci, 1991). However, teachers must provide students with direct instruction in calculator or computer usage, including skills necessary to estimate and to round answers.

Recently, several mathematics curricula have been developed to teach functional skills, as well as other essential math skills and concepts, to students with mild disabilities. These include DISTAR Arithmetic I and II, Connecting Math Concepts, Corrective Mathematics, Project Math, Real Life Math, the Strategic Math Series, Tic Tac Toe Math, and Touch Math.

DISTAR Arithmetic

DISTAR Arithmetic I and II, developed by Engelmann and Carnine (1972, 1976, 1976) and published by Science Research Associates, follows a rapid, highly sequenced, scripted, direct instructional format. Available as kits at two different instructional levels, the program is designed to teach basic arithmetic skills to children in small groups from kindergarten through grade 3. DISTAR I focuses on ordinal counting, addition, subtraction, multiplication, simple word problems, and the concepts of greater than and less than. In DISTAR II, target skills include addition and subtraction with regrouping, complex multiplication, division, operations with fractions, and the concepts of time, money, measurement, and negative numbers. (The reader may also wish to consult *Designing Effective Mathematics Instruction: A Direct Instruction Approach*, 3rd ed., Stein, Silbert, &

Carnine, 1997, for an excellent discussion of procedures for adapting the standard mathematics curriculum to a direct instructional format.)

Connecting Math Concepts

Appropriate for students in grades 1 through 6, Connecting Math Concepts is a scripted, direct instructional program to teach "difficult" ideas such as ratios, proportions, probability, coordinate systems, functions, and data analysis. The program carefully builds these ideas in small steps requiring repeated use across 6 levels. The program, developed by Engelmann, Carnine, Kelly, and Engelmann (1996), is available from Science Research Associates.

Corrective Mathematics

The Corrective Mathematics Program, developed by Engelmann and Steely (1981) and published by Science Research Associates, is a remedial mathematics program for students in grades 3 through 12. The program is also appropriate for adults who have not yet mastered basic arithmetic skills. It uses a highly sequenced, direct instructional format requiring only minimal reading skills. Included in the program are the addition, subtraction, multiplication, and division facts; regrouping concepts; and story problem solving.

Edmark

Edmark offers a number of programs appropriate for students who have extreme difficulty learning functional math skills such as telling time or using money. The Coin Skills Curriculum, Revised, for example, provides systematic direct instruction in naming coins, determining coin equivalence, selecting coins, and adding coins. Edmark Time Telling teaches students how to read both digital and analog clocks, as well as how to write time. Small steps and systematic repetition and review are built into both programs.

Project MATH

Project MATH (Cawley et al., 1976) is a total mathematics curriculum for children in preschool through grade 6. The program is designed to teach mathematics skills to children with mild disabilities who might otherwise be hindered by their poor reading ability. Included within Project MATH is a screening device, called the Mathematics Concept Inventory, that is helpful for assessing and placing students within the curriculum. The kits within the program cover sets, patterns, numbers, operations, fractions, geometry, and measurement. In addition, other units introduce topics such as calculators, metrics, and telephone use. The entire program emphasizes problem solving, connecting ideas, and reasoning and communicating about mathematics. Project MATH individualizes instruction for learners by utilizing "interactive units" that give students a variety of options for responding to information, including manipulating, displaying, saying, and writing (Cawley & Reines, 1996). The program emphasizes mastery of basic mathematics skills and advanced concepts and is adaptable for students at the secondary level. (See Cawley, Fitzmaurice-Hayes, & Shaw, 1988, for additional information on this curriculum.)

Real Life Math

Real Life Math (Schwartz, 1977) teaches functional mathematics skills to students aged 13 to 18 with learning problems. The program uses a unique role-playing format in which students set up businesses, handle billing, conduct transactions with a bank, and keep business-related records and files. The approach is quite motivating to older students with mild disabilities who must soon function independently as adults in the world of work. (Real Life Math is available through Pro-Ed.)

The Strategic Math Series

The Strategic Math Series (Mercer & Miller, 1992a) is a field-tested curriculum for basic computational skills. Students learn to solve and create word problems using the basic arithmetic facts. They also increase their computational speed, improve accuracy, and learn to generalize acquired mathematics skills. The program follows an eight-step instructional sequence: pretest, concrete, representation, mnemonics, abstract, posttest, practice to mastery, and review. Scripted lessons guide the teacher to present an advanced organizer, demonstrate skills, give guided practice, provide independent practice, help students create their own problems to solve, and give feedback on student progress. (The Strategic Math Series is available through Edge Enterprises, Lawrence, KS.)

Tic Tac Toe Math

Tic Tac Toe Math includes a set of instructional workbooks and videos that enable students of all ages to master math skills, including basic computation, fractions, decimals, percentages, and geometry. The program makes use of graph paper, mnemonics, and visual images illustrating patterns in numerical concepts. An emphasis of the program is developing number sense rather than rote memorization of isolated skills and facts. Developed by Dr. Richard Cooper, the materials are available through Learning Disabilities Resources, P.O. Box 716, Bryn Mawr, PA, 19010. (The reader may wish to order an introductory version of these materials, *Alternative Math Techniques: Instructional Guide*, Cooper, 1994, at 1-800-869-8336 or on the Web at: **www.learningdifferences.com**

Touch Math

Touch Math, originally developed by Bullock and her colleagues (see, for example, Bullock, 1994), is a field-tested program for teaching basic arithmetic skills to children at the elementary level. The program comes in a series of kits covering number concepts; addition, subtraction, multiplication, and division facts; story problems; place value; fractions; time; and money. Children first learn the numerals and their values through "touch points" (see Figure 13.1). The child learns addition as a "counting-on," then later, a

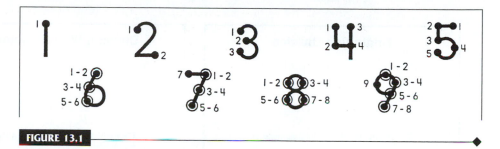

Touch Math Touch Points From: Bullock, J. (1994). *Touch Math: The touchpoint approach for teaching basic math: Computation (4th ed.).* Colorado Springs, CO: Innovative Learning Concepts, Inc. Reprinted with permission.

"counting-on-from-bigger-number" strategy. (For example, when solving the problem 4 + 7 = ____, the child says the larger number, 7, and then counts on 8, 9, 10, 11, while touching each of the touch points on the numeral 4.) Similarly, subtraction is introduced as a "counting-off" process. In addition, children learn to sequence count by ones, twos, threes, fours, fives, sixes, and so forth, in order to understand multiplication as a process of repeated addition. Later, multiplication and division are taught using "count-by" strategies, in which children count by the bottom number while touching the touch points on the top number during multiplication, or they count by the smaller number up to the larger number while making tally marks during division (see Figures 13.2 and 13.3). (Touch Math is available from Innovative Learning Concepts, 6760 Corporate Drive, Colorado Springs, CO 80919-1999.)

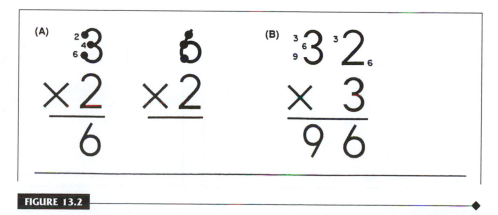

Touch Math Multiplication: Using the "Count-By" Strategy From: Bullock, J. (1994). *Touch Math: The touchpoint approach for teaching basic math: Computation (4th ed.).* Colorado Springs, CO: Innovative Learning Concepts, Inc. Reprinted with permission.

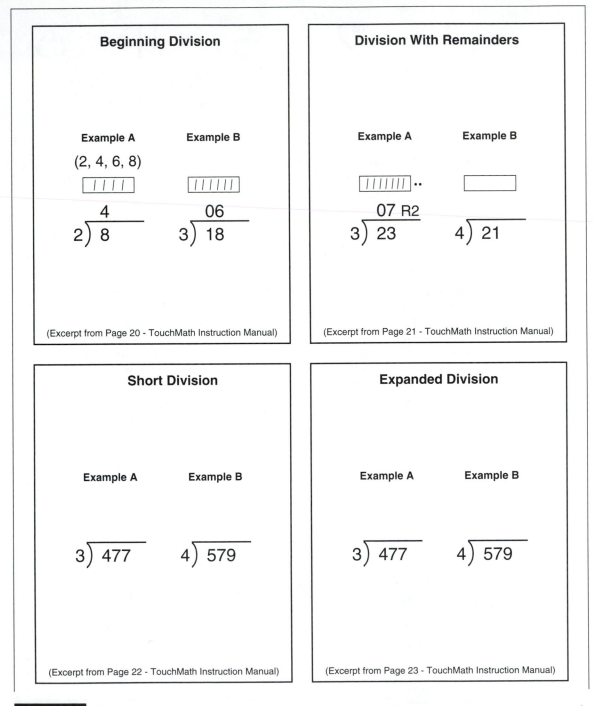

Beginning Division

Example A   Example B

(2, 4, 6, 8)

$$2\overline{)8} = 4$$

$$3\overline{)18} = 06$$

Division With Remainders

Example A   Example B

$$3\overline{)23} = 07 \text{ R2}$$

$$4\overline{)21}$$

(Excerpt from Page 20 - TouchMath Instruction Manual)

(Excerpt from Page 21 - TouchMath Instruction Manual)

Short Division

Example A   Example B

$$3\overline{)477}$$

$$4\overline{)579}$$

Expanded Division

Example A   Example B

$$3\overline{)477}$$

$$4\overline{)579}$$

(Excerpt from Page 22 - TouchMath Instruction Manual)

(Excerpt from Page 23 - TouchMath Instruction Manual)

FIGURE 13.3

Touch Math Division: Using the "Count-by" Strategy From: Bullock, J. (1994). *Touch Math: The touchpoint approach for teaching basic math: Computation (4th ed.).* Colorado Springs, CO: Innovative Learning Concepts, Inc. Reprinted with permission.

A Summary of Mathematics Programs ◆

Teachers of children with mild disabilities must prepare their students to function successfully and independently as adults. Therefore, functional math skills and the use of calculators and computers as problem-solving tools are essential elements of the mathematics curriculum for children with mild disabilities. In addition, teachers may select from among several mathematics programs designed for students in special education in order to meet individual needs.

Let's turn now to a discussion of instructional procedures that are effective for teaching a wide range of mathematics skills to youngsters with mild disabilities, regardless of the mathematics curriculum followed. ◆

Generalizable Procedures for Teaching Mathematics

Children with mild disabilities must understand all critical mathematics concepts and be able to apply them successfully. This means that the special education teacher must find ways to minimize the amount of memorization required when learning rote memory tasks, to maximize the child's motivation to develop automaticity with basic skills, and to enhance mathematical understandings and number sense. According to Lloyd and Keller (1989), Mercer and Miller (1992b), and Montague (1993), mathematics instruction for children with mild disabilities should include:

1. Curriculum-based assessment and error analysis to teach to mastery and to control task difficulty;
2. Concrete manipulatives to develop understanding of all important concepts;
3. Direct instructional teaching techniques;
4. Careful sequencing of skills and rule-based instruction in order to minimize memorization;
5. Strategy instruction built into teaching sequences to minimize memorization and increase independent performance;
6. Motivational devices to enhance drill-and-practice sessions, including self-monitoring, peer tutoring, computer-assisted instruction, games, and real-life math tasks; and
7. Teacher-student dialogues designed to develop an understanding of math concepts, to model strategies for problem solving, and to make connections between mathematical learning and the real world.

Curriculum-Based Assessment and Error Analysis

Students learn best when they are given math tasks at their instructional level (i.e., when their success rate is approximately 70% to 90%) (Wilson & Wesson, 1991). Teachers can use criterion-referenced, curriculum-based measures that assess performance at each level of a mathematics-skills hierarchy to determine the skills children have mastered (i.e., performance at or above the 90% success level) and those still requiring additional instruction and practice. Performance below the 70% success rate indicates a task on the hierarchy at the frustration level, one that is currently too difficult for the child.

Students with mild disabilities need many opportunities to use manipulatives and to relate math skills to real life.

To assess mathematics skills, teachers may construct probes or use a diagnostic interview. Recall from Chapter 6 that to use a probe the teacher must (a) examine the sequence of skills in the curriculum being used, (b) target a particular math skill, (c) construct a number of items clearly representing the targeted skill, (d) administer the probe either timed or untimed, (e) compute the student's performance rate if appropriate, and (f) analyze student errors. On the other hand, diagnostic interviews allow teachers to "tap" a student's thought processes. Using this procedure, the teacher might ask a student to explain how he or she derived an answer to a particular math problem or to draw a picture or use manipulatives to illustrate a specific math concept. Patterns of errors or gaps in a student's conceptual understanding of mathematics may become apparent during these exchanges.

For example, Joey may know the subtraction facts with 100% accuracy, and he may be able to subtract a two- or three-digit number from a three-digit number with no renaming. When given a similar problem requiring renaming, however, Joey's performance may fall below the frustration level. At this point, Ms. Lopez will need to analyze Joey's performance by carefully scrutinizing the errors he makes and by asking him to explain how he solves these problems. Joey may be (a) renaming when not required, (b) having difficulty renaming in the hundreds but not the tens place, (c) having difficulty renaming when required in both the hundreds and tens place, (d) having difficulty renaming when zeroes are involved, or (e) lacking understanding of place value. Ms. Lopez will need to teach or reteach the necessary skills to enable Joey to profit from instruction at this level of the hierarchy.

Through careful, ongoing assessment, teachers can provide children with tasks at the appropriate level of difficulty and teach skills to mastery. In addition, prompts and specific error-correction techniques, such as "slicing back" to reteach a lower skill on the task hierarchy based on observation of student errors, may also improve the child's success rate (Wilson & Wesson, 1991). That is, student performance improves when component prerequisite skills are taught first to mastery rather than concurrently with a new skill (Carnine, 1980).

Concrete-to-Semiconcrete-to-Abstract Sequencing

In order to develop an understanding of mathematics concepts, children with mild disabilities need many opportunities to work with concrete manipulatives. Students can, for example, manipulate buttons, beans, counters (available through school supply catalogs), or popsicle sticks to understand numeration or addition of sets (Paddock, 1992), or they can use base-10 blocks to understand place value and complex operations like long division. Travis and Joey, in the opening vignette for this chapter, are able to understand the concept of division as forming equivalent subsets by manipulating base-10 blocks (see Figure 13.4).

Unfortunately, most mathematics textbooks begin at either the semiconcrete (representational) level, at which pictures are used to represent mathematical concepts, or at the abstract level, at which only numerals and other mathematics symbols are used. Students with mild disabilities learn concepts like place value best, however, when a concrete-to-representational-to-abstract sequence is followed (Harris, Miller, & Mercer, 1995; Mercer & Miller, 1992a; Peterson et al., 1988). That is, concepts are introduced first with concrete

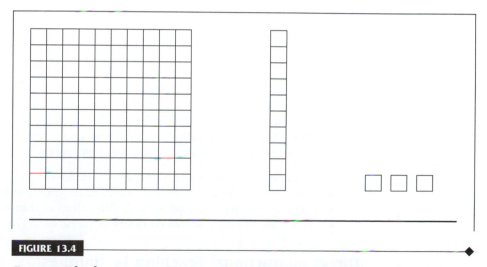

FIGURE 13.4

Base-10 Blocks From *Mathematics: With Manipulatives Teacher's Guide* by Marilyn Burns. © 1988 by Cuisenaire Company of America, an imprint of Pearson Learning. Used by permission.

objects, later with pictorial representations, and finally with number symbols only. Students with mild disabilities require repeated opportunities to manipulate concrete objects in order to learn important concepts in mathematics, including basic computational skills and problem solving (Harris et al., 1995; Marsh & Cooke, 1996).

In addition, teachers must take care to relate any manipulation of concrete objects or pictures immediately to the number symbols. This technique, called *parallel modeling,* enables youngsters with mild disabilities to make the transfer from the manipulatives or pictures to the actual number symbols. Ms. Lopez, for example, might place popsicle sticks on the table arranged in six rows of five sticks each:

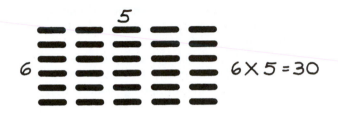

To illustrate multiplication as repeated addition of equal sets, she might ask "How many rows?" and "How many sticks in each row?" and write "6 × 5" immediately as the children give the answers. To answer the question, "How many in all?" or "6 × 5 = ?", Ms. Lopez may then help the children count by fives six times, writing the number 30 as the correct answer. Alternatively, Ms. Lopez could draw pictures to represent similar problems or use the number line to illustrate seven equal hops of three steps each. In each case, she would immediately use the number symbols necessary to express the concept illustrated: 7 × 3 = 21.

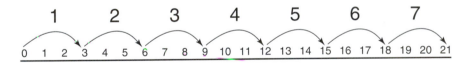

Because the goal of the concrete-to-semiconcrete-to-abstract sequence is to build understanding of mathematical concepts, teachers should provide a variety of different manipulatives and pictures for students to use. Systematically varying the manipulatives will help students generalize the concepts to be learned. In addition, Thornton and Toohey (1986) recommend that teachers:

◆ Ask questions as students manipulate the objects,
◆ Have students verbalize their thinking as they manipulate the objects,
◆ Help students write the problem being solved in numerical form, and
◆ Encourage students to use counters or pictures to check answers.

Direct Instructional Teaching Techniques

At the acquisition level of learning, students with mild disabilities learn best when instruction is focused, explicit, and interactive. Tasks are analyzed into appropriate substeps, clear examples are selected, questions are posed, and feedback is given to lead students to the correct response. Recall, for example, in Chapter 8, how Mr. Mathis taught his class to add decimal numbers with no regrouping required. He broke the task into three essential steps: (a) Write the numbers lining up the decimal points, (b) "Bring down" a decimal point into the answer line, and (c) Add the numbers together. These three steps became the focus for questions throughout the demonstration and guided-practice phase of the lesson.

In addition, following the demonstration of a skill or concept, teachers should provide a permanent model of the problem to be solved to which students can refer. Leaving on the chalkboard or on the top of a student's paper a clear example of the problem or a list of the steps to be followed improves student performance. Demonstration plus a permanent model is one simple teaching procedure that clearly improves the achievement on mathematics tasks of youngsters with mild disabilities (Smith & Lovitt, 1975).

Another procedure leading to a high success rate for students with mild disabilities is the time delay. Recall from Chapters 11 and 12 how a zero-second time delay was used to teach sight word vocabulary and spelling words. Cybriwsky and Schuster (1990) and Mattingly and Bott (1990) applied similar procedures to teach multiplication facts to students with learning problems. Initial instruction might begin, for example, with a zero-second delay between the presentation of the multiplication fact and the prompted answer. Later, the delay could be increased to 3, 4, or 5 seconds.

Teacher-directed instruction remains an effective means of helping students acquire basic math skills (Maccini & Hughes, 1997). Of course, as students master these skills, they need systematic practice in applying them in real-world contexts. When students are given only isolated practice of math facts on worksheets, for example, they are not likely to generalize the skill to solve problems in the workplace or in the home. Teachers can limit the procedural knowledge required to solve particular problems, or provide calculators, as students use their math skills to solve problems that appear in everyday contexts in the postsecondary work world (Woodward, 1999).

Sequencing and Rule-Based Instruction

Some authorities suggest that teachers should not be afraid to resequence the skills and concepts presented in the mathematics textbook if the sequences are not appropriate for the children in their special education programs (Silbert, Carnine, & Stein, 1990; Thornton & Toohey, 1985; Wilson & Wesson, 1991). Teachers may, for example, decide to work to mastery with all addition skills before moving on to subtraction. Similarly, within the addition-skills hierarchy, they may decide to teach the addition of "zero" facts early as a simple rule, "Any number plus zero means the number stays the same." Often, the addition of zero is taught as one of the last set of facts.

Rule-based instruction, like careful sequencing of skills, minimizes the amount of memorization that is necessary. Engelmann, Carnine, and Steely (1991) characterize mathematics instruction for low-performing students as explicit instruction about important samenesses. If, for example, when children learn about fractions they are taught the rule, "The bottom number tells how many parts are in each group and the top number tells how many parts you use," they will immediately be able to analyze fractions less than, equal to, or greater than one whole—provided that initial examples are used to illustrate clearly each of these possibilities. Similarly, teaching the commutative property of addition as a rule reduces the number of addition facts the child must memorize if he or she recognizes "3 + 5 = ____" and "5 + 3 = ____" as examples of the rule, as does teaching the commutative property of multiplication (e.g., 3 × 4 is the same as 4 × 3). Miller, Strawser, and Mercer (1996) suggest other rules that may lower the amount of memorization required of students:

1. Any number plus zero is always still that number.
2. Any number plus one means say the next number on the number line.
3. Any number minus zero is always still that number.
4. Any number minus itself is always zero.
5. Any number minus one means say the next smaller number on the number line.
6. Any number times zero is always zero.
7. Any number times 1 is always still that number.
8. Zero divided by any number is always zero.
9. Any number divided by 1 is always still that number.
10. Any number divided by itself is always 1.

Using rule-based instruction does not negate or contradict the need to develop understanding of the mathematical concepts involved. That is, teachers can begin with concrete objects and parallel modeling, later moving to semi-concrete representations, to demonstrate concepts and rules. Once the child understands the concept, the rule may be presented explicitly, practiced using direct instructional teaching techniques, and then applied to solve real-world problems.

Building Strategies into Teaching Sequences

Self-instructional and mnemonic strategies can be helpful to students with mild disabilities (Davis & Hajicek, 1985; Mastropieri, Scruggs, & Shiah, 1991). Teachers can provide strategies, when needed, to help children in special education programs complete math tasks independently. When incorporated into a direct instructional lesson, teachers can use these strategies to prompt students, thus improving their success rate. For example, the youngster might learn the "counting-on-from-bigger" strategy as an aid to completing addition problems independently (i.e., "Say the larger number and count up from that number, raising a finger each time you count, until you have the other number of fingers raised."), or a mnemonic, such as "Daddy, Mother, Sister, Brother" to remember the steps in a long division problem (i.e., Divide, Multiply, Subtract, and Bring down).

Cullinan, Lloyd, and Epstein (1981) suggest a "count-by" strategy to teach multiplication facts:

1. Read the problem: $2 \times 5 =$
2. Point to a number you can count by: 2

Counters and number lines help students understand basic operations like addition.

3. Make the number of marks indicated   /////
   by the other number:
4. Count by your number, touching a mark each time you count. Stop counting when you touch the last mark: 2, 4, 6, 8, 10
5. Write the last number you said: $2 \times 5 = \underline{10}$

     Such a strategy can easily be applied to forming a line of questioning for use during guided practice, providing a permanent model of task-completion steps to be left on the chalkboard or at the child's desk, and prompting the child when he or she is "stuck." Strategies of this type often provide a bridge between teacher-led and independent practice.

     Similarly, Thornton and Toohey (1985) describe a strategy for teaching addition facts containing doubles. Children learn to associate pictures with the addition doubles facts, giving them a visual representation of the fact and a way for the teacher to visually or verbally cue a correct response if the youngster has not yet mastered the facts. For example, $2 + 2$ can become the "bunny ears" or the "car" fact. Depending upon the age level of the child, a picture of two bunnies or of a car with two front and two rear tires can be presented to teach and/or cue the answer "four." The fact "$5 + 5 = 10$" can become the "hands" fact, "$6 + 6 = 12$" can become the "egg carton" fact, and so forth. Cooper (1994) also suggests using visual-imagery strategies to remember concepts such as *odd* and *even* (e.g., picture pairs of shoes for even numbers and pairs of shoes with an odd one left over for odd numbers) or procedures such as converting fractions to decimals (e.g., the top number dives into a swimming pool which becomes the division bracket).

Some authorities are concerned that an overemphasis on teaching specific strategies such as "counting-on" or "counting-by" may interfere with learning when the child attempts more complex operations (Hasselbring, Goin, & Bransford, 1987). If the child has only a very limited attentional capacity and he or she must devote a great deal of attention to arriving at the correct answer to a basic fact, the youngster will have only limited attention to devote to solving the complex operation. In other words, the efficient execution of lower-level skills, such as basic math facts, enhances the performance of higher level skills, such as completing multistep long division problems.

Teachers must remember that strategy instruction should be used only when needed by an individual child. The youngster with a mild disability will need to practice basic facts and operations until these become automatic. Strategy instruction does not obviate the need for drill-and-practice activities for mastery and maintenance of skills. If a strategy "makes sense" within an instructional sequence, however, and if it will enable students to solve a wide range of sample problems, the teacher should consider its use to facilitate the transition between teacher-directed guided practice and independent practice (Silbert et al., 1990). Moreover, if the child experiences severe difficulty with rote memorization, strategies can become useful tools to enable problem solving with a greater degree of independence. One might argue that the use of strategy instruction is similar to the use of calculators. For some children, the strategy serves as a useful tool until basic facts can be recalled without hesitation or error. On the other hand, for some children with mild disabilities, the strategy may be a necessity if progress on more complex tasks is to be made.

Providing Motivation for Practice

In order to become proficient with mathematics skills, children must engage in multiple practice sessions. Unfortunately, as students with mild disabilities become older, or as they come to believe they are not "good" at math, they are less motivated to participate in drill-and-practice activities. Sometimes simple procedures, such as including basic facts that are known among those to be practiced, can improve motivation. At other times, the teacher must be very creative to motivate students!

Games. Traditional game formats, like Bingo, War, or Concentration, can be adapted for active practice of basic mathematics skills by small groups of children (Wesson, Wilson, & Mandlebaum, 1988). For example, in Bingo, the teacher can present a math fact on a flashcard. The children would then write the fact and the correct answer in one of the spaces on a laminated, washable Bingo card. When playing War, addition-fact flashcards can be divided equally between pairs of children. The two children would turn their cards over simultaneously, and the one with the higher sum would keep both cards if he or she correctly stated the sum. In the case of equal sums or incorrectly-stated higher sums, both cards would be placed in a center pile to become an additional "kitty" for

Students can use concrete objects to recreate and solve word problems.

the next round of play. Concentration, or Memory, is played in the traditional manner; however, students would have to match a math fact to its answer in order to keep the cards.

If permitted by the school district, card games such as Blackjack may motivate older students to practice basic addition facts, such as adding to 21. Similarly, dice can be used to practice addition, subtraction, or multiplication facts. Board games can also be devised or adapted for practice of basic math skills. For example, the child would have to draw a card and state the correct product before moving that number of spaces on a game board, or the child would have to draw a card and state the correct quotient, sum, product, or so forth, before moving a game piece in checkers or chess. Additionally, teachers can encourage active games like "Math Basketball," in which a student would have to state the correct answer to a problem posed by the teacher in order to throw a ball at a goal and, hopefully, score a point for his or her team. Finally, many commercially-available games encourage the use of basic mathematics skills involving money, particularly games like Monopoly and Life.

When considering the use of games, teachers must ensure that the practice will be more important than the competition. Moreover, games can be used inappropriately to "fill time." They can also be overused or not enjoyed by some students. If used correctly, however, games can provide motivating practice opportunities for many children with mild disabilities. Even a "game" as simple as establishing a set of "Fast Facts" for the day (i.e., a small set of basic facts to be stated rapidly as a password before leaving the classroom or upon hearing the teacher say "Fast Facts") can give students additional motivating practice with essential skills (Hasselbring et al., 1987).

Relating Math to Real Life. Relating math skills to real life is another motivational technique particularly useful for older students with mild disabilities. Pupils can use the newspaper, for example, to find an affordable apartment given a specific "salary" and other living expenses. The newspaper can also be used to illustrate sales discounts, to calculate "best buys" on varying quantities of a given item such as quarts of oil, or to determine the average temperature in the community for a week. Similarly, access to the Internet can afford students many opportunities to obtain and analyze data related to real-world problems. Math skills can also be linked to vocational-technical school training (e.g., understanding linear measurement, perimeter, area, or the Pythagorean theorem as a means for producing a level tool shed of the proper size and with square corners). Telling time; reading bus, airplane, train, and television schedules; and reading and recording calendar dates are also functional real-life skills required by older students with mild disabilities.

All students, not just older ones, can profit from relating mathematics to everyday life. The National Council of Teachers of Mathematics (1989) recommends that students should use math to solve real-life problems. In addition, professionals in special education also encourage teachers to infuse problem solving throughout mathematics instruction and to create problems important to students in their daily lives so that children will learn math concepts and skills in a meaningful context (Cawley & Reines, 1996; Maccini & Hughes, 1997). Relating mathematics to real life, then, is not simply a motivational device, but also an important means of promoting student understanding in math.

Self-Monitoring and Goal Setting. Students with mild disabilities can be taught to monitor the number of arithmetic problems they complete correctly (Reith, Polsgrove, McLeskey, Payne, & Anderson, 1978). For example, the child can count and then record or graph the number of problems correctly answered on a 3-minute division-fact probe worksheet. On the next day, the child may attempt to "beat" his or her previous record by correctly answering a greater number of problems.

Students with mild disabilities may enjoy setting their own goals for the number of practice problems or pages to be completed, when given a range of appropriate goals from which to choose. Schunk (1985), for example, improved the subtraction skills of sixth-grade students with learning disabilities by allowing each child to determine the number of daily practice pages to be completed, given a range of from 4 to 10 pages per day. Similarly, Fuchs, Bahr, and Rieth (1989) improved the math fluency of adolescents with learning disabilities by allowing each student to set an individual goal for the number of digits to be correctly written during 1-minute timed trials.

Miller, Strawser, and Mercer (1996) suggest that teachers should hold goal-setting conferences privately with students, encourage them to set goals at the acquisition, proficiency, and maintenance levels of learning, and listen to students' ideas without interruption. Moreover, students can improve their math fluency when they are taught to self-monitor during math practice activities, even in heterogeneous classrooms (McDougall & Brady, 1998) (see Chapter 9). Finally, students may need instruction in positive attributions and self-talk to overcome negative attitudes about their mathematics performance (Corral & Antia, 1997). For example, teachers can help students replace negative self-talk (e.g., "I can't do these math problems; the teacher didn't explain it very well.") with positive statements (e.g., "I can probably do this problem because I've done similar ones before."; "I'll just have to try harder with this type of difficult problem and I'll probably be successful.").

Cooperative Learning and Peer Tutoring.

Cooperative Learning and Peer Tutoring. Both cooperative learning arrangements and peer tutoring may enhance mathematics practice for youngsters with mild disabilities. For example, Beirne-Smith (1991) trained cross-aged tutors to help elementary-level students with learning disabilities practice the basic addition facts. Tutors used either an explicit counting-on strategy or a rote memorization approach. In each case, addition-fact performance improved for the tutees. According to Kane and Alley (1980), peer tutoring is an effective method for providing additional interactive practice with computational mathematics for adolescent students with learning disabilities who have been incarcerated as juvenile delinquents. Miller, Barbetta, Drevno, Martz, and Heron (1996) maintain that peer tutoring in mathematics is not just an "add-on," but rather an important instructional methodology for increasing active student involvement in mathematics learning.

Cooperative learning arrangements offer yet another way to increase interactive mathematics practice sessions in both the special education and the mainstream classroom (Maccini & Hughes, 1997; Maheady, Sacca, & Harper, 1987). The teacher forms mixed-ability, cooperative learning groups within the class. Then, after the teacher has demonstrated new content, students within each group take turns as tutors and tutees. Tutors may, for example, present a set of multiplication facts to the tutees, checking their answers and giving them necessary feedback. Tutees earn points for their team for correct answers and bonus points from the teacher for appropriate practice behaviors. Tutors earn bonus points for giving corrective feedback to tutees. Such arrangements have been used successfully at both the elementary and secondary levels (Maheady, Sacca, & Harper). In addition, cooperative learning groups have been used to improve mathematics homework completion and beginning algebraic problem-solving skills for students with mild disabilities in middle and high school special education and inclusive classroom settings (Allsopp, 1997; O'Melia & Rosenberg, 1994).

Computer-Assisted Instruction. Drill-and-practice, tutorial, and educational games software abound in the area of mathematics and can provide students with motivating practice opportunities. Teacher-directed instruction, in combination with drill-and-practice or tutorial software, may enhance the math performance of students with mild disabilities (Howell, Sidorenko & Jurica, 1987; Trifiletti, Frith, & Armstrong, 1984). (See Table 13.2 for a list of tutorial and drill-and-practice mathematics software.)

Students with mental retardation can learn simple, single-digit addition by using a computer (Leung, 1994). Moreover, these students can use computers to learn problem-solving strategies, although these strategies may not generalize to similar problems requiring paper-and-pencil solutions. For example, Mastropieri, Scruggs, and Shiah (1997) used a computer tutorial program to teach students with mild mental retardation a problem-solving strategy: Read the problem, *Think* about the problem, *Decide* the operation sign, *Write* the math sentence, *Do* the problem, *Label* the answer, *Check* every step. Using the strategy, the students solved problems such as, "If Jean saw seven roses in her yard and then she saw seven more next door, how many roses did she see in all?" Both computational and problem-solving skills may be taught effectively through computer-assisted instruction (Jitendra & Xin, 1997; Xin & Jitendra, 1999).

When considering computer-assisted instruction, teachers must be sure that students have the prerequisite skills to make use of the chosen software and that the software employs appropriate options for branching to practice on critical, but weak, preskills. In addition, for students with selective attention problems, computer math games may provide too many distracting elements for the practice sessions to be beneficial (Christensen & Gerber, 1990).

Developing Understanding and Modeling Problem Solving through Teacher-Student Dialogues

Numerous researchers now maintain that it is not enough to teach children with mild disabilities isolated computational skills and strategies because these students cannot apply the skills and strategies they learn to solve real-world problems (see, for example, Cawley & Reines, 1996; Mercer, Jordan, & Miller, 1994, 1996; Miller & Mercer, 1997). Moreover, the NCTM (1989) considers mathematical reasoning and problem solving to be essential skills for students in the twenty-first century. Research is now suggesting that explicit teacher modeling of problem-solving strategies and teacher-student dialogues centered on understanding mathematical concepts may be important avenues for helping students reason and problem solve (Harris, Miller, & Mercer, 1995; Hutchinson, 1993; Miller & Mercer, 1997; Montague, 1992, 1997).

For example, Montague (1992) explicitly modeled a problem-solving strategy to middle school students with learning disabilities. Her strategy included the following steps: (a) Read for understanding; (b) Paraphrase in your own words; (c) Visualize a picture or diagram; (d) Hypothesize a plan to solve the problem;

Table 13.2 **Mathematics Computer Software**

Computer Drill and Instruction: Mathematics (Science Research Associates)	Covers all major skills in grades K to 9 math curriculum. Built-in assessment, placement, and record-keeping systems. Interactive tutorial gives help when needed. Teacher assistance for generating practice problems. Program also available for solving word problems. Sample skills: number readiness, whole numbers, basic operations, fractions, decimals, ratio, percent, measurement, beginning algebra.
Math Blasters (Davidson)	A software series covering mathematical concepts across the grade levels. Built-in record keeping and levels of difficulty allow teachers to individualize to meet student needs, and sound and visual effects are appealing to students. Series includes: *Math Blaster Jr., In Search of Spot, Secret of the Lost City, Math Blaster Mystery, Alge-Blaster 3,* and *What's My Angle?*
Math for the Real World (Davidson)	For grades 5 and up, the students go "on the road" with a band. Students learn to apply math skills in daily life using over 4,000 word problems developed around helping the band arrive at their destination, be on time, eat, and make a profit! Skills include fractions, decimals, weights and measures, recognizing patterns, thinking logically, and understanding time. Enjoyable games for two users with interesting visuals and sound.
Math Sequences (Milliken)	For grades 1 to 8, or adaptable for older students. All operations with whole numbers, fractions and decimals, measurement, and percents. Monitors skills mastery and advances or moves students back to proper levels. Keeps records for teacher use.
Mighty Math (Edmark)	A series of CD-ROMs for grades K through 10. Interesting visuals and sound effects. Covers basic number and computational skills through algebra and geometry. Includes *Zoo Zillions, Carnival Countdown, Number Heroes, Calculating Crew, Astro Algebra,* and *Cosmic Geometry.*
Show Me Math (Attainment)	Appropriate for all grades, students learn basic addition, subtraction, multiplication, and division facts. Students complete math sentences and can use the "Show Me" option to see and hear correct answers illustrated with visual and sound effects. Teachers can set preferences for problem displays and levels of difficulty. Assessment component tracks progress and keeps records.
Word Math (Milliken)	A series of programs to develop and give practice with word problem solving. For grades 2 to 8, each of the three programs contains tutorial assistance for incorrect answers and two different levels of difficulty. Includes *Primary WordMath, WordMath I,* and *WordMath II.*

(e) Estimate or predict the answer; (f) Compute the answer; and (g) Check to be sure everything is correct. To teach the strategy, Montague used not only teacher modeling, but also verbal rehearsal, specific feedback, guided practice, and checks to ensure mastery.

Similarly, Hutchinson (1993) taught secondary-level students with learning disabilities a self-questioning strategy for solving algebra problems. Teachers used explicit modeling and "think alouds" to guide students in asking themselves questions such as, "Have I read and understood the sentence?" and "Do I have a representation for this problem?" After learning the strategy, students generalized its use to other word problems.

Although in these two studies teachers were given scripted dialogues, Harris, Miller, and Mercer (1995) suggest that, with practice, the scripts are no longer needed. Teachers can learn to model the strategy while explicitly "thinking out loud," provide "scaffolded" practice giving students assistance until they are able to perform independently, and then offer elaborated feedback regarding student errors in private teacher-student dialogues (Miller, Strawser, & Mercer, 1996) (see Box 13.2). According to Scheid (1994), if students with mild disabilities are to understand mathematical concepts and problem solve, teachers must:

1. Identify the underlying concepts and relationships that students need to understand and explicitly teach these to students,
2. Draw connections between what students already know and understand and what they are learning,
3. Actively involve students in learning by presenting instruction from a problem-solving perspective,
4. Use questions and listen to students throughout instruction,
5. Involve students in groups to communicate about problem solving, and
6. Help students gain confidence in their ability to ask questions and use mathematical knowledge gleaned from daily living experiences.

A Summary of Generalizable Teaching Procedures ◆

Mathematics instruction for children with mild disabilities begins with careful, curriculum-based assessment and analysis of errors to determine appropriate tasks and student needs. Initial instruction proceeds using a concrete-to-semi-concrete-to-abstract sequence in order to maximize the child's understanding of new skills and concepts. In addition, a youngster's mastery of computational skills increases when his or her teacher uses explicit and focused direct instructional techniques and provides many motivating practice opportunities. Careful sequencing, rule-based instruction, and strategy training may help to minimize memorization and simplify procedural learning for students with mild disabilities. Finally, mathematics skills must be continuously set within the context of real life, interesting problems to solve, and teachers must engage students in dialogues regarding problem solutions. ◆

Procedures for Teaching Specific Skills and Concepts

Each of the procedures we have considered so far is useful for teaching a wide range of mathematics tasks. The reader is encouraged to keep these firmly in

Box 13.2

Modeling Problem Solving and Providing Elaborated Feedback

Ms. Lopez uses the following process when teaching Joey and Travis to problem solve:

Provide an Advanced Organizer

"Yesterday we learned the letters standing for a problem-solving strategy. Who remembers what those letters were? Yes, the letters were F,A,S,T,D,R,A,W—the FASTDRAW strategy. Just knowing the letters won't help us, though. So, let me show you what the letters stand for."

Explicitly Model Strategic Behavior and Think Aloud

"Let's see, the *F* means find what you're solving for, and the *A* means ask yourself, 'What are the parts of the problem?' *S* means set up the numbers and *T* means tie down the sign. The *D* stands for discover the sign. The *R* stands for read the equation. The *A* stands for answer or draw the problem and check, and the *W* stands for write the answer. (She points to the steps written on a chart as she talks.) Let's see. Let me use these steps to solve this problem (pointing to a problem written on the board). Travis has six marbles. Joey gives him five more marbles. How many marbles does Travis have now?"

"Okay, I can do this. The *F* means find what I'm solving for and *A* means ask myself, 'What are the parts of the problem?' Let's see, I have to solve for how many marbles Travis has now (pointing). The parts of the problem are six marbles and five more marbles. Okay, I can set up the numbers (writing) 6 and 5. Now, tie down the sign. I have to find out how many marbles Travis has. He had 6 and he got 5 more, so that must mean I have to find out how many he has altogether now. I think that's a plus sign, so (writing) 6 + 5 = ____."

"Hmmm, *D* is discover the sign. It's a plus sign, I know that. *R* means read the equation. Okay, 6 + 5 = what? *A* is answer the problem or draw a picture and check it. I can't remember what 6 + 5 equals. I can use my counting-on-from-bigger strategy though. Let's see. Six is the bigger number, so I'll make 5 marks on the paper. Now, I'll say 6 and count on touching my tally marks: 6, 7, 8, 9, 10, 11. 6 + 5 = 11. Let me check one more time to be sure (repeating the counting-on procedure). Yep, it's 11. Now, *W* means write the answer (writing 11)."

Give Guided or Scaffolded Practice

Ms. Lopez assists Joey and Travis in solving similar problems. Throughout the practice, she asks questions designed to focus her students on key parts of the strategy and the problem to be solved. For example, she asks questions such as these:
What is the first step in the strategy?
What does this mean we have to do?
What are we solving for?
What are the parts of the problem?

Provide Elaborated Feedback during Independent Practice

"Joey, for each of these problems you did a good job identifying what you're solving for and you found the parts of the problem quite well. Wow, you've set up the numbers, tied down and discovered the signs, and read the problems. (She begins with specific positive feedback. Then, in her corrective feedback, she avoids saying the word *you.*) Let's see, when we answer/check, let me show you how to add zero to a number. When zero is added to any number, the answer is always that number. Look at the second problem. 12 + 0 = how many? I start by counting my 12 action figures. Now, the second number is 0, so I can't count any more action figures. That's the same as counting nothing. The answer is all the action figures I've counted, or 12. So the answer is 12."

"Let's look at this fourth problem, 9 + 0 = how many? How many candies will you count first? Yep, 9 candies. Now how many more candies can you count? Right, you can't count any more candies. You have 0 and you don't have any more candies to count. So the answer will be all the candies you've counted, or? . . . Good job, 9 candies! Nice job adding 0 to these numbers. Now, let's see you finish the rest of these problems and I know you can use the strategy to add 0 to any number now!"

Provide Strategy Practice

Ms. Lopez reminds Joey of the rule, "Any number plus zero is always still that number." She gives him additional practice solving word problems using this rule and the FASTDRAW strategy. Later, she provides her students with a self-monitoring checklist for solving word problems:

My Word Problem Checklist
FASTDRAW

____Read the problem.

____What is the question the problem asks?

____To answer the question, do I have to:

    ___ ADD

    ___ SUBTRACT

    ___ MULTIPLY

    ___ DIVIDE

____What information is not needed?

____Write out the problem using numbers.

____Solve the problem.

____Check the answer.

Adapted with permission from: Miller, S.P., Strawser, S., & Mercer, C.D. (1996). Promoting strategic math performance among students with learning disabilities. *LD Forum, 21*(2), 34-40.

mind as we turn to a discussion of instructional tips for teaching specific math skills and concepts.

Basic Number Concepts and Number Sense

According to Gersten and Chard (1999), if children with mild disabilities are to make progress in mathematics, they must develop a number sense. That is, they must understand basic concepts about numerals and their meanings, and they must be able to look at the world mathematically. For example, students must develop an understanding of the relationship between numbers and objects (i.e., one-to-one correspondence), and they must be able to identify the numerals and their face value (i.e., numeration). In addition, an understanding of seriation (i.e., ordinal properties of objects) and place value is necessary if students are to perform complex operations.

One-to-one correspondence. One-to-one correspondence is a mathematics "readiness" skill included in all early childhood programs. Youngsters must understand that one object may be matched exactly to another object and that number words help us to identify this relationship and to "tag" objects as we count them. Typically, most children come to school with this number concept established. However, when students are having difficulty, teachers should engage them in activities such as the following to develop this concept:

1. Have children pass out common classroom supplies such as crayons, scissors, or paper, giving one item to each child. As children do this, say, "That's one for Joey, and one for Travis. That's two crayons," and so forth.
2. Provide children with egg cartons or muffin tins and have children place one raisin or one bean in each hole. Count the raisins or beans with the children.
3. Use common nursery rhymes for counting (e.g., "One, two, buckle my shoe . . ., or "Five little monkeys jumping on the bed . . .").
4. Give children counting sticks, such as popsicle sticks or plastic straws, or counters such as checkers or buttons. Count these saying the numbers out loud with the children. Begin by moving each item away from the others as you say the number. Later, help the child to touch and move each counter as he or she says the numbers with you. You may need to use physical prompting at this stage for some youngsters.
5. If children have difficulty establishing a counting "rhythm," clap or tap the table as the child counts. Alternatively, hold the child's hands and control his or her clapping as you count the claps with the child. Children can also count with you as you bounce a ball or jump.

Numeration. To help children understand cardinal numbers, teachers must provide opportunities for youngsters to identify numerals, recognize their value, and write them. Following are several suggestions for teaching numeration skills:

1. Give the child a card with a numeral or number word on it. Help the child place the correct number of blocks, buttons, or the like, on the card. Initially, you may need to begin with large dots on the card arranged in a recognizable pattern so that the child has a visual reference point for the number of items to be counted:

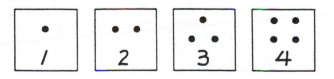

2. Give the child an egg carton, muffin tin, or set of paper cups with numerals written in the bottom of each. Have the child count the correct number of raisins, beans, buttons, or the like, to place in each.

3. Attach cards with numerals or number words to coat hangers. Have children place the correct number of clothespins on each hanger and hang each from a "clothesline" in a designated classroom space. Or, have children clip cards containing sets of dots or sets of pictures of objects to the correct coat hanger.

4. Using the felt board, have children match numerals or number words to sets of objects and vice versa.

5. Use trading tasks with the children. Tell the student, "Give me four beans and I'll give you the numeral four." Or, conversely, "Give me the numeral four and I'll give you four raisins."

6. Give each child a personal number line. For each numeral, 1 through 10, provide an illustration using patterns of dots (Mercer & Mercer, 1993):

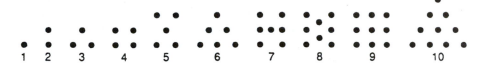

7. Teach children to write the numerals as they learn the manuscript alphabet. Use the procedures described in Chapter 12 for teaching handwriting skills. Provide children with the numerals 1 through 9 to trace, to trace over dots, and to copy from near point. Verbalize numeral names and the strokes as they are formed. Use directional arrows and color cues if these are necessary.

8. Arrange sets of objects on the table. Have the child hold up a card with the correct numeral or number word written on it. Or, have the child state or write the numeral that correctly represents the set. Arrange the sets in easily recognizable patterns; stress immediate recognition rather than counting of objects.

9. Place the numerals 1 through 9 on large cards. Have the children arrange the cards in correct sequence on the chalkboard tray or on the floor. Children may also enjoy holding the cards and arranging themselves in correct sequence.

10. Make self-correcting puzzles, each containing a numeral and a matching set of dots. Or have children complete a number-sequence puzzle by placing the numerals in correct sequence. On the back of the puzzle, draw sets of dots to represent each numeral:

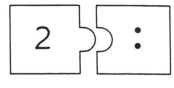

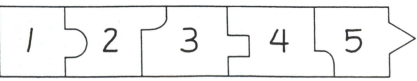

11. Teach the children the touch points for each numeral as used in *Touch Math* (Bullock et al., 1991).

12. Illustrate different quantities using concrete objects, and, later, pictured representations. For example, show students 1, 5, 10, 25, 50, and 100 pennies. Let them see how a stack of 25 pennies is much bigger than a stack of 5. Show them what a dozen looks like, and so forth. Have children stack counters or coins up along a number line in sequence: 1 coin, 2 coins, 3 coins, and so on.

Seriation. Children must understand that objects can be arranged by attributes such as length, height, weight, and so forth. The ordinal property of objects and numerals is essential to developing such concepts as more than/less than/equal to. To develop these concepts, teachers should engage students in the following types of activities:

1. Give students objects of varying lengths, such as Cuisenaire Rods (Davidson, 1969). Have the children arrange these in order from the shortest to the longest and from the longest to the shortest.

2. Fill jars with sand or water and have students arrange these in order from tallest to shortest, or have students stack books into piles from biggest to smallest (Bos & Vaughn, 1998).

3. Have students arrange themselves in order from the tallest to the shortest and vice versa.

4. Have children count their place in line as they line up during daily activities (e.g., first, second, third, and so forth).

Place value. Place value is a difficult concept for many students with mild disabilities. It is an essential concept, however, if students are to progress to complex operations involving regrouping. The following techniques are useful in developing an understanding of place value:

1. Bundle objects like popsicle sticks or pencils into groups of 10. Count the groups of 10 with students, saying, "Two 10's is twenty, five 10's is fifty," and so forth. Practice counting by 10's until students are firm with this skill.

2. Bundle objects like popsicle sticks or pencils into groups of 10. Keep 9 sticks or pencils loose to serve as 1's. Arrange groups of 10's and 1's on a large sheet of paper and have the children count the bundles of 10's and then the 1's with you. Write the numerals on the paper under the bundles of 10's and 1's. Later, arrange the paper into columns headed "tens" and "ones." Repeat the preceding activity, placing the sticks over the proper heading. Write the numerals in the columns, stressing to the children that only one digit can be written in each position or place.

3. Use base-10 blocks such as those available from school supply catalogs. (If your school cannot afford to purchase blocks, sets for each child can easily be made by purchasing contact shelf paper patterned with large squares. Fold the contact paper in half so that it sticks to itself and so that the same square pattern is visible on both sides. Then, cut out single squares, strips of 10 squares, and blocks of 100 squares.) Have children place the correct number of blocks on the table to form various numbers. Arrange the blocks

under the headings of "hundreds," "tens," and "ones" printed on paper lined with three columns. Write the corresponding numerals in each column directly beneath the blocks.

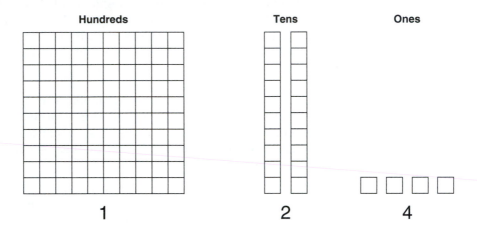

Hundreds	Tens	Ones
1	2	4

4. Place only numerals in columns headed by thousands, hundreds, tens, and ones. Have children identify the place value of each numeral. Later, write the numerals without the headings and have children again identify the place each numeral occupies. Later, write numbers such as 3,333 and ask the student to identify the 3 that is worth the most and the 3 that is worth the least.

5. Ask children to write the number representing seven 1,000's, three 100's, two 10's, and four 1's and to read the number he or she has written. If necessary, this can first be done using the headed column paper described in item 3.

6. Using the base-10 blocks, give children thirteen 1's and one 10-strip. Arrange these on column paper headed "tens" and "ones." Ask children to write the numerals to represent the number of blocks. Remind them that only one digit can be written in each place. Explain to the children that ten of the 1's blocks can be traded in for a 10-strip. Now, the child can write the numerals correctly. Repeat this procedure until children have mastered trading 1's for 10's. Use the same procedure, later, for trading ten 10-strips for a 100's square.

7. Children also must understand that zero can be used as a place holder, in addition to representing "nothing." Using the base-10 blocks and column paper, set up problems in which children must trade in ten 1's blocks for a 10-strip and have no 1's remaining (e.g., give students two 10-strips and ten 1's blocks). Arrange the blocks under the proper column headings and write the numerals to represent the number. Explain that the zero is used as a placeholder and remind children of the "three-10's-is-30" and counting-by-tens concept they have mastered. Later, arrange situations in which youngsters must trade in ten 10's strips for a 100's square and have zero in the tens place as a place holder.

8. Write numbers and have children identify incorrect zeroes. This can be done initially on the column paper described earlier if necessary. Teach

children this rule: Zero can never be the numeral farthest to the left in a whole number. Using the column paper, children can see that zero can be a numeral "in the middle" or the numeral "farthest to the right," serving as a place holder.

9. Give children dice of three different colors. Make each color represent one place value: 100's, 10's, or 1's. Children roll the dice and then write and/or read the number they roll. Column paper may be used as necessary. To change this practice into a game format, children may be paired and each child given his or her own set of dice. The children roll the dice, write/read the number, and score a point for the larger of the two numbers if it is written/read correctly.

10. For older students, the concept of place value may be practiced using an odometer or numbers from student textbooks or from the newspaper (Bos & Vaughn, 1998). Alternatively, "money" and a cashier's drawer may be used to practice place value, particularly trading pennies (1's) for dimes (10's) and trading dimes (10's) for dollars (100's).

11. The abacus is also a time-honored means for practicing place value. Students can see that when they have more than 10 beads on a row, they must trade for 1 bead on the next row. Help children to form, write, and read numbers using the abacus as a concrete aid along with color-coded column paper if necessary.

12. To develop number sense related to place value, Vacc (1995) recommends that teachers restructure the hundreds chart. Rather than the traditional hundreds chart in which rows of numbers go from left to right, she suggests arranging the chart from right to left in columns and including the number zero. Although students can see many important number patterns in the traditional hundreds chart (top of page 404), with the restructured chart they can consistently read and learn numbers in the right-to-left format. Thus, the restructured hundreds chart (bottom of page 404) may help them develop number sense:

Basic Facts and Operations

Proficiency with the basic facts and operations is as essential as understanding number concepts if students are to perform complex mathematics with ease. Automaticity with the basic addition, subtraction, multiplication, and division facts does not, of course, ensure that the student will be able to solve advanced problems easily; however, if they understand the operations and can immediately recall the basic facts, they will be better equipped to tackle more complex problems.

Addition. Addition is a basic operation involving the joining of two or more sets. The sums through 18 are the essential addition facts that children must master. Following are several suggestions for teaching addition to students with mild disabilities:

1. Begin with counters or sticks. Place these on the table in two groups (e.g., 3 sticks and 4 sticks). Together with the child, count the sticks in each group

Traditional Hundreds Chart

1	2	3	4	5	6	7	8	9	10
11	12	13	14	15	16	17	18	19	20
21	22	23	24	25	26	27	28	29	30
31	32	33	34	35	36	37	38	39	40
41	42	43	44	45	46	47	48	49	50
51	52	53	54	55	56	57	58	59	60
61	62	63	64	65	66	67	68	69	70
71	72	73	74	75	76	77	78	79	80
81	82	83	84	85	86	87	88	89	90
91	92	93	94	95	96	97	98	99	100

Restructured Hundreds Chart

90	80	70	60	50	40	30	20	10	0
91	81	71	61	51	41	31	21	11	1
92	82	72	62	52	42	32	22	12	2
93	83	73	63	53	43	33	23	13	3
94	84	74	64	54	44	34	24	14	4
95	85	75	65	55	45	35	25	15	5
96	86	76	66	56	46	36	26	16	6
97	87	77	67	57	47	37	27	17	7
98	88	78	68	58	48	38	28	18	8
99	89	79	69	59	49	39	29	19	9

and write the number on a sheet of paper beneath each group. Then, count all the sticks together and write the total number of sticks. Stress that 3 + 4 is another way to name 7. To move to the semiconcrete level, substitute tally marks or draw pictures to represent the number in each set.

2. Place patterns of dots on cards with numerals beneath each to represent addition facts from the 1's through the 5's. Place numerals on separate cards. Have children match the dots to the sums. Later, move to larger sums through 18.

3. Flexer (1989) suggests using 5- and 10-frames to enable children to visualize the basic addition facts. Once children recognize number patterns using the 5- and 10-frames (see Figure 13.5), they can use frames and counters to learn

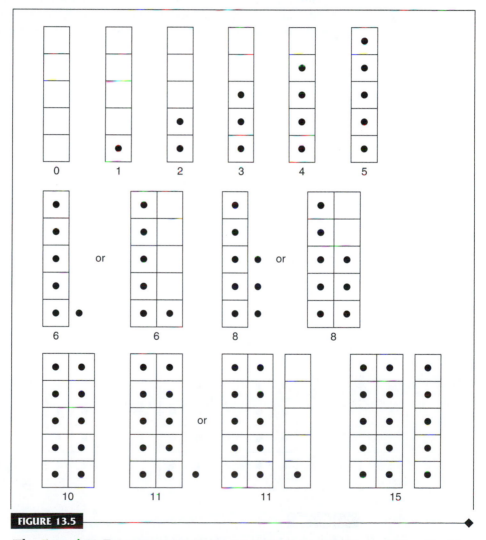

FIGURE 13.5

The 5- and 10-Frames From: Flexer, R.J. (1989). Conceptualizing addition. *Teaching Exceptional Children, 21*, p. 23. Copyright © 1989 by the Council for Exceptional Children. Reprinted with permission.

the addition facts. The child places frames on the table with counters, such as beans, to represent each addend. Counters are then moved from one frame to fill in any missing cells in the other frame, and the new configuration becomes the sum (see Figure 13.6). Jones, Thornton, and Toohey (1985) used a similar strategy to help children remember the "harder" facts. For example, the children visualized the 10-frame and used the strategy "make 10 and add on" to complete difficult addition facts like 9 + 4 = ___ (see Figure 13.7).

4. Thornton and Toohey (1985) suggest that students with mild disabilities must be given specific strategies for attacking unknown addition facts prior to drill. They also recommend using a teaching sequence based on recalling the sum rather than the traditional sequence based on the size of the sum. In the traditional sequence, "easy" facts are the 1's through the 5's because they sum to 9 or less; the "harder" facts sum to 18 (see Figure 13.8).

5. A program such as Touch Math (Bullock, 1994) can also be used to teach addition as "counting-on" or "counting-on-from-bigger." For example, students first touch the touch points on each numeral in turn while

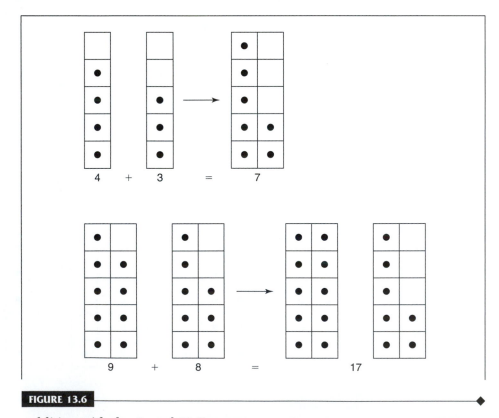

FIGURE 13.6

Addition with the 5- and 10-Frames From: Flexer, R.J. (1989). Conceptualizing addition. *Teaching Exceptional Children, 21,* p. 24. Copyright © 1989 by the Council for Exceptional Children. Reprinted with permission.

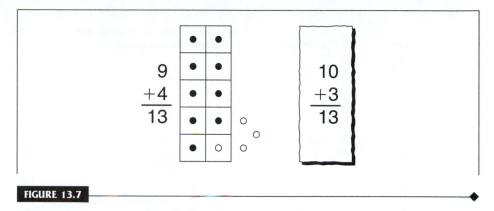

FIGURE 13.7

Using a 10-Frame for Difficult Addition Facts: "Making 10 and Adding On"
From: Jones, G.A., Thornton, C.A., & Toohey, M.A. (1985). A multi-option program for learning basic addition facts: Case studies and an experimental report. *Journal of Learning Disabilities, 18,* p. 324. Copyright © 1985 by PRO-ED, Inc. Reprinted with permission.

counting up. Later, children say the larger number while simultaneously crossing it out, then count on the remaining numerals by touching each touch point:

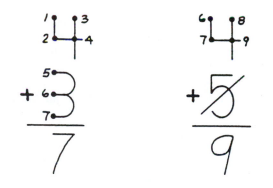

6. When students have mastered basic addition facts, they can practice column addition using three or four digits. The touch points and the "counting-on-from-bigger" strategy described in item 5 are also helpful for computing column addition problems. Additionally, teachers may draw blank lines to the side of column addition problems and cue children to break these into separate addition facts. For example:

7. Similarly, Cooper (1994) recommends that students be taught to look for "sums to 10" as a strategy for completing column addition. As students find numerals that sum to 10, they cross them out and write a 10 to the right of

Fact group	Examples	Most popular strategy for working out unknown answers	Sentence pattern (verbal prompt)
Count ons	(+1, +2, +3, facts)	"Feel" the count	Start BIG and count on.
Zero facts	(6 + 0, 0 + 4)	Show it	Plus zero stays the same.
Doubles	(4 + 4, 7 + 7)	Use pictures (e.g., 7 + 7 is the 2-week fact; 7 + 7 = 14)	Think of the picture.
10 sums	(especially 6 + 4)	Use 10-frame 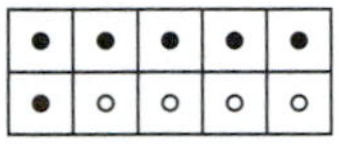	
9's	(4 + 9, 9 + 6)	Use pattern	What's the pattern?
Near doubles	(4 + 5, 7 + 8)	Relate to doubles (via pictures)	Think doubles to help.
4 last facts	(7 + 5, 8 + 4, 8 + 5, 8 + 6)	Make 10, add extra 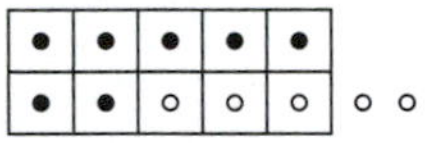	Use 10 to help.

(bracket at left spanning Count ons through Near doubles, labeled vertically: "No fingers needed!")

Note: Turnarounds (cummutatives of facts within each group would be learned before moving to a different group of facts.)

FIGURE 13.8

A Sequence for Teaching the Addition Facts: Grouping the Facts by Strategy for Recall
Adapted From: Thornton, C.A., & Toohey, M.A. (1985). Basic math facts: Guidelines for teaching and learning. *Learning Disabilities Focus, 1*, pp. 50 and 51. Reprinted with permission.

the addition problem. When all "sums to 10" are identified, the student adds the numbers in the new column created to the right. For example:

$$
\begin{array}{cc}
\cancel{2} & \\
\cancel{7} & 10 \\
\cancel{8} & \\
1 & 1 \\
+\cancel{3} & 10 \\
\hline
\end{array}
$$

8. Give students personal number lines to use for solving unknown addition facts. Begin with number lines 1 through 10 and advance to a line from 1 through 18. Teach children to find the larger addend on the line and count on the next addend touching a number along the line each time they count. Thus, 3 + 4 = ___ is represented as "Find 4 and count on three more":

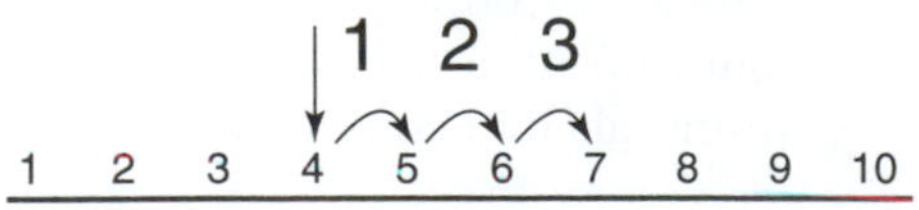

Similarly, $7 + 9 =$ ___ can become "Touch 9 and then count on seven more":

							1 2 3 4 5 6 7

1 2 3 4 5 6 7 8 9 10 11 12 13 14 15 16 17 18

For both addition and subtraction facts, Cohen and deBettencourt (1988) suggest a modified number line that highlights the size relationships among numbers (see Figure 13.9). For addition, the child places a marker on the smaller addend and then moves the marker down the number of spaces indicated by the larger addend. (Note: For subtraction, the child places the marker on the larger number and moves up.)

9. Students must also understand the concept of missing addends. Arrange addition problems in families and help children to find the addend.

$$2 + 3 = \text{\_\_\_} \qquad 2 + \text{\_\_\_} = 5 \qquad \text{\_\_\_} + 3 = 5$$
$$3 + 2 = \text{\_\_\_} \qquad 3 + \text{\_\_\_} = 5 \qquad \text{\_\_\_} + 2 = 5$$

10. Cooper (1994) suggests a simple strategy for students who have great difficulty remembering the sums to 10. He suggests teaching students to write the numerals 1 through 5 from left to right and then directly beneath to write the numerals 5 through 9 from right to left:

1 2 3 4 5
9 8 7 6 5

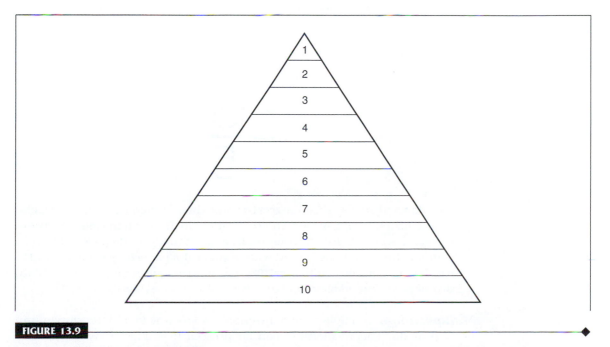

FIGURE 13.9

The "Triangle" Number Line From: Cohen, S., & deBettencourt, L. (1988). Teaching children to be independent learners: A step-by-step strategy. In E.L. Meyen, G.A. Vergason, & R.J. Whelan (Eds.), *Effective instructional strategies for exceptional children*, Denver, CO: Love, p. 328. Reprinted with permission.

Subtraction. Subtraction is relatively easy once students understand the operation of addition and know the basic addition facts. Teachers can, for example, help students use the missing-addends concept as they learn the "fact families" (i.e., If $2 + 3 = 5$ and $3 + 2 = 5$ then $5 - 2 = 3$ and $5 - 3 = 2$.). Following are several suggestions for teaching subtraction:

1. As was done with addition, begin with counters and later move to pictures to establish an understanding of the subtraction operation. Be sure to tie each set of counters or set of pictures immediately to the corresponding number symbols.

2. Students may use number lines starting with the larger number (i.e., the minuend) and count back the number of spaces indicated by the smaller number (i.e., the subtrahend) to find unknown differences. Similarly, the student can be taught to make tally marks for the minuend and then "minus" the number of tally marks indicated by the subtrahend. The difference is the number of tally marks remaining:

$$9 \quad - \quad 3 \quad = \quad 6$$

++†/ / / / / /

3. In Touch Math (Bullock , 1994), students learn to touch the touch points while "counting off." This means that students will first require time to practice counting in reverse, first from 10 down to zero and then from 18 down to zero:

$$
\begin{array}{r}
8 \\
- \, 3 \\
\hline
5
\end{array}
$$

4. Thornton and Toohey (1986) suggest a way to help students with mild disabilities visualize subtraction facts and relate these to the addition facts. For example, pictures are used to illustrate subtraction doubles (see Figure 13.10) and a "counting-on" technique is used with number dot patterns (see Figure 13.11). In addition, Thornton and Toohey (1986) present a unique triangular-shaped flash card for practice of addition- and subtraction-fact families (see Figure 13.12).

Multiplication. Multiplication is essentially a fast way to add the same number repeatedly. This relationship can be stressed to youngsters with mild disabilities as they first learn the operation of multiplication. Consider, for example, the following activities:

1. Arrange equal groups of counters in rows. Begin with simple groups and rows such as three rows of two. Count the number of counters in each group, then the number of rows, and write these numerals on paper. Count the total number of counters and write the product. Illustrate for the child how this is the same as the operation $2 + 2 + 2$. Later, move to pictures to represent the multiplication problems:

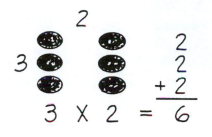

2. Use Geoboards to illustrate the concept of multiplication (Brosnan, 1997). Use pegs and rubber bands, or small cubes, to illustrate on the Geoboard patterns like 1×1, 2×2, 3×3, and so forth. Later, at the semiconcrete level, graph paper can be used to represent the squares on the Geoboard:

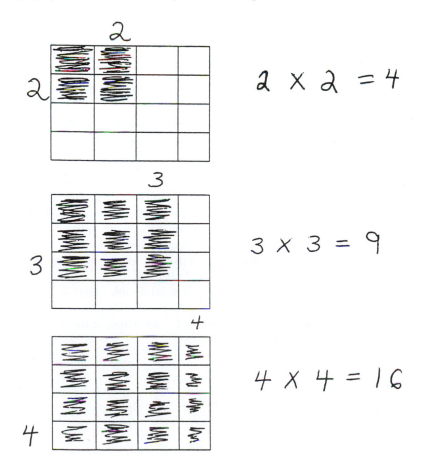

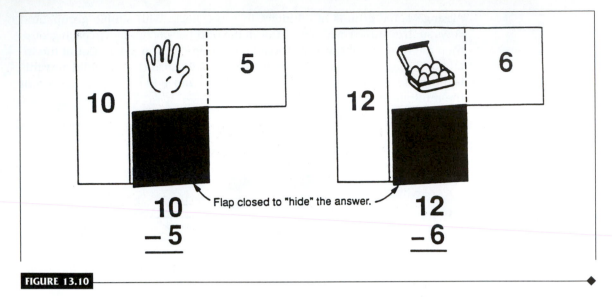

Flap closed to "hide" the answer.

10
− 5

12
− 6

FIGURE 13.10

Using Pictures to Teach Subtraction Doubles From: Thornton, C.A., & Toohey, M.A. (1986). Subtraction hide-and-seek cards can help. *Teaching Exceptional Children, 19,* p. 12. Copyright © 1986 by the Council for Exceptional Children. Reprinted with permission.

3. When children can sequence count, sometimes called "skip counting," by twos, threes, fours, fives, and so forth, they can learn the "count-by" strategy illustrated earlier in the chapter. In addition, programs like Touch Math (Bullock , 1994) use the "count-by" strategy to teach multiplication facts (refer to Figure 13.2).

4. Mercer and Mercer (1993) suggest a sensible sequence for teaching the multiplication facts, in which the amount of memorization required by the student is minimized:

    a) Teach as a rule that zero times any number is always zero.

    b) Teach as a rule that 1 times any number is always that same number.

    c) Teach that 2 times any number means double that number. Emphasize that 2 times a number is the same as the doubles facts in addition, so these are not really new facts to learn.

    d) Teach the child to use the "count-by" strategy, particularly for the 3's, 4's, and 5's.

    e) Group the multiplication doubles facts (e.g., 3 × 3, 4 × 4, etc.) as a family for learning.

    f) Teach the child "tricks" for learning the 9's, such as the inverse trick or the 9's using fingers:

Inverse Trick

0	9	(1 × 9)
1	8	(2 × 9)
2	7	
3	6	
4	5	

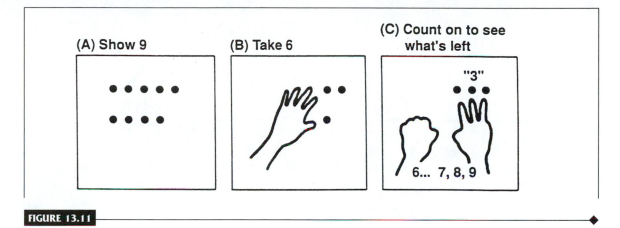

(A) Show 9

(B) Take 6

(C) Count on to see what's left

"3"

6... 7, 8, 9

FIGURE 13.11

Using a "Counting-On" Strategy to Subtract From: Thornton, C.A., & Toohey, M.A. (1986). Subtraction hide-and-seek cards can help. *Teaching Exceptional Children, 19,* p. 12. Copyright © 1986 by the Council for Exceptional Children. Reprinted with permission.

5	4
6	3
7	2
8	1
9	0

(10×9)

(Notice that the inverse-trick procedure also results in the sums to 9.)

Fingers Trick

The fingers are numbered 1 through 10 from left to right. To multiply any number by 9, count over on the fingers to that number and put that finger down. The fingers to the left are the 10's and the fingers to the right are the 1's. Thus, $3 \times 9 = 27$ is represented as follows:

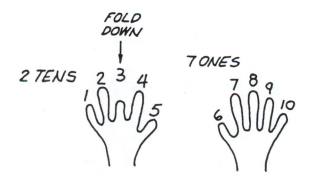

FOLD DOWN

2 TENS

7 ONES

Division. Division is the inverse of multiplication. Frequently, division becomes the most difficult of the four operations for students with mild disabilities to master. The task can be made easier if the teacher uses the following strategies:

1. Begin with base-10 blocks or other counters and have students divide these groups into equal piles. For example, students could be given nine 1's blocks

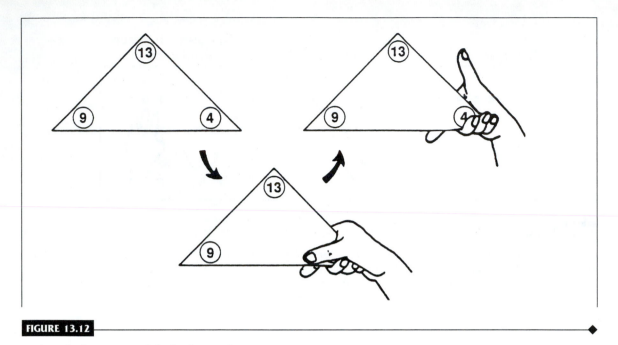

FIGURE 13.12

Triangle "Fact-Family" Flash Cards From: Thornton, C.A., & Toohey, M.A. (1986). Subtraction hide-and-seek cards can help. *Teaching Exceptional Children, 19,* p. 14. Copyright © 1986 by the Council for Exceptional Children. Reprinted with permission.

or counters and be asked to place these into piles containing the same number in each. The teacher would then write the symbols to illustrate that 9 can be divided into three equal groups (i.e., of three each). Stein, Silbert, and Carnine (1997) state that using this method of removing equivalent disjoint subsets can illustrate the inverse relationship between multiplication and division at the concrete level. Later, the teacher can use tally marks drawn on paper and ask children to circle equal groups of marks and count the groups. For example, 30 divided by 6 can be illustrated as follows:

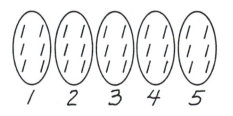

2. Similarly, at the semiconcrete level, some youngsters can remember the "easy" division facts by using a number line through 25. Students begin at the larger number (i.e., the dividend) and then hop back along the number line to zero in equal jumps indicated by the smaller number (i.e., the divisor). Using laminated number lines that are washable, the child then counts his or her number of "hops" to find the answer (i.e., the quotient). Thus, 20 divided

by 5 means start at 20 and hop back along the number line to zero in equal jumps of 5 (Stein et al., 1997).

The relationship along the number line of division to equal subtractions is also sometimes helpful for youngsters with mild disabilities.

3. Teach the child to use a "count-by" strategy to solve unknown division facts, such as that used in Touch Math (Bullock et al., 1991).
4. Make fact-family cards and worksheets so that students may practice multiplication and division families just as they did with addition and subtraction families.

Complex Operations and Algorithms

When students understand the basic operations and are automatic with basic facts, they are ready to learn more complex operations that involve step-by-step procedures. It should be emphasized, however, that to learn these procedures or algorithms, students must first understand the concept of place value. In order to complete many complex operations, regrouping (i.e., carrying and borrowing) is often required. The teacher should remember that more than one algorithm can be used to arrive at the correct answer. Although teachers must give students efficient and effective algorithms, they must also be "flexible" in selecting those that will best suit the needs of the individual child.

As students begin performing complex operations, teachers may find it helpful to have the child state the operation involved before solving the problem. This procedure focuses student attention on the relevant symbol; therefore, the youngster is more likely to perform the correct operation (Lovitt & Curtiss, 1968). For children who have difficulty aligning columns of numbers, a useful technique is to turn a sheet of notebook paper on its side. The lines then become columns to be used for writing numbers in their proper positions. Alternatively, graph paper with large squares is a helpful aid to some youngsters who must overcome alignment problems. Let's examine some additional ways in which to teach complex operations involving regrouping.

Addition with regrouping. If children with mild disabilities understand place value, they can easily learn to regroup for complex addition problems. Again, teachers must start with concrete manipulatives, such as base-10 blocks, to enable students to trade ten 1's for a 10-strip, ten 10-strips for a 100's square, and so forth. Moving these blocks across column paper and writing the numerals in the proper columns allows the child to "see" the operation performed. Some teachers also suggest that a small card be placed over the problem, uncovering only one column from right to left at a time. In this way, the child must focus on each vertical column of numbers for addition before moving on to the next column.

An alternative algorithm for addition with regrouping, useful as a transitional step for some youngsters with mild disabilities, is partial sums. In this algorithm, when adding the 1's digits together produces a sum greater than ten, that sum is written properly beneath the "tens" and "ones" columns. The student verbalizes "x 1's plus x 1's is ____" as he or she adds the numerals in the "ones" column. The 10's digits are then added using the verbalization "x 10's plus x 10's is ___." The sum for the "tens" column is then written underneath the sum for the "ones," with zero used as a placeholder in the "ones" column. The two partial sums are added with no regrouping required to find the actual sum for the problem.

```
   36
 +59
   15      (6 ones + 9 ones is 15 ones)
   80      (3 tens + 5 tens is 8 tens)
   95
```

Subtraction with Regrouping. As with addition, subtraction with regrouping begins with base-10 blocks and trading of one 10-strip for ten 1's and, later, trading of one 100's square for ten 10-strips. Again, youngsters can "see" the regrouping necessary to complete the operation as the manipulatives are moved across columns headed "hundreds," "tens," and "ones" on lined paper, and as the corresponding numbers are written to represent each.

For complex regrouping involving one or more zeros, teach the child to recognize and name a quantity of 10's or 100's. Thus, in the problem 405 − 37 = ___, the child can verbalize: "Forty 10's borrow one 10 is thirty-nine 10's," while crossing out the 4 and 0 and writing the 39 and "borrowed" 10 above the proper columns. Similarly, 4005 − 378 = ___ becomes "Four hundred 10's borrow one ten is three hundred ninety-nine 10's":

Multiplication. Complex multiplication involving regrouping can confuse many youngsters with mild disabilities. A partial-products algorithm may be a useful transitional step for some children when learning to multiply a 2- or 3-digit number by a 1-digit number with regrouping required. The student multiplies each digit in the multiplicand in turn by the multiplier, immediately recording each partial product beneath the problem. The partial products are then summed to produce the final product. An understanding of place value and of zero as a place holder is an essential prerequisite for a multiplication algorithm such as this.

```
   38
 × 2
   16      (2 times eight 1's is sixteen 1's)
 +60      (2 times three 10's is six 10's)
   76
```

Similarly,

$$
\begin{array}{r}
386 \\
\times\ 3 \\
\hline
18 \\
240 \\
+900 \\
\hline
1158 \\
\end{array}
$$

18   (3 times six 1's is eighteen 1's)
240   (3 times eight 10's is twenty-four 10's)
+900   (3 times three 100's is nine 100's)

Division. Long division can be an extremely difficult skill for some students with mild disabilities to master. Providing children with a mnemonic or visual reminder of the steps to be performed is helpful; however, for many youngsters, extensive manipulation of concrete aids such as base-10 blocks may be necessary. For example, given the problem $537 \div 4$, Ms. Lopez might place five 100's squares, three 10-strips, and seven 1's blocks under the appropriate headings on column paper. Then, she might write the division problem and say, "I have to divide 537 into equal groups of four. I'll start with the 100's. I can make one group of four 100's squares, that's 400." At this point, Ms. Lopez has written the 1 in the quotient in the hundreds place and the 400 beneath the problem. "Now, I have one 100's square, three 10-strips, and seven 1's left over." She draws a line beneath the 400 and writes 137 as she talks. "Now I must divide the 10's into groups of four, but I can't do that unless I trade in the one leftover 100's square for ten 10-strips. Now I have thirteen 10-strips, and I can divide these into three groups of four each. That's twelve 10's I used up." Ms. Lopez writes the 3 in the quotient in the tens place and the twelve 10's, or 120, under the 137. Continuing, she says, "I now have one 10-strip and seven 1's left over." She draws the line and writes 17. "Now, 17 divided into equal groups of four. Oops! I'll have to trade in my one 10-strip first to make seventeen 1's. Now, I can divide into four groups of four each, that's sixteen 1's that I used, and I only have one 1's block left, so that's my remainder." She completes the problem, writing the 4 in the quotient, the 16 below the 17, and the remainder, 1:

$$
\begin{array}{r}
134\ \text{R}1 \\
4\overline{)537} \\
\underline{400} \\
137 \\
\underline{120} \\
17 \\
\underline{16} \\
1 \\
\end{array}
$$

When students understand the long division process, they can learn the steps "Divide, Multiply, Subtract, Compare, and Bring down." At this stage, some teachers also suggest that arrows be drawn straight down in the long division problem to help students keep numbers lined up in the appropriate columns when "bringing them down." Thus, in the preceding problem the lines and cues might look like this:

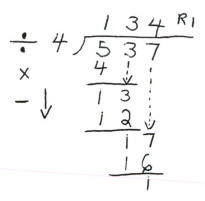

Other Essential Concepts and Skills

To function successfully as independent adults, students with mild disabilities must master fractions and decimals, as well as concepts of money, measurement, and time. Each of these skills may pose difficulty for learners in special programs.

Fractions. An understanding of fractions is necessary if students are to share items equally with one another, measure materials/ingredients for a hobby project or recipe, or solve a ratio problem. Kelly, Gersten, and Carnine (1990) maintain that the typical mathematics curriculum does not use essential design principles necessary for children with mild disabilities to master concepts like fractions. That is, mathematics textbooks often do not provide systematic practice in discriminating among related problem types (e.g., knowing when and when not to find a common denominator). Moreover, they fail to separate confusing elements or to give sufficient examples to illustrate concepts.

Similarly, Baroody and Hume (1991) argue that the typical mathematics curriculum fails to deliver instruction designed to ensure that youngsters with mild disabilities understand fractional concepts. These authors argue that teachers should first develop an understanding of fractions as a part of so many equal-sized parts. Thus, the child must first use many different manipulatives to see that this relationship applies whether the "whole" refers to a single unit (e.g., a candy bar divided into four equal parts) or to a set of discrete things (e.g., four cookies shared equally by two children). Baroody and Hume offer the following suggestions for teaching fractions:

1. Have children explicitly define the whole and emphasize that a fraction is a part of so many equal-sized parts. Use many different types of manipulatives to illustrate this relationship.
2. Engage children in "fair-sharing" activities. Have children divide groups of objects like toys or crackers equally among themselves. Have them divide whole objects, such as a pizza, equally.
3. When children understand the concept of a fraction as a part of so many equivalent parts, introduce the formal symbolism to represent the fractional

parts. Begin by labeling fractional parts such as ½, ⅓, and ¼. Using manipulatives during this stage can help students compare fractions and "see" that ½ is larger than ⅓, ⅓ is larger than ¼, and so on. At this point, teachers can help children understand that we cannot compare fractions like ⅓ and ¼ unless we identify the *whole* that is being defined.

4. When teaching youngsters to perform the four basic operations on fractional numbers, begin with concrete aids to develop an understanding of the concepts before teaching rules (e.g., "invert and multiply"). For some youngsters with mild disabilities, rule-based instruction may ultimately be necessary; however, the teacher should first emphasize understanding. For example, the teacher can have students represent fractions like 2½ with manipulatives (e.g., five ½-blocks) and then use these to demonstrate addition or subtraction of fractions with like denominators. Thus, 2½ plus 1½ becomes five ½-blocks plus three ½-blocks equals eight ½-blocks. The ½-blocks are then traded for "wholes," demonstrating that 2½ plus 1½ equals 4. Similarly, teachers can manipulate transparencies of different colors on the overhead projector to demonstrate the multiplication of fractions by shading in half the rows on a square grid and superimposing a similar square grid with columns shaded in to represent ¾. The product of ½ × ¾ is then shown by counting the total number of blocks in the grid for the denominator and the number of blocks that overlap in the grid for the numerator. Paper strips can also be used to demonstrate addition of fractions with unlike denominators (see Figure 13.13).

5. An interactive videodisc program, entitled *Mastering Fractions*, available from Systems Impact (1985), may be helpful in teaching operations with fractions to students with mild disabilities (see Lubke, Rogers, and Evans, 1989). A similar program is also available for mastering decimals and percents. According to Woodward, Baxter, and Robinson (1999), however, students with mild disabilities require much more time to learn rational number concepts such as decimals than previously believed.

Decimals. Students learn decimals best when instruction begins with concrete manipulatives. Thus, they first develop an understanding that decimals represent fractions with denominators of 10 or 100, and later, 1,000. Base-10 blocks can be used to illustrate this concept. That is, youngsters can place 1's blocks on a 10-strip to see the relationship between 1/10 (i.e., 1 part out of 10 equal parts), 2/10 (i.e., 2 parts out of 10 equal parts), and so forth. Similarly, students can place 1's blocks on the 100's square to illustrate the concept of hundredths. Initially, the teacher might emphasize visually the concept that decimal numerals are less than one whole by placing the 10-strip or 100's block to the right of a large decimal point. Later, children can examine equivalent amounts by such activities as comparing twenty 1's blocks on the 100's square (i.e., 20 parts out of 100 equal parts or .20) with two 10-strips on the 100's square (i.e., 2 parts out of 10 equal parts or two tenths). Similarly, youngsters can easily see, by manipulating the blocks, the relative size of decimals (e.g., .32 is greater than .30, but .30 is greater than .03). Teachers can construct column paper with the appropriate headings for decimal numerals and teach children to read and write these numerals following a procedure similar to that described for teaching place value.

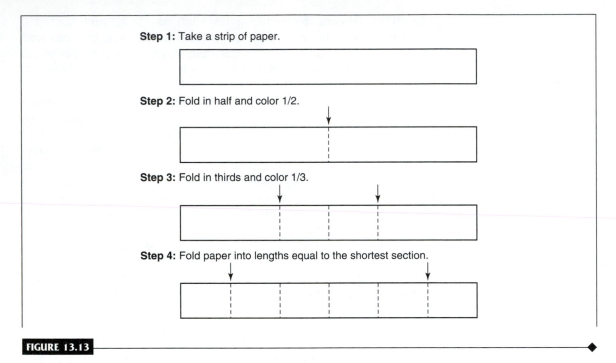

Step 1: Take a strip of paper.

Step 2: Fold in half and color 1/2.

Step 3: Fold in thirds and color 1/3.

Step 4: Fold paper into lengths equal to the shortest section.

FIGURE 13.13 ◆

Using Manipulatives to Teach Addition of Fractions with Unlike Denominators
The teacher can use a variety of manipulatives to teach difficult concepts like adding frac-
tions with unlike denominators. Above is one example of how paper strips can be used to
illustrate the problem $^1/_2 + ^1/_3 = ^5/_6$ *in a concrete manner.* From: Baroody, A.J., & Hume, J. (1991).
Meaningful mathematics instruction: The case of fractions. *Remedial and Special Education, 12*, p. 65.
Copyright © 1991 by the Council for Exceptional Children. Reprinted with permission.

Money, measurement, and time. Students with mild disabilities require
numerous opportunities to work with money in real-life contexts. Students must
practice counting coins and bills and making equivalent amounts. Browder and
Grasso (1998) suggest that teachers begin with instruction on making purchases
and simplify the academic demands of the task by allowing students like Susan
to use a calculator. For example, Ms. Lopez might challenge Joey to find all the
ways he can make 36 cents given pennies, nickels, dimes, and quarters. Setting
up a classroom store or using the newspaper to clip coupons and/or calculate
purchases are two additional ways teachers can provide youngsters with real-
life opportunities to practice money skills. For students who have difficulty determining the amount of correct change, teachers can begin by giving students
a preset amount such as $1.00 or $5.00 (Browder & Grasso, 1999). Mercer and
Mercer (1993) suggest a "money card." Based on a ten-dollar bill used to make a
purchase, the student simply crosses out the purchase amount on the card. The
remaining "money" on the card indicates the correct change. The change to be
returned from a ten-dollar bill, based on a purchase of $7.38, is determined as
follows:

$\cancel{\$}$ $\cancel{\$}$ $\cancel{\$}$ $\cancel{\$}$ $\cancel{\$}$ $\cancel{\$}$ $\cancel{\$}$ $\$$ $\$$

$\cancel{10}$ $\cancel{10}$ $\cancel{10}$ 10 10 10 10 10 10   **$2.62**

$\cancel{1}$ $\cancel{1}$ $\cancel{1}$ $\cancel{1}$ $\cancel{1}$ $\cancel{1}$ $\cancel{1}$ $\cancel{1}$ 1 1

Youngsters in special education programs also need many opportunities to measure familiar objects. Begin with simple rulers, measuring only to the inch. Later, students can measure to the $\frac{1}{2}$ inch, $\frac{1}{4}$ inch, and so forth, to complete art or hobby projects or to determine their height. Similarly, students can measure the width of the classroom in feet or the length of the hall in yards. Concepts such as area or perimeter can also be illustrated by using manipulatives like Geoboards (Brosnan, 1997). In addition, measurement of liquids and solids can easily be practiced by following recipes calling for cups, pints, quarts, pounds, ounces, and so forth. Youngsters also can weigh themselves or other objects, recording the weight in pounds and ounces. Concrete and realistic experiences with measurement are essential before children move to tasks involving comparisons and conversions of units of measure that require paper and pencil.

Children with mild disabilities also must understand the concept of time. The teacher can establish a basic understanding of time by sequencing events over the course of a class day or during a story and by pointing out, for example, "We go to P.E. first at 11:15, and then we go to lunch." Students can begin to understand the passage of time and relative lengths of time through concrete activities; for example, naming which of two familiar events is longer, reading time or snack time, or naming which student jumps for the longest time. In addition, daily routines involving the calendar highlight the everyday importance of time. Teachers can, for example, ask youngsters to name the day of the week on which they watch a favorite TV show or the day of the week on which they have music class.

Telling time can be a particularly difficult skill for some students with mild disabilities. Lipstreu and Johnson (1988) suggest that teachers use the "whole-clock" method rather than traditional methods that teach time to the hour, half hour, and quarter hour. These latter methods often confuse children with mild disabilities because of the terminology (e.g., "a quarter after six," "15 minutes before two"). To use the whole-clock method, students must be able to count by ones and by fives to 60 and identify the numerals 1 through 12. Children first learn to discriminate between the hour and minute hand and to tell time to the hour. At this step, teachers might choose to state the rule: "When the minute hand is pointing to the 12 and the hour hand is pointing to a number, we say the number and o'clock." Next, students practice 5 minutes after each hour, then 10 minutes, 15 minutes, and so on, through 55 minutes after the hour. In this way, children can focus on the movement of the minute hand and see that every hour has the same 5-minute intervals (Lipstreu & Johnson). Sometimes the teacher may find it necessary to highlight the proper hour on the clock face with color to help children discriminate the correct times after the half hour. When students master time in 5-minute intervals, they can learn to count on by ones up to the minute hand (e.g., 3:45, 3:46, 3:47), learning a predictable pattern for telling time.

This predictable pattern for telling time is also consistent with the use of digital clocks. Teachers can use this pattern as a starting point for direct instruction in telling time to the hour and to the minute with digital clocks. When students master time to the hour and to the minute, teachers may explicitly teach alternative language forms such as a "quarter before," a "quarter after," or "half past."

Algebra

Many students with mild disabilities must learn algebra for high school credit or for a college degree. Allsopp (1999) suggests teachers combine direct instruction, think-alouds, a concrete-to-representational-to-abstract sequence, and strategy instruction to improve student success in algebra. For example, Mr. Abel might teach Robert the FOIL (*First, Outside, Inside, Last* terms) strategy to help Robert remember the steps for multiplying binomials. Similarly, Mr. Abel might construct a concrete or representational illustration of an algebraic equation to be solved:

"The equation is like a balance scale. Each side of the equal sign has to have the same value or weight." [Mr. Abel illustrates the problem on the board]:

$$6a + 3 = 21$$

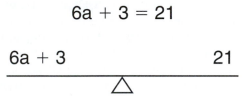

"If I take three counters away from the left side, the right side has more than the left. The equation is unequal." [Mr. Abel illustrates]:

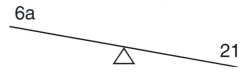

"So, to make the equation equal again, I have to take three counters away from the right side, too." [Mr. Abel completes the explanation]:

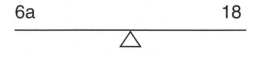

(Adapted from Allsopp, 1999, p. 78.)

Arithmetic Word Problems

One particularly difficult area for youngsters with mild disabilities is the solving of word problems. Cawley, Miller, and School (1987) suggest that much of this difficulty is due to mathematics textbooks that teach students to rely on "cue words" to solve only simple, direct word problems. For example, the text may state, "Mary has two candies. Bob gives her two more candies. How many candies does Mary have *altogether*?" Similarly, teachers may tell children that the "cue words" *left, gave away, ate,* and *lost* signal subtraction (Parmar & Cawley, 1994).

Rather than relying on cue words, these authors, among others, suggest that word problems about familiar subjects become the basis for learning computational skills in context from the first day of school (Cawley, Baker-Kroczynski, Urban, 1992; Cawley, Miller & School, 1987; Cawley & Parmar, 1992; National Council of Teachers of Mathematics, 1989). Although instruction should begin with direct word problems using relatively simple sentence structures, students need systematic instruction in more difficult word problems, including those that have an operation inconsistent with the "cue words" (e.g., "The girl had 3 apples left after she gave 2 apples to the boy. How many apples did the girl start with?"), those that require more than one step to solve (e.g., indirect problems such as "Mary had five candies after Bob gave her three. How many candies did Mary have before Bob gave her some?"), and those that contain extraneous information (Parmar & Cawley, 1994).

Cawley and Miller (1986) also suggest that teachers group story problems around familiar themes and that they use a series of questions to focus children's attention on the important information stated within the problem. Pictures and manipulatives can be used as aids to help children visualize and represent the actions within each word problem. According to Jitendra, Hoff, and Beck (1999), students with mild disabilities can learn to use schema-based strategies for problem solving. That is, they can draw diagrams to "map out" important information in particular types of word problems, facilitating the translation of these into equations to solve.

On the other hand, Stein (1987) applies the principles of effective instruction to the teaching of word problems. She maintains that students must learn rules and strategies for attacking word problems as teachers present carefully sequenced examples. According to Stein, Rule One is to determine whether or not the "big number" is given in the problem. If that number is not given, the operation is either addition or multiplication. If the big number is given, subtraction is used. Thus, in the problem "Doug has three dogs. He gives one dog to his best friend, Pete. How many dogs does Doug have now?" "three" is the "big number" that is given, resulting in subtraction as the chosen operation. Similarly, Rule Two is to multiply whenever a problem refers to the same number of equal-sized groups over and over again.

Although controversy exists regarding whether or not to teach children with mild disabilities to search for "cues" within word problems, numerous strategies appear in the literature. The teacher should first emphasize *understanding* the problem by re-creating it with concrete manipulatives or pictures, or engaging children in the actions detailed in the story (Cawley & Parmar, 1992). Teachers must also prepare a line of questions designed to elicit important information about the word problem as the teacher and student converse in order to transcribe information into the proper number symbols to represent the equation. Moreover, teachers must explicitly model strategies for solving word problems and give elaborated feedback to students as they problem solve. Finally, teachers can combine these techniques with strategies to help learners with mild disabilities solve word problems independently. Some of these strategies follow:

1. Study the question (Choate, 1990, p. 45)
   Scan for clues.
   Highlight the clues and the question.
   Revise the question. (Turn it into a fill-in-the-blank statement.)
   Read the statement and then reread the problem.
2. The SOLVE Strategy (Enright & Beattie, 1989, p. 58)
   Study the problem.
   Organize the facts.
   Line up a plan.
   Verify the plan/computation.
   Examine your answer.
3. The Problem Solving Prompt Card (Fleischner, Nuzum, & Marzola, 1987, p. 216)

READ	What is the question?
REREAD	What is the necessary information?
THINK	Putting together? (Add)
	Taking apart? (Subtract)
	Do I need all the information?
	Is it a two-step problem?
SOLVE	Write the equation.
CHECK	Recalculate.
	Label.
	Compare.

4. The SOLVE Strategy (Miller & Mercer, 1993)
   See the sign.
   Observe and answer (if unable to answer, keep
      going).
   Look and draw.
   Verify your answer.
   Enter your answer.

Summary

Children with mild disabilities are likely to have numerous deficits in mathematics. Related reading, handwriting, and language problems may hinder the child's progress when learning math skills and concepts. The spiral curriculum, the approach used by most of the major math textbook series, may also contribute to the difficulty that youngsters with mild disabilities experience in mathematics, particularly with the automatic recall of basic facts and the efficient execution of operations.

Students with mild disabilities must master essential skills if they are to function as independent adults. In addition to the basic facts and operations using whole numbers, fractions, and decimals, children must master concepts of money, measurement, and time to be successful in later life. One other necessary skill, problem solving, is receiving increasing emphasis in the mathematics curriculum for youngsters in special education. Several programs are available for teaching each of these essential skills to students with mild disabilities.

Some instructional procedures are useful for teaching a wide range of mathematics skills and concepts to youngsters. These include increasing the child's understanding of concepts through a concrete-to-semiconcrete-to-abstract sequence. Although teachers must help students achieve automaticity with basic facts and operations, they also must minimize rote memorization for children with mild disabilities. This can be accomplished through careful sequencing; explicit direct instruction of skills, identified by curriculum-based assessment and error analysis; and the provision of useful strategies for independent problem solving.

Other instructional procedures are specific for particular math skills and concepts. These include suggestions for teaching basic number sense and concepts like one-to-one correspondence, numeration, and place value, as well as tips for teaching basic facts and operations, complex operations and algorithms, and functional math skills.

Application Exercises

1. Assume the role of Mr. Abel during an IEP meeting for Susan. Justify the inclusion of the following provision on the IEP: Susan's use of a calculator in her math class with Mr. Mathis and her use of the calculator to complete a state-required competency test for graduation.

2. Examine two or three mathematics books used in nearby school districts. Explain the algorithms used to teach addition and subtraction with regrouping, complex multiplication, and long division. How could each of these algorithms be adapted and/or the instructional methods be changed to teach Joey and Travis these skills?

3. Make a set of base-10 blocks from paper. Illustrate how you might teach Joey and Travis to add and subtract with regrouping. Illustrate the long division problem 648 divided by 6 with the base-10 blocks. How would you explain the zero as a place holder?

4. Given the following word problem, explain how you might use manipulatives to improve Joey and Travis's performance: "Heather has eight cookies. If she has three friends, how many cookies can she give to each friend so that everyone has the same number of cookies?"

5. Select a problem-solving strategy described in this chapter. With a partner, demonstrate how you would use the strategy to teach Joey and Travis to solve the word problem in Exercise 4.

6. Using the Web sites described in Box 13.1, locate two or three lessons designed to implement the standards for a chosen grade level recommended by the National Council of Teachers of Mathematics. With a peer, review the lesson and determine what areas, if any, may be difficult for students with mild disabilities. Then, list specific suggestions to adapt or modify the lesson to meet individual student needs.

7. Browse InfoTrac for at least five articles related to the new mathematics standards. Write a statement of three or four paragraphs describing your position on the standards for students with mild disabilities. Use the articles you have located to justify your position.

CHAPTER
14

CONTENT INSTRUCTION IN THE INCLUSIVE CLASSROOM

Focus

As you read, think about the following questions:

◆ *What adaptations are "acceptable" to classroom teachers?*

◆ *What essential skills must be mastered by students with mild disabilities if they are to succeed in content-area instruction in the inclusive classroom?*

◆ *How can instruction be enhanced to support students with mild disabilities in content classrooms?*

◆ *How can textbooks, assignments, and tests be adapted to accommodate students with mild disabilities in the mainstream?*

◆ *What are some learning strategies and school survival skills that students with mild disabilities can use to enhance their performance in the classroom?*

Most low-achieving students, with or without identified disabilities, will complete much of their content-area instruction in the inclusive classroom. Often, special education teachers are not trained to teach vital content areas such as science, social studies, or health. In fact, special educators, intent on teaching the basic reading, language arts, and mathematics skills, may overlook these important areas of the curriculum (Patton, Polloway, & Cronin, 1987).

Classroom teachers, on the other hand, may be licensed to teach science, social studies, or other subject areas, but hesitate to accept students with learning and/or behavioral problems into large, heterogeneous classes. They may lack confidence in their ability to teach children with mild disabilities (Schumm, Vaughn, Gordon, & Rothlein, 1994), and often believe that these students require more instructional time than they are able to provide, given the size of many classrooms today (Martens, Peterson, Witt, & Cirone, 1986). Many classroom teachers also feel that they lack the instructional assistance necessary to support students with mild disabilities in the mainstream (Heron & Harris, 1987). Increasingly, special educators and classroom teachers must collaborate to ensure the full, successful participation of youngsters with mild disabilities in content classes. The following discussion between Mr. Abel and Mr. McNally illustrates the type of ongoing communication necessary to support students like Robert in geography class:

Mr. McNally: For Robert, Marcus, and the other students in world geography, the main concepts in Chapter 2 involve map and globe skills, as well as skill in interpreting charts and graphs. Many of my students, not just those in special education, have trouble understanding the vocabulary for this chapter.

Mr. Abel: All right. What are some of the important vocabulary terms the students need to know?

Mr. McNally: I usually require the students to know all the terms listed in the "Keys to Understanding" section at the start of each chapter. In this chapter, the vocabulary words are on page 34, and students should especially know how to use latitude and longitude to cite locations. The new words are always in boldface type when they first appear in the chapter, but the definition sometimes precedes the actual word. When the definition comes before the word itself, that's difficult for some of my students.

Mr. Abel: Robert does have difficulty with that type of text structure. I know you give students a study guide for each chapter. Would it be possible to list questions for the important terms and concepts in sequential order followed by a page number to serve as a student guide? For Robert, that would be very helpful. Also, I could teach the students a simple strategy to follow: read the question; find the page given; find the clue, like words in boldface type or headings and subheadings; skim above and below the clue for the answer; and finally, write the answer.

Mr. McNally: That sounds reasonable. Here's the study guide I've used before. I'll redo this using the page numbers.

Mr. Abel: Okay. You may want to put the steps of the strategy at the top of the study guide, too. When do you plan to begin the chapter?

Mr. McNally:	I'll introduce the chapter Wednesday, but I won't use the study guide until Thursday. I think it's a good idea to put the steps of the strategy on the study guide like you suggested. I think I'll do that.
Mr. Abel:	Okay. I'd like to start working with the students in class tomorrow on the study guide strategy. Can we plan in some time for that?
Mr. McNally:	Sure. Let's take some time at the start of the class period tomorrow. We'll be in a transition between topics anyway, so introducing the strategy then makes sense to me.
Mr. Abel:	Okay. I'll be ready. I think we need to give the students an overview of the upcoming topic so they'll see how everything is related. Also, we might want to start out having students discuss what they already know about latitude, longitude, and other concepts from the chapter before we actually begin.

Classroom teachers, like Mr. McNally, may be quite willing to adapt instruction to accommodate the needs of students with mild disabilities in the mainstream if they believe that the suggested intervention is likely to be effective (Whinnery, Fuchs, & Fuchs, 1991). However, because of limited time and resources across grade levels, regular educators consider most adaptations to be more desirable than feasible. According to Schumm and Vaughn (1991), adaptations involving the mainstreamed student in *whole-class* activities with positive reinforcement and encouragement are, not surprisingly, viewed more favorably by regular classroom teachers than are those adaptations requiring adjustment of long-range plans, materials, or scoring/grading criteria on an individual basis. Teachers are apparently unlikely to alter whole-group instructional strategies for individual students (Scott, Vitale, & Masten, 1998).

According to Fuchs, Fuchs, Hamlett, Phillips, and Karns (1995), teachers set instructional and classroom management routines early in the school year. These routines facilitate instruction but make flexibility and instructional adaptations difficult. Interventions that are the "least invasive," involving the fewest changes in the regular classroom routine while helping many students simultaneously, are those most likely to be embraced by teachers (Reisberg & Wolf, 1988). Thus, at the elementary and secondary levels, shortened assignments, preferential seating, peer-mediated instruction, and oral testing are examples of instructional modifications that many classroom teachers find "reasonable" (Bacon & Schulz, 1991).

In addition, teachers demonstrate distinct patterns in the types of modifications they use in the classroom according to the grade level they teach or the expectations they hold for students (Gelzheiser, Meyers, Slesinski, Douglas, & Lewis, 1997). Teachers at the secondary level, for example, are less likely to use small-group or individualized instructional adaptations than are teachers at the elementary level. Similarly, teachers who have uniform expectations regarding the performance of all students in the classroom are less likely to vary instructional arrangements to meet the needs of specific students than are those who have individualized expectations.

When recommending instructional modifications in the inclusive classroom, special education teachers must first understand the classroom teacher's view of the situation and what that teacher considers to be practical and possible (Margolis & McGettigan, 1988). Suggestions perceived by the regular educator as easy to employ, likely to work, and responsive to needs are accepted with the least amount of resistance. Margolis and McGettigan offer the following guidelines to assist special educators when collaborating with classroom teachers on behalf of mainstreamed youngsters:

1. Ascertain the strengths and perceived needs of the classroom teacher by observing, asking open-ended questions, and listening empathetically; .
2. Build upon what the teacher knows and does well;
3. Brainstorm alternatives with the teacher so that he or she becomes a central figure in the decision-making process and "owns" the modifications selected;
4. Provide support and feedback as instructional modifications are implemented;
5. Encourage teachers to change and adapt strategies to suit their teaching styles; and
6. Give teachers positive recognition for their efforts. (See Chapter 4 for additional suggestions for communicating with classroom teachers.)

According to Cohen and Lynch (1991), classroom teachers have a wide range of modification options from which to choose. These include modifying the physical and/or social environment of the classroom, altering the lesson structure or objective, selecting materials and activities to meet the needs of individual students, and changing the classroom-management or evaluation procedures used. The task of the special education teacher is to assist the regular educator in determining whether or not a problem exists, to clearly define the problem, and to select a modification that will be under the classroom teacher's control and within his or her level of comfort (Cohen & Lynch). For example, Mr. McNally might select modifications pertaining to the problem he identified from a "menu" of options and then rate the ones selected according to their likelihood of being effective (see Table 14.1 and Table 14.2). Later, after the modifications have been implemented, Mr. McNally would evaluate them along several dimensions, including degree of effectiveness, for future reference.

Table 14.1 Modification Options for the Regular Classroom: A Menu for the Teacher

1. Study carrels	11. Give both oral and written directions
2. Room dividers	12. Have student repeat directions
3. Headsets to muffle noise	13. Have student repeat lesson objective
4. Seat child away from doors/windows	14. Ask frequent questions
5. Seat near model (student or teacher)	15. Change question level
6. Time out area	16. Change response format (e.g., from verbal to physical: from saying to pointing)
7. Rearrange student groups (according to instructional needs, role models, etc.)	17. Provide sequential directions (label as first, second, etc.)
8. Group for cooperative learning	18. Use manipulatives
9. Vary working surface (e.g., floor or vertical surface such as blackboards)	19. Alter objective criterion level
10. Simplify/shorten directions	20. Provide functional tasks (relate to child's environment)

21. Reduce number of items in a task
22. Highlight relevant words/features
23. Use rebus (picture) directions
24. Provide guided practice
25. Provide more practice trials
26. Increase allotted time
27. Use a strategy approach
28. Change reinforcers
29. Increase reinforcement frequency
30. Delay reinforcement
31. Provide error drill
32. Increase wait-time
33. Use firm-up activities
34. Use specific rather than general praise
35. Have a peer-tutor program
36. Provide frequent review
37. Have student summarize at end of lesson
38. Use self-correcting materials
39. Adapt test items for differing response modes
40. Provide mnemonic devices
41. Provide tangible reinforcers
42. Use behavioral contracts
43. Establish routines for handing work in, heading papers, etc.
44. Use timers to show allotted time
45. Teach self-monitoring
46. Provide visual cues (posters, desktop number lines, etc.)
47. Block out extraneous stimuli on written material
48. Tape record directions
49. Tape record student responses
50. Use a study guide
51. Provide critical vocabulary list for content material
52. Provide essential fact list
53. Use clock faces to show classroom routine times
54. Use dotted lines to line up math problems or show margins
55. Use cloze procedure to test comprehension
56. Provide transition directions
57. Assign only one task at a time
58. Provide discussion questions before reading
59. Use word markers to guide reading

60. Alter sequence of presentation
61. Enlarge or highlight key words on test items
62. Provide daily and weekly assignment sheets
63. Post daily/weekly schedule
64. Use graph paper for place value or when adding/subtracting 2-digit numbers, or turn notebook paper horizontally
65. Provide anticipation cues
66. Establish rules and review frequently
67. Teach key direction words
68. Use distributed practice
69. Provide pencil grips
70. Tape paper to desk
71. Shorten project assignment into daily tasks
72. Segment directions
73. Number (order) assignments to be completed
74. Change far-point to near-point material for copying or review
75. Put desk close to blackboard
76. Incorporate currently popular themes/ characters into assignments for motivation
77. Repeat major points
78. Use physical cues while speaking (1, 2, 3, etc.)
79. Pause during speaking
80. Use verbal cues ("don't write this down; this is important")
81. Change tone of voice, whisper, etc.
82. Use an honor system
83. Collect notebooks weekly (periodically) to review student notes
84. Reorganize tests to go from easy to hard
85. Color code place value tasks
86. Use self-teaching materials
87. Do only odd- or even-numbered items on a large task sheet
88. Use a large print font to create written material
89. Provide organizers (cartons/bins) for desk material
90. Teach varied reading rates (scanning, skimming, etc.)
91. Provide content/lecture summaries

From: Cohen, S.B., & Lynch, D.K. (1991). Instructional Modification Menu, Unpublished Manuscript. Reprinted with permission.

Table 14.2 A Modification Rating Scale

Directions: Rate the modification according to the value given for each item. Priority should be given to those items receiving the highest total scores.

1. In my estimation the potential impact of this modification is (1 low–5 high)	1	2	3	4	5
2. In my experience the use of the modification has been successful (1 seldom–5 often)	1	2	3	4	5
3. I feel comfortable in my ability to apply this modification (1 strongly disagree–5 strongly agree)	1	2	3	4	5
4. The estimated time needed for this modification to be effective is (1 long–5 short)	1	2	3	4	5
5. The number of additional resources needed to implement this modification is (1 many–5 few)	1	2	3	4	5

Total score _____

Modification	Total Score	Ranking
_____	_____	_____
_____	_____	_____
_____	_____	_____
_____	_____	_____
_____	_____	_____

From: Cohen, S.B., & Lynch, D.K. (1991). An instructional modification process. *Teaching Exceptional Children*, 23, p. 15. Copyright © 1991 by the Council for Exceptional Children. Reprinted with permission.

Special education teachers also must consider how their students feel about instructional modifications. Feedback from mainstreamed students with mild disabilities and their peers regarding the "acceptability" of various accommodation strategies may help the teachers select strategies and implement them to the best advantage. In fact, Schumm and Vaughn (1991) report that students perceive teacher adaptations in instructional procedures, student grouping, and special assistance positively. On the other hand, they view adaptations of assignments, tests, and textbooks negatively. Apparently, students view adaptations as being unfair when they change or shorten an assignment or change the way in which grades are determined because these adaptations help students who might not deserve better grades to get them anyway (Bursuck, Munk, & Olson, 1999; Polloway, Bursuck, Jayanthi, Epstein, & Nelson, 1996). Conversely, making changes in the response mode (e.g., giving oral tests or assignments) or giving extra help are seen as positive accommodations that help students learn. Students with mild disabilities want to be like their peers. If students and teachers are to use adaptations when appropriate in the content classroom, special educators must consider student preferences and needs, as well as those of the classroom teacher.

Finally, special education teachers must assess the student's ability to meet regular classroom demands (Putnam, 1992a, 1992b). Asking Robert specific questions about how his teachers teach, evaluating him in content classes, and observing how he prepares for and takes tests may give Mr. Abel valuable information for helping Robert perform successfully in those classes. Mr. Abel may ascertain, for example, the types of tests that are given and the relative importance of tests, notebooks, and assignments in determining grades. He may also determine Robert's reading rate and knowledge of vocabulary by having him orally read passages from the textbook and match new words to their definitions, two effective measures for predicting student performance on content-area tasks (Espin & Foegen, 1996). Moreover, informally analyzing Robert's notebook, his actual performance on tests, and his ability to use the textbook may provide Mr. Abel with data regarding effective strategies for learning that Robert may or may not be using (Wiener, 1991).

What are the essential skills needed by learners with mild disabilities if they are to succeed in the regular classroom? How can curriculum, instruction, materials, and assignments be modified to accommodate mainstreamed students? These questions are the focus for the remainder of this chapter. Although much of our discussion centers on students at the secondary level in science and social studies classes, elementary teachers may find many of the suggested modifications applicable to their students as well. In addition, most of the recommended procedures are also appropriate for content classes other than science and social studies.

Factors Affecting Success in the Regular Classroom

Before making a decision to "include" a student for content-area instruction, the Individualized Education Program (IEP) team must consider the demands of a *specific* classroom environment, the ability of the student to meet those demands, and the types of supports necessary (Monda-Amaya, Dieker, & Reed, 1998). To be successful in the regular classroom, youngsters with mild disabilities must possess not only adequate academic skills but also certain "school survival skills" and learning strategies. In addition, the regular curriculum must be well organized and the instructional methods appropriate for students with mild disabilities.

School Survival Skills

Students with mild disabilities may lack many of the so-called school survival skills that seem to come naturally for "good" students. Many of these skills are nonacademic. For example, in a survey of skills critical for school success (Schaeffer, Zigmond, Kerr, & Farra, 1990), principals, teachers, and students listed the following six items as most important:

1. Going to class each day.
2. Being on time to school.
3. Bringing pencils, paper, and books to class.
4. Turning work in on time.
5. Talking to teachers without using "back talk."
6. Reading and following directions.

Similarly, regular classroom teachers consider vital for success in the mainstream such nonacademic skills as asking for help when needed, interacting appropriately with peers and teachers, obeying classroom rules, following oral and written instructions, attending class, beginning tasks promptly, and working independently. Employers, too, expect similar attitudes and behaviors from their employees. Unfortunately, special educators and classroom teachers sometimes differ in their perceptions of the degree to which students with mild disabilities possess these critical school survival skills (Downing, Simpson, & Myles, 1990). That is, a youngster may demonstrate these skills within the special education classroom, but fail to generalize or transfer them to the regular classroom.

Moreover, students with mild disabilities may receive more positive teacher attention and feedback in the special education classroom than in the content classroom (Baker & Zigmond, 1990). Because feedback and praise are related to a child's performance, students must be taught how to obtain positive attention from their teachers. According to Alber, Heward, and Hippler (1999), when students with mild disabilities are taught how to recruit positive teacher attention, the rate of instructional feedback received by students increases, as does the accuracy with which they complete their work.

Academic Skills and Learning Strategies

Although many special education students, particularly those with learning disabilities, may be able to get passing grades in their content-area classes, they may not learn or perform well in these classes (Rieth & Polsgrove, 1994). For example, Donahoe and Zigmond (1990) found that ninth-grade youngsters with learning disabilities received lower grades than did low-achieving peers in the same mainstreamed social studies and health classes. Both groups, however, received primarily below C-level grades in science. Astoundingly, 20% of the students with learning disabilities failed the ninth grade, while 79% earned a D or lower in social studies, 69% earned a D or below in science, and 63% received a D or lower in health. These grades do not reflect the intelligence and potential for success of most youngsters with learning disabilities.

Similarly, students with mild disabilities, particularly those with learning disabilities, are retained in grades at a higher rate than those who have not been labeled (McLeskey, Lancaster, & Grizzle, 1995). Immaturity, social/behavioral problems, and low academic achievement make students with mild disabilities more likely than peers to be retained in one or more grades. Yet, retention in a grade is not related to improved academic performance, but rather to the risk of dropping out of school.

Apparently, many students with mild disabilities exhibit academic deficits that impede their progress in the mainstream. In fact, some students with severe deficits in reading may make virtually no progress in the regular classroom (Klingner, Vaughn, Hughes, Schumm, & Elbaum, 1998). Warner, Schumaker, Alley, and Deshler (1980) note that many students with learning disabilities plateau at about the fourth- to sixth-grade level in reading and mathematics by grade 10. These students may not be able to read content-area textbooks, to listen and take notes in class, to produce coherent written work, or to take tests.

Furthermore, students with mild disabilities may lack the experiences, vocabulary, and study strategies necessary for school success. Yet, Moran (1980) reports that teachers often rely on lectures, textbooks, and written tests as the primary means of delivering and evaluating instruction in content-area classrooms. Teachers expect students to read at grade level, obtain information from the textbook and lectures, and memorize this material for tests. Unfortunately, these are all language-based skills with which students with mild disabilities have considerable difficulty and that hinder their progress in content-area classes (Parmar, Deluca, & Janczak, 1994).

Donahoe and Zigmond (1990) suggest that the typical resource-room program at the high school level, one in which students receive remedial instruction in English, reading, or mathematics, may not be providing youngsters with the learning strategies they need to be successful in the regular curriculum. In addition, departmental models, in which special education teachers provide instruction in science, social studies, and other content areas, may violate standards for accreditation and licensure if teachers are leading classes outside their area of expertise. Finally, classroom teachers may not be receiving the support they need to adapt instruction for their special learners.

According to Ellis (1997, 1998), rather than adapting instruction for students with mild disabilities, a practice which he believes often results in lowered expectations and performance, support should be provided to help teachers "water up" the curriculum for adolescents with mild disabilities. In a watered-up curriculum, topics are covered in depth, students construct their own knowledge and elaborate on their learning, and more emphasis is placed on understanding broad concepts and patterns and relating knowledge to real-world contexts. In addition, students are expected to develop higher-order thinking skills and learning strategies. Of critical importance, then, is the nature of the regular classroom curriculum and whether or not the "standard" curriculum is appropriate for students with mild disabilities and their low-achieving peers (Gersten, 1998).

The Standard Curriculum and Instructional Approaches

As in mathematics, professionals in the areas of science and social studies are debating what and how to teach their discipline as new national standards are developed and implemented in the schools (see, for example, Wineburg, 1999, for a discussion of debates regarding the history standards). The National Science Teachers Association (NSTA) recommends that science instruction should be activity-driven and inquiry-based (Doran & Sentman, 1994). Rather than teaching scientific areas as discrete topics with little depth, the NSTA suggests that broad themes such as *systems* or *change* should be emphasized, purposefully integrated, and explored in depth. Similarly, the National Council for the Social Studies (NCSS) suggests ten themes such as *culture* and *global connections* for providing integrated and meaningful instruction in social studies. (See Box 14.1 for Web sites containing information on standards for teaching social studies, history, and science.)

Box 14.1

Web Watch

Standards and Instructional Methods for Science, Social Studies, and History

Center for Civic Education

http://www.civiced.org
Standards, links to related sites, activities and lesson plans.

History/Social Studies Web Site for K-12 Teachers

http://www.execpc.com/~dboals/boals.html
Many different lesson plans, activities, and suggestions for history and social studies teachers across the grade levels.

National Center for History in the Schools

http://www.sscnet.ucla.edu/nchs/
Standards, links to other related sites, activities and lesson plans.

National Center to Improve the tools of Educators (NCITE)

http://www.darkwing.uoregon.edu/~ncite/index.html
A site offering six major principles of instructional design that can be applied to varied content areas. Practices for improving instructional tools such as textbooks, videodisks, multimedia systems, and other curricular materials.

National Council for Geographic Education

http://www.ncge.org
Activities, lesson plans, related links, standards

National Council for the Social Studies (NCSS)

http://www.ncss.org
Standards, links to other related sites, activities and lesson plans.

National Council on Economic Education

http://www.nationalcouncil.org
Links to related sites, standards, activities and lesson plans.

National Science Teachers Association (NSTA)

http://www.nsta.org/
Resources, links to other sites, standards, lesson plans, and professional activities. The main professional site for teachers of science K-12.

Instruction in science, social studies, and other subject areas has been, and still is, dominated by daily use of the textbook (Armento, 1986; Mastropieri & Scruggs, 1994). Critics argue that this traditional instructional approach is overly dependent upon curricular materials that are often poorly organized. When combined with administrative pressure to "cover" the curriculum during an academic year and pass "high stakes" standards tests, the "textbook" approach results in superficial learning of isolated facts rather than a deeper understanding of the overall structure and related nature of the concepts involved (Kinder & Bursuck, 1991; Woodward, 1994). Thus, students with mild disabilities may fail to see the "connectedness" of the many facts they learn, soon becoming disenchanted with the endless and, for them, difficult memorization of details.

According to Gersten (1998), an overemphasis on learning the "basics" prevents many students with mild disabilities from engaging in creative and cognitively complex activities. Instead these students are exposed to an unstimulating and unmotivating curriculum. Moreover, with a focus on the lecture-textbook-written test approach to instruction, students who have difficulty reading and taking notes or tests quickly become discouraged and disengaged from learning. In effect, they lack meaningful access to the more challenging curriculum offered to their nondisabled peers.

Although a degree of rote learning of basic facts is necessary in any discipline, many authorities are now calling for a reorganization of the "standard curriculum" to promote higher-order thinking skills both for students with low achievement and for those with mild disabilities (Carnine, 1991; Ellis, 1997, 1998). Whereas current curricular materials often present content rapidly, superficially, and in a fragmented manner, a "smart" curriculum would highlight the organizational structure of a discipline so that facts always become connected for learners. As pointed out by Prawat (1989), Brophy (1990), and Carnine, all of science involves the noting of similarities and the development of interwoven networks of knowledge rather than the memorization of unrelated bits of information. These authorities suggest that if teachers teach both facts and concepts "efficiently" to all youngsters in the regular classroom, students with mild disabilities may experience a reduced memory load as new knowledge is constantly connected to old (Carnine).

For example, Kinder and Bursuck (1991, 1993) describe a unified social studies curriculum in which students are first taught a strategy for analyzing historical events according to a "problem-solutions-effects" network (see Figure 14.1). Using this framework, youngsters can see how history revolves around human reactions to problems that lead to solutions, which often lead to other problems. Moreover, these problems and solutions often involve similar issues such as economics, religion, or human rights. Also within this curriculum, students make timelines for historical events, learn a strategy for defining vocabulary from the textbook, and are continually challenged by the question *why* to explain their statements.

Similarly, in two videodisc programs, *Earth Science* and *Understanding Chemistry and Energy*, both available from Systems Impact, Woodward and Noell (1991) illustrate how seemingly unrelated facts in science can become integrated as concepts for low-achieving students. For example, when students understand how convection cells work, they can apply this knowledge to understanding movement in the atmosphere, the ocean, or the Earth's mantle because this link is made explicit for them. Thus, youngsters with mild disabilities can be challenged to use higher-order thought processes to solve complex problems through deductive reasoning.

```
                    CHAPTER 4  MAKING A LIVING
                    SECTION 2  COLONIAL TRADE

        Problem                Solution                  Effect

 England was unhappy    The Navigation Acts        The shipbuilding grew.
   cause Dutch was      They started a thing called   They had to sell their
   getting all the        the Navigation acts they    goods for lower prices.
   money.                 said.                        Had to pay more for
                       1. The English ships had        foreign goods.
                          to carry all goods
                       2. They had to sell the
                          goods only to England
                       3. They put a tax on some
                          goods shipped from
                          foreign colonies

 The colonists had to   They smuggled goods in     Englands too far away
   pay more than what     and out of the USA.        to stop them.
   they got back.
```

FIGURE 14.1 ───◆

Problems-Solutions-Effect Framework From: Kinder, D., & Bursuck, W. (1991).
The search for a unified social studies curriculum: Does history really repeat itself?
Journal of Learning Disabilities, 24, p. 274. Copyright © 1991 by PRO-ED, Inc. Reprinted
with permission.

In addition, authorities recommend that instruction be *situated* or *anchored* in a real-world problem to solve (see, for example, Ferretti & Okolo, 1996; Gersten, 1998; Gersten & Baker, 1998; McCleery & Tindal, 1999). After viewing a videodisc of the film "To Kill a Mockingbird," for example, Kinzer, Gabella, and Rieth (1994) anchored abstract concepts discussed during the year, such as justice and equality, to specific events in the movie. Similarly, Hollingsworth and Woodward (1993) taught important biology and health concepts to adolescents with learning disabilities by giving them scenarios or health profiles of various individuals. The students were to describe and prioritize the problems and then offer steps to be taken to avert serious difficulty later.

As teachers implement new standards to promote higher-order thinking and learning, many will move away from textbooks and adopt curricular materials using an inquiry, or discovery, approach to instruction. In this approach, the teacher serves as a facilitator, guiding children to ask questions, discover solutions to real-world problems, and formulate generalizations. Although inquiry approaches to instruction in science and social studies create more "student-directed" opportunities for learning, most youngsters with mild disabilities do not learn well inductively (Carnine, 1991). For these students, an inquiry approach may still result in children learning isolated bits of information, with no understanding of how this information is connected. Moreover, students with mild disabilities often lack vocabulary and background information necessary for understanding complex social or scientific concepts, and they have trouble organizing information and persisting to complete difficult tasks.

To overcome these challenges, professionals recommend teachers combine anchored or situated learning with explicit instruction (Gersten & Baker, 1998; McCleery & Tindal, 1999). Thus, special educators can provide instructional support for students with mild disabilities in the content classroom by:

- Preteaching important vocabulary prior to its use in a lesson.
- Preteaching important rules, strategies, or essential facts explicitly.
- Helping classroom teachers identify, organize, and connect the "big ideas" (Kameenui & Carnine, 1998) or important concepts to be learned through procedural facilitators such as graphic organizers, flow charts, mnemonics, or content enhancement routines (Ellis, 1997; Tralli, Colombo, Deshler, & Schumaker, 1996).
- Providing explicit guidance, or scaffolding, to students during anchored or situated learning activities.
- Providing sufficient review following a lesson to ensure that material is learned and maintained.

Although many students with mild disabilities can be challenged to demonstrate higher-order thinking skills, the reader must remember that a "connected" curriculum, such as those just described, will not be appropriate for all youngsters in special education programs. Activity-oriented instructional approaches will necessitate *increased* support for special education students in the mainstream (Mastropieri & Scruggs, 1994), as well as altered forms of assessing instructional outcomes (Tindal, Rebar, Nolet, & McCollum, 1995). Moreover, such curricula are only now in the formative stages. Until "user-friendly" curricula are developed, special educators will still need to help classroom teachers adapt textbooks, tests, instructional presentations, and assignments while simultaneously teaching students with mild disabilities those learning strategies and school survival skills essential for their successful performance in a particular classroom environment.

Adapting Instruction, Textbooks, Tests, and Assignments

After a decision has been made to include a student with mild disabilities into the regular classroom for science, social studies, health, or any other content area, the special education teacher must not assume that instruction then becomes the sole responsibility of the classroom teacher. Although not all youngsters with mild disabilities will require modifications in order to achieve in the regular classroom, the special educator must ensure that those who do are given the special assistance they need. Moreover, special education teachers have an obligation to assist and support regular classroom teachers in providing necessary modifications to ensure that the quality of education received by *all* youngsters in the classroom will remain high. Teachers must, of course, be provided with adequate time to plan together, as well as individually, and they must specify their roles and responsibilities clearly (see Chapter 4).

Fortunately, those modifications designed to help students with mild disabilities perform successfully in the regular classroom often help other children as well. These include adapting the instructional presentation, adapting the textbook, and modifying assignments and/or tests.

Adapting Instruction

How teachers organize and present information in the content classroom profoundly affects student learning. Typically, teachers at the secondary level convey information through lectures, discussions, group projects, and supportive media such as videotapes or computer software programs. Teachers who engage in certain content enhancement routines, procedures to organize learning and present concepts, can improve learning for their students (Tralli et al., 1996). The following suggestions may help classroom teachers adapt their instructional presentations to suit the needs of learners with mild disabilities.

Advance organizers and organizational routines. Advance organizers refer to preteaching events that structure the learning situation (Ausubel & Robinson, 1969) and provide for low-achieving students a framework for integrating new knowledge with old. They also can involve steps taken by students themselves to organize for learning. Teachers can provide structure for learning in numerous ways, some of which are listed in Table 14.3.

Advance organizers, then, can be visual reminders (e.g., a topical outline on the board) or verbal statements made by the teacher regarding the task or topic. In addition, according to Tralli, Columbo, Deshler, and Schumaker (1996), teachers can use four different organizational strategies as content enhancement routines to facilitate learning:

- ◆ A Course Organizer Routine to show students the "big ideas" and the plan for units to be covered during the course;
- ◆ A Unit Organizer Routine (Boudah, Lenz, Bulgren, Schumaker, & Deshler, 2000) to show how a unit relates to the overall course and to illustrate relationships among major parts within the unit;
- ◆ A Chapter Survey Routine to orient students to a new chapter in the textbook; and
- ◆ A Lesson Organizer Routine to orient students to an upcoming lesson, to illustrate the relationship between the new lesson and other lessons, and to highlight the major parts of the lesson.

Lenz, Alley, and Schumaker (1987), for example, used advance organizers to help secondary-level content-area teachers improve the quality of their instruction, as well as the performance of their students with learning disabilities. First, however, the students themselves had to be trained to recognize and to use the advance organizers provided by their teachers. To train students, Mr. McNally might organize his geography lesson by placing a topical outline on an overhead transparency, by referring to previous learning and the topic for the current class session, by saying, for example, "This is important," or by using words like *first, next,* and *finally* throughout the discussion. In addition, Mr. McNally might write important vocabulary or concepts on the overhead as he talks and remind students to write these on their own copies of the outline. If Robert does not recognize these organizational clues, however, he cannot use them to his advantage

Table 14.3 Suggestions for Advance Organizers

Lenz, Alley, and Schumaker (1987, p. 56) suggest that teachers use the following behaviors as advance organizers to structure learning for students in their content area classrooms:

1. Tell the learner the purpose for the advance organizer;
2. Clarify the actions to be taken by the teacher;
3. Clarify the actions to be taken by the students;
4. Identify the topic for the learning task;
5. Identify the subtopics related to the learning task;
6. Provide essential background information;
7. State the concepts to be learned;
8. Clarify the concepts to be learned through examples, nonexamples, or cautions about possible errors;
9. Motivate students to learn by pointing out relevance to their lives;
10. Introduce and repeat new vocabulary;
11. Give students an organizational framework for the learning task such as an outline, a list, or a general overview of the topic presented verbally/visually; and,
12. State the outcomes expected from the learning activity.

to facilitate learning. Thus, Mr. Abel might support Mr. McNally's instruction by teaching Robert the importance of the advance organizers used in his classes.

When teachers present well-organized lectures and discussions, student learning and note taking become easier. In addition to providing written outlines, teachers can improve their lesson effectiveness by preteaching vocabulary, writing important terms or directions on the chalkboard, varying their voice tone and position in the classroom as they make key points, raising questions to test comprehension, pausing periodically to allow students to ask questions or to write important information in their notes, and using pictures or diagrams to represent the relationships among key ideas and concepts.

Graphic organizers and concept routines. In our previous discussion regarding the science and social studies curriculum, we noted the importance of explicitly linking facts in order to build concepts and promote higher-order thinking skills. One way to accomplish this task is through the use of graphic organizers (Anders & Bos, 1984; Dye, 2000). Graphic organizers sometimes take the form of flow charts and timelines (Donahue & Baumgartner, 1997) or *semantic maps* (Pearson & Johnson, 1978). In addition, content enhancement routines such as *concept diagrams* (Bulgren, Schumaker, & Deshler, 1988; Tralli et al., 1996) can be used to introduce new concepts, to tie new concepts to those already known, and to compare and contrast concepts. Graphic organizers and concept routines involve visual displays clearly representing the relationships among the facts, vocabulary, and concepts to be developed (see Figures 14.2 and 14.3).

To prepare a graphic organizer or concept diagram, the teacher must first precisely state the concepts to be learned. Next, the teacher must list all vocabulary or facts that learners must know in order to understand the

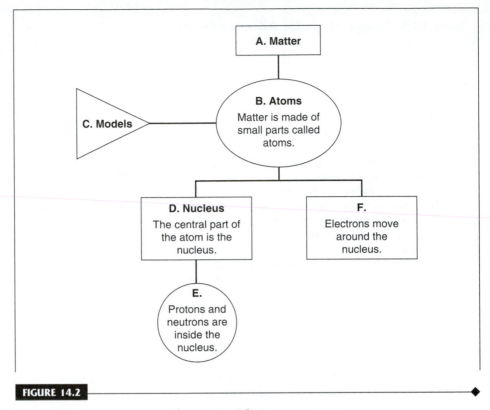

FIGURE 14.2

A Graphic Organizer on the Topic of Matter From: Kameenui, E.J., &
Simmons, D.C. (1990). Designing instructional strategies: The prevention of learning
problems. Columbus, OH: Merrill, p. 335. Reprinted with permission.

concept. McKeown and Beck (1988) suggest that teachers focus on important
terms that are related not only to the specific concept, but also to other concepts and lessons within the discipline. For example, as illustrated in Figure
14.1, rather than learning about the Navigation Acts or the Stamp Act as separate facts or events, the student would gain an understanding of the larger
concept: The basic problem leading to the American Revolution was that
Great Britain wanted control of production, taxation, and navigation in order
to benefit economically from the colonies (Kinder & Bursuck, 1991). The
problem-solutions-effects framework serves as one vehicle for graphically
representing this concept.

Once the teacher has selected the important concepts and related vocabulary, these are arranged visually to highlight their relationships. The
teacher might, for example, construct a concept diagram illustrating characteristics that "always," "sometimes," and "never" relate to the concept of
democracy. The teacher might also state examples of democracy and compare and contrast these with other forms of government. Bulgren,
Schumaker, and Deshler (1988) improved the performance in their content
classes of high school students with learning disabilities by using the

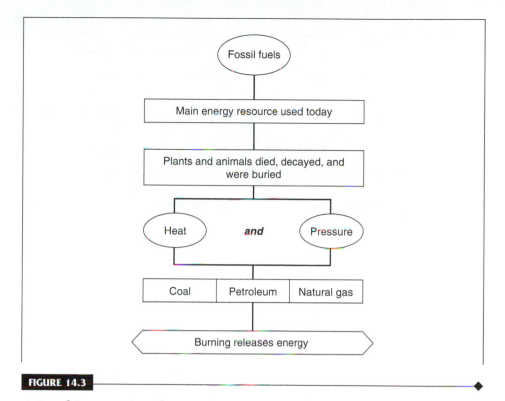

FIGURE 14.3

A Graphic Organizer from Robert's Science Class From: Kameenui, E.J., &
Simmons, D.C. (1990). Designing instructional strategies: The prevention of learning
problems. Columbus, OH: Merrill, p. 357. Reprinted with permission.

concept diagram illustrated in Figure 14.4. When using this diagram, the authors suggest that teachers incorporate the following instructional routine:

1. Provide the advance organizer.
2. Elicit from the students a list of keywords from the chapter and write the
   words on the board.
3. Review the symbols on the concept diagram.
4. Name the concept.
5. Define the concept.
6. Discuss the "always" characteristics.
7. Discuss the "sometimes" characteristics.
8. Discuss the "never" characteristics.
9. Discuss one example of the concept.
10. Discuss one nonexample of the concept.
11. Link the example to each of the characteristics.
12. Link the nonexample to each of the characteristics.
13. Test potential examples and nonexamples to determine whether or not they
    are members of the concept class.
14. Provide a postorganizer.

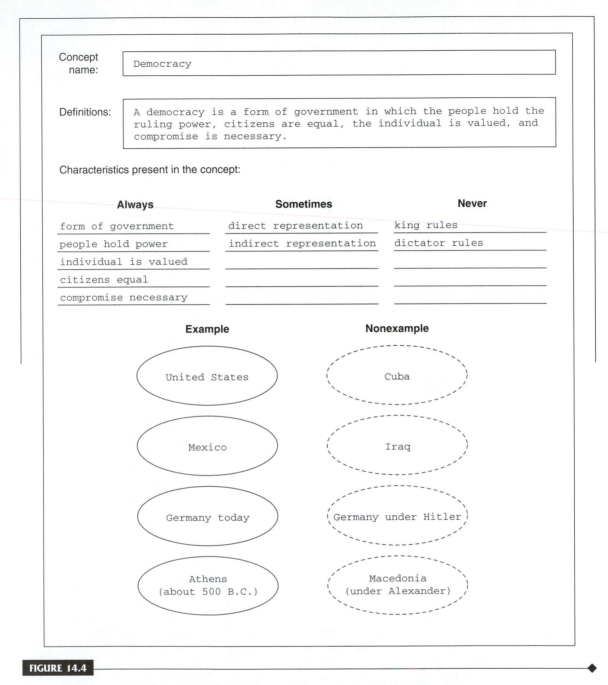

Concept name: Democracy

Definitions: A democracy is a form of government in which the people hold the ruling power, citizens are equal, the individual is valued, and compromise is necessary.

Characteristics present in the concept:

Always	Sometimes	Never
form of government	direct representation	king rules
people hold power	indirect representation	dictator rules
individual is valued		
citizens equal		
compromise necessary		

Example

United States

Mexico

Germany today

Athens (about 500 B.C.)

Nonexample

Cuba

Iraq

Germany under Hitler

Macedonia (under Alexander)

FIGURE 14.4

A Concept Diagram from Social Studies From: Bulgren, J., Schumaker, J.B., & Deshler, D.D. (1988). Effectiveness of a concept teaching routine in enhancing the performance of LD students in secondary level mainstream classes. *Learning Disability Quarterly, 11,* pp. 5-6. Reprinted with permission.

Secondary-level classroom teachers expressed satisfaction with the concept diagrams and concept teaching routines (Bulgren, Schumaker, & Deshler, 1988). When they completed blank concept diagrams on the chalkboard or on an overhead transparency as they progressed through the concept teaching routine, they also facilitated note taking by students who completed identical diagrams individually.

Ellis (1997) also describes methods for constructing semantic maps and concept diagrams. When using semantic maps, Ellis suggests that teachers place the topic name on a "sticky note." Students are then placed in small groups,

Computer software enhances science and geography lessons and gives the teacher a tool for producing study guides and test questions.

given pads of sticky notes and asked to brainstorm words or ideas they know about the topic. After the groups write one word or idea on each sticky note, the teacher gathers them and places them in a column on the chalkboard. Students are asked to explain an item from the column and suggest where it might belong relative to the main topic. The sticky notes are rearranged, combined, and added to as the topic under study is developed.

To construct concept diagrams, Ellis (1997) suggests looking for archetypal patterns to illustrate. He calls one of these the *Tension/Reaction/Spin-off Tensions* pattern. For example, events in history, economics, and politics are often the result of tensions, which result in certain reactions that create additional spin-offs resulting in other tensions. Students can be taught to analyze events through this archetypal pattern and link historical or other events in "flow chart" style.

Similarly, Bos and her colleagues used an interactive teaching strategy, the semantic feature analysis, to improve the vocabulary and reading comprehension of high school students with learning disabilities in their special education social studies classes (Bos, Anders, Filip, & Jaffe, 1989). Teachers first listed key concepts and vocabulary from the text and arranged these on a relationship chart (see Figure 14.5). The superordinate concept became the name of the chart, the coordinate concepts (the important ideas) became the column heads, and the subordinate concepts and terms (related vocabulary) formed the left-hand column, or stub.

To implement the interactive teaching strategy using the semantic feature analysis, Mr. Abel gave each of his students a copy of the relationship chart and also drew the chart on an overhead transparency. He then introduced the chart by its title and helped his students define all important ideas and related vocabulary. As students defined the vocabulary, they predicted the relationship between the vocabulary and each important idea as positive, negative, no relationship, or unknown. When the class achieved consensus on the relationship, it was recorded on the chart. Later, Mr. Abel's students read content-area passages to confirm or clarify predictions and amended their relationship charts.

According to Bos, Anders, Filip, and Jaffe (1989), students with learning disabilities who completed the semantic feature analysis evidenced superior performance on a multiple-choice comprehension test when compared with a group of peers who looked up the vocabulary words in a dictionary and wrote sentences using the terms. The authors suggested that the interactive nature of the strategy may help students with learning disabilities overcome their "passive" approach to learning, as well as facilitate storage and retrieval of information from memory.

Mnemonics. Teachers can make use of various mnemonics to help learners with mild disabilities actively store information in memory and retrieve it. For example, Mr. McNally might give his students a first-letter acronym, HOMES, to help them remember the names of the Great Lakes (i.e., **H**uron, **O**ntario, **M**ichigan, **E**rie, and **S**uperior). Similarly, Ms. Stone might give the students in her ninth-grade earth science class a first-letter acronym for remembering the planets by using the sentence, "Mary's violet eyes make John stay up nights permanently." Although first-letter acronyms are well-known devices, other

IMPORTANT IDEAS

LEGEND:
+ = Positive relationship
− = Negative relationship
0 = No relationship
? = Uncertain

RELATED VOCABULARY

	Citizen's right to privacy *versus* Society needs to keep law and order		Police search with a search warrant	Police search without a search warrant	Evidence allowed in court
search and seizure					
unreasonable search and seizure					
probable cause to search					
your property and possessions					
absolute privacy					
you give consent					
hot pursuit					
moving vehicle					
stop-and-frisk					
plain view					
during an arrest					
evidence					
exclusionary rule					

FIGURE 14.5

A Semantic Relationship Chart From: Bos, C.S., Anders, P.L., Filip, D., & Jaffe, L.E. (1989). The effects of an interactive instructional strategy for enhancing reading comprehension and content area learning for students with learning disabilities. *Journal of Learning Disabilities, 22,* p. 386. Copyright © 1989 by PRO-ED, Inc. Reprinted with permission.

mnemonic strategies include the keyword method, reconstructive elaborations, and the pegword method.

In the keyword method, students form mental pictures in which new information to be learned is related in an unusual manner to known information in order to form an association for memory. The keyword is often an acoustic reconstruction. That is, a "sound-alike" word is used to form the mental image (Scruggs & Mastropieri, 1990). For example, to remember that *trace* means a narrow trail used by the pioneers, students might use the similar sounding but more familiar word race to form a mental image of pioneers racing on a narrow road, as shown in Figure 14.6 (Mastropieri & Scruggs, 1989a). Or, to remember that an herbivore is an animal that eats plants, students might picture animals in herds (the keyword), eating only plants (Mastropieri, Emerick, & Scruggs, 1988). Mastropieri and Scruggs (1998) and Mastropieri, Scruggs, Whittaker, and Bakken (1994) report that students successfully learn content and enjoy instruction when their teachers incorporate such mnemonic devices into lessons.

For those terms or concepts more familiar to students, mimetic, or literal representational, pictures can be used. Students may be familiar, for example, with concrete words such as *soldier* and *trench*. Thus, to remember that during World War I many soldiers became ill or died because of unhealthy living conditions in the trenches, students might simply be told to picture soldiers getting sick or dying in trenches (Mastropieri & Scruggs, 1989b). When information is more abstract, however, *reconstructive elaborations* as symbolic representations might be more useful. For example, students could picture Uncle Sam, as a symbolic representation of the United States, looking over Europe and stating, "It's not my war," in order to remember America's initial policy of neutrality during World War I.

King-Sears, Mercer, and Sindelar (1992) describe an interesting strategy for teaching students to produce keywords in science class. The authors use a

FIGURE 14.6

A Keyword Mnemonic Using an Acoustic Reconstruction From: Mastropieri, M.A., & Scruggs, T.E. (1989). Mnemonic social studies instruction: Classroom applications. *Remedial and Special Education, 10,* p. 43. Reprinted with permission.

first-letter acronym, IT FITS, to help students with mild disabilities recall the steps in the strategy:

Identify the term.
Tell the definition of the term.
Find a keyword.
Imagine the definition doing something with the keyword.
Think about the definition doing something with the keyword.
Study what you imagined until you know the definition.

Pegwords are helpful when students must remember ordered information or numbers associated with unfamiliar terms. To implement this mnemonic strategy, students first learn a rhyming poem in which familiar concrete objects are associated with numbers (e.g., one—sun or bun; two—shoe; three—bee or tree; four—door or floor; and so forth). Then, to produce the visual image, students picture the information to be remembered in association with the familiar object. For example, in Ms. Stone's earth science class, Robert might remember that wolframite is 4 on the Mohs hardness scale, is black in color, and is used for making light bulbs, by picturing a *wolf* standing on a *black floor* (i.e., the pegword for *four*) surrounded by light bulbs, as shown in Figure 14.7 (Scruggs, Mastropieri, Levin, & Gaffney, 1985).

Students with mild disabilities require explicit and structured presentations of mnemonic devices if they are to use them to increase their recall of important information in content classes. Thus, teachers should incorporate recall-enhancement routines into their lessons to help students with mild disabilities remember information and improve their performance on tests (Bulgren, Deshler, & Schumaker, 1997; Bulgren, Schumaker, & Deshler, 1994). According to Bulgren and her colleagues, Mr. McNally might use the following critical elements for the memory enhancement routine during his lesson on the Great Lakes:

- Cueing the importance of the information to be remembered ("You need to remember the names of the five Great Lakes.")
- Cueing students to write the memory device and the set of facts to be remembered in their notes ("Be sure to write the acronym and the name of each lake in your notes.")
- Naming the mnemonic device ("To remember the names of the five Great Lakes, we'll use the acronym HOMES.")
- Presenting the mnemonic device and linking it to the information to be remembered (While writing, Mr. McNally says, "H stands for Huron, O stands for Ontario, M stands for Michigan, E stands for Erie, and S stands for Superior. The acronym HOMES will help you remember the names of the Great Lakes. To remember the acronym, just think about the sentence, 'Many people build HOMES around the Great Lakes.'")
- Reviewing the mnemonic device at the end of the session (Mr. McNally asks "What device will you use to remember the names of the Great Lakes?" Then he elicits the meaning of each letter of the acronym HOMES from his students.)

Although still requiring additional research, mnemonic strategy instruction appears to hold promise for students with mild disabilities in content-area

FIGURE 14.7

Using a Pegword Mnemonic in Science From: Scruggs, T.E., Mastropieri, M.A., Levin, J.R., & Gaffney, J.S. (1985). Facilitating the acquisition of science facts in learning disabled students. *American Educational Research Journal, 22*, p. 580. Reprinted with permission.

classes (Forness, Kavale, Blum, & Lloyd, 1997; Mastropieri & Scruggs, 1988, 1998; Mastropieri, Scruggs et al., 1994; Pressley, Scruggs, & Mastropieri, 1989). In particular, mnemonic instruction appears superior to the use of visual-spatial displays and/or direct instruction alone for enhancing the memory performance of youngsters with mild disabilities (Scruggs, Mastropieri, Levin, & Gaffney, 1985; Scruggs, Mastropieri, Levin, McLoone, Gaffney, & Prater, 1985). Keywords and pegwords do, however, require students to generate and remember complex illustrations. Moreover, some abstract concepts may not lend themselves to meaningful images or pegwords likely to be retained by students. Finally, teachers may not have the time or training to implement mnemonic devices successfully in the classroom. Nevertheless, teachers should consider these strategies and use them when appropriate to facilitate learning for their students with mild disabilities.

Technology. Increasingly, teachers are using modern technology to improve instructional presentations. Traditional media, such as films or filmstrips, are rapidly being replaced by videos, videodiscs, and computer software.

Carnine (1989) describes how such technology can incorporate essential features of instructional design and mastery learning to improve the performance of students with mild disabilities in science, health, chemistry, and other cognitively complex content areas. Using a laser videodisc in earth science, for example, Ms. Stone can "play" a video, but stop instantly to display any given video frame, enabling her students to focus on key ideas. With the ease of a remote control, she can move to a new section on the videodisc to review difficult concepts, to provide students with additional information, or to engage students in simulations anchoring the concepts to real life.

Experiments or demonstrations that may be too expensive or impractical to conduct in Ms. Stone's classroom can be presented using the graphics and sound effects available on laser videodisc, CD-ROM, or the World Wide Web. Moreover, students can access up-to-date information (e.g., news reports or weather information) and numerous data banks through the Internet. Many organizations such as the National Geographic Society and NASA have interactive sites on the World Wide Web. On these sites, students can gather information, converse with other students or experts around the world, and participate in contributing data or analyzing challenging problems (see, for example, **http://www.nationalgeographic.com** or **http://www.quest.arc.nasa.gov/**).

Computer software can also be used to produce study guides and corresponding test questions. Students with learning disabilities who make use of computerized study guide questions, answers, and corresponding multiple-choice tests do better on these tests than students who use standard note-taking procedures (Lovitt & Horton, 1994).

Adapting Textbooks

Teachers value textbooks because they provide a guide for making decisions about curriculum and instruction (Bean, Zigmond, & Hartman, 1994). Classroom teachers report that they use the textbook a great deal, although they may skip sections or change the order in which information is covered. They also maintain that the readability of textbooks, particularly the vocabulary, is too difficult for their problem readers, and others critique the content stating that it "lacks meat," is boring, or covers too much information. According to Fiore and Cook (1994), the textbook adoption process frequently fails to consider the needs of students with disabilities in inclusive classrooms. Moreover, Ciborowski (1995) asserts that the teacher's editions of textbooks lack adequate suggestions for teachers as to how to motivate their students to read, comprehend, and engage in critical thinking about the topic.

Thus, content-area textbooks are currently receiving much criticism. For example, according to Beck, McKeown, and Gromoll (1989); Crabtree (1989); and Tyson and Woodward (1989), textbooks in history and social studies are poorly written and cover many topics superficially without providing analyses and connectives to tie events and concepts together for learners. Science textbooks, too, are densely packed with concepts and terms that are often not repeated, and they frequently assume considerable background knowledge that learners may or may not possess (Lovitt & Horton, 1994; Tyson & Woodward, 1989).

Teachers must not assume that textbooks prepared for a given grade level are at the appropriate reading level for students. Many factors other than sentence length and word length/difficulty affect the overall readability of a textbook. For example, well-organized texts contain clear headings, subheadings, introductory paragraphs, summary paragraphs, highlighted vocabulary or key concepts, marginal notes, and pictures, charts, and graphs related to the topic. Moreover, key concepts are linked together through connective words and phrases in order to clarify relationships in the content.

In an attempt to provide relevant and age-appropriate content-area materials that are written at an appropriate reading level for students with mild disabilities, some teachers use "high-interest/low-vocabulary" materials as a substitute for or a supplement to the regular textbook (see Table 14.4). For example, Mr. Abel might give Robert an earth science text written at the fifth-grade reading level but that covers the same ninth-grade curriculum as Ms. Stone's normal textbook. Such an approach may be appropriate for some students with mild disabilities, particularly those in departmentalized special education content classes or those with mild mental retardation. Many adolescents with mild disabilities, however, prefer to use the same text as their peers. Furthermore, reducing the reading level of the text by decreasing the sentence length, sentence complexity, and vocabulary may produce a fragmented text that is difficult to comprehend because important connective words and ideas have been eliminated (Bean et al., 1994).

To permit students with mild disabilities to read the textbook used in the regular classroom, some teachers tape record the textbook or order prerecorded versions of the text. Although recording services may require a nominal registration fee, they can provide copies of most major textbooks used in the

---

Table 14.4 Publishers of High-Interest/Low-Vocabulary Materials

Curriculum Associates
P.O. Box 2000
North Billerica, MA 01862

Fearon/Janus/Quercus
4350 Equity Drive
Columbus, OH 43228

Globe Fearon Educational Publishers
& Modern Curriculum Press
P.O. Box 2649
Columbus, OH 43216

High Noon Books
Academic Therapy Publications
20 Commercial Boulevard
Novato, CA 94949

Scholastic, Inc.
2931 E. McCarty Street
P.O. Box 7502
Jefferson City, MO 65102

Science Research Assoc.
Macmillan/McGraw-Hill
860 Taylor Station Road
P.O. Box 543
Blacklick, OH 43004

Stanfield Publishing Company
P.O. Box 41058
Santa Barbara, CA 93140
Steck-Vaughn Publishing Co.
1-800-531-5015

schools or they can make copies of texts not in frequent use. Teachers must make advanced arrangements, though, if they are to receive textbooks for their students in a timely manner. For information on one such service, contact Recordings for the Blind & Dyslexic, 20 Roszel Road, Princeton, NJ 08540 or **http://www.rfbd.org**.

Although tape recording may be a useful adaptation for some students with mild disabilities, the procedure can also be a time-consuming one for teachers. The following suggestions may be helpful for teachers who choose to record textbooks for their students:

1. Enlist the aid of student, parent, or community volunteer groups as readers.
2. Use clear directions on the tape so that students will know when to move from one page to the next or from one paragraph/section to the next.
3. Use colors or symbols to highlight important information or to indicate movement through the text.
4. Periodically pause and insert questions to keep the listener actively engaged with the text.
5. Give students an advance organizer (i.e., a topical outline or study guide) to structure the reading selection.

Many effective "textbook adaptations" are really not modifications of the textbook at all. Rather, they are changes in the teacher's instructional presentation that enhance the student's involvement with the text (see Chapter 11 for other suggestions, such as "Think-Pair-Share" and K-W-L). Teachers can begin each new chapter or section of a textbook with a systematic overview to preview the reading selection and activate background knowledge. Mr. McNally, for example, might have students in his class go through the pages of a new chapter, locating headings, subheadings, boldfaced or highlighted terms, and pictures, charts, or graphs. As students scan the text, Mr. McNally might ask, "What do you think this section will be about?" or "What do you think that word means?" He can challenge students to define vocabulary or facts they know and identify words or concepts that are unknown to them. According to Ciborowski (1995), Mr. McNally might construct a semantic map, like the one that follows, to organize vocabulary, concepts, and facts for his students prior to reading:

WORDS YOU WILL SEE IN THIS CHAPTER ON _____

People——————**Ideas**—————**Places**

_____	_____	_____
_____	_____	_____
_____	_____	_____
_____	_____	_____

Following this structured overview, the students and Mr. McNally might engage in guided reading (i.e., reading aloud) of the text selection, with Mr. McNally interjecting questions between short segments of text. To keep students actively engaged, they can be challenged to name as many facts as they can remember without looking back at the passage. As students offer information, Mr. McNally can arrange their contributions on the chalkboard in a concept diagram, flow chart, or graphic organizer to link related concepts and to facilitate note taking. Or, Mr. McNally might choose to use a cooperative learning strategy, such as Numbered Heads Together (Kagan, 1989), described in Chapter 9, to increase student involvement during textbook reading. Finally, Mr. McNally might use a pause procedure (Ruhl, Hughes, & Schloss, 1987), stopping periodically at logical points of a lecture or textbook selection while students work in pairs to clarify complex information, fill in notes/partial outlines, or complete study guides.

Study guides or graphic organizers can also help to structure textbook reading assignments and improve reading comprehension, just as they facilitate understanding during lectures or classroom discussions. Billingsley and Wildman (1988) improved the textbook comprehension of high school students with learning disabilities by giving them a structured visual overview of the major ideas in a passage prior to reading it. Similarly, Horton and Lovitt (1989) found that remedial students and youngsters with learning disabilities achieve higher social studies and science test scores when textbook reading is accompanied by study guides containing comprehension questions or graphics and visual/verbal clues, such as page numbers to locate answers (see Figure 14.8).

Lovitt and Horton (1994) suggest that the study guide is the most important tool that teachers can use to adapt the textbook. They maintain that study guides are versatile and easy to construct, particularly with computerized assistance. However, these authorities do offer six approaches for efficiently modifying instructional materials:

- ◆ Modify only the textbook chapters or passages within chapters that actually prove difficult for students or those that obviously lack organization;
- ◆ Collaborate with other teachers using the same text to divide the modification load and share materials;
- ◆ Use curriculum-based assessments before instruction to determine who can read the text and who will need materials modifications;
- ◆ Computerize the materials adaptation process in order to develop a continuous store of materials;
- ◆ Encourage coteaching of subjects so that special educators and classroom teachers can modify materials cooperatively; and
- ◆ Urge teachers on textbook adoption committees to demand that publishers offer study guides, graphic organizers, vocabulary exercises, and computer programs or other adaptations of materials in addition to the basic textbook and supplementary materials (p. 115).

Finally, when preparing study guides or other handouts for students, teachers must take care to use a readable typographic design. Hoener, Salend, and Kay (1997) recommend that teachers construct study guides with the following elements in mind:

- ◆ Fonts—Use those with which students are familiar.
- ◆ Type size—Ensure size is appropriate for grade level (e.g., 18 point for grade 1, 14 point for grade 3, 11 point for grade 6, and so forth).
- ◆ Proportional spacing—Spaces between letters vary rather than having the same spacing between all letters.

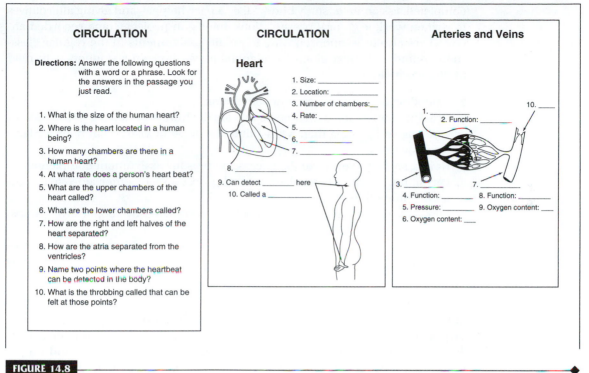

◆ Left justification—Text is justified on the left side with a "ragged" margin on the right.

◆ Boldfaced or italicized characters—Use these styles, rather than underlining, for emphasis.

◆ Contrast—Black type on white paper rather than color.

◆ Spacing—Examine carefully to ensure that there is adequate spacing between lines on the page and that all parts are clear.

Adapting Assignments and Tests and Modifying Grades

Assignments can be modified in numerous ways to suit the needs of learners with mild disabilities. For example, teachers can post directions for assignments in a designated area of the classroom and use a consistent format for written work. Obtaining attention before giving directions, providing clear examples and steps for completing the task, and clearly defining the requirements (e.g., "Your assignment is finished when all six problems have been completed, checked, and corrected.") are three additional ways to support students with mild disabilities in completing assignments. Reducing the quantity of items to be completed, assigning a "study buddy" (i.e., a peer helper), and giving alternatives to written work (e.g., oral presentations, hands-on projects, tape-recorded answers) are also time-honored ways to modify assignments in the regular classroom. Additional suggestions for adapting assignments for students with mild disabilities include:

1. Extending time for assignment completion;
2. Breaking down long assignments into small chunks, reviewing the steps with students and posting them with a timeline or other visual reminder for later reference;
3. Having students verbalize the necessary steps for assignment completion;
4. Permitting the use of calculators, word processors, or other aides to assignment completion;
5. Allowing some written assignments to be completed by cooperative groups; and
6. Reducing the amount of written material to be copied by providing the student with a copy of the text page to write on instead of having him or her copy a problem from the text.

Similarly, teachers can vary the requirements of tests used to evaluate the outcome of instruction. Some teachers give, for example, frequent small tests, or practice tests, to alleviate "test anxiety" and to review essential information. Such practice and structured study opportunities improve grades and relieve test anxiety for students with mild disabilities (Swanson & Howell, 1996). In addition, telling students the types of questions to expect on a test (i.e., true/false, multiple-choice, short-answer, matching, essay) and providing them with a study guide can help low-achieving students prepare for tests. In fact, student performance on tests can be positively influenced by structured preteaching activities, called the *learning set*, during which teachers review previous content, link the review to new material, state lesson objectives and performance expectations, and give a reason to learn the material (Hudson, 1996).

Teachers believe test modifications that are effective and easy to implement and those that maintain academic integrity to be the most acceptable (Gajria, Salend, & Hemrick, 1994). Other testing accommodations that classroom teachers may find helpful and acceptable follow:

1. Use multiple-choice items with fewer choices (e.g., three instead of four or five alternatives);
2. Arrange matching items so that related information is grouped together with no more than five or six items in a group;
3. Provide a list of terms or phrases from which students can choose for short-answer tests;
4. Provide a partial outline for students to complete when giving essay tests;
5. Permit the student to tape-record answers to test questions or take the test on a computer;
6. Underline important directions or keywords on the student's test paper;
7. Allow extended time for test taking;
8. Use clear, readable, uncluttered test forms and permit students to place answers on the test rather than on an answer sheet; and

9. Consider alternative forms of assessment, such as performance assessment or portfolios, to evaluate what the student produces or can actually do.

Of critical importance in today's world of educational reform are accommodations on "high stakes" tests for students with mild disabilities. The Individuals with Disabilities Education Act (IDEA) (1997) requires that students with disabilities participate, whenever possible, in state- or district-wide testing programs. The IEP team must decide whether or not the student will participate, and if so, what accommodations will be necessary to enable his or her participation. Generally, local or state educational agencies determine the types of accommodations or modifications permissible on large-scale assessments of student progress. Elliott, Ysseldyke, Thurlow, and Erikson (1998) suggest teachers and administrators consider three questions to ensure fairness and equity for all students taking these assessments:

1. What test accommodations does the student need to take the test without the impact of his or her disability?
2. Has the student had sufficient opportunity to learn what is on the test?
3. Does the student have the necessary test-taking skills?

Hollenbeck, Tindal, and Almond (1998) define an accommodation as a method that provides access to, but does not change, a test. On the other hand, a modification is a change in the test itself. According to Thurlow, Ysseldyke, and Silverstein (1995), much research is needed regarding the types of accommodations made for students with mild disabilities on large-scale tests and the effects of these accommodations on student performance as well as test validity.

Having an examiner orally read the test, for example, does appear to improve a student's score on state-wide tests (Tindal, Heath, Hollenbeck, Almond, & Harniss, 1998). Research suggests, however, that teachers lack knowledge of allowable accommodations, and they often do not use accommodations consistently (Hollenbeck, Tindal, & Almond, 1998). Nevertheless, teachers do frequently mention those accommodations listed in Table 14.5.

Table 14.5 Testing Accommodations

According to Hollenbeck, Tindal, and Almond (1998), teachers lack knowledge on allowable testing accommodations. Accommodations often used include:

Extending time	Reading math tests
Testing over several sessions	Providing a calculator
Testing in a separate location	Allowing arithmetic tables
Testing in a small group in a separate location	Allowing dictated responses
Minimizing distractions	Using masks or markers
Clarifying directions	Allowing an alternate response
Assisting students to understand writing prompts	Providing an alternate form
Providing a dictionary	Marking on the test booklet rather than on a
Providing a Franklin Speller	"bubble" sheet

Finally, teachers must carefully consider grading options for students with mild disabilities in inclusive classrooms. Bradley and Calvin (1998) report that many classroom teachers believe that if grading criteria are modified, the standards and course integrity suffer. Others believe that students who can't pass the class using the same materials and tests as others haven't really mastered the course content. If students with mild disabilities are to learn the content and pass the courses necessary for receiving a high school diploma, special educators and classroom teachers must collaborate to determine fair and equitable practices consistent with state and local policy.

Munk and Bursuck (1997/1998) caution, however, that students do not always agree that teachers should modify grades. For example, most students believe grading some students on a different scale, passing all students, and giving pass-fail grades are unfair practices. Although some students feel giving two grades, one for effort and one for achievement, to be fair, the majority of students still disapprove of this option. If teachers use grading adaptations, they should expect students to notice and be prepared to justify their use.

Christiansen and Vogel (1998) maintain that effective grading practices are consistent with school policy, meet the communication needs of the grading process, reflect the theoretical orientations of the teachers involved, and are consistent with a student's IEP. Similarly, Bradley and Calvin (1998) recommend that teachers assess students frequently and use this information to make ongoing achievement reports to parents. If teachers give modified grades, they may wish to consider the guidelines suggested by several authorities (Bradley & Calvin; Bursuck et al., 1996; Munk & Bursuck, 1998/1998):

◆ Use points and percentages, rather than letter grades, to grade differentiated assignments.
◆ Avoid changing the grading scale for only one individual.
◆ Avoid posting grades and scores.
◆ Match grading criteria with IEP goals and objectives.
◆ Provide opportunities for students to grade themselves.
◆ Develop scoring rubrics detailing the standards for completing assignments and for grading them. (Build in differentiated assignments for students with mild disabilities.)
◆ Use a variety of approaches to determine grades, including portfolios and other direct measures of performance.
◆ Avoid grading strictly on effort, but consider one grade for the process (i.e., effort) and another for the product (i.e. the outcome, test score).
◆ Base grades on meeting the requirements of behavioral or academic contracts.
◆ Adjust grading weights so that projects and participation count more than test grades.

Summary of Adaptation Techniques

Special education teachers can help classroom teachers adapt their instructional presentations through content enhancement routines to assist students with mild disabilities in the classroom. Advance organizers and other organizational routines can give students a learning set resulting in improved performance. In addition, graphic organizers and concept diagrams can be used to provide students with a framework by which they can integrate new information with old. Mnemonics, recall-enhancement routines, and technological aids may also improve the comprehension and retention of content-area information by special learners.

In addition, teachers can adapt textbooks to assist students who are having problems with reading. Often, effective textbook adaptations involve alterations in instructional procedures that increase active involvement with textbooks before, during, and after the reading process. Similarly, modifications in assignments, tests, and grading also can improve the content-area performance of youngsters with mild disabilities. ◆

Teaching Learning Strategies and School Survival Skills

In major research projects conducted at the University of Kansas (Deshler & Schumaker, 1986) and the University of Pittsburgh (Zigmond, Kerr, Schaeffer, Brown, & Farra, 1986), researchers examined the demands of secondary schools and the characteristics of adolescents with learning disabilities. Not surprisingly, findings indicated that adolescents with mild disabilities do not adjust well to such complex demands of the secondary school environment as meeting due dates for multiple assignments and demonstrating active interest or participation in seven or eight different content classes (Kerr, Zigmond, Schaeffer, & Brown, 1986). Rather, these students are passive in their approach to learning and deficient in the study skills and strategies needed for success in secondary schools (Deshler, Schumaker, Alley, Warner, & Clark, 1982). Moreover, they do not seem to generalize the strategies and study skills learned in the special education setting to appropriate use in the regular classroom (Alley, Deshler, Clark, Schumaker, & Warner, 1983).

As students with mild disabilities are increasingly included in content-area classrooms, such learner characteristics as these will present challenges to both special educators and classroom teachers. To overcome these challenges, Deshler, Schumaker, and their colleagues at the University of Kansas (see, for example, Alley & Deshler, 1979; Deshler, 1998; Deshler & Schumaker, 1986; Tralli et al., 1996) recommend that teachers use a *Strategic Instruction Model* (SIM) to help students with mild disabilities cope with the many demands of the secondary school. The SIM has three major components: Learning Strategy Interventions, Content-Enhancement Routines, and Empowerment Interventions. *Content-Enhancement Routines* are, as previously described, the organizational and conceptual routines that content-area teachers use to improve their instruction and student understanding of important information. On the other hand, Learning Strategies and Empowerment Interventions are routines students must master to become more effective and independent learners in the classroom.

Learning strategies involve teaching students procedures or rules to help them "learn how to learn" and become more active and self-directed in their content classes. Immediately useful strategies for acquiring and storing content-area information, as well as strategies for expressing or demonstrating competence with the information, are the essential elements of the learning strategies curriculum. (See Chapter 9 for additional discussion of the Learning Strategies Curriculum and the Strategic Instruction Model.) For example, Mr. Abel might help his students learn specific strategies for completing their current assignments, or he might teach his students strategies to prepare for classes, take notes, read textbooks, or take various types of tests.

Empowerment strategies help students perform to their best ability and establish positive relationships with peers and teachers. Strategies for self-advocacy are essential for students with mild disabilities in inclusive classrooms. So, too, are motivational and social strategies enabling students to enjoy positive interactions with others.

Not all students with mild disabilities will require new strategies in order to be successful in their content-area instruction. For those who do, however, strategy instruction must involve a coordinated effort over an extended period of time rather than simply a "one-shot," haphazard approach (Deshler, 1998; Deshler & Schumaker, 1993). According to Ellis, Deshler, Lenz, Schumaker, and Clark (1991), the critical features of learning strategy instruction are daily and sustained instruction, many opportunities to practice the strategy in a variety of situations, individualized feedback, and required mastery of the strategy. Schumaker, Deshler, Alley, and Warner (1983) and Ellis, Deshler, Lenz, Schumaker and Clarke (1991) describe the following eight-step teaching procedure as essential:

Step 1: Pretest the student and point out the student's strengths and weaknesses on the task for which a new learning strategy is being considered. Discuss with the student the need for a more effective strategy and *obtain the student's commitment to try a new method.* Select for instruction only the tasks for which the student or the teacher has identified a true need for a new strategy.

Step 2: Break the strategy into separate parts. Describe each step of the strategy for the student, telling the student why each part is important and where the strategy might be useful.

Step 3: Model the new strategy for the student. Make overt and explicit all of the thought processes that are a part of the strategy by "thinking aloud."

Step 4: Require the student to rehearse each step of the strategy verbally until he or she can self-instruct without error.

Step 5: Have the student practice the new strategy using controlled materials that are closer to his or her current performance level than are the regular classroom materials. Provide the student with positive and corrective feedback throughout the practice trials until he or she performs to a specified criterion level.

Step 6: Increase the difficulty level of the practice materials until it approximates that of the regular classroom. Require the student to perform to a specified criterion level each time before moving to harder practice materials.

Step 7: Posttest the student and state specific information regarding performance gains.

Step 8: Help the student generalize the strategy to the regular classroom. This step requires careful planning and monitoring by the teacher, including:

◆ Helping the student to verbalize where and under what conditions the strategy might be useful in his or her content-area classes;

◆ Encouraging the student to use the strategy in the regular classroom and, if appropriate, informing the classroom teacher of the strategy so that he or she can privately reward the student for using it; and

◆ Continuing with periodic follow-up to make sure that the strategy is still appropriate, that the student is still using it correctly, and that the student is setting personal goals for strategy use.

Several cautions are in order when teaching learning strategies. First, steps 1 through 3 are critical for student success. Of particular importance are obtaining the student's commitment to try a potentially useful new approach and deliberately making apparent to students the cognitive process and rationale underlying each part of the new strategy (see Box 14.2). Steps 4 through 7 may vary depending upon the skill and maturity level of the individual student. Often, however, students require extensive controlled and grade-appropriate practice in order to master learning strategies (Deshler, 1998).

Second, the teacher must not assume that the student will automatically use the new strategy in his or her content classes. Generalization to the regular classroom is still problematic within the Strategic Instruction Model. Teachers must plan systematically for generalization if it is to occur as suggested in step 8. Edmunds (1999) even suggests that teachers may need to make "cognitive credit cards" for students—small, wallet-sized cards containing strategy steps and reminders regarding when or how to use particular strategies in the classroom. Finally, the teacher must refrain from teaching learning strategies to particular students if there is no need to do so. Learning strategies should never be taught merely for the sake of teaching a "new" and "different" curriculum.

As larger numbers of students with mild disabilities are included in content classrooms, the proficiency of classroom teachers in the use of the Strategic Instruction Model is becoming more important. Although teaching learning strategies in context may help students become aware of the usefulness of strategies, and thus make generalization easier to accomplish, classroom teachers may not have sufficient training or time to explicitly teach strategies to mastery. Content teachers are under constant pressure to "cover the curriculum"; therefore, they may not always engage in critical teaching behaviors or provide sufficient opportunities for students to practice, master and apply strategies (Scanlon, Deshler, & Schumaker, 1996). Special educators will need to provide instructional support within the content classroom and the resource room in order for students to become independent, strategic learners.

Box 14.2

Mr. Abel Teaches Robert a Learning Strategy

Mr. Abel is about to introduce Robert to a "better way" to write sequence paragraphs in his content area classes. First, Mr. Abel reviews Robert's current level of performance when writing sequence paragraphs and gives Robert a reason to learn a "better way" to write these. After obtaining Robert's commitment to learn the new strategy, Mr. Abel describes and then models the strategy for Robert using a "think aloud" procedure. Let's listen to the conversation as Mr. Abel begins the learning strategies teaching sequence:

Mr. Abel: Remember yesterday in class you wrote a sequence paragraph similar to the ones you have to write for Mr. McNally and Ms. Stone. Here's the paragraph you wrote. You used a nice topic sentence for your paragraph, but I had difficulty following the order of your thoughts. For example, I didn't see words or phrases to help me, as the reader, see how the events took place in a certain order. You know how Mr. McNally and Ms. Stone are always giving you lower marks on tests and on the homework you turn in when you don't show things occurring in the proper order?

Robert: Yeah, sometimes I forget the order. But, I do know it lots of times. I just don't do good on written tests and homework.

Mr. Abel: I know a way to help you write better sequence paragraphs like this one for Mr. McNally and Ms. Stone. Would you like to give it a try?

Robert: Okay, I guess so.

Mr. Abel: Fantastic! The strategy goes like this. Write a topic sentence. Write three or four sentences about the topic, but make these sentences each start with "First," "Next," "Then," and "Finally" in that order. End with a "clincher" sentence that says the same thing as the topic sentence but in different words. (Mr. Abel writes the steps to the strategy on the board as he talks: Topic Sentence

First, . . .
Next, . . .
Then, . . .
Finally, . . .
Clincher Sentence.)

It's important to use the words like "first," "next," "then," and "finally" because these are the words that tell the reader the exact sequence in your paragraph.

Robert: That doesn't look too hard.

Mr. Abel: It's not. Watch me do an example. In earth science with Ms. Stone, you've been talking about convection. That process takes place in a certain sequence, so I can write a paragraph about that using the steps in this strategy. (Mr. Abel "thinks aloud" as he writes the sample paragraph on the chalkboard.) Let's see, I have to write a topic sentence. I know what convection means, so I'll use that in my topic sentence. "Convection is the movement of molecules caused by heating." Now, I have to write a sentence about the convection process that begins with the word

"First". "First, molecules are heated, move faster, and become less dense." Hmmm . . . now I need a sentence starting with "Next". "Next, these buyoant molecules move up, forming an area of high pressure." Let's see, now a sentence starting with "Then" . . . "Then, the molecules move across the top from the area of high pressure to an area of low pressure." Now, I need a sentence using "Finally". "Finally, as the molecules move across the top, they cool and slow down, become less dense, and sink back down." Let's see, the last step is to write a clincher sentence: "Convection is one way to explain the movement of molecules." (Mr. Abel writes the last sentence.)

Robert: The other day in class, we had to write an answer to tell about convection like that.

Mr. Abel: Yeah, I think you can use this strategy in earth science and in geography. You might be able to use it in health, too. You can use it any time you must write a paragraph to explain how something happens in a specific order. Now, tell me the steps to follow when you write a sequence paragraph . . .

Mr. Abel moves the lesson to verbal rehearsal and guided practice with the steps in the strategy. Later, he will help Robert apply the strategy to write sequence paragraphs using curricular materials from Robert's earth science and geography classes. When Robert masters this paragraph-writing strategy, Mr. Abel will assist Robert to plan and evaluate his independent use of the strategy in content classes.

Based on the following source:
Additional information about Paragraph Writing Strategies can be found in: Moran, M., Schumaker, J.B., & Vetter, A. (1981). *Teaching a paragraph organization strategy to learning disabled adolescents.* Lawrence, KS: University of Kansas Institute for Research in Learning Disabilities.

♦

In addition, the Strategic Instruction Model is receiving criticism on the grounds that it is still teacher-directed rather than student-directed (Ellis, 1986). That is, some authorities argue that students are merely taught rote procedures for completing specific tasks, precluding their active involvement in the construction of knowledge (Poplin, 1988). Although the goal of learning strategies instruction is to produce students who function strategically and independently as learners in their content-area classes, it is the teacher who most often assumes the responsibility for evaluating and selecting appropriate strategies for use. To begin addressing this difficulty, Ellis, Deshler, and Schumaker (1989) designed an executive strategy procedure to enable students to produce their own strategies likely to be effective in novel situations. Students learn to employ the SUCCESS strategy following this eight-step teaching sequence:

S = Sort out the most important demand or problem.
U = Unarm the problem by identifying the critical trouble spots.
C = Cash in on your old strategies, experiences, and observations of others.
C = Create a strategy for solving this problem that will work on all similar problems.
E = Echo your strategy (use substrategy ECHO).
    E = Evaluate the strategy as you try it.

C = Change the strategy to make it work better for future use.
H = Have another try and reevaluate it.
O = Overlearn your strategy.
S = See how well your strategy works in different situations.
S = Save your strategy.

Although the effectiveness of strategy instruction in the inclusive classroom requires further investigation, the technique appears promising for students with mild disabilities. "Good" strategy instruction is interactive, involving on-going dialogue and collaboration between students and their teachers to produce individualized strategies that meet specific needs of learners in their content classes (Harris & Pressley, 1991). (Additional information about the Strategic Instruction Model and specific training in its use may be obtained from The University of Kansas Center for Research on Learning, 3061 Dole Building, The University of Kansas, Lawrence, Kansas 66045 or at **www.ku-crl.org**.) Although many of the strategies we will now examine have been designed for adolescents with mild disabilities, some are also appropriate for elementary-level students.

Class Preparation and Assignment Completion Strategies

Robert constantly loses study guides, books, and assignments. He complains that he never has time to finish his homework and he frequently makes the excuse that he didn't know an assignment was due. Robert feels that his teachers pick on him. Like many students with mild disabilities, he has difficulty organizing himself and his time in order to come to class prepared and to complete the work required by Mr. McNally, Ms. Stone, and his other teachers.

Shields and Heron (1989) suggest that teachers have students like Robert use assignment logs or calendars. When assignments are given, students write down the present date, the nature of the assignment, its due date, and other pertinent information in columns on the assignment log. Similarly, students can use a weekly or monthly calendar and a "to do today" list. On these calendars, students note assignments with due dates, estimate time for assignment completion, and "block out" time in increments in order to complete both short- and long-range projects. First, however, they may need to complete a time log, monitoring exactly how they spend their time for a week, in order to see "where time goes." Students who monitor their time and use daily calendars increase their fulfillment of academic responsibilities (Flores, Schloss, & Alper, 1995).

Ellis (1998) suggests a "calendar" approach to help students complete their responsibilities when assignments involve group projects. Students are taught the PROJECT Planning Strategy:

P = Preview the task
R = Rough out a plan

O = Organize tasks and resources
J = Jot down job assignments
E = Examine obstacles and develop strategies
C = Commit to goals
T = Target timelines (p.96)

Students can then plan as a team according to each of the steps of the strategy. The project task to be completed is analyzed and roughed out, and the steps are listed in order on the left side of a "calendar." The resources needed for each step are listed in the second column. In the next column, the job assignments are listed specifically so that each student knows the pieces of the job task or the resources for which he or she is responsible. Due dates for procuring resources or completing job tasks are also placed in this column beside the student's name and his or her responsibility. Finally, in the right-hand column, possible obstacles are listed, such as an inability to obtain a particular resource, and possible strategies to overcome the problems are listed.

Having a notebook with pockets large enough to hold standard notebook paper also enables students to keep track of work to be completed and work to be turned in during the day. Teachers who require students to keep notebooks and who spend time helping students organize them are using their time wisely. In addition, teachers are advised to check notebooks frequently and to help students reorganize them periodically.

Students may also require specific strategies to ensure that they arrive in class with work completed, fully prepared to participate. Four specific strategies for classroom preparation and assignment completion are PREPARE, PREP, WATCh and HOW.

PREPARE. PREPARE (Ellis & Lenz, 1987, p. 100) cues the student to bring both materials and a positive attitude to the class session. In addition, the student reminds himself or herself to review the previous day's lesson before class begins:

P = Plan locker visits.
R = Reflect on what you need and get it.
E = Erase personal needs.
P = PSYC (substrategy).
     P = Pause for an attitude check.
     S = Say a personal goal related to the class.
     Y = Yoke in your negative thoughts.
     C = Challenge yourself to good performance.
A = Ask yourself where class has been and where class is going.
R = Review notes and study guides.
E = Explore the meaning of the teacher's introduction.

PREP. PREP (Ellis, 1989, p. 36) is a strategy designed to engage the student in thought about an upcoming lesson before the lesson actually begins. This strategy also ensures that the student brings a positive attitude, as well as materials, to content-area classes.

P = Prepare materials.

    Get notebook, study guide, pencil, and textbooks ready for class. Mark difficult parts of the textbook, notes, and study guide.

R = Review what you know.

    Read notes, study guide, and textbook cues and relate these to what you already know about the topic. List at least three things you know about the topic.

E = Establish a positive mindset.

    Tell yourself to learn. Suppress "put downs" and make a positive statement.

P = Pinpoint goals.

    Decide what you want to find out and note your participation goals.

WATCh. WATCh (Glomb & West, 1990, p. 236) is a strategy designed to help students with behavior disorders complete their assignments neatly, accurately, and on time.

W = Write down the assignment, the due date, and any special requirements in an "assignment planner."

A = Ask yourself if you understand the assignment, and ask for clarification if necessary.

T = Task-analyze the assignment and schedule the task over the days available to complete the assignment.

Ch = Check each task as you do it with CAN (substrategy).

    C = Completeness.

    A = Accuracy.

    N = Neatness.

HOW. HOW (Archer, 1988, p. 56; Archer & Gleason, 1989) is actually part of a larger strategy intended to help elementary-level students with mild disabilities complete content-area assignments accurately and on time. The strategy requires that students read directions and check assignments for neatness.

Step 1: *Plan it.*

    Read the directions and circle the words that tell you what to do.

    Get out the materials you need.

    Tell yourself what to do.

Step 2: *Complete it.*

    Do all the items.

    If you can't do an item, go to the next one or ask for help.

    Use HOW (substrategy for how your paper should look.)

        H = Heading.

        Name, date, subject, page number.

        O = Organized.

        On the front side of the paper, left and right margins, at least one blank line at the top and bottom, good spacing.

        W = Written neatly.

        Words or numbers written neatly and on the lines. Neat erasing.

Step 3: *Check it.*
>Did you do everything?
>Did you get the right answers?
>Did you proofread?

Step 4: *Turn it in.*

Class Participation Strategies

In addition to completing work and coming to class prepared, Robert must actively participate in his classes if he is to be successful. Class participation entails listening to the teacher and to class discussions, reflecting on what is being said, asking relevant questions or making comments in an appropriate manner, and taking notes. Three specific empowerment strategies for class participation are SLANT, RELATE, and WISE.

SLANT. SLANT (Ellis, 1989, p. 37) is a strategy designed to help students with mild disabilities increase nonverbal "teacher-pleasing" behaviors in the content class.

S = Sit up.
L = Lean forward.
A = Act like you're interested.
N = Nod your head.
T = Track the teacher with your eyes.

RELATE. RELATE (Ellis, 1989, p. 37) gives students a specific strategy for verbal participation during a class session. Students learn, for example, how to listen for "alert" words that signal important information, such as reasons, examples, or comparisons, as well as opportunities for students to contribute by asking questions or making comments (see Table 14.6).

R = Reveal reasons.
>Listen for alert words and reasons. Paraphrase the reasons back to the teacher.

E = Echo examples.
>Listen for alert words and examples. Paraphrase the examples back to the teacher.

L = Lasso comparisons.
>Listen for alert words and comparisons. Paraphrase the similarities and/or differences back to the teacher.

A = Ask questions.
>Ask yourself if the information makes sense. If not, ask a question at an appropriate pause.

T = Tell the main idea.
>Listen for alert words and a main-idea statement. Paraphrase the main idea.
>(Or, tell what you think the main idea is and see if others agree with you.)

E = Examine importance.
>Ask the teacher to say what is most important.

Table 14.6 Alert Words for Classroom Discussions

Alert words that may be signaling that reasons are being offered:

because	deduct	effect	explanation
purpose	reasons	since	therefore

Alert words that may be signaling that examples of things/ideas are being offered:

example	instance	model	pattern
sample	type		

Alert words and phrases that may be signaling that things/ideas are being compared:

associated	contrast	differences	with relation to
opposite	parallel	resemblance	similarities
on the other hand . . .			

Alert words and phrases that may be signaling that main-idea statements are being offered:

basically . . .	driving at . . .	drift is . . .	in essence . . .
in conclusion . . .	in summary . . .	key point . . .	significance of this is . . .
the gist is . . .	the most important . . .		

Alert words that may be signaling that lists of important information are being offered:

categories	characteristics	classes	divisions
features	first, second, etc.	groups	kinds
many	members	parts	roles
steps	stages	ways	

From: Ellis, E.S. (1989). A metacognitive intervention for increasing class participation. *Learning Disabilities Focus, 5* (1), p. 38. Reprinted with permission.

Or, decide what you think is most important. Tell what you think is most important and see if others agree with you.

WISE. WISE (Ellis, 1989, p. 37) is a strategy to help students "think back on" class sessions to monitor their learning and remember information.

W = Were goals met?
Did you learn what you wanted to learn?
Did you meet your participation goals?
I = Itemize important information.
Review the study guide, notes, or the textbook and mark key information.
S = See how information can be remembered.
Draw graphic displays, create study cards, or make up mnemonics.
E = Explain what was learned to somebody.
Use your notes to teach somebody about the topic.

Teachers may need to model, or have other students model, appropriate ways to ask questions and make comments in the regular classroom. Modeling how to ask and/or answer questions and providing students with practice opportunities and specific feedback may enhance the generalization of this essential skill to the content classroom (Knapcyzk, 1991). Moreover, teachers may need to demonstrate and give students practice using different formats for taking notes in content classes. To implement instruction, special education teachers may first need to use controlled lectures so that students have an opportunity to listen for clue words in well-organized presentations and to practice various note-taking formats. Later, the teacher may use videotaped or audiotaped sessions from actual content-area classes to increase speed and proficiency.

Some note-taking formats are particularly useful to secondary-level students with mild disabilities. In the two-column format, Devine (1987) recommends that students write the date and topic at the top of the notebook page and divide the page into two columns. Writing only on the front of the page, students take notes in simple outline form in the far right-hand column and then later label the key ideas in the left-hand column. The student follows a similar procedure using the three-column format; however, the third column (i.e., now the one on the far right) permits the student to return and add related notes from the textbook next to the corresponding information from class sessions.

Bos and Vaughn (1998) suggest several ways to help students become proficient note takers:

1. Skip lines in notes to indicate changes in ideas.
2. Write ideas or key phrases rather than complete sentences.
3. Use pictures and diagrams.
4. Use abbreviations or symbols consistently.
5. Underline or asterisk information stressed by the teacher.
6. Include in notes any information written on the chalkboard or shown on an overhead transparency.
7. If you miss an idea or fact, draw a blank line so that you can fill it in later. Look up the information in the textbook or ask about it later.
8. If you can't remember how to spell a word, spell it the way it sounds or the way you think it looks. Look the word up or ask about it later.
9. Review your notes as soon as possible after a class session.

Scanlon, Deshler, and Schumaker (1996) also suggest a strategy to help students identify and organize the important information in their class notes. The ORDER strategy uses the following steps:

O = Open your mind and take notes.
R = Recognize the structure.
D = Design an organizer. (Use the substrategy FLOW to create a box and word or a pictorial flow chart.) (See Figure 14.9.)
    F = Find and list
    L = Look and check
    O = Organize the information.
    W = Work out an organizer.
E = Explain it.
R = Recycle it (p. 45).

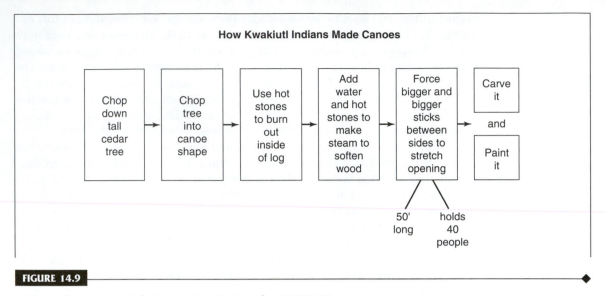

How Kwakiutl Indians Made Canoes

Chop down tall cedar tree → Chop tree into canoe shape → Use hot stones to burn out inside of log → Add water and hot stones to make steam to soften wood → Force bigger and bigger sticks between sides to stretch opening → Carve it / and / Paint it

50' long   holds 40 people

FIGURE 14.9

A Sample Sequential Organizer Using the FLOW Strategy From: Scanlon, D., Deshler, D.D., & Schumaker, J.B. (1996). Can a strategy be taught and learned in secondary inclusive classrooms? *Learning Disabilities Research & Practice*, 11(1), p.45.

Similarly, Boyle (1996), Boyle and Weishaar (1997), and Boyle and Yeager (1997) offer a strategy to help students produce organized semantic or cognitive maps from lectures or textbook passages. Students who produce their own cognitive organizers comprehend information better than those who do not generate them. Using the acronym TRAVEL, students complete the following steps to construct a cognitive map:

T = Topic—write down the main topic and circle it.
R = Read—read the first paragraph or remain alert to listen to the lecture.
A = Ask yourself what the main idea and three details are and write these down.
V = Verify—circle the main idea and draw a line from the main idea to each detail.
E = Examine—repeat the R, A, V steps with each successive paragraph or with each idea in the lecture.
L = Link—draw lines to link together the main ideas that are related.

Textbook Strategies

Students with mild disabilities often have difficulty reading and comprehending their content-area textbooks. At the same time, they are expected to study their texts to prepare for tests. In addition to adapting the textbook, the strategies we will examine next may help youngsters obtain important information from their texts. The reader also may wish to review the comprehension strategies discussed in Chapter 11, including RAM (Clark, Deshler, Schumaker, Alley, & Warner, 1984), RAP, and RIDER (Ellis & Lenz, 1987).

FIST (or FAST). In the FIST strategy (Ellis & Lenz, 1987, p. 98), students cue themselves to self-question while reading textbook passages in order to improve their comprehension.

F = First sentence in the paragraph is read.
I = Indicate (or Ask) a question based on information in the first sentence.
S = Search for the answer to the question.
T = Tie the answer to the question with a paraphrase.

Chapter-Question Strategy. Archer and Gleason (1989) suggest a strategy to help students with mild disabilities answer specific questions from a textbook chapter or from a study guide. First, students practice turning a question into a statement containing part of the answer. For example, if the question is "What is latitude?" Robert might state, "*Latitude* means . . . ". Next, students practice locating the section of the chapter in which the answer is likely to be found. These two steps force students to think about what exactly the question is asking and the type of information to be given in the answer (e.g., a name, event, date, or place) *before* attempting to answer the question. Finally, students learn the complete strategy:

Step 1: Read the question carefully.
Step 2: Change the question into part of the answer.
Step 3: Locate the section of the chapter that discusses the topic.
Step 4: Read the section of the chapter until you find the answer.
Step 5: Complete the answer.

Other strategies give students with mild disabilities procedures for reading content-area textbooks while extracting and organizing important information for note- taking. These strategies also use the familiar techniques of paraphrasing, self-questioning, and forming first-letter acronyms.

LISTS. LISTS (Ellis & Lenz, 1987, p. 99) gives students a specific technique for taking notes from content-area textbooks and recalling information for tests. The strategy focuses student attention on textual clues that signal important information and provides a first-letter acronym for arranging the information in a format to promote study and memorization. The LISTS strategy allows students to create paired associates that can be placed on the front and back of index cards and recalled through mnemonic devices (Bulgren, Hock, Schumaker, & Deshler, 1995). For example, after LISTing authors and their works, students can improve their recall of an author (e.g., Jack London) and his or her literature (e.g., To Build a Fire). By placing the questions "Who wrote To Build a Fire?" and "What short story did Jack London write?" on the front and back of index cards, students might link this information for memory by picturing a man building a fire in London. LISTS consists of the following steps:

L = Look for clues.
I = Investigate the items. (Be sure they all relate to the topic and are parallel.)
S = Select a mnemonic device using FIRST (substrategy).

F = Form a word.

I = Insert letters to form a word.

R = Rearrange the letters to form a word.

S = Shape a sentence.

T = Try combinations.

T = Transfer information to a study card.

S = Self-test.

The Self-Questioning Summarization Strategy. The self-questioning summarization strategy (Wong, Wong, Perry, & Sawatsky, 1986, p. 24-26) consists of a series of questions used as prompts for finding the main idea of a textbook paragraph and rewriting it.

Question 1: In this paragraph, is there anything I don't understand?

Question 2: In this paragraph, what's the most important sentence (main idea sentence)? Let me underline it.

Question 3: Let me summarize the paragraph. To summarize, I rewrite the main idea sentence and add important details.

Question 4: Now, does my summary statement link up with the chapter sub-heading?

Question 5: When I have written summary statements for a whole subsection,

    a. Let me review my summary statements for the subsection. (A subsection consists of several paragraphs under the same sub-heading.)

    b. Do my summary statements link up with each other?

    c. Do they all link up with the subheading?

Question 6: At the end of an assigned reading section, let me see if I am aware of all the themes. If I am, let me predict the teacher's test question on this section. If I'm not, let me go back to item 4.

Columnar Note Taking With Tip Sheets. In a technique devised by Horton, Lovitt, and Christensen (1991), middle school and high school students with mild disabilities improved their ability to take notes from their social studies and science textbooks. In this form of note taking, four columns are used: "Heading," "What," "Special Terms," and "Facts" (see Figure 14.10). In the "Heading" column, students write each of the headings and subheadings from the chapter. To complete the "What" column, students formulate a main-idea statement for each paragraph. In order to find main ideas, they learn four specific strategies:

Level 1: Use the first sentence of the paragraph if it does a good job of describing the main point of the paragraph. If it doesn't, try Level 2.

Level 2: Use the first sentence of the paragraph and add other information from the paragraph to it to make a "what" statement. It should still be one sentence. It helps sometimes to join sentences by using the word *and*. If this doesn't work, go to Level 3.

Level 3: Look for a sentence other than the first sentence that describes the main point of the paragraph and use it as your "what" statement. If this doesn't work, try Level 4.

HEADING	WHAT	SPECIAL TERMS	FACTS
Name: _____ Period: _____ Date: _____ **WHAT:** One statement of the main point of the paragraph. **SPECIAL TERMS:** Unusual words and their definitions. **FACTS:** Up to three short pieces of important information			
	During the early 1500s: The conquistadores won for Spain control of much of Latin America	N/A	—the Spanish language and Christianity were imposed on all who lived there —the economic policies were Spanish, as were the social and political ideas
The Spanish Colonies	Thousands of Spanish colonists came to the New World after the conquistadores opened the lands for settlement	Colony: An area ruled by a foreign country	—settlers or colonists from the ruling country came to live in the colony —the King gave land grants to nobles, army officers, and priests
Towns	Spanish settlers built towns in the New Worl patterned after Spanish towns	Plaza: Central square in the center of each town	—Spanish settlers brought their customs and traditions to the New World —plaza was the center of the town's business and religious life —Catholic church and government buildings were on the plaza

FIGURE 14.10

Columnar Notetaking From Textbooks From: Horton, S.V., Lovitt, T.C., & Christensen, C.C. (1991). *Notetaking from textbooks: Effects of a columnar format on three categories of secondary students.* Exceptionality, 2, p. 25. Copyright © 1991 by Springer-Verlag. Reprinted with permission.

Level 4: Use your own words to make a "what" statement.

"Special Terms" are defined as any unusual words and their definitions. Students look for words that are written in boldfaced, italicized, or colored print. The "Facts" column consists of any items that support the main-idea statement. Students cue themselves to write at least one fact for each paragraph, but never more than three facts.

A Note-Taking Strategy Using Index Cards. Rooney (1988) describes a similar strategy for note taking from content-area textbooks. In her strategy, however, students place their notes on index cards using the following steps:

Step 1: Read the subtitle and the section under the subtitle. While reading, write on *separate* index cards names of people and places, important numbers, and important terms. Write only two or three words per card. Do this for each paragraph in the section.

Step 2: Go back to the subtitle and turn it into the best test question you can. Write this question on one side of an index card and the answer on the other side. You now have a set of main-idea and detail cards from a chapter section.

Step 3: Repeat steps 1 and 2 for all the sections to be covered.

Step 4: Study the cards by looking at them one at a time. For detail cards, ask yourself "How is this related to the material?" Try to answer the main-idea question cards from memory.

Study and Test-Taking Strategies

Closely related to preceding strategies are several others designed to help youngsters with mild disabilities study for and take tests in their content classes. When students in special programs receive instruction on how to take specific types of tests, their performance in the regular classroom improves (Scruggs & Marsing, 1987).

EASY. EASY (Ellis & Lenz, 1987, p. 99) is a relatively straightforward strategy that enables students with mild disabilities to prepare for tests systematically, for example, by organizing and then prioritizing the information for study.

E = Elicit "WH" questions to identify important information (i.e., who, what, when, where, why).

A = Ask yourself which information is the least troublesome.

S = Study the easy parts first and the hardest parts last.

Y = Say *Yes* to self-reinforcement.

READ. READ (Marks, Van Laeys, Bender, & Scott, 1996, p. 37) is a teacher-designed strategy students can use while taking objective tests. Students can be given cards containing the four steps of the strategy prior to beginning a test:

R = Read the questions carefully.

E = Examine each answer choice.

A = Accent important words by underlining them.

D = Decide on the correct answer.

SPLASH. SPLASH (Simmonds, Luchow, Kaminsky, & Cottone, 1989, p. 101) offers a systematic method for taking tests.

S = Skim the entire test. Note easy and hard parts, directions, and point values so that you can best allocate the available time.

P = Plan your strategy once you have a general idea of the test.

L = Leave out difficult questions in a planned manner. (Teachers may wish to cue students to mark items skipped over with an asterisk.)

A = Attack immediately those questions you know.

S = Systematically guess after exhausting other strategies (Here teachers must first instruct students to look for clues and answers on the test to help answer unknown questions. If there is no penalty for guessing, students should be told to guess the best choice after eliminating incorrect choices.)

H = House cleaning (Leave 5% to 10% of your allotted time to making sure all answers are filled in, cleaning up erasures, and checking answers.)

PIRATES. Hughes, Schumaker, Deshler, & Mercer (1987) describe a similar test-taking strategy called PIRATES. Using this strategy, students establish a positive mindset for the test, read the instructions, and look for clues systematically.

P = Prepare to succeed.
   Put the acronym PIRATES and your name on the test.
   Prioritize test sections and allot time. Say something positive and start within 2 minutes.
I = Inspect the instructions.
   Read all of the instructions and underline how and where to answer. Also, notice any special requirements.
R = Read, remember, reduce.
   Read the whole question. Remember it with memory strategies and reduce your alternatives.
A = Answer or Abandon.
   If you know the answer, write it. If you're not sure, abandon the question for the moment.
T = Turn back.
   Go back to abandoned items at the end of the test and tell yourself to earn more points.
E = Estimate.
   Estimate unknown answers using the substrategy ACE:
   A = Avoid absolutes (e.g. "All").
   C = Choose the longest or most detailed alternative.
   E = Eliminate identical alternatives.
S = Survey.
   Survey the test to be sure all items are answered and switch answers only if you are sure they are wrong.

   Teachers can give students practice tests of various types, gradually increasing the difficulty level, as students learn strategies like SPLASH. In addition, students can apply several important general rules when taking tests in order to improve their performance:

1. When taking true/false tests, look for clue words like *Always, Never, None, No,* and *All.* These words frequently signal an item that is false. Conversely, words like *Sometimes* and *Usually* may signal items that are true. Although clue words are not foolproof, they may improve your odds to greater than chance if you do not know the correct answer.
2. On multiple choice tests, one or two alternatives for items are usually clearly incorrect. Eliminate these by marking them. In addition, learn to look for and underline keywords like *except* and *not* on multiple-choice tests and always read all the alternatives first before attempting an answer.
3. Essay tests contain directional words like *compare, contrast, describe, explain, evaluate,* or *illustrate.* Be sure you know what these words mean and underline them before taking essay tests. You may find it helpful to sketch a simple outline on your test paper before beginning to write answers to essay items.

4. Never change your answers unless you are certain they are incorrect. If you must guess, go with your first instinct after exhausting all possible clues. Unless there is a penalty for guessing, never leave items unanswered.

5. Write down information that you are likely to forget immediately upon receiving your test paper. For example, students can write a first-letter acronym in a margin of the test paper before they begin the test.

Empowerment Strategies

Students need to engage in teacher-pleasing behaviors using strategies such as those described previously. According to Ellis (1998), they also must learn ways to self-advocate, solve problems with teachers and peers, and participate in their own IEP conferences. Three strategies, ASSERT, PROACT and SHARE, may increase student participation in these important activities.

ASSERT. ASSERT (King, 2000) is a simple strategy designed to help students with mild disabilities recall the steps in a self-advocacy routine. To assert himself or herself, the student must be fully aware of his or her disability as well as his or her strengths and limitations. The ASSERT steps are:

A = Awareness of disability
S = State disability
S = State strengths and limitations
E = Evaluate problem and solutions
R = Role play situations
T = Try it in the real setting

PROACT. PROACT is a self-advocacy strategy designed by Ellis (1998, p. 99). The strategy enables youngsters to be proactive in the classroom environment rather than reacting to problems as they arise.

P = PLAN (Substrategy)
  *P*rofile your strengths/weaknesses.
  *L*ist problems of the specific situation.
  *A*nalyze why they are happening.
  *N*ote what needs to happen instead.
R = Rehearse
  Rehearse explaining your disability.
  Rehearse explaining how the disability is becoming a handicap.
  Rehearse making the request.
  Rehearse what to say if the response is positive and if it's negative.
O = Organize
  Evidence of disability
  Letters from professionals
  Paper/pencils
A = Ask
  Ask if this is a good time to talk.
  State something positive, your goal, problem and request.

Keep the focus on possible solutions.

C = Confirm

Confirm what you will do.

Confirm what the other person has agreed to do.

Confirm your appreciation.

T = Think back

What was agreed to? What wasn't?

Do you need to try again another time?

Will the other person need reminders?

What should be done differently next time?

SHARE. SHARE (see Tralli et al., 1996, p. 212) is a strategy designed to help students participate in their own IEP conferences. Effective participation is dependent on the following SHARE behaviors:

S = Sit up straight.

H = Have a pleasant tone of voice.

A = Activate your thinking.

Tell yourself to pay attention.

Tell yourself to participate.

Tell yourself to compare ideas.

R = Relax

Don't look uptight.

Tell yourself to stay calm.

E = Engage in eye communication.

A Summary of Strategies

A number of strategies have proved effective in helping students with mild disabilities succeed in content-area classes. These strategies may not turn students with mild disabilities into "star pupils"; however, they may make the difference between an F or D and a passing grade. Teachers must remember to teach only those strategies that are needed by an individual student and to elicit the student's commitment to learn the strategy before proceeding. In addition, teachers must follow the critical steps for teaching learning strategies, including those for generalization to the regular classroom. Special educators will need to collaborate to increase their level of effective instructional support for content-area teachers in inclusive classrooms. ◆

Summary

Many students with mild disabilities will complete their content-area instruction in the inclusive classroom. Increasingly, special education teachers are collaborating with regular educators in an effort to adapt instructional presentations to suit the needs of special learners. Content enhancement routines such as advance organizers, graphic organizers or concept diagrams, planned mnemonic devices, and technological aids all may be employed in the regular classroom to enhance the learning of youngsters with mild disabilities. In addition, the teacher may adapt textbooks, assignments, and tests to improve student performance. Although not an easy task, content-area teachers are willing to make such modifications if they are likely to benefit many students simultaneously and if the necessary support from special education personnel is available.

Teachers also must make sure that students with mild disabilities have the school survival skills essential for success in the regular classroom. Many learning strategies are available to teach youngsters how to organize and prepare for class, how to participate in class, and how to complete assignments, take notes, read textbooks, study, and take tests. Empowerment strategies also may help students become self-advocates and improve their relationships with peers and teachers. These strategies are not a panacea; however, they may be effective in helping many youngsters cope with the complex demands of the content classroom from the elementary level through the secondary grades.

Application Exercises

1. Examine textbooks for two different grade levels from a nearby school district. Choose one social studies text at each level and one science text at each level. Describe how each text is organized. Describe the vocabulary and concept load using specific examples from each text. Then, state whether or not each text will be difficult for students with mild disabilities to read and comprehend. Justify your opinion. Give at least five ways in which each textbook could be adapted to improve student performance.

2. Interview a special education teacher and a regular classroom teacher at a chosen grade level who "share" students. What adaptations are typically used to assist students with mild disabilities in the content class? Are there any differences between suggestions made by the special educator and those made by the regular educator? If so, how would you account for the differences?

3. Assume you are Mr. Abel assisting Robert in his geography class with Mr. McNally. What learning strategies would you recommend for Robert in this class? Justify your recommendations.

4. Using a textbook from a chosen grade level, analyze the content of one chapter for important concepts, ideas, and vocabulary. Then, prepare a graphic organizer or concept diagram to illustrate the relationship among the key concepts and ideas you identified in your analysis.

5. Ms. Stone says, "Robert never seems to listen in earth science. He doesn't take notes, and his test grades are low." Assume the role of Mr. Abel. What information do you need to gather? How will you obtain it? What strategies will you teach Robert to increase his participation in Ms. Stone's class?

6. Browse the Web sites listed in Box 14.1. What evidence do you see that the needs of students with disabilities in inclusive classrooms were considered in the various content-area standards? Examine four or five lesson plans from the different web sites. What parts of each lesson are likely to create difficulty for students with mild disabilities? What content enhancement routines or learning strategies might be used to improve the performance of these students? Be specific.

7. Locate at least five articles from InfoTrac regarding the Strategic Instruction Model. In approximately one page, summarize the information available regarding how teachers use interventions from the model in the inclusive classroom environment. Then, on an additional page, make recommendations regarding the special educator's role in helping classroom teachers implement the Strategic Instruction Model. With your peers, list important elements of instructional support for special educators collaborating with colleagues in content-area classrooms.

CHAPTER
15

INSTRUCTION IN SOCIAL AND INDEPENDENT LIVING SKILLS

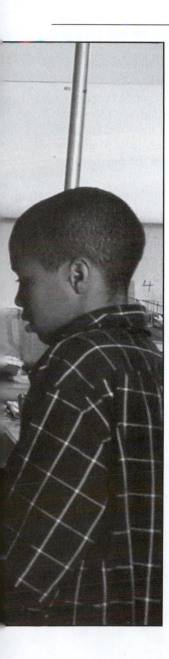

Focus

As you read, think about the following questions:

◆ *Why is instruction in social skills an important component of the curriculum for students with mild disabilities?*

◆ *What are some important ways to teach social skills?*

◆ *What is meant by* transition planning?

◆ *What is meant by* assistive technology devices and services?

◆ *How can teachers help their students with mild disabilities prepare to live independently as adults?*

Students with mild disabilities often lack the social and independent living skills they need in order to function as productive members of their mainstreamed classrooms and as contributing citizens during adulthood. Classroom teachers, for example, report that students with mild disabilities do not demonstrate the social behaviors that are necessary for success in their classes (Fad, 1990). Special educators must focus educational programming on critical skills that enable students with mild disabilities to function independently in the school and community. Let's take a look at some activities Ms. Lopez and Mr. Abel engage in to deal with these concerns.

Ms. Lopez evaluates Joey's recent performance in the classroom. Although Joey is now remaining in his seat for longer periods at a time, he still calls out the moment he has a question. If Ms. Lopez ignores Joey's rudeness, he becomes even more disruptive in an attempt to gain attention. Ms. Lopez decides that Joey may not know how to gain teacher attention appropriately. She defines "Getting the Teacher's Attention the Right Way" as a three-step process: (a) Raise your hand; (b) Wait quietly for the teacher to call on you; and (c) Ask a question using a polite tone of voice. Ms. Lopez writes these steps on a small card, demonstrates each step for Joey, and asks him to practice each step. Then, she rewards Joey with points and specific praise each time he gets the teacher's attention the right way.

Mr. Abel knows that Susan will need assistance if she is to live independently as an adult. Susan has no marketable job skill, poor personal hygiene, and little self-confidence. She has no idea of what type of job she might enjoy after leaving school. Because Susan will turn 14 in one month, Mr. Abel discusses his concerns with Mrs. Friend, Susan's guidance counselor and the chair of her Individualized Education Program (IEP) team. Mrs. Friend will obtain permission for Susan to have a thorough evaluation of her vocational interests and abilities at a nearby vocational evaluation center. In addition, Mrs. Friend suggests that it might be useful for the local representative from the state's vocational rehabilitation agency to join the IEP team once Susan moves to the high school in an effort to plan appropriate goals and objectives for her transition to post-secondary services and/or employment.

Students with mild disabilities, like Joey and Susan, often lack social skills, daily living skills, or vocational skills. Without appropriate social skills, Joey will not be successful in the regular classroom. Moreover, if he fails to learn important social skills such as how to follow directions, to accept criticism, or to make requests politely, he may have problems finding and keeping a job once he has left school. In addition, if Susan does not receive instruction in the daily living and vocational skills necessary for her adulthood, it is unlikely that she will be able to earn an adequate income or live independently.

In this chapter, we will first examine the social behavior of students with mild disabilities. Next, we will explore instructional methods and programs for teaching critical social skills to special children and youth. Finally, we will discuss independent living skills and the transitioning of students with mild disabilities into post-secondary settings.

Social Skills and Students with Mild Disabilities

Professionals define the term *social skills* in different ways. Hollinger (1987), for example, defines social skills as those skills needed for successful interactions with others and acceptance by peers. Walker and his colleagues (1983) view social skills as a collection of competencies that allow children to initiate and maintain positive interpersonal relationships and to cope with different social situations and environments. Despite the different definitions of *social skills*, those students who possess them are likely to meet with peer and teacher acceptance, while those who do not are likely to experience isolation, rejection, and limited opportunities for learning and friendship (Hollinger).

According to McFall (1982), *social skills* are specific strategies that individuals use to accomplish important social tasks, such as joining in activities or greeting an acquaintance. On the other hand, *social competence* means the judgments that parents, teachers, or peers make regarding the effectiveness of an individual's strategies for achieving desired social outcomes (Strain, Odom, & McConnell, 1984). Socially competent students, then, engage in the right social skills at the right time, and the positive interactions they experience increase the likelihood of additional positive interactions and judgments from others of social competence in the future. Effective social skills enable students to interact positively and competently with peers, teachers, and others in the community.

Teachers must realize that social skills and judgments of social competence are situation specific. For example, judgments of social competence may vary by differing cultural, ethnic, or social standards across different settings. Maag (1990) suggests that the same social behavior may be either appropriate or inappropriate depending on the context. That is, Marcus might offer a special handshake as an appropriate greeting to a friend in the hallway, but that greeting would most likely be inappropriate for his school principal.

Thus, teachers must understand the social requirements of particular situations and the intended outcomes behind a child's behavior (Neel & Cessna, 1990). If, for example, Joey steals a ball from peers on the playground, his intended outcome might be to join the game. Teaching Joey relevant social skills like asking to play or joining a group might help him to achieve his desired outcome and be perceived as more socially competent. Nelson, Drummond, Martella, and Marchand-Martella (1997) caution, however, that students may accurately assess the outcomes of their positive or negative behaviors in particular social situations, but fail to understand the long-term importance of negative interpersonal interactions for social outcomes in the future.

Social skills that are relevant and that improve a child's competence in particular social settings are considered to be *socially valid* (Wolf, 1978). Important social outcomes, like peer acceptance and popularity, are closely related to whether or not students demonstrate socially valid social skills (Gresham, 1986). Hence, the social validity of a social skill is measured by its significance to others in the child's immediate environment.

Students with mild disabilities often spend the majority of their school day in the inclusive classroom. Therefore, how teachers and peers view them with respect to social skills may be critical to their classroom success. For example, teachers rate compliant, nondisruptive pupil behavior, the ability to cope with failure, and the ability to function independently as essential skills for classroom success (Kauffman, Wong, Lloyd, Hung, & Pullen, 1991). According to McLeod, Kolb, and Lister (1994), high school students and their teachers do not always agree on important social skills for success. Teachers rate appropriate work habits, respecting others and their property, and following school rules as more important than do students with learning disabilities. On the other hand, students with learning disabilities believe making friends with other students and exhibiting a sense of humor to be important high school social skills. (See Table 15.1 for specific social skills identified by classroom teachers as necessary for success in the mainstream.)

Despite the importance of adequate social skills, students with mild disabilities often demonstrate numerous inappropriate behaviors (Fad, 1990). According to Center and Wascom (1987), regular classroom teachers perceive students with behavioral disorders as exhibiting more antisocial behaviors and fewer prosocial behaviors than normal peers. Moreover, teacher ratings of poor social skills at the elementary level are predictive of arrest status for boys with conduct disorders by the middle and high school years (Walker & Stieber, 1998). Students with learning disabilities are also rated by teachers as demonstrating fewer appropriate social skills (Bursuck, 1989); having greater pragmatic language deficits (Lapadat, 1991); and exhibiting increased levels of off-task behavior, conduct disorders, distractibility, and shyness (Bender & Smith, 1990; McKinney, 1989) when compared with same-age peers. Furthermore, poor social relationships for students with learning disabilities are related to depression (Maag & Behrens, 1989) and suicide (Peck, 1985). Teachers rate children and youth with learning disabilities, mild mental retardation, and behavior disorders alike as below peers in almost all critical social skills (Bryan, 1997; Gresham, Elliott, & Black, 1987; Vaughn & Haager, 1994).

The teacher's perception of the classroom behavior of mainstreamed students with mild disabilities also may be an important factor affecting the educational placement, social status, and achievement levels for these youngsters (Roberts & Zubrick, 1992). For example, the perceived "teachability" of students with mild disabilities may influence instructional opportunities and long-term academic outcomes (Osborne, Schulte, & McKinney, 1991). That is, children who exhibit more off-task, distractable, dependent, maladaptive classroom behaviors may receive different amounts or types of instruction than their peers (McKinney, 1989). This difference in instruction may, in turn, contribute to the low academic achievement of students in the mainstream, as well as those who remain in resource-room special education programs (Osborne et al.).

Students with mild disabilities may also experience lower social status when compared with same-age peers. Students with behavioral disorders and mild mental retardation are often rejected by their peers in the regular classroom (Sabornie, Kauffman, & Cullinan, 1990). Moreover, children and youth with behavioral disorders are likely to reject their peers as well (Sabornie, 1987). On the other hand, studies examining the social acceptance of students with learning disabilities have yielded mixed results. According to some authorities, children with learning disabilities form fewer friendships (Bursuck, 1989) and experience more social rejection or neglect (Stone & La Greca, 1990) than do their same-age

Table 15.1   Critical Social Skills Identified by Regular Classroom Teachers

Teachers identify many social skills critical for success in the regular classroom. The following list does not imply a particular hierarchy of skills; however, it does illustrate those skills considered by regular educators to be important in their classrooms.

Coping Skills
Is able to express anger without physical aggression or yelling.
Copes in an acceptable way if someone takes something that belongs to him or her.
Copes appropriately if someone insults him or her.
Copes in an acceptable way when someone gives orders or bosses him or her around.
Avoids an argument when another student is provoking one.
Can handle being lied to.
Copes with being blamed for something he or she did not do.
Copes appropriately if someone is upset with him or her.
Copes with aggression in an appropriate way (walking away, seeking assistance, or defending himself or herself).
Is able to cope with someone calling him or her a name.

Work Habits
Completes homework assignments on time.
Completes classwork on time.
Is on task most of the time.
Pays attention during class discussions.
Uses class time efficiently.
Listens carefully to teacher directions.
Listens carefully during direct instruction.
Follows written directions.
Is an independent worker.
Promptly follows teacher's requests.

Peer Relationships
Knows how to join a group activity already in progress.
Develops and maintains individual friendships with more than one significant peer.
Maintains friendships over an extended period of time.
Interacts with a variety of children on a regular basis.
Shares laughter and jokes with peers.
Will initiate conversations with peers.
Initiates play activities with other children.
Can express feelings of affection or friendship toward peers.
Appears to make friends easily.
Regularly compliments others.

From: Fad, K.S. (1990). The fast track to success: Social-behavioral skills. *Intervention in School and Clinic*, 26 (1), p. 41. Copyright © 1990 by PRO-ED, Inc. Reprinted by permission.

peers. Roberts and Mather (1995), for example, assert that students with learning disabilities are not achieving the goal of social acceptance and integration through inclusion. Other researchers, however, argue that some students with learning disabilities may form appropriate peer relationships, particularly in regular classroom settings (for example, Madge, Affleck, & Lowenbraun, 1990; Sabornie et al.). When students with learning disabilities drop out of school, however, they often cite feelings of social alienation toward classmates and teachers as a factor in their decision to leave (Seidel & Vaughn, 1991).

Not all children and youth with mild disabilities will require assistance with social skills. For those students who possess age-appropriate verbal and non-verbal skills enabling them to interact successfully with others, social skills instruction is unnecessary. However, for many youngsters, specific instruction is essential if they are to be accepted by peers and teachers, to grow in their self-confidence, and to succeed at school and/or on the job (Black & Langone, 1997).

Teaching Social Skills

As stated, not every student with a mild disability will require instruction in social skills. Moreover, some students will require less intensive instruction and practice than others. All students who need social skills instruction, however, will require a carefully constructed and individualized program. Although commercially available social skills training programs vary in the specific skills taught, teachers should ensure that the ones they choose incorporate the following teaching procedures:

1. Select for instruction only those skills that will maximize the child's success. That is, teach age- and situation-appropriate skills observed and validated as critical for success (Meadows, Neel, Parker, & Timo, 1991). Educators may determine skills likely to impact positively on valued social outcomes through a combination of ratings by peers and/or teachers using social skills checklists or rating systems (e.g., The Social Skills Rating System developed by Gresham & Elliott, 1990, available through American Guidance Services); direct observation in natural settings or during role playing; sociometric techniques, such as peer nomination; or interviews (Maag, 1989).
2. Provide clear statements regarding the skill to be learned and the importance of learning this skill to improve interactions with peers and teachers. For example, Ms. Lopez might tell Joey, "Today, we are going to learn how to get the teacher's attention the right way. When you get the teacher's attention the right way, your teachers will know that you want help and that you know how to ask for help politely. Getting the teacher's attention the right way means raising your hand, waiting quietly for the teacher to call on you, and asking your question using a polite tone of voice." Ms. Lopez might also ask Joey to state why or where this skill might be important.
3. Model the new skill for the student. Modeling may be conducted using videotapes, audiotapes, or live demonstrations by peers or teachers. To increase the probability of success, the model must be of high or expert status and of the same age/sex/race as the learner. In addition, the model must appear to receive reinforcement for engaging in the modeled skill (Goldstein, 1981). Moreover, demonstration sequences must be clear, detailed, and well sequenced.
4. Provide numerous examples and nonexamples of the social skill. For example, Ms. Lopez might demonstrate for Joey several instances of getting the

teacher's attention appropriately and inappropriately. Then, she might ask Joey to identify several additional examples as either appropriate or inappropriate "teacher-attention-getting" techniques.

5. Construct role-playing and practice opportunities in which the student can receive teacher coaching and feedback regarding the correct use of the social skill. During role playing and practice, the teacher must be specific as to the steps students perform correctly and the ways in which to correct those performed incorrectly. For example, Ms. Lopez might ask a student to play the role of a teacher and ask Joey to practice getting the teacher's attention the right way. She might tell Joey, "You did a good job of raising your hand and waiting quietly until you were called on, but you need to remember to use a polite tone of voice. Now, watch me do it." After demonstrating, Ms. Lopez might ask Joey to practice the skill with her and then repeat the role play again with his peer.

6. Provide reinforcement contingent on successful demonstration of each skill during practice and in the classroom.

Although students with mild disabilities can learn appropriate social skills through direct systematic instruction, social skills training is not a panacea for all of the behavioral and social difficulties experienced by youngsters outside their special education classrooms (Berler, Gross, & Drabman, 1982). In fact, systematic approaches to teaching social skills are now drawing criticism from authorities (see, for example, Gresham, 1998; Mathur & Rutherford, 1996; Mathur, Kavale, Quinn, Forness, & Rutherford, 1998). These authorities charge that the skills taught in many social skills curricula lack validity in specific classrooms, and furthermore, teachers may not have the time or resources to implement direct instruction of social skills when students are placed in inclusive classroom (Odom, McConnell, & Chandler, 1993). The criticism most often leveled at social-skills programs, however, is that students will demonstrate appropriate social skills in the controlled context of role playing within the special class, but they may not use these skills when necessary in other classrooms or settings (Schloss, Schloss, Wood, & Kiehl, 1986).

Special education teachers must plan carefully for generalization if they are to help their students learn to use newly acquired social skills appropriately in the inclusive classroom (Blackbourn, 1989; Stokes & Baer, 1977). Mathur and colleagues (Mathur et al., 1998; Mathur & Rutherford, 1996), Gresham (1998), and O'Reilly and Glynn (1995) all suggest that for generalization of social skills to occur teachers must capitalize on incidental learning opportunities in the natural context of the classroom, community, or job. The following suggestions may help teachers promote the transfer of social skills outside the special education classroom:

1. Target skills and select role-playing examples that are relevant for individual youngsters. Elicit from students, parents, and teachers necessary social skills and examples for realistic role-playing activities. Ensure that all skills and examples are socially valid.

2. Inform parents, teachers, and other school personnel of the trained social skill. Involve parents and teachers in role-playing and practice activities

whenever possible. Ask for their assistance in prompting and reinforcing the student's appropriate use of the skill outside the special education setting.

3. Encourage peer support for social skills. Peers can participate in role-playing activities and learn to initiate interactions with children with mild disabilities so that targeted students will experience increased opportunities to practice and receive reinforcement for appropriate social skills (Strain & Odom, 1986).

4. Require students with mild disabilities to complete "homework assignments" in which they document their use of new social skills (Armstrong & McPherson, 1991). These homework assignments might take the form of logs, diaries, journals, checklists of skills used on a particular day, or self-monitoring forms. For example, Ms. Lopez might provide Joey with a self-monitoring form on which to list each instance of his getting the teacher's attention the right way in Ms. Kirk's classroom (see Figure 15.1).

5. Harness opportunities for teaching social skills that occur in the classroom. Ms. Lopez, for example, might engage in structured teaching interactions (see Getting Along with Others described on page 489) with Joey to help him learn the expected social behavior as it is needed in context.

Social Skills Programs

Numerous programs are now available for teaching social skills to children and youth with mild disabilities. Carter and Sugai (1989) and Sugai and Fuller (1991) offer excellent suggestions for choosing an appropriate social-skills curriculum. For example, they suggest that teachers examine commercially available curricula to determine whether or not (a) structured teaching procedures are used, (b) the social skills included are relevant for their students, (c) assessment

---

Name: Joey   Date: October 16, 2000

Skill: <u>Getting the Teacher's Attention the Right Way</u>

My homework assignment is to practice: <u>Getting my teacher's attention the right way</u>. Each time I get Ms. Kirk's attention the right way today, I will write down the period when it happened, what I did, and what happened next.

<u>Getting the Teacher's Attention the Right Way means:</u>

1. Raise my hand.
2. Wait quietly in my seat for the teacher to call on me.
3. Ask for assistance using a polite tone of voice.

<u>What Class Period?</u>   <u>What Did I Do?</u>   <u>What Happened?</u>

How Did I Do?_____

_____

FIGURE 15.2 ◆

Joey's Homework Form

procedures and social validation data are included, and (d) strategies for maintenance and generalization of skills are included. In addition, teachers must consider the cost of the materials and the time required for them to learn and implement the curriculum.

Several commercially available social-skills curricula meet most of the aforementioned criteria. These include *Skillstreaming* (Goldstein & McGinnis, 1997; McGinnis & Goldstein, 1997), *The Walker Social Skills Curriculum* (Walker et al., 1983; Walker, Todis, Holmes, & Horton, 1988), and *Getting Along with Others* (Jackson, Jackson, & Monroe, 1983).

Skillstreaming. *Skillstreaming* is available for the young child, for the elementary school youngster, and for the adolescent. At the elementary level, McGinnis and Goldstein (1997) provide teachers with a checklist with which to form structured learning groups consisting of children with similar social skills and needs across six skills clusters (see Figure 15.2). Each social skill is broken down into small steps and then taught through modeling, role playing, and specific performance feedback. In addition, children are given homework assignments enabling them to practice newly learned social skills in context.

With adolescents, teachers are again encouraged to group youngsters by need. Goldstein and McGinnis (1997) list 6 skill clusters and 50 social skills for adolescents. Modeling, role playing, performance feedback, and structured homework assignments remain as key elements of the approach (see Figure 15.3). (The *Skillstreaming* programs may be obtained from Research Press, P.O. Box 9177, Champaign, IL 61826.)

The Walker Social Skills Curriculum. This curriculum is available at two levels appropriate for students with mild disabilities. The *ACCEPTS Program* (i.e., A Curriculum for Children's Effective Peer and Teacher Skills) (Walker et al., 1983) is designed for elementary-aged youngsters. Five skill areas are included in the program: Classroom Skills, Basic Interaction Skills, Getting Along, Making Friends, and Coping Skills. A pretest, teaching scripts, a behavior-management system, and optional videotapes are components of the curriculum. Modeling and role playing are, again, the key instructional features of this curriculum.

The *ACCESS Program* (i.e., Adolescent Curriculum for Communication and Effective Social Skills) (Walker et al., 1988) provides teachers with role-playing activities and structured homework assignments appropriate for middle school and high school students. Peer, adult, and self-related skills are the focus of 31 lessons in ACCESS. In addition, a placement test and student contracts are helpful features of the curriculum. (*The Walker Social Skills Curriculum* is available through Pro-Ed, 8700 Shoal Creek Blvd., Austin, TX 78758.)

Getting Along with Others. Although originally intended for elementary school children, *Getting Along with Others* (Jackson, Jackson, & Monroe, 1983) is adaptable for students with mild disabilities at the middle school level. Scripted social-skills lessons, role-playing activities, relaxation exercises, and homework assignments are components of the program. The curriculum also provides teachers with excellent strategies, or "teaching interactions," for teaching social skills continuously within the classroom once students learn the steps for a

I. Classroom survival skills	Student name			
1. Listening				
2. Asking for help				
3. Saying thank you				
4. Bringing materials to class				
5. Following instructions				
6. Completing assignments				
7. Contributing to discussions				
8. Offering help to an adult				
9. Asking a question				
10. Ignoring distractions				
11. Making corrections				
12. Deciding on something to do				
13. Setting a goal				
II. Friendship-making skills				
14. Introducing yourself				
15. Beginning a conversation				
16. Ending a conversation				
17. Joining in				
18. Playing a game				
19. Asking a favor				
20. Offering help to a classmate				
21. Giving a compliment				
22. Accepting a compliment				
23. Suggesting an activity				
24. Sharing				
25. Apologizing				
III. Skills for dealing with feelings				
26. Knowing your feelings				
27. Expressing your feelings				
28. Recognizing another's feelings				
29. Showing understanding of another's feelings				
30. Expressing concern for another				

III. Skills for dealing with feelings (cont.)	Student name			
31. Dealing with your anger				
32. Dealing with another's anger				
33. Expressing affection				
34. Dealing with fear				
35. Rewarding yourself				
IV. Skill alternatives to aggression				
36. Using self-control				
37. Asking permission				
38. Responding to teasing				
39. Avoiding trouble				
40. Staying out of fights				
41. Problem solving				
42. Accepting consequences				
43. Dealing with accusation				
44. Negotiating				
V. Skills for dealing with stress				
45. Dealing with boredom				
46. Deciding what caused a problem				
47. Making a complaint				
48. Answering a complaint				
49. Dealing with losing				
50. Being a good sport				
51. Dealing with being left out				
52. Dealing with embarrassment				
53. Reacting to failure				
54. Accepting no				
55. Saying no				
56. Relaxing				
57. Dealing with group pressure				
58. Dealing with wanting something that isn't yours				
59. Making a decision				
60. Being honest				

FIGURE 15.2

Skillstreaming the Elementary School Child: Grouping Chart From: McGinnis, E., & Goldstein, A.P. (1997). *Skillstreaming the elementary school child: New strategies and perspectives for teaching prosocial skills.* Champaign, IL: Research Press. Copyright 1997 by the authors. Reprinted by permission.

specific social skill. These interactions can easily be used along with any structured curriculum for teaching social skills, and they harness opportunities for teaching these skills, which occur naturally in the classroom. (*Getting Along with Others* is available through Research Press, P.O. Box 9177, Champaign, IL 61826.)

The first teaching interaction, called "effective praise," serves two purposes: to inform students about appropriate behaviors that should be repeated, and to reward them for correct behavior. Effective praise begins with an expression of affection (e.g., smiling or saying the child's name) and ends with a specific statement of praise telling the student exactly what he or she did correctly. For example, Ms. Lopez might praise Joey for getting the teacher's attention

I. Beginning social skills			
1. Listening			
2. Starting a conversation			
3. Having a conversation			
4. Asking a question			
5. Saying thank you			
6. Introducing yourself			
7. Introducing other people			
8. Giving a compliment			
II. Advanced social skills			
9. Asking for help			
10. Joining in			
11. Giving instructions			
12. Following instructions			
13. Apologizing			
14. Convincing others			
Group III. Skills for dealing with feelings			
15. Knowing your feelings			
16. Expressing your feelings			
17. Understanding the feelings of others			
18. Dealing with someone else's anger			
19. Expressing affection			
20. Dealing with fear			
21. Rewarding yourself			
Group IV. Skill alternative to aggression			
22. Asking permission			
23. Sharing something			
24. Helping others			
25. Negotiation			
26. Using self-control			
27. Standing up for your rights			
28. Responding to teasing			
29. Avoiding trouble with others			
30. Keeping out of fights			

Group V. Skills for dealing with stress			
31. Making a complaint			
32. Answering a complaint			
33. Being a good sport			
34. Dealing with embarrassment			
35. Dealing with being left out			
36. Standing up for a friend			
37. Responding to persuasion			
38. Responding to failure			
39. Dealing with contradictory messages			
40. Dealing with an accusation			
41. Getting ready for a difficult conversation			
42. Dealing with group pressure			
Group VI. Planning skills			
43. Deciding on something to do			
44. Deciding what caused a problem			
45. Setting a goal			
46. Deciding on your abilities			
47. Gathering information			
48. Arranging problems by importance			
49. Making a decision			
50. Concentrating on a task			

FIGURE 15.3

Skillstreaming for the Adolescent From: Goldstein, A.P., & McGinnis, E. (1997). *Skillstreaming the adolescent: New strategies and perspectives for teaching prosocial skills.* Champaign, IL: Research Press. Copyright 1997 by the authors. Reprinted by permission.

appropriately by saying, "Joey (an expression of affection), that was a good job of getting my attention the right way. You raised your hand, waited quietly for me to call on you, and used a polite tone of voice (specific praise). You may certainly be line leader today" (reward for correct behavior).

The second strategy, called the "teaching interaction," is used to interrupt a student's inappropriate behavior and to prompt a student to practice the appropriate social skill (Jackson, Jackson, & Monroe, 1983). The teaching interaction begins with an expression of affection in order to start the instructional episode on a positive note. Often, this expression of affection is either a statement of empathy or one of initial praise for something the student has done properly. This is followed by a description of the inappropriate behavior and an explanation of the appropriate social skill. Finally, the student is requested to practice the correct social skill and is given general praise for doing so.

The goal of this second strategy is to take positive action in order to teach the child the appropriate behavior when it is actually needed in a specific situation. In the previous example, if Joey were to leave his seat and start toward the classroom door, Ms. Lopez might interrupt his inappropriate behavior by stating, "Joey, I understand that you want to be line leader for lunch today (an expression of affection and empathy), but you just forgot to get my attention the right way (a description of the inappropriate behavior). What you need to do is stay in your seat, raise your hand, and wait for me to call on you (a description of the appropriate behavior). Please go back to your seat, raise your hand, and wait quietly for me to call on you" (a request for practice of the appropriate social skill). When Joey returns to his seat, Ms. Lopez will give him general praise by stating, "Thank you, Joey. That was a good job of getting my attention the right way!"

Whenever a teacher enters a teaching interaction with a student and the student becomes argumentative, begins to display his or her temper, or becomes noncompliant, the teacher initiates the third strategy. The "direct prompt" (Jackson, Jackson, & Monroe, 1983) is a short statement telling the student exactly what he or she must do in order to behave appropriately. Here, the teacher calmly issues a "You need to . . ." statement. If the student complies, the teacher delivers effective praise. However, if the student continues to display inappropriate behavior, the teacher issues an "If . . . then . . ." statement and follows through with the consequence for noncompliance if necessary. The consequences for noncompliance must, of course, be preestablished and clearly explained to students before they are used.

Ms. Lopez, in the previous example, might enter a teaching interaction with Joey by stating, "Joey, I understand that you want to be line leader for lunch today, but you just forgot to get my attention the right way." Joey, however, continues to march toward the door mumbling, "It's my turn for line leader. You never let me be line leader and it's my turn!" At this point, Ms. Lopez issues a direct prompt, saying, "You need to get my attention appropriately so I can call on you to be line leader." If Joey complies, Ms. Lopez might deliver "effective praise" along with a point loss and gain: "Joey, that was excellent. You followed my instructions by returning to your seat and waiting for me to call on you. You lost 100 points for forgetting to get my attention appropriately, but you've earned back 50 points for following my instructions." If Joey were to fail to comply following the direct prompt, however, Ms. Lopez might state, "Joey, if you do not return to your seat and get my attention appropriately, then you will choose to lose 100 points." Ms. Lopez must, of course, follow through with the point loss for continued noncompliance.

A Summary of Social Skills Instruction ◆

Special education teachers must provide social skills instruction for many of their students. Although such instruction is not necessary for every child, several social-skills curricula do exist for those youngsters requiring practice in this area. Teachers must take care to supplement curricula using direct, systematic teaching procedures, such as modeling, role playing, and specific feedback, with planned activities to promote the generalization of the social skills that are learned. Harnessing opportunities for teaching social skills in context may be one way to promote the generalization of social skills to the inclusive classroom. ◆

Independent Living Skills

Recall, at the beginning of this chapter, Mr. Abel's concern for Susan's ability to live independently as an adult. Like Susan, many students in special education programs do not have the basic daily living and vocational skills necessary for adult functioning. In fact, some authorities suggest that children like Susan who are currently placed in programs for students with mild mental retardation have more serious deficits than those identified in years past (Patton, Beirne-Smith, & Payne, 1990). Students like Robert, Travis, Joey, and Taylor will also require assistance as they get older and prepare to leave high school. For individuals with mild disabilities, the technology and "information age" of the twenty-first century will present significant barriers unless teachers prepare students for these challenges and unless supports are made available to them as information and technology rapidly change (Wircenski & Wircenski, 1997). These students require instruction and support in functional daily-living, vocational, and social skills (Smith & Puccini, 1995).

Adult Outcomes and Transitioning

Recent reports to Congress (U.S. Department of Education, 1997) indicate that 28.24% of students with disabilities over the age of fourteen exited school during the 1994-95 year. Of these students, 4.94% dropped out and another 3.49% exited with "unknown" status. That is, these students stopped attending school but were not known to have enrolled in a new school district. For students aged 14 and older, with learning disabilities, emotional/behavioral disorders, and mental retardation, combined percentages for dropping out and "unknown" status were 7.97%, 15.85%, and 6.29% respectively. Only 7.58% of all students in special education programs completed high school and earned an actual diploma.

Numerous reports suggest that when students with disabilities leave school, either with or without a high school diploma, they remain unemployed or work at part-time jobs or in positions that offer little opportunity for advancement (Edgar, 1987; Wagner, 1989). Data in a national longitudinal study of 8,000 youngsters aged 13 to 21, who were enrolled in special education programs in the 1985-86 school year, indicate that only one third of these former students were employed full-time 1 year after exiting school (Wagner). According to Wagner and Blackorby (1996) and Blackorby and Wagner (1996), employment rates improve to 57% when students have been out of high school from 3 to 5 years; however, 36% were still not working and an additional 17% were not looking for work. Moreover, youth with disabilities were more likely to be living at home 3 to 5 years after high school than were their peers.

Edgar (1987) reports that among special education graduates, only 18% were earning minimum wage or better. Moreover, females were more likely to be unemployed than males (Levine & Edgar, 1994; Lichtenstein, 1996). Females with learning disabilities were also more likely than peers without disabilities to be unmarried and parenting but not working or attending school (Murray, Goldstein, & Edgar, 1997). Three to five years after leaving high school, 60% of youth with disabilities were earning less than $6.00 per hour (Blackorby & Wagner, 1996; Wagner & Blackorby, 1996). Twice as many males as females, and three times as many white youth as African-American youth, were earning at the $6.00 or more wage level. High school graduates and students without disabilities were more likely to be earning the higher wage than those who did not graduate or those with disabilities.

One possible explanation for the difference in wages earned by students with and without disabilities is their rate of enrollment in postsecondary education programs (Goldstein, Murray, & Edgar, 1998). Blackorby and Wagner (1996) and Wagner and Blackorby (1996) report that almost 70% of youth without disabilities are involved in some type of postsecondary school education (i.e., 2-year or 4-year college or a technical school program); whereas, among youth with disabilities, only 26.7% are similarly engaged. Surprisingly, only 30% of students with learning disabilities enroll in postsecondary education programs 3 to 5 years after leaving high school, despite their intellectual ability, and the percentages of students with emotional disturbance or mental retardation entering postsecondary schools are even lower (25.6% and 12.8%, respectively). Moreover, students with learning disabilities hold lower occupational aspirations than their peers without disabilities, whether they aspire to a high school diploma, an advanced college degree, or less than a high school diploma (Rojewski, 1996).

Post-school outcomes such as these are problematic for students with mild mental retardation (Patton et al., 1996) and learning disabilities (Goldstein et al., 1998; Murray et al., 1997). Unfortunately, the statistics are even worse for students with emotional and/or behavioral disorders, who continue to lag far behind their peers without disabilities (Frank & Sitlington, 1997). Not only do few of these students go on to attend postsecondary education programs or obtain degrees, but 50% of these youth also drop out of high school (Malmgren, Edgar, & Neel, 1998). According to Mattison, Spitznagel, and Felix (1998), increasing age, conduct or oppositional disorder, presence of a depressive or anxiety disorder, and low verbal IQ are predictive of whether or not a student with an emotional/behavioral disorder is at risk of dropping out of school and experiencing reduced adult outcomes. Furthermore, although students with behavioral disorders perceive a need to "change their attitudes," they believe teachers and administrators should also improve their attitudes, teaching styles, policies, and interactions with students to keep more young people in school (Habel, Bloom, Ray, & Bacon, 1999; Kortering & Braziel, 1999a, 1999b).

Clearly, teachers must plan ways to help their students with mild disabilities stay in school and learn those skills essential for adulthood. Research suggests that the following factors are related to staying in school and obtaining more successful post-school outcomes:

- Parents actively involved in the youth's educational program (Sample, 1998).
- Higher family income and socioeconomic status (Heal & Rusch, 1995).

- Appropriate instruction and accommodations enabling academic achievement (Rylance, 1997, 1998).
- Having self-care and daily living skills (Heal & Rusch, 1995), as well as job-related social skills (Benz, Yovanoff, & Doren, 1997).
- Having access to a functional life-skills curriculum (Patton, Cronin, & Jairrels, 1997; Patton et al., 1996).
- Participation in school-based counseling and vocational education programs (Malian & Love, 1998; Rylance, 1997, 1998) to improve self-determination (Wehmeyer & Schwartz, 1997), career self-efficacy (Panagos & DuBois, 1999), and "success attributes" (Raskind, Goldberg, Higgins, & Herman, 1999).
- Continued support and follow-up after leaving school programs (Patton et al., 1996).
- Community-based instructional programs (see, for example, Beakley & Yoder, 1998).
- School-based and work-based work experience as part of a coordinated school-to-work transition program (Benz et al., 1997).

In 1984, as a result of such dismal statistics as those mentioned previously, transitioning became a national priority (Will, 1984). In 1990, with the reauthorization of PL 94-142, the Individuals with Disabilities Education Act, and PL 101-476, transitioning became a national mandate (U.S. Congress, 1990). Along with IDEA (1997), the School to Work Opportunities Act of 1994 increased the importance of school-to-work transitions and work-based learning for all students (see, for example, Goldberger & Kazis, 1996; Grubb, 1996; Hamilton & Hamilton, 1997a, 1997b; Hartoonian & Van Scotter, 1996).

According to IDEA (1997), the term *transition services* refers to coordinated and outcome-oriented activities that "promote movement from school to post-secondary education, vocational training, continuing or adult education, employment, adult services, independent living, or community participation." Transition services "must be based on an individual student's needs, preferences, and interests, and must include instruction, related services, and community experiences leading to the development of employment or other post-school adult living objectives, and, when appropriate, the acquisition of daily living skills and functional vocational evaluation." School districts are now adopting models for teaching critical life skills to youngsters while they are still in special education programs and are also involving other appropriate service agencies in planning for the post-secondary needs of these youth before they make the transition from school to the adult world.

Transitioning Services

As students with disabilities leave high school and move to employment or adult settings, they leave a protected environment in which the school is responsible for their special education program under IDEA (1997). Instead, they enter a world in which they must seek out the services and accommodations they need under Section 504 and the Americans with Disabilities Act of 1990 (Gartin, Rumrill, & Serebreni, 1996). Without advanced preparation, many may not obtain the services or accommodations to which they are entitled under law.

Recall that Section 504 of the Rehabilitation Act Amendments and the Americans with Disabilities Act of 1990 prohibit discrimination against "otherwise qualified" individuals with disabilities. Section 504 pertains specifically to agencies of state and local government that receive federal funding, such as public schools, colleges, universities or technical schools. On the other hand, the ADA broadens the scope of protection to include not only agencies of state and local government, but also private employers, transportation, private businesses, and telecommunications. In order to access the protection afforded under these laws, however, individuals with disabilities must recognize their rights and develop the skills to advocate for them.

For example, professionals in Taylor's school have recognized that under Section 504 Taylor has a "substantial limitation" (her AD/HD) in one or more "major life activities" (learning and full participation in school). They have developed an accommodation plan, also called a Section 504 plan or an ADA plan, to prohibit discrimination and afford Taylor equal treatment and access to her education while she is in the public schools. Blazer (1999) suggests that parents, students, and teachers systematically and collaboratively plan necessary accomodations in the physical, instructional, and behavioral environment. Physical accomodations, for example, might include posting schedules or classroom rules; using preferential seating, quiet study areas, or standing work stations; or organizing the workspace and using color codes. Instructional accomodations might range from repeating and simplifying oral directions, to providing directions in written form, to individualizing homework or other assignments. Modified testing and technological learning aids such as computers are additional forms of instructional accomodations often noted on Section 504 plans. Finally, behavioral accomodations include using positive reinforcement, goal setting, leadership opportunities, and consistency to promote appropriate behaviors, and communicating with parents and teachers through letters, meetings, phone calls, and so forth. (See Appendix A for a copy of Taylor's Section 504 Plan.)

When Taylor leaves high school and goes to college, however, she will have to take the initiative to obtain similar services. To help students like Taylor make the transition to college, some high schools link the student and his or her family with the "Section 504 Officer" on the college campus. This individual, in turn, develops an accommodation plan to enable the student to participate fully in college classes and college life. It is the student's responsibility, though, to ask for the necessary accommodations as they are needed. Teachers may also take students to visit college campuses and teach them the skills they will need to be proactive and serve effectively as their own advocates (CEC, 1997). Without advanced preparation such as this, students with learning disabilities may not have meaningful access to Section 504 or other services, such as those provided through a college's career development office (deBettencourt, Bonaro, & Sabornie, 1995).

For some students with mild disabilities, college will not be an option. These students require specific instruction in skills that will qualify them for well-paying jobs. Moreover, many youth with mild disabilities also need instruction in the appropriate social and advocacy skills necessary to access or maintain employment and enjoy the protections afforded them under the ADA. Still others will need ongoing support through adult service agencies in order to remain employed and to live independently. As the individual student progresses through school, members of the IEP team must consider his or her *future educational, vocational, and daily living needs*.

Although schools are implementing transition services for students with disabilities, there is still room for improvement. According to the Council for Exceptional Children (CEC) (1997), students with disabilities and their families may face the following barriers to a successful transition:

♦ Teachers who believe students with disabilities lack the academic skills to participate in technical or apprenticeship programs;

♦ Teachers who believe students with mild disabilities do not need transition services;

♦ Schools that discontinue vocational programs and emphasize only higher standards and college attendance;

♦ Eroding public support and funding for vocational programs; and

♦ Bias that fails to provide the same opportunities in the job market for females or members of ethnic groups as are offered to white males.

Therefore, several elements are critical for the success of transitioning efforts. Furney, Hasazi, and DeStefano (1997) report that states successfully implementing transitioning programs have developed collaborative structures to promote systemic change, such as creating interagency teams at the local and state level. In addition, Repetto and Correa (1996) encourage school personnel to help students and parents successfully plan for multiple transitions from early childhood to elementary school, from elementary to middle school, from middle to high school, and from high school to the postsecondary world.

For successful transitioning to occur, teachers also must consider the wishes and needs of parents and the students with disabilities themselves. For example, cultural factors may impact the types of occupations parents esteem (Syzmanski, 1994), and parents of students with disabilities may experience more anxiety and pessimism as their offspring leave high school than do parents of students without disabilities (Whitney-Thomas & Hanley-Maxwell, 1996). Moreover, students with disabilities believe that parental support and involvement is crucial, but that their parents must support them in their early efforts at self-determination if they are to become autonomous as they get older (Morningstar, Turnbull, & Turnbull, 1995). Although student and parental involvement are seen as critical elements for the success of transitioning, this participation is not always easy to obtain (Lehmann, Bassett, & Sands, 1999). For students, instruction in self-determination and advocacy skills is essential if they are to have a meaningful voice in the construction of their transition plan (Collet-Klingenberg, 1998; Thomas, 1999).

Individualized Transition Plans

One requirement of the Individuals with Disabilities Education Act (1997) is a statement on the IEP, made no later than age 14, and before age 14 whenever appropriate, of transition services needed for students in special education programs. An additional requirement on the IEP is a statement at least one year before the age of majority under a state's law that the child has been informed of his or her rights and that these rights will transfer to the child on reaching the age of majority. Thus, students, parents, teachers, counselors, and representatives from adult service agencies all must be involved in transitioning efforts. The complexity of transition planning will necessitate new responsibilities for special educators who serve as transition coordinators (Asselin, Todd-Allen, deFur, 1998) (see Table 15.2).

The Individualized Transition Plan (ITP) becomes a part of the student's IEP and describes interagency linkages and responsibilities if necessary. For example, the ITP promotes collaboration among special educators and state vocational rehabilitation counselors, professionals who often serve persons with disabilities after they leave school. Providing information about adult service agencies to students and their families and establishing early links to these agencies may be critical if students with mild disabilities are to make use of available services when they leave school (DeFur & Taymans, 1995; Smith, 1992). In addition to vocational rehabilitation, linkages can be established, for example, with:

◆ Local social service agencies,
◆ Centers for independent living or assisted living,
◆ Rehabilitation engineering services,
◆ Mental health, mental retardation, and substance abuse services, and
◆ Section 504 officers from local colleges or universities.

Whereas the IEP details educational or social goals, objectives, and services, the ITP must describe essential skills and services required by the student when he or she is no longer in school. Therefore, the ITP should include *functional and measurable* goals and objectives designed to help students succeed on the job, at home, or in the community (Davis & Bates, 1997). Using leisure time wisely, managing money, getting along with coworkers, traveling about the community, and home maintenance are representative skills that might be included on the ITP. Moreover, involvement of appropriate adult service agencies to document responsibilities for job training, placement, and follow-up services is a vital part of the ITP process. (See Figure 15.4 for a sample ITP designed for Susan.)

Miner and Bates (1997) encourage school personnel to engage in "person-centered" transition planning. Working with Susan and her mother and grandmother, for example, they might obtain the following information to be used in transition planning:

◆ Susan's "Circle of Support"—Susan's name is placed in the center circle. Then, the names of others are placed in successive concentric circles around her name including (a) her closest relatives (i.e., her mother, grandmother, uncle, aunt, and three cousins), (b) other close relations (e.g., distant family members or friends), (c) situational relationships (e.g., those at school or in recreational programs), and (d) paid care providers.
◆ Susan's "Community Presence Map"—A web of where Susan goes and what she does daily, weekly, or occasionally is constructed. For example, branching out from Susan's home are daily attendance at school, weekly attendance at a county recreational program and at church, and occasional trips to the grocery store or the mall in a nearby city.

Table 15.2   **Responsibilities of a Transition Coordinator**

1. Intraschool Linkage
    A. Disseminate transition information to teachers/administrators
    B. Present inservice training
    C. Assist families, parents, and students to access transition services
    D. Facilitate communication between special and vocational education teachers
    E. Serve as a liaison between vocational school and special education teachers to monitor student progress
    F. Serve as a liaison to identify appropriate accomodations
    G. Serve as a liaison to screen for student placement
    H. Facilitate appropriate referrals to school-based programs
    I. Assist school staff in interpreting assessment results and recommending appropriate placements
    J. Assist school staff in understanding strengths and weaknesses and modifications
    K. Assist vocational teachers in adapting curriculum
    L. Provide technical assistance to school staff

2. Interagency/Business Linkages
    A. Identify, establish, maintain linkages with community agencies and businesses
    B. Educate adult service agencies about school programs/procedures
    C. Write cooperative agreements
    D. Facilitate referrals to other agencies
    E. Lead interagency transition meetings
    F. Initiate and maintain collaboration between and among different local education agencies
    G. Link students with postsecondary and special support coordinators

3. Assessment and Career Counseling
    A. Identify and refer students for vocational assessment within the school
    B. Identify and refer students for vocational assessment at regional centers
    C. Facilitate implementation of recommendations of reports by communicating and interpreting results with parents, teachers, and others
    D. Coordinate the development of career awareness and exploration activities as part of the career counseling process
    E. Collaborate with guidance for student participation in career fairs and job fairs

4. Transition Planning
    A. Identify transition services provided by community agencies
    B. Attend/participate in team and IEP meetings
    C. Assist in planning and placement decisions
    D. Identify appropriate assistive technology
    E. Monitor adherence to federal laws
    F. Oversee the development of postsecondary employment or training plans

5. Education and Community Training
    A. Promote self-advocacy activities and curriculum
    B. Train special education teachers and employers to understand the need for self-advocacy
    C. Prepare students for self-advocacy
    D. Coordinate school and community work-based learning opportunities (job shadowing, mentorship, internship, cooperative education, student apprenticeship)
    E. Identify job placements

Table 15.2   **Responsibilities of a Transition Coordinator—*continued***

   F. Develop community-based training sites and school-based training
   G. Provide technical support/assistance to employers and supervisors
   H. Implement job support services for work adjustment and success
    I. Identify/coordinate transportation options
   J. Manage/coordinate job coaches
   K. Monitor/coordinate job coaching activities
   L. Coordinate community-based instruction
   M. Coordinate teaching of daily living skills
   N. Examine/identify postsecondary training and education options
   O. Conduct various tours of employment/vocational training/education options

6. Family Support and Resources
   A. Inform parents/families of community resources—understanding services
   B. Develop and provide parent training
   C. Promote understanding of laws, eligibility requirements, availability of services
   D. Assist students/families in understanding the system and accessing services
   E. Mediate between school and families
   F. Counsel and communicate with parents regarding parent/student changing roles

7. Public Relations
   A. Disseminate information (videos, print material) to employers, parents (variety of audiences)
   B. Write newspaper articles and public service announcements
   C. Hold awareness events/presentations to employers, teachers, parents, students, service organizations
   D. Develop business partnerships (guest speakers, field trips, equipment, mentorship programs, etc.)
   E. Promote work-based learning opportunities with businesses, and recruit businesses
   F. Serve on a variety of community committees: Mayor's Committee for Persons with Disabilities, CSBS
     (disability services), employment network, Tech Prep, regional transition committees, postsec-
     ondary committee, business/school alliance
   G. Coordinate/sponsor transition fairs

8. Program Development
   A. Develop process in transition planning
   B. Develop system guidelines, programs, and procedures
   C. Develop and revise precedures and forms
   D. Develop and manipulate transition curriculum
   E. Collaborate with agencies for program development
   F. Propose new ideas for grant development
   G. Write grants for supplemental services

9. Program Evaluation
   A. Carry out school and community needs assessment
   B. Identify gaps in transition services
   C. Devise evaluation forms
   D. Conduct follow-up studies on students who exit the program
   E. Analyze and use information gained from evaluations
   F. Complete annual reports

Name: Susan Moyler   **Date:** 8/5/00

Current Age: 13   **Expected Date of Graduation:** 6/07

Transition Service Area	Person Responsible	Date Begun
Occupational Preparation Goals: Susan will acquire work experience in food services (unpaid) for at least one semester	Cafeteria staff in the Middle School with assistance from Mr. Abel	_____
Daily Living Goals: Susan will demonstrate good habits of personal hygiene on a daily basis including: bathing, washing hair, brushing teeth, wearing clean clothing, and applying deodorant	Mr. Abel Home Economics teacher P.E. teacher	_____
Personal/Social Goals: Susan will work independently for at least 10-minute intervals	Mr. Abel Mrs. Friend Ms. Booker	_____
Recreation/Leisure Goals: Susan will participate in one recreation program sponsored by Apple County on Saturday mornings	Mrs. Friend Apple County Recreation Department	_____

Signed:

Name	Title	Date
Mr. Abel	Spec. Educ. Teacher	9/5/2000
Martha Moyler	Mother	9-5-2000
Susan Moyler		9/5/2000
Mrs. Friend	Counselor	9-5-2000

FIGURE 15.4

Selected Goals from the Transition Component of Susan's IEP (See Appendix A for the remainder of Susan's IEP)

◆ Susan's Preferences—A list is made of "things that work" for Susan (e.g., watching television, playing with her cousins) and "things that don't work" for Susan (e.g., speaking to people she does not know, reading).

◆ Susan's Gifts and Capacities—Susan's positive attributes and strengths are listed (e.g., good with children, loving, likes to do things correctly).

◆ Susan's Desired Future Lifestyle—Questions such as these are asked: Where will Susan live? What does she want to do? What will she do for fun and recreation?

After this personal profile is created, a plan is devised for taking action. The activities necessary to bring about these desired outcomes, such as participation in a work-experience program, and the persons responsible for each activity are listed. Necessary changes in the service and support system are also considered in devising her transition plan.

Appropriate goals and objectives for the ITP planning process may also be developed through both formal and informal assessments. For example, special education teachers can gather much career-relevant information from the cumulative files (e.g., attendance data, health status, parent occupations) and from the confidential files (e.g., educational performance levels, family responsibilities, leisure-time interests) that are kept for each child in a special program. In addition, adaptive behavior scales such as those described in Chapter 6 offer teachers valuable information about social and independent living skills requiring instruction. Moreover, teachers can use criterion-referenced measures, such as the Brigance Series available from Curriculum Associates, to assess important life skills like completing checks, filling out job applications, or successfully interviewing for a job (see, for example, the *Brigance Inventory of Essential Skills: 1-6* and *6-Adult*; the *Brigance Life Skills Inventory*, and the *Brigance Employability Skills Inventory*). Other measures also can help students to determine potential career interests (e.g., *The Reading-Free Vocational Interest Inventory*, Becker, 1987).

Teachers may wish to conduct a "job readiness inventory" (Knight & Aucoin, 1999). Critical skills needed to function independently in the local community or on the job can be determined through systematic observation. When constructing these inventories, teachers might consider life skills such as proper grooming and personal hygiene; affective skills like following directions, accepting authority, or showing respect for others and their property; and employability skills such as working independently and being punctual. Parents, employers, and teachers can all be invited to rate students using these inventories. Once the skills that students do or do not possess are identified, task analyses may be conducted and the resulting lists used to pinpoint instructional needs for individual students.

Finally, teachers can use an "ecological inventory" to help students determine the requirements of actual jobs in the community. Robert can, for example, be helped to construct a set of questions to use during an interview with an employer. Actual job qualifications, duties, and social skills and behaviors necessary for job success can be included on the questionnaire as well as routine questions regarding the pay scale and hours for work. Robert's job-readiness skills can then be compared to the job requirements to enable him to prepare more successfully for those jobs most interesting to him.

As students prepare to search for jobs and make the transition from school, teachers can facilitate the process in many other ways. For example, students can gain work experience in school through school-based business enterprises such as an "Apple Cart Espresso Bar" (Lindstrom, Benz, & Johnson, 1997). Moreover, job clubs that meet at a regularly scheduled, convenient time and location can help students explore needed job skills as well as provide information about jobs that are actually available in the community (Lindstrom, Benz, & Johnson, 1996). Teachers can also facilitate the process by teaching students the independent living and "employability skills" they will need to be successful on the job, such as dressing appropriately for interviews or for work, job attendance, or completing job applications (Knight & Rieck, 1997; Patton, de la Garza, & Harmon, 1997) (see Table 15.3).

Independent Living Skills Instruction

Teachers must prepare their students to function independently as adults. This preparation must include more than just attaining a particular vocational or occupational skill. As Brolin (1995) suggests, career education must emphasize all roles and responsibilities of adulthood, both paid and unpaid work responsibilities, and family, civic, and leisure-time roles. Furthermore, career education must begin early in special education programs, preferably during the primary grades, if youngsters are to gain the necessary skills, habits, and experiences they will need later in life. When teachers wait until students enter middle school or become eligible for high school vocational or technical programs to begin career education, many opportunities for discovering work interests and for establishing work-oriented values and attitudes are lost.

Often, special education programs are oriented toward academic achievement alone, despite the student's need for a more functional curriculum. Teachers can and should make academic-skills instruction relevant and meaningful for students by providing a career orientation to subject-area instruction. For example, Mr. Abel might help Susan relate measurement skills in mathematics to following cooking recipes or patterns for sewing in her home economics class. He might also extend Susan's learning activities to include exploration of potential occupations that would require the use of measurement skills.

Integrating or infusing career education skills into subject-area instruction in school is an effective way of helping students learn independent living skills. Systematic planning is critical, however, if all essential skills are to be mastered. To determine whether or not skills to be taught are functional, Clark (1994) suggests teachers ask the following questions:

- ◆ Is the content appropriate for meeting the student's personal-social, daily-living, and occupational-adjustment needs?
- ◆ Does the content focus on knowledge and skills necessary to function as independently as possible in the home, school, or community?
- ◆ Does the content provide a scope and sequence for meeting future needs?
- ◆ Do the student's parents think the content is important for both current and future needs?
- ◆ Does the student think the content is important for both current and future needs?
- ◆ Is the content appropriate for the student's chronological age and current intellectual, academic, or behavioral performance level(s)?
- ◆ What are the consequences to the student of not learning the concepts and skills?

Teachers also must involve students with special needs in *community-based instruction*. Community-based instruction requires teachers to identify relevant

---

Table 15.3 **Employability Skills Instructional Units**

Unit 1: Preparing to Look for a Job
Lesson 1: Orientation to the course
Lesson 2: Obtaining documentation
Lesson 3: Key parts of a resume
Lesson 4: References
Lesson 5: Preparing a resume
Lesson 6: Learning about job applications
Lesson 7: Completing a job application

Unit 2: What Kind of Work Would I Like?
Lesson 1: Why should I work?
Lesson 2: Finding out about different kinds of work
Lesson 3: What am I interested in?
Lesson 4: What conditions would I like to work in?

Unit 3: Finding Out About Job Openings
Lesson 1: Job leads
Lesson 2: Organizing job lead information
Lesson 3: Locating and using classified want ads
Lesson 4: Reading classified want ads
Lesson 5: Using the yellow pages as a resource
Lesson 6: Using the white pages as a resource

Unit 4: Contacting Employers
Lesson 1: Making a good first impression
Lesson 2: Practicing telephone skills
Lesson 3: Telephoning employers
Lesson 4: Visiting an employer

Unit 5: How Do I Interview for a Job?
Lesson 1: Preparing for a job interview
Lesson 2: Dressing for a job interview
Lesson 3: Preparing for interview questions
Lesson 4: Practicing job interviews
Lesson 5: Following up a job interview

Unit 6: Handling Paperwork
Lesson 1: Understanding the key parts of your paycheck stub
Lesson 2: Understanding deductions from your pay
Lesson 3: Reading a work schedule
Lesson 4: Reading and completing a timecard
Lesson 5: Becoming familiar with state and federal tax returns

Unit 7: What Makes a Good Employee?
Lesson 1: Positive worker traits
Lesson 2: Starting a job
Lesson 3: Dressing and grooming appropriately on the job
Lesson 4: Taking initiative on the job

Table 15.3   **Employability Skills Instructional Units—*continued***

Unit 8: Getting Along with Others
Lesson 1: Understanding the role of a supervisor
Lesson 2: Accepting criticism from a supervisor
Lesson 3: What makes a good co-worker?
Lesson 4: Social skill, "greeting your co-workers"
Lesson 5: Dealing with customers

Unit 9: What If I Can't Make It to Work?
Lesson 1: The four rules of good attendance
Lesson 2: Whom to notify and when
Lesson 3: Notifying your supervisor when you must be absent
Lesson 4: Being on time

Unit 10: How Will I Get to Work?
Lesson 1: Telephoning for bus route information
Lesson 2: Reading maps and schedules (location to location)
Lesson 3: Reading maps and schedules (reading time schedules)
Lesson 4: Selecting a bus or trolley route
Lesson 5: Planning to transfer
Lesson 6: Safe and appropriate behavior when using public transit
Lesson 7: Solving transportation problems

Unit 11: Managing Your Personal Finances
Lesson 1: Banking services
Lesson 2: Choosing a bank
Lesson 3: Opening a savings account
Lesson 4: Making a deposit
Lesson 5: Withdrawing money from your savings account
Lesson 6: Reading your bank statement
Lesson 7: Using your automated teller machine (ATM)

Unit 12: Making Positive Job Changes
Lesson 1: Positive ways to handle stress and "bad" days at work
Lesson 2: Ending a job in a positive way
Lesson 3: Giving written notice of your resignation

Unit 13: What Are My Goals for the Future?
Lesson 1: Thinking about your future
Lesson 2: Guidelines for setting goals and making a plan
Lesson 3: The individualized transition meeting
Lesson 4: Being an effective self-advocate

From: Patton, P.L., de la Garza, B., & Harmon, C. (1997). Successful employment: Employability skills +. *Teaching Exceptional Children*, 29(3), p. 10. Copyright © 1997 by the Council for Exceptional Children. Reprinted by permission.

independent living skills in the local community and then teach these skills in the community setting. For example, Mr. Abel might determine that Susan needs instruction in making purchases and counting her change. In addition to instruction and practice in the classroom and school environments, such as the school store or cafeteria, Mr. Abel might arrange for opportunities to accompany Susan to local stores or restaurants to give her supervised practice in making purchases and counting change in her community.

For those students requiring extended assistance in obtaining a job in the community, schools sometimes employ a job coach for supported employment (Wehman, West, & Kregel, 1999). That is, a professional might train Susan on the job, ensuring her employer that the job will be performed satisfactorily during the training period. As Susan performs her job with increasing competence, her coach slowly fades from the job site while making systematic follow-up contacts to ensure that Susan's performance remains acceptable. Although supported employment requires additional research, particularly in using "natural supports" provided by coworkers and others in the job environment, the model shows promise for helping individuals like Susan to remain successfully employed.

Several career-education models also exist to help teachers provide students with the necessary skills for a successful transition to adult life. These include the Life Skills Instruction model (Cronin & Patton, 1993), the Life-Centered Career Education model (Brolin, 1993), and the Comprehensive Transition Education Model (Sitlington, Clark, & Kolstoe, 2000).

Life Skills Instruction. The Life Skills Instruction curricular model (Cronin & Patton, 1993) is designed to teach low-performing students the competencies and skills needed for survival in common situations they will encounter as adults. Six major domains of adulthood make up the Life Skills curriculum. These are employment and education, home and family, leisure pursuits, community involvement, physical and emotional health, and personal responsibility and relationships. Within the standard curriculum, then, basic reading, writing, listening/speaking, computation, problem-solving, and interpersonal skills are applied across the six domains to content areas covered in the regular classroom.

Concrete activities and tasks for attaining each of the life skills are also provided. At the elementary level, for example, students might apply basic writing skills to the domain of community involvement or leisure pursuits by filling out an application to play on a little league team. Similarly, at the middle school or junior high school level, youngsters apply interpersonal skills by asking a salesperson for help when making a particular purchase. Appropriate high school tasks include using reading skills in the area of health to interpret directions on a bottle of cough syrup or learning how the body fights disease in a science class (Helmke, Havekost, Patton, & Polloway, 1994). (See Figure 15.5 for examples of functional tasks at the secondary level.) The authors of this curriculum encourage school personnel to adapt the program to respond to technological advances and to current needs and resources of the local community as an integral part of transition education (Patton, Cronin, & Jairrels, 1997).

Life-Centered Career Education. The Life-Centered Career Education model (LCCE) (Brolin, 1993) is a competency-based model that has been adopted by numerous school districts across the United States. It has also received the support of the Council for Exceptional Children. Brolin (1993, 1995) views career education as a lifelong process, culminating in successful functioning in school, family, and community roles. In Figure 15.6, he identifies 22 competencies and 97 subcompetencies across 3 major domains: Daily Living Skills, Personal/Social

	Employment Education	Home and Family	Leisure Pursuits	Community Involvement	Emotional– Physical Health	Personal Responsibility Relationships
Reading	Reading classified ads for jobs	Interpreting bills	Locating and understanding movie information in a newspaper	Following directions on tax forms	Comprehending directions on medication	Reading letters from friends
Writing	Writing a letter of application for a job	Writing checks	Writing for information on a city to visit	Filling in a voter registration form	Filling in your medical history on forms	Sending thank you notes
Listening	Understanding oral directions of a procedure change	Comprehending directions	Listening to a weather forecast to plan an outdoor activity	Understanding campaign ads	Attending lectures on stress	Taking turns in conversation
Speaking	Asking your boss for a raise	Discussing morning routines with family	Inquiring about tickets for a concert	Stating your opinion at the school board meeting	Describing symptoms to a doctor	Giving feedback to a friend
Math applications	Understanding difference between net and gross pay	Computing the cost of doing laundry in a laundromat versus home	Calculating the cost of a dinner out versus eating at home	Obtaining information for a building permit	Using a thermometer	Planning the costs of a date
Problem solving	Settling a dispute with a coworker	Deciding how much to budget for rent	Role-playing appropriate behaviors for various places	Knowing what to do if you are the victim of fraud	Selecting a doctor	Deciding how to ask someone for a date
Survival skills	Using a prepared career planning packet	Listing emergency phone numbers	Using a shopping-center directory	Marking a calendar for important dates (e.g., recycling, garbage collection)	Using a system to remember to take vitamins	Developing a system to remember birthdays
Personal/social	Applying appropriate interview skills	Helping a child with homework	Knowing the rules of a neighborhood pool	Locating self-improvement classes	Getting a yearly physical exam	Discussing how to negotiate a price at the flea market

FIGURE 15.5 ◆

Life Skills Instruction: Examples of Tasks across Six Adult Domains at the Secondary Level
From: Cronin, M.E., & Patton, J.R. (1993). *Life skills instruction for students with special needs: A practical guide for integrating real life topics into the curriculum.* Austin, TX: Pro-Ed., p. 33. Reprinted with permission.

Curriculum Area	Competency	Subcompetency: The student will be able to:		
DAILY LIVING SKILLS	1. Managing Personal Finances	1. Count money and make correct change	2. Make responsible expenditures	
	2. Selecting and Managing a Household	7. Maintain home exterior/interior	8. Use basic appliances and tools	
	3. Caring for Personal Needs	12. Demonstrate knowledge of physical fitness, nutrition and weight	13. Exhibit proper grooming and hygiene	
	4. Raising Children and Meeting Marriage Responsibilities	17. Demonstrate physical care for raising children	18. Know psychological aspects of raising children	
	5. Buying, Preparing and Consuming Food	20. Purchase food	21. Clean food preparation areas	
	6. Buying and Caring for Clothing	26. Wash/clean clothing	27. Purchase clothing	
	7. Exhibiting Responsible Citizenship	29. Demonstrate knowledge of civil rights and responsibilities	30. Know nature of local, state and federal governments	
	8. Utilizing Recreational Facilities and Engaging in Leisure	33. Demonstrate knowledge of available community resources	34. Choose and plan activities	
	9. Getting Around the Community	38. Demonstrate knowledge of traffic rules and safety	39. Demonstrate knowledge and use of various means of transportation	
PERSONAL-SOCIAL SKILLS	10. Achieving Self-Awareness	42. Identify physical and psychological needs	43. Identify interests and abilities	
	11. Acquiring Self-Confidence	46. Express feelings of self-worth	47. Describe other's perception of self	
	12. Achieving Socially Responsible Behavior—Community	51. Develop respect for the rights and properties of others	52. Recognize authority and follow instructions	
	13. Maintaining Good Interpersonal Skills	56. Demonstrate listening and responding skills	57. Establish and maintain close relationships	
	14. Achieving Independence	59. Strive toward self-actualization	60. Demonstrate self-organization	
	15. Making Adequate Decisions	62. Locate and utilize sources of assistance	63. Anticipate consequences	
	16. Communicating with Others	67. Recognize and respond to emergency situations	68. Communicate with understanding	
OCCUPATIONAL GUIDANCE AND PREPARATION	17. Knowing and Exploring Occupational Possibilities	70. Identify remunerative aspects of work	71. Locate sources of occupational and training information	
	18. Selecting and Planning Occupational Choices	76. Make realistic occupational choices	77. Identify requirements of appropriate and available jobs	
	19. Exhibiting Appropriate Work Habits and Behaviors	81. Follow directions and observe regulations	82. Recognize importance of attendance and punctuality	
	20. Seeking, Securing and Maintaining Employment	88. Search for a job	89. Apply for a job	
	21. Exhibiting Sufficient Physical-Manual Skills	94. Demonstrate stamina and endurance	95. Demonstrate satisfactory balance and coordination	
	22. Obtaining Specific Occupational Skills			

FIGURE 15.6

Life-Centered Career Education Competencies and Subcompetencies From: Brolin, D.E. (1993). *Life Centered Career Education: A competency-based approach (4th ed.).* Reston, VA: Council for Exceptional Children, pp. 12-13. Copyright © 1993 by the Council for Exceptional Children. Reprinted with permission.

3. Keep basic financial records	4. Calculate and pay taxes	5. Use credit responsibly	6. Use banking services	
9. Select adequate housing	10. Set up household	11. Maintain home grounds		
14. Dress appropriately	15. Demonstrate knowledge of common illness, prevention and treatment	16. Practice personal safety		
19. Demonstrate marriage responsibilities				
22. Store food	23. Prepare meals	24. Demonstrate appropriate eating habits	25. Plan/eat balanced meals	
28. Iron, mend and store clothing				
31. Demonstrate knowledge of the law and ability to follow the law	32. Demonstrate knowledge of citizen rights and responsibilities			
35. Demonstrate knowledge of the value of recreation	36. Engage in group and individual activities	37. Plan vacation time		
40. Find way around the community	41. Drive a car			
44. Identify emotions	45. Demonstrate knowledge of physical self			
48. Accept and give praise	49. Accept and give criticism	50. Develop confidence in oneself		
53. Demonstrate appropriate behavior in public places	54. Know important character traits	55. Recognize personal roles		
58. Make and maintain friendships				
61. Demonstrate awareness of how one's behavior affects others				
64. Develop and evaluate alternatives	65. Recognize nature of a problem	66. Develop goal-seeking behavior		
69. Know subtleties of communication				
72. Identify personal values met through work	73. Identify societal values met through work	74. Classify jobs into occupational categories	75. Investigate local occupational and training opportunities	
78. Identify occupational aptitudes	79. Identify major occupational interests	80. Identify major occupational needs		
83. Recognize importance of supervision	84. Demonstrate knowledge of occupational safety	85. Work with others	86. Meet demands for quality work	87. Work at a satisfactory rate
90. Interview for a job	91. Know how to maintain post-school occupational adjustment	92. Demonstrate knowledge of competitive standards	93. Know how to adjust to changes in employment	
96. Demonstrate manual dexterity	97. Demonstrate sensory discrimination			
There are no specific subcompetencies as they depend on skill being taught				

Skills, and Occupational Guidance and Preparation. Competencies and sub-competencies are infused into the regular curriculum, whenever possible, as well as into practice activities at home and in the community. The LCCE is available from the Council for Exceptional Children.

Brolin (1993, 1995) has expanded the notion of Life-Centered Career Education to encompass transitioning requirements as well. His LCCE Transition Model, illustrated in Figure 15.7, spans kindergarten through adulthood and focuses on the attainment of essential LCCE competencies and sub-competencies. To implement this model, Berkell and Brown (1989) suggest that successful career education and transition planning should be based on twelve propositions as follows:

1. Early experiences are essential if students with disabilities are to develop a "work personality" (i.e., one's unique collection of abilities, needs, habits, and values with respect to work).
2. A career encompasses unpaid work and other productive pursuits at home and in the community.
3. Career development occurs across four stages: from career awareness to career exploration, career preparation,and career placement, follow-up, and continuing education.
4. In addition to daily living, personal/social, and occupational skills, fundamental academic skills such as reading, writing, and computing are essential for a successful, independent adulthood.
5. Career education should be infused into subject-area instruction rather than taught as separate courses or curricula.
6. Successful career development and transitioning depends on coordinated and interrelated efforts of schools, parents, businesses, and community agencies rather than on school instruction alone.
7. Hands-on, real-life experiences are critical for instruction in the LCCE curriculum.
8. Mainstreaming and community integration are vital aspects of career development and transitioning.
9. Cooperative learning methods can help students with disabilities achieve social and interpersonal skills necessary for successful participation in the classroom and in the community.
10. Both formal and informal career and vocational assessment play an important role in successful career development and transition planning.
11. Local transition teams, including special and vocational educators and vocational rehabilitation counselors, must monitor and carry out career and transition programs.
12. Interagency agreements and cross-agency inservices are necessary to ensure that all appropriate personnel will be involved in career education and transitioning.

Comprehensive Transition Education Model. The Comprehensive Transition Education Model (Sitlington, Clark, & Kolstoe, 2000) also infuses career-education concepts and skills into the special and/or regular curriculum (see Figure 15.8). Beginning in the infant and preschool years and

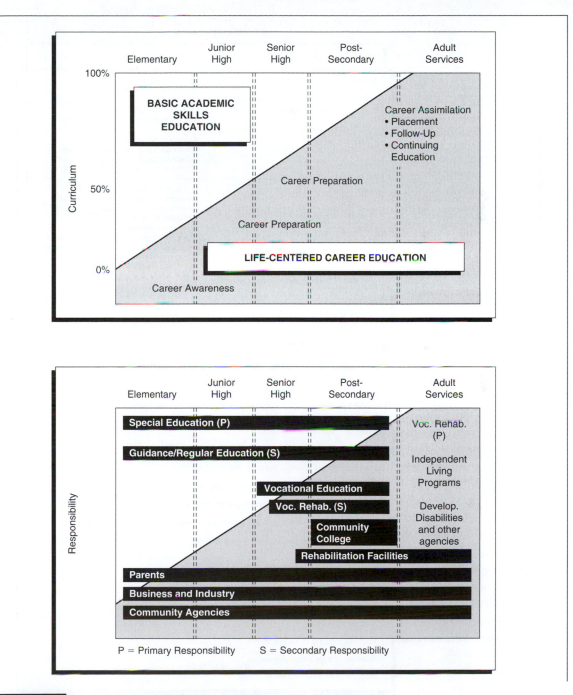

Top chart:

| | Elementary | Junior High | Senior High | Post-Secondary | Adult Services |

Curriculum (y-axis): 100%, 50%, 0%

BASIC ACADEMIC SKILLS EDUCATION

Career Assimilation
• Placement
• Follow-Up
• Continuing Education

Career Preparation

Career Preparation

LIFE-CENTERED CAREER EDUCATION

Career Awareness

Bottom chart:

| | Elementary | Junior High | Senior High | Post-Secondary | Adult Services |

Responsibility (y-axis)

Special Education (P) — Voc. Rehab. (P)

Guidance/Regular Education (S) — Independent Living Programs

Vocational Education

Voc. Rehab. (S) — Develop. Disabilities and other agencies

Community College

Rehabilitation Facilities

Parents

Business and Industry

Community Agencies

P = Primary Responsibility   S = Secondary Responsibility

FIGURE 15.7

Life-Centered Career Education Transition Model From: Council for Exceptional Children. (1993). *Life-Centered Career Education: Professional development activity book.* Reston, VA: CEC, p. 43 Reprinted with permission.

Exit Points and Outcomes

Developmental/Life Phases	Exit Points
Infant/toddler and home training	Exit to preschool programs and integrated community participation
Preschool and home training	Exit to elementary school programs and integrated community participation
Elementary school	Exit to middle school/junior high school programs, age-appropriate self-determination, and integrated community participation
Middle school/junior high school	Exit to high school programs, entry-level employment, age-appropriate self-determination, and integrated community participation
High school	Exit to postsecondary education or entry-level employment, adult and continuing education, full-time homemaker, self-determined quality of life, and integrated community participation
Postsecondary education	Exit to specialized, technical, professional, or managerial employment, graduate or professional school programs, adult and continuing education, full-time homemaker, self-determined quality of life, and integrated community participation

Knowledge and Skills Domains

Communication and Academic Performance

Self-Determination

Interpersonal Relationships

Integrated Community Participation

Health and Fitness

Independent/Interdependent Daily Living

Leisure and Recreation

Employment

Further Education and Training

Education and Service Delivery Systems

Knowledge and Skills Domains

Communication and Academic Performance

Self-Determination

Interpersonal Relationships

Integrated Community Participation

Health and Fitness

Independent/Interdependent Daily Living

Leisure and Recreation

Employment

Further Education and Training

Home and neighborhood

Family and friends

Public and private infant/toddler programs

General education with related and support services

Special education with related and support services

Generic community organization and agencies (employment, health, legal, housing, financial)

Specific community organization and agencies (crisis services, time-limited services, ongoing services)

Apprenticeship programs

School and community work-based learning programs

Postsecondary vocational or applied technology programs

Community colleges

Four-year colleges and universities

Graduate or professional schools

Adult and continuing education/training

FIGURE 15.8

Comprehensive Transition Education Model From: Sitlington, P.L., Clark, G.M., & Kolstoe, O.P. (2000). *Transition education & services for adolescents with disabilities* (3rd ed.). Boston, MA: Allyn and Bacon. (pp. 27–28) continuing throughout postsecondary education and adulthood, the following areas are given special emphasis across multiple education and service delivery systems:

1. Communication skills and academic performance
2. Self-determination
3. Interpersonal Relationships
4. Integrated community participation
5. Health and fitness
6. Independent/interdependent daily living
7. Leisure and recreation
8. Employment
9. Further education and training

Assistive Technology

In order to profit from instruction in academic or independent living skills and to function effectively in school, at home, in the community, or on the job, students with disabilities may need the benefits of assistive technology. The Assistive Technology Act of 1998 is one piece of federal legislation designed to increase the availability of assistive technology for individuals with disabilities. Moreover, an additional requirement of IDEA (1997) is that students are to be provided with *assistive technology devices and services* if these are necessary. Because assistive technology can be provided either as a form of special education or as a related service, a statement of needed assistive technology and services is to be placed on the student's IEP (Menlove, 1996).

According to IDEA (1997), *assistive technology* "means any item, piece of equipment, or product system, whether acquired commercially off the shelf, modified, or customized, that is used to increase, maintain, or improve functional capabilities of a child with a disability." Assistive technology services are any services designed to help "a child with a disability in the selection, acquisition, or use of an assistive technology device."

Parette (1997) suggests that assistive technology can be either "low-tech" or "high–tech" depending upon an individual student's needs. He defines assistive technology as any tool that is used on a daily basis and which has the potential to increase the functional abilities of a child. For many students with mild disabilities, assistive technology may be relatively "low-tech." Susan, for example, might benefit from adapted books to enable her to participate in reading activities in Ms. Booker's class. On the other hand, Robert might benefit from a small laptop computer for note taking or homework assignments in his classes. Appropriate assistive technology and services are to be determined by the IEP team. (See Box 15.1 for Web sites giving information on assistive technology and funding sources. See also Lahm and Nickels [1999] for assistive technology competencies needed by special educators.)

A Summary of Independent Living Skills Instruction ◆

Currently, most effective programs for career education, transition planning, or instruction in independent living skills have several features in common. They

Box 15.1

Web Watch

Assistive Technology Resources

Alliance for Technology Access

http://www.ataccess.org/

A wealth of information on assistive technology resources and advocacy for obtaining assistive technology devices and services.

Rehabilitative Engineering and Assistive Technology Society of North America (RESNA)

http://www.resna.org/

A wonderful resource containing links to many sites offering information on assistive technology and funding for assistive technology and services. Includes a link to the Assistive Technology Act of 1998.

Trace Research and Development Center

http://www.trace.wisc.edu/tcel/

Databases, links to websites, and documents providing information on assistive technology devices and services, funding, and legislation.

emphasize collaboration among professionals, coordination of services, and early planning as essential elements. In addition, effective programs infuse instruction across the curriculum and include instruction in community settings. Whenever necessary, assistive technology devices and services that will enhance a child's ability to function in his or her environment are provided.

Like social-skills instruction, however, career education and transition planning are not panaceas for all students with disabilities. As Halpern (1992) cautions, we still have a long way to go to improve what we teach, how we teach, and where we teach our students with disabilities. All too often career education and instruction in independent living skills are offered only within the confines of a classroom. Unfortunately, too, transition planning for some school districts means little more than choosing a career goal to write on a student's IEP. Such approaches are not likely to result in important and lasting benefits for youngsters in special education programs. ◆

Summary

Like Joey and Susan, many students in special education programs require social-skills instruction if they are to engage in successful interpersonal relationships with peers and teachers. Direct, systematic instructional techniques, using modeling, role playing, and specific feedback, are the most commonly used methods for teaching social skills. Teachers may choose from among several social skills programs based on these methods. In addition, special educators must plan for the generalization of social skills to natural settings by using realistic role-playing scenarios and by giving students self-monitoring sheets or other relevant homework assignments. Moreover, teachers must make use of the many opportunities for teaching social skills that occur naturally throughout the day during interactions in the classroom.

Transition planning and instruction in independent living skills are two related areas requiring attention by special educators. If students in special programs are to learn those life skills necessary for successful performance on the job, in the home, and in the community, career education must begin during the preschool years. Moreover, appropriate personnel from adult service agencies must become a part of the IEP/ITP process while students are still in school in order to plan and coordinate necessary goals, objectives, and services for these youngsters. Finally, the IEP team must request assistive technology and services if these will help a student function more effectively in school or beyond.

Application Exercises

1. Examine a social-skills curriculum used by your local school district. Does this curriculum include the techniques of modeling, role playing, providing specific feedback, and planning for the transfer of skills learned?

2. Ms. Kirk gives Joey 10 math problems and asks him to complete them in the next 15 minutes before lunch. Assume Joey begins the assignment immediately. If you were Ms. Kirk, how would you give Joey effective praise? Now assume that Joey does not follow your instructions right away. How will you phrase a teaching interaction with Joey? (Hint: You will first need to define "following your instructions!") Suppose Joey becomes argumentative during your teaching interaction. How will you issue a direct prompt?

3. Examine an ITP for a student in a local school district. What are the stated goals, objectives, and services? Be sure to obtain permission to examine the document first and to protect the confidentiality of the information.

4. Assume you are Mr. Abel participating in the IEP/ITP process on behalf of Robert. What would you suggest as appropriate independent living goals and objectives for him? What adult services might Robert need, if any, after he leaves school?

5. Ask a special education teacher in a local school district to describe the types of assistive technology devices and services provided to his or her students. How was funding obtained for these items and services?

6. Browse the Web sites listed in Box 15.1. Make a list of sources for funding assistive technology devices and services. Share this list with your colleagues. Then, assume you are conducting a workshop for parents on assistive technology. Prepare a list of important points to be considered when selecting assistive technology that you plan to share with these parents.

7. Locate four or five articles from InfoTrac regarding effective social skills instructions or locate four or five articles from InfoTrac regarding components of successful transition programs. Prepare a one-page checklist of important considerations for successful transition programs or the effective teaching of social skills. Distribute this checklist to your colleagues.

DETAILED INFORMATION ON THE STUDENTS

Psychoeducational Assessment for Travis

Name: Travis Johnson
School: Oak Hill Elementary
Date of Birth: 3-20-92
Date(s) of Evaluation: 10/25/00-10/27/00
Chronological Age: 8 years, 7 months
Current Grade Placement: 3.2
Examiners: Deborah Detail, School Psychologist; George Skillful, Educational Diagnostician; Susan Lopez, Special Education Teacher.
Tests Administered: *Wechsler Intelligence Scale for Children—III; Woodcock-Johnson Revised Tests of Achievement, Standard Battery; Woodcock Reading Mastery Tests—Revised; Key Math—Revised.*
Other Evaluative Information: Student work samples, classroom behavioral observations, teacher and parent interviews.

Background Information and Referral

Travis was referred for psychoeducational assessment by his third-grade teacher after several weeks of intervention strategies had been employed. According to his teacher, Travis is a bright youngster, but he has a difficult time in all areas of language arts and basic math skills. Travis's teacher feels that he does not pay attention to much of the group instruction and seems to work better in small groups or in a one-on-one situation.

Travis lives in an environment that appears to be warm and supportive. His mother, Mrs. Johnson, is concerned that Travis does not seem to be making progress in school and that he has a more difficult time with his studies than did his two older sisters. Mrs. Johnson believes that Travis is as smart as his sisters, but that he is sometimes forgetful. She also reports that Travis does not always finish what he begins at home, such as chores, games, or homework. He typically starts something new before finishing the original task. Mrs. Johnson also reports that Travis is not as neat and organized as his sisters. She believes that education is important and states that she will do whatever it takes to help her son achieve in school.

Test Results

Wechsler Intelligence Scale for Children—III
Verbal IQ: 102
Performance IQ: 127
Full Scale IQ: 119

Woodcock–Johnson Revised Tests of Achievement: Standard Battery

Subtest	Standard Score	Percentile Rank
Letter-word identification	83	13
Passage comprehension	87	19
Calculation	85	16
Applied problems	84	14
Dictation	84	14
Writing samples	67	1
Science	98	45
Social studies	104	61
Humanities	100	50

Standard Battery Clusters	Standard Score	Percentile Rank
Broad reading	85	16
Broad mathematics	82	12
Broad written language	77	7
Broad knowledge	100	50
Skills	80	9

Woodcock Reading Mastery Tests—Revised

Subtest	Grade Equivalent	Standard Score	Percentile Rank
Visual-auditory learning	1.8	91	26
Letter identification	2.6	88	20
Word identification	1.7	68	2
Word attack	1.2	65	1
Word comprehension	1.7	73	4
Passage comprehension	1.9	78	7
Readiness cluster	2.8	84	14
Basic skills cluster	1.5	66	1
Reading comprehension cluster	1.8	73	4
TOTAL READING CLUSTER	1.6	70	2

KeyMath—Revised

Subtest	Scaled Scores	Percentile Rank
Numeration	8	25
Rational Numbers	—	—
Geometry	4	2
Addition	8	25
Subtraction	9	37
Multiplication	7	16
Division	10	50
Mental Computation	9	37
Measurement	5	5
Time and Money	9	37
Estimation	9	37
Interpreting Data	8	25
Problem solving	7	16

Standard Battery Clusters	Grade Equivalent	Standard Score	Percentile Rank
Basic concepts area	1.4	77	6
Operations area	2.8	93	32
Applications area	2.1	84	14
TOTAL TEST	2.2	84	14

Analysis of Test Results

According to measures of intellectual ability, Travis is currently functioning in the above-average range. The discrepancy between his Verbal and Performance IQ scores may be significant. Analysis of subtest scores reveals that Travis seems to have significant weaknesses in attention skills and short-term auditory memory. Travis has relative strengths in the areas of visual memory, nonverbal skills, and general intellectual ability according to his performance on the WISC-III. The low score obtained on the coding subtest may indicate difficulty in fine-motor skills.

Travis is currently functioning one to two grade levels below expectancy for his age in word-attack skills, word identification, and areas of comprehension according to his performance on the Woodcock Reading Mastery Tests—Revised, and subtests of the Woodcock-Johnson Revised Tests of Achievement.

Travis's performance on the KeyMath indicates that he has the basic understanding of math concepts necessary to perform everyday math, as measured by skills on the Time and Money, Measurement, and Estimation subtests. He also has a basic understanding of elementary geometry. He exhibits weaknesses on the Operations subtests on items that require regrouping, algorithms, and multiple-step operations. In addition, he has difficulty retaining the data provided in order to answer some of the orally presented items of the Problem Solving and Interpreting Data subtests.

Summary and Recommendations

Although Travis is currently functioning within the above-average range of intellectual ability, he continues to struggle with grade-level school work. Travis seems to have academic weaknesses in the areas of reading, handwriting, and mathematics. His reading and math achievement may be influenced by significant deficits in attention and auditory memory. Classroom observations reveal that Travis finds it hard to pay attention and to follow directions.

Travis also has problems with the fine-motor skills necessary for handwriting. Student work samples display evidence of this difficulty. His weak organizational skills may influence his ability to complete assignments effectively.

The following recommendations are suggested to promote a successful academic experience for Travis:

1. Resource room support is recommended for language arts and math. Travis will benefit from small-group instruction and the classroom environment of the resource room.
2. Travis will benefit from direct instruction of organizational skills and a management program that promotes self-monitoring of organizational skills. Behavior management to increase time on task in the resource room and the regular classroom should begin as soon as possible. These efforts will help to preserve Travis's healthy self-esteem.
3. Travis may need additional time and support to master handwriting. In the computer lab, he should receive instruction in typing and word processing. The resource-room teacher should determine when Travis is ready to begin this process and may wish to allow a majority of Travis's work to be typed once he feels comfortable with the computer and keyboarding.
4. Support should be provided by the resource-room teacher to maintain Travis in the regular classroom for the remainder of his academic instruction. Completing work on the computer, extended time and a distraction-free environment during testing, structured reviews of directions for assignments, and a peer "buddy" system may be supports necessary to maintain Travis in the classroom.

Classroom Observation 1

Name of Student: Travis Johnson

Teacher: Mrs. Smith

Name of Observer: Deborah Detail

Grade: 3.2

Date: 10/25/00

Time: 9:30 AM

Class: Language Arts

Travis is seated with five other students in his reading group. Mrs. Smith calls on individual students to read short sentences of the story. Travis is unable to read when asked to do so. When Mrs. Smith verbally prompts him by providing the initial consonant sounds of the words, Travis is able to orally decode two of the five words in his sentence. He seems to be somewhat frustrated with the task and expresses relief when Mrs. Smith calls on another student to read. As the students alternate reading, Travis looks around the room rather than following along in his book. He turns to the next page only after he notices that the other students have already done so. Travis quickly jumps up from his chair when Mrs. Smith announces that reading time is over for the day.

The students return to their desks and most make the transition to the handwriting activity fairly easily. Other students in the class get their handwriting workbooks from beneath their desks when Mrs. Smith gives the visual cue of writing the letters for the day on the chalkboard. Travis spends more time looking beneath his desk, which has several ragged-edge papers sticking out of it. After several minutes, he is able to locate his booklet. The other students are well into copying the letters from the boards as Travis labors over the first letter. He seems to be concentrating very hard. As he finishes the first letter, his pencil lead breaks and he hops up to the pencil sharpener. He churns away at the sharpener until Mrs. Smith asks him to return to his seat, assuring him that his pencil is sharp enough for the task. Travis struggles with the second letter and is not quite able to copy it satisfactorily. He erases the letter and begins again, but this effort, too, is not satisfactory. Finally, he erases too hard and tears the paper. Mrs. Smith walks over to Travis's desk and quietly calms him by placing her hand on his shoulder. She turns to a clean page in his booklet and instructs him to start again.

Classroom Observation 2

Name of Student: Travis Johnson

Teacher: Mrs. Smith

Name of Observer: Deborah Detail

Grade: 3.2

Date: 10/26/00

Time: 1:15 PM

Class: Math

The students sit quietly as Mrs. Smith reviews the lesson from the previous day. Travis attends to Mrs. Smith initially but seems to be somewhat distracted by activities outside the window (another class is playing ball during P.E.). Mrs. Smith asks a question that involves a two-digit addition problem with regrouping. Travis raises his hand, along with several other students. Mrs. Smith calls on Travis and he responds incorrectly. Mrs. Smith reminds him that the number must be brought over to the tens column in this particular problem. Travis looks a little puzzled. Mrs. Smith begins the next problem on the chalkboard. Travis turns his head toward the window again and watches the other students outside.

Behavioral Observation

Name of Student: Travis Johnson   Teacher: Mrs. Smith
Name of Observer: Deborah Detail   Grade: 3.2
Date: 10/26/00
Time: 1:30
Class: Math
Behavior Observed: On Task
Intervals: 30 seconds

1	2	3	4	5	6	7	8	9	10	11	12	13	14	15	16	17	18	19	20
+	+	−	−	+	−	+	−	−	+	−	−	+	−	+	+	−	+	+	−

10 intervals/20 intervals = 50% intervals on task

Date: 10/27/00
Time: 9:45
Class: Language Arts
Behavior Observed: On Task
Intervals: 30 seconds

1	2	3	4	5	6	7	8	9	10	11	12	13	14	15	16	17	18	19	20
+	+	+	−	−	−	+	+	+	−	+	−	+	−	+	−	−	+	+	+

12 intervals/20 intervals = 60% intervals on task

Date: 10/27/00
Time: 11:00
Class: Science
Behavior Observed: On Task
Intervals: 30 seconds

1	2	3	4	5	6	7	8	9	10	11	12	13	14	15	16	17	18	19	20
−	−	−	+	+	−	+	+	+	+	+	+	+	+	−	+	−	+	−	−

12 intervals/20 intervals = 60% intervals on task

Teacher Interview

Name of Student: Travis Johnson
Name of Interviewer: George Skillful
Teacher: Mrs. Smith
Date: 10/25/00

Q: In what areas does Travis have difficulty?

A: Reading—especially reading new words. Mrs. Smith feels that Travis doesn't read well enough to comprehend sentences or remember details or story sequence. He also has difficulty with handwriting. Travis has been able to learn to spell and recognize a few short sight words. He hasn't yet mastered regrouping in addition or subtraction, although he does know his basic math facts 1 through 10.

Q: What are Travis's strengths?

A: Travis likes science and social studies best. He makes his highest grades in science. He likes math, but he hasn't yet mastered the organizational skills he needs to compute the more complex math problems.

Q: Describe Travis's typical behavior during a school day.

A: Travis likes school, and he likes his peers. He seems to be eager to begin each day and he volunteers to answer questions from time to time, although he doesn't always answer correctly. He has a real interest in science, especially now that the class has begun to study a unit on insects. Travis brought some bugs to school in a container and he enthusiastically explained to the class how he caught each bug. When Mrs. Smith informed the class that they would next study a unit on fish, Travis volunteered that his family had an aquarium and several books on tropical fish.

Travis seems to have difficulty attending to large-group instruction. He does better in smaller groups or in one-on-one instruction. He becomes frustrated with some of his seatwork assignments, especially handwriting activities.

Mrs. Smith reports that Travis does not display any aggressive or acting-out behaviors. He is able to quietly resolve any conflicts he may have with peers and is generally well-liked. Travis occasionally gets reprimanded for not following instructions or for not paying attention, although Mrs. Smith tries to "catch" Travis by calling on him whenever she notices his attention beginning to drift.

Psychoeducational Assessment for Joey Greenhill—Triennial Review

Name: Joey Greenhill

School: Oak Hill Elementary

Date of Birth: 9/4/90

Date(s) of Evaluation: 10/9/2000-10/11/2000

Chronological Age: 10 years, 1 month

Current Grade Placement: 4.2

Examiners: Deborah Detail, School Psychologist; George Skillful, Educational Diagnostician; Susan Lopez, Special Education Teacher

Tests Administered: *Wechsler Intelligence Scale for Children—III; Woodcock-Johnson Revised Tests of Achievement: Behavior Rating Profile—2: Parent, Teacher, Student*

Other Evaluative Information: Classroom Behavioral Observations

Background Information:

After being retained in kindergarten, Joey was referred and evaluated for special education eligibility in the first grade. He began receiving special education services during the first-grade year. This triennial review was completed to review Joey's progress. The IEP team decided to readminister the same tests initially used for placement to determine whether or not Joey is making adequate progress under the provisions of his IEP.

Joey's teachers feel that he has made some progress; however, they believe that he continues to need the support services provided through the special education teacher. Joey's teachers report that he needs support services in order to maximize both academic and behavioral skills. The IEP team believes that Joey continues to be eligible for special education services.

During Joey's initial evaluation and subsequent eligibility meeting it was determined that he would benefit from placement in the regular classroom for science, social studies, health, music, art, and P.E., and that he should receive resource-room support for reading and math. Support for the development of social skills and a positive behavior intervention plan would be provided in both the resource room and the regular classroom by the special education teacher.

Ms. Kirk, Joey's fourth-grade teacher, reports that he continues to have difficulty controlling his acting-out behaviors. He has had some episodes of aggressive behavior, including fighting and name calling. He may also react to conflict by crying.

Test Results

Wechsler Intelligence Scale for Children—III
Verbal IQ 102
Performance IQ 109
Full Scale IQ 105

Woodcock–Johnson Revised Tests of Achievement

Subtest	Standard Score	Percentile Rank
Letter-word identification	76	5
Passage comprehension	82	12
Calculation	63	1
Applied problems	81	10
Dictation	83	13
Writing Samples	82	12
Science	86	18
Social Studies	85	16
Humanities	90	25

Standard Battery Clusters	Standard Score	Percentile Rank
Broad reading	79	8
Broad mathematics	70	2
Broad written language	77	6
Broad knowledge	85	16

Behavior Rating Profile—2

Scale	Standard Score	Percentile Rank
Student rating scale	6	9
	4	2
	4	2
Teacher rating scale	5	4
Parent rating scale	3	1

Joey's classroom teacher, Mrs. Kirk, and his mother both rated the following behaviors as very typical of Joey's behavior:

- ◆ Is verbally aggressive
- ◆ Doesn't follow directions
- ◆ Doesn't follow rules

In addition, Ms. Kirk feels that he does not respect the rights of others, disrupts the classroom, and bullies other children. He says that other children don't like him. Ms. Kirk reports that Joey has no friends among his classmates. She rates him as overactive, restless, and an academic underachiever. Joey is considered to be "messy" in his personal space and he lacks organizational skills.

Joey's mother, Mrs. Greenhill, feels that he is sometimes verbally abusive to his parents and that he lies to avoid punishment. He obeys them only with reluctance. Furthermore, Mrs. Greenhill reports that Joey demands immediate gratification, is overly sensitive to teasing, makes "put-down" remarks about himself, and demands excessive parental attention. Among his peers, he is not a leader.

Joey completed the student version of the Behavior Rating Profile—2. His responses indicate that he has low self-esteem. He is aware that he is argumentative and that he is not liked by others at school. He admits that he tries to avoid his chores at home and breaks rules, but he believes that his parents treat him like a baby and do not allow him enough freedom. His responses indicate that he has difficulty concentrating in class and that he is really not interested in what his teachers have to say to him.

Summary and Recommendations

Joey's mother, teacher, and Joey himself are in general agreement that Joey is neither a popular student nor a strong one academically. He responds inappropriately to everyday occurrences and does not follow rules or instructions. In addition, his self-esteem is low. Joey is currently functioning within the average range of intellectual ability according to his performance on the WISC-III. His academic functioning continues to be somewhat depressed in terms of his intellectual potential. Based on these results, as well as his current educational functioning, it is recommended that he continue placement in the resource room and fourth-grade classroom with the same schedule. It is further recommended that appropriate, positive behavior management strategies be implemented in all school situations. Joey's parents may wish to meet with the school psychologist, guidance counselor, and teachers to develop a home/school behavior intervention plan.

Individual and/or group therapy with the school psychologist or guidance counselor is an additional strategy that may help Joey develop a more positive self-concept and learn better anger-management skills.

Parent Interview

Name of Student: Joey Greenhill
Name of Interviewer: Deborah Detail
Date: 10/10/2000

Joey's mother reports that he seems to be doing somewhat better since he has been receiving help in special education. Joey's grades continue to fluctuate, but he has not failed any subjects in about a year, and she is pleased with his progress.

Joey's mother does not feel that he has made much progress in developing appropriate social skills. She is aware that Joey is behaving a little better in some school situations, but he has not been able to improve much at home. (See the Behavior Rating Profile—2, Parent Rating Scale.)

Mrs. Greenhill wants Joey to be happy and wants very much to have a normal home environment. She stated that at times the entire household seems to revolve around Joey's behavior. If Joey is having a "bad day," all family schedules and events may have to be changed. She would like more guidance about how to handle Joey and additional instruction in social skills for her son.

Student Interview

Name: Joey Greenhill
Name of Interviewer: Deborah Detail
Date: 10/11/2000

Joey was asked to comment on his feelings about school prior to completing the Behavior Rating Profile—2. He remarked that he thought school was "okay," but that he would rather be at home. He said that he didn't like the kids in his class and that he wasn't interested in any particular subject.

During the interview, Joey spoke quietly with his head lowered. He did not maintain much eye contact. He was eager to begin the BRP-2 questionnaire rather than continue answering questions posed by the examiner.

Individualized Education Programs and Section 504 Plan

On the following 28 pages, you will find sample pages from the Individualized Education Programs (IEP's) for Robert, Travis, Joey, and Susan. On page 556, you will find a sample Section 504 plan developed for Taylor for her sixth-grade school year.

Confidential Information INDIVIDUALIZED EDUCATION PROGRAM School Year 2000-2001

Name Robert Richardson DOB 8-7-1985 School Apple County High School Grade 9

Disability Learning Disability Date of IEP Meeting 9-6-2000 Notification to parent 8-16-2000

Initiation and anticipated duration of services 9-6-00 6-9-01 Eligibility/Triennial 10-6-2002 Plan to be reviewed no later than 9-5-2001

M-Y to M-Y   M-D-Y   M-D-Y

Services Provided (Type and Intensity of Service)

Special Education and Related Services	Frequency/Duration Per Week	Date to Begin	Date to Complete	Location and Provider	Percent of Time
Study Skills and	5 days/week	9-6-2000	6-9-2001	Resource Room – Mr. Abel	15%
Use computer in	1 period/day				
resource room					

Transportation [√] Regular [ ] Special Describe: _____

Extent of Participation with Non-disabled Students

Subject and/or Activity

All academic subjects, Health/P.E., and Industrial Arts

in regular classroom with teacher support provided by

Mr. Abel.

Frequency and Duration Per Week

5 days/week

5½ hours/day

Does the program designed above ensure 6 1/2 hours of instruction or training per day? Yes

For High School student only:

This student is a candidate for: [√] High School Diploma [ ] Special Education Certificate [ ] GED Equivalency Diploma

Current Level of Performance

Achievement (Woodcock-Johnson) – Percentiles

Passage Comprehension – 7

Calculation – 11

Applied Problems – 10

Writing Samples – 7

Broad Reading – 7

Broad Math – 10

Broad Written Language – 8

Study Skills

Mainstreaming checklists and observation indicate Robert does not bring necessary materials or homework to class on a daily basis. He does not budget time to complete assignments.

Confidential Information   INDIVIDUALIZED EDUCATION PROGRAM   School Year _2000-2001_

Goals and Objectives Section: Must Relate Directly to Present Level of Educational Performance. (Use additional sheets as needed)

Area of Instruction: _Study Skills/Learning Strategies_

Area Goal: _Robert will demonstrate appropriate study skills in all of his content area classes by June._

Short Term Objective	Evaluation Schedule	Evaluation Procedure	Evaluation Criteria	Date Mastered
Robert will identify the materials needed for each class on a daily basis.	Daily	Mainstreaming checklists	100%	
Robert will take all materials needed to each class on a daily basis.	Daily	Mainstreaming checklists	100%	
Given an assignment book, Robert will write all assignments from each class correctly into the book on a daily basis.	Daily	Mainstreaming checklists; Daily checks by Mr. Abel.	100%	
Given strategies for studying for tests, Robert will apply the strategies to earn grades of "C" or better on weekly tests in Geography and Earth Science.	Weekly	Mainstreaming checklists; weekly test grades.	"C" or better on weekly tests	
Given a word processing program and computer available in the resource room, Robert will apply the "Paragraph Writing" strategy to write a coherent paragraph containing a topic sentence, 4-5 supporting sentences related to the topic, and no spelling errors.	Weekly	Mainstreaming checklists; work samples from English 9.	Topic sentence 4-5 related detail sentences No spelling errors.	

Confidential Information   INDIVIDUALIZED EDUCATION PROGRAM   School Year _2000-2001_

Goals and Objectives Section: Must Relate Directly to Present Level of Educational Performance. (Use additional sheets as needed)

Area of Instruction: _Transitioning_

Area Goal: _Robert will state 3-4 career options of interest to him by May._

Short Term Objective	Evaluation Schedule	Evaluation Procedure	Evaluation Criteria	Date Mastered
Given participation in 8 different units offered in the Industrial Arts class (carpentry skills, small engine repair, electricity, heating/refrigeration basics, basic plumbing, home maintenance, car repair, and basic masonry), Robert will state 3-4 which he enjoyed the most and why he enjoyed these.	9 weeks	Teacher interviews with Robert; Teacher observation	Statement of 3-4 preferences and rationale	

Confidential Information   INDIVIDUALIZED EDUCATION PROGRAM   School Year 2000-2001

Student Name: Robert Richardson

Student Number: _____

Are modifications to the Instructional Program required to implement this IEP?   _____ Yes or _____ No

Accommodations in Test Format:

Audio-Cassette
[ ] Math
[ ] Writing
[ ] Reading*

Braille
[ ] Math
[ ] Writing
[ ] Reading

Large Print
[ ] Math
[ ] Writing
[ ] Reading

Oral Administration
[✓] Math
[✓] Writing
[✓] Reading*

Accommodations by Use of Aids:

Answers Recorded by Proctor
[✓] Math
[ ] Reading

Braille-Writer Abacus
[ ] Math
[ ] Writing
[ ] Reading

Dictation to a Scribe
[ ] Writing*

Dictation into a Tape Recorder
[ ] Writing
(for pre-writing only)

Electric Calculations and Other Calculation Devices
[✓] Math*

Sign Language, Interpretation Directions
[ ] Math
[ ] Writing
[ ] Reading

Magnification
[ ] Math
[ ] Writing
[ ] Reading

Marking Responses in Test Booklet
[✓] Math
[ ] Writing

Place Keepers, Trackers, Pointers
[ ] Math
[ ] Writing
[ ] Reading

Typewriter, Word Processor, Augmented Communication
[✓] Writing

Written Directions
[ ] Math
[ ] Writing
[ ] Reading

Other: _____
[ ] Math
[ ] Writing
[ ] Reading

Hospital/Home Setting
[ ] Math
[ ] Writing
[ ] Reading

Multiple Sessions
[✓] Math
[✓] Reading

Testing in a Separate Room
[✓] Math
[✓] Writing
[✓] Reading

Other: _____
[ ] Math
[ ] Writing
[ ] Reading

** Designated Nonstandard Administration, but will not affect pass/fail or eligibility for high school diploma.

Confidential Information INDIVIDUALIZED EDUCATION PROGRAM School Year 2000-2001

Student Name: Robert Richardson Student Number: _____

Placement Justification Form

Check the following items YES or NO. A written explanation must be provided for items checked NO in 1 through 10.

	YES	NO
1. The school the student would normally attend, if not disabled, is the recommended placement or is the placement. Placement is as close as possible to the student's home school.	✓	
2. The student is educated in the regular class with the use of supplementary aids and services.	✓	
3. The student is educated in a special education class in the regular school building.	✓	
4. The quality of services which the disabled student requires to meet IEP goals is provided by the placement.	✓	
5. The placement providing educational services required to meet the student's IEP goals is appropriate taking into account the potential harmful effects to the disabled student.	✓	
6. The student is educated with chronologically age-appropriate peers (age-appropriate to school and class).	✓	
7. The student will participate in a regular physical education program with non-disabled, chronologically age-appropriate peers.	✓	
8. The amount of travel time and distance to and from school is appropriate.	✓	
9. The student is educationally integrated with non-disabled chronologically age-appropriate peers.	✓	
10. The placement in a more restrictive environment is based on the individual needs of the student.	✓	

Student will participate in the State Assessment Program: [✓] YES [ ] NO
If no, list any component(s) to be excluded. _____

Student will participate in local option testing: [✓] YES [ ] NO
If no, give reason(s) _____

** In the state of _____, the awarding of a high school diploma is based upon achievement. A student must earn the number of credits prescribed by the Board of Education and attain minimum competencies.

The implications of not taking or not passing the State Assessment Program have been explained to me and I understand them.

Mr. Richardson   _9/6/2000_   _Robert Richardson_   _9/6/2000_
Parent Signature   Date   Student Signature (as appropriate)   Date

Confidential Information   INDIVIDUALIZED EDUCATION PROGRAM   School Year _2000-2001_

Student Name: _Robert Richardson_   Student Number: _____

Signature of Participants	Relationship to Student	Date
Mr. Abel	_Teacher - Special Education_	_9/6/2000_
Mrs. Church	_Principal_	_9/6/2000_
Mrs. Wells	_Counselor_	_9/6/2000_
Mr. Richardson	_Father_	_9/6/2000_
Robert Richardson	_Student_	_9/6/2000_
H.S. Stone	_Teacher_	_9/6/2000_

I give permission for my child, _Robert Richardson_, to be enrolled in the special education program described in the Individualized Education Program (IEP). I understand the contents of this document and I have been informed of my due process rights. I understand that I have the right to review my child's record and to request a change in the IEP at any time. I also understand that I have the right to refuse this placement and to have my child continue in his/her present placement pending exhaustion of due process procedures. I have received a copy of the IEP.

_9/6/2000_   _Mr. Richardson_
Date   Signature of Parent/Guardian/Surrogate

I do not give permission for my child, _____, to be enrolled in the special education program described in the Individualized Education Program (IEP). I understand that I have the right to review his/her records and request another placement. I understand that the action described above will not take place without my permission or until due process procedures have been exhausted. I understand that if my decision is appealed, I will be notified of my process rights in this procedure. I have received a copy of the IEP.

_____   _____
Date   Signature of Parent/Guardian/Surrogate

Confidential Information

INDIVIDUALIZED EDUCATION PROGRAM

School Year 2000-2001

Name Travis Johnson   DOB 3/20/91   School Oak Hill Elementary   Grade 4

Disability Learning Disability   Date of IEP Meeting 9/7/2000   Notification to parent 8-22-2000
                                                    M-D-Y   M-D-Y

Initiation and anticipated duration of services 9-7-00 6-16-01 Eligibility/Triennial 10-29-2002 Plan to be reviewed no later than 9-6-2001
                                                M-Y to M-Y   M-D-Y   M-D-Y

Services Provided (Type and Intensity of Service)

Special Education and Related Services	Frequency/Duration Per Week	Date to Begin	Date to Complete	Location and Provider	Percent of Time
Reading and Math	5 days/week	9-7-2000	6-16-2001	Resource Room – Ms. Lopez	30%
in Resource Room	2 hours/day				

Transportation   [√] Regular   [ ] Special   Describe: N/A

Extent of Participation with Non-disabled Students

Subject and/or Activity

All other subjects and activities will be in the regular

4th grade classroom with in-class support provided by

Ms. Lopez.

Frequency and Duration Per Week

5 days/week

4 1/2 hours/day

Does the program designed above ensure 6 1/2 hours of instruction or training per day? Yes

For High School student only:

This student is a candidate for: [ ] High School Diploma   [ ] Special Education Certificate   [ ] GED Equivalency Diploma

Current Level of Performance

Reading (Woodcock Reading Mastery – Revised) – G.E.   Math (Key Math – Revised) – G.E.
  Word identification – 1.7   Readiness cluster – 2.8   Basic Concepts – 1.4
  Word attack – 1.2   Basic skills cluster – 1.5   Operations – 2.8
  Word comprehension – 1.7   Reading comprehension – 1.8   Applications – 2.1
  Passage comprehension – 1.9

Goals and Objectives Section: Must Relate Directly to Present Level of Educational Performance. (Use additional sheets as needed)

Area of Instruction: _Reading_

Area Goal: _Travis will complete the second-level reader by the end of the academic year._

Short Term Objective	Evaluation Schedule	Evaluation Procedure	Evaluation Criteria	Date Mastered
Given 100 vocabulary words from the 2^1 reader presented in phrases from stories in the reader, Travis will state the words with at least 90% accuracy by January.	Weekly Probes	Phrase probe— untimed	90% mastery	
Given 5 comprehension questions at the literal level following each story in the 2^1 reader, Travis will orally answer the questions with at least 80% accuracy by January.	Weekly	Oral testing by teacher	80% acc.	
Given a story read silently from the 2^1 reader, Travis will state the main idea of the story correctly with no teacher assistance.	Weekly	Oral testing by teacher	100% acc.	
Given 100 new vocabulary words from the 2^2 reader presented in phrases from stories in the reader, Travis will state the words with at least 90% accuracy by June.	Weekly Probes	Untimed Phrase probes	90% mastery	

Goals and Objectives Section: Must Relate Directly to Present Level of Educational Performance. (Use additional sheets as needed)

Area of Instruction: _Math_

Area Goal: _Travis will write the sum for 2-digit plus 2-digit addition problems with regrouping._

Short Term Objective	Evaluation Schedule	Evaluation Procedure	Evaluation Criteria	Date Mastered
Given a probe with 50 2-digit plus 2-digit addition problems with no regrouping, Travis will write the sum with 100% accuracy in 3 minutes.	Weekly	Timed, 3-minute probes	100%	9/22/2000
Given base-10 blocks and any 2-digit plus 2-digit addition problem requiring regrouping from the ones to the tens, Travis will demonstrate how to exchange 10 one-blocks for 1 ten block correctly within 15 seconds.	Weekly	Timed, 15-second trials with base-10 blocks	100%	10/3/2000
Given a probe sheet with 50 2-digit plus 2-digit addition problems with regrouping from the ones to the tens, Travis will write the sums with 100% accuracy within 3 minutes.	Weekly	Timed, 3-minute probes	100%	10/9/2000
Given a probe sheet with any 50 2-digit plus 2-digit addition problems requiring regrouping from the 10's or the 100's place, Travis will write the sums with at least 90% accuracy within 3 minutes.	Weekly	Timed, 3-minute probes	90%	

Confidential Information   INDIVIDUALIZED EDUCATION PROGRAM   School Year _2000-2001_

Goals and Objectives Section: Must Relate Directly to Present Level of Educational Performance. (Use additional sheets as needed)

Area of Instruction: _Math_

Area Goal: _Travis will write the product for multiplication facts through the nines._

Short Term Objective	Evaluation Schedule	Evaluation Procedure	Evaluation Criteria	Date Mastered
Given a probe with multiplication facts through the fives presented in random order, Travis will write the products with 100% accuracy within 2 minutes.	Weekly	Timed, 2-minute probes	100%	
Given a probe with multiplication facts from the sixes through the nines presented in random order, Travis will write the products with 100% accuracy within 2 minutes.	Weekly	Timed, 2-minute probes	100%	

Confidential Information   INDIVIDUALIZED EDUCATION PROGRAM   School Year _2000-2001_

Student Name: _Travis Johnson_   Student Number: _____

Are modifications to the Instructional Program required to implement this IEP?   ___ Yes   or   ___ No

Accommodations in Test Format:

Audio-Cassette
[ ] Math
[ ] Writing
[ ] Reading*

Braille
[ ] Math
[ ] Writing
[ ] Reading

Large Print
[ ] Math
[ ] Writing
[ ] Reading

Oral Administration
[ ] Math
[ ] Writing
[✓] Reading*

Accommodations by Use of Aids:

Answers Recorded by Proctor
[✓] Math
[✓] Reading

Braille-Writer Abacus
[ ] Math
[ ] Writing
[ ] Reading

Dictation to a Scribe
[✓] Writing*

Dictation into a Tape Recorder
[✓] Writing
(for pre-writing only)

Electric Calculations and Other Calculation Devices
[ ] Math*

Sign Language, Interpretation Directions
[ ] Math
[ ] Writing
[ ] Reading

Magnification
[ ] Math
[ ] Writing
[ ] Reading

Marking Responses in Test Booklet
[✓] Math
[✓] Writing

Place Keepers, Trackers, Pointers
[✓] Math
[✓] Writing
[✓] Reading

Typewriter, Word Processor, Augmented Communication
[✓] Writing

Written Directions
[ ] Math
[ ] Writing
[ ] Reading

Other: _____
[ ] Math
[ ] Writing
[ ] Reading

Hospital/Home Setting
[ ] Math
[ ] Writing
[ ] Reading

Multiple Sessions
[✓] Math
[✓] Reading

Testing in a Separate Room
[✓] Math
[✓] Writing
[✓] Reading

Other: _____
[ ] Math
[ ] Writing
[ ] Reading

** Designated Nonstandard Administration, but will not affect pass/fail or eligibility for high school diploma.

Confidential Information   INDIVIDUALIZED EDUCATION PROGRAM   School Year _2000-2001_

Student Name: _Travis Johnson_   Student Number: _____

Placement Justification Form

Check the following items YES or NO. A written explanation must be provided for items checked NO in 1 through 10.

	YES	NO
1. The school the student would normally attend, if not disabled, is the recommended placement or is the placement. Placement is as close as possible to the student's home school.	✓	
2. The student is educated in the regular class with the use of supplementary aids and services.	✓	
3. The student is educated in a special education class in the regular school building.	✓	
4. The quality of services which the disabled student requires to meet IEP goals is provided by the placement.	✓	
5. The placement providing educational services required to meet the student's IEP goals is appropriate taking into account the potential harmful effects to the disabled student.	✓	
6. The student is educated with chronologically age-appropriate peers (age-appropriate to school and class).	✓	
7. The student will participate in a regular physical education program with non-disabled, chronologically age-appropriate peers.	✓	
8. The amount of travel time and distance to and from school is appropriate.	✓	
9. The student is educationally integrated with non-disabled chronologically age-appropriate peers.	✓	
10. The placement in a more restrictive environment is based on the individual needs of the student.	✓	

Student will participate in the State Assessment Program: [✓] YES   [ ] NO
If no, list any component(s) to be excluded. _____

Student will participate in local option testing: [✓] YES   [ ] NO
If no, give reason(s) _____

** In the state of _____, the awarding of a high school diploma is based upon achievement. A student must earn the number of credits prescribed by the Board of Education and attain minimum competencies.

The implications of not taking or not passing the State Assessment Program have been explained to me and I understand them.

Mrs. L. Johnson   _9/7/2000_   _____
Parent Signature   Date   Student Signature (as appropriate)   Date

Confidential Information   INDIVIDUALIZED EDUCATION PROGRAM   School Year _2000-2001_

Student Name: _Travis Johnson_   Student Number: _____

Signature of Participants	Relationship to Student	Date
Susan Lopez	_Special Education Teacher_	_9/7/2000_
Ms. Kirk	_4th grade teacher_	_9/7/2000_
Mr. Grier	_Principal_	_9/7/2000_
Mrs. L. Johnson	_Mother_	_9/7/2000_

I give permission for my child, _Travis Johnson_, to be enrolled in the special education program described in the Individualized Education Program (IEP). I understand the contents of this document and I have been informed of my due process rights. I understand that I have the right to review my child's record and to request a change in the IEP at any time. I also understand that I have the right to refuse this placement and to have my child continue in his/her present placement pending exhaustion of due process procedures. I have received a copy of the IEP.

_9/7/2000_   _Mrs. L. Johnson_
Date   Signature of Parent/Guardian/Surrogate

_____

I do not give permission for my child, _____, to be enrolled in the special education program described in the Individualized Education Program (IEP). I understand that I have the right to review his/her records and request another placement. I understand that the action described above will not take place without my permission or until due process procedures have been exhausted. I understand that if my decision is appealed, I will be notified of my process rights in this procedure. I have received a copy of the IEP.

_____   _____
Date   Signature of Parent/Guardian/Surrogate

Confidential Information INDIVIDUALIZED EDUCATION PROGRAM School Year 2000-2001

Name _Joey Greenhill_ DOB _9-4-90_ School _Oak Hill Elementary_ Grade _4_

Disability _Emotional Disturbance/Behavior Disorder_ Date of IEP Meeting _9-8-2000_ Notification to parent _8-22-2000_
   M-D-Y   M-D-Y

Initiation and anticipated duration of services _9-8-00 6-16-01_ Eligibility/Triennial _10-15-2000_ Plan to be reviewed no later than _10-15-2000_
   M-Y to M-Y   M-D-Y   M-D-Y

Services Provided (Type and Intensity of Service)

Special Education and Related Services	Frequency/Duration Per Week	Date to Begin	Date to Complete	Location and Provider	Percent of Time
Reading, Math & Social Skills in	5 days/week	9-8-2000	6-16-2001	Resource Room – Ms. Lopez	30%
Resource Room	2 hours/day				

Transportation [✓] Regular [ ] Special Describe: _N/A_

Extent of Participation with Non-disabled Students

Subject and/or Activity

All other subjects and activities will be in the 4th

grade classroom with in-class support provided by

Ms. Lopez.

Frequency and Duration Per Week

5 days/week

4 1/2 hours/day

Does the program designed above ensure 6 1/2 hours of instruction or training per day? _Yes_

For High School student only:

This student is a candidate for: [ ] High School Diploma [ ] Special Education Certificate [ ] GED Equivalency Diploma

Current Level of Performance

Achievement (Woodcock-Johnson) – Percentiles
   Passage Comprehension – 12   Writing Samples – 12
   Calculation – 1   Broad Reading – 8
   Applied Problems – 10   Broad Math – 2
   Dictation – 13   Broad Written Language – 6

Behavior (BRP-2) – Standard Scores
   Student rating scale – 6,4,4
   Teacher rating scale – 5
   Parent rating scale – 3

Goals and Objectives Section: Must Relate Directly to Present Level of Educational Performance. (Use additional sheets as needed)

Area of Instruction: _Social Skills_

Area Goal: _Joey will demonstrate the first 3 social skills in the "Essential Social Skills" curriculum in all classroom interactions by June._

Short Term Objective	Evaluation Schedule	Evaluation Procedure	Evaluation Criteria	Date Mastered
Given a request presented orally by Joey's teacher or another staff member in the school, Joey will comply with the request 100% of the time within 30 seconds by saying "Okay" and beginning the request.	Daily	Teacher observation	100% in 30 seconds	
When Joey needs the teacher's attention, he will remain in his seat and raise his hand quietly until the teacher acknowledges him 100% of the in-seat requests made.	Daily	Teacher observation	100%	
When Joey makes a request, he will say "Please" 100% of the time.	Daily	Teacher observation	100%	

Confidential Information INDIVIDUALIZED EDUCATION PROGRAM School Year 2000-2001

Goals and Objectives Section: Must Relate Directly to Present Level of Educational Performance. (Use additional sheets as needed)

Area of Instruction: Social Skills -- Anger Management

Area Goal: Joey will demonstrate positive strategies for anger management by May.

Short Term Objective	Evaluation Schedule	Evaluation Procedure	Evaluation Criteria	Date Mastered
When Joey encounters a frustrating task in the 4th grade classroom, he will use the "anger management strategy" 100% of the time.	Daily	Teacher observation	Joey uses the strategy 100% time	
When Joey is provoked by peers in the 4th grade classroom, he will correctly use the steps in the "Dealing with Teasing" strategy to control his anger 100% of the time.	Daily	Teacher observation	Joey uses the strategy each time peers provoke him.	

Confidential Information   INDIVIDUALIZED EDUCATION PROGRAM   School Year <u>2000-2001</u>

Goals and Objectives Section: Must Relate Directly to Present Level of Educational Performance. (Use additional sheets as needed)

Area of Instruction: <u>Reading</u>

Area Goal: <u>Joey will correctly decode 90% of the words in the third grade reader by June.</u>

Short Term Objective	Evaluation Schedule	Evaluation Procedure	Evaluation Criteria	Date Mastered
Given any vowel or consonant digraph, Joey will state the most common sound for the digraph with 100% accuracy within 15 seconds.	Weekly	15-second timed probes using flashcards of digraphs.	100%	
Given a list of 50 new sight words from the 3rd grade reader, Joey will state the words with 100% accuracy in 3 minutes.	Weekly	List of sight words—timed 3 minute probe.	100% in 3 minutes	
When Joey encounters a word he does not know in the 3rd grade reader, he will correctly apply the "Word Attack strategy" 100% of the time.	Daily	Teacher Observation	Uses strategy each time an unknown word is encountered.	

Confidential Information   INDIVIDUALIZED EDUCATION PROGRAM   School Year _2000-2001_

Goals and Objectives Section: Must Relate Directly to Present Level of Educational Performance. (Use additional sheets as needed)

Area of Instruction: _Math_

Area Goal: _Joey will write answers for all division facts by the end of May._

Short Term Objective	Evaluation Schedule	Evaluation Procedure	Evaluation Criteria	Date Mastered
Given a probe with the division facts for divisors up to 5 and dividends to 50, Joey will correctly write the answers with 100% accuracy in 2 minutes.	Weekly	2-minute timed probe	100% in 2 minutes	
Given a probe with the division facts for divisors 6 - 9 and dividends to 90, Joey will correctly write the answers with 100% accuracy in 2 minutes.	Weekly	2-minute timed probe	100% in 2 minutes	
Given all of the basic division facts presented in random order, Joey will correctly write the answers with 100% accuracy within 3 minutes.	Weekly	3-minute timed probe	100% in 3 minutes	

Confidential Information   INDIVIDUALIZED EDUCATION PROGRAM   School Year _2000-2001_

Student Name: _Joey Greenhill_   Student Number: _____

Are modifications to the Instructional Program required to implement this IEP?   ✓ Yes or _____ No

Accommodations in Test Format:

Audio-Cassette
[ ] Math
[ ] Writing
[ ] Reading*

Braille
[ ] Math
[ ] Writing
[ ] Reading

Large Print
[ ] Math
[ ] Writing
[ ] Reading

Oral Administration
[ ] Math
[ ] Writing
[✓] Reading*

Accommodations by Use of Aids:

Answers Recorded by Proctor
[ ] Math
[ ] Reading

Braille-Writer Abacus
[ ] Math
[ ] Writing
[ ] Reading

Dictation to a Scribe
[ ] Writing*

Dictation into a Tape Recorder
[ ] Writing
(for pre-writing only)

Electric Calculations and Other Calculation Devices
[ ] Math*

Sign Language, Interpretation Directions
[ ] Math
[ ] Writing
[ ] Reading

Magnification
[ ] Math
[ ] Writing
[ ] Reading

Marking Responses in Test Booklet
[ ] Math
[ ] Writing

Place Keepers, Trackers, Pointers
[ ] Math
[ ] Writing
[ ] Reading

Typewriter, Word Processor, Augmented Communication
[✓] Writing

Written Directions
[ ] Math
[ ] Writing
[ ] Reading

Other: _____
[ ] Math
[ ] Writing
[ ] Reading

Hospital/Home Setting
[ ] Math
[ ] Writing
[ ] Reading

Multiple Sessions
[✓] Math
[✓] Reading

Testing in a Separate Room
[✓] Math
[✓] Writing
[✓] Reading

Other: _____
[ ] Math
[ ] Writing
[ ] Reading

** Designated Nonstandard Administration, but will not affect pass/fail or eligibility for high school diploma.

Confidential Information   INDIVIDUALIZED EDUCATION PROGRAM   School Year _2000-2001_

Student Name: _Joey Greenhill_   Student Number: _____

Placement Justification Form

Check the following items YES or NO. A written explanation must be provided for items checked NO in 1 through 10.

	YES	NO
1. The school the student would normally attend, if not disabled, is the recommended placement or is the placement. Placement is as close as possible to the student's home school.	✓	
2. The student is educated in the regular class with the use of supplementary aids and services.	✓	
3. The student is educated in a special education class in the regular school building.	✓	
4. The quality of services which the disabled student requires to meet IEP goals is provided by the placement.	✓	
5. The placement providing educational services required to meet the student's IEP goals is appropriate taking into account the potential harmful effects to the disabled student.	✓	
6. The student is educated with chronologically age-appropriate peers (age-appropriate to school and class).	✓	
7. The student will participate in a regular physical education program with non-disabled, chronologically age-appropriate peers.	✓	
8. The amount of travel time and distance to and from school is appropriate.	✓	
9. The student is educationally integrated with non-disabled chronologically age-appropriate peers.	✓	
10. The placement in a more restrictive environment is based on the individual needs of the student.	✓	

Student will participate in the State Assessment Program: [✓] YES   [ ] NO
If no, list any component(s) to be excluded. _____

Student will participate in local option testing: [✓] YES   [ ] NO
If no, give reason(s) _____

** In the state of _____, the awarding of a high school diploma is based upon achievement. A student must earn the number of credits prescribed by the Board of Education and attain minimum competencies.

The implications of not taking or not passing the State Assessment Program have been explained to me and I understand them.

Mrs. Greenhill   _9/8/2000_   _____
Parent Signature   Date   Student Signature (as appropriate)   Date

Confidential Information

INDIVIDUALIZED EDUCATION PROGRAM

School Year _2000-2001_

Student Name: _Joey Greenhill_

Student Number: _____

Signature of Participants	Relationship to Student	Date
Susan Lopez	_Special Education Teacher_	_9/8/2000_
Ms. Kirk	_4th grade teacher_	_9/8/2000_
Mr. Grier	_Principal_	_9/8/2000_
Mrs. Greenhill	_Mother_	_9/8/2000_

I give permission for my child, _Joey Greenhill_, to be enrolled in the special education program described in the Individualized Education Program (IEP). I understand the contents of this document and I have been informed of my due process rights. I understand that I have the right to review my child's record and to request a change in the IEP at any time. I also understand that I have the right to refuse this placement and to have my child continue in his/her present placement pending exhaustion of due process procedures. I have received a copy of the IEP.

_9/8/2000_   _Mrs. Greenhill_

Date   Signature of Parent/Guardian/Surrogate

_____

I do not give permission for my child, _____, to be enrolled in the special education program described in the Individualized Education Program (IEP). I understand that I have the right to review his/her records and request another placement. I understand that the action described above will not take place without my permission or until due process procedures have been exhausted. I understand that if my decision is appealed, I will be notified of my process rights in this procedure. I have received a copy of the IEP.

_____

Date   Signature of Parent/Guardian/Surrogate

Confidential Information INDIVIDUALIZED EDUCATION PROGRAM School Year 2000-2001

Name _Susan Moyler_ DOB _5/5/87_ School _Apple County Middle School_ Grade _6_

Disability _Mild Mental Retardation_ Date of IEP Meeting _9-5-2000_ Notification to parent _8-16-2000_
                                                              M-D-Y   M-D-Y

Initiation and anticipated duration of services _9-5-00 6-9-01_ Eligibility/Triennial _11-10-02_ Plan to be reviewed no later than _9-4-2001_
                                                  M-Y to M-Y   M-D-Y   M-D-Y

Services Provided (Type and Intensity of Service)

Special Education and Related Services	Frequency/Duration Per Week	Date to Begin	Date to Complete	Location and Provider	Percent of Time
Reading and Social Skills in Resource Room	5 days/week 2 hours/day	9-5-2000	6-9-2001	Resource Room – Mr. Abel	30%
Adapted P.E.	1 hour/day 5 days/week	9-5-2000	6-9-2000	P.E. classroom – Ms. Fit (weight control and hygiene)	15%

Transportation [✓] Regular [ ] Special Describe: _____

Extent of Participation with Non-disabled Students

Subject and/or Activity

Social Studies, Language Arts, Math, Health, Science
in regular classroom with support provided by Mr. Abel.

Frequency and Duration Per Week

5 days/week
3.5 hours/day

Does the program designed above ensure 6 1/2 hours of instruction or training per day? _Yes_

For High School student only:
This student is a candidate for: [ ] High School Diploma [ ] Special Education Certificate [ ] GED Equivalency Diploma

Current Level of Performance

Reading (Woodcock Reading Mastery – Revised) – G.E.
Word identification – 2.9   Basic skills cluster – 2.3
Word attack – 2.4   Reading comprehension – 2.2
Word comprehension – 2.9
Readiness cluster – 2.9
Passage comprehension – 2.3

Math (Key Math – Revised) – G.E.
Basic Concepts – 3.5
Operations – 4.3
Applications – 4.1

Social Skills
Checklist indicates
problems in self-
confidence and personal
appearance.

Confidential Information INDIVIDUALIZED EDUCATION PROGRAM School Year 2000–2001

Goals and Objectives Section: Must Relate Directly to Present Level of Educational Performance. (Use additional sheets as needed)

Area of Instruction: _Reading_

Area Goal: _Susan will increase oral reading rate and passage comprehension skills._

Short Term Objective	Evaluation Schedule	Evaluation Procedure	Evaluation Criteria	Date Mastered
Given any 200-word passage written at the 3rd grade level, Susan will orally read the passage at a rate of at least 150 words per minute with fewer than 2 errors.	Weekly	Timed probes from high interest/low reading level materials	150+ wpm; fewer than 2 errors	
Given a passage written at the 3rd grade level, Susan will orally answer comprehension questions at the literal level, after silently reading the passage, with at least 80% accuracy.	Daily	Oral questions at literal level from high interest/low reading level passages.	80% accuracy	
Given a passage written at the 3rd grade level, read silently, Susan will correctly state the main idea without teacher assistance.	Daily	Prompt: "What is the main idea?"	100% with no teacher assistance	

Confidential Information   INDIVIDUALIZED EDUCATION PROGRAM   School Year _2000-2001_

Goals and Objectives Section: Must Relate Directly to Present Level of Educational Performance. (Use additional sheets as needed)

Area of Instruction: _Social/Independent Living Skills_

Area Goal: _Susan will complete assignments independently by June._

Short Term Objective	Evaluation Schedule	Evaluation Procedure	Evaluation Criteria	Date Mastered
Given any seatwork assignment at the appropriate level and oral and written directions and/or demonstration by the teacher, Susan will complete the task with no more than one request for assistance by the teacher.	Daily	Mainstreaming checklists; Teacher observation	Begins task immediately and asks for help no more than one time.	

INDIVIDUALIZED EDUCATION PROGRAM   School Year <u>2000-2001</u>

Goals and Objectives Section: Must Relate Directly to Present Level of Educational Performance. (Use additional sheets as needed)

Area of Instruction: <u>Social/Independent Living Skills</u>

Area Goal: <u>Susan will improve her personal appearance and hygiene.</u>

Short Term Objective	Evaluation Schedule	Evaluation Procedure	Evaluation Criteria	Date Mastered
Given a weight control and exercise program in adapted P.E./Health, Susan will attain the appropriate weight for her height and build and will maintain that weight.	Daily	Self-monitoring form to record her weight.	Appropriate weight given by physician (120 lbs.)	
Susan will shower using warm water and soap and shampoo on a daily basis applying soap to all body areas and thoroughly rinsing.	Daily	Daily checks by Susan's adapted P.E. teacher.	Uses soap and water on all body parts.	
Susan will apply deodorant on a daily basis immediately after showering.	Daily	Daily checks by adapted P.E. teacher in Homeroom.	Deodorant applied under both arms.	

Confidential Information   INDIVIDUALIZED EDUCATION PROGRAM   School Year _2000–2001_

Student Name: _Susan Moyler_   Student Number: _____

_____ Yes   or   _____ No

Are modifications to the Instructional Program required to implement this IEP?

Accommodations in Test Format:

Audio-Cassette
[ ] Math
[ ] Writing
[ ] Reading*

Braille
[ ] Math
[ ] Writing
[ ] Reading

Large Print
[ ] Math
[ ] Writing
[ ] Reading

Oral Administration
[✓] Math
[✓] Writing
[✓] Reading*

Accommodations by Use of Aids:

Answers Recorded by Proctor
[✓] Math
[✓] Reading

Braille-Writer Abacus
[ ] Math
[ ] Writing
[ ] Reading

Dictation to a Scribe
[✓] Writing*

Dictation into a Tape Recorder
[✓] Writing
(for pre-writing only)

Electric Calculations and Other Calculation Devices
[✓] Math*

Sign Language, Interpretation Directions
[ ] Math
[ ] Writing
[ ] Reading

Magnification
[ ] Math
[ ] Writing
[ ] Reading

Marking Responses in Test Booklet
[✓] Math
[✓] Writing

Place Keepers, Trackers, Pointers
[✓] Math
[✓] Writing
[✓] Reading

Typewriter, Word Processor, Augmented Communication
[✓] Writing

Written Directions
[ ] Math
[ ] Writing
[ ] Reading

Other: _____
[ ] Math
[ ] Writing
[ ] Reading

Hospital/Home Setting
[ ] Math
[ ] Writing
[ ] Reading

Multiple Sessions
[✓] Math
[✓] Reading

Testing in a Separate Room
[✓] Math
[✓] Writing
[✓] Reading

Other: _____
[ ] Math
[ ] Writing
[ ] Reading

** Designated Nonstandard Administration, but will not affect pass/fail or eligibility for high school diploma.

Confidential Information INDIVIDUALIZED EDUCATION PROGRAM School Year _2000-2001_

Student Name: _Susan Moyler_ Student Number: _____

Placement Justification Form

Check the following items YES or NO. A written explanation must be provided for items checked NO in 1 through 10.

	YES	NO
1. The school the student would normally attend, if not disabled, is the recommended placement or is the placement. Placement is as close as possible to the student's home school.	✓	
2. The student is educated in the regular class with the use of supplementary aids and services.	✓	
3. The student is educated in a special education class in the regular school building.	✓	
4. The quality of services which the disabled student requires to meet IEP goals is provided by the placement.	✓	
5. The placement providing educational services required to meet the student's IEP goals is appropriate taking into account the potential harmful effects to the disabled student.	✓	
6. The student is educated with chronologically age-appropriate peers (age-appropriate to school and class).	✓	
7. The student will participate in a regular physical education program with non-disabled, chronologically age-appropriate peers.	✓	
8. The amount of travel time and distance to and from school is appropriate.	✓	
9. The student is educationally integrated with non-disabled chronologically age-appropriate peers.	✓	
10. The placement in a more restrictive environment is based on the individual needs of the student.	✓	

Student will participate in the State Assessment Program: [ ] YES ✓[ ] NO
If no, list any component(s) to be excluded. _Susan will receive alternative assessment of progress indicators for daily living skills._

Student will participate in local option testing: [ ] YES ✓[ ] NO
If no, give reason(s) _Susan is receiving a functional, independent living skills curriculum. Her skills are too low for meaningful_
assessment of 6th grade competencies for promotion.

** In the state of _____, the awarding of a high school diploma is based upon achievement. A student must earn the number of credits prescribed by the Board of Education and attain minimum competencies.

The implications of not taking or not passing the State Assessment Program have been explained to me and I understand them.

Martha Moyler   _9/5/2000_   _Susan Moyler_   _Sept. 5, 2000_
Parent Signature   Date   Student Signature (as appropriate)   Date

Confidential Information INDIVIDUALIZED EDUCATION PROGRAM School Year 2000-2001

Student Name: Susan Moyler Student Number: _____

Signature of Participants	Relationship to Student	Date
Mr. Abel	Special Education Teacher	9/5/2000
Mrs. Friend	Counselor	9/5/2000
Ms. Clean	Adapted P.E. Teacher	9-5-2000
Martha Moyler	Mother	9-5-2000
Susan Moyler	Student	9/5/2000
Ms. Booker	Teacher	9/5/2000

I give permission for my child, _Susan Moyler_, to be enrolled in the special education program described in the Individualized Education Program (IEP). I understand the contents of this document and I have been informed of my due process rights. I understand that I have the right to review my child's record and to request a change in the IEP at any time. I also understand that I have the right to refuse this placement and to have my child continue in his/her present placement pending exhaustion of due process procedures. I have received a copy of the IEP.

_9-5-2000_   _Martha Moyler_
Date   Signature of Parent/Guardian/Surrogate

_____

I do not give permission for my child, _____, to be enrolled in the special education program described in the Individualized Education Program (IEP). I understand that I have the right to review his/her records and request another placement. I understand that the action described above will not take place without my permission or until due process procedures have been exhausted. I understand that if my decision is appealed, I will be notified of my process rights in this procedure. I have received a copy of the IEP.

_____   _____
Date   Signature of Parent/Guardian/Surrogate

(Note to the reader: Please see the Individualized Transition Plan, a part of Susan's IEP, in Chapter 15.)

Section 504 Accommodation Plan

Confidential

Name of Student: <u>Taylor Winfree</u>
Date of Birth: <u>April 12, 1990</u>
Current Age: <u>10 years 5 months</u>
Current Grade: <u>6</u>
School: <u>Apple County Middle School</u>
Effective Dates of Plan: <u>9/5/2000 through 6/16/2001</u>
Section 504 Plan to be Monitored by: <u>Mrs. M. Friend</u>

As diagnosed by her physician, Taylor has an Attention Deficit/Hyperactivity Disorder. She receives medication (Ritalin) for this disorder under her doctor's care. This disorder significantly impacts Taylor's ability to focus and maintain attention to instruction during class lectures and discussion. In addition, Taylor's AD/HD affects her ability to remain attentive in order to complete tests, homework, and in-class assignments. The following accommodations are to be made to support Taylor in her sixth-grade classes:

- Permit Taylor to leave 5 minutes early from her math class so that she may report to the clinic to receive her medication before going to her language arts class.
- Preferential Seating—Seat Taylor away from hallway doors, windows, or areas of high traffic to minimize distractions.
- Permit Taylor extended time on assignments.
- Break longer assignments into smaller parts and set deadlines for each part.
- Check to be sure Taylor writes down all assignments in her assignment book.
- Assist Taylor to set short-term goals in each of her classes and to record these in her assignment book.
- Permit Taylor extended time on tests.

Signatures:

_____   _____

_____   _____

_____   _____

_____   _____

MATERIALS AND ORGANIZATIONS

Materials

Academic Therapy Publications
20 Commercial Boulevard
Novato, CA 94949
1-800-422-7249
E-mail: **atpub@aol.com**
Web: **www.atpub.com**

American Guidance Service
4201 Woodland Road #11279
Circle Pines, MN 55014
1-800-328-2560
E-mail: **ags@skypoint.com**
Web: **www.agsnet.com**

Apple Office of Special Education Programs
1 Infinite Loop
Cupertino, CA 95014
408-996-1010
Web: **www.apple.com**

Attainment Company Inc.
P.O. Box 930160
Verona, WI 53593-0160
1-800-327-4269
Web: **www.attainment-inc.com**

Beckley Cardy Group
100 Paragon Parkway
Mansfield, OH 44903
1-888-222-1332
Web: **www.beckleycardy.com**

Communication Skill Builders
555 Academic Court
San Antonio, TX 78204
1-800-228-0752

Conover Company
1050 Witzel Ave.
Osh Kosh, WI 54901
1-800-933-1933
Web: **www.conovercompany.com**

Constructive Playthings
13201 Arrington Road
Grandview, MO 64030-2886
1-800-448-4115
E-mail: **ustoy@ustoyco.com**

Cuisenaire * Dale Seymour Publications
P.O. Box 5026
White Plains, NY 10602-5026
1-800-872-1100
Web: **www.cuisenaire.com**

Curriculum Associates
P.O. Box 2001
N. Billerica, MA 01862
1-800-225-0248
E-mail: **cainfo@curriculumassociates.com**
Web: **www.curriculumassociates.com**

Ebsco Curriculum Materials
P.O. Box 486
Birmingham, AL 35201
1-800-633-8623
Web: **www.ecmtest.com**

Edmark Associates
P.O. Box 97021
Redmond, WA 98073-9721
1-800-362-2890
Web: **www.edmark.com**

Educators Publishing Service
31 Smith Place
Cambridge, MA 02138
1-800-225-5750
E-mail: **epsbooks@epsbooks.com**
Web: **www.epsbooks.com**

Fearon/Janus/Quercus
4350 Equity Dr.
Columbus, OH 43228
1-800-877-4283
Web: **www.globefearon.com**

Globe Fearon Educational Publishers
P.O. Box 2649
Columbus, OH 43216
1-800-848-9500

Harcourt Brace and Company
Web: **www.harcourtbrace.com**

Innovative Learning Concepts
Touch Math
6760 Corporate Dr.
Colorado Springs, CO 80919-1999
1-800-888-9191
Web: **www.touchmath.com**

LinguiSystems, Inc.
Exclusively LD
3100 4thAvenue
East Moline, IL 61244-9700
1-800-PRO IDEA
Web: **www.linguisystems.com**

Modern Curriculum Press
P.O. Box 2649
Columbus, OH 43216
1-800-321-3106
Web: **www.mcschool.com**

Pro-Ed
8700 Shoal Creek Boulevard
Austin, TX 78758
512-451-3246
Web: **www.proedinc.com**

Research Press
P.O. Box 9177
Champaign, IL 61826
217-352-3273
E-mail: **rp@researchpress.com**
Web: **www.researchpress.com**

Scholastic, Inc.
2931 E. McCarty St.
P.O. Box 7502
Jefferson City, MO 65102
1-800-325-6149
Web: **www.scholastic.com**

Silver Burdett Ginn
4350 Equity Drive
P.O. Box 2649
Columbus, OH 43216
1-800-848-9500
Web: **www.sbgschool.com**

Slosson Educational Publications, Inc.
P.O. Box 280
East Aurora, NY 14052-0280
1-888-SLOSSON
E-mail: slosson@slosson.com

Special Times—Cambridge Development Lab
86 West St.
Waltham, MA 02451
1-800-637-0047
Web: **www.cdl-cambridge.com**

SRA (Science Research Associates)
Macmillan/McGraw-Hill
860 Taylor Station Road
P.O. Box 543
Blacklick, OH 43004
1-800-621-0476

Stanfield Publishing Company
P.O. Box 41058
Santa Barbara, CA 93140
1-800-421-6534
Web: **www.stanfield.com**

Steck-Vaughn Publishing Co.
1-800-531-5015
Web: **www.steckvaughn.com**

Sunburst Communications, Inc.
101 Castleton Street, P.O. Box 100
Pleasantville, NY 10570-0100
1-800-321-7511
Web: **www.SUNBURST.com**

Zaner-Bloser
2200 W. 5thAve.
P.O. Box 16764
Columbus, OH 43216-6764
1-800-421-3018
Web: **www.zaner-bloser.com**

Organizations:

American Association on
   Mental Retardation
444 North Capitol St., NW
Suite 846
Washington, D.C. 20001-1512
1-800-424-3688
E-mail: **mailbox@aamr.org**
Web: **www.aamr.org**

American Psychological Association
750 First St., NE
Washington, D.C. 20002-4242
202-336-5500
Web: **www.apa.org**

Association for Career and
   Technology Education
1410 King St.
Alexandria, VA 22314
1-800-826-9972
E-mail: **acte@acteonline.org**
Web: **www.avaonline.org**

Association for Supervision and
   Curriculum Development
1703 North Beauregard St.
Alexandria, VA 22311-1714
1-800-933-ASCD
Web: **www.ascd.org**

Council for Exceptional Children/
Council for Children with Behavior Disorders/
Division for Learning Disabilities/
Division on Career Development/
Division on Mental Retardation/
Division on Research, Technology and Media
1920 Association Drive
Reston, VA 20191-1589
1-888-CEC-SPED
Web: **www.cec.sped.org**

Council for Learning Disabilities
P.O. Box 40303
Overland Park, KS 66204
913-492-8755

Federation of Families for Children's
   Mental Health
1021 Prince St.
Alexandria, VA 22314
703-684-7710
E-mail: **ffcmh@crosslink.net**
Web: **www.ffcmh.org**

International Reading Association
800 Barksdale Road
P.O. Box 8139
Newark, DE 19714-8139
302-731-1600
Web: **www.ira.org**

Learning Disabilities Association of America
4156 Library Road
Pittsburgh, PA 15234-1349
412-341-1515
E-mail: **ldanatl@usaor.net**
Web: **www.ldanatl.org**

The Arc of the United States
500 East Border St., Suite 300
Arlington, TX 76010
817-261-6003
E-mail: **thearc@metronet.com**
Web: **http://thearc.org**

National Council of Teachers of Math
1906 Association Dr.
Reston, VA 22091
1-800-235-7566
Web: **www.nctm.org**

National Education Association
1210 16thSt., NW
Washington, D.C. 20036
202-833-4000
Web: **www.nea.org**

The International Dyslexia Association
   (formerly the Orton Dyslexia Society)
   National Office
8600 LaSalle Road
Chester Building, Suite 382
Baltimore, MD 21286
Messages: 1-800-ABCD123
Phone: 410-296-0232
E-mail: **info@interdys.org**
Web: **www.iser.com/orton.html**

The University of Kansas Center for
   Research on Learning
3061 Dole
Lawrence, KS 66045
Order desk: 785-864-0617
Main phone number: 785-864-4780
Web: **www.ku-crl.org**

National Information Center for
   Handicapped Children and
   Youth-NICHCY
P.O. Box 1492
Washington, D.C. 20013-1492
1-800-695-0285
Web: **www.nichcy.org**

Recording for the Blind and Dyslexic
1-800-803-7201
Web: **www.rfbd.org**

Chapter One

Americans with Disabilities Act, 42 U.S.C. § 12101 12213 (1990).

Carnegie Council on Adolescent Development. (1989). *Turning points: Preparing American youth for the 21st century.* New York: Carnegie.

Dwyer, K., Osher, D., & Warger, C. (1998). *Early warning, timely response: A guide to safe schools.* Washington, D.C.: U.S. Department of Education.

Eitzen, D.S. (1992). Problem students: The sociocultural roots. *Phi Delta Kappan, 73,* 584-590.

Goals 2000: Educate America Act, P.L. 102-227, (1994).

Hallahan, D.P., & Kauffman, J.M. (1977). Labels, categories, behaviors: ED, LD, and EMR reconsidered. *Journal of Special Education, 11,* 139-149.

Harris, L. & Associates, Inc. (1989). *The metropolitan life survey of the American teacher 1989: Preparing schools for the 1990's.* New York: Author.

Henley, M., Ramsey, R.S., & Algozzine, R.F. (1996). *Characteristics of and strategies for teaching students with mild disabilities.* Boston, MA: Allyn and Bacon.

Individuals with Disabilities Education Act, 20 U.S.C. § 1400 et seq. (1997).

McDonnell, L.M., McLaughlin, M.J., & Morison, P. (Eds.). (1997). *Educating one and all: Students with disabilities and standards-based reform.* Washington, D.C.: National Academy Press.

National Assessment of Educational Progress. (1985). *The reading report card: Progress toward excellence in our schools; trends in reading over four national assessments, 1971-1984.* Princeton, NJ: Author.

National Center for Children in Poverty. (1998). *Fact Sheet.* Washington, D.C.: Author.

National Center for Education Statistics. (1990). *The condition of education: Volume I. Elementary and secondary education.* Washington, D.C.: Author.

National Center for Education Statistics. (1991). *Dropout rates in the United States: 1990.* Washington, D.C.: Author.

National Center for Education Statistics. (1998). *The Condition of Education.* Washington, D.C.: Author.

National Coalition for the Homeless. (1998). *Fact Sheet # 3.* Washington, D.C.: Author.

National Commission on Excellence in Education. (1983). *A nation at risk: The imperative for educational reform.* Washington, D.C.: U.S. Government Printing Office.

National Governor's Association. (1986). *Time for results: The governors' report on education.* Washington, D.C.: Author.

Puma, M., Karweit, N., Price, C., Ricciuti, A., Thompson, W., Vaden-Kiernan, M. (1997). *Prospects: Final report on student outcomes.* Washington, D.C.: U.S. Department of Education.

Rehabilitation Act, Section 504, 29 U.S.C. (1975).

Reid, R., & Katsiyannis, A. (1995). Attention-deficit/hyperactivity disorder and Section 504. *Remedial and Special Education, 16*(1), 44-52.

Rose, L.C., & Gallup, A.M. (1998). The 30th annual Phi Delta Kappa/Gallup Poll of the public's attitudes toward the public schools. *Kappan, 80*(1), 41-56.

Slavin, R.E., Karweit, N.L., & Madden, N.A. (1989). *Effective programs for students at risk.* Boston, MA: Allyn & Bacon.

U.S. Centers for Disease Control and Prevention. (1997). *Youth risk behavior survey.* Washington, D.C.: Author.

U.S. Department of Education. (1997). *Nineteenth annual report to Congress on the implementation of the Individuals with Disabilities Education Act.* Washington, D.C.: Author.

Ysseldyke, J., & Algozzine, B. (1982). *Critical issues in special and remedial education.* Boston, MA: Houghton Mifflin.

Chapter Two

Algozzine, B., & Korinek, L. (1985). Where is special education for students with high prevalence handicaps going? *Exceptional Children, 51,* 388–394.

Algozzine, B., Ysseldyke, J.W., & McGue, M. (1995). Differentiating low-achieving students: Thoughts on setting the record straight. *Learning Disabilities Research & Practice, 10,* 140–144.

Allington, R., & McGill-Franzen, A. (1989). Different programs, indifferent instruction. In D.K. Lipsky & A. Gartner (Eds.), *Beyond separate education: Quality education for all* (pp. 75–98). Baltimore: Paul H. Brookes.

American Psychiatric Association. (1994). *Diagnostic and statistical manual of mental disorders* (4th ed., DSM-IV). Washington, D.C.: Author.

Ashbaker, M.H., & Swanson, H.L. (1996). Short-term memory and working memory operations and their contribution to reading in adolescents with and without learning disabilities. *Learning Disabilities Research & Practice, 11,* 206–213.

Baker, J.M., & Zigmond, N. (1995). The meaning and practice of inclusion for students with learning disabilities: Themes and implications from the five cases. *The Journal of Special Education, 29,* 163–180.

Bateman, B. (1992). Learning disabilities: The changing landscape. *Journal of Learning Disabilities, 25,* 29–36.

Beirne-Smith, M., Ittenbach, R.E., & Patton, J.R. (1998). *Mental retardation* (5th ed.). Upper Saddle River, NJ: Merrill/Prentice Hall.

Bender, W.N., Scott, K., & McLaughlin, P.J. (1993). A model for noncategorical service delivery for students with mild disabilities. In R.C. Eaves & P.J. McLaughlin (Eds.), *Recent advances in special education and rehabilitation* (pp. 127–145). Boston, MA: Andover Medical Publishers.

Berninger, V.W., & Stage, S.A. (1996). Assessment and intervention for writing problems of students with learning disabilities or behavioral disabilities. *B.C. Journal of Special Education, 20*(2), 5–23.

Bower, E. M. (1981). *Early identification of emotionally handicapped children in school* (3rd ed.). Springfield, IL: Charles C. Thomas.

Brooks, P.H., & McCauley, C. (1984). Cognitive research in mental retardation. *American Journal of Mental Deficiency, 88,* 479–486.

Bryan, T.H. (1986). Self-concept and attributions of the learning disabled. *Learning Disabilities Focus, 1,* 82–89.

Bussing, R., Zima, B.T., Belin, T.R., & Forness, S.R. (1998). Children who qualify for LD and SED programs: Do they differ in level of ADHD symptoms and comorbid psychiatric conditions? *Behavioral Disorders, 23,* 85–97.

Carpenter, D. (1983). Spelling error profiles of able and disabled readers. *Journal of Learning Disabilities, 16,* 102–104.

Cawley, J.F., & Parmar, R.S. (1992). Arithmetic programming for students with disabilities: An alternative. *Remedial and Special Education, 13,* 6–18.

Cawley, J.F., Parmar, R.S., Yan, W.F., & Miller, J.H. (1996). Arithmetic computation abilities of students with learning disabilities: Implications for instruction. *Learning Disabilities Research & Practice, 11,* 230–237.

Christenson, S.L., Ysseldyke, J.E., & Thurlow, M.L. (1989). Critical instructional factors for students with mild handicaps: An integrative review. *Remedial and Special Education, 10,* 21–31.

Committee on the Prevention of Reading Difficulties in Young Children. (1998). *Preventing reading difficulties in young children.* Washington, D.C.: National Academy Press.

Deno, S., Marston, D., & Mirkin, P. (1982). Valid measurement procedures for continuous evaluation of written expression. *Exceptional Children, 48,* 368–371.

Deshler, D.D., & Schumaker, J.B. (1988). An instructional model for teaching students how to learn. In J.L. Graden, J.E. Zins, & M.J. Curtis (Eds.), *Alternative educational delivery systems: Enhancing educational options for all students* (pp. 391–412). Silver Spring, MD: National Association of School Psychologists.

Downing, J.A., Simpson, R.L., & Myles, B.S. (1990). Regular and special educator perceptions of nonacademic skills needed by mainstreamed students with behavioral disorders and learning disabilities. *Behavioral Disorders, 15*, 217–226.

Duncan, B.B., Forness, S.R., & Hartsough, C. (1995). Students identified as seriously emotionally disturbed in day treatment classrooms: Cognitive, psychiatric, and special education characteristics. *Behavioral Disorders, 20*, 221–237.

Englert, C.S., Raphael, T., Fear, K., & Anderson, H. (1988). Students' metacognitive knowledge about how to write informational texts. *Learning Disability Quarterly, 11*, 18–46.

Espin, C.A., Deno, S.L., & Albayrak-Kaymak, D. (1998). Individualized education programs in resource and in-clusive settings: How "individualized" are they? *The Journal of Special Education, 32*, 164–174.

Fister, S., & Kemp, K. (1993). Translating research: Classroom application of validated instructional strategies. In R.C. Eaves & P.J. McLaughlin (Eds.), *Recent advances in special education and rehabilitation* (pp. 107–126). Boston, MA: Andover Medical Publishers.

Flavell, J.H. (1979). Metacognition and cognitive monitoring: A new area of cognitive-developmental inquiry. *American Psychologist, 34*, 906–911.

Fletcher, J.M., Francis, D.J., Shaywitz, S.E., Lyon, G.R., Foorman, B.R., Stuebing, K.K., & Shaywitz, B.A. (1998). Intelligent testing and the discrepancy model for children with learning disabilities. *Learning Disabilities Research & Practice, 13*, 186–203.

Forness, S.R., & Kavale, K.A. (1993). Strategies to improve basic learning and memory deficits in mental retar-dation: A meta-analysis of experimental studies. *Education and Training in Mental Retardation, 28*, 99–110.

Forness, S.R., Keogh, B.K., MacMillan, D.L., Kavale, K.A., & Gresham, F.M. (1998). What is so special about IQ: The limited explanatory power of cognitive abilities in the real world of special education. *Remedial and Special Education, 19*, 315–322.

Forness, S.R., Ramey, S.L., Ramey, C.T., Hsu, C., Brezausek, C.M., MacMillan, D.L., Kavale, K.A., & Zima, B.T. (1998). Head Start children finishing first grade: Preliminary data on school identification of children at risk for special education. *Behavioral Disorders, 23*, 111–124.

Frankenberger, W., & Fronzaglio, K. (1991). A review of states' criteria and procedures for identifying chil-dren with learning disabilities. *Journal of Learning Disabilities, 24*, 495–500.

Fuchs, D., & Fuchs, L.S. (1995). What's special about special education? *Phi Delta Kappan, 76*, 522–530.

Fuchs, L.S., & Fuchs, D. (1998). Treatment validity: A unifying concept for reconceptualizing the identification of learning disabilities. *Learning Disabilities Research & Practice, 13*, 204–219.

Gardner, H., & Hatch, T. (1989). Multiple intelligences go to school: Educational implications of the theory of multiple intelligences. *Educational Researcher, 18*(8), 4–9.

Glassberg, L.A., Hooper, S.R., & Mattison, R.E. (1999). Prevalence of learning disabilities at enrollment in spe-cial education students with behavioral disorders. *Behavioral Disorders, 25*(1), 9–21.

Graham, S. (1990). The role of production factors in learning disabled students' compositions. *Journal of Educational Psychology, 80*, 781–791.

Graham, S. (1992). Issues in handwriting instruction. *Focus on Exceptional Children, 25*(2), 1–14.

Graham, S., Harris, K.R., & Sawyer, R. (1987). Composition instruction with learning disabled students: Self-instructional strategy training. *Focus on Exceptional Children, 20* (4).

Gresham, F.M., MacMillan, D.L., & Bocian, K.M. (1996). Learning disabilities, low achievement and mild men-tal retardation: More alike than different? *Journal of Learning Disabilities, 29*, 570–581.

Grossman, H.J. (Ed.). (1983). *Classification in mental retardation*. Washington, D.C.: American Association on Mental Deficiency.

Gunter, P.L., & Coutinho, M.J. (1997). Negative reinforcement in classrooms: What we're beginning to learn. *Teacher Education and Special Education, 20*, 249–264.

Halgren, D.W., & Clarizio, H.F. (1993). Categorical and programming changes in special education services. *Exceptional Children, 59*, 547–555.

Hallahan, D.P., & Kauffman, J.M. (1977). Labels, categories, behaviors: ED, LD, and EMR reconsidered. *Journal of Special Education, 11,* 139–149.

Hallahan, D.P., Kauffman, J.M., & Lloyd, J.W. (1985). *Introduction to learning disabilities.* Englewood Cliffs, NJ: Prentice–Hall.

Hammill, D.D. (1990). On defining learning disabilities: An emerging consensus. *Journal of Learning Disabilities, 23,* 74–84.

Hammill, D.D., Leigh, J.E., McNutt, G., & Larsen, S.C. (1981). A new definition of learning disabilities. *Learning Disability Quarterly, 4,* 336–342.

Heiman, T., & Margalit, M. (1998). Loneliness, depression, and social skills among students with mild mental retardation in different educational settings. *The Journal of Special Education, 32,* 154–163.

Henley, M., Ramsey, R.S., & Algozzine, R.F. (1996). *Characteristics of and strategies for teaching students with mild disabilities* (2nd ed.). Boston, MA: Allyn and Bacon.

Horton, S.V., Lovitt, T.C., & White, O.R. (1992). Teaching mathematics to adolescents classified as educable mentally handicapped: Using calculators to remove the computational onus. *Remedial and Special Education, 13,* 36–46.

Individuals with Disabilities Education Act, 20 U.S.C., § 1400 et seq. (1997).

Isaacson, S.L. (1987). Effective instruction in written language. *Focus on Exceptional Children, 19* (6), 1–12.

Isaacson, S., & Gleason, M.M. (1997). Mechanical obstacles to writing: What can teachers do to help students with learning problems? *Learning Disabilities Research & Practice, 12,* 188–194.

Jitendra, A.K., & Xin, Y. (1997). Mathematical word-problem-solving instruction for students with mild disabilities and students at risk for math failure: A research synthesis. *The Journal of Special Education, 30,* 412–438.

Kauffman, J.M. (1997). *Characteristics of emotional and behavioral disorders of children and youth* (6th ed.). Columbus, OH: Merrill/Prentice Hall.

Kavale, K.A. (1995). Setting the record straight on learning disability and low achievement: The tortuous path of ideology. *Learning Disabilities Research & Practice, 10,* 145–152.

Kavale, K.A, Fuchs, D., & Scruggs, T.E. (1994). Setting the record straight on learning disability and low achievement: Implications for policymaking. *Learning Disabilities Research & Practice, 9,* 70–77.

Licht, B.G. (1984). Cognitive-motivational factors that contribute to the achievement of learning–disabled children. *Annual Review of Learning Disabilities, 2,* 119–126.

Lloyd, J. (1984). How shall we individualize instruction: Or should we? *Remedial and Special Education, 5,* 7–15.

Lloyd, J.W., & Keller, C.E. (1989). Effective mathematics instruction: Development, instruction, and programs. *Focus on Exceptional Children, 21* (7), 1–10.

Luckasson, R., Coulter, D.L. Polloway, E.A., Reiss, S., Schalock, L.L., Snell, M.E., Spitalnik, D.M., & Stark, J.A. (1992). *Mental retardation: Definition, classification, and systems of support.* Washington, D.C.: American Association on Mental Retardation.

Maag, J.W., & Reid, R. (1994). The phenomenology of depression among students with and without learning disabilities: More similar than different. *Learning Disabilities Research & Practice, 9,* 91–103.

MacMillan, D.L., & Forness, S.R. (1998). The role of IQ in special education placement decisions: Primary and determinative or peripheral and inconsequential? *Remedial and Special Education, 19,* 239–253.

MacMillan, D.L., Gresham, F.M., Bocian, K.M., & Lambros, K.M. (1998). Current plight of boderline students: Where do they belong? *Education and Training in Mental Retardation and Developmental Disabilities, 33,* 83–94.

Mastropieri, M.A., Scruggs, T.E., & Shiah, S. (1991). Mathematics instruction for learning disabled students: A review of research. *Learning Disabilities Research & Practice, 6,* 89–98.

McKinney, J.D. (1987). Research on conceptually and empirically derived subtypes of specific learning disabilities. In M.C. Wang, M.C. Reynolds, & H.J. Walberg (Eds.), *Handbook of special education: Research and practice.* Elmsford, NY: Pergamon.

McKinney, J.D. (1989). Longitudinal research on the behavioral characteristics of children with learning disabilities. *Journal of Learning Disabilities, 22,* 141–150.

Mercer, C.D., & Miller, S.P. (1992). Teaching students with learning problems in math to acquire, understand, and apply basic math facts. *Remedial and Special Education, 13*(3), 19–35, 61.

National Joint Committee on Learning Disabilities. (1988). Unpublished letter to member organizations.

Rehabilitation Act, Section 504, 29 U.S.C. (1975).

Reid, D.K., Hresko, W.P., & Swanson, H.L. (Eds.). (1996). *Cognitive approaches to learning disabilities* (3rd ed.). Austin, TX: Pro–Ed.

Reid, R., Maag, J.W., Vasa, S.F., & Wright, S.F. (1994). Who are the children with attention deficit-hyperactivity disorder? A school–based survey. *The Journal of Special Education, 28,* 117–137.

Reynolds, M.C., & Heistad, D. (1997). 20/20 analysis: Estimating school effectiveness in serving students at the margins. *Exceptional Children, 63,* 439–449.

Riccio, C.A., Gonzalez, J.J., & Hynd, G.W. (1994). Attention-deficit hyperactivity disorder (ADHD) and learning disabilities. *Learning Disability Quarterly, 17,* 311–322. Samuels, S.J. (1988). Decoding and automaticity: Helping poor readers become automatic at word recognition. *The Reading Teacher, 41,* 756–760.

Scarborough, H.S. (1998). Early identification of children at risk for reading disabilities: Phonological awareness and some other promising predictors. In B.K. Shapiro, P.J. Accardo, & A.J. Capute (Eds.), *Specific reading disability: A view of the spectrum* (pp. 77–121). Timonium, MD: York Press.

Scruggs, T.E., & Laufenberg, R. (1986). Transformational mnemonic strategies for retarded learners. *Education and Training of the Mentally Retarded, 21,* 165–173.

Shores, R.E., Gunter, P.L., Denny, R.K., & Jack, S.L. (1993). Classroom influences on aggressive and disruptive behaviors of students with emotional and behavioral disorders. *Focus on Exceptional Children, 26,* 1–10.

Siperstein, G.N., & Leffert J.S. (1999). Managing limited resources: Do children with learning problems share? *Exceptional Children, 65,* 187–199.

Slavin, R.E., Karweit, N.L., & Madden, N.A. (1989). *Effective programs for students at risk.* Boston, MA: Allyn & Bacon.

Smith, S.W. (1990). Comparison of Individualized Education Programs (IEP's) of students with behavioral disorders and learning disabilities. *The Journal of Special Education, 24,* 85–100.

Stanovich, K. (1986). Matthew effects in reading: Some consequences of individual differences in the acquisition of literacy. *Reading Research Quarterly, 31,* 360–406.

Stanovich, P.J., Jordan, A., & Perot, J. (1998). Relative differences in academic self-concept and peer acceptance among students in inclusive classrooms. *Remedial and Special Education, 19,* 120–126.

Sternberg, R.J. (1997). What does it mean to be smart? *Educational Leadership, 54*(6), 20–24.

Swanson, H.L. (1994). Short-term memory and working memory: Do both contribute to our understanding of academic achievement in children and adults with learning disabilities? *Journal of Learning Disabilities, 27,* 34–50.

Torgesen, J.K., & Kail, R.V. (1980). Memory processes in exceptional children. In B. Keogh (Ed.), *Advances in special education, Volume I: Basic constructs and theoretical orientations.* Greenwich, CN: J.A.I. Press.

Torgesen, J.K., & Wagner, R.K. (1998). Alternative diagnostic approaches for specific developmental reading disabilities. *Learning Disabilities Research & Practice, 13,* 220–232.

Tur-Kaspa, H., & Bryan, T. (1994). Social information-processing skills of students with learning disabilities. *Learning Disabilities Research & Practice, 9*(1), 12–23.

U.S. Department of Education. (1997). *Nineteenth annual report to Congress on the implementation of the Individuals with Disabilities Education Act.* Washington, D.C.: Author.

Wallace, G., & McLoughlin, J.A. (1988). *Learning disabilities: Concepts and characteristics.* (3rd ed.). Columbus, OH: Merrill.

Weintraub, N. & Graham, S. (1998). Writing legibly and quickly: A study of children's ability to adjust their handwriting to meet common classroom demands. *Learning Disabilities Research & Practice, 13,* 146–152.

Weiss, E. (1984). Learning disabled childrens' understanding of social interactions of peers. *Journal of Learning Disabilities, 17,* 612–615.

Wiig, E.H. (1990). Language disabilities in school-age children and youth. In G.H. Shames & E.H. Wiig (Eds.), *Human communication disorders.* Columbus, OH: Merrill.

Ysseldyke, J.E. (1987). Classification of handicapped students. In M.C. Wang, M.C. Reynolds, & H.J. Walberg (Eds.), *Handbook of special education: Research and practice* (pp. 253–271). Elmsford, NY: Pergamon.

Ysseldyke, J.E., Algozzine, B., & Thurlow, M.L. (1992). *Critical issues in special education* (2nd ed.). Boston, MA: Houghton-Mifflin.

Ysseldyke, J.F., O'Sullivan, P.J., Thurlow, M.L., & Christenson, S.L. (1989). Qualitative differences in reading and math instruction received by handicapped students. *Remedial and Special Education, 10,* 14–20.

Zigmond, N., & Baker, J.M. (1995). Concluding comments: current and future practices in inclusive schooling. *The Journal of Special Education, 29,* 245–250.

Chapter Three

Affleck, J.Q., Madge, S., Adams, A., & Lowenbraun, S. (1988). Integrated classroom versus resource model: Academic viability and effectiveness. *Exceptional Children, 54,* 339–348.

Alberto, P.A., & Troutman, A.C. (1999). *Applied behavior analysis for teachers (5th ed.).* Columbus, OH: Merrill/Prentice Hall.

Anderson, J.R., Reder, L.M., & Simon, H.A. (1996). Situated learning and education. *Educational Researcher, 25,* 5–11.

Anderson, L.W., & Pellicer, L.O. (1990). Synthesis of research on compensatory and remedial education. *Educational Leadership, 48,* 10–16.

Aronson, E., Blaney, N., Stephan, C., Sikes, J., & Snapp, M. (1978). *The jigsaw classroom.* Beverly Hills, CA: Sage.

Ayres, A.J. (1978). Learning disabilities and the vestibular system. *Journal of Learning Disabilities, 11,* 18–29.

Baker, J.M., & Zigmond, N. (1995). The meaning and practice of inclusion for students with learning disabilities: Themes and implications from the five cases. *Journal of Special Education, 29,* 163–180.

Beakley, B.A., & Yoder, S.L. (1998). Middle schoolers learn community skills. *Teaching Exceptional Children, 30*(3), 16–21.

Bereiter, C., & Engelmann, S. (1966). *Teaching disadvantaged children in the preschool.* Englewood Cliffs, NJ: Prentice Hall.

Bottge, B., & Hasselbring, T. (1993). A comparison of two approaches for teaching complex, authentic mathematical problems to adolescents in remedial math classes. *Exceptional Children, 56,* 556–566.

Bulgren, J.A., & Carta, J.J. (1993). Examining the instructional contexts of students with learning disabilities. *Exceptional Children, 59,* 182–191.

Carbo, M. (1983). Research in reading and learning style: Implications for exceptional children. *Exceptional Children, 49,* 486–494.

Carbo, M. (1987). Reading styles research: What works isn't always phonics. *Phi Delta Kappan, 68,* 431–445.

Carbo, M. (1988). Debunking the great phonics myth. *Phi Delta Kappan, 70,* 226–239.

Carbo, M., Dunn, R., & Dunn, K. (1986). *Teaching students to read through their individual learning styles.* Englewood Cliffs, NJ: Prentice Hall.

Carnine, D.W., & Engelmann, S. (1981). *Corrective mathematics.* Chicago, IL: Science Research Associates.

Carnine, D., Silbert, J., & Kameenui, E.J. (1990). *Direct instruction reading* (2nd ed.). Columbus, OH: Merrill.

Chalfant, J.C., Pysh, M.V., & Moultrie, R. (1979). Teacher assistance teams: A model for within building problem solving. *Learning Disability Quarterly, 2,* 85–96.

Cruickshank, W.M. (1975). The learning environment. In W.M. Cruickshank & D.P. Hallahan (Eds.), *Perceptual and learning disabilities in children, Volume I: Psychoeducational practices.* Syracuse, NY: Syracuse University Press.

Cruickshank, W.M., Bentzen, F.A., Ratzeburg, F.H., & Tannhauser, M.T. (1961). *A teaching method for brain–injured and hyperactive children.* Syracuse, NY: Syracuse University Press.

Delquadri, J., Greenwood, C.R., Whorton, D., Carta, J.J., & Hall, R.V. (1986). Classwide peer tutoring. *Exceptional Children, 52,* 535–542.

Deno, S.L., Foegen, A., Robinson, S., & Espin, C.A. (1996). Commentary: Facing the realities of inclusion: Students with mild disabilities. *Journal of Special Education, 62,* 497–514.

Deshler, D.D., Ellis, E.S., & Lenz, B.K. (1996). *Teaching adolescents with learning disabilities.* Denver, CO: Love.

Deshler, D.D., & Schumaker, J.B. (1986). Learning strategies: An instructional alternative for low–achieving adolescents. *Exceptional Children, 52,* 583–590.

Dunn, R. (1988). Teaching students through their perceptual strengths or preferences. *Journal of Reading, 31,* 304–309.

Engelmann, S., & Bruner, E. (1995). *Reading mastery: Level I/II.* Blacklick, OH: Science Research Associates.

Engelmann, S., Johnson, G., & Carnine, L. (1999). *Corrective reading: Decoding.* Blacklick, OH: Science Research Associates.

Englert, C.S. (1984). Examining effective direct instruction practices in special education settings. *Remedial and Special Education, 5,* 38–47.

Feingold, B.F. (1976). Hyperkinesis and learning disabilities linked to the ingestion of artificial food color and flavors. *Journal of Learning Disabilities, 9,* 551–559.

Fernald, G.M. (1943). *Remedial techniques in basic school subjects.* New York: McGraw-Hill.

Flavell, J.H. (1979). Metacognition and cognitive monitoring: A new area of cognitive-developmental psychology. *American Psychologist, 34,* 906–911.

Forness, S.R., & Kavale, K.A. (1988). Psychopharmacologic treatment: A note on classroom effects. *Journal of Learning Disabilities, 21,* 144–147.

Forness, S.R., Swanson, J.M., Cantwell, D.P., Guthrie, D., & Sena, R. (1992). Response to stimulant medication across six measures of school-related performance in children with ADHD and disruptive behavior. *Behavioral Disorders, 18,* 42–53.

Forness, S.R., Sweeney, D.P., & Toy, K. (1996). Psychopharmacologic medication: What teachers need to know. *Beyond Behavior, 7*(2), 4–11.

Fuchs, D., & Fuchs, L.S. (1995). What's 'special' about special education? *Phi Delta Kappan, 76,* 522–530.

Gartner, A., & Lipsky, D.K. (1987). Beyond special education: Toward a quality system for all students. *Harvard Educational Review, 57,* 367–395.

Gerber, M.M. (1988). Cognitive-behavioral training in the curriculum: Time, slow learners, and basic skills. In E.L. Meyen, G.A. Vergason, & R.J. Whelan (Eds.), *Effective instructional strategies for exceptional children* (pp. 45–64). Denver, CO: Love.

Gerber, M.M. (1995). Inclusion at the high-water mark? Some thoughts on Zigmond and Baker's case studies of inclusive education programs. *Journal of Special Education, 29,* 181–191.

Gillingham, A., & Stillman, B. (1956). *Remedial training for children with special disability in reading, spelling, and penmanship.* Cambridge, MA: Educator's Publishing Service.

Gorton, C.E. (1972). The effects of various classroom environments on performance of a mental task by mentally retarded and normal children. *Education and Training of the Mentally Retarded, 7,* 32–38.

Hallahan, D.P., & Cruickshank, W.M. (1973). *Psychoeducational foundations of learning disabilities.* Englewood Cliffs, NJ: Prentice Hall.

Hallahan, D.P., & Kauffman, J.M. (1975). Research on the education of distractible and hyperactive children. In W.M. Cruickshank & D.P. Hallahan (Eds.), *Perceptual and learning disabilities in children, Volume II: Research and theory.* Syracuse, NY: Syracuse University Press.

Hallahan, D.P., Lloyd, J.W., & Stoller, L. (1982). *Improving attention with self–monitoring: A manual for teachers.* Charlottesville, VA: University of Virginia Learning Disabilities Research Institute.

Hock, M.F., Schumaker, J.B., & Deshler, D.D. (1993). Training strategic tutors to enhance learning independence: A new conceptualization of the process. *Preventing School Failure, 38*(1), 43–49.

Houck, C.K., & Rogers, C.J. (1994). The special/general education integration initiative for students with specific learning disabilities: A "snapshot" of program change. *Journal of Learning Disabilities, 27,* 435–453.

Hunter, M. (1982). *Mastery teaching.* El Segundo, CA: TIP Publications.

Individuals with Disabilities Education Act, 20 U.S.C. § 1400 et seq. (1997).

Irlen, H. (1983, August). *Successful treatment of learning disabilities.* Paper presented at the 91st annual convention of the American Psychological Association, Anaheim, CA.

Jenkins, J.R., Gorrafa, Q., & Griffiths, S. (1972). Another look at isolation effects. *American Journal of Mental Deficiency, 76,* 591–593.

Jenkins, J., & Jenkins, L. (1988). Peer tutoring in elementary and secondary programs. In E.L. Meyen, G.A. Vergason, & R.J. Whelan (Eds.), *Effective instructional strategies for exceptional children* (pp. 335–354). Denver, CO: Love Publishing Co.

Jenkins, J.R., Jewell, M., Leicester, N., O'Connor, R.E., Jenkins, L.M., & Troutner, N.M. (1994). Accommodations for individual differences without classroom ability groups: An experiment in school restructuring. *Exceptional Children, 60,* 344–358.

Johnson, D.W., & Johnson, R.T. (1986). Mainstreaming and cooperative learning strategies. *Exceptional Children, 52,* 553–561.

Johnson, D.W., & Johnson, R.T. (1987). *Learning together and alone: Cooperative, competitive, and individualistic learning*(2nd ed.). Englewood Cliffs, NJ: Prentice Hall.

Johnson, L.J., Pugach, M.C., & Hammitte, D.J. (1988). Barriers to effective special education consultation. *Remedial and Special Education, 9,* 41–47.

Kauffman, J.M. (1995). Why we must celebrate a diversity of restrictive environments. *Learning Disabilities Research & Practice, 10,* 225–232.

Kauffman, J.M. (1996). Research to practice issues. *Behavioral Disorders, 22*(1), 55–60.

Kauffman, J.M. (1999). Commentary: Today's special education and its messages for tomorrow. *The Journal of Special Education, 32,* 244–254.

Kavale, K.A., & Forness, S.R. (1987). Substance over style: Assessing the efficacy of modality testing and teaching. *Exceptional Children, 54,* 228–239.

Kavale, K.A., Hirshoren, A., & Forness, S.R. (1998). Meta–analytic validation of the Dunn and Dunn model of learning–style preferences: A critique of what was Dunn. *Learning Disabilities Research & Practice, 13*(2), 75–80.

Kerr, M.M., & Nelson, C.M. (1998). *Strategies for managing behavior problems in the classroom (3rd ed.).* Columbus, OH: Merrill/Prentice Hall.

Kline, F.M., Schumaker, J.B., & Deshler, D.D. (1991). The development and validation of feedback for instructing students with learning disabilities. *Learning Disability Quarterly, 14,* 191–207.

Lloyd, J.W. (1984). How shall we individualize instruction: Or should we? *Remedial and Special Education, 5,* 7–15. Lloyd, J.W. (1988). Direct academic interventions in learning disabilities. In M.C. Wang, M.C. Reynolds, & H.J. Walberg (Eds.), *Handbook of special education: Research and practice: Volume II: Mildly handicapped conditions.* New York: Pergamon Press.

MacMillan, D.L., Gresham, F.M., & Forness, S.R. (1995). Full inclusion: An empirical perspective. *Behavioral Disorders, 21,* 145–159.

Maheady, L., & Harper, G.F. (1987). A classwide peer tutoring program to improve the spelling test performance of low income, third and fourth grade students. *Education and Treatment of Children, 10,* 120–133.

Maheady, L., Sacca, M.K., & Harper, G.F. (1988). Classwide peer tutoring with mildly handicapped high school students. *Exceptional Children, 55,* 52–59.

Marston, D. (1996). A comparison of inclusion only, pull-out only, and combined service models for students with mild disabilities. *Journal of Special Education, 30,* 121–132.

Mastropieri, M.A., & Scruggs, T.E. (1989). Constructing more meaningful relationships: Mnemonic instruction for special populations. *Educational Psychology Review, 1,* 83–111.

Mather, N., & Roberts, R. (1995). Sold out?: A response to McLeskey and Pugach. *Learning Disabilities Research & Practice, 10,* 239–249.

Mathes, P., Fuchs, D., Fuchs, L.S., Henley, A.M., & Sanders, A. (1994). Increasing strategic reading practice with Peabody classwide peer tutoring. *Learning Disabilities Research & Practice, 8,* 233–243.

McLeskey, J., & Pugach, M.C. (1995). The real sellout: Failing to give inclusion a chance: A response to Roberts and Mather. *Learning Disabilities Research & Practice, 10,* 233–238.

Meichenbaum, D. (1977). *Cognitive-behavior modification: An integrative approach.* New York: Plenum.

Minke, K.M., Bear, G.G., Deemer, S.A., & Griffin, S.M. (1996). Teachers' experiences with inclusive classrooms: Implications for special education reform. *Journal of Special Education, 30,* 152–186.

Morsink, C.V., Thomas, C.C., & Correa, V.I. (1991). *Interactive teaming: Consultation and collaboration in special programs.* New York: Merrill/Macmillan.

Palincsar, A.S. (1986). Metacognitive strategy instruction. *Exceptional Children, 53,* 118–124.

Pelham, W.E., Swanson, J.M., Furman, M.B., & Schwindt., H. (1995). Pemoline effects on children with ADHD: A time-response by dose-response analysis on classroom measures. *Journal of the American Academy of Child and Adolescent Psychiatry, 34,* 1504–1513.

Phillips, V., & McCullough, L. (1990). Consultation-based programming: Instituting the collaborative ethic in schools. *Exceptional Children, 56,* 291–304.

Pressley, M., Burkell, J., Cariglia-Bull, T., Lysynchuk, L., McGoldrick, J.A., Schneider, B., Snyder, B.L., Symons, S., & Woloshyn, V.E. (1990). *Cognitive strategy instruction that really improves children's academic performance.* Cambridge, MA: Brookline Books.

Pugach, M.C., & Wesson, C.L. (1995). Teachers' and students' view of team teaching of general education and learning-disabled students in two fifth-grade classes. *Elementary School Journal, 95,* 279–295.

Rapp, D.J. (1986). *The impossible child in school and at home.* Buffalo, NY: Life Sciences Press.

Reynolds, M.C., Wang, M.C., & Walberg, H.J. (1987) The necessary restructuring of special and regular education. *Exceptional Children, 53,* 391–398.

Roberts, R., & Mather, N. (1995). The return of students with learning disabilities to regular classrooms: A sellout? *Learning Disabilities Research & Practice, 10*(1), 46–58.

Rosenshine, B. (1976). Classroom instruction. In N.L. Gage (Ed.), *The psychology of teaching methods: Seventy–seventh yearbook of the National Society for the Study of Education.* Chicago, IL: University of Chicago Press.

Rost, K.J., & Charles, D.C. (1967). Academic achievement of brain injured and hyperactive children in isolation. *Exceptional Children, 34,* 125–126.

Sabornie, E.J. (1985). Social mainstreaming of handicapped students: Facing an unpleasant reality. *Remedial and Special Education, 6,* 12–16.

Scanlon, D., Deshler, D.D., & Schumaker, J.B. (1996). Can a strategy be taught and learned in secondary inclusive classrooms? *Learning Disabilities Research & Practice, 11*(1), 41–57.

Scruggs, T.E., & Mastropieri, M.A. (1996). Teacher perceptions of mainstreaming/inclusion, 1958–1995: A research synthesis. *Exceptional Children, 63*(1), 59–74.

Scruggs, T.E., & Richter, L. (1985). Tutoring learning disabled students: A critical review. *Learning Disability Quarterly, 8,* 286–298.

Self, H., Benning, A., Marston, D., & Magnusson, D. (1991). Cooperative teaching project: A model for students at risk. *Exceptional Children, 58,* 26–34.

Semmel, M.I., Abernathy, T.V., Butera, G., & Lesar, S. (1991). Teacher perceptions of the Regular Education Initiative. *Exceptional Children, 58,* 9–24.

Shores, R.E., & Haubrich, P.A. (1969). Effects of cubicles in educating emotionally disturbed children. *Exceptional Children, 36,* 21–26.

Silver, L.B. (1995). Controversial therapies. *Journal of Child Neurology, 10* (Supplement 1), 96–100.

Slavin, R.E. (1988). *Educational psychology: Theory into practice.* Englewood Cliffs, NJ: Prentice Hall.

Slavin, R.E. (1990). *Cooperative learning: Theory, research and practice.* Englewood Cliffs, NJ: Prentice Hall.

Slavin, R.E., Karweit, N.L., & Madden, N.A. (1989). *Effective programs for students at risk.* Boston, MA: Allyn and Bacon.

Sommerville, J.W., Warnberg, L.S., & Bost, D.E. (1973). Effects of cubicles versus increased stimulation on task performance by first-grade males perceived as distractible and nondistractible. *The Journal of Special Education, 7,* 169–185.

Stainback, W., Stainback, S., & Bunch, G. (1989). Introduction and historical background. In S. Stainback, W. Stainback, & M. Forest (Eds.), *Educating all students in the mainstream of regular education* (pp. 3–14). Baltimore, MD: Paul Brookes.

Stokes, T.F., & Baer, D.M. (1977). An implicit technology of generalization. *Journal of Applied Behavior Analysis, 10,* 349–367.

Strauss, A.A., & Lehtinen, L.E. (1947). *Psychopathology and education of the brain–injured child.* New York: Grune & Stratton.

Taylor, S. (1988). Caught in the continuum: A critical analysis of the principle of least restrictive environment. *Journal of the Association for Persons with Severe Handicaps, 13*(1), 41–53.

Thousand, J.S., & Villa, R.A. (1989). Enhancing success in heterogeneous schools. In S. Stainback, W. Stainback, & M. Forest (Eds.), *Educating all students in the mainstream of regular education* (pp. 89–103). Baltimore, MD: Paul Brookes.

Torgesen, J.K. (1982). The learning disabled child as an inactive learner: Educational implications. *Topics in Learning and Learning Disabilities, 2*(1), 45–52.

U.S. Department of Education. (1997). *Nineteenth annual report to Congress on the implementation of the Individuals with Disabilities Education Act.* Washington, D.C.: Author.

Vaughn, S., Schumm, J.S., Jallad, B., Slusher, J., & Saumell, S. (1996). *Learning Disabilities Research & Practice, 11*(2), 96–106.

Villa, R.A., Thousand, J.S., Paolucci-Whitcomb, P., & Nevin, A. (1990). In search of new paradigms for collaborative consultation. *Journal of Educational and Psychological Consultation, 1,* 279–292.

Wang, M.C., & Birch, J.W. (1984). Effective special education in regular classes. *Exceptional Children, 50,* 391–398.

Wehman, P. (1996). *Life beyond the classroom.* Baltimore: Paul Brookes.

Whalen, C.K. (1989). Attention deficit and hyperactivity disorders. In T. Ollendick & M. Hersen(Eds.), *Handbook of child psychopathology*(pp. 131–169). New York: Plenum.

Wiedmeyer, D., & Lehman, J. (1991). Approach to collaborative teaching and consultation. *Teaching Exceptional Children, 23*(3), 6–10.

Will, M.C. (1986). Educating children with learning problems: A shared responsibility. *Exceptional Children, 52,* 411–415.

Wilson, M.S. (1991). Support services professionals' evaluation of current services for students with learning disabilities and low achieving students without learning disabilities: More grist for the reform mill. *School Psychology Review, 20,* 67–80.

Yoder, D.I., Retish, E., & Wade, R. (1996). Service learning: Meeting student and community needs. *Teaching Exceptional Children, 28*(4), 14–18.

Zirpoli, T.J., & Melloy, K.J. (1997). *Behavior management: Applications for teachers and parents* (2nd ed.). Columbus, OH: Merrill/Prentice Hall.

Chapter Four

Bauwens, J., & Hourcade, J.J. (1995). *Cooperative teaching: Rebuilding the schoolhouse for all students.* Austin, TX: Pro–Ed.

Bauwens, J., & Hourcade, J.J., (1997). Cooperative teaching: Pictures of possibilities. *Intervention in School and Clinic, 33*(2), 81–85, 89.

Beale, A., & Beers, C.S. (1982). What do you say to parents after you say hello? *Teaching Exceptional Children, 15*(1), 34–38.

Boomer, L. (1980). Special education paraprofessionals: A guide for teachers. *Teaching Exceptional Children, 12,* 146–149.

Boomer, L.W. (1981). Meeting common goals through effective teacher-paraprofessional communication. *Teaching Exceptional Children, 13,* 51–53.

Boomer, L. (1982). The paraprofessional: A valued resource for special children and their teachers. *Teaching Exceptional Children, 14,* 194–197.

Boudah, D.J., Schumaker, J.B., Deshler, D.D. (1997). Collaborative instruction: Is it an effective option for inclusion in secondary classrooms? *Learning Disability Quarterly, 20,* 293–316.

Buck, G.H., Bursuck, W.D., Polloway, E.A., Nelson, J., Jayanthi, M.J., & Whitehouse, F.A. (1996). Homework-related communication problems: Perspectives of special educators. *Journal of Emotional and Behavioral Disorders, 4*(2), 105–113.

Chan, S. (1987). Parents of exceptional Asian children. In M.K. Kitano & P.C. Chinn (Ed.), *Exceptional Asian children and youth* (pp. 36–53). Reston, VA: The Council for Exceptional Children.

Council for Exceptional Children. (1997). Working with paraeducators. *CEC Today, 4*(3), 1,5.

deBettencourt, L.U. (1987). How to develop parent relationships. *Teaching Exceptional Children, 19*(2), 26–27.

Donaldson, R., & Christiansen, J. (1990). Consultation and collaboration: A decision-making model. *Teaching Exceptional Children, 22,* 22–25.

Epstein, M.H., Polloway, E.A., Buck, G.H., Bursuck, W.D., Wissinger, L.M., Whitehouse, F., & Jayanthi, M. (1997). Homework–related communication problems: Perspectives of general education teachers. *Learning Disabilities Research & Practice, 12,* 221–227.

Everson, J.M. (1990). A local team approach. *Teaching Exceptional Children, 23,* 44–46.

Fimian, M., Fafard, M.B., & Howell, K. (1984). *A teacher's guide to human resources in special education: Paraprofessionals, volunteers, and peer tutors.* Boston, MA: Allyn & Bacon.

Fisher, D., Pumpian, I., & Sax, C. (1998). Parent and caregiver impressions of different educational models. *Remedial and Special Education, 19,* 173–180.

French, N.K. (1998). Working together: Resource teachers and paraeducators. *Remedial and Special Education, 19,* 357–368.

French, N.K. (1999). Paraeducators: Who are they and what do they do? *Teaching Exceptional Children, 32*(1), 65–69.

French, N.K., & Pickett, A.L. (1997). Paraprofessionals in special education: Issues for teacher educators. *Teacher Education and Special Education, 20*(1), 61–73.

Freschi, D.F. (1999). Guidelines for working with one–to–one aides. *Teaching Exceptional Children, 31*(4), 42–45.

Garcia, S.B., & Malkin, D.H. (1993). Toward defining programs and services for culturally and linguistically diverse learners in special education. *Teaching Exceptional Children, 26*(1), 52–58.

Giangreco, M.F., Edelman, S.W., Luiselli, T.E., & MacFarland, S.Z.C. (1997). Helping or hovering? Effects of instructional assistant proximity on students with disabilities. *Exceptional Children, 64*(1), 7–18.

Gilliam, H.V., & Van Den Berg, S. (1980). Different levels of eye contact: Effects on black and white college students. *Urban Education, 15,* 83–92.

Gonder, S. (1998). Parents: Friend or foe? *CEC Today, 4* (6), 12.

Gutkin, T.B. (1996). Core elements of consultation service delivery for special service personnel: Rationale, practice, and some directions for the future. *Remedial and Special Education, 17,* 333–340.

Gutkin, T.B., & Curtis, M.J. (1990). School–based consultation: Theory, techniques and research. In C.R. Reynolds & T.B. Gutkin (Eds.), *The handbook of school psychology (2nd ed.).* New York: John Wiley & Sons.

Harry, B., Allen, N., & McLaughlin, M. (1995). Communication versus compliance: African American parents' involvement in special education. *Exceptional Children, 61,* 364–377.

Hobbs, T., & Westling, D.L. (1998). Promoting successful inclusion through collaborative problem-solving. *Teaching Exceptional Children, 31*(1), 12–19.

Idol, L. (1993). *Special educator's consultation handbook (2nd ed.).* Austin, TX: Pro–Ed.

Idol, L., Nevin, A., & Paolucci–Whitcomb, P. (1994). *Collaborative consultation (2nd ed.)* Austin, TX: Pro–Ed.

Idol-Maestas, L., & Ritter, S. (1985). A follow-up study of resource/consulting teachers. *Teacher Education and Special Education, 8,* 121–131.

Individuals with Disabilities Education Act, 20 U.S.C. § 1400 et seq. (1997).

Jayanthi, M., Bursuck, W., Epstein, M.H., & Polloway, E.A. (1997). Strategies for successful homework. *Teaching Exceptional Children, 30*(1), 4–7.

Jayanthi, M., Sawyer, V., Nelson, J.S., Bursuck, W.D., & Epstein, M.H. (1995). Recommendations for homework-communication problems from parents, classroom teachers, and special education teachers. *Remedial and Special Education, 16,* 212–225.

Johnson, L.J., Pugach, M.C., & Devlin, S. (1990). Professional collaboration. *Teaching Exceptional Children, 22,* 9–11.

Johnson, L.J., Pugach, M.C., & Hammitte, D.J. (1988). Barriers to effective special education consultation. *Remedial and Special Education, 9,* 41–47.

Jones, K.H., & Bender, W.N. (1993). Utilization of paraprofessional in special education: A review of the literature. *Remedial and Special Education, 14*(1), 7–14.

Klingner, J.K., Vaughn, S., Hughes, M.T., Schumm, J.S., & Elbaum, B. (1998). Outcomes for students with and without learning disabilities in inclusive classrooms. *Learning Disabilities Research & Practice, 13,* 153–161.

Knoff, H.M., McKenna, A.F., & Riser, K. (1991). Toward a consultant effectiveness scale: Investigating the characteristics of effective consultants. *School Psychology Review, 20,* 81–96.

Linan-Thompson, S., & Jean, R.E. (1997). Completing the parent participation puzzle: Accepting diversity. *Teaching Exceptional Children, 30*(2), 46–50.

Marion, R. (1979). Minority parent involvement in the IEP process: A systematic model approach. *Focus on*

Exceptional Children, 10 (8), 1–15.

Marks, S.U., Schrader, C., & Levine, M. (1999). Paraeducator experiences in inclusive settings: Helping, hovering, or holding their own? *Exceptional Children, 65*, 315–328.

McKenzie, R.G., & Houk, C.S. (1986). The paraprofessional in special education. *Teaching Exceptional Children, 19*, 246–252.

Meyers, J., Gelzheiser, L.M., & Yelich, G. (1991). Do pull-in programs foster teacher collaboration? *Remedial and Special Education, 12*(2), 7–15.

Miramontes, O.B. (1990). Organizing for effective paraprofessional services in special education: A multilingual/multiethnic instructional service team model. *Remedial and Special Education, 12*(1), 29–36.

Morsink, C.V., Thomas, C.C., & Correa, V.I. (1991). *Interactive teaming: Consultation and collaboration in special programs.* New York: Merrill/Macmillan.

Perl, J. (1995). Improving relationship skills for parent conferences. *Teaching Exceptional Children, 28*(1), 29–31.

Phillips, V., & McCullough, L. (1990). Consultation-based programming: Instituting the collaborative ethic in schools. *Exceptional Children, 56*, 291–304.

Polsgrove, L., & McNeil, M. (1989). The consultation process: Research and practice. *Remedial and Special Education, 10*(1), 6–13.

Pugach, M.C., & Johnson, L.J. (1988). Peer collaboration. *Teaching Exceptional Children, 20*, 75–77.

Pugach, M.C., & Johnson, L.J. (1995). *Collaborative practitioners: Collaborative schools.* Denver, CO: Love.

Reinhiller, N. (1996). Coteaching: New variations on a not-so-new practice. *Teacher Education and Special Education, 19*(1), 34–48.

Runge, A., Walker, J., & Shea, T.M. (1975). A passport to positive parent-teacher communications. *Teaching Exceptional Children, 7*, 91–92.

Saint-Laurent, L., Dionne, J., Giasson, J., Royer, E., Simard, C., Pierard, B. (1998). Academic achievement effects of an in-class service model on students with and without disabilities. *Exceptional Children, 64*, 239–253.

Salend, S.J., Johansen, M., Mumper, J., Chase, A.S., Pike, K.M., & Dorney, J.A. (1997). Cooperative teaching: The voices of two teachers. *Remedial and Special Education, 18*(1), 3–11.

Salzberg, C.L., & Morgan, J. (1995). Preparing teachers to work with paraeducators. *Teacher Education and Special Education, 18*(1), 49–55.

Shea, T.M., & Bauer, A.M. (1985). *Parents and teachers of exceptional students: A handbook for involvement.* Newton, MA: Allyn & Bacon.

Shea, T.M., & Bauer, A.M. (1991). *Parents and teachers of children with exceptionalities: A handbook for collaboration (2nd ed.).* Boston, MA: Allyn & Bacon.

Sheridan, S.M., Welch, M., & Orme, S.F. (1996). Is consultation effective? A review of outcome research. *Remedial and Special Education, 17*, 341–354.

Simpson, R.L. (1982). *Conferencing parents of exceptional children.* Rockville, MD: Aspen.

Sonnenschein, P. (1981). Parents and professionals: An uneasy relationship. *Teaching Exceptional Children, 14*, 62–65.

Thorkildsen, R., & Stein, M.R.S. (1998). Is parent involvement related to student achievement? Exploring the evidence. *Research Bulletin*, No. 22, Phi Delta Kappa Center for Evaluation, Development, and Research.

Thousand, J.S., & Villa, R.A. (1989). Enhancing success in heterogeneous schools. In S. Stainback, W. Stainback, & M. Forest, (Eds.), *Educating all students in the mainstream of regular education* (pp. 89–103). Baltimore, MD: Paul Brookes.

Turnbull, A.P., & Turnbull, H.R. (1997). *Families, professionals, and exceptionality: A special partnership (3rd ed.).* Columbus, OH: Merrill/Prentice Hall.

Vaughn, S., Schumm, J.S., & Arguelles, M.E. (1997). The ABCDE's of co–teaching. *Teaching Exceptional Children, 30*(2), 4–10.

Villa, R.A., Thousand, J.S., Nevin, A.I., & Malgeri, C. (1996). Instilling collaboration for inclusive schooling as a way of doing business in public schools. *Remedial and Special Education, 17*, 169–181.

Voltz, D.L., Elliott, R.N., & Harris, W.B. (1995). Promising practices in facilitating collaboration between resource room teachers and general education teachers. *Learning Disabilities Research & Practice, 10*,

129–136.

Walther-Thomas, C.S. (1997). Co–teaching experiences: The benefits and problems that teachers and principals report over time. *Journal of Learning Disabilities, 30*, 395–407.

West, J.F. (1990). Educational collaboration in the restructuring of schools. *Journal of Educational and Psychological Consultation, 1*(1), 23–40.

Westling, D.L. (1996). What do parents with moderate and severe mental disabilities want? *Education and Training in Mental Retardation and Developmental Disabilities, 31*, 86–114.

Williams, V.I., & Cartledge, G. (1997). Passing notes to parents. *Teaching Exceptional Children, 30*(1), 30–34.

Winton, P.J., & Turnbull, A.P. (1981). Parent involvement as viewed by parents of preschool handicapped children. *Topics in Early Childhood Special Education, 1*(3), 11–19.

Wood, M.(1998). Whose job is it anyway? Educational roles in inclusion. *Exceptional Children, 64*, 181–195.

Chapter Five

Alberto, P.A., & Troutman, A.C. (1999). *Applied behavior analysis for teachers* (5th ed.). Columbus, OH: Merrill/Prentice Hall.

Armstrong, S.W., & Kauffman, J.M. (1999). Functional behavioral assessment: Introduction to the series. *Behavioral Disorders, 24*, 167–168.

Bakken, J.P., & Aloia, G.F. (1998). Evaluating the World Wide Web. *Teaching Exceptional Children, 30*(5), 48–52.

Berliner, D.C. (1984). The half-full glass: A review of research on teaching. In P.L. Hosford (Ed.), *Using what we know about teaching* (pp. 51–77). Alexandria, VA: Association for Supervision and Curriculum Development.

Blackhurst, A.E. (1989). Using *AppleWorks* to improve personal productivity. *Teaching Exceptional Children, 21*, 68–70.

Charles, C.M. (1999). *Building classroom discipline* (6th ed.). NY: Addison Wesley Longman.

Clarke, S., Dunlay, G., Foster-Johnson, L., Childs, K.E., Wilson, D., & Vera, A. (1995). Improving the conduct of students with behavioral disorders by incorporating student interests into curricular activities. *Behavioral Disorders, 20*, 221–237.

Cohen, S.B., & Hart-Hester, S. (1987). Time management strategies. *Teaching Exceptional Children, 20*(1), 56–57.

Cohen, S.B., & Hearn, D. (1988). Reinforcement. In R. McNergney (Ed.), *Guide to Classroom Teaching,* Boston, MA: Allyn & Bacon.

Curwin, R., & Mendler, A. (1988). *Discipline with dignity.* Alexandria, VA: Association for Supervision and Curriculum Development.

Deluke, S.V., & Knoblock, P. (1987). Teacher behavior as preventive discipline. *Teaching Exceptional Children, 19* (4), 18–24.

DePaepe, P.A., Shores, R.E., Jack, S.L., & Denny, R.K. (1996). Effects of task difficulty on the disruptive and on-task behavior of students with severe behavioral disorders. *Behavioral Disorders, 21*, 216–225.

Freiberg, H.J. (1998). Measuring school climate: Let me count the ways. *Educational Leadership, 56*(1), 22–26.

Gallagher, P.A. (1979). *Teaching students with behavior disorders: Techniques for classroom instruction.* Denver, CO: Love.

Gallagher, P.A. (1997). Promoting dignity: Taking the destructive d's out of behavioral disorders. *Focus on Exceptional Children, 29*(9), 1–19.

Gartland, D. (1990). Classroom management: Preventive discipline. *LD Forum, 15*(3), 24–25.

Gartland, D., & Rosenberg, M.S. (1987). Managing time in the LD classroom. *LD Forum, 12*(2), 8–10.

Gast, D., & Nelson, C.M. (1977a). Legal and ethical considerations for the use of timeout in special education settings. *The Journal of Special Education, 11*, 457–467.

Gast, D., & Nelson, C.M. (1977b). Time out in the classroom: Implications for special education. *Exceptional Children, 43*, 461–464.

Guernsey, M.A. (1989). Classroom organization: A key to successful management. *Academic Therapy, 25*(1), 55–58.

Gunter, P.L., Shores, R.E., Jack, S.L., Rasmussen, S.K., & Flowers, J. (1995). On the move: Using teacher/student proximity to improve students' behavior. *Teaching Exceptional Children, 28*(1), 12–13.

Hannaford, A.E. (1993). Computers and exceptional individuals. In J.D. Lindsey (Ed.), *Computers and exceptional individuals* (2nd ed.). Austin, TX: Pro-Ed.

Hoffman, E. (1988). Time management from the kitchen. *Academic Therapy, 23*(3), 275–277.

Individuals with Disabilities Education Act, 20 U.S.C. § 1400 et seq. (1997).

Johns, B., Guetzloe, E., & Yell, M. (1997). The Individuals with Disabilities Education Act Amendments of 1997: Update on disciplinary provisions. *Beyond Behavior, 8*(2), 4–9.

Katsiyannis, A., & Maag, J.W. (1998). Disciplining students with disabilities: Issues and considerations for implementing IDEA '97. *Behavioral Disorders, 23,* 276–289.

Maher, G.B. (1989). "Punch Out": A behavior management technique. *Teaching Exceptional Children, 21*(2), 74.

Meese, R.L. (1996). *Strategies for teaching students with emotional and behavioral disorders.* Pacific Grove, CA: Brooks/Cole.

Minner, S., & Prater, G. (1989). Arranging the physical environment of special education classrooms. *Academic Therapy, 25*(1), 91–96.

Myles, B.S., & Hronek, L.J. (1990). Transition activities: A classroom management tool. *LD Forum, 15*(3), 20–22.

O'Connor, S. (1988). Affective climate. In R. McNergney (Ed.), *Guide to classroom teaching.* Boston, MA: Allyn & Bacon.

Olson, J. (1989). Managing life in the classroom: Dealing with the nitty gritty. *Academic Therapy, 24*(5), 545–553.

O'Melia, M.C., & Rosenberg, M.S. (1989). Classroom management: Preventing behavior problems in classrooms for students with learning disabilities. *LD Forum, 15(1),* 23–26.

Reynolds, C.J., Salend, S.J., & Beahan, C.L. (1989). Motivating secondary students: Bringing in the reinforcements. *Academic Therapy, 25*(1), 81–89.

Sabatino, D.A. (1987). Preventive discipline as a practice in special education. *Teaching Exceptional Children, 19*(4), 8–11.

Salpeter, J. (1997). Industry snapshot: Where are we headed? *Technology & Learning, 17*(6), 22–24, 28–32.

Stage, S.A. (1997). A preliminary investigation of the relationship between in-school suspension and the disruptive classroom behavior of students with behavioral disorders. *Behavioral Disorders, 23*(1), 57–76.

Stainback, W., Stainback, S., & Froyen, L. (1987). Structuring the classroom to prevent disruptive behaviors. *Teaching Exceptional Children, 19*(4), 12–16.

Yell, M. (1994). Timeout and students with behavior disorders: A legal analysis. *Education and Treatment of Children, 17,* 293–301.

Yell, M.L. (1997). Teacher liability for student injury and misconduct. *Beyond Behavior, 8*(1), 4–9.

Chapter Six

Alberto, P.A., & Troutman, A.C. (1999). *Applied behavior analysis for teachers* (5th ed.). Columbus, OH: Merrill.

Allinder, R.M. (1996). When some is not better than none: Effects of differential implementation of curriculum-based measurement. *Exceptional Children, 62,* 525–535.

Barnett, D., Zins, J., & Wise, L. (1984). An analysis of parental participation as a means of reducing bias in the education of handicapped children. *Special Services in the Schools, 1,* 71–84.

Bennett, R.E. (1982). Cautions for the use of informal measures in the educational assessment of exceptional children. *Journal of Learning Disabilities, 15,* 337–339.

Blankenship, C.S. (1985). Using curriculum-based assessment data to make instructional decisions. *Exceptional Children, 52,* 233–238.

Bos, C.S., & Reyes, E.I. (1996). Conversations with a Latina teacher about education for language-minority students with special needs. *Elementary School Journal, 96,* 343–351.

Bradley, D.F., & Calvin, M.B. (1998). Grading modified assignments: Equity or compromise? *Teaching Exceptional Children, 31*(2), 24–29.

Brantlinger, E. (1987). Making decisions about special education placement: Do low income parents have the information they need? *Journal of Learning Disabilities, 20,* 94–101.

Brigance, A.H. (1999). *Brigance comprehensive inventory of basic skills* (Rev. ed.). North Billerica, MA: Curriculum Associates.

Bursuck, W.D., Munk, D.D., & Olson, M.M. (1999). The fairness of report card grading adaptations: What do students with and without learning disabilities think? *Remedial and Special Education, 20*(2), 84–92, 105.

Bursuck, W., Polloway, E.A., Plante, L., Epstein, M.H., Jayanthi, M., & McConeghy, J. (1996). Report card grading and adaptations: A national survey of classroom practices. *Exceptional Children, 62,* 301–318.

Chalfant, J.C., Pysh, M.V., & Moultrie, R. (1979). Teacher assistance teams: A model for within-building problem solving. *Learning Disability Quarterly, 2,* 85–96.

Chinn, P.C., & Hughes, S. (1987). Representation of minority students in special education classes. *Remedial and Special Education, 8* (4), 41–46.

Choate, J.S., Enright, B.E., Miller, L.J., Poteet, J.A., & Rakes, T.A. (1992). *Curriculum-based assessment and programming* (2nd ed.). Boston, MA: Allyn and Bacon.

Christiansen, J., & Vogel, J.R. (1998). A decision model for grading students with disabilities. *Teaching Exceptional Children, 31*(2), 30–35.

Council for Exceptional Children. (1997). Making assessments of diverse students meaningful. *CEC Today, 4*(4), 1,9.

Coutinho, M., & Malouf, D. (1992, November). *Performance assessment and children with disabilities: Issues and possibilities.* Washington, D.C.: U.S. Department of Education.

Craig, S., Hull, K., Haggart, A.G., & Perez-Selles, M. (2000). Promoting cultural competence through teacher assistance teams. *Teaching Exceptional Children, 32*(3), 6–12.

Dalton, B., Tivnan, T., Riley, M.K., Rawson, P., & Dias, D. (1995). Revealing competence: Fourth-grade students with and without learning disabilities show what they know on paper-and-pencil and hands-on performance assessments. *Learning Disabilities Research & Practice, 10,* 198–214.

Daub, D., & Colarusso, R.P. (1996). The validity of the WJ-R, PIAT-R, and DAB-2 reading subtests with students with learning disabilities. *Learning Disabilities Research & Practice, 11*(2), 90–95.

Deno, S.L. (1985). Curriculum-based measurement: The emerging alternative. *Exceptional Children, 52,* 219–231.

Dickinson, D.J. (1980). The direct assessment: An alternative to psychometric testing. *Journal of Learning Disabilities, 13* (9), 8–12.

Elliott, J., Ysseldyke, J., Thurlow, M. & Erickson, R. (1998). What about assessment and accountability? Practical implications for educators. *Teaching Exceptional Children, 31*(1), 20–27.

Elliott, S.N. (1998). Performance assessment of students' achievement: Research and practice. *Learning Disabilities Research & Practice, 13,* 233–241.

Elliott, S.N., Kratochwill, T.R., & Schulte, A.G. (1998). The assessment accommodation checklist. *Teaching Exceptional Children, 31*(2), 10–14.

Erickson, R., Ysseldyke, J., Thurlow, M., & Elliott, J. (1998). Inclusive assessments and accountability systems: Tools of the trade in educational reform. *Teaching Exceptional Children, 32*(2), 4–9.

Fagley, N.S. (1984). Behavioral assessment in the schools: Obtaining and evaluating information for individualized programming. *Special Services in the Schools, 1*(2) 45–57.

Fuchs, D., Fuchs, L.S., & Bahr, M.W. (1990). Mainstream assistance teams: A scientific basis for the art of consultation. *Exceptional Children, 57,* 128–139.

Fuchs, L.S. (1986). Monitoring progress among mildly handicapped pupils: Review of current practice and research. *Remedial and Special Education, 7* (5), 5–12.

Fuchs, L.S. (1993). Enhancing instructional programming and student achievement with curriculum-based measurement. In J.J. Kramer (Ed.), *Curriculum-based assessment: Examining old problems, evaluating new solutions* (pp. 65–103). Lincoln, NE: Buros Institute of Mental Measurements.

Fuchs, L.S., & Deno, S.L. (1994). Must instructionally useful performance assessment be based in the curriculum? *Exceptional Children, 61*(1), 15–24.

Fuchs, L.S., & Fuchs, D. (1996). Combining performance assessment and curriculum-based measurement to strengthen instructional planning. *Learning Disabilities Research & Practice, 11,* 183–192.

Fuchs, L.S., Fuchs, D., & Hamlett, C.L. (1989). Effects of alternative goal structures within curriculum-based measurement. *Exceptional Children, 55,* 429–438.

Fuchs, L.S., Fuchs, D., & Stecker, P. (1989). Effects of curriculum-based measurement on teachers' instructional planning. *Journal of Learning Disabilities, 22*(1), 51–59.

Gersten, R., & Woodward, J. (1994). The language-minority student and special education: Issues, trends, and paradoxes. *Exceptional Children, 60,* 310–322.

Glickman, C.D. (1990). *Supervision of instruction: A developmental approach* (3rd ed.). Boston, MA: Allyn and Bacon.

Good, R.H., & Salvia, J. (1988). Curriculum bias in published norm-referenced reading tests: Demonstrable effects. *School Psychology Review, 17*(1), 51–60.

Graden, J., Casey, A., & Bonstrom, O. (1985). Implementing a prereferral intervention system: Part II. The data. *Exceptional Children, 51,* 487–496.

Gresham, F.M., & Elliott, S.N. (1990). *The social skills rating system.* Circle Pines, MN: American Guidance Service.

Guerin, G., & Maier, A. (1983). *Informal assessment in education.* Palo Alto, CA: Mayfield Publishing Company.

Harry, B., Allen, N., & McLaughlin, M. (1995). Communication versus compliance: African-American parents' involvement in special education. *Exceptional Children, 61,* 364–377.

Hodge, J.P., & Shriner, J.G. (1997). Special education mediation: A workable solution to impasses between parents and school districts. *Beyond Behavior, 8*(2), 20–24.

Howell, K.W. (1985). Task analysis and the characteristics of tasks. *Journal of Special Education Technology, 6,* 5–14.

Howell, K.W. (1986). Direct assessment of academic performance. *School Psychology Review, 15,* 324–335.

Individuals with Disabilities Education Act, 20 U.S.C. § 1400 et seq. (1997).

King-Sears, M.E., Burgess, M., & Lawson, T.L. (1999). Curriculum-based assessment in inclusive settings. *Teaching Exceptional Children, 32*(1), 30–38.

Leung, B.P. (1996). Quality assessment practices in a diverse society. *Teaching Exceptional Children, 28*(3), 42–45.

Linan-Thompson, S., & Jean, R.E. (1997). Completing the parent participation puzzle: Accepting diversity. *Teaching Exceptional Children, 30*(2), 46–50.

Marston, D., & Magnusson, D. (1985). Implementing curriculum-based measurement in special and regular education settings. *Exceptional Children, 52,* 266–276.

Marston, D., & Magnusson, D. (1988). Curriculum-based measurement: District level implementation. In J.Z. Graden & M. Curtis (Eds.), *Alternative educational delivery systems: Enhancing instructional options for all students.* Washington, D.C.: National Association of School Psychologists.

Marston, D., & Tindal, G. (1995). Performance monitoring. In A. Thomas & J. Grimes (Eds.), *Best practices in school psychology III* (pp. 597–608). Washington, D.C.: The National Association of School Psychologists.

Oswald, D.P., Coutinho, M.J., Best, A.M., & Singh, N.N. (1999). Ethnic representation in special education: The influence of school-related economic and demographic variables. *The Journal of Special Education, 32,* 194–206.

Pike, K., & Salend, S.J. (1995). Authentic assessment strategies: Alternatives to norm-referenced testing. *Teaching Exceptional Children, 28*(1), 15–20.

Polloway, E.A., Epstein, M.H., Bursuck, W., Roderique, T.W., McConeghy, J.L., & Jayanthi, M. (1994). Classroom grading: A national survey of policies. *Remedial and Special Education, 15,* 162–170.

Ramey, P., & Robbins, P. (1989). Professional growth and support through peer coaching. *Educational Leadership, 46*(8), 35–38.

Reschly, D.J. (1987). Learning characteristics of mildly handicapped students: Implications for classification, placement, and programming. In M.C. Wang, M.C. Reynolds, & H.J. Walberg (Eds.), *Handbook of special education: Research and practice, Volume I: Learner characteristics and adaptive education.* New York: Pergamon Press.

Rueda, R., & Garcia, E. (1997). Do portfolios make a difference for diverse students? The influence of type of data on making instructional decisions. *Learning Disabilities Research & Practice, 12,* 114–122.

Safran, S.P., & Safran, J.S. (1996). Intervention assistance programs and prereferral teams: Directions for the twenty-first century. *Remedial and Special Education, 17,* 363–369.

Salend, S.J. (1998). Using portfolios to assess student performance. *Teaching Exceptional Children, 31*(2), 36–43.

Salvia, J., & Hughes, C. (1990). *Curriculum-based assessment: Testing what is taught.* New York: Macmillan.

Salvia, J., & Ysseldyke, J. (1998). *Assessment: In special and remedial education* (7th ed.). Boston, MA: Houghton Mifflin.

Schumm, J.S., & Vaughn, S. (1991). Making adaptations for mainstreamed students: General classroom teachers' perspectives. *Remedial and Special Education, 12,* 18–27.

Shinn, M.R. (1988). Development of curriculum–based local norms for use in special education decision-making. *School Psychology Review, 17*(1), 61–80.

Shinn, M.R. (Ed.). (1989). *Curriculum-based measurement: Assessing special children.* New York: Guilford Press.

Shinn, M.R., Tindal, G.A., & Stein, S. (1988). Curriculum-based measurement and the identification of mildly handicapped students: A research review. *Professional School Psychology, 3*(1), 69–85.

Simpson, R.L., Ormsbee, C.K., & Myles, B.S. (1997). General and special educators' perceptions of preassessment-related activities and team members. *Exceptionality, 7,* 157–167.

Slate, J.R. (1996). Interrelations of frequently administered achievement measures in the determination of specific learning disabilities. *Learning Disabilities Research & Practice, 11*(2), 86–89.

Slate, J.R., Jones, C.H., Graham, L.S., & Bower, J. (1994). Correlations of WISC-III, WRAT-R, KM-R, and PPVT-R scores in students with specific learning disabilities. *Learning Disabilities Research & Practice, 9,* 104–107.

Telzrow, C. (1988). Debate over usefulness of IQ. *Communique, 17,* 4–6.

Thurlow, M.L. (1998). Assessment: A key component of education reform. *Peer Information Brief.* Boston, MA: The Federation for children with Special Needs.

Thurlow, M.L., Ysseldyke, J.E., & Silverstein, B. (1995). Testing accommodations for students with disabilities. *Remedial and Special Education, 16,* 260–270.

U.S. Department of Education. (1997). *Nineteenth Annual Report to Congress on the Implementation of the Individuals with Disabilities Education Act.* Washington, D.C.: Author.

Valdes, K.A., Williamson, C.L., & Wagner, M.M. (1990). *The national longitudinal transition study of special education students* (Vol. I). Menlo Park, CA: SRI International.

Vaughn, S., Bos, C., Harrell, J., & Lasky, B. (1988). Parent participation in the initial IEP conference ten years after mandated involvement. *Journal of Learning Disabilities, 21,* 82–89.

Walker, H. & McConnell, S. (1988). *The Walker-McConnell Scale of Social Competence and School Adjustment,* Austin, TX: Pro-Ed.

Welch, M., Brownell, K., & Sheridan, S.M. (1999). What's the score and game plan on teaming in schools? A review of the literature on team teaching and school-based problem-solving teams. *Remedial and Special Education, 20*(1), 36–49.

Ysseldyke, J., & Olsen, K. (1999). Putting alternate assessments into practice: What to measure and possible sources of data. *Exceptional Children, 65,* 175–185.

Chapter Seven

Airasian, P.W. (1991). *Classroom assessment.* New York: McGraw-Hill.

Baker, J., Young, M., & Martin, M. (1990). The effectiveness of small-group versus one-to-one remedial instruction for six students with learning disabilities. *The Elementary School Journal, 91*(1), 65–76.

Bennett, N., & Desforges, C. (1988). Matching classroom tasks to students' attainments. *The Elementary School Journal, 88*(3), 221–234.

Billingsley, F. (1984). Where are the generalized objectives? An examination of instructional objectives. *Journal of the Association for Persons with Severe Handicaps, 9,* 186–192.

Billingsley, F.F., Burgess, D., Lynch, V.W., & Matlock, B.L. (1991). Toward generalized outcomes: Considerations and guidelines for writing instructional objectives. *Education and Training in Mental Retardation, 26,* 351–360.

Blackhurst, A.E. (1997). Perspectives on technology in special education. *Teaching Exceptional Children, 29*(5), 41–48.

Bloom, B.S., Englehart, M.B., Furst, E.J., Hill, W.H., & Krathwohl, O.R. (1956). *Taxonomy of educational objectives: The classification of educational goals. Handbook I: The cognitive domain.* New York: Longman.

Brown, D.S. (1988). Twelve middle-school teachers' planning. *The Elementary School Journal, 89*(1), 69–87.

Cohen, S.G., & deBettencourt, L.V. (1991). Dropout: Intervening with the reluctant learner. *Intervention in School and Clinic, 26*(5), 263–271.

de la Cruz, R.E., Cage, C.E., & Lian, M.J. (2000). Let's play mancala and sungka! Learning math and social skills through ancient multicultural games. *Teaching Exceptional Children, 32*(3), 38–42.

Dyck, N., Sundbye, N., & Pemberton, J. (1997). A recipe for efficient co-teaching. *Teaching Exceptional Children, 30*(2), 42–45.

Englert, C.S. (1984). Effective direct instruction practices in special education settings. *Remedial and Special Education, 5*(2), 38–47.

Forness, S.R., Kavale, K.A., Blum, I.M., & Lloyd, J.W. (1997). Mega-analysis of meta-analysis: What works in special education and related services. *Teaching Exceptional Children, 29*(6), 4–9.

French, N.K. (1999a). Paraeducators and teachers: Shifting roles. *Teaching Exceptional Children, 32*(2), 69–73.

French, N.K. (1999b). Paraeducataors: Who are they and what do they do? *Teaching Exceptional Children, 32*(1), 65–69.

Fuchs, L.S., Fuchs, D., & Bishop, N. (1992). Teacher planning for students with learning disabilities: Differences between general and special educators. *Learning Disabilities Research & Practice, 7,* 120–128.

Giek, K.A. (1992). Monitoring student progress through efficient record keeping. *Teaching Exceptional Children, 24*(3), 22–26.

Individuals with Disabilities Education Act, 20 U.S.C. § 1400 et seq. (1997).

Kameenui, E.J., & Simmons, D.C. (1990). *Designing instructional strategies: The prevention of academic learning problems.* Columbus, OH: Merrill.

Keel, M.C., & Gast, D.L. (1992). Small-group instruction for students with learning disabilities: Observational and incidental learning. *Exceptional Children, 58*(4), 357–368.

Kroeger, S.D., Leibold, C.K., & Ryan, B. (1999). Creating a sense of ownership in the IEP process. *Teaching Exceptional Children, 32*(1), 4–9.

Lloyd, J.W. (1988). Direct academic intervention in learning disabilities. In M. Want, M. Reynolds, & H. Walberg (Eds.), *Handbook of special education research and practice, Volume 2* (pp. 345–366). New York: Pergamon.

Maheady, L., Sacca, M.K., & Harper, G.F. (1988). Classwide peer tutoring with mildly handicapped high school students. *Exceptional Children, 55*(1), 52–59.

McConnell, M.E. (1999). Self-monitoring, cueing, recording, and managing: Teaching students to manage their own behavior. *Teaching Exceptional Children, 32*(2), 14–21.

Rappaport, S.R. (1991). Diagnostic-prescriptive teaming: The road less traveled. *Reading, Writing, and Learning Disabilities, 7,* 183–199.

Rosenshine, B. (1986). Synthesis of research on explicit teaching. *Educational Leadership, 43*(7), 60–69.

Sands, D.J., Adams, L., & Stout, D.M. (1995). A statewide exploration of the nature and use of curriculum in special education. *Exceptional Children, 62*(1), 68–83.

Santos, K.E., & Rettig, M.D. (1999). Going on the block: Meeting the needs of students with disabilities in high schools with block scheduling. *Teaching Exceptional Children, 31*(3), 54–59.

Schumm, J.S., & Vaughn, S. (1992). Planning for mainstreamed special education students: Perceptions of general classroom teachers. *Exceptionality, 3,* 81–98.

Schumm, J.S., Vaughn, S., Haager, D., McDowell, J., Rothlein, L., & Saumell, L. (1995). General education teacher planning: What can students with learning disabilities expect? *Exceptional Children, 61,* 335–353.

Schumm, J.S., Vaughn, S., & Harris, J. (1997). Pyramid power for collaborative planning. *Teaching Exceptional Children, 29*(6), 62–66.

Searcy, S., & Maroney, S.A. (1996). Lesson planning practices of special education teachers. *Exceptionality, 6,* 171–187.

Shure, A., Morocco, C.C., DiGisi, L.L., & Yenkin, L. (1999). Pathways to planning: Improving student achievement in inclusive classrooms. *Teaching Exceptional Children, 32*(1), 48–54.

Slavin, R.E. (1990). *Cooperative learning: Theory, research and practice.* Englewood Cliffs, NJ: Prentice Hall.

Slavin, R.E. (1991). *Educational psychology* (3rd ed.). Englewood Cliffs, NJ: Prentice Hall.

Slavin, R., & Madden, N. (1989). What works for students at risk: A research synthesis. *Educational Leadership, 46,* 4–13.

Stinson, D.M., Gast, D.L., Wolery, M., & Collins, B.C. (1991). Acquisition of nontargeted information during small-group instruction. *Exceptionality, 2*(2), 65–80.

Stokes, T.F., & Baer, D.M. (1977). An implicit technology of generalization. *Journal of Applied Behavior Analysis, 10,* 349–367.

Taylor, S.V. (2000). Multicultural is who we are: Literature as a reflection of ourselves. *Teaching Exceptional Children, 32*(3), 24–29.

Vaughn, S., & Schumm, J.S. (1994). Middle school teachers' planning for students with learning disabilities. *Remedial and Special Education, 15*(3), 152–161.

Wolery, M., Bailey, D.B., & Sugai, G.M. (1988). *Effective teaching: Principles and procedures of applied behavior analysis with exceptional students.* Boston, MA: Allyn and Bacon.

Chapter Eight

Adams, G.L., & Engelmann, S. (1996). *Research on direct instruction: 25 years beyond DISTAR.* Seattle, WA: Educational Achievement Systems.

Anderson, G.L., & Barrera, I. (1995). Critical constructivist research and special education: Expanding our lens on social reality and exceptionality. *Remedial and Special Education, 16,* 142–149.

Bereiter, C., & Engelmann, S. (1966). *Teaching disadvantaged children in the preschool.* Englewood Cliffs, NJ: Prentice Hall.

Berliner, D.C. (1984). The half-full glass: A review of research on teaching. In P. L. Hosford (Ed.), *Using what we know about teaching* (pp. 51–77). Alexandria, VA: Association for Supervision and Curriculum Development.

Brophy, J., & Good, T.L. (1986). Teacher behavior and student achievement. In M.C. Wittrock (Ed.), *Handbook of research on teaching.* New York: MacMillan.

Carnine, D., Silbert, J., & Kameenui, E.J. (1990). *Direct instruction reading* (2nd ed.). Columbus, OH: Merrill.

Echevarria, J., & McDonough, R. (1995). An alternative reading approach: Instructional conversations in a bilingual special education setting. *Learning Disabilities Research & Practice, 10*(2), 108–119.

Englert, C.S. (1983). Measuring special education teacher effectiveness. *Exceptional Children, 50,* 247–254.

Englert, C.S. (1984). Effective direct instruction practices in special education settings. *Remedial and Special Education, 5,* 38–47.

Englert, C.S., & Mariage, T.V. (1996). A sociocultural perspective: Teaching ways-of-thinking and ways-of-talking in a literacy community. *Learning Disabilities Research & Practice, 11*(3), 157–167.

Englert, C.S., Raphael, T.E., Anderson, L.M., Anthony, H.M., & Stevens, D.D. (1991). Making strategies and self-talk visible: Writing instruction in regular and special education classrooms. *American Educational Research Journal, 28,* 337–373.

Forness, S.R., Kavale, K.A., Blum, I.A., & Lloyd, J.W. (1997). A mega-analysis of meta-analysis: What works in special education and related services. *Teaching Exceptional Children, 29*(6), 4–9.

Fueyo, V. (1997). Below the tip of the iceberg: Teaching language-minority students. *Teaching Exceptional Children, 30*(1), 61–65.

Gersten, R. (1998). Recent advances in instructional research for students with learning disabilities: An overview. *Learning Disabilities Research & Practice, 13,* 162–170.

Gersten, R., & Keating, T. (1987). Long-term benefits from direct instruction. *Educational Leadership, 44,* 28–31.

Good, T.L., Grouws, D.A., & Backerman, T. (1978). Curriculum pacing: Some empirical data in mathematics. *Journal of Curriculum Studies, 10,* 75–82.

Goodman, Y.M. (1989). Roots of the whole-language movement. *The Elementary School Journal, 90*(2), 113–127.

Graham, S., & Harris, K.R. (1994). Implications of constructivism for teaching writing to students with special needs. *The Journal of Special Education, 28,* 275–289.

Greenwood, C.R., Delquadri, J.C., & Hall, R.V. (1984). Opportunity to respond and student academic performance. In W.L. Heward, T.E. Heron, D.S. Hill, & J. Trap-Porter (Eds.), *Focus on behavior analysis in education* (pp. 58–88). Columbus, OH: Merrill.

Harris, K.R., & Graham, S. (1994). Constructivism: Principles, paradigms, and integration. *Journal of Special Education, 28,* 233–247.

Harris, K.R., & Graham, S. (1996a). Constructivism and students with special needs: Issues in the classroom. *Learning Disabilities Research & Practice, 11,* 134–137.

Harris, K.R., & Graham, S. (1996b). Memo to constructivists: Skills count too. *Educational Leadership, 53,* 26–29.

Haynes, M.C., & Jenkins, J.R. (1986). Reading instruction in special education resource rooms. *American Educational Research Journal, 23,* 161–190.

Heshusius, L. (1989). The Newtonian mechanistic paradigm, special education, and contours of alternatives: An overview. *Journal of Learning Disabilities, 22,* 403–415.

Heward, W.L., Gardner, R., Cavanaugh, R.A., Courson, F.H., Grossi, T.A., & Barbetta, P.M. (1996). Everyone participates in this class: Using response cards to increase active student responding. *Teaching Exceptional Children, 28*(2), 4–10.

Hunter, M. (1982). *Mastery teaching.* El Segundo, CA: TIP Publications.

Kline, F.M., Schumaker, J.B., & Deshler, D.D. (1991). Development and validation of feedback routines for instructing students with learning disabilities. *Learning Disability Quarterly, 14,* 191–207.

Kronick, D. (1990). Holism and empiricism as complementary paradigms. *Journal of Learning Disabilities, 23*(1), 5–8, 10.

Lenz, B.K., Alley, G.R., & Schumaker, J.B. (1987). Activating the inactive learner: Advance organizers in the secondary content classroom. *Learning Disability Quarterly, 10,* 53–68.

Lloyd, J.W. (1988). Direct academic interventions in learning disabilities. In M.C. Wang, M.C. Reynolds, & H.J. Walberg (Eds.), *Handbook of special education: Research and practice: Volume II: Mildly handicapped conditions.* New York: Pergamon Press.

Mastropieri, M.A., & Scruggs, T.E. (1987). *Effective instruction for special education.* Boston, MA: College-Hill Press.

Mercer, C.D., Jordan, L., & Miller, S.P. (1996). Constructivistic math instruction for diverse learners. *Learning Disabilities Research & Practice, 11,* 147–156.

Northwest Regional Educational Laboratory. (1990). *Effective schooling practices: A research synthesis 1990 update.* Portland, OR: Author.

Palincsar, A.S. (1986). Metacognitive strategy instruction. *Exceptional Children, 53*(2), 118–124.

Poplin, M.S. (1988). Holistic/constructivist principles of the teaching/learning process: Implications for the field of learning disabilities. *Journal of Learning Disabilities, 21,* 401–416.

Pressley, M., Hogan, K., Wharton-McDonald, R., Mistretta, J., & Ettenberger, S. (1996). The challenges of instructional scaffolding: The challenges of instruction that supports student thinking. *Learning Disabilities Research & Practice, 11,* 138–146.

Resnick, L. (1987). Constructing knowledge in school. In L. Liben (Ed.), *Development and learning: Conflict or congruence?* (pp. 19–50). Hillsdale, NJ: Erlbaum.

Rojewski, J.W., & Schell, J.W. (1994). Cognitive apprenticeship for learners with special needs: An alternate framework for teaching and learning. *Remedial and Special Education, 15,* 234–243.

Rosenshine, B.V. (1983). Teaching functions in instructional programs. *Elementary School Journal, 83,* 335–352.

Rosenshine, B. (1986). Synthesis of research on explicit teaching. *Educational Leadership, 43*(7), 60–69.

Sindelar, P.T., Smith, M.A., Harriman, N.E., Hale, R.L., & Wilson, R.J. (1986). Teacher effectiveness in special education programs. *Journal of Special Education, 20,* 195–207.

Skrtic, T.M. (1995). The special education knowledge tradition: Crisis and opportunity. In E.L. Meyen & T.M. Skrtic (Eds.), *Special education and student disability: Traditional, emerging, and alternative perspectives* (pp. 609–672). Denver, CO: Love.

Slavin, R.E., Karweit, N.L., & Madden, N.A. (1989). *Effective programs for students at risk.* Boston, MA: Allyn and Bacon.

Stallings, J.A. (1985). A study of implementation of Madeline Hunter's Model and its effects on students. *Journal of Educational Research, 78,* 325–337.

Stallings, J. (1987). *Longitudinal findings for early childhood programs: Focus on direct instruction.* (ERIC 297 874, pp. 1–10.)

Stevens, R., & Rosenshine, B. (1981). Advances in research on teaching. Exceptional Education Quarterly, 2(1), 1–9.

Stokes, T.F., & Baer, D.M. (1977). An implicit technology of generalization. *Journal of Applied Behavior Analysis, 10,* 349–367.

U.S. Department of Education. (1997). *Nineteenth Annual Report to Congress on the Implementation of the Individuals with Disabilities Education Act.* Washington, D.C.: Author.

Vygotsky, L.S. (1978). *Mind in society: The development of higher psychological processes.* Cambridge, MA: Harvard University Press.

Werts, M.G., Wolery, M., Gast, D.L., & Holcombe, A. (1996). Sneak in some extra learning by using instructive feedback. *Teaching Exceptional Children, 28*(3), 70–71.

White, W.A.T. (1988). A meta-analysis of effects of direct instruction in special education. *Education and Treatment of Children, 11,* 364–373.

Wittrock, M.C. (Ed.). (1986). *Handbook of research on teaching* (3rd ed.). New York: MacMillan.

Wolery, M., Bailey, D.B., & Sugai, G.M. (1988). *Effective teaching: Principles and procedures of applied behavior analysis with exceptional students.* Boston, MA: Allyn & Bacon.

Ysseldyke, J.E., Christenson, S.L., & Thurlow, M.L. (1987). *Instructional factors that influence student achievement: An integrative review* (Monograph No. 7). Minneapolis, MN: University of Minnesota.

Chapter Nine

Alley, G., & Deshler, D. (1979). *Teaching the learning disabled adolescent: Strategies and methods.* Denver, CO: Love.

Allsopp, D.H. (1997). Using classwide peer tutoring to teach beginning algebra problem-solving skills in heterogeneous classrooms. *Remedial and Special Education, 18,* 367–379.

Boudah, D.J., Lenz, B.K., Bulgren, J.A., Schumaker, J.B., & Deshler, D.D. (2000). Don't water down! Enhance content learning through the unit organizer routine. *Teaching Exceptional Children, 32*(3), 48–56.

Center for Special Education Technology. (September, 1990). *Computers and cooperative learning.* Reston, VA: The Council for Exceptional Children.

Clees, T.J. (1995). Self-recording of students' daily schedules of teachers' expectancies: Perspectives on reactivity, stimulus control, and generalization. *Exceptionality, 5*(3), 113–129.

Cohen, E.G. (1998). Making cooperative learning equitable. *Educational Leadership, 56*(1), 18–21.

Deshler, D.D., Alley, G.R., Warner, M.N., & Schumaker, J.B. (1981). Instructional practices for promoting skill acquisition and generalization in severely learning disabled adolescents. *Learning Disability Quarterly, 4,* 415–421.

Deshler, D.D., & Schumaker, J.B. (1988). An instructional model for teaching students how to learn. In J.L. Graden, J.E. Zins, & M.J. Curtis (Eds.), *Alternative educational delivery systems: Enhancing instructional options for all students* (pp. 391–411). Washington, D.C.: National Association of School Psychologists.

DiGangi, S.A., & Maag, J.W. (1992). A component analysis of self-management training with behaviorally disordered youth. *Behavioral Disorders, 17,* 281–290.

Dunlap, L.K., Dunlap, G., Koegel, L.K., & Koegel, R.L. (1991). Using self-monitoring to increase independence. *Teaching Exceptional Children, 23*(3), 17–22.

Eiserman, W.D. (1988). Three types of peer tutoring: Effects on the attitudes of students with learning disabilities and their regular class peers. *Journal of Learning Disabilities, 21*(4), 249–252.

Ellis, E.S., Deshler, D.D., Lenz, B.K., Schumaker, J.B., & Clark, F.L. (1991). An instructional model for teaching learning strategies. *Focus on Exceptional Children, 24*(1), 1–14.

Fad, K.S., Ross, M., & Boston, J. (1995). We're better together: Using cooperative learning to teach social skills to young children. *Teaching Exceptional Children, 27*(4), 28–34.

Forness, S.R., Kavale, K.A., Blum, I.M., & Lloyd, J.W. (1997). Mega-analysis of meta-analysis: What works in special education and related services. *Teaching Exceptional Children, 29*(6), 4–9.

Fuchs, D., Fuchs, L.S., Mathes, P.G., & Simmons, D.C. (1997). Peer-assisted learning strategies: Making classrooms more responsive to academic diversity. *The American Educational Research Journal, 34,* 174–206.

Glomb, N., & West, R.P. (1990). Teaching behaviorally disordered adolescents to use self-management skills for improving the completeness, accuracy, and neatness of creative writing homework assignments. *Behavioral Disorders, 15*(4), 233–242.

Graham, S., Harris, K.R., & Reid, R. (1992). Developing self–regulated behaviors. *Focus on Exceptional Children, 24*(6), 1–16.

Greenwood, C.R. (1991). CWPT: Longitudinal effects on the reading, language, and mathematics achievement of at-risk students. *Reading, Writing, and Learning Disabilities International, 7*(2), 105–123.

Greenwood, C.R., Delquadri, J.C., & Hall, R.V. (1989). Longitudinal effects of CWPT. *Journal of Educational Psychology, 81*(3), 371–383.

Hallahan, D.P., Lloyd, J., Kosiewicz, M.M., & Kauffman, J.M. (1979). Self-monitoring of attention as a treatment for a learning disabled boy's off-task behavior. *Learning Disability Quarterly, 2*(1), 24–32.

Hallahan, D.P., Lloyd, J.W., & Stoller, L. (1982). *Improving attention with self-monitoring.* Charlottesville, VA: University of Virginia Learning Disabilities Research Institute.

Hayes, S.C., Rosenfarb, I., Wulfert, E., Munt, E.D., Korn, Z., & Zettle, R.D. (1985). Self-reinforcement effects: An artifact of social standard setting? *Journal of Applied Behavior Analysis, 18,* 201–214.

Henrico County Public Schools. (1989). *Tutoring: Lending a helping hand.* Richmond, VA: Author.

Hogan, S., & Prater, M.A. (1993). The effects of peer tutoring and self-management training on on-task academic and disruptive behaviors. *Behavioral Disorders, 18*(2), 118–128.

Johnson, D.W., & Johnson, R.T. (1986). Mainstreaming and cooperative learning strategies. *Exceptional Children, 52*(6), 553–562.

Johnson, L.R., & Johnson, C.E. (1999). Teaching students to regulate their own behavior. *Teaching Exceptional Children, 31*(4), 6–10.

Kagan, S. (1990). *Cooperative learning: Resources for teachers.* San Juan Capistrano, CA: Resources for Teachers.

Luria, A.R. (1961). *The role of speech in the regulation of normal and abnormal behaviors.* New York: Liveright.

Maag, J.W., Reid, R., & DiGangi, S.A. (1993). Differential effects of self-monitoring attention, accuracy, and productivity. *Journal of Applied Behavior Analysis, 26*(3), 329–344.

Maheady, L., & Harper, G.F. (1987). A class-wide peer tutoring program to improve the spelling test performance of low-income third-and fourth-grade students. *Education and Treatment of Children, 10*(2), 120–133.

Maheady, L., Mallett, B., Harper, G.F., & Sacca, K. (1991). Heads together: A peer-mediated option for improving the academic achievement of heterogeneous learning groups. *Remedial and Special Education, 12*(2), 25–33.

Maheady, L., Sacca, M.K., & Harper, G.F. (1988). CWPT with mildly handicapped high school students. *Exceptional Children, 55*(1), 52–59.

Martin, K.F., & Manno, C. (1995). Use of a check-off system to improve middle school students' story composition. *Journal of Learning Disabilities, 28,* 139–149.

Mastropieri, M.A., & Scruggs, T.E. (1991). *Teaching students ways to remember: Strategies for learning mnemonically.* Cambridge, MA: Brookline.

Mastropieri, M.A., & Scruggs, T.E. (1998). Constructing more meaningful relationships in the classroom: Mnemonic research into practice. *Learning Disabilities Research & Practice, 13,* 138–145.

Mastropieri, M.A., & Scruggs, T.E. (2000). *The inclusive classroom: Strategies for effective instruction.* Upper Saddle River, NJ: Merrill/Prentice Hall.

Mastropieri, M.A., Scruggs, T.E., Levin, J.R., Gaffney, J., & McLoone, B. (1985). Mnemonic vocabulary instruction for learning disabled students. *Learning Disability Quarterly, 8,* 57–63.

Mastropieri, M.A., Scruggs, T.E., Whittaker, M.E.S., & Bakken, J.P. (1994). Applications of mnemonic strategies with students with mild mental disabilities. *Remedial and Special Education, 15*(1), 34–43.

Mathes, M.Y., & Bender, W.N. (1997). The effects of self-monitoring on children with attention-deficit/hyperactivity disorder who are receiving pharmacological interventions. *Remedial and Special Education, 18*(2), 121–128.

Mathes, P.G., Fuchs, D., & Fuchs, L.S. (1997). Cooperative story mapping. *Remedial and Special Education, 18*(1), 20–27.

Mathes, P.G., Fuchs, D., Fuchs, L.S., Henley, A.M., & Sanders, A. (1994). Increasing strategic reading practice with Peabody classwide peer tutoring. *Learning Disabilities Research & Practice, 9*(1), 44–48.

Mathes, P.G., & Fuchs, L.S. (1994). The efficacy of peer tutoring in reading for students with mild disabilities: A best-evidence synthesis. *School Psychology Review, 23*(1), 59–80.

Mathes, P.G., Grek, M.L., Howard, J.K., Babyak, A.E., & Allen, S.H. (1999). Peer-assisted learning strategies for first-grade readers: A tool for preventing early reading failure. *Learning Disabilities Research & Practice, 14*(1), 50–60.

McDougall, D. (1998). Research on self-management techniques used by students with disabilities in general education settings: A descriptive review. *Remedial and Special Education, 19*(5), 310–320.

McDougall, D., & Brady, M.P. (1998). Initiating and fading self-management interventions to increase math fluency in general education classes. *Exceptional Children, 64*(2), 151–166.

Meichenbaum, D. (1977). *Cognitive behavior modification: An integrative approach.* New York: Plenum.

Meichenbaum, D. (1981). Cognitive behavior modification with exceptional children: A promise yet unfulfilled. *Exceptional Education Quarterly, 1,* 83–88.

O'Leary, S.G., & Dubey, D.R. (1979). Applications of self-control procedures by children: A review. *Journal of Applied Behavior Analysis, 12,* 449–465.

Peck, G. (1989). Facilitating cooperative learning: A forgotten tool gets it started. *Academic Therapy, 25*(2), 145–150.

Pomplun, M. (1997). When students with disabilities participate in cooperative groups. *Exceptional Children, 64*(1), 49–58.

Prater, M.A., Bruhl, S., & Serna, L.A. (1998). Acquiring social skills through cooperative learning and teacher-directed instruction. *Remedial and Special Education, 19,* 160–172.

Reddy, S.S., Utley, C.A., Delquadri, J.C., Mortweet, S.L., Greenwood, C.R., & Bowman, V. (1999). Peer tutoring for health and safety. *Teaching Exceptional Children, 31*(3), 44–52.

Rooney, K.J., & Hallahan, D.P. (1985). Future directions for cognitive behavior modification research: The quest for cognitive change. *Remedial and Special Education, 6,* 46–51.

Sainato, D.M., Strain, P.S., Lefebvre, D., & Rapp, N. (1990). Effects of self-evaluation on the independent work skills of preschool children with disabilities. *Exceptional Children, 56,* 540–549.

Scanlon, D., Deshler, D.D., & Schumaker, J.B. (1996). Can a strategy be taught and learned in secondary inclusive classrooms? *Learning Disabilities Research & Practice, 11*(1), 41–57.

Schrader, B., & Valus, A. (1990). Disabled learners as able teachers: A cross-age tutoring project. *Academic Therapy, 25*(5), 589–597.

Scruggs, T.E., & Mastropieri, M.A. (1989). Reconstructive elaborations: A model for content area learning. *American Educational Research Journal, 26,* 311–327.

Slavin, R.E. (1987). *Cooperative learning: Student teams* (2nd ed.). Washington, D.C.: National Education Association.

Slavin, R.E. (1991). Synthesis of research on cooperative learning. *Educational Leadership, 48*(6), 71–82.

Tralli, R., Colombo, B., Deshler, D.D., & Schumaker, J.B. (1996). The Strategies Intervention Model: A model for supported inclusion at the secondary level. *Remedial and Special Education, 17,* 204–216.

Veit, D., Scruggs, T.E., & Mastropieri, M.A. (1986). Extended mnemonic instruction with learning disabled students. *Journal of Educational Psychology, 78,* 300–308.

Vygotsky, L. (1962). *Thought and language.* New York: Wiley.

Wehrung-Schaffner, L., & Sapona, R.H. (1990). May the FORCE be with you: A test preparation strategy for learning disabled adolescents. *Academic Therapy, 25*(3), 291–300.

Williams, R.M., & Rooney, K.J. (1986). *A handbook of cognitive behavior modification procedures for teachers.* Charlottesville, VA: University of Virginia Learning Disabilities Research Institute.

Yasutake, D., Bryan, T., & Dohrn, E. (1996). The effects of combining peer tutoring and attribution training on students' perceived self-competence. *Remedial and Special Education, 17*(2), 83–91.

Chapter Ten

Adams, M.J. (1990). *Beginning to read: Thinking and learning about print.* Cambridge, MA: MIT Press.

Adams, M.J., Foorman, B.R., Lundberg, I., & Beeler, T. (1998). *Phonemic awareness in young children.* Baltimore, MD: Paul H. Brookes.

August, D., & Hakuta, K. (Eds.) (1997). *Improving schooling for language-minority children: A research agenda.* Washington, D.C.: National Academy Press.

Bashir, A.S., & Scavuzzo, A. (1992). Children with language disorders: Natural history and academic success. *Journal of Learning Disabilities, 25*(1), 53–65.

Bloom, L., & Lahey, M. (1978). *Language development and language disorders.* New York: John Wiley.

Bryan, T., Donahue, M., & Pearl, R. (1981). Studies of learning disabled children's pragmatic competence. *Topics in Learning and Learning Disabilities, 1,* 29–41.

Chamot, A., & O'Malley, J.M. (1994). The CALLA Handbook: How to implement the cognitive academic language learning approach. In K. Spangenberg-Urbschat & R. Pritchard (Eds.), *Kids come in all languages: Reading instruction for ESL students* (pp. 82–103). Newark, DE: International Reading Association.

Correa, W.I., & Heward, W.L. (1996). Special education in a culturally and linguistically diverse society. In W.L. Heward (Ed.), *Exceptional Children* (5th ed.) (pp. 91–129). Englewood Cliffs, NJ: Merrill.

Cummins, J. (1989). A theoretical framework for bilingual special education. *Exceptional Children, 56,* 111–119.

Cummins, J. (1994). The acquisition of English as a second language. In K. Spangenberg-Urbschat & R. Pritchard (Eds.), *Kids come in all languages: Reading instruction for ESL students* (pp. 36–62). Newark, DE: International Reading Association.

Dunn, L.M., Smith, J.O., Dunn, L.M., & Horton, K.B. (1981). *Peabody language development kits* (Rev. Ed.). Circle Pines, MN: American Guidance Service.

Elkonin, D.B. (1973). USSR. In J. Downing (Ed.), *Comparative reading: Cross-national studies of behavior and processes in reading and writing* (pp. 551–579). New York: Macmillan.

Fueyo, V. (1997). Below the tip of the iceberg: Teaching language-minority students. *Teaching Exceptional Children, 30*(1), 61–65.

German, D.J. (1992). Word-finding intervention for children and adolescents. *Topics in Language Disorders, 13*(1), 33–50.

Gersten, R. (1999). The changing face of bilingual education. *Educational Leadership, 56*(7), 41–45.

Gollnick, D.M., & Chinn, P.C. (1998). *Multicultural education in a pluralistic society* (5th ed.). Upper Saddle River, NJ: Merrill/Prentice Hall.

Juel, C., Griffith, P.L., & Gough, P.B. (1986). Acquisition of literacy: A longitudinal study of children in first and second grades. *Journal of Educational Psychology, 78,* 243–255.

Liberman, I.Y., & Shankweiler, D. (1985). Phonology and the problems of learning to read. *Remedial and Special Education, 6*(6), 8–17.

Liberman, I.Y., Shankweiler, D., Fischer, F.W., & Carter, B. (1974). Explicit syllable and phoneme segmentation in the young child. *Journal of Experimental child Psychology, 18,* 201–212.

McCormick, L., & Schiefelbusch, R.L. (1990). *Early language intervention: An introduction.* Upper Saddle River, NJ: Merrill/Prentice Hall.

McDonough, K.M. (1989). Analysis of the expressive language characteristics of emotionally handicapped students in social interactions. *Behavior Disorders, 14,* 127–139.

McIntyre, T., & Battle, J. (1998). The traits of "Good Teachers" as identified by African-American and white students with emotional and/or behavioral disorders. *Behavioral Disorders, 23*(2), 134–142.

McLaughlin, S. (1998). *Introduction to language development.* San Diego, CA: Singular.

Owens, R.E. (1995). *Language disorders: A functional approach to assessment and intervention* (2nd ed.). New York: Merrill/Macmillan.

Robertson, C., & Salter, W. (1995). *The phonological awareness kit.* Moline, IL: LinguiSystems.

Robertson, C., & Salter, W. (1997). *The phonological awareness test.* Moline, IL: LinguiSystems.

Ruiz, N.T. (1989). An optimal learning environment for Rosemary. *Exceptional Children, 56,* 130–144.

Salends, S.J., Dorney, J.A., & Mazo, M. (1997). The roles of bilingual special educators in creating inclusive classrooms. *Remedial and Special Education, 18*(1), 54–64.

Scarborough, H.S. (1998). Early identification of children at risk for reading disabilities: Phonological awareness and some other promising predictors. In B.K. Shapiro, P.J. Accardo, & A. J. Capute (Eds.), *Specific reading disability: A view of the spectrum* (pp. 77–121). Timonium, MD: York Press.

Scott, C.M., & Stokes, S.L. (1995). Measures of syntax in school-age children and adolescents. *Language, Speech, and Hearing Services in Schools, 26,* 309–319.

Shaywitz, B., Escobar, M.D., Shaywitz, B.A., Fletcher, J.M., & Makuch, R. (1992). Evidence that dyslexia may represent the lower tail of a normal distribution of reading ability. *New England Journal of Medicine, 326,* 145–150.

Sileo, T.W., & Prater, M.A. (1998). Creating classroom environments that address the linguistic and cultural backgrounds of students with disabilities: An Asian Pacific American perspective. *Remedial and Special Education, 19,* 323–337.

Snow, C.E., Burns, M.S., & Griffin, P. (1998). *Preventing reading difficulties in young children.* Washington, D.C.: National Academy Press.

Snyder, L.S., & Downey, D.M. (1997). Developmental differences in the relationship between oral language deficits and reading. *Topics in Language Disorders, 17*(3), 27–40.

Torgesen, J.K. (1995). *Phonological awareness: A critical factor in dyslexia.* Monograph in the Orton Emeritus Series. Orton Dyslexia Society.

Wagner, R., Torgesen, J., & Rashotte, C. (1994). Development of reading-related phonological processing abilities: New evidence of bidirectional causality from a latent variable longitudinal study. *Developmental Psychology, 30,* 73–87.

Wiig, E.H., & Secord, W.A. (1994). Language disabilities in school-age children and youth. In G.H. Shames, E.H. Wiig, & W.A. Secord (Eds.), *Human communication disorders* (4th ed.) (pp. 212–247). New York: Merrill.

Wiig, E.H., & Semel, E.M. (1984). *Language assessment and intervention for the learning disabled* (2nd ed.). Boston: Allyn & Bacon.

Wilcox, M.J. (1986). Developmental language disorders: Preschoolers. In J.M. Costello & A.L. Holland (Eds.), *Handbook of speech and language disorders* (pp. 643–670). San Diego, CA: College-Hill Press.

Chapter Eleven

Adams, G.L., & Engelmann, S. (1996). *Research on direct instruction: 25 years beyond DISTAR.* Seattle, WA: Educational Achievement Systems.

Adams, M.J. (1990). *Beginning to read: Thinking and learning about print.* Cambridge, MA: MIT Press.

Anderson, D.D. (1995). *Moving toward change: The literature-based first-grade basals.* Paper presented at the Annual Meeting of the American Educational Research Association, San Francisco, CA, April 18–22. (ERIC ED 384 000)

Anderson, R.C., Hiebert, E.H., Scott, J.A., & Wilkinson, I.A.G. (1985). *Becoming a nation of readers.* Champaign, IL: Center for the Study of Reading.

Archer, A., & Gleason, M. (1989). *Skills for school success.* N. Billerica, MA: Curriculum Associates.

Ashbaker, M.H., & Swanson, H.L. (1996). Short-term memory and working memory operations and their contribution to reading in adolescents with and without learning disabilities. *Learning Disabilities Research & Practice, 11,* 206–213.

Baumann, J.F., & Heubach, K.M. (1994). *Do basal readers deskill teachers?* Reading research report No. 26. National Reading Research Center, University of Georgia and University of Maryland. (ERIC ED 378 557)

Baumann, J.F., & Heubach, K.M. (1996). Do basal readers deskill teachers? A national survey of educators' use and opinions of basals. *The Elementary School Journal, 5,* 511–526.

Billingsley, B.S., & Wildman, T.M. (1988). The effects of prereading activities on the comprehension monitoring of learning disabled adolescents. *Learning Disabilities Research, 4,* 36–44.

Boehnlein, M. (1987). Reading intervention for high-risk first-graders. *Educational Leadership, 44,* 32–37.

Bos, C.S. (1982). Getting past decoding: Using modeled and repeated readings as a remedial method for learning disabled students. *Topics in Learning and Learning Disabilities, 1,* 51–57.

Bos, C.S., & Vaughn, S. (1998). *Strategies for teaching students with learning and behavior problems* (4th ed.). Boston, MA: Allyn and Bacon.

Browder, D.M., Hines, C., McCarthy, L.J., & Fees, J. (1984). A treatment package for increasing sight word recognition for use in daily living skills. *Education and Training of the Mentally Retarded, 19,* 191–200.

Butler, A. (1987). *The elements of whole language.* Crystal Lake, IL: Rigby.

Carlisle, J.F. (1993). Selecting approaches to vocabulary instruction for the reading disabled. *Learning Disabilities Research & Practice, 8*(2), 97–105.

Carnine, D., & Silbert, J. (1979). *Direct instruction reading.* Columbus, OH: Merrill.

Carnine, D., Silbert, J., & Kameenui, E.J. (1997). *Direct instruction reading* (3rd ed.). Upper Saddle River, NJ: Prentice-Hall.

Center, Y., Wheldall, K., Freeman, L., Outhred, L., & McNaught, M. (1995). An evaluation of Reading Recovery. *Reading Research Quarterly, 30,* 240–263.

Chall, J.S. (1967). *Learning to read: The great debate.* New York: McGraw-Hill.

Chall, J.S. (1983). *Stages of reading development.* New York: McGraw-Hill.

Chall, J.S. (1989). Learning to read: The great debate 20 years later—A response to 'Debunking the great phonics myth'. *Phi Delta Kappan, March,* 521–538.

Clark, F.L., Deshler, D.D., Schumaker, J.B., Alley, G.R., & Warner, M.M. (1984). Visual imagery and self-questioning: Strategies to improve comprehension of written material. *Journal of Learning Disabilities, 17,* 145–149.

Clay, M.M. (1993). *Reading Recovery: A guidebook for teachers in training.* Portsmouth, NH: Heinemann.

Coutinho, M.J. (1986). Reading achievement of students identified as behaviorally disordered at the secondary level. *Behavioral Disorders, 11,* 200–207.

Cullinan, B.E. (1987). Inviting readers to literature. In B.E. Cullinan (Ed.), *Children's literature in the reading program* (pp. 2–14). Newark, DE: The International Reading Association.

Dixon, R. (1987). Strategies for vocabulary instruction. *Teaching Exceptional Children, 19,* 61–63.

Deshler, D.D., Alley, G.R., Warner, M.M., & Schumaker, J.B. (1981). Instructional practices for promoting skill acquisition and generalization in severely learning disabled adolescents. *Learning Disability Quarterly, 4,* 415–421.

Dyck, N., & Sundbye, N. (1988). The effects of text explicitness on story understanding and recall by learning disabled children. *Learning Disabilities Research, 3,* 68–77.

Edmark Reading Program. (1972). Bellevue, WA: The Edmark Corporation.

Ehri, L.C. (1995). Phases of development in learning to read words by sight. *Journal of Research in Reading, 18,* 116–125.

Ehri, L.C., & McCormick, S. (1998). Phases of word learning: Implications for instruction with delayed and disabled readers. *Reading and Writing Quarterly: Overcoming Learning Difficulties, 14*(2), 135–163.

Ellis, E.S., Deshler, D.D., Lenz, B.K., Schumaker, J.B., & Clark, F.L. (1991). An instructional model for teaching learning strategies. *Focus on Exceptional Children, 24*(1), 1–14.

Engelmann, S., & Bruner, E.C. (1995). *Reading Mastery Rainbow Edition: Levels I, II, Fast Cycle.* Blacklick, OH: Science Research Associates.

Engelmann, S., Engelmann, O., & Davis, K.L.S. (1997). *Horizons: Learning to read, Fast track, A-B teacher's guide.* Blacklick, OH: Science Research Associates.

Engelmann, S., Engelmann, O., & Davis, K.L.S. (1998). *Horizons: Learning to read, Level A teacher's guide.* Blacklick OH: Science Research Associates.

Engelmann, S., Haddox, P., & Hanner, S. (1999). *SRA: Comprehension corrective reading, A.* Blacklick, OH: Science Research Associates.

Engelmann, S., & Hanner, S. (1998). *Horizons: Learning to read, Fast track, C-D teacher's guide.* Blacklick, OH: Science Research Associates.

Englemann, S., Johnson, G., & Carnine, L. (1999). *SRA: Decoding corrective reading program, A.* Blacklick, OH: Science Research Associates.

Englert, C.S., & Mariage, T.V. (1991). Shared understandings: Structuring the writing experience through dialogue. *Journal of Learning Disabilities, 24,* 330–342.

Fernald, G.M. (1943). *Remedial techniques in basic school subjects.* New York: McGraw-Hill.

Fessler, M.A., Rosenberg, M.S., & Rosenberg, L.A. (1991). Concomitant learning disabilities and learning problems among students with behavioral/emotional disorders. *Behavioral Disorders, 16,* 97–106.

Fletcher, J.M., & Lyon, G.R. (1998). Reading: A research-based approach. In W. Evers (Ed.), *What's wrong in America's classrooms?* (pp. 49–90). Stanford University, Hoover Institution.

Foorman, B.R., & Liberman, D. (1989). Visual and phonological processing of words: A comparison of good and poor readers. *Journal of Learning Disabilities, 22,* 349–355.

Fry, E. (1980). The New Instant Word List. *The Reading Teacher, 34,* 284–289.

Gast, D.L., Wolery, M., Morris, L.L., Doyle, P.M., & Meyer, S. (1990). Teaching sight word reading in a group instructional arrangement using constant time delay. *Exceptionality, 1,* 81–96.

Gersten, R., & Dimino, J. (1990). *Reading instruction for at-risk students: Implications of current research* (OSSC Bulletin Volume 33, Number 5). Eugene, OR: Oregon School Study Council.

Gillingham, A., & Stillman, B.W. (1973). *Remedial training for children with specific disability in reading, spelling, and penmanship.* Cambridge, MA: Educators Publishing Service.

Goodman, K.S. (1970). Behind the eye: What happens in reading. In K.S. Goodman & O.S. Niles (Eds.), *Reading process and program.* Urbana, IL: National Council of Teachers of Reading.

Goodman, K.S. (1986). *What's whole in whole language?* Portsmouth, NH: Heineman.

Graves, A.W. (1986). Effects of direct instruction and metacomprehension training on finding main ideas. *Learning Disabilities Research, 1,* 90–100.

Graves, A.W. (1987). Improving comprehension skills. *Teaching Exceptional Children, 19,* 63–65.

Griffey, Q.L., Zigmond, N., & Leinhardt, G. (1988). The effects of self-questioning and story structure training on the reading comprehension of poor readers. *Learning Disabilities Research, 4,* 45–51.

Gunning, T.G. (1996). *Creating reading instruction for all children* (2nd ed.). Boston, MA: Allyn and Bacon.

Gurney, D., Gersten, R., Dimino, J., & Carnine, D. (1990). Story grammar: Effective literature instruction for high school students with learning disabilities. *Journal of Learning Disabilities, 23,* 335–342.

Guszak, F.J. (1972). *Diagnostic reading instruction in the elementary school.* New York: Harper & Row.

Guyer, B.P., & Sabatino, D. (1989). The effectiveness of a multisensory alphabetic phonetic approach with college students who are learning disabled. *Journal of Learning Disabilities, 22,* 430–434.

Hanau, L. (1974). *The study game: How to play and win with statement-pie.* New York: Barnes & Noble.

Hargis, C.H. (1982). Word recognition development. *Focus on Exceptional Children, 14* (9), 1–8.

Harris, T., Creekmore, M., & Greenman, M. (1967). *Phonetic keys to reading.* Oklahoma City, OK: Economy Company.

Henk, W.A., Helfeldt, J.P., & Platt, J.M. (1986). Developing reading fluency in learning disabled students. *Teaching Exceptional Children, 18,* 202–206.

Herman, R. (1975). *The Herman Method for Reversing Reading Failure.* Sherman Oaks, CA: Romar Publications.

Higgins, K., & Boone, R. (1990). Hypertext: A new vehicle for computer use in reading instruction. *Intervention in School and Clinic, 26,* 26–31.

Hoffman, J.V., McCarthey, S.J., Abbott, J., Christian, C., Corman, L., Curry, C., Dressman, M., Elliott, B., Matherne, D., & Stahle, D. (1994). So what's new in the new basals? A focus on first grade. *Journal of Reading Behavior, 26*(1), 47–73.

Hoffman, J.V., McCarthey, S.J., Bayles, D., Price, D., Elliott, B., Dressman, M., & Abbott, J. (1995). *Reading instruction in first-grade classrooms: Do basals control teachers?* (Reading Research Report No. 43). National Reading Research Center. (ERIC ED 387 792)

Hoffman, J.V., McCarthey, S.J., Elliott, B., Bayles, D.L., Price, D.P., Ferree, A., & Abbott, J.A. (1998). The literature-based basals in first-grade classrooms: Savior, Satan, or same-old, same-old? *Reading Research Quarterly, 33*(2), 168–197.

Idol, L. (1987). Group story mapping: A comprehension strategy for both skilled and unskilled readers. *Journal of Learning Disabilities, 20,* 196–205.

Invernizzi, M., Juel, C., & Rosemary, C.A. (1997). A community volunteer tutorial that works. *The Reading Teacher, 50,* 304–311.

Jenkins, J.R., Stein, M.L., & Osborn, J.R. (1981). What next after decoding? Instruction and research in reading comprehension. *Exceptional Education Quarterly, 2,* 27–39.

Johnson, D.D. (1971). The Dolch list reexamined. *The Reading Teacher, 24,* 455–456.

Kameenui, E.J., & Simmons, D.C. (1990). *Designing instructional strategies: The prevention of academic learning problems.* Columbus, OH: Merrill.

Keel, M.C., & Gast, D.L. (1992). Small-group instruction for students with learning disabilities: Observational and incidental learning. *Exceptional Children, 58,* 357–368.

Kirk, S.A., Kirk, W.D., & Minskoff, E.H. (1985). *Phonic remedial reading lessons.* Novato, CA: Academic Therapy Publications.

Kleinert, H.L., & Gast, D.L. (1982). Teaching a multihandicapped adult manual signs using a constant time delay procedure. *Journal of the Association of the Severely Handicapped, 6*(4), 25–32.

Kuder, S.J. (1990). Effectiveness of the DISTAR Reading Program for children with learning disabilities. *Journal of Learning Disabilities, 23,* 69–71.

Kuder, S.J. (1991). Language abilities and progress in a direct instruction reading program for students with learning disabilities. *Journal of Learning Disabilities, 24,* 124–127.

LaBerge, D., & Samuels, S.J. (1974). Toward a theory of automatic information processing in reading. *Cognitive Psychology, 6,* 293–323.

Laughton, J., & Morris, N.T. (1989). Story grammar knowledge of learning disabled students. *Learning Disabilities Research, 4,* 87–95.

Learning First Alliance (1998). *Every child reading: An action plan of the Learning First Alliance.* Washington, D.C.: Author.

Lenchner, O., Gerber, M.M., & Routh, D.K. (1990). Phonological awareness tasks as predictors of decoding ability: Beyond segmentation. *Journal of Learning Disabilities, 23,* 240–247.

Lenz, B.K., & Hughes, C.A. (1990). A word identification strategy for adolescents with learning disabilities. *Journal of Learning Disabilities, 23,* 149–158.

Lenz, B.K., Schumaker, J.B., Deshler, D.D., & Beals, V.L. (1984). *Learning strategies curriculum: The word identification strategy.* Lawrence, KS: University of Kansas Institute for Research on Learning Disabilities.

Levy, B.A., Abello, B., & Lysynchuk, L. (1997). Transfer from word training to reading in context: Gains in reading fluency and comprehension. *Learning Disability Quarterly, 20*(3), 173–188.

Liberman, I.Y., & Shankweiler, D. (1985). Phonology and the problems of learning to read and write. *Remedial and Special Education, 6,* 8–17.

Lundberg, I. (1995). The computer as a tool of remediation in the education of students with reading disabilities—A theory-based approach. *Learning Disability Quarterly, 18,* 89–100.

Mann, V.A., Cowin, E., & Schoenheimer, J. (1989). Phonological processing, language comprehension, and reading ability. *Journal of Learning Disabilities, 22,* 76–89.

Mastropieri, M.A., & Scruggs, T.E. (1991). *Teaching students ways to remember: Strategies for learning mnemonically.* Cambridge, MA: Brookline.

Mastropieri, M.A., & Scruggs, T.E. (1997). Best practices in promoting reading comprehension in students with learning disabilities: 1976 to 1996. *Remedial and Special Education, 18,* 197–213.

McCarthey, S.J., & Hoffman, J.V. (1995). The new basals: How are they different? *The Reading Teacher, 49*(1), 72–75.

McCarthey, S.J., Hoffman, J.V., Christian, C., Corman, L., Elliott, B., Matherne, D., & Stahle, D. (1994). Engaging the new basal readers. *Reading Research and Instruction, 33,* 233–256.

McGill-Franzen, A., & Allington, R.L. (1991). The gridlock of low reading achievement: Perspectives on practice and policy. *Remedial and Special Education, 12,* 20–30.

McNamara, T.P., Millder, D.L., & Bransford, J.D. (1991). Mental models and reading comprehension. In R. Barr, M.L. Kamil, P. Mosenthal, & P.D. Pearson (Eds.), *Handbook of reading research, Volume II* (pp. 490–511). New York: Longman.

Merrill Linguistic Reading Program (4th ed.). (1986). Columbus, OH: Merrill.

Noll, E., & Goodman, K. (1995). "Using a howitzer to kill a butterfly": Teaching literature with basals. *The New Advocate, 8,* 243–254.

Ogle, D.M. (1986). K-W-L: A teaching model that develops active reading of expository text. *The Reading Teacher, 39,* 564–570.

Palincsar, A.S., & Brown, A.L. (1984). Reciprocal teaching of comprehension fostering and comprehension monitoring activities. *Cognition and Instruction, 1,* 117–175.

Paul, P.V., & O'Rourke, J.P. (1988). Multimeaning words and reading comprehension: Implications for special education students. *Remedial and Special Education, 9,* 42–52.

Peterson, S.K., Scott, J., & Sroka, K. (1990). Using the language experience approach with precision. *Teaching Exceptional Children, 22,* 28–31.

Pinnell, G.S. (1990). Success for low achievers through reading recovery. *Educational Leadership, 48,* 17–21.

Polloway, E.A., Epstein, M.H., Polloway, C., Patton, J.R., & Ball, D.W. (1986). Corrective reading program: An analysis of effectiveness with learning disabled and mentally retarded students. *Remedial and Special Education, 7,* 41–47.

Poplin, M.S. (1988). The reductionist fallacy in learning disabilities: Replicating the past by reducing the present. *Journal of Learning Disabilities, 21,* 389–400.

Pressley, M., Brown, R., El-Dinary, P.B., & Afflerbach, P. (1995). The comprehension instruction that students need: Instruction fostering constructively responsive reading. *Learning Disabilities Research & Practice, 10,* 215–224.

Quigley, S.P., McAnally, P.L., King, C.M., & Rose, S. (Eds.) (1991). *Reading Milestones.* Austin, TX: Pro–Ed.

Rashotte, C.A., & Torgesen, J.K. (1985). Repeated reading and reading fluency in learning disabled children. *Reading Research Quarterly, 20,* 180–188.

Reutzel, D.R., & Cooter, R.B., (1996). *Teaching children to read: From basals to books* (2nd ed.). Englewood Cliffs, NJ: Prentice Hall.

Reutzel, D.R., & Larsen, N.S. (1995). Look what they've done to read children's books in the new basal readers! *Language Arts, 72*(7), 495–507.

Robinson, R.P. (1941). *Effective study.* New York: Harper & Row.

Rooney, K. (1988). *Independent strategies for efficient study.* Richmond, VA: J.R. Enterprises.

Rose, T.L. (1984). Effects of previewing on the oral reading of mainstreamed behaviorally disordered students. *Behavioral Disorders, 10,* 33–39.

Rose, T.L., & Sherry, L. (1984). Relative effects of two previewing procedures on the oral reading performance of learning disabled adolescents. *Learning Disability Quarterly, 7,* 39–44.

Rosenshine, B., & Meister, C. (1994). Reciprocal teaching: A review of the research. *Review of Educational Research, 64,* 479–530.

Routman, R. (1988). *Transitions: From literature to literacy.* Portsmouth, NH: Heineman.

Rumelhart, D. (1984). Understanding understanding. In J. Flood (Ed.), *Understanding reading comprehension* (pp. 1–20). Newark, DE: International Reading Association.

Samuels, S.J. (1979). The method of repeated readings. *Reading Teacher, 32,* 403–408.

Samuels, S.J. (1981). Some essentials of decoding. *Exceptional Education Quarterly, 2,* 11–25.

Samuels, S.J. (1987). Information processing abilities and reading. *Journal of Learning Disabilities, 20,* 18–22.

Schoolfield, L.D., & Timberlake, J.B. (1974). *The phonovisual method* (Rev. Ed.). Rockville, MD: Phonovisual Products.

Schumaker, J.B., Denton, P.H., & Deshler, D.D. (1984). *The paraphrasing strategy (Learning Strategies Curriculum).* Lawrence, KS: University of Kansas.

Schumaker, J.B., Deshler, D.D., Alley, G.R., Warner, M.M., & Denton, P.H. (1982). Multipass: A learning strategy for improving reading comprehension. *Learning Disability Quarterly, 5,* 295–304.

Schumm, J.S., Vaughn, S., Haager, D., & Klingner, J.K. (1994). Literacy instruction for mainstreamed students: What suggestions are provided in basal reading series? *Remedial and Special Education, 15*(1), 14–20.

Schworm, R.W. (1988). Look in the middle of the word. *Teaching Exceptional Children, 20,* 13–17.

Scruggs, T.E., & Mastropieri, M.A. (1986). Academic characteristics of behaviorally disordered and learning disabled students. *Behavioral Disorders, 11,* 184–190.

Seidenberg, P.L. (1989). Relating text-processing research to reading and writing instruction for learning disabled students. *Learning Disabilities Focus, 5,* 4–12.

Shake, M.C., Allington, R.L., Gaskins, R., & Marr, M.B. (1989). How remedial teachers teach vocabulary. *Remedial and Special Education, 10,* 51–57.

Shannon, P. (1992). *Becoming political: Readings and writings in the politics of literacy education.* Portsmouth, NH: Heinemann.

Shannon, P., & Crawford, P. (1997). Manufacturing descent: Basal readers and the creation of reading failures. *Reading & Writing Quarterly: Overcoming Learning Difficulties, 13*(3), 227–245.

Simmons, D.C., Fuchs, D., & Fuchs, L.S. (1991). Instructional and curricular requisites of mainstreamed students with learning disabilities. *Journal of Learning Disabilities, 24,* 354–360.

Simmons, D.C., & Kameenui, E.J. (1990). The effect of task alternatives on vocabulary knowledge: A comparison of students with and without learning disabilities. *Journal of Learning Disabilities, 23,* 291–297.

Simms, R.B., & Falcon, S.C. (1987). Teaching sight words. *Teaching Exceptional Children, 20,* 30–33.

Sindelar, P.T. (1982). The effects of cross-aged tutoring on the comprehension skills of remedial reading students. *Journal of Special Education, 16,* 199–206.

Slavin, R.E., Karweit, N.L., & Madden, N.A. (1989). *Effective programs for students at risk.* Boston, MA: Allyn and Bacon.

Smith, F. (1971). *Understanding reading.* New York: Holt, Rinehart, & Winston.

Snider, V. (1997). Transfer of decoding skills to a literature basal. *Learning Disabilities Research & Practice, 12*(1), 54–62.

Snow, C.E., Burns, M.S., & Griffin, P. (Eds.)(1998). *Preventing reading difficulties in young children.* Washington, D.C.: National Academy Press.

Spalding, R.B., & Spalding, W.T. (1962). *The writing road to reading.* New York: Morrow.

Spear, L.D., & Sternberg, R.J. (1986). An information processing framework for understanding reading disability. In S. Ceci (Ed.), *Handbook of cognitive, social, and neuropsychological aspects of learning disabilities* (pp. 3–31). Hillsdale, NJ: Erlbaum.

Spiro, R., & Myers, A. (1984). Individual differences and underlying cognitive processes. In P.D. Pearson (Ed.), *Handbook of reading research* (pp. 471–504). New York: Longman.

Stahl, S.A., Duffy-Hester, A.M., & Stahl, K.A.D. (1998). Everything you wanted to know about phonics (but were afraid to ask). *Reading Research Quarterly, 33,* 338–355.

Stahl, S.A., & Fairbanks, M.M. (1986). The effects of vocabulary instruction: A model-based meta-analysis. *Review of Educational Research, 56*(1), 72–110.

Stahl, S.A., Heubach, K., & Cramond, B. (1997). Fluency-oriented reading instruction. Paper presented at the 44th Annual Meeting of the National Reading Conference, San Diego, CA, Nov. 30–Dec. 3. (ERIC ED 379 610)

Stahl, S., & Miller, P.D. (1989). Whole language and language experience approaches for beginning reading: A quantitative research synthesis. *Review of Educational Research, 59,* 87–116.

Stallings, J.A. (1974). *Follow through classroom observation evaluation 1972–1973* (Executive Summary SRI Project URU–7370). Menlo Park, CA: Stanford Research Institute.

Stanovich, K. (1980). Toward an interactive-compensatory model of individual differences in the development of reading fluency. *Reading Research Quarterly, 16,* 32–71.

Stanovich, K. (1986a). Explaining the variance in reading ability in terms of psychological processes: What have we learned? *Annals of Dyslexia, 35,* 67–996.

Stanovich, K. (1986b). Matthew effects in reading: Some consequences of individual differences in the acquisition of literacy. *Reading Research Quarterly, 21,* 360–406.

Stanovich, K., & Stanovich, P. (1995). How research might inform the debate about early reading acquisition. *Journal of Research in Reading, 18*(2), 87–105.

Stauffer, R.G. (1970). *The language-experience approach to the teaching of reading.* New York: Harper & Row.

Stein, M.L. (1993). *The beginning reading instruction study.* Washington, D.C.: U.S. Government Printing Office.

Stein, M., Johnson, B., & Gutlohn, L. (1999). Analyzing beginning reading programs: The relationship between decoding and text. *Remedial and Special Education, 20*(5), 272–287.

Stein, M.L., & Trabasso, T. (1982). What's in a story?: An approach to comprehension and instruction. In R. Glaser (Ed.), *Advances in instructional psychology, Vol. II* (pp. 213–267). Hillsdale, NJ: Erlbaum.

Stevens, K.B., & Schuster, J.W. (1988). Time delay: Systematic instruction for academic tasks. *Remedial and Special Education, 9,* 16–21.

Taylor, B., Harris, L.A., Pearson, P.D., & Garcia, G. (1995). *Reading difficulties: Instruction and assessment* (2nd ed.). New York: McGraw-Hill.

Tindall, G., & Marston, D. (1996). Technical adequacy of alternative reading measures as performance assessments. *Exceptionality, 6*(4), 201–230.

Torgesen, J.K., & Barker, T.A. (1995). Computers as aids in the prevention and remediation of reading disabilities. *Learning Disability Quarterly, 18,* 76–88.

Touchette, P.E. (1971). Transfer of stimulus control: Measuring the moment of transfer. *Journal of Experimental Analysis of Behavior, 15,* 347–354.

Touchette, P.E., & Howard, J.S. (1984). Errorless learning: Reinforcement contingencies and stimulus control transfer in delayed prompting. *Journal of Applied Behavior Analysis, 17,* 175–188.

Traub, N., & Bloom, F. (1990). *Recipe for reading* (3rd ed.). Cambridge, MA: Educators Publishing Service.

Wilson, B.A. (1996). *The Wilson Reading System* (3rd ed.). Millbury, MA: Wilson Language Training Corporation.

Wolery, M., Ault, M.J., Gast, D.L., Doyle, P.M., & Mills, B.M. (1990). Use of choral and individual attentional responses with constant time delay when teaching sight word reading. *Remedial and Special Education, 11,* 47–58.

Wong, B., & Jones, W. (1982). Increasing metacomprehension in learning disabled and normally-achieving students through self-questioning training. *Learning Disability Quarterly, 5,* 228–240.

Yoshimoto, R. (1997). Phonemes, phonetics, and phonograms: Advanced language structures for students with learning disabilities. *Teaching Exceptional Children, 29*(3), 43–48.

Chapter Twelve

Ashton, T.M. (1999). Spell checking: Making writing meaningful in the inclusive classroom. *Teaching Exceptional Children, 32*(2), 24–27.

Barbe, W., Milone, M., & Wasylyk, T. (1983). Manuscript is the "write" start. *Academic Therapy, 18,* 397–406.

Bereiter, C., & Scardamalia, M. (1982). From conversation to composition: The role of instruction in a developmental process. In R. Glaser (Ed.), *Advances in instructional psychology, Volume 2* (pp. 1–64). Hillsdale, NJ: Erlbaum.

Berninger, V.W., Abbott, R.D., Whitaker, D., Sylvester, & Nolen, S.B. (1995). Integrating low-and high-level skills in instructional protocols for writing disabilities. *Learning Disability Quarterly, 18,* 293–309.

Berninger, V.W., & Stage, S.A. (1996). Assessment and intervention for writing problems of students with learning disabilities or behavioral disabilities. *B.C. Journal of Special Education, 20*(2), 5–23.

Bos, C.S. (1988). Process-oriented writing: Instructional implications for mildly handicapped students. *Exceptional Children, 54,* 521–577.

Bos, C.S., & Vaughn, S. (1998). *Strategies for teaching students with learning and behavior problems* (4th ed.). Needham Heights, MA: Allyn & Bacon.

Brown, A.S. (1988). Encountering misspellings and spelling performance: Why wrong isn't right. *Journal of Educational Psychology, 80,* 488–494.

Bryant, N.D., Drabin, I.R., & Gettinger, M. (1981). Effects of varying unit size on spelling achievement in learning disabled children. *Journal of Learning Disabilities, 14,* 200–203.

Carnine, D., & Kinder, B.D. (1985). Teaching low-performing students to apply generative and schema strategies to narrative and expository material. *Remedial and Special Education, 6,* 20–30.

Carpenter, D., & Miller, L.J. (1982). Spelling ability of reading disabled LD students and able readers. *Learning Disability Quarterly, 5,* 65–70.

Clarke, L.K. (1988). Invented versus traditional spelling in first grader's writings: Effects on learning to spell and read. *Research in the Teaching of English, 22,* 281–309.

Dangel, H.L. (1987). The coach's spelling approach. *Teaching Exceptional Children, 19,* 20–22.

DeLaPaz, S., & Graham, S. (1997). Strategy instruction in planning: Effects on the writing performance and behavior of students with learning difficulties. *Exceptional Children, 63*(2), 167–181.

DeMaster, V.K., Crossland, C.L., & Hasselbring, T.S. (1986). Consistency of learning disabled students' spelling performance. *Learning Disability Quarterly, 9,* 89–96.

Dixon, R.C. (1991). The application of sameness analysis to spelling. *Journal of Learning Disabilities, 24,* 285–291.

Dobbie, L., & Askov, E.N. (1995). Progress of handwriting research in the 1980's and future prospects. *Journal of Educational Research, 88,* 339–351.

Dowis, C.L., & Schloss, P. (1992). The impact of mini-lessons on writing skills. *Remedial and Special Education, 13*(5), 34–42.

Ehri, L.C. (1989). The development of spelling knowledge and its role in reading acquisition and reading disability. *Journal of Learning Disabilities, 22,* 356–365.

Ekwall, E.E. (1989). *Locating and correcting reading difficulties* (5th ed.). Columbus, OH: Merrill.

Ellis, E.S., & Lenz, B.K. (1987). A component analysis of effective learning strategies for LD students. *Learning Disabilities Focus, 2,* 94–107.

Englert, C.S. (1992). Writing instruction from a sociocultural perspective: The holistic, dialogic, and social enterprise of writing. *Journal of Learning Disabilities, 25,* 153–172.

Englert, C.S., & Raphael, T.E. (1990). Developing successful writers through cognitive strategy instruction. In J. Brophy (Ed.), *Advances in research on teaching.* Greenwich, CT: JAI Press.

Englert, C.S., Raphael, T.E., Anderson, L.M., Anthony, H.M., Fear, K.L., & Gregg, S.L. (1988). A case for writing intervention: Strategies for writing informational text. *Learning Disabilities Focus, 3,* 98–113.

Englert, C.S., Raphael, T.E., Anderson, L.M., Anthony, H.M., & Stevens, D.D. (1991). Making strategies and self-talk visible: Writing instruction in regular and special education classrooms. *American Educational Research Journal, 23,* 337–373.

Fernald, G.M. (1943). *Remedial techniques in basic school subjects.* New York: McGraw-Hill.

Fuchs, L.S., Allinder, R.M., Hamlett, C.L., & Fuchs, D. (1990). An analysis of spelling curricula and teachers' skills in identifying error types. *Remedial and Special Education, 11,* 42–52.

Fuchs, L.S., Fuchs, D., Hamlett, C.L., & Allinder, R.M. (1991). The contribution of skills analysis to curriculum-based measurement in spelling. *Exceptional Children, 57,* 443–452.

Fulk, B.M. (1997). Think while you spell: A cognitive motivational approach to spelling instruction. *Teaching Exceptional Children, 29*(4), 70–71.

Gallegos, A.Y., & Gallegos, M.L. (1990). A student's perspective on good teaching: Michael. *Intervention in School and Clinic, 26,* 14–15.

Gentry, J.R. (1982). An analysis of developmental spellings in Gnys at Wrk. *The Reading Teacher, 36,* 192–200.

Gerber, M.M. (1984). Orthographic problem-solving ability of learning-disabled and normally achieving students. *Learning Disability Quarterly, 17,* 157–164.

Gillingham, A., & Stillman, B.W. (1973). *Remedial training for children with specific disability in reading, spelling, and penmanship.* Cambridge, MA: Educators Publishing Service.

Gleason, M.M. (1995). Using direct instruction to integrate reading and writing for students with learning disabilities. *Reading & Writing Quarterly: Overcoming Learning Difficulties, 11*(1), 91–108.

Gordon, J., Vaughn, S., & Schumm, J.S. (1993). Spelling intervention: A review of literature and implications for instruction for students with learning disabilities. *Learning Disabilities Research & Practice, 8,* 175–181.

Graham, S. (1992). Issues in handwriting instruction. *Focus on Exceptional Children, 25*(2), 1–14.

Graham, S. (1993/94). Are slanted manuscript alphabets superior to the traditional manuscript alphabet? *Childhood Education, 70*(2), 91–95.

Graham, S., & Harris, K.R. (1988). Instructional recommendations for teaching writing to exceptional students. *Exceptional Children, 54,* 506–512.

Graham, S., & Harris, K.R. (1989a). Components analysis of cognitive strategy instruction: Effects on learning disabled students' compositions and self-efficacy. *Journal of Educational Psychology, 81,* 353–361.

Graham, S., & Harris, K.R. (1989b). Improving learning disabled students' skills at composing essays: Self-instructional strategy training. *Exceptional Children, 56,* 201–214.

Graham, S., Harris, K.R., & Loynachan, C. (1996). The directed spelling thinking activity: Application with high-frequency words. *Learning Disabilities Research & Practice, 11*(1), 34–40.

Graham, S., Harris, K.R., & Sawyer, R. (1987). Composition instruction with learning disabled students: Self-instructional strategy training. *Focus on Exceptional Children, 20* (4), 1–11.

Graham, S., Loynachan, C., & Harris, K. (1993). The basic spelling vocabulary list. *Journal of Educational Research, 86,* 363–368.

Graham, S., & MacArthur, C. (1988). Improving learning disabled students' skills at revising essays produced on a word processor: Self-instructional strategy training. *The Journal of Special Education, 22,* 133–152.

Graham, S., & Miller, L. (1979). Spelling research and practice: A unified approach. *Focus on Exceptional Children, 12*(2), 1–16.

Graves, D.H. (1985). All children can write. *Learning Disability Focus, 1,* 36–43.

Graves, D.H., & Hansen, J. (1983). The author's chair. *Language Arts, 60,* 176–183.

Greene, G. (1994). Research into practice: The magic of mnemonics. *LD Forum, 19*(3), 34–37.

Greenland, R., & Polloway, E.A. (1994). *Handwriting and students with disabilities: Overcoming first impressions.* Unpublished position paper. Lynchburg, VA. (ERIC ED 378 757)

Hackney, C., & Lucas, V. (1993). *Zaner-Bloser handwriting: A way to self-expression.* Columbus, OH: Zaner-Bloser.

Hagood, B.F. (1997). Reading and writing with help from story grammar. *Teaching Exceptional Children, 29*(4), 10–14.

Hallenbeck, M.J. (1996). The cognitive strategy in writing: Welcome relief for adolescents with learning disabilities. *Learning Disabilities Research & Practice, 11*(2), 107–119.

Hanover, S. (1983). Handwriting comes naturally? *Academic Therapy, 18,* 407–412.

Hayes, J., & Flower, L. (1986). Writing research and the writer. *American Psychologist, 41,* 1106–1113.

Hoffmeister, A.M. (1981). *Handwriting resource book: Manuscript/cursive.* Allen, TX: DLM Teaching Resources.

Hunt-Berg, M., Rankin, J.L., & Beukelman, D.R. (1994). Ponder the possibilities: Computer-supported writing for struggling writers. *Learning Disabilities Research & Practice, 9*(3), 169–178.

Idol, L. (1987). Group story mapping: A comprehension strategy for both skilled and unskilled readers. *Journal of Learning Disabilities, 20,* 196–205.

Isaacson, S.L. (1988a). Effective instruction in written language. In E.L. Meyen, G.A. Vergason, & R.J. Whelan (Eds.), *Effective instructional strategies for exceptional children* (pp. 288–306). Denver, CO: Love.

Isaacson, S. (1988b). Assessing the written product: Qualitative and quantitative measures. *Exceptional Children, 54,* 528–534.

Isaacson, S.L. (1992). Volleyball and other analogies: A response to Englert. *Journal of Learning Disabilities, 25,* 173–177.

Isaacson, S., & Gleason, M.M. (1997). Mechanical obstacles to writing: What can teachers do to help students with learning problems? *Learning Disabilities Research & Practice, 12,* 188–194.

Johnson, D.J., & Carlisle, J.F. (1996). A study of handwriting in written stories of normal and learning disabled children. *Reading and Writing: An Interdisciplinary Journal, 8*(1), 45–59.

Johnson, D.J., & Myklebust, H.R. (1967). *Learning disabilities: Educational principles and practices.* New York: Grune & Stratton.

Kauffman, J.M., Hallahan, D.P., Haas, K., Brame, T., & Boren, R. (1978). Imitating children's errors to improve their spelling performance. *Journal of Learning Disabilities, 11,* 217–222.

Korinek, L., & Bulls, J.A. (1996). SCORE A: A student research paper writing strategy. *Teaching Exceptional Children, 28*(4), 60–63.

Lewis, E.R., & Lewis, H.P. (1965). An analysis of errors in the formation of manuscript letters by first grade children. *American Educational Research Journal, 2,* 25–35.

Lewis, R.B., Graves, A.W., Ashton, T.M., & Kieley, C.L. (1998). Word processing tools for students with learning disabilities: A comparison of strategies to increase text entry speed. *Learning Disabilities Research & Practice, 13*(2), 95–108.

MacArthur, C.A., Graham, S., Haynes, J.B., & DeLaPaz, S. (1996). Spelling checkers and students with learning disabilities: Performance comparisons and impact on spelling. *The Journal of Special Education, 30*(1), 35–57.

MacArthur, C., Graham, S., Schwartz, S., & Schafer, W. (1995). Evaluation of a writing instruction model that integrated a process approach, strategy instruction, and word processing. *Learning Disability Quarterly, 18,* 278–291.

Mann, V., & Liberman, I. (1984). Phonological awareness and verbal short-term memory. *Journal of Learning Disabilities, 17,* 592–599.

Mercer, C.D. (1997). *Students with learning disabilities* (5th ed.). Upper Saddle River, NJ: Merrill/Prentice Hall.

Montague, M., & Leavell, A.G. (1994). Improving the narrative writing of students with learning disabilities. *Learning Disabilities Research & Practice, 15*(1), 21–33.

Newcomer, P.L., & Barenbaum, E.M. (1991). The written composing ability of children with learning disabilities: A review of the literature from 1980-1990. *Journal of Learning Disabilities, 24*, 578–593.

Newland, T.E. (1932). An analytical study of the development of illegibilities in handwriting from the lower grades to adulthood. *Journal of Educational Research, 26*, 249–258.

Oldrieve, R.M. (1997). Success with reading and spelling: Students internalize words through structured lessons. *Teaching Exceptional Students, 29*(4), 57–61.

O'Shea, L.J., Sindelar, P.T., & O'Shea, D.J. (1985). The effects of repeated readings and attentional cues on reading fluency and comprehension. *Journal of Reading Behavior, 17*, 129–141.

Roberts, R., & Mather, N. (1997). Orthographic dyslexia: The neglected subtype. *Learning Disabilities Research & Practice, 12*(4), 236–250.

Rooney, K. (1988). *Independent strategies for efficient study.* Richmond, VA: J.R. Enterprises.

Schumaker, J.B., Nolan, S.M., & Deshler, D.D. (1985). *Learning strategies curriculum: The error monitoring strategy.* Lawrence, KS: University of Kansas Institute for Research on Learning Disabilities.

Sexton, M., Harris, K., & Graham, S. (1998). Self-regulated strategy development and the writing process: Effects on essay writing and attributions. *Exceptional Children, 64*, 295–311.

Shanker, J.L., & Ekwall, E.E. (1998). *Locating and correcting reading difficulties* (7th ed.). Upper Saddle River, NJ: Merrill/Prentice Hall.

Snow, C.E., Burns, M.S., & Griffin, P. (Eds.) (1998). *Preventing reading difficulties in young children.* Washington, D.C.: National Academy Press.

Stevens, K.B., & Schuster, J.W. (1987). Effects of a constant time delay procedure on the written spelling performance of a learning disabled student. *Learning Disability Quarterly, 10*, 9–16.

Strauss, A., & Lehtinen, L. (1947). *Psychopathology and education of the brain-injured child.* New York: Grune & Stratton.

Templeton, S. (1986). Synthesis of research on the learning and teaching of spelling. *Educational Leadership, 43*, 73–78.

Thomas, C.C., Englert, C.S., & Gregg, S. (1987). An analysis of errors and strategies in the expository writing of learning disabled students. *Remedial and Special Education, 8*, 21–30.

Thurber, D.N. (1993). *D'Nealian handwriting.* Glenview, IL: Scott-Foresman.

Thurber, D.N. (1995). *D'Nealian handwriting versus circle-stick print.* Paper presented at the Annual Convention of the Council for Exceptional Children, San Antonio, TX, April, 1993. (ERIC ED 381 911)

Tovey D. (1978). Sound-it-out: A reasonable approach to spelling? *Reading World, 17*, 220–233.

Troia, G.A., Graham, S., & Harris, K.R. (1999). Teaching students with learning disablities to mindfully plan when writing. *Exceptional Children, 65*(2), 235–252.

Vacc, N.N. (1987). Word processor versus handwriting: A comparative study of writing samples produced by mildly mentally handicapped students. *Exceptional Children, 54*, 156–165.

Vallecorsa, A.L., & Garriss, E. (1990). Story composition skills of middle-grade students with learning disabilities. *Exceptional Children, 57*, 48–54.

Vallecorsa, A.L., Ledford, R.R., & Parnell, G.G. (1991). Strategies for teaching composition skills to students with learning disabilities. *Teaching Exceptional Children, 23*, 52–55.

Wallace, G.W., & Bott, D.A. (1989). Statement-Pie: A strategy to improve the paragraph writing skills of adolescents with learning disabilities. *Journal of Learning Disabilities, 22*, 541–543.

Weintraub, N., & Graham, S. (1998). Writing legibly and quickly: A study of children's ability to adjust their handwriting to meet common classroom demands. *Learning Disabilities Research & Practice, 13*, 146–152.

Welch, M., & Jensen, J.B. (1990). Write, P.L.E.A.S.E.: A video-assisted strategic intervention to improve written expression of inefficient learners. *Remedial and Special Education, 12*, 37–47.

Whitt, J., Paul, P.V., & Reynolds, C.J. (1988). Motivate reluctant learning disabled writers. *Teaching Exceptional Children, 20*, 37–39.

Winterling, V. (1990). The effects of constant time delay, practice in writing or spelling, and reinforcement on sight word recognition in a small group. *Journal of Special Education, 24*, 101–116.

Wirtz, C.L., Gardner, R., Weber, K., & Bullara, D. (1996). Using self–correction to improve the spelling performance of low-achieving third graders. *Remedial and Special Education, 17*(1), 48–58.

Wong, B.Y.L., Butler, D.L., Ficzere, S.A., & Kuperis, S. (1997). Teaching adolescents with learning disabilities and low achievers to plan, write, and revise compare-and-contrast essays. *Learning Disabilities Research & Practice, 12*(1), 2–15.

Wong, B.Y.L., Wong, R., Darlington, D., & Jones, W. (1991). Interactive teaching: An effective way to teach revision skills to adolescents with learning disabilities. *Learning Disabilities Research & Practice, 6,* 117–127.

Zipprich, M.A. (1995). Teaching web making as a guided planning tool to improve student narrative writing. *Remedial and Special Education, 16*(1), 3–15,52.

Chapter Thirteen

Allsopp, D.H. (1997). Using classwide peer tutoring to teach beginning algebra problem-solving skills in heterogeneous classrooms. *Remedial and Special Education, 18,* 367–379.

Allsopp, D.H. (1999). Using modeling, manipulatives, and mnemonics with eigth-grade math students. *Teaching Exceptional Children, 32*(2), 74–81.

Baroody, A.J., & Hume, J. (1991). Meaningful mathematics instruction: The case of fractions. *Remedial and Special Education, 12,* 54–68.

Battista, M.T. (1999). The mathematical miseducation of America's youth: Ignoring research and scientific study in education. *Phi Delta Kappan, 80*(6), 424–433.

Beirne–Smith, M. (1991). Peer tutoring in arithmetic for children with learning disabilities. *Exceptional Children, 57,* 330–337.

Bishop, W. (1999). The California mathematics standards: They're not only right; They're the law. *Phi Delta Kappan, 80*(6), 439–440.

Bos, C.S., & Vaughn, S. (1998). *Strategies for teaching students with learning and behavior problems* (4th ed.). Boston, MA: Allyn and Bacon.

Browder, D.M., & Grasso, E. (1999). Teaching money skills to individuals with mental retardation: A research review with practical applications. *Remedial and Special Education, 20*(5), 297–308.

Brosnan, P.A. (1997). Visual mathematics using geoboards. *Teaching Exceptional Children, 29*(3), 18–22.

Bullock, J. (1994). *TOUCHMATH: The touchpoint approach for teaching basic math computations* (4th ed.). Colorado Springs, CO: Innovative Learning Concepts, Inc.

Carnine, D. (1980). Preteaching versus concurrent teaching of the component skills of a multiplication algorithm. *Journal for Research in Mathematics Education, 11,* 375–379.

Carnine, D., Jitendra, A.K., & Silbert, J. (1997). A descriptive analysis of mathematics curricular materials from a pedagogical perspective: A case study of fractions. *Remedial and Special Education, 18*(2), 66–81.

Cawley, J.F., Baker-Kroczynski, S., & Urban, A. (1992). Seeking excellence in mathematics education for students with mild disabilities. *Teaching Exceptional Children, 24,* 40–43.

Cawley, J.F., Fitzmaurice, A.M., Goodstein, H.A., Lepore, A.V., Sedlak, R., & Althaus, V. (1976). *Project MATH.* Tulsa, OK: Educational Development Corporation.

Cawley, J.F., Fitzmaurice-Hayes, A.M., & Shaw, R. (1988). *Mathematics for the mildly handicapped: A guide to curriculum and instruction.* Boston, MA: Allyn and Bacon.

Cawley, J.F., Kahn, H., & Tedesco, A. (1989). Vocational education and students with learning disabilities. *Journal of Learning Disabilities, 22,* 630–634.

Cawley, J.F., & Miller, J.H. (1986). Selected views on metacognition, arithmetic problem solving, and learning disabilities. *Learning Disabilities Focus, 2,* 36–48.

Cawley, J.F., Miller, J.H., & School, B.A. (1987). A brief inquiry of arithmetic word-problem-solving among learning disabled secondary students. *Learning Disabilities Focus, 2,* 87–93.

Cawley, J.F., & Parmar, R.S. (1992). Arithmetic programming for students with disabilities: An alternative. *Remedial and Special Education, 13,* 6–18.

Cawley, J.F., Parmar, R.S., Yan, W.F., & Miller, J.H. (1996). Arithmetic computation abilities of students with learning disabilities: Implications for instruction. *Learning Disabilitis Research & Practice, 11,* 230–237.

Cawley, J.F., Parmar, R.S., Yan, W.F., & Miller, J.H. (1998). Arithmetic computation performance of students with learning disabilities: Implications for curriculum. *Learning Disabilities Research & Practice, 13*(2), 68–74.

Cawley, J.F., & Reines, R. (1996). Mathematics as communication: Using the interactive unit. *Teaching Exceptional Children, 28*(2), 29–34.

Choate, J.S. (1990). Study the problem. *Teaching Exceptional Children, 22*, 44–46.

Christensen, C.A., & Gerber, M.M. (1990). Effectiveness of computerized drill and practice games in teaching basic math facts. *Exceptionality, 1*, 149–165.

Cohen, S., & deBettencourt, L. (1988). Teaching children to be independent learners: A step-by-step strategy. In E.L. Meyen, G.A. Vergason, & R.J. Whelan (Eds.), *Effective instructional strategies for exceptional children* (pp. 319–334). Denver, CO: Love.

Cooper, R. (1994). *Alternative math techniques: Instructional guide*. Bryn Mawr, PA: Learning Disabilities Resources.

Corral, N., & Antia, S.D. (1997). Self-talk: Strategies for success in math. *Teaching Exceptional Children, 29*(4), 42–45.

Cossey, R. (1999). Are California's math standards up to the challenge? *Phi Delta Kappan, 80*(6), 441–443.

Cullinan, D., Lloyd, J., & Epstein, M.H. (1981). Strategy training: A structured approach to arithmetic instruction. *Exceptional Education Quarterly, 2*, 41–49.

Cybriwsky, C.A., & Schuster, J.W. (1990). Using constant time delay procedures to teach multiplication facts. *Remedial and Special Education, 11*, 54–59.

Davidson, J. (1969). *Using the Cuisenaire Rods*. New Rochelle, NY: Cuisenaire Company of America.

Davis, R.W., & Hajicek, J.O. (1985). Effects of self-instructional training and strategy training on a mathematics task with severely behaviorally disordered students. *Behavioral Disorders, 10*, 275–282.

Dunn, C., & Rabren, K. (1996). Functional mathematics instruction to prepare students for adulthood. *LD Forum, 21*(3), 34–40.

Engelmann, S., & Carnine, D. (1972, 1975, 1976). *DISTAR Arithmetic: I & II*. Blacklick, OH: Science Research Associates.

Engelmann, S., Carnine, D., Kelly, B., & Engelmann, O. (1996). *Connecting math concepts: Level A*. Blacklick, OH: Science Research Associates.

Engelmann, S., Carnine, D., & Steely, D.G. (1991). Making connections in mathematics. *Journal of Learning Disabilities, 24*, 292–303.

Engelmann, S., & Steeley, D. (1981). *Corrective mathematics program*. Blacklick, OH: Science Research Associates.

Englert, C.S., Culatta, B.E., & Horn, D.G. (1987). Influence of irrelevant information in addition word problems on problem solving. *Learning Disability Quarterly, 10*, 29–36.

Enright, B., & Beattie, J. (1989). Problem solving step by step in math. *Teaching Exceptional Children, 22*, 58–59.

Epstein, M.H., Kinder, D., & Bursuck, B. (1989). The academic status of adolescents with behavioral disorders. *Behavioral Disorders, 14*, 157–165.

Fleischner, J.E., Nuzum, M.B., & Marzola, E.S. (1987). Devising an instructional program to teach arithmetic problem-solving skills to students with learning disabilities. *Journal of Learning Disabilities, 20*, 214–217.

Flexer, R.J. (1989). Conceptualizing addition. *Teaching Exceptional Children, 21*, 20–25.

Fuchs, L.S., Bahr, C.M., & Rieth, H.J. (1989). Effects of goal structures and performance contingencies on math performance of adolescents with learning disabilities. *Journal of Learning Disabilities, 22*, 554–560.

Geary, D.C. (1993). Mathematical disabilities: Cognitive, neuropsychological, and genetic components. *Psychological Bulletin, 114*, 345–362.

Gersten, R., & Chard, D. (1999). Number sense: Rethinking arithmetic instruction for students with mathematical disabilities. *The Journal of Special Education, 33*(1), 18–28.

Harris, C.A., Miller, S.P., & Mercer, C.D. (1995). Teaching initial multiplication skills to students with disabilities in general education classrooms. *Learning Disabilities Research & Practice, 10*(3), 180–195.

Hasselbring, T.S., Goin, L.I., & Bransford, J.D. (1987). Developing automaticity. *Teaching Exceptional Children, 19*, 30–33.

Hasselbring, T.S., Goin, L., & Bransford, J.D. (1988). Developing math automaticity in learning handicapped children: The role of computerized drill and practice. *Focus on Exceptional Children, 20*, 1–7.

Hembree, R. (1986). Research gives calculators a green light. *Arithmetic Teacher, 34*, 18–21.

Hofmeister, A.M. (1993). Elitism and reform in school mathematics. *Remedial and Special Education, 14*(6), 8–13.

Horton, S.V., Lovitt, T.C., & White, O.R. (1992). Teaching mathematics to adolescents classified as educable mentally handicapped: Using calculators to remove the computational onus. *Remedial and Special Education, 13,* 36–61.

Howell, R., Sidorenko, E., & Jurica, J. (1987). The effects of computer use on the acquisition of multiplication facts by a student with learning disabilities. *Journal of Learning Disabilities, 20,* 336–341.

Hutchinson, N.L. (1993). Students with disabilities and mathematics education reform—Let the dialogue begin. *Remedial and Special Education, 14*(6), 20–23.

Jitendra, A.K., Hoff, K., & Beck, M.M. (1999). Teaching middle school students with learning disabilities to solve word problems using a schema-based approach. *Remedial and Special Education, 20*(1), 50–64.

Jitendra, A., & Xin, Y.P. (1997). Mathematical word-problem-solving instruction for students with mild disabilities and students at risk for math failure: A research synthesis. *The Journal of Special Education, 30,* 412–438.

Jones, G.A., Thornton, C.A., & Toohey, M.A. (1985). A multi-option program for learning basic addition facts: Case studies and an experimental report. *Journal of Learning Disabilities, 18,* 319–325.

Jordan, N.C. (1995). Clinical assessment of early mathematics disabilities: Adding up the research findings. *Learning Disabilities Research & Practice, 10*(1), 59–69.

Jordan, N.C., & Montani, T.O. (1997). Cognitive arithmetic and problem solving: A comparison of children with specific and general mathematics difficulties. *Journal of Learning Disabilities, 30,* 624–634, 684.

Kane, B.J., & Alley, G.R. (1980). A peer tutored instructional management program in computational mathematics for incarcerated learning disabled juvenile delinquents. *Journal of Learning Disabilities, 13,* 39–42.

Kelly, B., Gersten, R., & Carnine, D. (1990). Student error patterns as a function of curriculum design: Teaching fractions to remedial high school students and high school students with learning disabilities. *Journal of Learning Disabilities, 23,* 23–29.

Kirby, J.R., & Becker, L.D. (1988). Cognitive components of learning problems in arithmetic. *Remedial and Special Education, 9,* 7–16.

Kitz, W.R., & Thorpe, H.W. (1995). A comparison of the effectiveness of videodisc and traditional algebra instruction for college-age students with learning disabilities. *Remedial and Special Education, 16*(5), 295–306.

Leung, J. (1994). Teaching simple addition to children with mental retardation using a microcomputer. *Journal of Behavioral Education, 4,* 355–367.

Light, J.G., & DeFries, J.C. (1995). Comorbidity of reading and mathematics disabilities: Genetic and environmental etiologies. *Journal of Learning Disabilities, 28,* 96–106.

Lipstreu, B.L., & Johnson, M.K. (1988). Teaching time using the whole clock method. *Teaching Exceptional Children, 20,* 10–12.

Lloyd, J.W., & Keller, C.E. (1989). Effective mathematics instruction: Development, instruction, and programs. *Focus on Exceptional Children, 21*(7), 1–10.

Lovitt, T.C., & Curtiss, K. (1968). Effects of manipulating an antecedent event on mathematics response rate. *Journal of Applied Behavior Analysis, 1,* 329–333.

Lubke, M.M., Rogers, B., & Evans, K.T. (1989). Teaching fractions with videodiscs. *Teaching Exceptional Children, 21,* 55–56.

Maccini, P., & Hughes, C.A. (1997). Mathematics interventions for adolescents with learning disabilities. *Learning Disabilities Research & Practice, 12*(3), 168–176.

Maheady, L., Sacca, M.K., & Harper, G.F. (1987). Classwide student tutoring teams: The effects of peer mediated instruction on the academic performance of secondary mainstreamed students. *Journal of Special Education, 21,* 107–121.

Malouf, D.B., Jamison, P.J., Kercher, M.H., & Carlucci, C.M. (1991). Integrating computer software into effective instruction. *Teaching Exceptional Children, 23,* 54–56.

Marsh, L.G., & Cooke, N.L. (1996). The effects of using manipulatives in teaching math problem solving to students with learning disabilities. *Learning Disabilities Research & Practice, 11*(1), 58–65.

Mastropieri, M.A., Scruggs, T.E., & Shiah, R. (1991). Mathematics instruction for learning disabled students: A review of research. *Learning Disabilities Research & Practice, 6,* 89–98.

Mastropieri, M.A., Scruggs, T.E., & Shiah, R. (1997). Can computers teach problem-solving strategies to students with mild mental retardation? A case study. *Remedial and Special Education, 18*(3), 157–165.

Mattingly, J.C., & Bott, D.A. (1990). Teaching multiplication facts to students with learning problems. *Exceptional Children, 56,* 438–449.

McCloskey, M., & Macaruso, P. (1995). Representing and using numerical information. *American Psychologist, 50,* 351–363.

McDougall, D., & Brady, M.P. (1998). Initiating and fading self-management interventions to increase math fluency in general education classes. *Exceptional Children, 64*(2), 151–166.

McLeod, T., & Armstrong, S. (1982). Learning disabilities in mathematics-skills deficits and remedial approaches at the intermediate and secondary grades. *Learning Disability Quarterly, 5,* 305–311.

Mercer, C.D., Harris, C.A., & Miller, S.P. (1993). Reforming reforms in mathematics. *Remedial and Special Education, 14*(6), 14–19.

Mercer, C.D., Jordan, L., & Miller, S.P. (1994). Implications of constructivism for teaching math to students with moderate to mild disabilities. *The Journal of Special Education, 28,* 290–306.

Mercer, C.D., Jordan, L., & Miller, S.P. (1996). Constructivist math instruction for diverse learners. *Learning Disabilities Research & Practice, 11*(3), 147–156.

Mercer, C.D., & Mercer, A.R. (1993). *Teaching students with learning problems* (4th ed.). Upper Saddle River, NJ: Merrill/Prentice Hall.

Mercer, C.D., & Miller, S.P. (1992a). *Strategic math series.* Lawrence, KS: Edge Enterprises.

Mercer, C.D., & Miller, S.P. (1992b). Teaching students with learning problems in math to acquire, understand, and apply basic math facts. *Remedial and Special Education, 13,* 19–35, 61.

Miller, A.D., Barbetta, P.M., Drevno, G.E., Martz, S.A., & Heron, T.E. (1996). Math peer tutoring for students with specific learning disabilities. *LD Forum, 21*(3), 21–28.

Miller, S.P., & Mercer, C.D. (1993). Mnemonics: Enhancing the math performance of students with learning difficulties. *Intervention in School and Clinic, 29,* 78–82.

Miller, S.P., & Mercer, C.D. (1997). Educational aspects of mathematics disabilities. *Journal of Learning Disabilities, 30*(1), 47–56.

Miller, S.P., Strawser, S., & Mercer, C.D. (1996). Promoting strategic math performance among students with learning disabilities. *LD Forum, 21*(2), 34–40.

Montague, M. (1992). The effects of cognitive and metacognitive strategy instruction on the mathematical problem solving of middle school students with learning disabilities. *Journal of Learning Disabilities, 25,* 230–248.

Montague, M. (1993). Student-centered or strategy-centered instruction: What is our purpose? *Journal of Learning Disabilities, 26,* 433–437, 481.

Montague, M. (1996). Assessing mathematical problem solving. *Learning Disabilities Research & Practice, 11,* 238–248.

Montague, M. (1997). Student perception, mathematical problem solving, and learning disabilities. *Remedial and Special Education, 18*(1), 46–53.

Montague, M., & Applegate, B. (1993). Middle school students' mathematical problem solving: An analysis of think–aloud protocols. *Learning Disability Quarterly, 16,* 19–30.

Montague, M., Bos, C., & Doucette, M. (1991). Affective, cognitive, and metacognitive attributes of eighth-grade mathematical problem solvers. *Learning Disabilities Research & Practice, 6,* 145–151.

National Assessment of Educational Progress. (1992). *Mathematics report card for the nation and states* (Report No. 23–STO2). Washington, D.C.: National Center for Education Statistics.

National Council of Teachers of Mathematics. (1989). *Curriculum and evaluation standards for school mathematics.* Reston, VA: Author.

National Research Council. (1989). *Everybody counts: A report to the nation on the future of mathematic education.* Washington, D.C.: National Academy Press.

Nelson, J.R., Smith, D.J., Dodd, J.M., & Gilbert, C. (1991). The time estimation skills of students with emotional handicaps: A comparison. *Behavioral Disorders, 16,* 116–119.

O'Brien, T.C. (1999). Parrot math. *Phi Delta Kappan, 80*(6), 434–438.

O'Melia, M.C., & Rosenberg, M.S. (1994). Effects of cooperative homework teams on the acquisition of mathematics skills by secondary students with mild disabilities. *Exceptional Children, 60,* 538–548.

Paddock, C. (1992). Ice cream stick math. *Teaching Exceptional Children, 24,* 50–51.

Parmar, R.S., & Cawley, J.F. (1994). Structuring word problems for diagnostic teaching: Helping teachers meet the needs of children with mild disabilities. *Teaching Exceptional Children, 26*(4), 16–21.

Parmar, R.S., Cawley, J.F., & Frazita, R.R. (1996). Word problem-solving by students with and without mild disabilities. *Exceptional Children, 62,* 415–429.

Parmar, R.S., Cawley, J.F., & Miller, J.H. (1994). Differences in mathematics performance between students with learning disabilities and students with mild retardation. *Exceptional Children, 60,* 549–563.

Patton, J.R., Cronin, M.E., Bassett, D.S., & Koppel, A.E. (1997). A life skills approach to mathematics instruction: Preparing students with learning disabilities for the real-life math demands of adulthood. *Journal of Learning Disabilities, 30*(2), 178–187.

Pellegrino, J.W., & Goldman, S.R. (1987). Information processing and elementary mathematics. *Journal of Learning Disabilities, 20,* 23–32, 57.

Peterson, S.K., Mercer, C.D., & O'Shea, L. (1988). Teaching learning disabled students place value using the concrete to abstract sequence. *Learning Disabilities Research, 4,* 52–56.

Porter, A. (1989). A curriculum out of balance: The case of elementary school mathematics. *Educational Researcher, 18,* 9–15.

Ratnesar, R. (1997). This is math? Suddenly, math becomes fun and games. *Time, 25* (August), 66–67.

Reith, H.J., Polsgrove, L., McLeskey, J., Payne, K., & Anderson, R. (1978). The use of self-recording to increase the arithmetic performance of severely behaviorally disordered students. In R.B. Rutherford & A.G. Prieto (Eds.), *Severe behavior disorders of children and youth* (pp. 50–58.). Arizona State University, Monograph in Behavioral Disorders.

Reys, B., Robinson, E., Sconiers, S., & Mark, J. (1999). Mathematics curricula based on rigorous national standards: What, why, and how? *Phi Delta Kappan, 80*(6), 454–456.

Rivera, D.M. (1993). Examining mathematics reform and the implications for students with mathematics disabilities. *Remedial and Special Education, 14*(6), 24–27.

Scheid, K. (1994). Cognitive-based methods for teaching mathematics. *Teaching Exceptional Children, 26*(3), 6–10.

Schoen, H.L., Fey, J.F., Hirsch, C.R., & Coxford, A.F. (1999). Issues and options in the math wars. *Phi Delta Kappan, 80*(6), 444–453.

Schunk, D.H. (1985). Participation in goal setting: Effects on self-efficacy and skills of learning disabled children. *The Journal of Special Education, 19,* 307–317.

Schwartz, S.E. (1977). *Real life math program.* Chicago, IL: Hubbard.

Scruggs, T.E., & Mastropieri, M.A. (1986). Academic characteristics of behaviorally disordered and learning disabled students. *Behavioral Disorders, 11,* 184–190.

Siegler, R. (1988). Individual differences in strategy choices: Good students, not-so-good students, and perfectionists. *Child Development, 59,* 833–851.

Siegler, R. (1991). In young children's counting, procedures precede principles. *Educational Psychology Review, 3,* 127–135.

Silbert, J., Carnine, D., & Stein, M. (1990). *Direct instruction mathematics* (2nd ed.). Columbus, OH: Merrill.

Smith, D.D., & Lovitt, T.C. (1975). The use of modeling techniques to influence the acquisition of computational arithmetic skills in learning-disabled children. In E. Ramp & G. Semb (Eds.), *Behavior analysis: Areas of research and application* (pp. 283–308). Englewood Cliffs, NJ: Prentice–Hall.

Stein, M. (1987). Arithmetic word problems. *Teaching Exceptional Children, 19,* 33–35.

Stein, M., Silbert, J., & Carnine, D. (1997). *Designing effective mathematics instruction: A direct instruction approach.* Upper Saddle River, NJ: Merrill/Prentice Hall.

Swanson, H.L., & Rhine, B. (1985). Strategy transformations in learning disabled children's math performance: Clues to the development of expertise. *Journal of Learning Disabilities, 18,* 596–603.

Systems Impact, Inc. (1985). *Mastering fractions.* Washington D.C.: Author.

Thornton, C.A., & Toohey, M.A. (1985). Basic math facts: Guidelines for teaching and learning. *Learning Disabilities Focus, 1*, 44–57.

Thornton, C.A., & Toohey, M.A. (1986). Subtraction hide and seek cards can help. *Teaching Exceptional Children, 19*, 10–14.

Trifiletti, J.J., Frith, G.H., & Armstrong, S. (1984). Microcomputers versus resource rooms for LD students: A preliminary investigation of the effects on math skills. *Learning Disability Quarterly, 7*, 69–76.

Vacc, N.N. (1995). Gaining number sense through a restructured hundreds chart. *Teaching Exceptional Children, 28*(1), 50–55.

Wesson, C., Wilson, R., & Mandlebaum, L.H. (1988). Learning games for active student responding. *Teaching Exceptional Children, 20*, 12–14.

Wilson, R., & Wesson, C. (1991). Increasing achievement of learning disabled students by measuring and controlling task difficulty. *Learning Disabilities Research & Practice, 6*, 34–39.

Woodward, J. (1991). Procedural knowledge in mathematics: The role of the curriculum. *Journal of Learning Disabilities, 24*, 242–251.

Woodward, J. (1999). Redoing the numbers: Secondary math for a postsecondary work world. *Teaching Exceptional Children, 31*(4), 74–79.

Woodward, J., & Baxter, J. (1997). The effects of an innovative approach to mathematics on academically low-achieving students in inclusive settings. *Exceptional Children, 63*, 373–388.

Woodward, J., Baxter, J., & Robinson, R. (1999). Rules and reason: Decimal instruction for academically low achieving students. *Learning Disabilities Research & Practice, 14*(1), 15–24.

Woodward, J., & Howard, L. (1994). The misconceptions of youth: Errors and their mathematical meaning. *Exceptional Children, 61*, 126–136.

Xin, Y.P., & Jitendra, A.K. (1999). The effects of instruction in solving mathematical word problems for students with learning problems: A meta-analysis. *The Journal of Special Education, 32*, 207–225.

Chapter Fourteen

Alber, S.R., Heward, W.L., & Hippler, B.J. (1999). Teaching middle school students with learning disabilities to recruit positive teacher attention. *Exceptional Children, 65*(2), 253–270.

Alley, G.R., & Deshler, D.D. (1979). *Teaching the learning disabled adolescent: Strategies and methods.* Denver, CO: Love.

Alley, G.R., Deshler, D.D., Clark, F.L., Schumaker, J.B., & Warner, M.M. (1983). Learning disabilities in adolescent and adult populations: Research implications (Part II). *Focus on Exceptional Children, 15*(9), 1–14.

Anders, P.L., & Bos, C.S. (1984). In the beginning: Vocabulary instruction in content classrooms. *Topics in Learning and Learning Disabilities, 3*(4), 53–65.

Archer, A.L. (1988). Strategies for responding to information. *Teaching Exceptional Children, 20*, 55–57.

Archer, A., & Gleason, M. (1989). *Skills for school success.* Billerica, MA: Curriculum Associates.

Armento, B. (1986). Research on teaching social studies. In M. Witrock (Ed.), *Handbook of research on teaching* (3rd ed.) (pp. 942–951). New York: Macmillan.

Ausubel, D.P., & Robinson, F.G. (1969). *School learning: An introduction to educational psychology.* New York: Holt, Rinehart, & Winston.

Bacon, E.H., & Schulz, J.B. (1991). A survey of mainstreaming practices. *Teacher Education and Special Education, 14*, 144–149.

Baker, J.M., & Zigmond, N. (1990). Are regular education classes equipped to accommodate students with learning disabilities? *Exceptional Children, 56*, 515–526.

Bean, R.M., Zigmond, N., & Hartman, D.K. (1994). Adapted use of social studies textbooks in elementary classrooms: Views of classroom teachers. *Remedial and Special Education, 15*, 216–226.

Beck, I.L., McKeown, M., & Gromoll, E.W. (1989). Learning from social studies texts. *Cognition and Instruction, 6*(2), 99–153.

Bergerud, D., Lovitt, T.C., & Horton, S. (1988). The effectiveness of textbook adaptations in Life Science for high school students with learning disabilities. *Journal of Learning Disabilities, 21*, 70–76.

Billingsley, B.S., & Wildman, T.M. (1988). The effects of prereading activities on the comprehension monitoring of learning disabled adolescents. *Learning Disabilities Research, 4*(1), 36–44.

Bos, C.S., Anders, P.L., Filip, D., & Jaffe, L.E. (1989). The effects of an interactive instructional strategy for enhancing reading comprehension and content area learning for students with learning disabilities. *Journal of Learning Disabilities, 22*, 384–390.

Bos, C.S., & Vaughn, S. (1998). *Strategies for teaching students with learning and behavior problems* (4th ed.). Boston, MA: Allyn and Bacon.

Boudah, D.J., Lenz, B.K., Bulgren, J.A., Schumaker, J.B., & Deshler, D.D. (2000). Don't water down! Enhance content learning through the unit organizer routine. *Teaching Exceptional Children, 32*(3), 48–56.

Boyle, J.R. (1996). The effects of a cognitive mapping strategy on the literal and inferential comprehension of students with mild disabilities. *Learning Disability Quarterly, 19*, 86–98.

Boyle, J.R., & Weishaar, M. (1997). The effects of expert-generated versus student-generated cognitive organizers on the reading comprehension of students with learning disabilities. *Learning Disabilities Research & Practice, 12*(4), 228–235.

Boyle, J.R., & Yeager, N. (1997). Blueprints for learning: Using cognitive frameworks for understanding. *Teaching Exceptional Children, 29*(4), 26–31.

Bradley, D.F., & Calvin, M.B. (1998). Grading modified assignments: Equity or compromise? *Teaching Exceptional Children, 31*(2), 24–29.

Brophy, J. (1990). Teaching social studies for understanding and higher–order applications. *The Elementary School Journal, 90*, 351–417.

Bulgren, J.A., Deshler, D.D., & Schumaker, J.B. (1997). Use of a recall enhancement routine and strategies in inclusive secondary classes. *Learning Disabilities Research & Practice, 12*(4), 198–208.

Bulgren, J.A., Hock, M.F., Schumaker, J.B., & Deshler, D.D. (1995). The effects of instruction in a paired associates strategy on the information mastery performance of students with learning disabilities. *Learning Disabilities Research & Practice, 10*(1), 22–37.

Bulgren, J., Schumaker, J.B., & Deshler, D.D. (1988). Effectiveness of a concept teaching routine in enhancing the performance of LD students in secondary-level mainstream classes. *Learning Disability Quarterly, 11*, 3–16.

Bulgren, J.A., Schumaker, J.B., & Deshler, D.D. (1994). The effects of a recall enhancement routine on the test performance of secondary students with and without learning disabilities. *Learning Disabilities Research & Practice, 9*(1), 2–11.

Bursuck, W.D., Munk, D.D., & Olson, M.M. (1999). The fairness of report card grading adaptations: What do students with and without learning disabilities think? *Remedial and Special Education, 20*(2), 84–92.

Bursuck, W., Polloway, E.A., Plante, L., Epstein, M.H., Jayanthi, M., & McConeghy, J. (1996). Report card grading and adaptations: A national survey of classroom practices. *Exceptional Children, 62*, 301–318.

Carnine, D. (1989). Teaching complex content to learning disabled students: The role of technology. *Exceptional Children, 55*, 524–533.

Carnine, D. (1991). Curricular interventions for teaching higher order thinking to all students: Introduction to the special series. *Journal of Learning Disabilities, 24*, 261–269.

Christiansen, J., & Vogel, J.R. (1998). A decision model for grading students with disabilities. *Teaching Exceptional Children, 31*(2), 30–35.

Ciborowski, J. (1995). Using textbooks with students who cannot read them. *Remedial and Special Education, 16*(2), 90–101.

Clark, F.L., Deshler, D.D., Schumaker, J.B., Alley, G.R., & Warner, M.M. (1984). Visual imagery and self-questioning: Strategies to improve comprehension of written material. *Journal of Learning Disabilities, 17*, 145–149.

Cohen, S.B., & Lynch, D.K. (1991). An instructional modification process. *Teaching Exceptional Children, 23*, 12–18.

Crabtree, C. (1989). Improving history in the schools. *Educational Leadership, 47*(3), 25–28.

Deshler, D.D. (1998). Grounding interventions for students with learning disabilities in "power ideas." *Learning Disabilities Research & Practice, 13*(1), 29–34.

Deshler, D.D., & Schumaker, J.B. (1986). Learning strategies: An instructional alternative for low-achieving adolescents. *Exceptional Children, 52*, 583–590.

Deshler, D.D., & Schumaker, J.B. (1993). Strategy mastery by at-risk students: Not a simple matter. *Elementary School Journal, 94,* 153–167.

Deshler, D.D., Schumaker, J.B., Alley, G.R., Warner, M.M., & Clark, F.L. (1982). Learning disabilities in adolescent and young adult populations: Research implications. *Focus on Exceptional Children, 15*(1), 1–12.

Devine, T.G. (1987). *Teaching study skills: A guide for teachers* (2nd ed.). Boston, MA: Allyn and Bacon.

Donahoe, K., & Zigmond, N. (1990). Academic grades of ninth-grade urban learning-disabled students and low-achieving peers. *Exceptionality, 1,* 17–27.

Donahue, M.L., & Baumgartner, D. (1997). Having the timeline of my life. *Teaching Exceptional Children, 29*(6), 38–41.

Doran, R.L., & Sentman, J.R. (1994). Science and special education: A science education perspective. *Remedial and Special Education, 15*(2), 128–133.

Downing, J.A., Simpson, R.L., & Myles, B.S. (1990). Regular and special educator perceptions of nonacademic skills needed by mainstreamed students with behavioral disorders and learning disabilities. *Behavioral Disorders, 15,* 217–226.

Dye, G.A. (2000). Graphic organizers to the rescue! Helping students link–and remember–informaation. *Teaching Exceptional Children, 32*(3), 72–76.

Edmunds, A.L. (1999). Cognitive credit cards: Acquiring learning strategies. *Teaching Exceptional Children, 31*(4), 68–73.

Elliott, J., Ysseldyke, J., Thurlow, M., & Erikson, R. (1998). What about assessment and accountability? Practical implications for educators. *Teaching Exceptional Children, 31*(1), 20–27.

Ellis, E.S. (1986). The role of motivation and pedagogy on the generalization of cognitive training by the mildly handicapped. *Journal of Learning Disabilities, 19,* 66–70.

Ellis, E.S. (1989). A metacognitive intervention for increasing class participation. *Learning Disabilities Focus, 5,* 36–46.

Ellis, E.S. (1997). Watering up the curriculum for adolescents with learning disabilities: Goals of the knowledge dimension. *Remedial and Special Education, 18,* 326–346.

Ellis, E.S. (1998). Watering up the curriculum for adolescents with learning disabilities—Part 2: Goals of the affective dimension. *Remedial and Special Education, 19*(2), 91–105.

Ellis, E.S., Deshler, D.D., Lenz, B.K., Schumaker, J.B., & Clarke, F.L. (1991). An instructional model for teaching learning strategies. *Focus on Exceptional Children, 24*(1), 1–14.

Ellis, E.S., Deshler, D.D., & Schumaker, J.B. (1989). Teaching adolescents with learning disabilities to generate and use task-specific strategies. *Journal of Learning Disabilities, 22,* 108–119.

Ellis, E.S., & Lenz, B.K. (1987). A component analysis of effective learning strategies for LD students. *Learning Disabilities Focus, 2,* 94–107.

Espin, C.A., & Foegen, A. (1996). Validity of general outcome measures for predicting secondary students' performance on content-area tasks. *Exceptional Children, 62,* 497–514.

Ferretti, R.P., & Okolo, C. (1996). Authenticity in learning: Multimedia design projects in the social studies for students with LD. *Journal of Learning Disabilities, 29,* 450–460.

Fiore, T.A., & Cook, R.A. (1994). Adopting textbooks and other instructional materials: Policies and practices that address diverse learners. *Remedial and Special Education, 15,* 333–347.

Flores, D.M., Schloss, P.J., & Alper, S. (1995) The use of a daily calendar to increase responsibilities fulfilled by secondary students with special needs. *Remedial and Special Education, 16*(1), 38–43.

Forness, S.R., Kavale, K.A., Blum, I.M., & Lloyd, J.W. (1997). Mega-analysis of meta-analysis: What works in special education and related services. *Teaching Exceptional Children, 29*(6), 4–9.

Fuchs, L.S., Fuchs, D., Hamlett, C.L., Phillips, N.B., & Karns, K. (1995). General educators' specialized adaptation for students with learning disabilities. *Exceptional Children, 61,* 440–459.

Gajria, M., Salend, S.J., & Hemrick, M.A. (1994). Teacher acceptability of testing modifications for mainstreamed students. *Learning Disabilities Research & Practice, 9,* 236–243.

Gelzheiser, L.M., Meyers, J., Slesinski, C., Douglas, C., & Lewis, L. (1997). Patterns in general education teachers' integration practices. *Exceptionality, 7,* 207–228.

Gersten, R. (1998). Recent advances in instructional research for students with learning disabilities: An overview. *Learning Disabilities Research & Practice, 13*(3), 162–170.

Gersten, R., & Baker, S. (1998). Real world use of scientific concepts: Integrating situated cognition with explicit instruction. *Exceptional Children, 65*(1), 23–25.

Glomb, N., & West, R.P. (1990). Teaching behaviorally disordered adolescents to use self-management skills for improving the completeness, accuracy, and neatness of creative writing homework assignments. *Behavioral Disorders, 15,* 233–242.

Harris, K.R., & Pressley, M. (1991). The nature of cognitive strategy instruction: Interactive strategy construction. *Exceptional Children, 57,* 392–404.

Heron, T.E., & Harris, K.C. (1987). *The educational consultant* (2nd ed.). Austin, TX: Pro-Ed.

Hoener, A., Salend, S., & Kay, S.I. (1997). Creating readable handouts, worksheets, overheads, tests, review materials, study guides, and homework assignments through effective typographic design. *Teaching Exceptional Children, 29*(3), 32–35.

Hollenbeck, K., Tindal, G., & Almond, P. (1998). Teachers' knowledge of accommodations as a validity issue in high-stakes testing. *The Journal of Special Education, 32*(3), 175–183.

Hollingsworth, M., & Woodward, J. (1993). Integrated learning: Explicit strategies and their role in problem-solving instruction. *Exceptional Children, 59,* 444–455.

Horton, S.V., & Lovitt, T.C. (1989). Using study guides with three classifications of secondary students. *The Journal of Special Education, 22,* 447–462.

Horton, S.V., Lovitt, T.C., & Christensen, C.C. (1991). Notetaking from textbooks: Effects of a columnar format on three categories of secondary students. *Exceptionality, 2,* 19–40.

Hudson, P. (1996). Using a learning set to increase the test performance of students with learning disabilities in social studies classes. *Learning Disabilities Research & Practice, 11*(2), 78–85.

Hughes, C.A., Schumaker, J.B., Deshler, D.D., & Mercer, C. (1987). *The test-taking strategy.* Lawrence, KS: Excel Enterprises.

Kagan, S. (1989). *Cooperative learning resources for teachers.* San Juan Capistrano, CA: Resources for Teachers.

Kameenui, E., & Carnine, D. (1998). *Effective teaching strategies that accommodate diverse learners.* Upper Saddle River, NJ: Prentice Hall.

Kameenui, E.J., & Simmons, D.C. (1990). *Designing instructional strategies: The prevention of academic learning problems.* Columbus, OH: Merrill.

Kerr, M.M., Zigmond, N., Schaeffer, A.L., & Brown, G. (1986). An observational follow-up study of successful and unsuccessful high school students. *High School Journal, 71,* 20–32.

Kinder, D., & Bursuck, W. (1991). The search for a unified social studies curriculum: Does history really repeat itself? *Journal of Learning Disabilities, 24,* 270–275.

Kinder, D., & Bursuck, W. (1993). History strategy instruction: Problem-solution-effect analysis, timeline, and vocabulary instruction. *Exceptional Children, 59,* 324–335.

King-Sears, M.E., Mercer, C.D., & Sindelar, P.T. (1992). Toward independence with keyword mnemonics: A strategy for science vocabulary instruction. *Remedial and Special Education, 13*(5), 22–33.

Kinzer, C.K., Gabella, M.S., & Rieth, H.J. (1994). An argument for using multimedia and anchored instruction to facilitate mildly disabled students' learning of literacy and social studies. *Technology and Disability, 3,* 117–128.

Kling, B. (2000). ASSERT yourself: Helping students of all ages develop self-advocacy skills. *Teaching Exceptional Children, 32*(3), 66–70.

Klingner, J.K., Vaughn, S., Hughes, M.T., Schumm, J.S., & Elbaum, B. (1998). Outcomes for students with and without learning disabilities in inclusive classrooms. *Learning Disabilities Research & Practice, 13*(3), 153–161.

Knapczyk, D. (1991). Effects of modeling in promoting generalization of student question asking and question answering. *Learning Disabilities Research & Practice, 6,* 75–82.

Lenz, B.K., Alley, G.R., & Schumaker, J.B. (1987). Activating the inactive learner: Advance organizers in the secondary content classroom. *Learning Disability Quarterly, 10,* 53–67.

Lovitt, T.C., & Horton, S.V. (1994). Strategies for adapting science textbooks for youth with learning disabilities. *Remedial and Special Education, 15*(2), 105–116.

Margolis, H., & McGettigan, J. (1988). Managing resistance to instructional modifications in mainstreamed environments. *Remedial and Special Education, 9,* 15–21.

Marks, J.W., Van Laeys, J., Bender, W.N., & Scott, K.S. (1996). Teachers create learning strategies: Guidelines for classroom creation. *Teaching Exceptional Children, 28*(4), 34–38.

Martens, B.K., Peterson, R.L., Witt, J.C., & Cirone, S. (1986). Teacher perceptions of school-based interventions. *Exceptional Children, 53,* 213–223.

Mastropieri, M.A., Emerick, K., & Scruggs, T.E. (1988). Mnemonic instruction of science concepts. *Behavioral Disorders, 14,* 48–56.

Mastropieri, M.A., & Scruggs, T.E. (1988). Increasing content area learning of learning disabled students: Research implementation. *Learning Disabilities Research, 4,* 17–25.

Mastropieri, M.A., & Scruggs, T.E. (1989a). Mnemonic social studies instruction: Classroom applications. *Remedial and Special Education, 10,* 40–46.

Mastropieri, M.A., & Scruggs, T.E. (1989b). Reconstructive elaborations: Strategies that facilitate content learning. *Learning Disabilities Focus, 4,* 73–77.

Mastropieri, M.A., & Scruggs, T.E. (1994). Text versus hands-on science curriculum: Implications for students with disabilities. *Remedial and Special Education, 15*(2), 72–85.

Mastropieri, M.A., & Scruggs, T.E. (1998). Constructing more meaningful relationships in the classroom: Mnemonic research into practice. *Learning Disabilities Research & Practice, 13*(3), 138–145.

Mastropieri, M.A., Scruggs, T.E., Whittaker, M.E.S., & Bakken, J.P. (1994). Applications of mnemonic strategies with students with mild mental disabilities. *Remedial and Special Education, 15*(1), 34–43.

McCleery, J.A., & Tindal, G.A. (1999). Teaching the scientific method to at-risk students and students with learning disabilities through concept anchoring and explicit instruction. *Remedial and Special Education, 20*(1), 7–18.

McKeown, M.G., & Beck, I.L. (1988). Learning vocabulary: Different ways for different goals. *Remedial and Special Education, 9,* 42–52.

McLeskey, J., Lancaster, M., & Grizzle, K.L. (1995). Learning disabilities and grade retention: A review of issues with recommendations for practice. *Learning Disabilities Research & Practice, 10*(2), 120–128.

Monda-Amaya, L.E., Dieker, L., & Reed, F. (1998). Preparing students with learning disabilities to participate in inclusive classrooms. *Learning Disabilities Research & Practice, 13*(3), 171–182.

Moran, M.R. (1980). *An investigation of the demands on oral language skills of learning disabled students in secondary classrooms* (Research Report No. 1). Lawrence, KS: University of Kansas Institute for Research in Learning Disabilities.

Munk, D.D., & Bursuck, W.D. (1997/1998). Can grades be helpful and fair? *Educational Leadership, 55*(4), 44–47.

Parmar, R.S., Deluca, C.B., & Janczak, T.M. (1994). Investigations into the relationship between science and language abilities of students with mild disabilities. *Remedial and Special Education, 15*(2), 117–126.

Patton, J.R., Polloway, E.A., & Cronin, M.E. (1987). Social studies instruction for mildly handicapped students: A status report. *The Social Studies, 71,* 131–135.

Pearson, P.D., & Johnson, D.D. (1978). *Teaching reading comprehension.* New York: Holt, Rinehart, & Winston.

Polloway, E.A., Bursuck, W.D., Jayanthi, M., Epstein, M.H., & Nelson, J.S. (1996). Treatment acceptability: Determining appropriate interventions within inclusive classrooms. *Intervention in School and Clinic, 31,* 133–144.

Poplin, M. S. (1988). The reductionist fallacy in learning disabilities: Replicating the past by reducing the present. *Journal of Learning Disabilities, 21,* 389–400.

Prawat, R.S. (1989). Promoting access to knowledge, strategy, and disposition in students: A research synthesis. *Review of Educational Research, 59,* 1–42.

Pressley, M., Scruggs, T.E., & Mastropieri, M.A. (1989). Memory strategy research in learning disabilities: Present and future directions. *Learning Disabilities Research, 4,* 68–77.

Putnam, M.L. (1992a). Characteristics of questions on tests administered by mainstream secondary classroom teachers. *Learning Disabilities Research & Practice, 7,* 129–136.

Putnam, M.L. (1992b). The testing practices of mainstream secondary classroom teachers. *Remedial and Special Education, 13*(5), 11–21.

Reisberg, L., & Wolf, R. (1988). Instructional strategies for special education consultants. *Remedial and Special Education, 9,* 29–40.

Rieth, H.J., & Polsgrove, L. (1994). Curriculum and instructional issues in teaching secondary students with learning disabilities. *Learning Disabilities Research & Practice, 9*(2), 118–126.

Rooney, K. (1988). *Independent strategies for efficient study.* Richmond, VA: J.R. Enterprises.

Ruhl, K.L., Hughes, C.A., & Schloss, P.J. (1987). Using the pause procedure to enhance lecture recall. *Teacher Education and Special Education, 10*(1), 14–18.

Scanlon, D., Deshler, D.D., & Schumaker, J.B. (1996). Can a strategy be taught and learned in secondary inclusive classrooms? *Learning Disabilities Research & Practice, 11*(1), 41–57.

Schaeffer, A.L., Zigmond, N., Kerr, M.M., & Farra, H.E. (1990). Helping teenagers develop school survival skills. *Teaching Exceptional Children, 23,* 6–9.

Schumaker, J.B., Deshler, D.D., Alley, G.R., & Warner, M.M. (1983). Toward the development of an intervention model for learning disabled adolescents: The University of Kansas Institute. *Exceptional Education Quarterly, 4,* 45–74.

Schumm, J.S., & Vaughn, S. (1991). Making adaptations for mainstreamed students: General classroom teachers' perspectives. *Remedial and Special Education, 12,* 18–27.

Schumm, J.S., Vaughn, S., Gordon, J., & Rothlein, L. (1994). General education teachers' beliefs, skills, and practices in planning for mainstreamed students with learning disabilities. *Teacher Education and Special Education, 17*(1), 22–37.

Scott, B.J., Vitale, M.R., & Masten, W.G. (1998). Implementing instructional adaptations for students with disabilities in inclusive classrooms: A literature review. *Remedial and Special Education, 19*(2), 106–119.

Scruggs, T.E., & Marsing, L. (1987). Teaching test-taking skills to behaviorally disordered students. *Behavioral Disorders, 13,* 240–244.

Scruggs, T.E., & Mastropieri, M.A. (1990). Mnemonic instruction for students with learning disabilities: What it is and what it does. *Learning Disability Quarterly, 13,* 271–280.

Scruggs, T.E., Mastropieri, M.A., Levin, J.R., & Gaffney, J.S. (1985). Facilitating the acquisition of science facts in learning disabled students. *American Educational Research Journal, 22,* 575–586.

Scruggs, T.E., Mastropieri, M.A., Levin, J.R., McLoone, B., Gaffney, J.S., & Prater, M.A. (1985). Increasing content–area learning: A comparison of mnemonic and visual-spatial direct instruction. *Learning Disabilities Research, 1*(1), 18–31.

Shields, J.M., & Heron, T.E. (1989). Teaching organizational skills to students with learning disabilities. *Teaching Exceptional Children, 21,* 8–13.

Simmonds, E.P.M., Luchow, J.P., Kaminsky, S., & Cottone, V. (1989). Applying cognitive learning strategies in the classroom: A collaborative training institute. *Learning Disabilities Focus, 4,* 96–105.

Swanson, S., & Howell, C. (1996). Test anxiety in adolescents with learning disabilities and behavior disorders. *Exceptional Children, 62,* 389–397.

Thurlow, M.L., Ysseldyke, J.E., & Silverstein, B. (1995). Testing accommodations for students with disabilities. *Remedial and Special Education, 16,* 260–270.

Tindal, G., Heath, B., Hollenbeck, K., Almond, P., & Harniss, M. (1998). Accommodating students with disabilities on large-scale tests: An experimental study. *Exceptional Children, 64,* 439–450.

Tindal, G., Rebar, M., Nolet, V., & McCollum, S. (1995). Understanding instructional outcome options for students with special needs in content classes. *Learning Disabilities Research & Practice, 10*(2), 72–84.

Tralli, R., Colombo, B., Deshler, D.D., & Schumaker, J.B. (1996). The strategies intervention model: A model for supported inclusion at the secondary level. *Remedial and Special Education, 17*(4), 204–216.

Tyson, H., & Woodward, A. (1989). Why students aren't learning very much from textbooks. *Educational Leadership, 47*(3), 14–17.

Warner, M.M., Schumaker, J.B., Alley, G.R., & Deshler, D.D. (1980). Learning disabled adolescents in public schools: Are they different from other low achievers? *Exceptional Education Quarterly, 1*(2), 27–36.

Whinnery, K.W., Fuchs, L.S., & Fuchs, D. (1991). General, special, and remedial teachers' acceptance of behavioral and instructional strategies for mainstreaming students with mild handicaps. *Remedial and Special Education, 12,* 6–17.

Wiener, J. (1991). Alternatives in the assessment of the learning disabled adolescent: A learning strategies approach. *Learning Disabilities Focus, 1,* 97–107.

Wineburg, S. (1999). Historical thinking and other unnatural acts. *Phi Delta Kappan, 80,* 488–499.

Wong, B.Y.L., Wong, R., Perry, N., & Sawatsky, D. (1986). The efficacy of a self–questioning summarization strategy for use by underachievers and learning disabled adolescents in social studies. *Learning Disabilities Focus, 2*(2), 20–35.

Woodward, J. (1994). The role of models in secondary science instruction. *Remedial and Special Education, 15*(2), 94–104.

Woodward, J., & Noell, J. (1991). Science instruction at the secondary level: Implications for students with learning disabilities. *Journal of Learning Disabilities, 24,* 277–284.

Zigmond, N., Kerr, M.M., Schaeffer, A., Brown, G., & Farra, H. (1986). *The school survival skills curriculum.* Pittsburgh, PA: University of Pittsburgh.

Chapter Fifteen

Armstrong, S.W., & McPherson, A. (1991). Homework as a critical component in social skills instruction. *Teaching Exceptional Children, 24,* 45–47.

Asselin, S.B., Todd-Allen, M., & deFur, S. (1998). Transition coordinators define yourselves. *Teaching Exceptional Children, 30*(3), 11–15.

Beakley, B.A., & Yoder, S.L. (1998). Middle schoolers learn community skills. *Teaching Exceptional Children, 30*(3), 16–21.

Becker, R.L. (1987). *Reading-free vocational interest inventory.* Monterey, CA: Publishers Test Service.

Bender, W.N., & Smith, J.K. (1990). Classroom behavior of children and adolescents with learning disabilities: A meta-analysis. *Journal of Learning Disabilities, 23,* 298–305.

Benz, M.R., Yovanoff, P., & Doren, B. (1997). School-to-work components that predict postschool success for students with and without disabilities. *Exceptional Children, 63*(2), 151–165.

Berkell, D.E., & Brown, J.M. (1989). *Transition from school to work for persons with disabilities.* White Plains, NY: Longman.

Berler, E.S., Gross, A.M., & Drabman, R.S. (1982). Social skills training with children: Proceed with caution. *Journal of Applied Behavior Analysis, 15,* 41–53.

Black, R.S., & Langone, (1997). Social awareness and transition to employment for adolescents with mental retardation. *Remedial and Special Education, 18,* 214–222,232.

Blackbourn, J.M. (1989). Acquisition and generalization of social skills in elementary-aged children with learning disabilities. *Journal of Learning Disabilities, 22,* 28–34.

Blackorby, J., & Wagner, M. (1996). Longitudinal postschool outcomes of youth with disabilities: Findings from the National Longitudinal Transition Study. *Exceptional Children, 62*(5), 399–413.

Blazer, B. (1999). Developing 504 classroom accommodation plans: A collaborative, systematic parent-student-teacher approach. *Teaching Exceptional Children, 32*(2), 28–33.

Brolin, D.E. (1993). *Life-centered career education: A competency-based approach* (4th ed.). Reston, VA: Council for Exceptional Children.

Brolin, D.E. (1995). *Career education: A functional life skills approach* (3rd ed.) Englewood Cliffs, NJ: Merrill/Prentice Hall.

Bryan, T. (1997). Assessing the personal and social status of students with learning disabilities. *Learning Disabilities Research & Practice, 12*(1), 63–76.

Bursuck, W. (1989). A comparison of students with learning disabilities to low achieving and higher achieving students on three dimensions of social competence. *Journal of Learning Disabilities, 22,* 188–194.

Carter, J., & Sugai, G. (1989). Social skills curriculum analysis. *Teaching Exceptional Children, 22,* 36–39.

Center, D.B., & Wascom, A.M. (1987). Teacher perceptions of social behavior in behaviorally disordered and socially normal children and youth. *Behavioral Disorders, 12,* 200–206.

Clark, G.M. (1994). Is a functional curriculum approach compatible with an inclusive education model? *Teaching Exceptional Children, 26*(2), 36–39.

Collet–Klingenberg, L.L. (1998). The reality of best practices in transition: A case study. *Exceptional Children, 65*(1), 67–78.

Council for Exceptional Children. (1997). Transition programs help students with disabilities succeed. *CEC Today, 3*(9), 1, 15.

Cronin, M.E. & Patton, J.R. (1993). *Life skills instruction for students with special needs: A practical guide for integrating real life topics into the curriculum.* Austin, TX: Pro-Ed.

Davis, P.K., & Bates, P. (1997). Transition-related IEP objectives: Ensuring their functionality, technical adequacy, and generality. *Exceptionality, 7*(1), 37–60.

deBettencourt, L.U., Bonaro, D.A., & Sabornie, E.J. (1995). Career development services offered to postsecondary students with learning disabilities. *Learning Disabilities Research & Practice, 10*(2), 102–107.

DeFur, S.H., & Taymans, J.M. (1995). Competencies needed for transition specialists in vocational rehabilitation, vocational education, and special education. *Exceptional Children, 62*(1), 38–51.

Edgar, E. (1987). Secondary programs in special education: Are any of them justifiable? *Exceptional Children, 53*, 555–561.

Fad, K.S. (1990). The fast track to success: Social-behavioral skills. *Intervention in School and Clinic, 26*(1), 39–43.

Frank, A.R., & Sitlington, P.L. (1997). Young adults with behavioral disorders—Before and after IDEA. *Behavioral Disorders, 23*(1), 40–56.

Furney, K.S., Hasazi, S.B., & DeStefano, L. (1997). Transition policies, practices, and promises: Lessons from three states. *Exceptional Children, 63*(3), 343–355.

Gartin, B.C., Rumrill, P., & Serebreni, R. (1996). The higher education transition model: Guidelines for facilitating college transition among college-bound students with disabilities. *Teaching Exceptional Children, 29*(1), 30–33.

Goldberger, S., & Kazis, R. (1996). Revitalizing high schools: What the school-to-career movement can contribute. *Phi Delta Kappan, 77*(8), 547–554.

Goldstein, A.P. (1981). Social skills training. In A.P. Goldstein, E.G. Carr, W.S. Davidson, & P. Weher (Eds.), *In response to aggression: Methods of control and prosocial alternatives.* New York: Pergamon Press.

Goldstein, A.P., & McGinnis, E. (1997). *Skillstreaming the adolescent: New strategies and perspectives for teaching prosocial skills.* Champaign, IL: Research Press.

Goldstein, D.E., Murray, C., & Edgar, E. (1998). Employment earnings and hours of high school graduates with learning disabilities through the first decade after graduation. *Learning Disabilities Research & Practice, 13*(1), 53–64.

Gresham, F. (1986). Conceptual issues in the assessment of social competence in children. In P.S. Strain, M.J. Guralnick, & H.M. Walker (Eds.), *Children's social behavior: Development, assessment, and modification* (pp. 143–179). Orlando, FL: Academic Press.

Gresham, F.M. (1998). Social skills training: Should we raze, remodel, or rebuild? *Behavioral Disorders, 24*(1), 19–25.

Gresham, F.M., & Elliott, S.N. (1990). *Social Skills Rating System (SSRS).* Circle Pines, MN: American Guidance Service.

Gresham, F.M., Elliott, S.N., & Black, F.L. (1987). Teacher-rated social skills of mainstreamed mildly handicapped and nonhandicapped children. *School Psychology Review, 16*, 78–88.

Grubb, W.N. (1996). The new vocationalism: What it is, What it could be. *Phi Delta Kappan, 77*(8), 535–546.

Habel, J., Bloom, L.A., Ray, M.S., & Bacon, E. (1999). Consumer resports: What students with behavior disorders say about school. *Remedial and Special Education, 20*(2), 93–105.

Halpern, A.S. (1992). Transition: Old wine in new bottles. *Exceptional Children, 58*, 202–211.

Hamilton, M.A., & Hamilton, S.F. (1997a). When is work a learning experience? *Phi Delta Kappan, 78*(9), 682–689.

Hamilton, S.F., & Hamilton, M.A. (1997b). When is learning work-based? *Phi Delta Kappan, 78*(9), 676–681.

Hartoonian, M., & Van Scotter, R. (1996). School-to-work: A model for learning a living. *Phi Delta Kappan, 77*(8), 555–560.

Heal, L.W., & Rusch, F.R. (1995). Predicting employment for students who leave special education high school programs. *Exceptional Children, 61*(5), 472–487.

Helmke, L.M., Havekost, D.M., Patton, J.R., & Polloway, E.A. (1994). Life skills programming: Development of a high school science course. *Teaching Exceptional Children, 26*(2), 49–53.

Hollinger, J.D. (1987). Social skills for behaviorally disordered children as preparation for mainstreaming. *Remedial and Special Education, 8*(1), 17–27.

Jackson, N.F., Jackson, D.A., & Monroe, C. (1983). *Getting along with others: Teaching social effectiveness to children.* Champaign, IL: Research Press.

Kauffman, J.M., Wong, K.L.H., Lloyd, J.W., Hung, L., & Pullen, P.L. (1991). What puts pupils at risk? An analysis of classroom teachers' judgments of pupils' behavior. *Remedial and Special Education, 12*, 7–16.

Knight, D., & Aucoin, L. (1999). Assessing job-readiness skills: How students, teachers, and employers can work together to enhance on-the-job training. *Teaching Exceptional Children, 31*(5), 10–17.

Knight, D., & Rieck, W. (1997). Contracts for careers. *Teaching Exceptional Children, 29*(6), 42–46.

Kortering, L.J., & Braziel, P.M. (1999a). School dropout from the perspective of former students. *Remedial and Special Education, 20*(2), 78–83.

Kortering, L.J., & Braziel, P.M. (1999b). Staying in school: The perspective of ninth-grade students. *Remedial and Special Education, 20*(2), 106–113.

Lahm, E.A., & Nickels, B.L. (1999). What do you know? Assistive technology competencies for special educators. *Teaching Exceptional Children, 32*(1), 56–63.

Lapadat, J.C. (1991). Pragmatic language skills of students with language and/or learning disabilities: A quantitative synthesis. *Journal of Learning Disabilities, 24*, 147–158.

Lehmann, J.P., Bassett, D.S., & Sands, D.J. (1999). Students' participation in transition-related actions: A qualitative study. *Remedial and Special Education, 20*(3), 160–169.

Levine, P., & Edgar, E. (1994). An analysis of gender of long-term postschool outcomes for youth with and without disabilities. *Exceptional Children, 61*(3), 282–300.

Lichtenstein, S. (1996). Gender differences in the education and employment of young adults. *Remedial and Special Education, 17*(1), 4–20.

Lindstrom, L.E., Benz, M.R., & Johnson, M.D. (1996). Developing job clubs for students in transition. *Teaching Exceptional Children, 29*(2), 18–21.

Lindstrom, L.E., Benz, M.R., & Johnson, M.D. (1997). From school grounds to coffee grounds: An introduction to school-based enterprises. *Teaching Exceptional Children, 29*(4), 20–24.

Maag, J.W. (1989). Assessment in social skills training: Methodological and conceptual issues for research and practice. *Remedial and Special Education, 10*, 6–17.

Maag, J.W. (1990). Social skills training in schools. *Special Services in the Schools, 6*, 1–19.

Maag, J.W., & Behrens, J.T. (1989). Depression and cognitive self-statements of learning disabled and seriously emotionally disturbed adolescents. *Journal of Special Education, 23*(1), 17–27.

Madge, S., Affleck, J., & Lowenbraun, S. (1990). Social effects of integrated classrooms and resource room/regular class placements on elementary students with learning disabilities. *Journal of Learning Disabilities, 23*, 439–445.

Malian, I.M., & Love, L.L. (1998). Leaving high school: An ongoing transition study. *Teaching Exceptional Children, 30*(3), 4–10.

Malmgren, K., Edgar, E., & Neel, R.S. (1998). Postschool status of youths with behavioral disorders. *Behavioral Disorders, 23*(4), 257–263.

Mathur, S.R., Kavale, K.A., Quinn, M.M., Forness, S.R., & Rutherford, R.B. (1998). Social skills interventions with students with emotional and behavioral problems: A quantitative synthesis of single-subject research. *Behavioral Disorders, 23*, 193–201.

Mathur, S.R., & Rutherford, R.B. (1996). Is social skills training effective for students with emotional or behavioral disorders? Research issues and needs. *Behavioral Disorders, 22*(1), 21–28.

Mattison, R.E., Spitznagel, E.L., & Felix, B.C. (1998). Enrollment predictors of the special education outcomes for students with SED. *Behavioral Disorders, 23*(4), 243–256.

McFall, R. (1982). A review and reformulation of the concept of social skills. *Behavioral Assessment, 4*, 1–33.

McGinnis, E., & Goldstein, A.P. (1997). *Skillstreaming the elementary school child: New strategies and perspectives for teaching prosocial skills*. Champaign, IL: Research Press.

McKinney, J.D. (1989). Longitudinal research on the behavioral characteristics of children with learning disabilities. *Journal of Learning Disabilities, 22,* 141–150.

McLeod, T.M., Kolb, T.L., & Lister, M.O. (1994). Social skills, school skills, and success in the high school: A comparison of teachers' and students' perceptions. *Learning Disabilities Research & Practice, 9*(3), 142–147.

Meadows, N., Neel, R.S., Parker, G., & Timo, K. (1991). A validation of social skills for students with behavioral disorders. *Behavioral Disorders, 16,* 200–210.

Menlove, M. (1996). A checklist for identifying funding sources for assistive technology. *Teaching Exceptional Children, 28*(3), 20–24.

Miner, C.A., & Bates, P.E. (1997). Person-centered transition planning. *Teaching Exceptional Children, 30*(1), 66–69.

Morningstar, M.E., Turnbull, A.P., & Turnbull, H.R. (1995). What do students with disabilities tell us about the importance of family involvement in the transition from school to adult life? *Exceptional Children, 62*(3), 249–260.

Murray, C., Goldstein, D.E., & Edgar, E. (1997). The employment and engagement status of high school graduates with learning disabilities through the first decade after graduation. *Learning Disabilities Research & Practice, 12*(3), 151–160.

Neel, R.S., & Cessna, K.K. (1990). Maybe this behavior does make sense. In R.B. Rutherford & S.A. DiGangi (Eds.), *Severe behavior disorders of children and youth: Volume 13* (pp. 18–22). Reston, VA: Council for Children with Behavioral Disorders.

Nelson, J.R., Drummond, M., Martella, R., & Marchand-Martella, N. (1997). The current and future outcomes of interpersonal social interactions: The views of students with behavioral disorders. *Behavioral Disorders, 22,* 141–151.

Odom, S.L., McConnell, S.R., & Chandler, L.K. (1993). Acceptability and feasibility of classroom–based social interaction interventions for young children with disabilities. *Exceptional Children, 60*(3), 226–236.

O'Reilly, M.F., & Glynn, D. (1995). Using a process social skills training approach with adolescents with mild intellectual disabilities in a high school setting. *Education and Training in Mental Retardation and Developmental Disabilities, 30*(3), 187–198.

Osborne, S.S., Schulte, A.C., & McKinney, J.D. (1991). A longitudinal study of students with learning disabilities in mainstream and resource programs. *Exceptionality, 2,* 81–95.

Panagos, R.J., & DuBois, D.L. (1999). Career self-efficacy development and students with learning disabilities. *Learning Disabilities Research & Practice, 14*(1), 25–34.

Parette, H.P. (1997). Assistive technology devices and services. *Education and Training in Mental Retardation and Developmental Disabilities, 32*(4), 267–280.

Patton, J.R., Beirne-Smith, M., & Payne, J.S. (1990). *Mental Retardation* (3rd ed.). Columbus, OH: Merrill.

Patton, J.R., Cronin, M.E., & Jairrels, V. (1997). Curricular implications of transition: Life skills instruction as an integrated part of transition education. *Remedial and Special Education, 18*(5), 294–306.

Patton, J.R., Polloway, E.A., Smith, T.E.C., Edgar, E., Clark, G.M., & Lee, S. (1996). Individuals with mild mental retardation: Postsecondary outcomes and implications for educational policy. *Education and Training in Mental Retardation and Developmental Disabilities, 31*(2), 75–85.

Patton, P.L., de la Garza, B., & Harmon, C. (1997). Successful employment: Employability skills +. *Teaching Exceptional Children, 29*(3), 4–10.

Peck, M. (1985). Crisis intervention treatment with chronically and acutely suicidal adolescents. In M. Peck, N.L. Farberow, & R.E. Litman (Eds.), *Youth suicide* (pp. 112–122). New York: Springer.

Raskind, M.H., Goldberg, R.J., Higgins, E.L., & Herman, K.L. (1999). Patterns of change and predictors of success in individuals with learning disabilities: Results from a twenty-year longitudinal study. *Learning Disabilities Research & Practice, 14*(1), 35–49.

Repetto, J.B., & Correa, V.I. (1996). Expanding views on transition. *Exceptional Children, 62*(6), 551–563.

Roberts, C., & Zubrick, S. (1992). Factors influencing the social status of children with mild academic disabilities in regular classrooms. *Exceptional Children, 59,* 192–202.

Roberts, R., & Mather, N. (1995). The return of students with learning disabilities to regular classrooms: A sellout? *Learning Disabilities Research & Practice, 10*(1), 46–58.

Rojewski, J.W. (1996). Educational and occupational aspirations of high school seniors with learning disabilities. *Exceptional Children, 62*(5), 463–476.

Rylance, B.J. (1997). Predictors of high school graduation or dropping out for youths with severe emotional disturbances. *Behavioral Disorders, 23*(1), 5–17.

Rylance, B.J. (1998). Predictors of post-high school employment for youth identified as severely emotionally disturbed. *The Journal of Special Education, 32*(3), 184–192.

Sabornie, E.J. (1987). Bi–directional social status of behaviorally disordered and nonhandicapped elementary school pupils. *Behavioral Disorders, 13*, 45–57.

Sabornie, E.J., Kauffman, J.M., & Cullinan, D.A. (1990). Extended sociometric status of adolescents with mild handicaps: A cross-categorical perspective. *Exceptionality, 1*, 197–209.

Sample, P.L. (1998). Postschool outcomes for students with significant emotional disturbance following best–practice transition services. *Behavioral Disorders, 23*(4), 2331–242.

Schloss, P.J., Schloss, C.N., Wood, C.E., & Kiehl, W.S. (1986). A critical review of social skills research with behaviorally disordered students. *Behavioral Disorders, 12*, 1–14.

Seidel, J.F., & Vaughn, S. (1991). Social alienation and the learning disabled school dropout. *Learning Disabilities Research & Practice, 6*, 152–157.

Sitlington, P.L., Clark, G.M., & Kolstoe, O.P. (2000). *Transition education and services for adolescents with disabilities* (3rd ed.). Boston, MA: Allyn & Bacon.

Smith, J.O. (1992). Falling through the cracks: Rehabilitation services for adults with learning disabilities. *Exceptional Children, 58*, 451–460.

Smith, T.E.C., & Puccini, I.K. (1995). Position statement: Secondary curricula and policy issues for students with mental retardation. *Education and Training in Mental Retardation and Developmental Disabilities, 30*(4), 275–282.

Stokes, T.F., & Baer, D.M. (1977). An implicit technology of generalization. *Journal of Applied Behavior Analysis, 10*, 349–367.

Stone, W.L., & La Greca, A.M. (1990). The social status of children with learning disabilities: A reexamination. *Journal of Learning Disabilities, 23*, 32–37.

Strain, P.S., & Odom, S.L. (1986). Peer social initiations: Effective intervention for social skills development of exceptional children. *Exceptional Children, 52*, 543–551.

Strain, P.S., Odom, S.L, & McConnell, S. (1984). Promoting social reciprocity of exceptional children: Identification, target behavior selection, and intervention. *Remedial and Special Education, 5*(1), 21–28.

Sugai, G., & Fuller, M. (1991). A decision model for social skills curriculum analysis. *Remedial and Special Education, 12*, 33–42.

Szymanski, E.M. (1994). Transition: Life-span and life-space considerations for empowerment. *Exceptional Children, 60*(5), 402–410.

Thomas, C.A. (1999). Supporting student voice in transition planning. *Teaching Exceptional Children, 31*(5), 4–9.

U.S. Congress. (1990). *PL 101–476: Individuals with Disabilities Education Act (IDEA)*. Washington, D.C.: Author.

U.S. Department of Education. (1997). Seventeeth annual report to Congress on the implementation of the Individuals with Disabilities Education Act. Washington, D.C.: Author.

Vaughn, S., & Haager, D. (1994). Social competence as a multifaceted construct: How do students with learning disabilities fare? *Learning Disability Quarterly, 17*, 253–266.

Wagner, M. (1989). *The transition experience of youth with disabilities: A report from the national longitudinal transition study*. Menlo Park, CA: SRI International.

Wagner, M.M., & Blackorby, J. (1996). Transition from high school to work or college: How special education students fare. *The Future of Children, Spring*, 103–120.

Walker, H.M., McConnell, S., Holmes, D., Todis, B., Walker, J., & Golden, N. (1983). *The Walker social skills curriculum: The ACCEPTS program*. Austin, TX: Pro-Ed.

Walker, H.M., & Stieber, S. (1998). Teacher ratings of social skills as longitudinal predictors of long-term arrest status in a sample of at-risk males. *Behavioral Disorders, 23*, 222–230.

Walker, H.M., Todis, B., Holmes, D., & Horton, G. (1988). *The Walker social skills curriculum: The ACCESS program.* Austin, TX: Pro-Ed.

Wehman, P., West, M., & Kregel, J. (1999). Supported employment program development and research needs: Looking ahead to the year 2000. *Education and Training in Mental Retardation and Developmental Disabilities, 34*(1), 3–19.

Wehmeyer, M., & Schwartz, M. (1997). Self-determination and positive adult outcomes: A follow-up study of youth with mental retardation or learning disabilities. *Exceptional Children, 63*(2), 245–255.

Whitney-Thomas, J., & Hanley-Maxwell, C. (1996). Packing the parachute: Parents' experiences as their children prepare to leave high school. *Exceptional Children, 63*(1), 75–87.

Will, M. (1984). *OSERS programming for the transition of youth with disabilities: Bridges from school to working life.* Washington, D.C.: Office of Special Education and Rehabilitative Services.

Wircenski, J.L., & Wircenski, M.D. (1997). Beyond 2000: Preparing individuals from special populations for the next millenium. *Journal for Vocational Special Needs Education, 19*(3), 128–131.

Wolf, M.M. (1978). Social validity: The case for subjective measurement or how applied behavior analysis is finding its heart. *Journal of Applied Behavior Analysis, 11*, 203–214.

Employment linkages, 499
Empowerment strategies, 460, 476–477
Encouragement, 67
English
    oral proficiency in, 266
    as a second language (ESL), 232, 265–270
Enrollment, 10
Environment, physical, 97–98
Errors
    analysis in mathematics, 383–385
    analysis steps, 138
    analyzing, 136–139
    fear of, 34
ESL. *See* English, as a second language
Evaluation mandates, 153–154
Expressive language, 251
Extinction, 119–120

F
Fads, 49–54
Fairness, 101
Family structure, 6
FAPE. *See* Free appropriate public
    education
FAST, 471
Feedback
    conferences, 209
    giving, 208–210
    during guided practice, 208
    prompts and, 210
    on student performance, 202–205
Fernald's Multisensory Approach,
    302–303
First Thousand Words, 301
FIST, 471
FLOW strategy, 470
Fluency, 310–312
FORCE, 243–244
Form, 251–253, 259–263
Fractions, 418–419
    manipulatives for, 420
Frameworks, 198
Free appropriate public education (FAPE), 10
Fry's New Instant Word List, 296–297
Functional academics, 43
Functional and measurable goals and objec-
    tives, 498
Future goals, 505

G
Generalization
    planning for, 487
    stage, 178–179
Getting Along with Others, 489–490
Gillingham-Stillman Method, 290–291
Goals
    annual, 170
    functional and measurable, 498
    future, 505
    long-range, 167
Goals 2000: Educate America Act (1994),
    7
Go Fish, 260
Grading, 149–151
    criteria, 150–151
    modifying, 455–459
    practice changes, 150
    responsibility for, 150
Graphic organizers, 441–446
    instructional routines and,
        443
    in science, 442–443
Gray-area students, 149
Grazing, 77
Grouping
    arrangements, 60
    options, 173–176
    process, 223
Guided practice, 206–210
Guideline beliefs, 4

H
Handwriting, 339–345
    aligning letters, 343
    cursive or manuscript, 340
    instruction, 340, 345
    letter formation, 343
    programs, 341
    reversals, 344
    speed, 343
    transitional approach, 341
Hangman, 336
Health problems, 156
Help, routines for, 105
HELPERS in Writing, 355
Herman Method for Reversing Reading
    Failure, 291–292

Homework, communication about, 83–84
HOW, 466–467
Hypothesis-testing, 313

I

IDEA. *See* Individuals with Disabilities
    Education Act Amendment
IEP. *See* Individualized Education Program
Imagery, 300
Inclusion, 44–49
    in action, 47
    collaborative teaching and, 77–78
    factors for successful, 49
    at secondary level, 47
Inclusionists, 46
Independent living skills, 482
    adult outcomes, 493–495
    assistive technology for, 513
    individualized transition plans, 497–503
    linkages to community for, 499–500
    teaching, 503–513
    transitioning to, 493–495
    transitioning services for, 495–497
Independent practice, 210–211
    directions for, 212
Individualized Education Program (IEP),
    37–38, 74, 123, 220, 482
    annual goal with objectives, 183
    backward planning and, 182
    planning and, 180–185
    services information, 37
    short-term objectives, 183
Individualized Transition Plan (ITP)
    goals and objectives, 498
    process development, 502
Individuals with Disabilities Education Act
    (IDEA), 7
    behavior considerations, 123–126
    compliance with, 133
    disabilities covered under, 10
    mandates, 78
Informal Reading Inventory (IRI), 306–307
Information, organizing and retrieving, 29
Information superhighway, 114
Input organization, 298
Instruction. *See also* specific subject areas, i.e.,
    Language arts,

Mathematics, Spelling, etc.
    adapting, 440–457
    anchoring, 58
    approaches, 435–439
    clarity of, 201
    cognitive strategy for, 56
    daily, 168
    direct, 201–205
    elements of, 44
    evaluating, 212
    grouping for, 35
    individualizing, 35–37
    intensity of, 201
    issues in, 44–49
    method implications, 173
    modality-based, 52
    modifying, 454
    one-on-one, 220
    options, 173–176
    planning, 38
    practices, 60
    quality, 62, 201
    research-based approaches,
        54–57
    resources, 59
    setting, 24, 62
    standard curriculum and,
        435–439
Integration, guidelines for,
    214–215
Intellectual ability, 27–28
Intelligence
    average, 16
    below-average, 15
    construct of, 27–28
    low to average, 17
    tests for, 154
Interactions, 69
Interdependence, positive, 221, 223
Internet use, 113–114
Interruptions, minimizing, 107
Intervention strategies, 152
IQ and achievement, 27
IRI. *See* Informal Reading Inventory
Isolation, 121
IT FITS strategy, 449
ITP. *See* Individualized Transition Plan

M

Main idea, 314–315

Mainstreaming, 44
  checklist for, 75
  guidelines for, 430

Maintenance stage, 178

Major life activities learning, 496

Management, discipline and, 96–97

Manifestation Determination Review, 123–126

Materials, routines for, 104

Mathematics, 33. *See also* specific function,
    i.e., Addition, Subtraction,etc.
  abstract sequencing, 385–386
  algorithms, 415–418
  basal deficiencies, 372
  building strategies, 388–390
  calculator and computer use, 378
  complex operations, 415–418
  computation, 375–376
  conceptual knowledge, 371
  curriculum, 371–373
  for daily living, 376–377
  deficits. *See* Mathematics deficits
  elaborated feedback, 397–398
  empiricist and constructivist debate, 374
  essential concepts and skills, 375, 418–422
  instruction. *See* Mathematics instruction
  lowering memorization, 388
  manipulatives, 386
  modeling problem solving, 397–398
  number concepts. *See* Mathematics number
    concepts and instruction
  numeration, 375
  performance factors, 368–369
  procedural knowledge, 371
  programs, 375
  sequencing, 387–388
  skills. *See* Mathematics skills
  standards, 371–373
  strategies. *See* Mathematics strategies
  word problems, 422–424

Mathematics deficits, 371
  attitude, 370
  automaticity, 370
  computation, 370
  language and, 369
  motivation, 370

Mathematics deficits—cont'd
  procedural difficulties, 369
  representational difficulties, 369
  strategies, 370
  word problems, 370

Mathematics instruction, 368
  computer software, 395
  direct instructional teaching techniques,
    386–387
  general procedures, 383–396
  rule-based instruction, 387–388
  specific skills and concepts, 396–398
  teaching sequences, 388–390

Mathematics number concepts and sense,
    398–403
  addition, 403–409
  basic facts and operations, 403–415
  5- and 10- frames, 405
  hundreds chart, 404
  numeration, 399–401
  one-to-one correspondence, 399
  place value, 401–403
  seriation, 401

Mathematics skills
  assessment and error analysis, 383–385
  concepts, 396–424
  practice motivation, 390–394
  teaching specific, 396–398

Mathematics strategies
  computer-assisted instruction, 394
  cooperative learning, 393–394
  games, 390–392
  goal setting, 392–393
  modeling problem solving, 394–396
  relating to real life, 392
  self-monitoring, 392–393
  teacher-student dialogues, 394–396
  word problems, 391

Math war, 374

Measurement, 420–422

Medications, 53

Meetings, consultative or collaborative,
    69

Memory, 260
  deficits, 30
  enhancement routine, 449
  skills, 29–31

PHOTO CREDITS